Handbook of Research on Discrete Event Simulation Environments:
Technologies and Applications

Evon M. O. Abu-Taieh
Arab Academy for Banking and Financial Sciences, Jordan

Asim Abdel Rahman El Sheikh
Arab Academy for Banking and Financial Sciences, Jordan

INFORMATION SCIENCE REFERENCE

Hershey · New York

Director of Editorial Content:	Kristin Klinger
Senior Managing Editor:	Jamie Snavely
Assistant Managing Editor:	Michael Brehm
Publishing Assistant:	Sean Woznicki
Typesetter:	Michael Killian, Sean Woznicki
Cover Design:	Lisa Tosheff
Printed at:	Yurchak Printing Inc.

Published in the United States of America by
Information Science Reference (an imprint of IGI Global)
701 E. Chocolate Avenue
Hershey PA 17033
Tel: 717-533-8845
Fax: 717-533-8661
E-mail: cust@igi-global.com
Web site: http://www.igi-global.com/reference

Library of Congress Cataloging-in-Publication Data

Handbook of research on discrete event simulation environments : technologies and applications / Evon M.O. Abu-Taieh and Asim Abdel Rahman El Sheikh, editors.
    p. cm.
  Includes bibliographical references and index.
  Summary: "This book provides a comprehensive overview of theory and practice in simulation systems focusing on major breakthroughs within the technological arena, with particular concentration on the accelerating principles, concepts and applications"--Provided by publisher.

  ISBN 978-1-60566-774-4 (hardcover) -- ISBN 978-1-60566-775-1 (ebook) 1.
Discrete-time systems--Computer simulation. I. Abu-Taieh, Evon M. O. II. El
Sheikh, Asim Abdel Rahman.
  T57.62H365 2012
  003'.830113--dc22
                              2009019592

British Cataloguing in Publication Data
A Cataloguing in Publication record for this book is available from the British Library.

All work contributed to this book is new, previously-unpublished material. The views expressed in this book are those of the authors, but not necessarily of the publisher.

Editorial Advisory Board

List of Contributors

Table of Contents

Table of Contents

Chapter 1
Istvan Molnar, Bloomsburg University of Pennsylvania, USA

Chapter 1, *Simulation: Body of Knowledge*, attempts to define the knowledge body of simulation and describes the underlying principles of simulation education. It argues that any programs in Modelling and Simulation should recognize the multi-and interdisciplinary character of the field and realize the program in wide co-operation. The paper starts with the clarification of the major objectives and principles of the Modelling and Simulation Program and the related degrees, based on a broad business and real world perspective. After reviewing students' background, especially the communication, interpersonal, and team skills, the analytical and critical thinking skills, furthermore some of the additional skills leading to a career, the employer's view and possible career paths are examined. Finally, the core knowledge body, the curriculum design and program related issues are discussed. The author hopes to contribute to the recent discussions about modelling and simulation education and the profession.

Chapter 2
*Evon M. O. Abu-Taieh, Civil Aviation Regulatory Commission and Arab Academy for
     Financial Sciences, Jordan
Jeihan M. O. Abutayeh, World Bank, Jordan*

Chapter 2, *Simulation Environments as Vocational and Training Tools,* investigates over 50 simulation packages and simulators used in vocational and course training in many fields. Accordingly, the 50 simulation packages were categorized in the following fields: Pilot Training, Chemistry, Physics, Mathematics, Environment and ecological systems, Cosmology and astrophysics, Medicine and Surgery training, Cosmetic surgery, Engineering – Civil engineering, architecture, interior design, Computer and communication networks, Stock Market Analysis, Financial Models and Marketing, Military Training and Virtual Reality. The incentive for using simulation environments as vocational and training tools is to save live, money and effort.

    Brian L. Heath, Wright State University, USA
    Raymond R. Hill, Air Force Institute of Technology, USA

Chapter 3, *Agent-Based Modeling: A Historical Perspective and a Review of Validation and Verification Efforts*, traces the historical roots of agent-based modeling. This review examines the modern influences of systems thinking, cybernetics as well as chaos and complexity on the growth of agent-based modeling. The chapter then examines the philosophical foundations of simulation verification and validation. Simulation verification and validation can be viewed from two quite different perspectives: the simulation philosopher and the simulation practitioner. Personnel from either camp are typically unaware of the other camp's view of simulation verification and validation. This chapter examines both camps while also providing a survey of the literature and efforts pertaining to the verification and validation of agent-based models.

    Sattar J. Aboud, Middle East University for Graduate Studies, Jordan
    Mohammad Al-Fayoumi, Middle East University for Graduate Studies, Jordan
    Mohamed Alnuaimi, Middle East University for Graduate Studies, Jordan

Chapter 4, *Verification and Validation of Simulation Models*, discusses validation and verification of simulation models. The different approaches to deciding model validity are presented; how model validation and verification relate to the model development process are discussed; various validation techniques are defined; conceptual model validity, model verification, operational validity, and data validity; superior verification and validation technique for simulation models relied on a multistage approach are described; ways to document results are given; and a recommended procedure is presented.

    Thomas Wutzler, Max Planck Institute for Biogeochemistry, Germany
    Hessam Sarjoughian, Arizona Center for Integrative Modeling and Simulation, USA

Chapter 5, *DEVS-Based Simulation Interoperability*, introduces the usage of DEVS for the purpose of implementing interoperability across heterogeneous simulation models. It shows that the DEVS framework provides a simple, yet effective conceptual basis for handling simulation interoperability. It discusses the various useful properties of the DEVS framework, describes the Shared Abstract Model (SAM) approach for interoperating simulation models, and compares it to other approaches. The DEVS approach enables formal model specification with component models implemented in multiple programming languages. The simplicity of the integration of component models designed in the DEVS, DTSS, and DESS simulation formalisms and implemented in the programming languages Java and C++ is demonstrated by a basic educational example and by a real world forest carbon accounting model. The authors hope, that readers will appreciate the combination of generalness and simplicity and that readers will consider using the DEVS approach for simulation interoperability in their own projects.

Chapter 6

Lucia Cassettari, University of Genoa, Italy
Roberto Mosca, University of Genoa, Italy
Roberto Revetria, University of Genoa, Italy

Chapter 6, *Experimental Error Measurement in Monte Carlo Simulation*, describes the set up step series, developed by the Genoa Research Group on Production System Simulation at the beginning of the '80s, as a sequence, through which it is possible at first statistically validate the simulator, then estimate the variables which effectively affect the different target functions, then obtain, through the regression meta-models, the relations linking the independent variables to the dependent ones (target functions) and, finally, proceed to the detection of the optimal functioning conditions. The authors pay great attention to the treatment, the evaluation and control of the Experimental Error, under the form of Mean Square Pure Error (MS_{PE}), a measurement which is always culpably neglected in the traditional experimentation on the simulation models but, that potentially can consistently invalidate with its magnitude the value of the results obtained from the model.

Chapter 7

Pedro J. A. Sebastião, Instituto de Telecomunicações, Portugal
Francisco A. B. Cercas, Instituto de Telecomunicações, Portugal
Adolfo V. T. Cartaxo, Instituto de Telecomunicações, Portugal

Chapter 7, *Efficient Discrete Simulation of Coded Wireless Communication Systems*, presents a simulation method, named Accelerated Simulation Method (ASM), that provides a high degree of efficiency and accuracy, namely for lower BER, where the application of methods like the Monte Carlo simulation method (MCSM) is prohibitive, due to high computational and time requirements. The present work generalizes the application of the ASM to a Wireless Communication System's (WCS) modelled as a stochastic discrete channel model, considering a real channel, where there are several random effects that result in random energy fluctuations of the received symbols. The performance of the coded WCS is assessed efficiently, with soft-decision (SD) and hard-decision (HD) decoding. The authors show that this new method already achieves a time efficiency of two or three orders of magnitude for SD and HD, considering a BER = 1×10^{-4} when compared to MCSM. The presented performance results are compared with the MCSM, to check its accuracy.

Chapter 8

Hana Kubátová, Czech Technical University in Prague, Czech Republic

Chapter 8, *Teaching Principles of Petri Nets in Hardware Courses and Student's Projects*, presents the principles of using Petri Net formalism in hardware design courses, especially in the course "Architecture of peripheral devices". Several models and results obtained by student individual or group projects are mentioned. First the using of formalism as a modeling tool is presented consecutively from Place/Transition nets to Coloured Petri nets. Then the possible Petri Nets using as a hardware specification for direct hardware implementation (synthesized VHDL for FPGA) is described. Implementation and simulation results of three directly implemented models are presented

Chapter 9

Lorenzo Capra, Università degli Studi di Milano, Italy
Walter Cazzola, Università degli Studi di Milano, Italy

Chapter 9, *An Introduction to Reflective Petri Nets*, introduces Reflective Petri nets, a formal model for dynamic discrete-event systems. Based on a typical reflective architecture, in which functional aspects are cleanly separated from evolutionary ones, that model preserves the description effectiveness and the analysis capabilities of Petri nets. On the short-time perspective of implementing a discrete-event simulation engine, Reflective Petri nets are provided with timed state-transition semantics.

Chapter 10

Lorenzo Capra, Università degli Studi di Milano, Italy
Walter Cazzola, Università degli Studi di Milano, Italy

Chapter 10, *Trying out Reflective Petri Nets on a Dynamic Workflow Case*, proposes a recent Petri net-based reflective layout, called Reflective Petri nets, as a formal model for dynamic workflows. A localized open problem is considered: how to determine what tasks should be redone and which ones do not when transferring a workflow instance from an old to a new template. The problem is efficiently but rather empirically addressed in a workflow management system. The proposed approach is formal, may be generalized, and is based on the preservation of classical Petri nets structural properties, which permit an efficient characterization of workflow's soundness.

Chapter 11

Ari Korhonen, Helsinki University of Technology, Finland

Chapter 11, *Applications of Visual Algorithm Simulation*, represent a novel idea to promote the interaction between the user and the algorithm visualization system called visual algorithm simulation. As a proof of concept, the chapter represents an application framework called Matrix that encapsulates the idea of visual algorithm simulation. The framework is applied by the TRAKLA2 learning environment in which algorithm simulation is employed to produce algorithm simulation exercises. Moreover, the benefits of such exercises and applications of visual algorithm simulation in general are discussed.

Chapter 12

Ghada Al-Hudhud, Al-Ahlyia Amman University, Jordan

Chapter 12, *Virtual Reality: New Era of Simulation And Modelling*, represent a novel idea to promote the interaction between the user and the algorithm visualization system called visual algorithm simulation.

As a proof of concept, the chapter represents an application framework called Matrix that encapsulates the idea of visual algorithm simulation. The framework is applied by the TRAKLA2 learning environment in which algorithm simulation is employed to produce algorithm simulation exercises. Moreover, the benefits of such exercises and applications of visual algorithm simulation in general are discussed.

Chapter 13

Gyorgy Lipovszki, Budapest University of Technology and Economics, Hungary
Istvan Molnar, Bloomsburg University of Pennsylvania, USA

Chapter 13, *Case Study: Implementation of a DES Environment*, describes a program system that implements a Discrete Event Simulation (DES) development environment. The simulation environment was created using the LabVIEW graphical programming system; a National Instruments software product. In this programming environment the user can connect different procedures and data structures with "graphical wires" to implement a simulation model, thereby creating an executable simulation program. The connected individual objects simulate a discrete event problem. The chapter describes all simulation model objects, their attributes and methods. Another important element of the discrete event simulator is the task list, which has also been created using task type objects. The simulation system uses the "next event simulation" technique and refreshes the actual state (attribute values of all model objects) at every event. The state changes are determined by the entity objects, their input, current content, and output. Every model object can access (read) all and modify (write) a selected number of object attribute values. This property of the simulation system provides the possibility to build a complex discrete event system using predefined discrete event model objects.

Chapter 14

Andreas Tolk, Old Dominion University, USA

Chapter 14, *Using Simulation Systems for Decision Support*, describes the use of simulation systems for decision support in support of real operations, which is the most challenging application domain in the discipline of modeling and simulation. To this end, the systems must be integrated as services into the operational infrastructure. To support discovery, selection, and composition of services, they need to be annotated regarding technical, syntactic, semantic, pragmatic, dynamic, and conceptual categories. The systems themselves must be complete and validated. The data must be obtainable, preferably via common protocols shared with the operational infrastructure. Agents and automated forces must produce situation adequate behavior. If these requirements for simulation systems and their annotations are fulfilled, decision support simulation can contribute significantly to the situational awareness up to cognitive levels of the decision maker.

Chapter 15

David Gamez, Imperial College, UK

Chapter 15, *Discrete Event Simulation of Spiking Neural Networks*, is an overview of the simulation of spiking neural networks that relates discrete event simulation to other approaches. To illustrate the issues surrounding this work, the second half of this chapter presents a case study of the SpikeStream neural simulator that covers the architecture, performance and typical applications of this software along with some recent experiments.

Chapter 16

Chapter 16, *An Integrated Data Mining and Simulation Solution*, we will propose an intelligent DSS framework based on data mining and simulation integration. The main output of this framework is the increase of knowledge. Two case studies are presented, the first one on car market demand simulation. The simulation model was built using neural networks to get the first set of prediction results. Data mining methodology used named ANFIS (Adaptive Neuro-Fuzzy Inference System). The second case study demonstrates how applying data mining and simulation in assuring quality in higher education

Chapter 17

Chapter 17, *Modeling and Simulation of IEEE 802.11g using OMNeT++*, aims to provide a tutorial on OMNeT++ focusing on modeling and performance study of the IEEE 802.11g wireless network. Due to the complex nature of computer and telecommunication networks, it is often difficult to predict the impact of different parameters on system performance especially when deploying wireless networks. Computer simulation has become a popular methodology for performance study of computer and telecommunication networks. This popularity results from the availability of various sophisticated and powerful simulation software packages, and also because of the flexibility in model construction and validation offered by simulation. While various network simulators exist for building a variety of network models, choosing a good network simulator is very important in modeling and performance analysis of wireless networks. A good simulator is one that is easy to use; more flexible in model development, modification and validation; and incorporates appropriate analysis of simulation output data, pseudo-random number generators, and statistical accuracy of the simulation results. OMNeT++ is becoming one of the most popular network simulators because it has all the features of a good simulator.

Chapter 18

Chapter 18, *Performance Modeling of IEEE 802.11 WLAN using OPNET: A Tutorial*, aims to provide a tutorial on OPNET focusing on the simulation and performance modeling of IEEE 802.11 wireless local area networks (WLANs). Results obtained show that OPNET provides credible simulation results close to a real system.

Chapter 19

Chapter 19, *On the Use of Discrete-Event Simulation in Computer Networks Analysis and Design,* describes a newly developed research-level computer network simulator, which can be used to evaluate the performance of a number of flooding algorithms in ideal and realistic mobile ad hoc network (MANET) environments. It is referred to as MANSim.

Chapter 20

Chapter 20, *Queuing Theory and Discrete Events Simulation for Health Care: From Basic Processes to Complex Systems with Interdependenciess,* objective is twofold: (i) to illustrate practical limitations of queuing analytic (QA) compared to Discrete-event simulation (DES) by applying both of them to analyze the same problems, and (ii) to demonstrate practical application of DES models starting from simple examples and proceeding to rather advanced models.

Chapter 21

Chapter 21, *Modelling a Small Firm in Jordan Using System Dynamics,* objective of this chapter is to introduce new performance measures using systems thinking paradigm that can be used by the Jordanian banks to assess the credit worthiness of firms applying for credit. A simulator based on system dynamics methodology which is the thinking tool presented in this chapter. The system dynamics methodology allows the bank to test "What If" scenarios based on a model which captures the behavior of the real system over time.

Chapter 22

Chapter 22, *The State of Computer Simulation Applications in Construction,* presents an overview of computer simulation efforts that have been performed in the area of construction engineering and management. Also, it presents two computer simulation applications in construction; earthmoving and construction of bridges' decks. Comprehensive case studies are worked out to illustrate the practicality of using computer simulation in scheduling construction projects, taking into account the associated uncertainties inherited in construction operations.

Preface

The Chinese Proverb cites that "I hear and I forget. I see and I remember. I do and I understand", in this context, Simulation is the next best thing after the "I do" part, as it is the nearest thing to giving real life picture to images in the mind. Mirrors reflect real life into no existing picture, whereas simulation embodies our notions and ideas into a picture that cannot only be seen, but played and experimented with as well. Simulation environments exist on a number of dimensions in the market.

The desirable features in Discrete Event Simulation environments are taxonomiesed as modeling features, simulation systems features, and implementation features. While the modeling features include modularity, reuse and the hierarchical structure of the model, the simulation systems features include the scalability, portability, and interoperability of the simulation system, and the implementations features include distribution execution, execution over the internet, and ease of use. In order to accomplish the aforementioned desirable features, many components must be examined, while taking into account the market supply and demand factors. Actually, the race to accomplish such desirable features is as old as simulation itself. The components to be examined in this book are: Methodologies, Simulation language, Tutorials, Statistical analysis packages, Modeling, Animation, Interface, interoperability standards, Uses and Applications, Stochastic / Deterministic, Time handling, and History.

In **Handbook of Research on Discrete Event Simulation Environments: Technologies and Applications**, simulation is discussed from within the different features of theory and application. The goal of this book is not to look at simulation from traditional perspectives, but to illustrate the benefits and issues that arise from the application of simulation within other disciplines. This book focuses on major breakthroughs within the technological arena, with particular concentration on the accelerating principles, concepts and applications.

The book caters to the needs of scholars, PhD candidates, researchers, as well as, graduate level students of computer science, operations research, and economics disciplines. The target audience for this book also includes academic libraries throughout the world that are interested in cutting edge research. Another important segment of readers are students of Master of Business Administration (MBA) and Master of Public Affairs (MPA) programs, which include information systems components as part of their curriculum. To make the book accessible to all, a companion website was developed, which can be reached through the link (http://www.computercrossroad.org/).

This book is organized in 22 chapters. On the whole, the chapters of this book fall into five categories, while crossing paths with different disciplines, of which the first, *Simulation Prelude*, concentrates on simulation theory, while the second concentrates on *Petri Nets*, whereas the third section concentrates on *Monte Carlo*, besides the fourth section that sheds light on *visualization and real-time simulation*, likewise, the fifth section, *living simulation*, gives color to the black and white picture. The fifth section discusses simulation applications in neural networks, data mining, networks, banks, construction, thereby aiming to enrich this book with others knowledge, experience, thought and insight.

Chapter 1, *Simulation: Body of Knowledge*, attempts to define the knowledge body of simulation and describes the underlying principles of simulation education. It argues that any programs in Modelling and Simulation should recognize the multi-and interdisciplinary character of the field and realize the program in wide co-operation. The chapter starts with the clarification of the major objectives and principles of the Modelling and Simulation Program and the related degrees, based on a broad business and real world perspective. After reviewing students' background, especially the communication, interpersonal, and team skills, the analytical and critical thinking skills, furthermore some of the additional skills leading to a career, the employer's view and possible career paths are examined. Finally, the core knowledge body, the curriculum design and program related issues are discussed. The author hopes to contribute to the recent discussions about modelling and simulation education and the profession.

Chapter 2, *Simulation Environments as Vocational and Training Tools,* investigates over 50 simulation packages and simulators used in vocational and course training in many fields. Accordingly, the 50 simulation packages were categorized in the following fields: Pilot Training, Chemistry, Physics, Mathematics, Environment and ecological systems, Cosmology and astrophysics, Medicine and Surgery training, Cosmetic surgery, Engineering – Civil engineering, architecture, interior design, Computer and communication networks, Stock Market Analysis, Financial Models and Marketing, Military Training and Virtual Reality. The incentive for using simulation environments as vocational and training tools is to save live, money and effort.

Chapter 3, *Agent-Based Modeling: A Historical Perspective and a Review of Validation and Verification Efforts*, traces the historical roots of agent-based modeling. This review examines the modern influences of systems thinking, cybernetics as well as chaos and complexity on the growth of agent-based modeling. The chapter then examines the philosophical foundations of simulation verification and validation. Simulation verification and validation can be viewed from two quite different perspectives: the simulation philosopher and the simulation practitioner. Personnel from either camp are typically unaware of the other camp's view of simulation verification and validation. This chapter examines both camps while also providing a survey of the literature and efforts pertaining to the verification and validation of agent-based models.

Chapter 4, *Verification and Validation of Simulation Models*, discusses validation and verification of simulation models. The different approaches to deciding model validity are presented; how model validation and verification relate to the model development process are discussed; various validation techniques are defined; conceptual model validity, model verification, operational validity, and data validity; superior verification and validation technique for simulation models relied on a multistage approach are described; ways to document results are given; and a recommended procedure is presented.

Chapter 5, *DEVS-Based Simulation Interoperability*, introduces the usage of DEVS for the purpose of implementing interoperability across heterogeneous simulation models. It shows that the DEVS framework provides a simple, yet effective conceptual basis for handling simulation interoperability. It discusses the various useful properties of the DEVS framework, describes the Shared Abstract Model (SAM) approach for interoperating simulation models, and compares it to other approaches. The DEVS approach enables formal model specification with component models implemented in multiple programming languages. The simplicity of the integration of component models designed in the DEVS, DTSS, and DESS simulation formalisms and implemented in the programming languages Java and C++ is demonstrated by a basic educational example and by a real world forest carbon accounting model. The authors hope, that readers will appreciate the combination of generalness and simplicity and that readers will consider using the DEVS approach for simulation interoperability in their own projects.

The second section concentrates on, *Monte Carlo Simulation* where it is covered in chapter 6 and 7 as follows:

Chapter 6, *Experimental Error Measurement in Monte Carlo Simulation*, describes the set up step series, developed by the Genoa Research Group on Production System Simulation at the beginning of the '80s, as a sequence, through which it is possible at first statistically validate the simulator, then estimate the variables which effectively affect the different target functions, then obtain, through the regression meta-models, the relations linking the independent variables to the dependent ones (target functions) and, finally, proceed to the detection of the optimal functioning conditions. The authors pay great attention to the treatment, the evaluation and control of the Experimental Error, under the form of Mean Square Pure Error (MS_{PE}), a measurement which is always culpably neglected in the traditional experimentation on the simulation models but, that potentially can consistently invalidate with its magnitude the value of the results obtained from the model.

Chapter 7, *Efficient Discrete Simulation of Coded Wireless Communication Systems*, presents a simulation method, named Accelerated Simulation Method (ASM), that provides a high degree of efficiency and accuracy, namely for lower BER, where the application of methods like the Monte Carlo simulation method (MCSM) is prohibitive, due to high computational and time requirements. The present work generalizes the application of the ASM to a Wireless Communication System's (WCS) modelled as a stochastic discrete channel model, considering a real channel, where there are several random effects that result in random energy fluctuations of the received symbols. The performance of the coded WCS is assessed efficiently, with soft-decision (SD) and hard-decision (HD) decoding. The authors show that this new method already achieves a time efficiency of two or three orders of magnitude for SD and HD, considering a BER = 1×10^{-4} when compared to MCSM. The presented performance results are compared with the MCSM, to check its accuracy.

The third part of the book concentrates on *Petri Nets*. The chapters 8 through 10 cover this part as follows:

Chapter 8, *Teaching Principles of Petri Nets in Hardware Courses and Student's Projects*, presents the principles of using Petri Net formalism in hardware design courses, especially in the course "Architecture of peripheral devices". Several models and results obtained by student individual or group projects are mentioned. First the using of formalism as a modeling tool is presented consecutively from Place/Transition nets to Coloured Petri nets. Then the possible Petri Nets using as a hardware specification for direct hardware implementation (synthesized VHDL for FPGA) is described. Implementation and simulation results of three directly implemented models are presented

Chapter 9, *An Introduction to Reflective Petri Nets*, introduces Reflective Petri nets, a formal model for dynamic discrete-event systems. Based on a typical reflective architecture, in which functional aspects are cleanly separated from evolutionary ones, that model preserves the description effectiveness and the analysis capabilities of Petri nets. On the short-time perspective of implementing a discrete-event simulation engine, Reflective Petri nets are provided with timed state-transition semantics.

Chapter 10, *Trying out Reflective Petri Nets on a Dynamic Workflow Case*, proposes a recent Petri net-based reflective layout, called Reflective Petri nets, as a formal model for dynamic workflows. A localized open problem is considered: how to determine what tasks should be redone and which ones do not when transferring a workflow instance from an old to a new template. The problem is efficiently but rather empirically addressed in a workflow management system. The proposed approach is formal, may be generalized, and is based on the preservation of classical Petri nets structural properties, which permit an efficient characterization of workflow's soundness.

The fourth section of the book concentrates on visualization and real-time simulation. The chapters 11 through 14 cover this part as follows:

Chapter 11, *Applications of Visual Algorithm Simulation*, represent a novel idea to promote the interaction between the user and the algorithm visualization system called visual algorithm simulation. As a proof of concept, the chapter represents an application framework called Matrix that encapsulates the idea of visual algorithm simulation. The framework is applied by the TRAKLA2 learning environment in which algorithm simulation is employed to produce algorithm simulation exercises. Moreover, the benefits of such exercises and applications of visual algorithm simulation in general are discussed.

Chapter 12, *Virtual Reality: A New Era of Simulation And Modelling*, represent a novel idea to promote the interaction between the user and the algorithm visualization system called visual algorithm simulation. As a proof of concept, the chapter represents an application framework called Matrix that encapsulates the idea of visual algorithm simulation. The framework is applied by the TRAKLA2 learning environment in which algorithm simulation is employed to produce algorithm simulation exercises. Moreover, the benefits of such exercises and applications of visual algorithm simulation in general are discussed.

Chapter 13, *Implementation of a DES Environment*, describes a program system that implements a Discrete Event Simulation (DES) development environment. The simulation environment was created using the LabVIEW graphical programming system; a National Instruments software product. In this programming environment the user can connect different procedures and data structures with "graphical wires" to implement a simulation model, thereby creating an executable simulation program. The connected individual objects simulate a discrete event problem. The chapter describes all simulation model objects, their attributes and methods. Another important element of the discrete event simulator is the task list, which has also been created using task type objects. The simulation system uses the "next event simulation" technique and refreshes the actual state (attribute values of all model objects) at every event. The state changes are determined by the entity objects, their input, current content, and output. Every model object can access (read) all and modify (write) a selected number of object attribute values. This property of the simulation system provides the possibility to build a complex discrete event system using predefined discrete event model objects.

Chapter 14, *Using Simulation Systems for Decision Support*, describes the use of simulation systems for decision support in support of real operations, which is the most challenging application domain in the discipline of modeling and simulation. To this end, the systems must be integrated as services into the operational infrastructure. To support discovery, selection, and composition of services, they need to be annotated regarding technical, syntactic, semantic, pragmatic, dynamic, and conceptual categories. The systems themselves must be complete and validated. The data must be obtainable, preferably via common protocols shared with the operational infrastructure. Agents and automated forces must produce situation adequate behavior. If these requirements for simulation systems and their annotations are fulfilled, decision support simulation can contribute significantly to the situational awareness up to cognitive levels of the decision maker.

The final part of the book, *living simulation*, The chapters 15 through 22 cover this part as follows:

Chapter 15, *The Simulation of Spiking Neural Networks*, is an overview of the simulation of spiking neural networks that relates discrete event simulation to other approaches. To illustrate the issues surrounding this work, the second half of this chapter presents a case study of the SpikeStream neural simulator that covers the architecture, performance and typical applications of this software along with some recent experiments.

Chapter 16, *An Integrated Data Mining and Simulation Solution*, we will propose an intelligent DSS framework based on data mining and simulation integration. The main output of this framework is the increase of knowledge. Two case studies are presented, the first one on car market demand simulation. The simulation model was built using neural networks to get the first set of prediction results. Data mining methodology used named ANFIS (Adaptive Neuro-Fuzzy Inference System). The second case study demonstrates how applying data mining and simulation in assuring quality in higher education

Chapter 17, *Modeling and Simulation of IEEE 802.11g using OMNeT++*, aims to provide a tutorial on OMNeT++ focusing on modeling and performance study of the IEEE 802.11g wireless network. Due to the complex nature of computer and telecommunication networks, it is often difficult to predict the impact of different parameters on system performance especially when deploying wireless networks. Computer simulation has become a popular methodology for performance study of computer and telecommunication networks. This popularity results from the availability of various sophisticated and powerful simulation software packages, and also because of the flexibility in model construction and validation offered by simulation. While various network simulators exist for building a variety of network models, choosing a good network simulator is very important in modeling and performance analysis of wireless networks. A good simulator is one that is easy to use; more flexible in model development, modification and validation; and incorporates appropriate analysis of simulation output data, pseudo-random number generators, and statistical accuracy of the simulation results. OMNeT++ is becoming one of the most popular network simulators because it has all the features of a good simulator.

Chapter 18, *Performance Modeling of IEEE 802.11 WLAN using OPNET: A Tutorial*, aims to provide a tutorial on OPNET focusing on the simulation and performance modeling of IEEE 802.11 wireless local area networks (WLANs). Results obtained show that OPNET provides credible simulation results close to a real system.

Chapter 19, *On the Use of Discrete-Event Simulation in Computer Networks Analysis and Design*, describes a newly developed research-level computer network simulator, which can be used to evaluate the performance of a number of flooding algorithms in ideal and realistic mobile ad hoc network (MANET) environments. It is referred to as MANSim.

Chapter 20, *Queuing Theory and Discrete Events Simulation for Health Care: From Basic Processes to Complex Systems with Interdependencies*, objective is twofold: (i) to illustrate practical limitations of queuing analytic (QA) compared to Discrete-event simulation (DES) by applying both of them to analyze the same problems, and (ii) to demonstrate practical application of DES models starting from simple examples and proceeding to rather advanced models.

Chapter 21, *Modelling a Small Firm in Jordan Using System Dynamics*, objective of this chapter is to introduce new performance measures using systems thinking paradigm that can be used by the Jordanian banks to assess the credit worthiness of firms applying for credit. A simulator based on system dynamics methodology which is the thinking tool presented in this chapter. The system dynamics methodology allows the bank to test "What If" scenarios based on a model which captures the behavior of the real system over time.

Chapter 22, *The State of Computer Simulation Applications in Construction*, presents an overview of computer simulation efforts that have been performed in the area of construction engineering and management. Also, it presents two computer simulation applications in construction; earthmoving and construction of bridges' decks. Comprehensive case studies are worked out to illustrate the practicality of using computer simulation in scheduling construction projects, taking into account the associated uncertainties inherited in construction operations.

In conclusion, it is worth reaffirming that this book is not meant to look at simulation from within the different features of theory and application, nor is the goal of this book to look at simulation from traditional perspectives, in fact this book points toward illustrating the benefits and issues that arise from the application of simulation within other disciplines. As such, this book is organized in 22 chapters, sorted into five categories, while crossing paths with different disciplines, of which the first, *Simulation Prelude*, concentrated on simulation theory, while the second concentrated on *Petri Nets*, whereas the third section concentrated on *Monte Carlo*, besides the fourth section that shed light on *visualization and real-time simulation*, concluding in the fifth section, *living simulation*, which gave color to the black and white picture, as it discussed simulation applications in neural networks, data mining, networks, banks, construction.

Acknowledgment

The editors would like to acknowledge the relentless support of the IGI Global team, as their help and patience have been infinite and significant. Moreover, the authors would like to extend their gratitude to Mehdi Khosrow-Pour Executive Director of the Information Resources Management Association and Jan Travers the Vice President. Likewise, the authors would like to extend their appreciation to the Development Division at IGI Global; namely Julia Mosemann- the Development Editor, Rebecca Beistline- the Assistant Development Editor and Christine Bufton- the Editorial Assistant.

In this regard, the authors would like to express their recognition to their respective organizations and colleagues for the moral support and encouragement that have proved to be indispensable. In the same token, the editors would like to thank the reviewers for their relentless work and for their constant demand for perfection.

More importantly, the authors would like to extend their sincere appreciation and indebtedness to their family for their love, support, and patience. Also, as 2009 is the International Year of Astronomy, we dedicated this work in memory of the Father of Modern Science Galileo Galilei who stated once "But it does move".

Evon M. Abu-Taieh, PhD
Asim A. El-Sheikh, PhD
Editors

Chapter 1
Simulation:
Body of Knowledge

Istvan Molnar
Bloomsburg University of Pennsylvania, USA

ABSTRACT

This chapter attempts to define the knowledge body of simulation and describes the underlying principles of simulation education. It argues that any programs in Modelling and Simulation should recognize the multi- and interdisciplinary character of the field and realize the program in wide co-operation. The chapter starts with the clarification of the major objectives and principles of the Modelling and Simulation Program and the related degrees, based on a broad business and real world perspective. After reviewing students' background, especially communication, interpersonal, team, analytical and critical thinking skills, furthermore some of the additional skills facilitating entering a career, the employer's view and possible career paths are examined. Finally, the core knowledge body, the curriculum design and program related issues are discussed. The author hopes to contribute to the recent discussions about modelling and simulation education and the profession.

INTRODUCTION

Since the 70s, simulation education has been in the focus of attention. The growing acceptance of modelling and simulation (M&S) across different scientific disciplines and different major application domains (e.g., military, industry, services) increased the demand for well-qualified specialists. The place and recognition of modelling and simulation, however, is not very well recognized by academics; M&S as scientific disciplines are "homeless". This reflects and underlines the interdisciplinary and multidisciplinary nature of M&S and at the same time causes special problems in educational program and curriculum development.

Recognizing controversial developments and the fact that actions are necessary, different stakeholders of the international simulation community started to attack the problems. As part of the actions, Rogers (1997) and Sargent (2000) aimed to define M&S

DOI: 10.4018/978-1-60566-774-4.ch001

as a discipline, describing the characteristics of the profession, while Oren (2002) aimed at establishing its code of professional ethics. As a consequence of these efforts, questions were raised by Nance (2000) and Crosbie (2000) about the necessity, characteristics and content of an internationally acceptable educational program of simulation for different levels of education (undergraduate, graduate, and postgraduate). The first steps triggered a new wave of discussions by Szczerbicka (2000), Adelsberger (2000), Altiok (2001), Banks (2001), Nance and Balci (2001), followed by Harmon (2002) and Fishwick (2002) around the 50th anniversary of the Society for Computer Simulation and these discussions are not finished yet (e.g., Birta (2003a), Paul et al. (2003), and others). At the turn of the century, 50 years after the professional field was established, special attention was devoted to the subject of the simulation profession and the professional "simulationist", as well. Definition of the profession, along with possible programs and curricula were published, as were attempts to define the knowledge body of simulation discussed (e.g., Birta, 2003b and Oren 2008).

The growth of simulation applications in industry, government and especially in the military in the US, led to a growing demand for simulation professionals in the 90's. Academic programs have been introduced and standardization efforts undertaken; moreover, new organizations have been established to maintain different aspects of simulation. Europe has been following these trends with a slight delay. The Bologna Process is a European reform process aimed at establishing a European Higher Education Area by 2010. It is a process, driven by the 46 participating countries in cooperation with a number of international organizations; it is not based on an intergovernmental treaty. "By 2010 higher education systems in European countries should be organized in such a way that:

- it is easy to move from one country to the other (within the European Higher Education Area) – for the purpose of further study or employment;
- the attractiveness of European higher education is increased, so many people from non-European countries also come to study and/or work in Europe;
- the European Higher Education Area provides Europe with a broad, high quality and advanced knowledge base, and ensures the further development of Europe as a stable, peaceful and tolerant community." (Bologna Process, 2008)

These facts and developments call for action and international efforts to introduce changes in higher education based on the Bologna Process. As a result of the globalization of business, science and also education, it is expected that fundamental questions of educational practice will be regulated within the framework of or in compliance with the Bologna principles.

The model curriculum for graduate degree programs in M&S, which is the focus of this paper, is based on the typical degree structure, which is in compliance with the Bologna principles. Nevertheless, a number of U.S. higher education organizations (around 20% of the graduate schools) still resist accepting bachelor degrees of countries that signed the Bologna Treaty and deny that there are implications for the U.S. (see Jaschik 2006 and CGS Report 2007). The author's opinion is that progress cannot be stopped, especially not without viable alternative program(s). Because of the identical degree structure applied in the Bologna Process regulated countries, the US and Canada, the presented suggestions can be widely applied.

This paper attempts to define the knowledge body of simulation and the underlying principles of M&S education in relation to a Master's Degree program. The content representation intends to support the introduction of a curriculum model rather than concentration or option in an MBA or MS program. Placing this model curriculum into a specific context and the examination of the reasoning behind the degree structure and course content descriptions, allows it to be applied by educational program designers across the globe and helps to avoid difficulties of having to compare a large number of different educational systems. In addition, students with different background can use the model curriculum to obtain an overview of the discipline. Professionals and managers of different application areas can get a basic understanding of the qualifications and skills they can expect from recently hired new graduates .

The major strength of this contribution is that it discusses the related subjects in a new global, multi-disciplinary and quality-oriented perspective, built on solid foundations and providing flexible but modular educational approach, serving different knowledge levels and professional groups. A significant part of the questions about the necessity, characteristics and content of the M&S education have already been discussed in their different aspects in the early 90's in Europe. This was also the time when within the framework of the Eastern-European economic transition, higher education was being transformed by adapting key technologies whilst preserving the qualitative aspects of their system. Can the experience gained during this transition be reused?

OBJECTIVES OF THE M&S PROGRAM

The model curriculum is designed to reflect current and future industry needs, serve current standards, which can be used by higher educational institutions worldwide in their curriculum design. By adopting this model curriculum, faculty, students, and employers can be assured that M&S graduates are competent in a set of professional knowledge and skills, know about a particular application

domain in detail and are able to apply a strong set of professional values essential for success in the field.

Similarly to the MSIS Model Curriculum (Gorgone et al., 2006), the skills, knowledge, and values of M&S graduates are summarized in Figure 1. Accordingly, the curriculum model is designed as a set of interrelated building blocks and applies the "sliding window" concept.

The course-supply (the number and content of courses offered), is dictated by institutional resource constraints, while the demand (the students' choice of courses and course content), is dictated by the background of the students and the program objectives. The program size of the entire model curriculum from fundamentals to the most advanced courses consists of 20 courses; however, 12 courses are sufficient to finish successfully the program.

M&S graduates will have to have the following skills, knowledge and values (see Figure 1):

- Sound theoretical knowledge of M&S
- A core of M&S technology and management knowledge
- Integration of M&S knowledge into a specific application domain (e.g., business, engineering, science, etc.)
- Broad business and real world perspective
- Communication, interpersonal and team skills
- Analytical and critical thinking skills
- Specific skills leading to a career

The specification of the curriculum includes four components:

- *M&S Theoretical Foundations*: Most of the foundation courses serve as pre-requisite for the rest of the curriculum and provide an in-depth knowledge of basic M&S knowledge. Courses are designed to accommodate a wide variety of students' needs.

Figure 1. Skills, knowledge, and values of M&S graduates

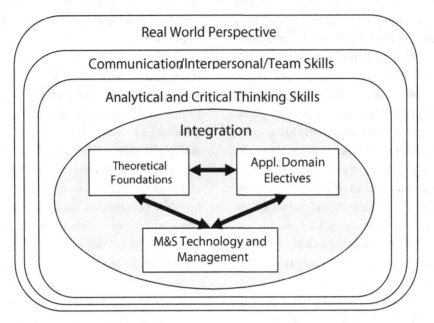

- *M&S Technology and Management:* These courses cover general and specific M&S related IT knowledge, furthermore educate students to work using collaboration and project management tools.
- *Integration*: An integration component is required after the core. This component addresses the increasing need to integrate a broad range of technologies and offers students the opportunity to synthesize theory and practice learned in a form of a capstone course, which also provides implementation experience for a comprehensive problem solution of a specific application domain.
- *Application Domain Electives (Career Tracks)*: High level flexibility can be achieved with courses that can be tailored to meet individual, group or institutional needs by selecting specific career tracks to address current needs.

A continuous assessment of the program must ensure that the objectives and expected outcomes of the M&S program are achieved. Quality assurance can take different forms and the measurement of student and program progress can use different methods; the emphasis should be rather on monitoring, analysis of the results and generating actions to further improve quality.

STUDENTS' BACKGROUND

It is often the case that students entering the M&S program have different backgrounds; students entering directly from undergraduate programs may have a BS or BA degree in Business (e.g., Information Systems), in Science (e.g., Computer Science), in Engineering (e.g., Electrical Engineering) or some other domain. The M&S program may also attract experienced professionals and people seeking career changes, who will study as part-time evening students and usually require access to the courses through a remote learning environment. With the rising volume of international student exchanges, international students' need must also be taken into account.

Table 1. Typical job objectives (career path) of M&S graduates

Engineer in design and development	Game designer/developer
Engineer in manufacturing and logistics planning	Systems analyst/designer
Engineer in energy production and dispatch	Supply chain manager
Engineer/Economist in BPR	Bank customer service analyst
Engineers/Scientist in aviation and space research	Military analyst
MDs and nurses in hospital operations	Researcher and Technical specialist
Financial (asset/liability/stock market) analyst	A Ph.D. program leading to research

The M&S program architecture accommodates a wide diversity of backgrounds and learning environments.

Background analysis usually does not cover any details about the quality aspects of the students' entry characteristics and related requirements, but quality concerns are strong, especially in mathematics and science in the US (see National Science Board 2008, pp.1: *"Relative ranking of U.S. students on international assessments gauges U.S. students performance against peers in other countries and economies. Among Organisation for Economic Co-operation and Development (OECD) nations participating in a recent assessment of how well 15-year-old students can use mathematics and science knowledge, U.S. students were at or near the bottom of the 29 OECD members participating."*). As a consequence, freshmen students' entry level knowledge can be very different (see PISA 2006), therefore solutions of the US universities should not be copied internationally without careful and critical analysis. Decisions, related to course content, must also take the above-mentioned facts in consideration.

CAREER PATHS

Applications are concentrated almost exclusively in government, military, large banks and industrial companies, as the M&S is rapidly gaining acceptance in major and mid-sized corporations. Career paths now include but are not restricted to:

- application domain related simulation model usage,
- simulation model development in a particular application domain (e.g., scientific research, government, military, industry, business and economics, education, etc.),
- simulation software development,
- consulting and systems integration.

Some of the typical job objectives of M&S graduates are listed in Table 1. The rapidly changing job market and the current demand can be best estimated by using job searching web-sites (e.g., http://careers.simplyhired.com/a/job-finder).

EMPLOYERS' VIEW

Because of the wide variety of M&S programs offered, employers are uncertain about the knowledge, skills, and values of new graduates. The students can ease employers' concerns by ensuring that they take a set of courses, which lays the foundation for practical experience in a particular simulation application domain.

It is a further advantage if students are able to help to overcome the skill shortage that exists in many of the major M&S application fields. It is a legitimate employer expectation that students graduating with an M&S degree should be able to take on job-related responsibilities (e.g., work independently on separate tasks or assignments) and also serve as mentor or middle-range manager to staff with lower level academic education (see Madewell and Swain, 2003).

PRINCIPLES OF M&S DEGREE

Author strongly believes that certain aspects of the specific M&S educational philosophy and principles need to be underlined separately. Based on (Molnar et al. 2008), some of these underlying philosophical aspects are listed as follows:

- *Simulation: Art or Science:* If we practice M&S, we certainly practice science and art at the same time; in different phases of the simulation modelling process different predominating elements of science and art appear. The whole process is always determined by time and space; we could say, determined by the "Zeitgeist" and "genus locii".
- *Central Role of Mathematical Modelling:* Because the strength of simulation will depend on the underlying model, mathematical modelling plays a crucial role in the M&S process. Creative thinking, holistic thinking and lateral thinking are important attributes that to a certain extent are innate but can be improved by practice and encouragement. In the process of modelling that uses the above skills, we contend that Art is a predominate factor.
- *Simulation software and applied technology:* One has to distinguish between developing simulation models and the use of ready-made simulation software. At the same time, the "mindless" use of ready-made simulation software, which only requires model computation and experimentation, is a kind of systematic, planned series of activities using a deterministic and finite machine, a computer, in order to search for conclusive evidence or for laws. Hence, this latter is exclusively a scientific

venture. Analysing the rough typology of computer simulation models to understand the implications for education, one can demonstrate that the use of simulation software tools and applied technologies need straightforward linear, convergent thinking. There is some technical and scientific expertise needed to make an appropriate selection of software or customise the software product itself; it might be time-consuming but relatively easy to learn and also to educate. The usage of simulation software and related applied technology increases programming efficiency and perhaps also overall project efficiency. It can also cause several problems and might be the source of significant errors. Nevertheless, the usage itself is not considered by the author as a central issue.

- *Skills needed for a good simulation:* Rogers (1997) classified several skills but only the most important are advocated by the author (see also Molnar, et al. 1996): good judgement, a thorough knowledge of mathematical statistics and probability theory; different ways of thinking; certain personal skills (e.g., communication skills, which also include listening to the person with the problem and translating those words into a model, ability to adapt and learn, learning to learn and life-long learning); some managerial expertise and team spirit. Supplementary issues related to general problems of the profession (e.g., responsibilities, value system, moral) are discussed in detail in Sargent (2000) and Oren (2002).

The philosophy discussed above serves as one element of the foundation of developing the M&S curriculum. In addition to this philosophy, some basic principles are also applied. These basic principles are a series of additional considerations, which are used to design the architecture of the

M&S program. The most important ones will be discussed briefly and cover the following:

- *Professional degree with added value:* The M&S is a professional degree, which adds value to students studying beyond the bachelor degree and integrates the information culture and the organizational culture. The investment of both the students and the employers will pay off.
- *Core courses:* The degree includes a standard set of core courses in M&S and related technology. Beside the core courses, the flexibility of the curriculum ensures the accommodation of students with differing background, skills, and objectives.
- *Career Tracks:* The curriculum focuses on current application domains and also provides great flexibility to include emerging concepts, "career tracks." This flexibility allows students to concentrate in a specific area within the competency of the faculty.
- *Integration of non-technical skills*: Ethics and professionalism, presentation skills (both, oral and written), negotiation, promotion of ideas, team and business skills, furthermore, customer orientation and real-world focus are integrated throughout the whole program.
- *Practicum:* A practicum is considered as a long project lasting one term and solves a real-world problem for a client within a given timeframe. It is recommended that institutions related to the application domain (e.g., industry) support the project by providing professional support and financial incentive, which increases the quality of the student output. The practicum can be applied as graduation requirement used instead or in addition of a master's thesis.
- *Capstone Integration:* The purpose of the capstone course is to integrate the program components and lead students into thinking about integration of M&S knowledge

and application-related technologies, policies and strategies.

- *Unit Requirements:* The program architecture is flexible and compatible with institutional unit requirements for an M&S degree. These requirements may range from 24 to 60 credit units, depending on the individual institution, program objectives, and student entry and exit characteristics.

THE DESCRIPTION OF THE M&S PROGRAM

The M&S program's building blocks are presented in Figure 2. The undergraduate courses are pre-requisites for the program. Students with missing pre-requisites or inadequate backgrounds are required to take additional courses.

The *M&S Core* defines the fundamental knowledge about M&S required from students and consists of two blocks the *M&S Theoretical Foundation* and *M&S Technology and Management* blocks. The core represents a standard that defines the M&S program and differentiates it from Computer Science, Information Systems or Science and Engineering programs and concentrations within these programs.

The *Integration* block is a one-semester capstone course and is fully devoted to a practical project.

The *Career Tracks* block consists of elective courses organized around careers.

According to Figure 2, the M&S program can be composed of different courses as the author suggests in Table 2. The pre-requisites are presented in three different versions based on students' professional orientation. Three typical M&S application domains are presented: Business and Economics, Engineering, and Computer Science.

The program's core courses are established rather along the scientific disciplines than the application domain, therefore the knowledge acquired by students is more flexible and portable.

Figure 2. Elements of the M&S program

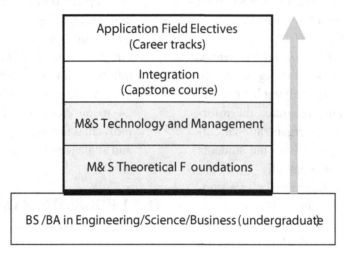

The sequence of the program blocks is strengthening the theoretical foundations and providing a learning path from the "general" theory to the "particular" application. This approach might serve well the described philosophy and helps to avoid application domain "blindness". Finally, this approach also supports the theoretically and methodologically founded applications of single application domains and beyond this, the multi- and interdisciplinary application domains. To increase learning efficiency, course-related knowl- edge body should be specified, paying special attention to control and restrict overlapping.

Table 2 also intends to provide a suggested course sequence within the blocks. This course sequence expresses a pre-requisite structure and can be used by students.

Table 3 clearly shows that students' choices depend on the individual institutional resources, the program objectives, and the student entry and exit characteristics. On the one hand, Table 3 is directly determined by the M&S knowledge body

Table 2. Pre-requisites for the M&S program

Pre-requisite	Additional application domain specific pre-requisites		
	Business and Economics	**Engineering**	**Computer Science**
BA/BS undergraduate degree	Critical Thinking	Critical Thinking	Critical Thinking
	Mathematical Thinking	Mathematical Thinking	Mathematical Thinking
	Programming, data and object structures	Programming, data and object structures	OO Programming Language
	Marketing or Organizational Behaviour	OO Systems Analysis and Design	OO Systems Analysis and Design
	Operations management	Software Engineering	Software Engineering
	IT Infrastructure	Systems Engineering	Mathematical Statistics
	Business Analysis	Dynamic Systems	IT Architectures
	Emerging Technologies	Emerging Technologies	Emerging Technologies
	Implications of Digitalization	Implications of Digitalization	Implications of Digitalization
	4-6 courses	*4-6 courses*	*4-6 courses*

Table 3. The complete M&S curriculum

M&S Theoretical Foundation	M&S Technology and Management	Integration	Application Domain Specific Electives
Systems Science	Model Description Formalisms		System Dynamics and Global Models
Mathematical Modelling	Simulation Languages a) Discrete, b) continuous, c) combined		Microsimulation and its Application
Computer Simulation	Symbolic Programming Languages a) Maple, b) Mathematica		Economic Dynamics and Macroeconomic Models
Computational Math. a) Numerical Methods	M&S Integrated Development Environments	I n t e g r a t i o n	Queuing Systems vs. Manufacturing (Logistics)
Computational Math. b) Stochastic Methods	Decision Support Systems		Training Simulators vs. Power Plant Application
Computational Math. c) Symbolic Computations	Distributed Systems		Game Simulators vs. Business Game
Simulation Data Analysis and Visualization	Software Quality Assurance		Dynamic Systems vs. Population Dynamics
Simulation Optimization	Project and Change Management		Embedded Simulation Systems vs.DSS
Emerging M&S related Technologies and Issues	Emerging M&S related Technologies and Issues		Emerging M&S related Application Domains
3-5 courses	*2-4 courses*	*1*	*2-4 courses*

and on the other hand its content helps to specify this knowledge body in details.

As indicated in Table 2, the M&S program can be minimum 24 units for well-prepared students and up to 60 units for students with no preparation, as described in Table 4.

The M&S knowledge body is heavily discussed (Birta 2003a, Birta 2003b and Oren, 2008). Sources evaluated clearly show that no consensus has been achieved yet. Table 2 reflects the author's professional values, perception and understanding of M&S and its education.

Table 5 demonstrates the details of four different courses in relation to the M&S knowledge body. The selected courses show a cross-sectional view and present one particular course with the knowledge body covered.

Based on the model curriculum presented, educational institutions can develop their own M&S program by following the basic steps described above.

Table 4. The "window size" of the program

Courses	Well prepared student	Student with no preparation
Core courses	15	27
Integration	3	3
Application domain	6	12
Additional required courses	-	18

Table 5. The rough course content used to define the detailed knowledge body

Computer Simulation	Emerging Technologies and Issues	Integrated Capstone	Implications of Digitization
Simulation modelling basics	Fuzzy modelling	Introduction to the M&S project	Ethics
Discrete, continuous and combined models	Agent-based modelling	Project realization based e.g., on prototyping life cycle	Virtual Work and Telecommuting
Random number generation	M&S of Business Processes	Project impact on the organization	Globalization and Outsourcing
Numerical integration	Data mining		Government. regulations
Simulation data analysis	SOA and Web Services		Implications of AI
Verification and validation	Mobile and Ubiquitous Computing		Intellectual Property
Experimental design, Sensitivity analysis	Business intelligence		Digital Divide
Simulation Optimization			Privacy

EDUCATIONAL PROBLEMS

Analysing the education of M&S, one can realize that the major difficulty lies in the "Janus-face" of simulation: both, artistic and scientific characteristics should be educated during the time available. The problems are discussed in detail in Molnar et al., 2008.

Within the frame of typical one semester simulation courses most lecturers are trying to teach different subjects, like system analysis, mathematical modelling, using simulation software, planning experiments and analysis of their results, and in addition to all these, specific knowledge of the application domain. Do we want too much?

Most of these courses are dedicated to students of different application domains (engineers, economists, etc.), sometimes even students of the broader field of computer science. None of the first group of students has deeper computer knowledge; none of the second group of students has deeper knowledge of the application domains. Worse, creative thinking is generally neglected in our present education systems. Following the organizational rules and the educational efficiency criteria can cause further problems (e.g., big class size).

Often raised question and a usual dilemma of many lecturers, how to create the curriculum for these courses, what phase of the simulation modelling process should be educated in detail, where the main point(s) of the course should be? Analysing the problem, basically two possibilities are given:

1. *Concentrate on mathematical modelling*: because of increasing complexity of real world systems and their mathematical models, one can put the question how to create mathematical models in the centre of the course. Instead of technical realisation and computational efforts, the lecturer can try to teach how to create a model, how to validate and use it.

2. *Concentrate on simulation software usage*: because of the complexity of modern simulation software tools, the education of simulation software and its usage is the main point of the course and can cover the whole semester if necessary. The main point of the course is how to use the software for simulation modelling purposes. In order to get the appropriate effect, the lecturer usually uses prepared models for demonstration

of software power. Thus, both mathematical models and simulation techniques are taught.

The lack of time makes the simultaneous teaching of mathematical modelling and software usage impossible. If the lecturer nevertheless tries to do so, she/he will be under continuous time pressure and have the feeling that the educational results are insufficient. Another problem addressed is the knowledge level of students (see national and international comparisons, e.g., National Science Board 2008 and PISA 2006).

The second solution, concentrating on software usage, is much more dangerous to implement, because it just transfers the actual technical level of knowledge (even though it is non-standardized and becomes quickly obsolete) and does not support the creative thinking process. The aggressive effort to cover the M&S life cycle in education does not make it possible to concentrate on the main problems of application. Nevertheless, following from the above, this concept is easier to teach.

Both approaches are having the fundamental disadvantage that the course is not delivered in co-operation and the interdisciplinary and multidisciplinary aspect of M&S education cannot prevail. Co-operation across departmental and college borders can help, but will never be able to resolve low enrolment problems or problems related to low student knowledge level, which also can further endanger the quality of the M&S program.

One can ask: is the profession 'simulationist' so difficult that one should teach both approaches at a high level of detail? Yes, the author thinks so, even if there are naturally endowed individual experts knowing both; these, however, usually work in teams! In order to teach both, the lecturer must introduce a curriculum that increases the quality of the mathematical modelling education and accept the fact that mathematical modelling and thus simulation is a kind of art and an intellectual challenge.

To achieve quality while keeping creative thinking, we suggest the introduction of a modular curriculum structure and use co-operation. In order to accomplish the educational goals, there is sometimes a possibility and organisational background to increase the time frame of the education and extend the curricula to more than one semester. An often accepted way of increasing the time frame of the M&S courses is the insertion of the first simulation course into the undergraduate curriculum, while maintaining the graduate and postgraduate level M&S courses. The extreme complexity of the M&S knowledge body, the inter- and multi-disciplinary nature of the different subjects and the large amount of different graduate courses are calling for institutional, even international co-operation (e.g., joint master curriculum, co-operation of MISS (McLeod Institute of Simulation Sciences) institutes, etc.).

The courses, offered based on a wide range of co-operation, can give an excellent possibility for meeting different student demands. Students have great freedom to choose one or more courses from the offered programs. In addition, the flexible course structure makes it possible to support important programs:

- Master programs (e.g., MBA or MS) in M&S
- PhD programs in M&S
- Retraining courses (for engineers and economists)
- Short-cycle retraining programs

CONCLUSION

It is a common problem in different countries to create simulation curricula that are able to cover the rapidly changing subject of M&S. Based on the long experience of the author in simulation education and in international curriculum development projects, a flexible, modular M&S model curriculum is suggested. The author sincerely hopes that this paper gives a flavour of M&S courses and readers are willing to rethink and discuss any of the points raised.

Finally, the author believes that all efforts to increase the quality of M&S education are well invested, because:

Seldom have so many independent studies been in such agreement: simulation is a key element for achieving progress in engineering and science. (Report of the National Science Foundation (NSF) Blue Ribbon Panel on Simulation-Based Engineering Science, May 2006)

REFERENCES

Adelsberger, H. H., Bick, M., & Pawlowski, J. M. (2000, December). *Design principles for teaching simulation with explorative learning environments.* In J. A. Joines, R. R. Barton, K. Kang & P. A. Fishwick (Eds.), *Proceedings of the 2000 Winter Simulation Conference*, Piscataway, NJ (pp. 1684-1691). Washington, DC: IEEE.

Altiok, T. (2001, December). Various ways academics teach simulation: are they all appropriate? In B. A. Peters, J. S. Smith, D. J. Medeiros, and M. W. Rohrer (Eds.), *Proceedings of the 2001 Winter Simulation Conference,* Arlington, VA, (pp. 1580-1591).

Banks, J. (2001, December). Panel session: Education for simulation practice – five perspectives. In B. A. Peters, J. S. Smith, D. J. Medeiros, & M. W. Rohrer (Eds.) *Proceedings of the 2001 Winter Simulation Conference,* Arlington, VA, (pp. 1571-1579).

Birta, L. G. (2003a). A Perspective of the Modeling and Simulation Body of Knowledge. *Modeling & Simulation Magazine, 2*(1), 16–19.

Birta, L. G. (2003b). *The Quest for the Modeling and Simulation Body of Knowledge.* Keynote presentation at the Sixth Conference on Computer Simulation and Industry Applications, Instituto Tecnologico de Tijuana, Mexico, February 19-21, 2003.

Bologna Process (2008). Strasbourg, France: Council of Europe, Higher Education and Research. Retrieved August 15, 2008, from http://www.coe.int/t/dg4/highereducation/EHEA2010/BolognaPedestrians_en.asp

Council of Graduate Schools. (2007). *Findings from the 2006 CGS International Graduate Admissions Survey, Phase III Admissions and Enrolment Oct. 2006, Revised March 2007.* Council of Graduate Schools Research Report, Council of Graduate Schools, Washington DC.

Crosbie, R. E. (2000, December). Simulation curriculum: a model curriculum in modeling and simulation: do we need it? Can we do it? In J. A. Joines, R. R. Barton, K. Kang & P. A. Fishwick, (Eds.) *Proceedings of the 2000 Winter Simulation Conference,* Piscataway, NJ, (pp. 1666-1668). Washington, DC: IEEE...

Fishwick, P. (2002). The Art of Modeling. *Modeling & Simulation Magazine, 1*(1), 36.

Gorgone, J. T., Gray, P., Stohr, E. A., Valacich, J. S., & Wigand, R. T. (2006). MSIS 2006. Model Curriculum and Guidelines for Graduate Degree Programs in Information Systems. *Communications of the Association for Information Systems, 17*, 1–56.

Harmon, S. Y. (2002, February-March). Can there be a Science of Simulation? Why should we care? *Modeling & Simulation Magazine, 1*(1).

Jaschik, S. (2006). Making Sense of 'Bologna Degrees.' *Inside Higher Ed.* Retrieved November 15, 2008 from http://www.insidehighered.com/news/ 2006/11/06/bologna

Madewell, C. D., & Swain, J. J. (2003, April-June). The Huntsville Simulation Snapshot: A Quantitative Analysis of What Employers Want in a Systems Simulation Professional. *Modelling and Simulation (Anaheim)*, *2*(2).

Molnar, I., Moscardini, A. O., & Breyer, R. (2009). Simulation – Art or Science? How to teach it? *International Journal of Simulation and Process Modelling*, *5*(1), 20–30. doi:10.1504/IJSPM.2009.025824

Molnar, I., Moscardini, A. O., & Omey, E. (1996, June). Structural concepts of a new master curriculum in simulation. In A. Javor, A. Lehmann & I. Molnar (Eds.), *Proceedings of the Society for Computer Simulation International on Modelling and Simulation ESM96*, Budapest, Hungary, (pp. 405-409).

Nance, R. E. (2000, December). Simulation education: Past reflections and future directions. In J. A. Joines, R. R. Barton, K. Kang & P. A. Fishwick, (Eds.) *Proceedings of the 2000 Winter Simulation Conference*, Piscataway, NJ (pp. 1595-1601). Washington, DC: IEEE.

Nance, R. E., & Balci, O. (2001, December). Thoughts and musings on simulation education. In B. A. Peters, J. S. Smith, D. J. Medeiros, & M. W. Rohrer (eds.), *Proceedings of the 2001 Winter Simulation Conference*, Arlington, VA (pp. 1567-1570).

National Science Board. (2008). *Science and Engineering Indicators 2008*. Arlington, VA: National Science Foundation.

Oren, T. I. (2002, December). Rationale for a Code of Professional Ethics for Simulationists. In E. Yucesan, C. Chen, J. L. Snowdon & J. M. Charnes (Eds.), *Proceedings of the 2002 Winter Simulation Conference*, San Diego, CA, (pp. 13-18).

Oren, T. I. (2008). *Modeling and Simulation Body of Knowledge*. SCS International. Retrieved May 31 2008 from http://www.site.uottawa.ca/~oren/MSBOK/ MSBOK-index.htm#coreareas

Paul, R. J., Eldabi, T., & Kuljis, J. (2003, December). Simulation education is no substitute for intelligent thinking. In S. Chick, P. J. Sanchez, D. Ferrin & D. J. Morrice (Eds.), *Proceedings of the 2003 Winter Simulation Conference*, New Orleans, LA, (pp. 1989-1993).

Program for International Student Assessment (PISA). (2006). *Highlights from PISA 2006*. Retrieved August 15, 2008 from Web site: http://nces.ed.gov/surveys/pisa/

Rogers, R. V. (1997, December) What makes a modelling and simulation professional? The consensus view from one workshop. In S. Andradottir, K. J. Healy, D. A. Whiters & B. L. Nelson (Eds.), *Proceedings of the 1997 Winter Simulation Conference*, Atlanta, GA (pp. 1375-1382). Washington, DC: IEEE...

Sargent, R. G. (2000, December). Doctoral colloquium keynote address: being a professional. In J. A. Joines, R. R. Barton, K. Kang and P. A. Fishwick (Eds.), *Proceedings of the 2000 Winter Simulation Conference*, Piscataway, NJ, (pp. 1595-1601). Washington, DC: IEEE.

Szczerbicka, H., et al. (2000, December). Conceptions of curriculum for simulation education (Panel). In J. A. Joines, R. R. Barton, K. Kang & P. A. Fishwick (Eds.), *Proceedings of the 2000 Winter Simulation Conference*, Piscataway, NJ (pp. 1635-1644). Washington, DC: IEEE.

KEY TERMS AND DEFINITIONS

Body of Knowledge (BoK): the sum of all knowledge elements of a particular professional field, defined usually by a professional organization.

Bologna Process: is a European reform process aiming to establish a European Higher Education Area by 2010. The process is driven by 46 participating countries and not based on an intergovernmental treaty.

Career Path: is a series of consecutive progressive achievements in professional life over an entire lifespan.

Curriculum: a set of courses offered by an educational institution. It means two things: on one hand, the curriculum defines a range of courses from which students choose, on the other hand the curriculum is understood as a specific learning program, which describes the teaching, learning, and assessment materials of a defined knowledge body available for a given course.

Education: refers to experiences in which students can learn, including teaching, training and instruction. Students learn knowledge, information and skills (incl. thinking skills) during the course of life. Learning process can include a teacher, a person who teaches.

Knowledge: the range of a person's information or understanding, or the body of truth, information, and principles acquired.

Model Curriculum or Curriculum Model: is an organized plan, a set of standards, defined learning outcomes, which describe systematically the curriculum.

Simulation Profession: it is a vocation based on specialised education or training in modeling and simulation, involves the application of systematic knowledge and proficiency of the modeling and simulation subject, field, or science to receive compensation. Modeling and simulation erose recently as a profession.

Skill: is a learned ability to do something in a competent way.

Chapter 2
Simulation Environments as Vocational and Training Tools

Evon M. O. Abu-Taieh
Civil Aviation Regulatory Commission and Arab Academy For Financial Sciences, Jordan

Jeihan M. O. Abutayeh
World Bank, Jordan

ABSTRACT

This paper investigates over 50 simulation packages and simulators used in vocational and course training in many fields. Accordingly, the 50 simulation packages were categorized in the following fields: Pilot Training, Chemistry, Physics, Mathematics, Environment and ecological systems, Cosmology and astrophysics, Medicine and Surgery training, Cosmetic surgery, Engineering – Civil engineering, architecture, interior design, Computer and communication networks, Stock Market Analysis, Financial Models and Marketing, Military Training and Virtual Reality. The incentive for using simulation environments as vocational and training tools is to save live, money and effort.

INTRODUCTION

Computer Simulation is widely used as an educational, as well as training tool in diverse fields; *inter alia* pilot training, chemistry, physics, mathematics, ecology, cosmology, medicine, engineering, marketing, business, computer communications networks, financial analysis etc., whereby computer simulation is used to train and teach students in many fields, not only to save: time, effort, lives, and money, but also to give them confidence in the matter at hand, in view that using computer simulation delivers the idea with sight and sound.

DOI: 10.4018/978-1-60566-774-4.ch002

Banks in 2000 summarized the incentives why we need simulation in the following reasons: Making correct choices, Compressing and expanding time, Understanding "Why?", Exploring possibilities, Diagnosing problems, Developing understanding, Visualizing the plan, Building consensus, Preparing for change. The reader can refer to (Banks, 2000) for more detailed study.

Moreover, computer simulation is considered a knowledge channel that transfers knowledge from an expert to newbie, thereby, training a pilot or a surgeon while using computer simulation, is in fact empowering the trainee with the knowledge of many expert pilots and expert surgeons. Accordingly, the

Figure 1. Simulation Applications in Educations and Training

paper shall discuss the simulation environments and packages used to train and teach in the following fields, as it is stipulated in (Figure 1):

1. Pilot Training.
2. Chemistry.
3. Physics.
4. Mathematics.
5. Environment and ecological systems.
6. Cosmology and astrophysics.
7. Medicine & Surgery training.
8. Cosmetic surgery.
9. Engineering – Civil engineering, architecture, interior design.
10. Computer and communication networks.
11. Stock market analysis, Financial Models, and Marketing.

12. Military Training and virtual reality.

In Pilot Training the paper discusses flight-safety, *Frasca*, *HAVELSAN*, and Thales. In Chemistry the simulators: Virtlab, REACTOR, ChemViz, ChemLab, NAMD and VMD are discussed. In regards to physics training Physics Simulator, PhET, Fission, RadSrc and CRY, ODE, Simbad, and TeamBots simulation packages will be discussed. In teaching mathematics by using simulation Matlab and STELLA are discussed in addition to statistical software like Fathom, DataDesk and Excel.

Environment and Ecological Systems, the paper will discuss SEASAM, The Agricultural Production Systems Simulator (APSIM), and Ecosim Pro simulation packages. In addition,

Table 1. Pilot training simulators

Simulator	Country of Origin	Website
FlightSafety International (FSI)	USA	www.flightsafety.com/
Frasca International, Inc.	USA	www.frasca.com/
Havelsan	Turkey	www.havelsan.com.tr/
Thales Group	France	www.thalescomminc.com
Rockwell Collins	USA	www.rockwellcollins.com
CAE Inc.	USA	www.cae.com/
Jeppesen	USA	www.jeppesen.com/

the five simulation packages: *Celestia, Computer Simulations of Cosmic Evolution, CLEA, Universe in a box: formation of large-scale structure*, and *WMAP Cosmology* will be discussed for Cosmology and Astrophysics. In the arena of Surgery training and Medicine: Human Patient Simulator (HPS), Emergency Care Simulator (ECS), and Laerdal SimMan will be discussed. Simulators used in Cosmetic Surgery that will be discussed in this paper include *Plastic Designer, LiftMagic, Virtual Cosmetic Surgery* and *MyBodyPart*.

In the Engineering simulation packages the paper discusses *EONreality, ANSYS,* and Full-Scale Virtual Walkthrough. The simulation packages used in computer and communication networks are: Anylogic and OptSim, and the paper will discuss both. In Stock Market Analysis, Financial Models and Marketing the simulation packages discussed are: Crews, Decision Script, Decision Pro, Crystalball and Anlaytica. For military training and virtual reality the following simulators will be discussed: World of Warcraft, Call of Duty, Disaster Response Trainer and Safety Solution.

PILOT TRAINING

Aircrafts simulators are used to train pilots fly. In this regard, there many types of simulators, as such, the National Aviation Authorities (NAA) for civil aircraft such as the U.S., the Federal Aviation Administration (FAA) and the European Aviation

Safety Agency (EASA) certify each category of simulators and test individual simulators within the approved categories. Simulators that pertain to aviation training can be categorized into two types: Flight Training Device (FTD) or Full Flight Simulator (FFS). In the same token, simulators are classified as Level 1-7 Flight Training Devices (FTD) or Level A-D full-flight simulators. The highest and most capable device is the Level D Full Flight Simulator, which can be used for the so-called Zero Flight Time (ZFT) conversions of already-experienced pilots from one type of aircraft to a type with similar characteristics. There many manufactures for such professional simulators as seen in Table 1.

FlightSafty is a product of FSI a corporation based in the USA. *FlightSafty* offers a wide range of simulation environments to many disciplines. *FlightSafty* trains pilots, aircraft maintenance technicians, ship operators, flight attendants and flight dispatchers using simulators that range from classroom-based desktop units to full-motion full flight simulators.

Frasca is a product of Frrasca International Incorporation and is also based in the USA. *Frasca* has products categories that include: general Aviation, Business Aircraft, Helicopters, Airlines, and Military (Fixed and rotary wings) and Visual systems.

HAVELSAN develops FAA Level C&D compatible Mission Simulators, Full Flight Simulators and Weapon System Trainers, in high fidelity, for cargo aircrafts, jet aircrafts and helicopters for military and civilian customers. In addition to full flight simulators; *HAVELSAN* provides maintenance, repair, operation, modification and supporting services. *HAVELSAN* is a product of *HAVELSAN* corporate which is based in Turkey.

Thales Group, Rockwell Collins and *CEA Inc.* all three compete in the army oriented kind of simulation environment in addition to civil aviation environment, whereas, Jeppesen is a subsidiary of Boeing Commercial Aviation Services and a unit of Boeing Commercial Airplanes.

CHEMISTRY

When tackling the subject of chemistry, the words *visualization, making sense, cognition, independence*, and *understanding* come to mind. Within this context, in the area of chemistry experiments, simulators work as a visualization tool or visual aid to both the teacher and the student, in view that molecules are too small to see and control. Likewise, conducting the experiment while using a simulator is considered safe in addition, it gives the student the needed independence, while the same experiment can be repeated over and over. In the same token, the student cognition may improve by repetition, especially for students with slow understanding rate, while giving the other students with faster rate of understanding the chance to explore other options in the experiment in a safe environment. The aforementioned is significantly preferred, in view that practicing the experiment before actually conducting it, would give the student the confidence needed. More importantly, another motivation for such simulators is distance learning, although the say is "seeing is believing", however, simulators may provide the student with the needed knowledge without actually conducting the experiment, thereby accentuating the intellectual capability of a student. In this regard, some of the well known simulators in this arena are Virtlab, REACTOR,

ChemViz, ChemLab, NAMD and VMD; which will be discussed next.

Virtlab (www.virtlab.com/) is web based simulator where teachers can use it as visual aid and students can experiment safely with chemicals, whereas, *REACTOR Prep Labs* from *Late Nite Labs* (www.latenitelabs.com/), students perform and analyze advanced hands-on simulations that are easy and enjoyable to use, and then enter the wet lab prepared, confident and ready to work.

ChemViz (Chemistry Visualization) is an interactive chemistry program which incorporates computational chemistry simulations and visualizations for use in the chemistry classroom (education.ncsa.uiuc.edu/products/chemviz/index.html).

ChemLab (www.soft14.com/Home_and_Education/Science/ChemLab_251_Review.html) originated from academic work in computer simulation and software design at McMaster University. It has continued to be developed with extensive input from educators interested in the possible application of computer simulations for classroom and distance learning. Model *ChemLab* incorporates both an interactive simulation and a lab notebook workspace with separate areas for theory, procedures and student observations. Commonly used lab equipment and procedures are used to simulate the steps involved in performing an experiment, whereby users step-through the actual lab procedure while interacting with animated equipment in a way that is similar to the real lab experience. Furthermore, *ChemLab* comes with a range of pre-designed lab experiments for general chemistry at the high school and college level, likewise, users can expand upon the original lab set using ChemLab's LabWizard development tools, thereby allowing for curriculum specific lab simulation development by educators, worthwhile to note that these user-designed simulations combine both text based instructions and the simulation into a single distributable file.

NAMD and its sister visualization program *VMD* (www.ks.uiuc.edu/Research/vmd/) helped scientists discern how plants harvest sunlight, how muscles stretch and how kidneys filter water. Both are used to teach and train students in the MIT. VMD (Virtual DNA Viewer) is a molecular visualization program for displaying, animating, and analyzing large bio-molecular systems using 3-D graphics and built-in scripting.

Conclusively, all five simulators: Virlab, REACTOR , ChemViz, ChemLab, NAMD and VMD allow the student/trainee to experiment in the chemistry world within the safety borders.

PHYSICS

It is known that the study of physics entails: Motion, Energy and power, Sound and waves, Heat and Thermo, Electricity, Magnets and circuits, light and radiation, as such, the use of simulation and multimedia-based systems provide the students with extensively rich source of educational material in a form that makes learning exciting. Pithily, the subsequent six simulators will be discussed: Physics Simulator, PhET, Fission, RadSrc and CRY, ODE, Simbad, and TeamBots

Physics Simulator (www.simtel.net/pub/pd/53712.shtml) simulates the dynamics of particles under the influence of their gravitational and/or electrostatic interactions.

The Physics Education Technology (PhET) (http://phet.colorado.edu/get_phet/index.php) project is an ongoing effort to provide an extensive suite of simulations for teaching and learning physics and chemistry and to make these resources both freely available from the *PhET* website and easy to incorporate into classrooms.

PhET simulations animate what is invisible to the eye, such as atoms, electrons, photons and electric fields. User interaction is encouraged by engaging graphics and intuitive controls that include click-and-drag manipulation, sliders and radio buttons. By immediately animating the response to any user interaction, the simulations are particularly good at establishing cause-and-effect and at linking multiple representations.

In the Computational Nuclear Physics Group (CNP) the Lawrence Livermore National Laboratory (LLNL) provide three distinct simulation codes (nuclear.llnl.gov/CNP/Home/CNP_Home.htm): cosmic-ray shower distributions near the Earth's surface, gamma-ray source spectra from nuclear decay of aged mixtures of radioisotopes, and discrete neutron and gamma-ray emission from *fission*.

Fission: Simulates discrete neutron and gamma-ray emission from the fission of heavy nuclei that is either spontaneous or neutron induced (Verbeke, Hagmann, & Wright, 2008). *RadSrc* Calculates intrinsic gamma-ray spectrum from the nuclear decay of a mixture of radioisotopes (Hiller, Gosnell, Gronberg, & Wright, 2007).

Cosmic-ray Shower (CRY): Generates correlated cosmic-ray particle showers at one of three elevations (sea level, 2100m, and 11300m) for use as input to transport and detector simulation codes (Hagmann, Lange, & Wright, 2008).

Open Dynamics Engine (ODE) (www.ode.org/) is an open source, high performance library for simulating rigid body dynamics. ODE is useful for simulating vehicles, objects in virtual reality environments and virtual creatures. It is currently used in many computer games, 3D authoring tools and simulation tools. ODE is BSD-licensed. (Russell, 2007)

Simbad (simbad.sourceforge.net/) is a Java 3D robot simulator for scientific and educational purposes. It is mainly dedicated to researchers/programmers who want a simple basis for studying Situated Artificial Intelligence, Machine Learning, and more generally AI algorithms, in the context of Autonomous Robotics and Autonomous Agents. It is not intended to provide a real world simulation and is kept voluntarily readable and simple. (Simbad Project Home, 2007).

TeamBots (www.cs.cmu.edu/~trb/TeamBots/) is a portable multi-agent robotic simulator that supports simulation of multi-agent control systems in dynamic environments with visualization, for example teams of soccer-playing robots. (Balch, 2000)

MATHEMATICS

Mathematics is multi-dimensional discipline that involves the study of quantity, structure, space and change, noting that mathematics, as well as statistics are considered an integral part of simulation, as such, simulation software is used to teach mathematics and statistics.

In addition, considering mathematics includes many sub-topics like: *Algebra and Number Theory, Geometry and Trigonometry, Functions and Analysis, Data Analysis, Statistics, and Probability, and Discrete Mathematics and Computer Science*–Graphs, trees, and networks; enumerative combinatorics; iteration and recursion; conceptual underpinnings of computer science, accordingly, (Nelson, 2002) has cited number of reasons that motivate teaching mathematics using simulation:

1. Visualization
2. Algorithmic Representation of Probability
3. Sensitivity or Insensitivity of Results to Assumptions
4. Connecting Probability to Statistics
5. Integrating Probability and Simulation Supports a Unified Treatment of Stochastic Modeling and Analysis

Matlab (www.mathworks.com/)is used in teaching Differential Equations, Linear Algebra, Multivariable Calculus, Finite Elements in Elastic Structures, Optimization, and Mathematical Theory of Waves among others.

STELLA (www.iseesystems.com/softwares/) offers a practical way to dynamically visualize and communicate how complex systems and ideas really work. STELLA helps visual learners discover relationships between variables in an equation. Verbal learners might surround visual

models with words or attach documents to explain the impact of a new environmental policy.

Other simulators like *Fathom* (www.keycollege.com/catalog/titles/fathom.html), *DataDesk* (www.datadesk.com/) and *Excel* (www.microsoft.com) are also used in the statistics arena.

ENVIRONMENT AND ECOLOGICAL SYSTEMS

The term ecosystem was coined in 1930 by Roy Clapham, to denote the physical and biological components of an environment considered in relation to each other as a unit. British ecologist Arthur Tansley later refined the term, describing it as "The whole system,… including not only the organism-complex, but also the whole complex of physical factors forming what we call the environment" (Tansley, 1935). Needless to say, when studying the ecosystem or environment there are many variables to consider; among them a very important element is TIME. Using simulators to teach and train students is an essential aspect, whereby, many simulators used for teaching and training ecosystems, mainly there are SEASAM, The Agricultural Production Systems Simulator (APSIM), and Ecosim Pro., which are all discussed next.

*SEASAM (*www.seasam.com/)is a software environment *SESAME* is a model development and analysis tool designed to facilitate the construction of ecological models using Fortran-77 on UNIX machines. (P. Ruardija, 1995).

The Agricultural Production Systems Simulator (APSIM) (www.apsim.info/) is a modular modeling framework that has been developed by the Agricultural Production Systems Research Unit in Australia. APSIM was developed to simulate biophysical process in farming systems, in particular where there is interest in the economic and ecological outcomes of management practice in the face of climatic risk. (B. A. Keating, 2003)

*Ecosim Pro (*www.ecosimpro.com*)* a powerful simulation environment for very complex hybrid systems (thermal fluid dynamics, chemical, mechanical, electrical, etc). *Ecosim* was used as real-time simulator for large scale cryogenic systems of CERN (European Organization for Nuclear Research) using helium refrigerators controlled by Programmable Logic Controllers (PLC). *Ecosim* Pro was used as a a tool to train the operators in this project. (Bradu, Gayet, & Niculescu, 2007).

Conclusively, the three simulators; SEASAM, The Agricultural Production Systems Simulator (APSIM), and Ecosim Pro; allow the student to experiment and test the different elements of environment within a safety net.

COSMOLOGY AND ASTROPHYSICS

Cosmology is the scientific study of the origin and evolution of the Universe. As such it obviously seeks to address some of the most profound questions in science. It is a lively and rapidly evolving field of inquiry. Technological improvements within the last decade have led to discoveries that have radically altered our understanding of the Universe. Software-based activities provide an interesting and effective way of engaging students and demonstrating some of the principles and technologies involved, in this regard, it is significant to note that there are several websites that can be browsed where supercomputer simulations of the formation of galaxies, star clusters and large-scale structure can be viewed. These are useful in conveying the role of simulation and mathematical modeling in modern cosmology and astrophysics.

Throughout the course of this paper, five Cosmology and astrophysics simulators are introduced: *Celestia, Computer Simulations of Cosmic Evolution, CLEA, Universe in a box: formation of large-scale structure, and WMAP Cosmology.*

Celestia: A 3D Space Simulator (www.shatters. net/celestia/) is an outstanding free software pack-

age with a wealth of add-ons, with a multi-platform package (Windows, Mac OS, Linux, Unix) that would allow the Solar System and galaxy to be visualized using real astronomical data, actually it would feel real, in terms of enabling the viewed to "fly" to other stars; visit the planets and even piggybank on any of the current or planned space probes, as such, this tool is considered an excellent educational add-ons, noting that there are interactive learning documents including one on stellar evolution available from another website (www.fsgregs.org/celestia/).

Computer Simulations of Cosmic Evolution (www.astro.washington.edu/weblinks/ Universe/ Simulations.html) provides over a dozen animations on galaxies and formation of large-scale structure.

Project CLEA (www.gettysburg.edu/academics/physics/clea/CLEAhome.html) allows the user to download free programs and manuals that allow user to simulate observing, obtaining and analyzing data. *The Hubble Redshift-Distance Relation* and *Large-Scale Structure of the Universe* are particularly relevant for this module whilst others are excellent for Astrophysics. These are excellent simulations that utilize real data.

Universe in a box: formation of large-scale structure (cosmicweb.uchicago.edu/sims.html) from the Center for Cosmological Physics at the University of Chicago has a set of pages and animations of supercomputer simulations on how large-scale structure forms, where it discusses cold dark matter models.

WMAP Cosmology 101: Our Universe (map. gsfc.nasa.gov/m_uni/uni_101ouruni.html) provides a clear introduction into modern cosmology, albeit it may be too detailed for most students, it is however useful for teachers and students who would want more details.

SURGERY TRAINING AND MEDICINE

"Combining the sense of touch with 3-D computer models of organs, researchers at Rensselaer Polytechnic Institute are developing a new approach to training surgeons, much as pilots learn to fly on flight simulators. With collaborators at Harvard Medical School, Albany Medical Center, and the Massachusetts Institute of Technology, the team is developing a virtual simulator that will allow surgeons to touch, feel, and manipulate computer-generated organs with actual tool handles used in minimally invasive surgery (MIS)." (ScienceDaily, 2006). Some of the well known medicine and surgery simulators are: Human Patient Simulator (HPS), Emergency Care Simulator (ECS), and Laerdal SimMan (www.cesei.org/simulators.php).

METI Human Patient Simulator (HPS): is full-sized mannequin is ultra sophisticated and highly versatile with programmed cardiovascular, pulmonary, pharmacological, metabolic, genitourinary (male and female), and neurological systems. It blinks, speaks and breathes; it has a heartbeat and a pulse, and accurately mirrors human responses to procedures such as CPR, intravenous medication, intubation, ventilation, and catheterization.

METI Emergency Care Simulator (ECS): Specially designed to support emergency care and trauma scenarios, this full-sized mannequin is portable, creating the opportunity to train learners in any environment. The ECS offers much of the same technology as the HPS, but optimizes emergency scenarios to expose students to the most complicated and high-risk situations.

Laerdal SimMan: is full-body mannequin offers scenarios similar to the METI simulators with the addition of an anatomically accurate bronchial tree, providing learners the opportunity to respond to airway complication scenarios and practice advanced procedures relative to the training needs of anesthesia, ACLS, ATLS, and difficult airway management.

COSMETIC SURGERY

Simulators used in cosmetic surgery applications can be a valuable tool for both the doctor and the patient, whereby the patient can see in advance if the results of a chosen procedure will suit their anatomical goals, in addition, they can experiment a variety of looks to make sure they are confident about the body aesthetic they really want to achieve. In retrospect, the doctor can use the process as a way to insure good communication with the patient. The doctor can actually see the result the patient wants and can save the image as a visual reference to be utilized during surgery. This virtual result makes it clear to both parties the exact look which is expected at the end of the healing process. Virtual reality can make the entire surgical process far easier for both doctor and patient and generally leads to more satisfying results with less pre-operative anxiety.

Plastic Designer (www.nausoft.net/eng/products/plastic/index.html) is new generation of plastic surgery software from NauSoft. *Plastic Designer* is plastic surgery imaging software allows physicians to work with a computer-based solution specifically to the needs of their practice. With the help of State-of-the-Art real time morphing algorithms, wide range of art tools (wrinkle smoother, skin pigment sprayer, sculpt builder and others) and multilevel undo functions, a physician can easily produce image modification in minimal time.

Plastic Designer plastic surgery makeover software provides: Aesthetic Imaging and Post-Operation outcome modeling, Laser resurfacing, Cosmetic surgery simulation, 3 powerful morphing algorithms, Automatic modeling for rihinopelasty, Pre-Operation Analysis, Automatically measures the main lengths, proportions and angles for Naso-facial operations, Manual measurements are available, Data Table shows the current dimensions, the individual norm and the difference, Operative Planning, Assessment list, Pre-Op list, Medical

Documentation, Medical Images processing and archiving, Slides Presentation.

LiftMagic (www.liftmagic.com/) is a software that is web based simulation program, where it allows the user to upload a frontal face image and then try out the different wanted procedures, as the software then shows the *before* and *after* affect of the procedures, thereby the software allows Face Processing Tools: Forehead enhancement, Eyebrow lift, Mid-brow enhancement, Around eyes enhancement, Beside eye enhancement, Tear trough enhancement, Inner cheek enhancement, Outer cheek enhancement, Cheek lift, Nose reduction, Outer lip lift, Lip augmentation, Jaw restoration, Weight reduction:

Virtual Cosmetic Surgery, which is a computer software that was developed to simulate an actual surgical procedure on the human body. First, the doctor will photograph patient and upload these images into the computer, then the doctor would discuss patient preferences for surgery and the look patient is trying to achieve, after that, the surgeon would enter these parameters into the computer which will adjust patient actual body image according to the doctor's commands. These alterations will simulate the exact methods used during actual plastic surgery and will give the patient a good idea of how s/her will look after undergoing the chosen operation.

MyBodyPart (www.mybodypart.com/), which can be downloaded to a PC and the patient, as well as, the surgeon can experiment with different scenarios. As such, the simulator allows the user to experiment with replacing different body parts rather than morphing the existing one.

ENGINEERING – CIVIL ENGINEERING, ARCHITECTURE, INTERIOR DESIGN

In engineering the National Science Foundation (NSF) supported research in the report "Revolutionizing Engineering Science through Simula-

tion" in May 2006 to emphasize the importance of using simulation in college curricula, in order to revolutionize the Engineering science (NSF-Panel, 2006).

In this regard, civil engineers use simulation software to guide design and construction as well as to solve a wide range of projects in: Building, Environmental engineering, Geotechnical engineering, Hydraulic engineering, Materials science, Structural engineering, Transportation engineering and Wind engineering.

One of the simulation software used for educational and training purposes in civil engineering arena is *EONreality* (www.eonreality.com/), noting that the applications of the *EONreality* are discussed by (Sampaio & Henriques, 2008) in their paper "Visual simulation of Civil Engineering activities: Didactic virtual models".

Another software is *ANSYS* (www.ansys.com/solutions/default.asp). *ANSYS* designs, develops, markets and globally supports engineering simulation solutions used to predict how product designs will behave in manufacturing and real-world environments. Its integrated, modular and extensible set of solutions addresses the needs of organizations in a wide range of industries. *ANSYS* solutions qualify risk, enabling organizations to know if their designs are acceptable or unacceptable not just that they will function as designed.

Full-Scale Virtual Walkthrough (www.world-viz.com/solutions/architecture.html): would literally allow a walk through the architectural designs in full scale and experience a stunning sense of the space in 3D.

COMPUTER AND COMMUNICATION NETWORKS

In order to learn about computer architecture and the tricks of the communication networks, there are professional simulation packages, such as *AnyLogic* and *OptSim*, which are both discussed next.

AnyLogic (www.xjtek.com)is based on UML and has big library of examples. *AnyLogic* is one of the few hybrid simulation packages, with application areas that include: Control Systems, Traffic, System Dynamics, Manufacturing, Supply Chain, Logistics, Telecom, Networks, Computer Systems, Mechanics, Chemical, Water Treatment, Military, and Education.

Optsim was known as *Artifex (*www.rsoftdesign.com*)*, is a tool based on Petri Nets. *Optsim* is one of the few packages that can handle both discrete and Continuous systems. *Optsim* applications are: Performance evaluation of the transmission level of Optical Communications systems, Network Modeling, Strategic analysis.

STOCK MARKET ANALYSIS, FINANCIAL MODELS AND MARKETING

There many simulation-based games that are used to learn how to trade in the stock exchange markets. In fact, students can "earn their Stock Broker License and then in turn apply for a business license to create their own investment company" as the schools website promises (Crews). Gwinnett County Public Schools the owner of the website is a public school that teaches children stock exchange, where the game is setup as part of computer science curriculum for eighth graders; the game is web-based simulation (www.crews. org/curriculum/ex/compsci/ 8thgrade/ stkmkt/ index.htm).

However, in order to learn Financial Planning & Modeling and Marketing in the real world, there are other more professional simulation packages like Decision Script, Decision Pro, Crystalball and Anlaytica.

DecisionScript along with *DecisionPro* (www. vanguardsw.com)are made by Vanguard except that *DecisionScript* is web based (vanguardsw), which provides applications that include: Military Financial Planning, Online Sales Assistance,

Management Reporting, Portfolio Simulation, Business Financial Modeling, Process Optimization, Decision-Making, Strategic Planning, Marketing, Finance Accounting, Operations, and Human Resources.

The package *Crystal Ball* (www.crystalball. com)has two versions that are sold commercially, one is standard, while the other is professional. *Crystal Ball* is an add-in for Microsoft Excel spreadsheet. The package is developed by using Visual Basic, based on the famous Monte Carlo, which offers applications that include: Business Planning And Analysis, Cost/Benefit Analysis, Risk Management, Petroleum Exploration, Portfolio Optimization, and Project Management (OR/ MS, 2003)

Analytica (www.lumina.com)is graphical user interface software that is used, among other things, for business modeling and decision and risk analysis, moreover, it is a visual tool for creating, analyzing, and communicating decision models" (Analytica, 2006). *Analytica* uses influence diagrams which Lumina claims to be "The perfect visual format for creating and communicating a common vision of objective issues, uncertainties and decisions" (Analytica, 2006)

MILITARY TRAINING AND VIRTUAL REALITY

Simulation is used to train military as well as disaster response teams, accordingly, many simulators are built for such purposes *inter alia*: MRE, World of Warcraft, Call of Duty, Disaster Response Trainer and Safety Solution.

Mission Rehearsal Exercise (MRE) is part of an elaborate high-tech simulator that is being developed by a contractor for the U.S. military to help train soldiers heading for combat, peacekeeping and humanitarian missions. This package actually reflects on a larger Pentagon policy to use technology to train the video game generation now entering the service. Additionally, the developers at the Institute of Creative Technologies (ICT) -- which created MRE -- are working in conjunction with storytellers from the entertainment industry; technologists and educators from the University of Southern California (USC); and Army military strategists, as well as the Los Angeles, California-based ICT was formed in 1999 to research the best types of simulators to be used by the military.(www.globalsecurity.org/education/index.html)

World of Warcraft and *Call of Duty* are additional VR Military training simulation packages, where *World of Warcraft* has more than eleven million subscribers for the game. Following is the website address that can provide the user with a trail version (https://signup.worldofwarcraft. com/trial/index.html;jsessionid=65296B939D4 3EA128E7243D9AFD9B5AC.app10_05). On the other hand *Call of Duty* is available on the website (www.callofduty.com/).

Disaster Response Trainer: Methodist University commissioned *WorldViz* to construct a turnkey solution for their new Environmental Simulation Center, as part of the university's Occupational Environmental Management Program. The center trains participants in environmental and Industrial disaster prevention and management. Using such simulation packages, the participants are given the opportunity to apply classroom knowledge in immersive virtual training environments. University students, local catastrophe response teams, industry employees, and Fort Bragg Army personnel will use the center.

Safety Solution: Simulate workplace environments, safety hazards, or machinery operation in ultra-realistic interactive 3D virtual environments, thereby making safety training more effective than before. Both *Disaster Response Trainer and Safety Solution* from (www.worldviz.com/)

CONCLUSION

This paper studied more than 50 simulation packages (simulators) used for the purpose of education and training in many fields. The 50 simulators were categorized in the following fields: Pilot Training, Chemistry, Physics, Mathematics, Environment and Ecological Systems, Cosmology and Astrophysics, Medicine & Surgery Training, Cosmetic Surgery, Engineering – Civil Engineering, Architecture, Interior Design, Computer and Communication Networks, Stock Market Analysis, Financial Models, and Marketing, Military Training and Virtual Reality.

In Pilot Training the paper discussed flight-safety, *Frasca, HAVELSAN*, and Thales. In Chemistry the simulators: Virtlab, REACTOR, ChemViz, ChemLab, NAMD and VMD were discussed. In regards to physics training Physics Simulator, PhET, Fission, RadSrc and CRY, ODE, Simbad, and TeamBots simulation packages were discussed. In teaching mathematics by using simulation Matlab and STELLA were discussed in addition to statistical software like Fathom, DataDesk and Excel.

Vis-à-vis Environment and Ecological Systems, the paper discussed SEASAM, The Agricultural Production Systems Simulator (APSIM), and Ecosim Pro simulation packages. In addition, the five simulation packages: *Celestia, Computer Simulations of Cosmic Evolution, CLEA, Universe in a box: formation of large-scale structure*, and *WMAP Cosmology* were discussed for Cosmology and Astrophysics. In the arena of Surgery training and Medicine: Human Patient Simulator (HPS), Emergency Care Simulator (ECS), and Laerdal SimMan were discussed. Simulators used in Cosmetic Surgery that are discussed in this paper include *Plastic Designer, LiftMagic, Virtual Cosmetic Surgery* and *MyBodyPart*.

In the Engineering simulation packages the paper discussed *EONreality, ANSYS,* and Full-Scale Virtual Walkthrough. The simulation packages used in computer and communication networks were: Anylogic and OptSim, and the paper tackled both. In Stock Market Analysis, Financial Models and Marketing the simulation packages discussed were: Crews, Decision Script, Decision Pro, Crystalball and Anlaytica. For military training and virtual reality the following simulators were discussed: World of Warcraft, Call of Duty, Disaster Response Trainer and Safety Solution.

Using computer simulation delivers the idea with sight and sound which gives the student confidence in the matter at hand. When training a pilot or a surgeon by using computer simulation, the trainee is actually given the knowledge of many expert pilots and expert surgeons. Therefore, computer simulation is a knowledge channel that transfers knowledge from an expert to newbie.

REFERENCES

Analytica. (2006). *Lumina*. Retrieved 2008, from Analytica: www.lumina.com

Balch, T. (2000, 4). *TeamBots*. Retrieved 10 2008, from Carnegie Mellon University - SCholl of Computer science: http://www.cs.cmu.edu/~trb/TeamBots/

Banks, J. (2000, December 10-13). *Introduction To Simulation*. In J. A. Joines, R. R. Barton, K. Kang, & P. A. Fishwick (Eds.), *Proceedings of the 2000 Winter Simulation Conference*, Orlando, FL, (pp. 510-517). San Diego, CA: Society for Computer Simulation International.

Bradu, B., Gayet, P., & Niculescu, S.-I. (2007). A Dynamic Simulator for Large-Scale Cryogenic Systems. In R. K. B. Zupančič (Ed.), *Proc. EU-ROSIM*, (pp. 1-8).

Crews, W. (n.d.). *Gwinnett County Public Schools*. Retrieved 2008, from Gwinnett County Public Schools, http://www.crews.org/curriculum/ex/compsci/8thgrade/stkmkt/index.htm

Hagmann, C., Lange, D., & Wright, D. (2008, 1). *Cosmic-ray Shower Library (CRY)*. Retrieved 10 2008, from Lawrence Livermore National Laboratory, http://nuclear.llnl.gov/

Hiller, L., Gosnell, T., Gronberg, J., & Wright, D. (2007, November). *RadSrc Library and Application Manual*. Retrieved October 2008, from http://nuclear.llnl.gov/

Keating, B. A., P. S. (2003). An overview of APSIM, a model designed for farming systems simulation. *European Journal of Agronomy*, *18*(3-4), 267–288. doi:10.1016/S1161-0301(02)00108-9

Nelson, B. L. (2002). Using Simulation To Teach Probability. In C.-H. C. E. Yücesan (Ed.), *Proceedings of the 2002 Winter Simulation Conference* (p. 1815). San Diego, CA: informs-cs.

NSF-Panel. (2006, May). *Revolutionizing Engineering Science through Simulation*. Retrieved 2008, from Report of the National Science Foundation Blue Ribbon Panel on Simulation-Based Engineering Science, http://www.nsf.gov/pubs/reports/sbes_final_report.pdf

OR/MS. (2003). *OR/MS*. Retrieved from OR/MS, www.lionhrtpub.com/orms/surveys/Simulation/Simulation.html

Ross, M. D. (n.d.). *3-D Imaging In Virtual Environment: A Scientific, Clinical And Teaching Tool*. Retrieved from United States National Library of Medicine- National Institiute of Health, http://biocomp.arc.nasa.gov/

Ruardija, P., J. W.-B. (1995). SESAME, a software environment for simulation and analysis of marine ecosystems. *Netherlands Journal of Sea Research*, *33*(3-4), 261–270. doi:10.1016/0077-7579(95)90049-7

Russell, S. (2007, May). *Open Dynamics Engine*. Retrieved October 2008, from Open Dynamics Engine, http://www.ode.org/

Sampaio, A., & Henriques, P. (2008). Visual simulation of Civil Engineering activities: Didactic virtual models. *International Conferences in Central Europe on Computer Graphics, Visualization and Computer Vision.* Czech Republic: University of West Bohemia.

ScienceDaily. (2006). Digital Surgery With Touch Feedback Could Improve Medical Training. *ScienceDaily.*

Simbad Project Home. (2007, Dec). Retrieved 1 2008, from Simbad Project Home: http://simbad.sourceforge.net/

vanguardsw. (n.d.). *vanguardsw.* Retrieved 2008, from vanguardsw: www.vanguardsw.com

Verbeke, J. M., Hagmann, C., & Wright, D. (2008, February 1). http://nuclear.llnl.gov/simulation/fission.pdf. Retrieved October 1, 2008, from Computational Nuclear Physics, http://nuclear.llnl.gov/simulation/

Chapter 3
Agent–Based Modeling:
A Historical Perspective and a Review of Validation and Verification Efforts

Brian L. Heath
Wright State University, USA

Raymond R. Hill
Air Force Institute of Technology, USA

ABSTRACT

Models and simulations have been widely used as a means to predict the performance of systems. Agent-based modeling and agent distillations have recently found tremendous success particularly in analyzing ground force employment and doctrine. They have also seen wide use in the social sciences modeling a plethora of real-life scenarios. The use of these models always raises the question of whether the model is correctly encoded (verified) and accurately or faithfully represents the system of interest (validated). The topic of agent-based model verification and validation has received increased interest. This chapter traces the historical roots of agent-based modeling. This review examines the modern influences of systems thinking, cybernetics as well as chaos and complexity on the growth of agent-based modeling. The chapter then examines the philosophical foundations of simulation verification and validation. Simulation verification and validation can be viewed from two quite different perspectives: the simulation philosopher and the simulation practitioner. Personnel from either camp are typically unaware of the other camp's view of simulation verification and validation. This chapter examines both camps while also providing a survey of the literature and efforts pertaining to the verification and validation of agent-based models. The chapter closes with insights pertaining to agent-based modeling, the verification and validation of agent-based models, and potential directions for future research.

INTRODUCTION TO THE CHAPTER

Simulation has long been a favored analytical technique. From early Monte Carlo (sampling) methods, through the powerful discrete-event paradigm, and with the more recent object-oriented and web-based simulation paradigms, simulation has continued to provide analysts a tool that provides valuable insight into many complex, real-world problems. Since many real-world systems feature an influen-

DOI: 10.4018/978-1-60566-774-4.ch003

tial human component, simulationists have often sought to implement simulation representations of that human component into their models, often with little success.

Agent-based modeling has emerged from the object-oriented paradigm with great potential to better model complex, real-world systems including those hard-to-model systems featuring the human component. However, the agent-based modeling paradigm struggles as do all other simulation paradigms with the question of whether the simulation accurately represents the system of interest. This is the simulation validation issue faced by any simulation model developer and user.

This chapter provides a historical perspective on the evolution of agent-based models. Our message is that this new paradigm has a series of historical scientific treads leading to the current state of agent-based modeling. We then delve into the various perspectives associated with verification and validation as a way to make the case for moving away from using "validation" and more towards the concept of model "sanctioning." We close with summary statements and concluding remarks.

INSIGHTS INTO THE EMERGENCE OF AGENT-BASED MODELING

Introduction

Over the years Agent-Based Modeling (ABM) has become a popular tool used to model and understand the many complex, nonlinear systems seen in our world (Ferber, 1999). As a result, many papers geared toward modelers discuss the various aspects and uses of ABM. The topics typically covered include an explanation of ABM, when to use it, how to build it and with what software, how results can be analyzed, research opportunities, and discussions of successful applications of the modeling paradigm. It is also typical to find within these papers brief discussions about the origins

of ABM, discussions that tend to emphasize the diverse applications of ABM as well as how some fundamental properties of ABM were discovered. However, these historical discussions often do not go into much depth about the fundamental theories and fields of inquiry that would eventually lead to ABM's emergence. Thus, in this chapter we re-examine some of the scientific developments in computers, complexity, and systems thinking that helped lead to the emergence of ABM, shed new light onto some old theories while connecting them to several key ABM principles of today. This chapter is not a complete account of the field, but does provide a historical perspective into ABM and complexity intended to provide a clearer understanding of the field, show the benefits of understanding the diverse origins of ABM, and hopefully spark further interest into the theories and ideas that laid the foundation for today's ABM paradigm.

The Beginning: Computers

The true origins of ABM can be traced back to when scientists first began discovering and attempting to explain the emergent and complex behavior seen in nonlinear systems. Some of these more familiar discoveries include Adam Smith's Invisible Hand in Economics, Donald Hebb's Cell Assembly, and the Blind Watchmaking in Darwinian Evolution (Axelrod & Cohen, 2000). In each of these theories simple individual entities interact with each other to produce new complex phenomena that seemingly just emerge. In Adam Smith's theory, this emergent phenomena is called the Invisible Hand, which occurs when each individual tries to maximize their own interests and as a result tend to improve the entire community. Similarly, Donald Hebb's Cell Assembly Theory states that individual neurons interacting together form a hierarchy that results in the storage and recall of memories in the human brain. In this case, the emergent phenomena is the memory formed by the relatively simple interactions of individual neurons. Lastly, the emergent phenomena in Darwinian evolution are that complex and specialized organisms resulted from the interaction of simple organisms and the principles of natural selection.

Although these theories were brilliant for their time, in retrospect, they appear marred by the prevalent scientific philosophy of the time. Newton's philosophy, which is still common today, posited that given an approximate knowledge of a system's initial condition and an understanding of natural law, one can calculate the approximate future behavior of the system (Gleick, 1987). Essentially, this view created the idea that nature is a linear system reducible into parts that eventually can be put back together to resurrect the whole system. Interestingly, it was widely known at the time that there were many systems where reductionism failed. These types of systems were called nonlinear because the sum output of the parts did not equal the output of the whole system. One of the more famous nonlinear systems is the Three Body Problem of classical mechanics, which shows that it is impossible to mathematically determine the future states of three bodies given the initial conditions.

Despite observing and theorizing about emergent behavior in systems, scientists of the time did not have the tools available to fully study and understand these nonlinear systems. Therefore, it was not until theoretical and technological advances were made that would lead to the invention of the computer that scientists could begin building models of these complex systems to better understand their behavior. Some of the more notable theoretical advances that led to the invention of the computer were first made by Gödel with his famous work in establishing the limitations of mathematics (Casti, 1995) and then by Turing in 1936 with his creation of the Turing Machine. The fundamental idea of the theoretical Turing Machine is that it can replicate any mathematical process, which was a big step in showing that machines were capable of repre-

senting systems. Furthermore, Turing and Church later developed the Church-Turing hypothesis which hypothesized that a machine could duplicate not only the functions of mathematics, but also the functions of nature (Levy, 1992). With these developments, scientists had the theoretical foundation onto which they could begin building machines to try and recreate the nonlinear systems they observed in nature.

Eventually, these machines would move from theoretical ideas to the computers of today. The introduction of the computer into the world has certainly had a huge impact, but its impact in science as more than just a high speed calculator or storage device is often overlooked. When the first computers were introduced, Von Neumann recognized their ability to "break the present stalemate created by the failure of the purely analytical approach to nonlinear problems" by giving scientists the ability to heuristically use the computer to develop theories (Burks & Neumann, 1966). The heuristic use of computers, as viewed by Von Neumann and Ulam, resembles the traditional scientific method except that the computer replaces or supplements the experimentation process (Burks & Neumann, 1966). By using a computer to replace real experiments, Von Neumann's process would first involve making a hypothesis based on information known about the system, building the model in the computer, running the computer experiments, comparing the hypothesis with the results, forming a new hypothesis, and repeating these steps as needed (Burks & Neumann, 1966). Essentially the computer serves as a proxy of the real system, which allows more flexibility in collecting data and controlling conditions as well as better control of the timeliness of the results.

The Synthesis of Natural Systems: Cellular Automata and Complexity

Once computers were invented and became established, several different research areas appeared with respect to understanding natural systems. One such area was focused primarily on synthesizing natural systems (Langton, 1989) and was led primarily by the work of Von Neumann and his theory on self-reproducing automata, which are self-operating machines or entities. In a series of lectures, Von Neumann presents a complicated machine that possesses a blueprint of information that controls how the machine acts, including the ability to self-reproduce (Burks & Neumann, 1966). This key insight by Von Neumann to focus not on engineering a machine, but instead on passing information was a precursor to the discovery of DNA which would later inspire and lead to the development of genetic algorithm computational search processes. However, despite his many brilliant insights, Von Neumann's machine was quite complicated since he believed that a certain level of complexity was required in order for organisms to be capable of life and self-reproduction (Levy, 1992). Although it is certainly true that organisms are fairly complex, Von Neumann missed the idea, later discovered, that global complexity can emerge from simple local rules (Gleick, 1987).

With the idea that complexity was needed to produce complex results, with reductionism still being the prevalent scientific methodology employed, and perhaps spurred on by the idea of powerful serial computing capabilities, many scientists began trying to synthesize systems using a top-down system design paradigm. As discussed earlier, top-down systems analysis takes global behavior, discomposes it into small pieces, understands those pieces, and then reassembles the pieces into a system to reproduce or predict future global behavior. This top-down paradigm was primarily employed in the early applications of Artificial Intelligence, where the focus was more on defining the rules of intelligence-looking and creating intelligent solutions rather than the structure that actually creates intelligence (Casti, 1995). Steeped in the tradition of linear systems, this approach did not prove to be extremely suc-

cessful in understanding the complex nonlinear systems found in nature (Langton, 1989).

Although Von Neumann believed that complexity was needed to represent complex systems, his colleague Ulam suggested that this self-reproducing machine could be easily represented using a Cellular Automata (CA) approach (Langton, 1989). As the name may suggest, CA are self-operating entities that exist in individual cells that are adjacent to one another in a 2-D space like a checkerboard and have the capability to interact with the cells around it. The impact of taking the CA approach was significant for at least two reasons. First, CA is a naturally parallel system where each cell can make autonomous decisions simultaneously with other cells in the system (Langton, 1989). This change from serial to parallel systems was significant because it is widely recognized that many natural systems are parallel (Burks & Neumann, 1966). Second, the CA approach had a significant impact on representing complex systems is that CA systems are composed of many locally controlled cells that together create a global behavior. This CA architecture requires engineering a cell's logic at the local level in hopes that it will create the desired global behavior (Langton, 1989). Ultimately, CA would lead to the bottom-up development paradigm now mainly employed by the field of Artificial Life because it is more naturally inclined to produce the same global behavior that is seen to emerge in complex, nonlinear systems.

Eventually Von Neumann and Ulam successfully created a paper-based self-reproducing CA system which was much simpler than Von Neumann's previous efforts (Langton, 1989). As a result, some scientists began using CA systems to synthesize and understand complexity and natural systems. Probably the most notable and famous use of CA was Conway's "Game of Life." In this CA system, which started out as just a Go Board with pieces representing the cells, only three simple rules were used by each cell to determine whether it would be colored white or black based on the color of cells around it. It was found that depending upon the starting configuration, certain shapes or patterns such as the famous glider would emerge and begin to move across the board where it might encounter other shapes and create new ones as if mimicking a very crude form of evolution. After some research, a set of starting patterns were found that would lead to self-reproduction in this very simple system (Levy, 1992). For more information on the "Game of Life," to see some of the famous patterns, and to see the game in action the reader can go to http://en.wikipedia.org/wiki/Conway's_Game_of_Life. However, this discovery that simple rules can lead to complex and unexpected emergent behavior was not an isolated discovery. Many others would later come to the same conclusions using CA systems, including Schelling's famous work in housing segregation which showed that the many micro-motives of individuals can lead to macro-behavior of the entire system (Schelling, 2006).

Upon discovering that relatively simply CA systems were capable of producing emergent behavior, scientists started conducting research to further determine the characteristics and properties of these CA systems. Wolfram published a series of papers in the 1980s on the properties and potential uses of 2-dimensional CA. In his papers (Wolfram, 1994), Wolfram creates four classifications into which different CA systems can be placed based on their long-term behavior. A description of these classifications is found in Figure 1. Langton would later take this research further and described that life, or the synthesis of life, exists only in class 4 systems, which is to say that life and similar complex systems exist between order and complete instability (Levy, 1992). As a result, it was concluded that in order to create complex systems that exhibit emergent behavior, one must be able to find the right balance between order and instability (termed the "edge of chaos") or else the system will either collapse on itself or explode indefinitely. It should be pointed out that the "edge of chaos" concept has been an issue of debate. In particular, there are arguments that suggest that it is not well defined and that experiments attempting to reproduce some of the earlier work concerning the "edge of chaos" have failed (Mitchell, Crutch & Hraber, 1994). Others, such as Czerwinski (1998), define nonlinear systems with three regions of behavior with his transition between the Complex behavior region and the Chaos region aligning with the "edge of chaos" concept. Hill et al. (2003) describe an ABM of two-sided combat whose behavior demonstrated the stage transitions described in (Epstein & Axtell, 1996). The debate, however, seems primarily focused on whether the particular trade-off mechanism used by natural systems is appropriately described by the "edge of chaos" and not on whether a trade-off mechanism exists (Axelrod & Cohen, 2000). Thus, until the debate comes to a conclusion, this paper takes the stance that the "edge of chaos" represents the idea of a trade-off mechanism that is thought to exist in natural systems.

Armed with these discoveries about synthesizing complex systems and emergent behavior, many scientists in the fields of ecology, biology, economics, and other social sciences began using CA to model systems that were traditionally very hard to study due to their nonlinearity (Epstein & Axtell, 1996). However, as technology improved, the lessons learned in synthesizing these nonlinear systems with CA would eventually lead to models where autonomous agents would inhabit environments free from restriction of their cells. Such a model includes Reynold's "boids" which exhibited the flocking behavior of birds. However, to better understand agents, their origins, and behaviors another important perspective of agents, the analysis of natural systems, should be examined.

Figure 1. cellular automata classifications

Class	Properties
1	Evolves to a homogeneous state, changes to the initial state have no impact on final state
2	Evolves into a set of simple periodic states, changes to the initial state have a finite regional impact on the final state
3	Evolves into patterns that grow indefinitely, changes to the initial state leads to large changes to the final state
4	Evolves to complex localized patterns that expand and contract with time, changes to the initial state leads to irregular changes to the final state

The Analysis of Natural Systems: Cybernetics and Chaos

While Von Neumann was working on his theory of self-reproducing automata and asking, 'what makes a complex system,' Wiener and others were developing the field of cybernetics (Langton, 1989) and asking the question, 'what do complex systems do (Ashby, 1956)?' Although these two questions are related, each is clearly focused on different aspects of the complexity problem and led to two different, but related, paths toward discovering the nature of complexity, the latter course of inquiry become cybernetics. According to Wiener, cybernetics is "the science of control and communication in the animal and the machine" (Weaver, 1948) and has it's origins in the control of the anti-aircraft firing systems of World War II (Langton, 1989). Upon fine tuning the controls, scientists found that feedback and sensitivity were very important and began formalizing theories about the control and communications of these systems having feedback. Eventually they would discover that the same principles found in the control of machines were also true for animals, such as the activity of recognizing and picking up an object (Weaver, 1948). This discovery would lead cybernetics to eventually be defined by Ashby as a "field concerned with understanding complexity and establishing foundations to study and understand it better" (Ashby, 1956), which includes the study of both machines and organisms as one system entity.

One of the main tools used in cybernetics to begin building theories about complex systems was Information Theory as it helped scientists think about systems in terms of coordination, regulation, and control. Armed with this new mathematical theory of the time, those studying cybernetics began to develop and describe many theories and properties of complex systems. One of these discoveries about complex systems was the importance of feedback on the long-term patterns and properties of complex systems. In general, complex systems consist of a large number of tightly coupled pieces that together receive feedback that influences the system's future behavior. Based on this information, Ashby explains that complex systems will exhibit different patterns depending upon the type of feedback found in the system. If the feedback is negative (i.e., the Lyapunov Exponent, $\lambda < 0$), then the patterns will become extinct or essentially reach a fixed point. If the feedback is zero ($\lambda = 0$), then the pattern will remain constant or essentially be periodic. Finally, if the feedback is positive ($\lambda > 0$), then the patterns would grow indefinitely and out of control (Ashby, 1956).

However, just as Von Neumann failed to make certain observations about complexity, the founders of cybernetics failed to consider what would happen if both positive and negative feedback simultaneously existed in a system. It was not until Shaw used Information Theory to show that if at least one component of a complex system has a positive Lyapunov Exponent, and was mixed with other components with varying exponent values, the system will exhibit chaotic patterns (Gleick, 1987). With Shaw's discovery that complex systems can exhibit chaotic behavior, scientists began considering what further impacts Chaos Theory might have on understanding complex systems.

In general, any system exhibiting chaos will appear to behave randomly with the reality being that the behavior is completely deterministic (Casti, 1995). However, this does not mean that the system is completely predictable. As Lorenz was first to discover with his simulation of weather patterns, it is impossible to make long-term predictions of a chaotic system with a simulated model because it is infeasible to record all of the initial conditions at the required level of significance (Gleick, 1987). This sensitivity to initial conditions results from the fact that the initial conditions are infinitely many random numbers, which implies they are incompressible and infinitely long. Therefore, collecting these initial conditions to the required level of significance is impossible without a measurement device capable of collecting an infinite number of infinitely long numbers as well as finding a computer capable of handling all of those infinitely long numbers.

It may seem that this property of chaos has at some level discredited the previously mentioned Church-Turing Hypothesis by suggesting that these types of natural complex systems cannot be duplicated by a machine. However, there are several other properties of chaos that help those attempting to model and understand these complex systems despite the inability to directly represent them. The first is that chaotic systems have a strange attractor property that keep these aperiodic systems within some definable region (Gleick, 1987). This is obviously good for those studying these complex systems because it limits the region of study into a finite space. The other property of these complex systems is that they can be generated using a very simple set of rules or equations. By using a small set of rules or equations, and allowing the results to act as a feedback

into the system, the complexity of these systems seems to emerge out of nowhere. As one can recall, the same discovery was made in CA when cells with simple rules were allowed to interact dynamically with each other (Gleick, 1987). Therefore, it appears that although natural complex systems cannot be modeled directly, some of the same emergent properties and behavior of these systems can be generated in a computer using simple rules (i.e., the bottom-up approach) without complete knowledge of the entire real system. Perhaps it is not surprising that the idea that complex systems can be represented sufficiently with a simpler model, often called a Homomorphic Model, has long been a fundamental concept when studying complex systems (Ashby, 1956).

Whenever discussing the idea that simple rules can be used to model complex systems it is valuable to mention fractals, which are a closely related to and often a fundamental component of Chaos Theory. First named by Mandelbrot, fractals are geometric shapes that regardless of the scale show the same general pattern (Mandelbrot, 1982).. The interesting aspect of fractals is that because of their scale-free, self-similar nature they can both fit within a defined space and have an infinite perimeter, which makes them complex and relates them very closely to the effect strange attractors can have on a system. Furthermore, forms of fractals can be observed in nature and, in turn, generated in labs using very simple rules, which shows that they also exhibit the same type of emergent behavior and properties as the previously discussed complex systems (Gleick, 1987) As a result, although fractals, chaos, and complex systems have a lot in common, fractals, due to their physical representation, provide an insightful look into the architecture of complexity. Essentially, fractals are composed of many similar subsystems of infinitely many more similar subsystems of the same shapes, which results in a natural hierarchy and the emergence of other, similar shapes. It is interesting to note that the architecture of fractals directly shows why reductionism does not work for nonlinear systems. With fractals, a scientist could forever break the fractal into smaller pieces and never be able to measure its perimeter. Another interesting aspect about the architecture of fractals is that they naturally form a hierarchy, which means the properties of hierarchies could possibly be exploited when attempting to model and understand complex systems. For example, the fact that Homomorphic models are effective at modeling complex systems could come from the fact that hierarchical systems are composed of subsystems such that the subsystems can be represented not as many individual entities but as a single entity (Simon, 1962).

There are other properties of chaos which give insight into complex natural systems and ABM. Since it is impossible to satisfactorily collect all of the initial conditions to obtain an exact prediction of a chaotic system, one might ask what would happen if the needed initial conditions were collected, but not to the infinite level of detail? It turns out that such a model, while close for the short term, would eventually diverge from the actual system being modeled. This example brings about another property of chaotic systems; they are very sensitive to the initial conditions (Casti, 1995). Because this sensitivity property of chaos ultimately leads to unreliable results when compared to the actual system and the models only being homomorphic, these computer models are unlikely to aid any decision about how to handle the real system. Instead, these models should be used to provide insights into the general properties of a complex system and not for forecasting 'hard' statistics like mean performance. Essentially, this methodology of using a computer for inference and insight harps back to Von Neumann's idea of using a computer to facilitate an experiment with hopes to gain insights about the system rather than using the computer to generate exact results about the future states of the system (Burks & Neumann, 1966).

The final property of chaos that can give insight into complex natural systems and ABM is that a strange attractor not only limits the state space of the system, but it also causes the system to be aperiodic. In other words, the system with a strange attractor will never return to a previous state; this results in tremendous variety within the system (Casti, 1995). In 1962, Ashby examined the issue of variety in systems and posited the Law of Requisite Variety, which simply states that the diversity of an environment can be blocked by a diverse system (Ashby, 1956). In essence, Ashby's law shows that in order to handle a variety of situations, one must have a diverse system capable of adapting to those various situations. As a result, it is clear that variety is important for natural systems given the diversity of the environment in which they can exist. In fact, it has been seen that entities within an environment will adapt to create or replace any diversity that have been removed, further enforcing the need and importance of diversity (Holland, 1995). However, it has also been found that too much variety can be counter productive to a system because it can grow uncontrollably and be unable to maintain improvements (Axelrod & Cohen, 2000). Therefore, it appears that complex natural systems that exhibit emergent behavior need to have the right balance between order and variety or positive and negative feedback, which is exactly what a strange attractor does in a chaotic system. By keeping the system aperiodic within definable bounds, chaotic systems show that the battle between order and variety is an essential part of complex natural systems. As a result, strange attractors provide systems with the maximum adaptability.

Towards Today's ABM: Complex Adaptive Systems

After learning how to synthesize complex systems and discovering some of their properties, the field of Complex Adaptive Systems (CAS), which is commonly referenced as the direct historical roots of ABM, began to take shape. The field of CAS draws much of its of inspiration from biological systems and is concerned mainly with how complex adaptive behavior emerges in nature from the interaction among autonomous agents (Macal & North, 2006). One of the fundamental contributions made to the field of CAS, and in turn ABM, was Holland's identification of the four properties and three mechanisms that compose all CAS (Holland, 1995). Essentially, these items have aided in defining and designing ABM as they are known today (Macal & North, 2006) because Holland takes many of the properties of complex systems discussed earlier and places them into clear categories, allowing for better focus, development, and research.

The first property of CAS discussed by Holland is Aggregation, which essentially states that all CAS can be generalized into subgroups and similar subgroups can be considered and treated the same. This property of CAS directly relates to the hierarchical structure of complex systems discussed early. Furthermore, not only in 1962 did Simon discussed this property of complex systems, he also discussed several other hierarchical ideas about the architecture of complex systems (Simon, 1962) that can be related to two of Holland's mechanisms of CAS. The first is Tagging, which is the mechanism that classifies agents, allows them to recognize each other, and allows their easier observation of the system. This classification means putting agents into subgroups within some sort of hierarchy. The second mechanism is Building Blocks, which is the idea that simple subgroups can be decomposed from complex systems that in turn can be reused and combined in many different ways to represent patterns. Besides being related to Simon's discussion of the decomposability of complex systems, this mechanism also reflects the common theme that simplicity can lead to emergent behavior and the theory behind modeling a complex system. Thus, the elements of Aggregation, Tagging, and Building Blocks can be related back to the results discovered by Simon when studying the architecture of complexity.

Another Holland property of CAS is Nonlinearity, the idea that the whole system output is greater than the sum of the individual component output. Essentially, the agents in a CAS come together to create a result such that it cannot be attributed back to the individual agents. This fundamental property, the inspiration behind synthesizing and analyzing complex systems, is the result of dynamic feedback and interactions. These causes of nonlinearity are related to two more of Holland's CAS elements. The first is the property of Flow, which states that agents in CAS communicate and that this communication changes with time. As the case in CA, having agents communicate with each other and their environment dynamically can lead to the nonlinearity of emergent behavior. Also, within the property of Flow, Holland discusses several interesting effects that can result from changes made to the flow of information such as the Multiplier Effect and the Recycling Effect. In short, the Multiplier Effect occurs when an input gets multiplied many times within a system. An example of the Multiplier Effect is the impact made on many other markets when a person builds a house. Similarly, the Recycling Effect occurs when an input gets recycled within the system and the overall output is increased. An example of the Recycling Effect is when steel is recycled from old cars to make new cars [Holland, 1995]. Interestingly enough, both of these effects can be directly related back to Information Theory and Cybernetics. The other element that relates to nonlinearity is the Internal Model Mechanism, which gives the agents an ability to perceive and make decisions about their environment. It is easy to think of this mechanism as being the rules that an agent follows in the model, such as turning colors based on its surroundings or moving away from obstacles. Even simple Internal Models can lead to emergent behavior in complex systems. The link between these three elements is the essential nature of complex systems: nonlinearity.

The final property discussed by Holland is Diversity. Holland states that agents in CAS are diverse, which means they do not all act the same way when stimulated by a set of conditions. With diverse agents, Holland argues that new interactions and adaptations can develop such that the overall system will be more robust. Of course, the idea that variety creates more robust systems relates directly back to Ashby's Law of Requisite Variety, which in turn relates back to strange attractors and Chaos Theory.

Summary

For all of positives of ABM there are often just as many, if not more, criticisms of ABM. For the modeler to successfully defend their model and have it be considered worth any more than a new and trendy modeling technique, the modeler needs to have a fundamental understanding of the many scientific theories, principles and ideas that lead to ABM and not just an understanding of the 'how to' perspective on emergence and ABM. By gaining deeper understandings of the history of ABM, the modeler can better contribute to transforming ABM from a potential modeling revolution (Bankes, 2002) to an actual modeling revolution with real life implications. Understanding that ABMs were the result of the lack of human ability to understand nonlinear systems allows the modeler to see where ABM fits in as a research tool. Understanding the role that computers play in ABM shows the importance of understanding the properties of computers and in turn their limitations. Understanding that the fundamental properties of CAS have their origins in many different fields (Computers, CA, Cybernetics, Chaos, etc) give the modeler the ability to better comprehend and explain their model. For example, understanding Chaos Theory can reveal why ABMs are thought to be incapable of providing anything more than insight into the model. By understanding each of these individual fields and how they are interrelated, a modeler can potentially make new discoveries and better analyze their model. For example, by understanding

the theory behind Cybernetics and Chaos Theory a modeler is better equipped in determining the impact that certain rules may have on the system or in trouble shooting why the system is not creating the desired emergent behavior. Finally, understanding the history of ABM presents the modeler with a better ability to discern between and develop new ABM approaches.

As it is often the case, examining history can lead to insightful views about the past, present, and the future. It is the hoped that this section has shed some light on the origins of ABM as well as the connections between the many fields from which it emerged. Starting with theories about machines, moving onto synthesis and analysis of natural systems, and ending with CAS, it is clear, despite this article being primarily focused on complexity, that many fields played an important role in developing the multidisciplinary field of ABM. Therefore, in accordance with the Law of Requisite Variety, it appears wise for those wishing to be successful in ABM to also be well versed in the many disciplines that ABM encompasses. Furthermore, many insights can be discovered about the present nature of ABM by understanding the theoretical and historical roots that compose the rules-of-thumb used in today's ABM. For example, knowing the theory behind Cybernetics and Chaos Theory could help a modeler in determining the impact that certain rules may have on the system or in trouble shooting why the system is not creating the desired emergent behavior. Finally, it could be postulated that understanding the history of ABM presents one with a better ability to discern between and develop new ABM approaches. In conclusion, this article has provided an abbreviated look into the emergence of ABM with respect to complexity and has made some new connections to today's ABM that can hopefully serve as a starting point for those interested in understanding the diverse fields that compose ABM.

SIMULATION AND AGENT-BASED MODELING VALIDATION: STRIVING TO OBTAIN THE UNOBTAINABLE?

Introduction

Since the introduction of the computer, simulations have become popular in many scientific and engineering disciplines. This is partly due to a computer simulation's ability to aid in the decision making and understanding of relatively complex and dynamic systems where traditional analytical techniques may fail or be impractical. As a result of this ability, the use of simulations can be found in just about every field of study. These fields can range anywhere from military applications (Davis, 1992) and meteorology (Küppers & Lenhard, 2005) to management science (Pidd, 2003), social science (Epstein & Axtell, 1996), nanotechnology (Johnson, 2006), and terrorism (Resnyansky, 2007). What can be inferred from this wide spread use is that not only are simulations robust in their application, but they are also practically successful. Due in large part to this robustness and success, simulations are becoming a fairly standard tool found in most analyst's toolbox. In fact, proof that simulations are becoming more of a generic analysis tool and less of a new technique can be found in the increasing number of published articles that use simulations but do not mention it in the title (Küppers, Lenhard, & Shinn, 2006).

However, despite their increasing popularity, a fundamental issue has continued to plague simulations since their inception (Naylor & Finger, 1967; Stanislaw, 1986): is the simulation an accurate representation of the reality being studied? This question is important because typically a simulation's goal is to represent some abstraction of reality and it is believed that if a simulation does not accomplish this representation, then information gained from the simulation is either worthless or at least not as valuable. Therefore, one can understand why answering the question of simulation validity is so important, because having an accurate simulation could mean that knowledge can be gained about reality without actually observing, experimenting, and dealing with the constraints of reality (Burks & Neumann, 1966). As a result of this potential, many articles over the years have been devoted to the topic of simulation validity and in particular they each tend to focus on some aspect of the following fundamental questions of simulation validity:

- Can simulations represent reality? If not, what can they represent?
- If a simulation cannot or does not represent reality, then is the simulation worth anything?
- How can one show that a simulation is valid? What techniques exist for establishing validity?
- What roles do or should simulations play today?

Given the considerable amount of time and effort spent on simulation validity, a reasonable question to ask is why is simulation validity still haunting simulationists today? In short, the fundamental reason why it is still an issue today, and will continue to be one, is that the question of a simulation's validity is really a philosophical question found at the heart of all scientific disciplines (Stanislaw, 1986). By considering the above questions, one will notice that they closely resemble some typical philosophy of science questions (Kincaid, 1998):

- Can scientific theories be taken as true or approximately true statements of what is true in reality?
- What methods, procedures, and practices make scientific theories believable or true?

Therefore, the philosophy of science perspective can shed light on the nature of simulation validity as it is known today as well as the nature of simulation itself. It is from this fundamental philosophy of science perspective that this section will give insights into the fundamental questions of simulation validity, where current practices in simulation validation fit into the general framework of the philosophy of science, and what role simulations play in today's world.

With this objective in mind, this section has four subsections. The first discusses how the relationship between reality and simulation is flawed such that all simulations do not represent reality. The second describes what is currently meant by the idea of simulation validation in practice. The third discusses the usefulness of simulations today and how simulations are becoming the epistemological tool of our time. In the fourth, the usefulness and role of Agent-Based Models as well as the special case they present to simulation validation is discussed.

Why All Simulations are Invalid

It is valuable to first define simulation and discuss how it is typically seen as related to reality. Although there are many definitions of simulation, for this section a simulation is defined as a numerical technique that takes input data and creates output data based upon a model of a system (Law, 2007) (for this section the distinction between theory and model will not be made, instead the term model will be used to represent them together). In essence, a simulation attempts to show the nature of a model as it changes over time. Therefore, it can be said that a simulation is a representation of a model and not directly a representation of reality. Instead, it is the model's job to attempt to represent some level of reality in a system. In this case, it would appear that a simulation's ability to represent reality really depends upon the model upon which it is built (Davis & Blumenthal, 1991). Although this relationship between a real system, a model, and a simulation has been described in many different

ways (Banks, Carson, Nelson, & Nicol, 2001; Law, 2007; Stanislaw, 1986; Winsberg, 1999), a simplified version of the cascading relationship is shown in Figure 2. It is also important to note that commonly simulations today are performed by computers because they are much more efficient at numerical calculations. Therefore, we assume that a simulation is constructed within a computer and that a simulation is a representation of a model which is in turn a representation of a real system (as shown in Figure 2).

Having defined the fundamental relationship between a real system, a model, and a simulation, the implications of this relationship can be examined. A simulation's ability to represent reality first hinges on the model's underlying ability to represent the real system. Therefore, the first step in determining a simulation's ability to represent reality is to examine the relationship between a real system and a model of that real system. To begin, it must be recognized that a real system is infinite in its input, how it processes the input, and its output, and that any model created must always be finite in nature given our finite abilities (Gershenson, 2002). From this statement alone it can be seen that a model can never be as real as the actual system and that instead all that can be hoped for is that the model is at least capable of representing some smaller component of the real system (Ashby, 1970). As a result, all models are invalid in the sense that they are not capable of representing reality completely.

The idea that all models are bad is certainly not a new idea. In fact, this is recognized by many people (Ashby, 1970; Gershenson, 2002; Stanislaw, 1986) and there are even articles written which discuss what can be done with some of these bad models to aid in our understanding and decision making (Hodges, 1991). However, if all models are bad at representing a real system and a model is only capable of representing a small portion of that real system, then how will it be known if a model actually represents what hap-

Figure 2. Relationship between a system, a theory/model, and a simulation

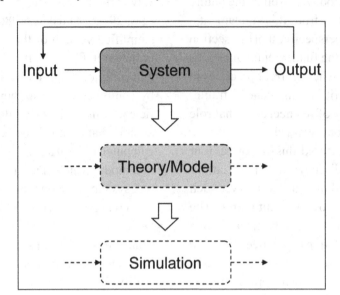

pens in the system? In essence, how can we prove that a model is valid at least in representing some subset of a real system?

The basic answer to this question is that a model can never be proven to be a valid representation of reality. This can be shown by examining several different perspectives. The first perspective involves using Gödel's Incompleteness Theorem (Gödel, 1931). In his theorem, Gödel showed that a theory cannot be proven from the axioms upon which the theory was based. By implication, this means that because every model is based upon some set of axioms about the real system, there is no way to prove that model is correct (Gershenson, 2002). Another perspective to consider is that there are an infinite number of possible models that can represent any system and it would therefore take an infinite amount of time to show that a particular model is the best representation of reality. Together these perspectives hearken back to one of the fundamental questions found in the philosophy of science: how can a model be trusted as representing reality?

Although a model cannot be proven to be a correct representation of reality, it does not mean that the second fundamental question of the philosophy of science (what methods and procedures make models believable?) has not been thoroughly explored. There actually exists many belief systems developed by famous philosophers that attempt to provide some perspective on this question (Kincaid, 1998; Kleindorfer & Ganeshan, 1993). For instance, Karl Popper believed that a theory could only be disproved and never proved (Falsificationism), others believe that a model is true if it is an objectively correct reflection of factual observations (Empiricism) (Pidd, 2003). However, no matter what one adopts as their philosophy, the fundamental idea that remains is that all models are invalid and impossible to validate. A shining example of this idea can be seen by the fact that although both are considered geniuses, Einstein still showed that Newton's model of the world was wrong and therefore it is likely that eventually someone will come up with a new model that seems to fit in better with our current knowledge of reality (Kincaid, 1998). Regardless of how correct a model may be believed to be, it is likely that there will always exist another model which is better.

The previous discussion on the relationship between a real system and a model lead to the following conjectures about models:

- Models cannot represent an infinite reality and therefore all models are invalid with respect to a complete reality;
- Models can only hope to represent some aspect of reality and be less incomplete;
- There are infinitely many models that could represent some aspect of reality and therefore no model can ever be proven to be the correct representation of any aspect of reality; and
- A better model than the current model is always likely to exist in the future.

From these conjectures, it appears that a simulation's capability to represent a real system is bleak based purely on the fact that a model is incapable of representing reality. However, there is another issue with trying to represent a model with a simulation. As seen graphically in Figure 2, another round of translation needs to occur before the transition from the system to the simulation is complete. At first glance, translating a model into a computer simulation seems relatively straightforward. Unfortunately, this does not appear to be the case even when programming (verification) issues are left out of the equation. This conclusion generally arises from to the limitations of the computer. For example, because computers are only capable of finite calculations, often times truncation errors may occur in the computer simulation when translating input into output via the model. Due to truncation errors alone, widely different results can be obtained from a simulation of a model with slightly different levels of detail. In fact this result is often seen in chaotic systems such as Lorenz's famous weather simulations, which would later lead to the idea of the Butterfly Effect (Gleick, 1987).

Suppose, however infeasible it may be, that advances in computers would make the issues of

memory storage and truncation errors obsolete, then the next issue in a computer simulation's ability to represent a model is the computer's processing speed. Given that computer processing speeds are getting increasingly faster, the question about whether a computer can process the necessary information, no matter how large and detailed the model, within an acceptable time seems to be answered by just waiting until technology advances. Unfortunately, there is a conjecture which states that there is a speed limit of any data processing system. This processing speed limit, better known as Bremermann's Limit (Ashby, 1970), is based upon Einstein's mass-energy relation and the Heisenberg Uncertainty Principle and conjectures that no data processing system whether artificial or living can process more than 2×10^{47} bits per second per gram of its mass (Bremermann, 1962). From this conjecture, it can be seen that eventually computers will reach a processing limit and that models and the amount of digits processed in a respectable amount of time will dwarf Bremermann's Limit. Consider for example how long it would take a computer approximately the size (6×10^{27} grams) and age (10^{10} years) of the Earth operating at Bremermann's Limit to enumerate all of the approximately 10^{120} possible move sequences in chess (Bremermann, 1962) or prove the optimal solution to a 100 city traveling salesperson problem (100! or approximately 9.33×10^{157} different routes). Given that this super efficient, Earth-sized computer would only be able to process approximately 10^{93} bits to date, it would take approximately 10^{27} and 9.33×10^{64} times longer than the current age of the Earth to enumerate all possible combinations for each problem, respectively. It would take entirely too long and be entirely too impractical to attempt to solve these problems using brute force.

Thus, it is challenging for a computer, given it's memory and processing limitations, to accurately represent a model or provide accurate results in a practical amount of time. To combat this issue of computing limitations, simulationists often build a simulation of a model that incorporates many assumptions, abstractions, distortions and non-realistic entities that are not in the model (Küppers & Lenhard, 2005; Morrison & Morgan, 1999; Stanislaw, 1986; Winsberg, 2001; Winsberg, 2003; Winsberg, 2006b). Such examples include breaking continuous functions into discrete functions (Küppers & Lenhard, 2005), introducing artificial entities to limit instabilities (Küppers & Lenhard, 2005), and creating algorithms which pass information from one abstraction level to another (Winsberg, 2006a). From these examples, we see that the limitations of computing makes translating a model into a simulation very unlikely to result in a completely valid representation of that model. This is why often simulation building is considered more of an art rather than a science, because getting a simulation to appear to represent a model in a computer requires a lot of tinkering that ends up with a simulation that only appears to represent the model. As a result of this discussion, it can be seen that not only are there an infinite number of models that can represent some aspect of reality, but there is probably also an infinite number of simulations that can represent some aspect of a model.

Given the above discussion, the following conjectures can be made about the ability of a computer simulation to represent a model:

- Computers are only capable of finite calculations and finite storage, therefore truncation errors and storage limitations may significantly impact the ability of a computer to represent a model;
- Computers can only process information at Bremermann's Limit, making it is impossible for them to process large amounts of information about a model in a practical amount of time;
- To attempt to represent a model with a computer simulation either requires sacrificing accuracy to get results or sacrificing time to get better accuracy;

- Given the limitations of computing and the trade off between accuracy and speed, there are many ways to try and represent a model with a simulation; and
- Because there are many possible simulations that can represent an aspect of a model, it is impossible to have a completely valid and still useful simulation of a model.

These conjectures illuminate why translating a model into a computer simulation is not a straightforward process and that many times a simulationist is simply trying to tinker with a simulation until it happens to be appear to have some representation of the model. This complexity with translating a model into a simulation only makes the question of a simulation's ability to represent reality more pressing.

A main goal of this section is to explain why all simulations are invalid representations of reality. By examining the relationship between the real system, the model attempting to represent the system, and the simulation attempting to represent the model, the following summary conjectures can be made about simulation validity:

1. A real system is infinite.
2. A model cannot represent an infinite real system and can only hope to be one of any infinite possible representations of some aspect of that real system.
3. As a result of 1 and 2, a model is an invalid representation of the real system and cannot be proven to be a valid representation of some aspect of the real system.
4. There are many possible computer simulations that can represent a model and each computer simulation has trade offs between the accuracy of the results and time it takes to obtain those results.
5. As a result of 4, a simulation cannot be said to be a completely valid representation of a model.

6. Therefore, a computer simulation is an invalid representation of a complete real system and at the very best cannot be proven to be a valid representation of some aspect of a real system.

The above conjectures lay out the issues with a simulation's ability to represent reality. Furthermore, it can be seen why simulation validation continues to be a major issue. If simulations cannot be proven to be valid and are generally invalid representations of a complete real system, then what value to they serve? However, this question is not the primary source of research in simulation validation. Instead, much of the focus still remains on how one can validate a simulation. Given the conjecture that all simulations are invalid, or impossible to prove to be valid, what possibly could all of these articles mean when discussing simulation validation?

What Does Simulation Validation Really Mean in Practice?

Even though it has been shown that generally all simulations are invalid with respect to a real system, there is still a fair amount of literature that continues to attempt to show how a simulation can be validated. It may initially appear that those practicing simulation building are unaware of the downfalls facing simulation's ability to represent reality, but this is not the case (Banks et al., 2001; Law, 2007). So what are these articles and books discussing when they are focused on simulation validation? Insight into what practitioner's really mean by simulation validation can be seen from their own definitions of validation:

Validation is the process of determining whether a simulation model is an accurate representation of the system, for the particular objectives of the study. (Fishman & Kiviat, 1968; Law, 2007)

Model Validation is substantiating that a model within its domain of applicability, behaves with satisfying accuracy consistent with the models and simulations objectives... (Balci, 1998; Sargent, 2005)

Validation is concerned with building the right model. It is utilized to determine that a model is an accurate representation of the real system. Validation is usually achieved through the calibration of the model, an iterative process of comparing the model to actual system behavior and using the discrepancies between the two, and the insights gained, to improve the model. This process is repeated until the model accuracy is judged to be acceptable. (Bankes et al., 2001)

Validation is the process of determining the manner in which and degree to which a model and its data is an accurate representation of the real world from the perspective of the intended uses of the model and the subjective confidence that should be placed on this assessment. (Davis, 1992)

These definitions indicate that in practice simulation validation takes on a somewhat subjective meaning. Instead of validation just being the process of determining the accuracy of a simulation to represent a real system, all of the above authors are forced to add the clause 'with respect to some objectives.' By adding this caveat, simulationists have inserted some hope that a model is capable of being classified as valid for a particular application, even though any model they create will at best be a less than perfect representation of reality. With the insertion of this clause, the issue of validation takes on a completely new meaning. No longer is the issue of absolute validity the problem, the problem is now proving the relative validity of a simulation model with respect to some set of objectives.

In order to address this new problem, many articles have been published which provide a different perspective of this relative validity problem. One of these perspectives is to attempt to evaluate the relative validity of the simulation by treating it not as a representation of a model/theory but as a miniature scientific theory by itself and then use the principles from the philosophy of science to aid in proving/disproving its validity (Kleindorfer & Ganeshan, 1993; Kleindorfer, O'Neill, & Ganeshan, 1998). As first introduced by Naylor and Finger in 1967 (Naylor & Finger, 1967), many authors have since thoroughly examined the many beliefs that have emerged from the philosophy of science and have related them to simulation validity (Barlas & Carpenter, 1990; A. H. Feinstein & Cannon, 2003; Klein & Herskovitz, 2005; Kleindorfer & Ganeshan, 1993; Pidd, 2003; Schmid, 2005). Often these authors provide insightful views into simulation validation because the philosophy of science has been actively discussing the validity of theories long before the inception of simulation (Kleindorfer & Ganeshan, 1993).

Although the introduction of scientific philosophy has certainly provided new perspectives and points of view on the subject of validity to simulationists (Kleindorfer & Ganeshan, 1993; Schmid, 2005), it could be said that overall the philosophy of science has brought with it more questions than answers. There are several key reasons for this. The first is that for every belief system in the philosophy of science there are both advantages and disadvantages. For example, simulation validation is often favorably compared to Falsificationism because it states that a simulation can only be proved false and that in order to have a simulation be considered scientific it must first undergo scrutiny to attempt to prove that it is false (Klein & Herskovitz, 2005). However, under this belief system it is difficult to determine whether a model was rejected based on testing and hypothesis errors or whether the model is actually false (Kincaid, 1998). Another source of concern for using the philosophy of science is that, as was discussed earlier, it is impossible to prove that a model/theory is valid at all. Therefore, using the

philosophy of science to aid in simulation validity is more applicable in providing insights into the fundamental philosophical questions stemming from validation as well as potential validation frameworks than in actually proving the validity of a simulation.

Besides this high-level look at the validation of simulation as miniature theories, another perspective considers methods and procedures which can aid simulationists in proving the relative validity of their simulation given the assumption that it can be proven. This assumption is by no means a radical one. It makes sense that if one defines the objective of the simulation to include the fact that it cannot completely represent the real system then it is possible for a simulation to meet the needs of a well defined objective and therefore have relative validity. With a goal in mind to find these methods and procedures, a plethora of techniques have been developed as well as when and how they should be applied within systematic frameworks to aid simulationists in validating their models (Balci, 1998; Sargent, 2005). As another indication of how much this field has been explored, even the idea of validation itself has been reduced to many different types of validation such as replicative, predictive, structural, and operational validity (A. H. Feinstein & Cannon, 2002; Zeigler, Praehofer, & Kim, 2000).

Clearly a lot of effort has been spent on summarizing and defining how one can go about validating a simulation given some objectives. It would be redundant to discuss all of them here in detail. However, to better understand what simulation validation means in practice it is worthwhile to consider what all of these techniques and ideas have in common. Whether the validation technique is quantitative, pseudo-quantitative, or qualitative, each technique has it's advantages, disadvantages, and is subjective to the evaluator. Although the statement that all of these techniques are subjective may seem surprising, it can actually be easily shown for all the validation techniques developed today. For example, when qualitatively/

pseudo-quantitatively comparing the behavior of the simulation and the real system, it is clear that a different evaluator may have a different belief about whether the behaviors of the two systems are close enough such that the simulation could be considered valid. For a quantitative example consider when statistically comparing two systems and the evaluator is required to subjectively select a certain level of significance for the particular hypothesis test used. For those familiar with statistical hypothesis testing, it is clear that different levels of significance may result in different conclusions regarding the validity of the simulation. From these examples, it can be seen that even though many techniques have been developed, none of them can serve as a definitive method for validating a simulation. They are all subjective to the evaluator.

Given there is no technique that can prove that the relative validity of a simulation is true, the fundamental question of this section resurfaces: what does simulation validation really mean in practice? In practice simulationists are not trying to validate that a simulation is a representation of a real system but are instead attempting to validate the simulation according to some objective, which also cannot be systematically proven to be true. Therefore, one must consider other alternatives when examining what is really occurring when a simulationist is trying to validate their model according to some objective. From the vast amount of techniques, guides, and systems proposed to validate a simulation, it can be conjectured that simulation validation in practice is really the process of persuading the evaluators to believe that the simulation is valid with respect to the objective. In other words, in practice whether a simulation is validated by the evaluators depends upon how well the simulationist can `sell' the simulation's validity by using the appropriate validation techniques that best appeals to the evaluator's sense of accuracy and correctness.

The idea that simulation validation in practice is really the process of selling the simulation to the evaluator may not appeal to scientists, engineers, and simulationists, but there is a fair amount of evidence that supports this conclusion. First of all, any simulation book or article focused on validation will frequently stress the importance of knowing the evaluator's expectations and getting the evaluator to buy into the credibility of the simulation (Banks et al., 2001), some will even go as far as to say explicitly that one must sell the simulation to the evaluator (Law, 2007). Others indicate that validating a simulation is similar to getting a judicial court system to believe in the validity of the simulation (A. H. Feinstein & Cannon, 2003). Generally those practicing simulation understand that validation is more about getting the evaluators to believe in the simulation's validity and less about getting a truly valid simulation (which is impossible anyway). From this statement, an interesting insight is that simulation validation is not completely removed from society and other social influences. In fact, it appears that simulation validation in practice requires the simulationist to have the ability to actively interact with the community of evaluators and attempt to persuade that community to accept the simulation as correct. As a result, some have argued that simulation validation in practice is similar to how any social group makes a decision (Pidd, 2003).

In trying to determine what simulation validation really means in practice, several fundamental points arise:

- In practice, a simulation is validated based on some objective and not on being a true representation of the real system;
- All of the techniques developed to prove the validity of a simulation in practice are subjective to the evaluator and therefore cannot systematically prove the relative validity of the simulation; and
- Validating a simulation in practice depends upon how well the simulationist sells the validity of the simulation by using

the appropriate validation techniques that best appeals to the evaluator's sense of accuracy and correctness. Furthermore, this means that simulation validation in practice is susceptible to the social influences permeating the society within which the simulation exists.

Simulation validation in practice really seems to have little to do with actual validation, where validation is the process of ensuring that a simulation accurately represents reality. Instead, simulation validation in practice is more concerned with getting approval from evaluators and peers of a community relative to some overall objective for the simulation; simulation validation in practice is really the process of getting the simulation sanctioned (Winsberg, 1999), not validated. Perhaps it is time for simulationists to consider adopting the term simulation sanctioning instead of simulation validation since sanctioning implies a better sense of what is actually occurring and validation implies that the truth is actually being conveyed in the simulation when it is not. However, it is unlikely that this transition will occur given the fact that simulation validation today is mainly concerned with getting evaluators to buy into the results of the simulation, the current paradigm in simulation has been established, and saying a simulation is valid sounds much better to a seller than does saying a simulation is sanctioned. This brings up an interesting dilemma for simulationists because if simulations cannot represent reality, then what good are they?

What Good are Simulations?

Since simulations in practice are sanctioned and not validated, the next logical question to ask is if simulations are incapable of representing reality and therefore are incapable of providing true results with respect to the system, then what good are simulations? To answer this question, it is first important to jump out of the world of logic

and philosophy and see that practically speaking simulation would not be growing in popularity if it did not provide some demonstrable good to those using the technique. In fact, it could be said that the continuing widespread use of simulation in practice, the number of commercial simulation software packages, and the number of academic publications meaning simulation are clear indications that simulation has provided enough robustness to be considered useful and indeed successful (Küppers et al., 2006).

At first glance, the success of simulation in practice may appear to be an contradiction to the previous statement that all simulations are invalid. However, this is resolved by making clear that all simulations are invalid with respect to an absolute real system, which does not mean that a simulation is not capable at some abstraction level to get relatively 'close' to representing a small portion of an absolute real system. For example, a simulation of a manufacturing system may come very close to representing the outcome of a process, but nevertheless it is still invalid with respect to actual system because of all the reasons discussed earlier. This same conclusion can also be related to purely scientific theories, such as Newton's laws of motion. Although they can produce reliable results in certain abstraction levels, overall they have been shown to not be completely correct representations of reality. Given the popularity of simulation it appears that in spite of the fact that they are not capable of representing an absolute real system, simulations are capable of getting close and robust enough results to become practically useful (Knuuttila, 2006; Küppers & Lenhard, 2006). Simulations are useful because they are capable of providing reliable results without needing to be a true representation of a real system (Winsberg, 2006b). However, this is often more true for some types of simulations and real systems than others.

In general, it can be said that the success of a simulation at obtaining reliable and predictable results depends upon how well the real system is understood and studied, because a well-understood system will result in better underlying theories that form the foundation of the simulation. When a simulation is used to represent a well-understood system, the reason for using the simulation is not solely to try to understand how the real system may operate but instead is to take advantage of the processing power and memory of the computer as a computational device. In this role, the simulation is likely to produce reliable results because it is simply being used to express the calculations that result from a well-established theory. A typical example of this can be found in a standard queuing simulation. Since queues have been extensively studied and well-established laws have been developed (Jensen & Bard, 2003), it would be likely that a sanctioned simulation of a queue would be capable of producing reliable results and predictions because the simulation's role is to simply be a calculator and data storage device. For these types of well-understood systems, simulation can provide predictive power. However, as less is known about the system, the likelihood of the simulation providing reliable data decreases to the point where the usefulness of the simulation takes on a new meaning.

A simulation takes on a new role of becoming a research instrument acting as a mediator between theory and the real system (Morrison & Morgan, 1999) when less is understood about the real system because the theories about the real system are not developed enough to truly provide reliable predictions about future states of that system. One can think of a simulation in this case as being a research tool in the same sense that a microscope is a research tool (Küppers & Lenhard, 2005). While the microscope provides insight into the real system, it does not directly reflect the nature of the real system and cannot directly provide reliable predictions about the real system. The microscope is only capable of providing a two-dimensional image of a dynamic three-dimensional real system. However, the microscope is capable of mediating between ex-

isting theories about the real system and the real system itself. Experiments can be designed and hypotheses tested based on information gained from the microscope. In this same way, a mediating simulation is capable of providing insight into the real system and the theory on which it was built without being a completely valid representation of that real system. Although only formally recognized recently (Morrison & Morgan, 1999), the idea that computers can be used to facilitate experiments and mediate between reality and theory has existed for a relatively long time. In the early years of computing, John von Neumann and Stanislaw Ulam espoused the heuristic use of the computer, as an alteration of the scientific method to replace real system experimentation with experiments performed within a computer (Burks & Neumann, 1966).

An interesting aspect of mediating simulations, which is valuable to consider, is the apparent interplay between the simulation and the real system. Just as a microscope started off as a relatively crude research tool that only provided a limited view of the real system and with time was improved to provide continuously deeper understandings of the real system, so too can a simulation of a real system be improved to gain better insights into that real system (Winsberg, 2003). Furthermore, as the real system is better understood, so can the simulation of that real system be improved to allow new insights to be gained about the real system. Examples of this mediating role of simulation can be seen in many different fields. One such example can be found in the field of nanotechnology where without computer simulations to aid in the complex and difficult experiments, certain advances in nanotechnology would not be possible (Johnson, 2006). Another example can be found in any complex production system, where the simulation provides insights into how the real system might behave under different circumstances. In the world of ABM, "toy models" such as ISAAC (Irreducible Semi-Autonomous Adaptive Combat) have been used as to explore and potentially exploit behavior that emerges in battlefield scenarios (Ilachinski, 2000). A final example can be seen in the field of physics where some ``think of sciences as a stool with three legs - theory, simulation, and experimentation - each helping us to understand and interpret the others'' (Latane, 1996).

It may seem odd to conduct an experiment using a computer simulation of a real system when the real system would seem to be the only way to guarantee that the conclusions obtained are impacted by the real system and not an error built into the simulation. However, since a real system is infinite in nature it makes error a natural aspect of any finite experiment conducted on that real system. For example, attempting to measure the impact different soils have on the growing rate of a plant will always have variation and error simply because the experimenter is trying to conduct a finite experiment and make finite measurements on an infinite system. Therefore, error is always present in experiments, regardless of whether they are done on the real system or a simulation of the real system (Winsberg, 2003). A huge difference is that simulation errors are largely repeatable giving the researcher greater control for potential insight into the real system. Nevertheless, this does not mean that the simulation should be not properly sanctioned prior to being used to facilitate an experiment. In order for a simulation to be a mediator in this sense, the simulation must contain some sort representation of the real system and be sanctioned by the evaluators, otherwise the results produced may not be reliable enough to provide any insight.

As the relationship between the real system, the theory, and the simulation blurs due to the lack of knowledge about the real system, what we mean by a simulation representing some part of reality also begins to become hazy. The more traditional belief is that for simulations to represent some aspect of a real system they should have at least some structural resemblance to the real system. However, even a simulation of a real system that is very well understood contains many built-in assumptions and falsifications, which do not match what is known about the structural aspects of the real system. This is especially true for simulations when not much is known about the real system because how can a simulation be a structural representation of a real system when the structure of the real system is not fully understood? This flaw of structural representation perhaps has led to one of the current paradigms in simulation where the performance of a simulation, i.e. how well the simulation translates realistic input into realistic output, and not accuracy is the fundamental benchmark in determining the usefulness of that simulation (Knuuttila, 2006; Küppers & Lenhard, 2005). Indeed, many of the technical validation techniques proposed today emphasize the use of this realistic output or black-box paradigm (Balci, 1995; Banks et al., 2001; Law, 2007; Sargent, 2005).

In general, this shift away from white-box evaluation (structural representation) towards black-box evaluation (output is all that matters) (Boumans, 2006) leads to several interesting conclusions. The first is this indicates the general acceptance of the idea found in Simon's The Sciences of the Artificial. Simon argues that artificial systems (ones man-made such as simulations) are useful because it is not necessary to understand the complete inner workings of a real system due to the fact that there are many possible inner workings of an artificial system that could produce the same or similar results (Simon, 1996). One way to think about this is to consider whether the differences between the inner workings of a digital clock and an analog clock really matter if they both provide the current time. Clearly, someone interested in knowing the correct time would be able to gain the same amount of information from either clock even though both clocks are structurally very different. This fundamental aspect of different structures producing the same or similar results should not be a complete surprise; as already discussed there are potentially an infinite number of possible models which can represent a single abstraction of a real system. Another conclusion drawn by the shift towards black-box evaluation is that simulations are beginning to catch up and pass the theoretical understanding of the systems that they are being built to represent. The question now becomes, what possible usefulness can a simulation be when little to nothing is known about the underlying principles of the real system of interest?

At first glance, the usefulness of a simulation for a system that is not well-understood appears to be nonexistent, because there is clearly nothing from which to build the simulation. But it is from this lack of underlying theory and understanding of the real system that the usefulness of this type of simulation becomes evident. Consider what a simulationist would encounter if asked to build a simulation of a poorly understood system. The first steps, besides trying to understand the needs of the evaluators, would be to observe the system and then attempt to generate the same behavior observed in the real system from within the simulation. This ability of a simulation to act as a medium in which new theories about a real system can be generated points to the third role of simulation, that of a theory or knowledge generator. Although certainly not a traditional means, using a simulation as a medium to generate new theories and ideas about the real system is no different in any way from using pencil and paper or simply developing mental simulations about the real system (Ashby, 1970). One could observe a system and attempt to test the implications of a theory by using pencil and paper or develop elaborate thought experiments as those made famous by Einstein just as easily as one could use a simulation to test whether a theory is capable of representing the real system. Examples of simulations being used for this role abound in the new simulation paradigm of ABM, where simulationists are typically trying to understand problems that are difficult for us to grasp due to the large amount of dispersed information and the

high number of interactions that occur in these systems (more about the special case that ABM simulations present to the world of simulation is discussed below) (Epstein & Axtell, 1996; Miller & Page, 2007; North & Macal, 2007).

There are several clear advantages for using simulations as generators, the most important of which is the ability of a simulation to create 'dirty' theories of systems where the simplicity of the real system eludes our grasp. Typically, scientific theories are often idealized for a particular case and do not allow for much deviations from these idealizations. It could be thought that these idealizations are partly the result or desire humans have to make simplifications and elegant equations to represent the complex world we live in. However, simulations allow a theorist to build a representation of a system within a simulation that is capable of having many non-elegant aspects, such as ad-hoc tinkering, engineering, and the addition of logic controls such as if-then statements (Küppers & Lenhard, 2006; Winsberg, 2006a). As a result of this flexibility, it could be predicted that as more problems venture into the realm of Organized Complexity (medium number of variables that organize into a highly interrelated organic whole) (Weaver, 1948) that the use of simulation to generate new 'dirty' theories about the real system will be needed because these systems are irreducible and typically hard to understand to the point that often simulationists are surprised about the results obtained from these systems (Casti, 1995).

By using simulations as theory generators, simulationists can attempt to generate a potential theory that explains the phenomena observed in the real system, just as a more traditional scientist would do but without the simulation medium. Therefore, there are no apparent implications of using a simulation as a generator to the philosophy of science (Frigg & Reiss, 2008). As a result, those using simulations in this manner should perhaps not consider themselves as disconnected from science because they are an engineer or computer

Figure 3. Different roles of simulation

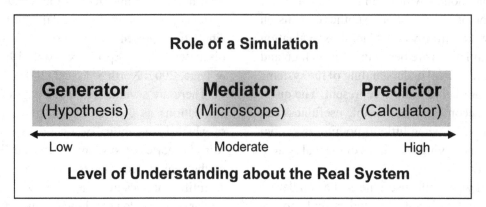

programmer by trade, but perhaps should attempt to ascribe to the practices, rigor, and roles taken on by scientists to make true progress in the practitioner's field of interest. Furthermore, as simulationists and scientists continue to push the limits of simulations beyond that of the current knowledge of some system of interest, it can be seen why some researchers are considering simulation to be the epistemological engine of our time (Ihde, 2006).

Despite the inability of a simulation to completely represent some abstraction of reality, simulation has still proven useful in several different ways. By making the connection between the level of understanding known about the real system and the simulation, a clearer picture is rendered about what simulation is capable of as well as where it fits into today's scientific and engineering endeavors. This continuous relationship, captured in Figure 3, means that when much is known about the system, the simulation tends to take on more of a predictor role, similar to that of a calculator. As less is known about the real system, the simulation takes on the role of a mediator between the system and the theory, much like the role a microscope plays a mediator between microscopic systems and the understanding of those systems. Finally, as the understanding of the system approaches almost nothing, the simulation can help generate potential theories about the nature of the system. Although

some of the implications of using simulations as generators have been discussed, it would be valuable to further breakdown the use of simulations as generators in order to better understand their relation to other simulations, the limitations they present, and to evaluate what might be lacking due the fact that the use of simulation in this manner is relatively new. Since ABM directly fits into this category, the deeper issues involved with generator simulations are discussed next.

What Good is ABM?

Despite the fact that any simulation paradigm could potentially be used as a generator, probably the most popular one used today is ABM. Emerging from Cellular Automata, Cybernetics, Chaos, Complexity, and Complex Adaptive Systems, ABM is used today to understand and explore complex, nonlinear systems where typically independent and autonomous entities interact together to form a new emergent whole. An example of such a system can be observed by the flocking behavior of birds (Levy, 1992). Although each bird is independent, somehow they interact together to form a flock, and seemingly without any leading entity, manage to stay in tight formations. With this in mind, simulationists using ABM attempt to discover the rules embedded in these individual entities that could lead to the emergent behavior and eventually attempt to make inferences about future states of these systems based on the simulations they developed. It can be clearly seen that ABM is indeed used as generators of hypotheses for these types of complex systems.

As expected, theories generated by ABM have many of the same problems encountered by more traditional methods of generating scientific theories. Such fundamental problems include whether the truth of a system be known and what methods can be used to sanction these theories. Although the issue of truth will always remain for any scientific theory, when it comes to the methods needed to sanction ABM it appears that several new problems begin, at least in terms of simulation, to emerge. These problems typically come from the fact that currently ABM is used to investigate problems where no micro level theory exists (it is not known how the individual entities operate) and where it is often very difficult to measure and collect macro level data (the emergent behavior) from a real system and compare it to the data generated from the simulation (Bankes, 2002; Levy, 1992; Miller & Page, 2007; North & Macal, 2007). Ultimately, this current characteristic of these complex problems means that the current traditional and accepted quantitative sanctioning techniques that promote risk avoidance based on performance and comparing outputs are not applicable (Shinn, 2006), since too little is known about these systems. Thus, several interesting conclusions can be made about ABM and generator simulations.

The first is that because ABM is relatively new as a paradigm, either accepted techniques to sanction these simulations have not yet been created to match the current sanctioning paradigm or a new sanctioning paradigm with new sanctioning techniques is needed for generator simulations. In order for the first statement to be the case, the underlying theory behind the real system being studied by these generator simulations needs to be known to the point that the simulation would no longer be a generator but instead be a

predictor; the current sanctioning paradigm has a majority of its interest is predictability and in turn has created sanctioning techniques that are mainly focused on this paradigm. Therefore, it is impossible for generator and ABM simulations by their nature to fit into the current predictive sanctioning paradigm. Furthermore, if an ABM simulation ever became predictable it would no longer be a generator simulation and traditional quantitative sanctioning techniques could be used. As a result, simulationists using ABM today as a generator should not be focused on meeting current predictive sanctioning paradigms, but should shift their focus to creating a new generator sanctioning paradigm and the development of new techniques to match. Attempting to create this new sanctioning paradigm will certainly not be an easy task, but it is absolutely necessary if ABM simulations as generators are to become acceptable for what they are: generators of hypotheses about complex systems. Only after this paradigm has been created can both simulationists and evaluators come to a firm conclusion about whether a generator simulation should be sanctioned as a scientific research tool or an engineering alternative analysis tool.

Although the overall lack of micro-level theory for these types of problems may push the current limits of today's simulation sanctioning for ABM, it should by no means be seen as a completely new problem. For almost every simulation the simulationist must make some assumption or build some theory about how the system works in order for the overall simulation to function appropriately. What ABM and generator simulations really do is take this engineering and ad-hoc notion to the extreme. As a result, it can be seen why that this departure from the engineering 'norm' in the world of simulation could produce a fair amount of skeptics. In fact, even von Neumann was skeptical about using a computer in this manner, even though he recognized the practical usefulness of this approach (Küppers & Lenhard, 2006). However, this type of skepticism is expected whenever pushing the limits of any paradigm accepted by a community (Pidd, 2003). Overall, what is needed to gain acceptance of generator simulations and a new sanctioning paradigm will be time and compelling evidence that eventually these ad-hoc simulations will move up the continuum of understanding about the real system such that they become mediators and then predictors.

Until the complex systems simulated by ABM are well understood, ABM simulations should be viewed practically for what they provide as strictly generator simulations. This means that ABM simulation should be viewed currently as a research tool, which is not only capable of providing insight into the real system but also points to what needs to be understood about the real system in order for a theory to be developed that can predict some aspect of the real system (Bankes, 2002). In order to know that the knowledge gained from ABM simulations is reliable, a new sanctioning paradigm is needed that is not based on predictability because it is impossible for the systems being studied with a generator simulation to be strictly predictable. Instead, this new sanctioning paradigm should be based on precision and understanding as it relates to the more traditional methods employed by scientists (Shinn, 2006). Furthermore, as this new sanctioning paradigm expands, new sanctioning techniques can be created which provide value to the generator simulationist such that the real system is understood to the point that generator simulation paradigms such as ABM can become mediator or predictor simulations.

Summary

As simulation continues to grow in popularity in scientific and engineering communities, it is invaluable to reflect upon the theories and issues that serve as the foundation for simulation as it is known today. With this in mind, this section attempted to add context and reconcile the practices of simulation with the theory of simulation.

In particular, we took fundamental philosophy of science issues related to simulation sanctioning and built a framework describing the crucial relationships that exist between simulation as a medium and real systems. The first relationship discussed is a simulation's inability to represent a complete abstraction of that real system. As a result, all simulations are invalid with respect to a complete real system. From this conclusion, the current practice of simulation validation was investigated to gain insights into what simulation validation really means. Despite the attempts of simulationists today, simulation validation really boils down to selling the simulation correctness to the evaluators of the simulation, since it is impossible to prove that a simulation is valid. With this in mind, it has been suggested that simulations are not really validated in practice but are instead sanctioned. In turn, this inability of a simulation to be validated brings into question the usefulness of simulations in general.

However, a simulation does not need to be a complete representation of some aspect of a real system to be useful. Therefore a general framework was developed that related the role of simulation based upon the level of understanding of the real system of interest. In this continuous framework, a simulation can take on the role of generator, mediator, or predictor as the level of understanding increases with regards to the real system. From this framework a clear set of expectations for a simulation can be distinguished based upon the level of understanding about the real system. Furthermore, it is hoped that this framework can further provide a base onto which new techniques and perceptions of a simulation's usefulness can be developed. Ultimately, this relationship shows partly why today simulation is becoming the research and knowledge-generating tool of choice. The epitome of this new use of simulation as a generator and research tool has emerged in the form of ABM, because ABM aids in the understanding of complex, nonlinear systems. However, because ABM is relatively new to simulation, the current practices developed to sanction simulations that are focused on predictive performances are not applicable. Therefore, simulationists using ABM should develop a new sanctioning paradigm for generator simulations that is focused on understanding and accuracy. With a new sanctioning paradigm, evaluators and simulationists can have better expectations of ABM and other generator simulations as a research tools that point to what is needed and what is possible. In the context of this framework and that as ABM improves the understanding of complex systems, perhaps eventually the level of understanding will increase concerning the real system and in turn allow ABM to take on the role of mediator or predictor.

CHAPTER SUMMARY, CONCLUSION AND FUTURE CHALLENGES

The growth of ABM requires collective critical thought pertainng to crucial aspects of the modeling paradigm. This chapter provided background information pertaining to the historical bases of ABM and to the philosophical positions regarding ABM and model validation. In the historical background section, key points made are that the current ABM paradigm grew out of multiple disciplines and that the proper use of an ABM is a function of the knowledge level associated with the current system or process. From the validation philosophy section, the bleak view is that true validation is impossible. Thus, we point out where models continue to provide benefits and lay out the case for model sanctioning as a function and model use and purpose.

The purpose of this chapter was to improve any reader's knowledge base with respect to the historical bases of ABM and the philosophical positions regarding model validation. Another purpose was to spark some debate regarding the meaning of the process of and the goals of model validation. Along this latter purpose a plethora of research questions arise. These include:

- Can a general purpose model be validated?
- If analyses are based on "un-validated" models, do the analyses provide any benefit?
- Are simulation developmental methods sufficiently precise to support model sanctioning?
- Are ABMs amenable to each simulation role we define via our Figure 3?
- What is a reasonable ABM sanctioning process?
- What kind of use cases are appropriate to test proposed ABM developmental methods as they purport to support model sanctioning?

REFERENCES

Ashby, W. R. (1970). Analysis of the system to be modeled. *The process of model-building in the behavioral sciences* (pp. 94-114). Columbus, OH: Ohio State University Press.

Axelrod, R., & Cohen, M. D. (2000). *Harnessing complexity: Organizational implications of a scientific*. New York: Basic Books.

Balci, O. (1995). Principles and techniques of simulation validation, verification. In *Proceedings of the 1995 Winter Simulation Conference*, eds. C. Alexopoulos, and K. Kang, 147-154. Piscataway, New Jersey: Institute of Electrical and Electronics Engineers, Inc.

Balci, O. (1998). Verification, validation, and accreditation. In *Proceedings of the 1998 Winter Simulation Conference*, eds. D. J. Medeiros, E. F. Watson, J. S. Carson and M. S. Manivannan, 41-48. Piscataway, New Jersey: Institute of Electrical and Electronics Engineers, Inc.

Bankes, S. C. (2002). Agent-based modeling: A revolution? *Proceedings of the National Academy of Sciences of the United States of America, 99*(10), 7199–7200. doi:10.1073/pnas.072081299

Banks, J., Carson, J. S., Nelson, B. L., & Nicol, D. M. (2001). *Discrete-event system simualtion* (3rd Ed.). Upper Saddle River, NJ: Prentice-Hall.

Barlas, Y., & Carpenter, S. (1990). Philosophical roots of model validation: Two paradigms. *System Dynamics Review, 6*(2), 148–166. doi:10.1002/sdr.4260060203

Boumans, M. (2006). The difference between answering a 'why' question and answering a 'how much' question. In G. K. Johannes Lenhard, & T. Shinn (Eds.), *Simulation: Pragmatic construction of reality; sociology of the sciences yearbook* (pp. 107-124). Dordrecht, The Netherlands: Springer.

Bremermann, H. J. (1962). Optimization through evolution and recombination. In F. T. J. M.C. Yovits, & G.D. Goldstein (Eds.), *Self-oganizing systems* (pp. 93-106). Washington D.C.: Spartan Books.

Burks, A. W., & Neumann, J. v. (1966). *Theory of self-reproducing automata*. Urbana and London: University of Illinois Press.

Casti, J. L. (1995). *Complexification: Explaining a paradoxical world through the science of surprise* (1st Ed.), New York: HarperPerennial.

Czerwinski, T. (1998). *Coping with the Bounds: Speculations on Nonlinearity in Military Affairs*. Washington, DC: National Defense University Press.

Davis, P. K. (1992). *Generalizing concepts and methods of verification, validation, and*. Santa Monica, CA: RAND.

Davis, P. K., & Blumenthal, D. (1991). *The base of sand problem: A white paper on the state of military*. Santa Monica, CA: RAND.

Epstein, J. M., & Axtell, R. (1996). *Growing artificial socieities: Social science from the bottom up*. Washington, DC: Brookings Institution Press.

Feinstein, A. H., & Cannon, H. M. (2002). Constructs of simulation evaluation. *Simulation & Gaming, 33*(4), 425–440. doi:10.1177/1046878102238606

Feinstein, A. H., & Cannon, H. M. (2003). A hermeneutical approach to external validation of simulation models. *Simulation & Gaming, 34*(2), 186–197. doi:10.1177/1046878103034002002

Ferber, J. (1999). *Multi-agent systems: An introduction to distributed artificial intelligence*. Harlow, UK: Addison-Wesley

Fishman, G. S., & Kiviat, P. J. (1968). The statistics of discrete-event simulation. *Simulation, 10*, 185–195. doi:10.1177/003754976801000406

Frigg, R., & Reiss, J. (2008). *The philosophy of simulation: Hot new issues or same old stew?* Gershenson, C. (2002). Complex philosophy. *The First Biennial Seminar on the Philosophical, Methodological*.

Gleick, J. (1987). *Chaos: Making a new science*. New York: Viking.

Gödel, K. (1931). Über formal unentscheidbare sätze der principia mathematica und verwandter. *Monatshefte Für Mathematik Und Physik, (38)*, 173-198.

Hill, R. R., McIntyre, G. A., Tighe, T. R., & Bullock, R. K. (2003). Some experiments with agent-based combat models. *Military Operations Research, 8*(3), 17–28.

Hodges, J. S. (1991). Six or so things you can do with a bad model. *Operations Research, 39*(3), 355–365. doi:10.1287/opre.39.3.355

Holland, J. H. (1995). *Hidden order: How adaptation builds complexity*. Cambridge, MA: Helix Books.

Ihde, D. (2006). Models, models everywhere. In G. K. Johannes Lenhard, & T. Shinn (Eds.), *Simulation: Pragmatic construction of reality; sociology of the sciences yearbook* (pp. 79-86). Dordrecht, The Netherlands: Springer.

Ilachinski, A. (2000). Irreducible semi-autonomous adaptive combat (ISAAC): An artificial-life approach to land warefare. *Military Operations Research, 5*(3), 29–47.

Jensen, P. A., & Bard, J. F. (2003). *Operations research models and methods*. Hoboken, NJ: John Wiley & Sons.

Johnson, A. (2006). The shape of molecules to come. In G. K. Johannes Lenhard, & T. Shinn (Eds.), *Simulation: Pragmatic construction of reality; sociology of the sciences yearbook* (pp. 25-39). Dordrecht, The Netherlands: Springer.

Kincaid, H. (1998). Philsophy: Then and now. In N. S. Arnold, T. M. Benditt & G. Graham (Eds.), (pp. 321-338). Malden, MA: Blackwell Publishers Ltd.

Klein, E. E., & Herskovitz, P. J. (2005). Philosophical foundations of computer simulation validation. *Simulation \& Gaming, 36*(3), 303-329.

Kleindorfer, G. B., & Ganeshan, R. (1993). The philosophy of science and validation in simulation. In *Proceedings of the 1993 Winter Simulation Conference*, ed. G.W. Evans, M. Mollaghasemi, E.C. Russell, and W.E. Biles, 50-57. Piscataway, New Jersey: Institute of Electrical and Electronic Engineers, Inc.

Kleindorfer, G. B., O'Neill, L., & Ganeshan, R. (1998). Validation in simulation: Various positions in the philosophy of science. *Management Science, 44*(8), 1087–1099. doi:10.1287/mnsc.44.8.1087

Knuuttila, T. (2006). From representation to production: Parsers and parsing in language. In G. K. Johannes Lenhard, & T. Shinn (Eds.), *Simulation: Pragmatic construction of reality; sociology of the sciences yearbook* (pp. 41-55). Dordrecht, The Netherlands: Springer.

Küppers, G., & Lenhard, J. (2005). Validation of simulation: Patterns in the social and natural sciences. *Journal of Artificial Societies and Social Simulation, 8*(4), 3.

Küppers, G., & Lenhard, J. (2006). From hierarchical to network-like integration: A revolution of modeling. In G. K. Johannes Lenhard, & T. Shinn (Eds.), *Simulation: Pragmatic construction of reality; sociology of the sciences yearbook* (pp. 89-106). Dordrecht, The Netherlands: Springer.

Küppers, G., Lenhard, J., & Shinn, T. (2006). Computer simulation: Practice, epistemology, and social dynamics. In G. K. Johannes Lenhard, & T. Shinn (Eds.), *Simulation: Pragmatic construction of reality; sociology of the sciences yearbook* (pp. 3-22). Dordrecht, The Netherlands: Springer.

Langton, C. G. (1989). Artificial life. *Artificial Life*, 1–48.

Latane, B. (1996). Dynamic social impact: Robust preditions from simple theory. In U. M. R. Hegselmann, & K. Triotzsch (Eds.), *Modelling and simulatiion in the social sciences fromthe philosophy of science point of view*. New York: Springer-Verlag.

Law, A. M. (2007). *Simulation, modeling, and analysis* (4th Ed.). New York: McGraw-Hill.

Levy, S. (1992). *Artificial life: A report from the frontier where computers meet*. New York: Vintage Books.

Macal, C. M., & North, M. J. (2006). Tutorial on agent-based modeling and simulation part 2: How to model. In *Proceedings of the 2006 Winter Simulation Conference*, eds. L. R. Perrone, F. P. Wieland, J. Liu, B. G. Lawson, D. M. Nicol, and R. M. Fujimoto, 73-83. Piscataway, New Jersey: Institute of Electrical and Electronics Engineers, Inc.

Mandelbrot, B. B. (1982). *The Fractal Geometry of Nature*. New York: W.H. Freeman.

Miller, J. H., & Page, S. E. (2007). *Complex adaptive systems: An introduction to computational models of social life*. Princeton, NJ: Princeton University Press.

Mitchell, M., Crutch, J. P., & Hraber, P. T. (1994). Dynamics, computation, and the "edge of chaos": A re-examination. In G. Cowan, D. Pines, & D. Melzner (Eds), *Complexity: Metaphors, Models and Reality*. Reading, MA: Addison-Wesley.

Morrison, M., & Morgan, M. S. (1999). Models as mediating instruments. In M. S. Morgan, & M. Morrison (Eds.), *Models as mediators* (pp. 10-37). Cambridge, UK: Cambridge University Press.

Naylor, T. H., & Finger, J. M. (1967). Verification of computer simulation models. *Management Science*, *14*(2), 92–106. doi:10.1287/mnsc.14.2.B92

North, M. J., & Macal, C. M. (2007). *Managing business complexity: Discovering strategic solutions with*. New York, NY: Oxford University Press.

Pidd, M. (2003). Tools for thinking: Modelling in management science. (2nd Ed., pp. 289-312) New York: John Wiley and Sons.

Resnyansky, L. (2007). *Integration of social sciences in terrorism modelling: Issues, problems*. Edinburgh, Australia: Australian Government Department of Defence, DSTO Command and Control.

Sargent, R. G. (2005). Verification and validation of simulation models. *The Proceedings of the 2005 Winter Simulation Conference*, (pp. 130-143).

Schelling, T. C. (2006). *Micromotives and macrobehavior* (2nd Ed.). New York: WW Norton and Company.

Schmid, A. (2005). What is the truth of simulation? *Journal of Artificial Societies and Social Simulation*, *8*(4), 5.

Shinn, T. (2006). When is simulation a research technology? practices, markets, and. In G. K. J. Lenhard, & T. Shinn (Eds.), *Simulation: Pragmatic construction of reality; sociology of the sciences yearbook* (pp. 187-203). Dordrecht, The Netherlands: Springer.

Simon, H. A. (1962). The architecture of complexity. *Proceedings of the American Philosophical Society*, *106*(6), 467–482.

Simon, H. A. (1996). *The sciences of the artificial* (3rd Ed.). Cambridge, MA: The MIT Press.

Stanislaw, H. (1986). Tests of computer simulation validation: What do they measure? *Simulation & Games*, *17*(2), 173–191. doi:10.1177/0037550086172003

Weaver, W. (1948). Science and complexity. *American Scientists, 36*.

Winsberg, E. (1999). Sanctioning models: The epistemology of simulation. *Science in Context*, *12*(2), 275–292. doi:10.1017/S0269889700003422

Winsberg, E. (2001). Simualtions, models, and theories: Complex physical systems and their. *Philosophy of Science*, *68*(3), 442–454. doi:10.1086/392927

Winsberg, E. (2003). Simulated experiments: Methodology for a virtual world. *Philosophy of Science*, *70*, 105–125. doi:10.1086/367872

Winsberg, E. (2006a). Handshaking your way to the top: Simulation at the nanoscale. In G. K. J. Lenhard, & T. Shinn (Eds.), *Simulation: Pragmatic construction of reality; sociology of the sciences yearbook* (pp. 139-151). Dordrecht, The Netherlands: Springer.

Winsberg, E. (2006b). Models of success versus the success of models: Reliability without. *Synthese*, *152*, 1–19. doi:10.1007/s11229-004-5404-6

Wolfram, S. (1994). *Cellular Automata and Complexity: Collected Papers.* Reading, MA: Addison-Wesley Publishing Company.

Zeigler, B. P., Praehofer, H., & Kim, T. G. (2000). *Theory of modeling and simulation* (2nd Ed.). New York: Academic Press.

KEY TERMS AND DEFINITIONS

Agent-Based Modeling: A computational model for simulating the actions and interactions of autonomous individuals in a network, with a view to assessing their effects on the system as a whole.

Verification: The act of reviewing, inspecting, testing, etc. to establish and document that a product, service, or system meets the regulatory, standard, or specification requirements.

Validation: The process of determining whether a simulation model is an accurate representation of a system.

Emergence: The process of coherent patterns of behavior arising from the self-organizing aspects of complex systems.

Cellular Automata: A discrete model consisting of a grip of cells each of which have a finite number of defined states where the state of a cells is a function of the states of neighboring cells and the transition among states is according to some predefined updating rule.

Cybernetics: The science of control and communication in the animal and the machine.

Complex Adaptive Systems: A complex, self-similar collection of interacting agents, acting in parallel and reacting to other agent behaviors within the system.

Nonlinearity: In terms of system output refers to the state wherein the system output as a collective is greater than the sum of the individual system component outputs.

Simulation: The imitation of some real thing, state of affairs, or process. The act of simulating something generally entails representing certain key characteristics or behaviors of a selected physical or abstract system.

Chapter 4
Verification and Validation of Simulation Models

Sattar J. Aboud
Middle East University for Graduate Studies, Jordan

Mohammad Al Fayoumi
Middle East University for Graduate Studies, Jordan

Mohamed Alnuaimi
Middle East University for Graduate Studies, Jordan

ABSTRACT

Unfortunately, cost and time are always restraints; the impact of simulation models to study the dynamic system performance is always rising. Also, with admiration of raising the network security models, the complexity of real model applications is rising too. As a result, the complexity of simulation models applications is also rising and the necessary demand for designing a suitable verification and validation systems to ensure the system reliability and integrality is very important. The key requirement to study the system integrity is to verify the system accuracy and to validate its legality regarding to pre-specified applications causes and validly principles. This needs different plans, and application phases of simulation models to be properly identified, and the output of every part is properly documented. This chapter discusses validation and verification of simulation models. The different approaches to deciding model validity are presented; how **model validation** *and verification relate to the* **model development process** *are discussed; various* **validation techniques** *are defined;* **conceptual model validity**, **model verification**, **operational validity**, *and* **data validity**; *superior verification and validation technique for simulation models relied on a* **multistage approach** *are described; ways to* **document** *results are given; and a recommended procedure is presented.*

INTRODUCTION

Regarding rigorous analysis of divers current ideas for verification and validation of simulation models, the specialists impression of model development and their knowledge in verification and validation of simulation models in organizations (Brade and Lehmann, 2002), within the topics of the Symposium in 2002 a developed structured verification and validation method, also denoted to as verification

DOI: 10.4018/978-1-60566-774-4.ch004

and validation triangle (Brade, 2003). This method deal with the following key points of successful verification and validation:

- Using the structured and **stepwise technique**
- Reengineering verification and validation throughout **model development**
- Testing intermediate results
- Constructing a chain of facts relied on verification and validation results
- supplying templates for **documentation** of verification and validation activities and findings
- Accomplish verification and validation activities separately.

To perform this aim, the standard **verification and validation triangle** provides:

- An outline of fault types that are probably is concealed in the intermediate result on which the verification and validation activities are concentrated.
- **Verification and validation stages** to measure the accuracy and validity of every intermediate result separately.
- **Verification and validation sub stages** with generic verification and validation goals to investigate the possible test of certain types of intermediate results and outside information.
- Guide point to implement verification and validation methods and to reuse formerly generated verification and validation results.
- Outline the dependence between various verification and validation goals and the effect of cyclic test on the integrity of the simulation model.

Simulation models are increasingly employed these days in solving difficulty and in decision making. Thus, a developers and consumers of these models, the decision makers with data resulting from a findings of the systems, and individuals affected via decisions relied on such systems are accurately concerned if the system and its finding are accurate. This matter is addressed during **model validation and verification**. Model validation is generally defined a corroboration that a computerized model with its area of applicability possesses an acceptable range of accuracy reliable with the planned use of a model and is a definition employed. Model verification is often defined as ensuring that a program of a computerized system and its performance are accurate, and is a definition accepted. The system becomes accredited during model accreditation. The system accreditation concludes if the system satisfies specified model accreditation measures consistent with the particular process. The related issue is system reliability. The system reliability is concerned with developing a confidence wanted via possible users in the system and in a data resulting from a system that they are eager to employ a system and a resulting data.

The model must be developed for a specific aim and its validity fixed with respect to that aim. When the aim of the system is to solve a selection of questions, a validity of a system wants to be fixed with respect to every question. Many collection of **experimental status** are usually needed to define the area of system **intended applicability**. The system can be valid for one collection of experimental status and invalid for another. The model is measured valid for a collection of experimental status when its precision is within its satisfactory range that is the amount of precision needed for a system intended aim. This usually needs the system result variables of interest that is a system variables employed in solving the questions that a system is being developed to answer is specified and that their needed amount of precision is specified. The amount of precision needed must be identified before to beginning the **development of a system** for each early in the system development process. When the variables of interest are arbitrary variables, then characteristic and functions of the arbitrary variables such as means and variances are usually is of main interest and are employed in fixing system validity. Some versions of the system are normally developed before to getting an acceptable valid system. The substantiation the model is valid, that is system verification and validation, is usually measured to be a process and is generally part of the system **development process**.

Entire documentation needs an obvious definition of the intermediate outcome that creates during system development. Data modeling is a lengthy and difficult work to accomplish, and some study stated that up to 33% of the complete time used in a simulation analysis can be used on data modeling (Wang and Lehmann, 2008). Moreover, the quality of data is also a vital factor for the reliability assessment of simulation models. Accordingly for the **verification and validation process**, truth and correctness of data gathering, analysis, and alteration is essential. But the data used must be measured in each **system development stage** and within the range of the standard of **verification and validation method**. This is not intended for as an independent matter, and not considered in depth. Though, in this chapter, we attempt to enhance the standard verification and validation method by attaching an extra consideration resultant from the advice feedback (Spieckermann, Lehmann and Rabe, 2004) which the verification and validation operation of data modeling is obviously managed. Furthermore, with an advanced fashion thought, we will show how this system can be modified according to the specific requirements of some known simulation systems.

It is always very costly and time consuming to determine that a system is completely valid over the entire field of its planned applicability. Instead, tests and assessments are guided until sufficient confidence is got that a system can be considered valid for its planned application (Sargent, 1999). The cost of system validation is generally very important, mainly if really high system confidence is needed.

VALIDATION PROCESS

There are three fundamental methods are employed in determining if the **simulation model** is valid or invalid. Every one of these methods needs a model development team to lead validation and verification as an element of a model **development process** that will be discussed in this section. The most common method for the development team is to create a decision as to if the system is valid. This is a subjective decision relied on a outcome of a different tests and assessments guided as an element of the model development process. Another method, usually named independent verification and validation, employs the third trusted party to determine if a model is valid. The third trusted party is independent from a model development team and a system user. Following the model is developed; a third trusted party leads an assessment to decide its validity. Relied on the validation, a third trusted party creates a particular decision on the validity of a system. This method is often employed if a large cost is linked with the difficulty a simulation model is being employed for and to assist in system reliability. The third trusted party is also generally employed for model authorization.

The assessment made in an independent verification and validation method ranges from just reviewing a verification and validation guided via a model development team to a entire verification and validation attempt. (Sagent, 2000) explains experiences over this range of assessment via the third trusted party on energy models. The conclusion that we reach is that an entire independent **verification and validation assessment** is very costly and time consuming for what is got. Researcher vision is that when the third trusted party is employed, it must be throughout a model development process. When a model has been developed, these authors consider that generally the third trusted party must assess just a verification and validation that has been done. The last method for deciding if the system is valid is to employ a scoring model (Balci, 1998). Scores are determined subjectively if performing different parts of a validation process and then combined to decide type scores and a total score for a simulation system. The simulation model is measured valid when its total and type scores are greater than certain passing scores. This method is uncommonly employed in practice. However, these researchers do not think in the employ of a scoring system for formative validity since:

- The subjective of this system tends to be unseen and therefore seems to be objective
- The scores should be determined in certain way generally subjective means
- The system could receive a passing score but have a fault that requires correction.
- The scores could results over trust in a system or is employed to claim that certain system is better than another one.

However, we now describe the validation and verification model regarding the development process. There are two general methods to observe this relationship. The first method employs certain kind of full model development process, and the second method employs certain kind of simple model development process. (Banks, Gerstein, and Searles, 1998) evaluated effort employing both of these methods we concluded that the simple method more obviously lights up validation and verification model. These researchers recommend the service of a simple method (Sargent, 1999). Consider the typical version of a system process in Figure 1.

The problem entity: Are a system suggested, thought, condition, policy, and phenomena to be formed.

The conceptual model: is the arithmetical or logical statement imitated of the problem entity developed for the specific report. The **computerized system** is the **conceptual model executed** on the machine. The conceptual model is developed during an analysis and prototype phase, the computerized system is developed during a **computer programming** and **executing phase**, and inferences regarding the problem entity are got via guiding machine experiments on a **computerized system** in an experimentation phase.

Conceptual model validity: is described as formative that hypothesizes and assumptions motivating a conceptual model are approved and that a model representation of a problem entity is realistic for an intended aim of a system.

Computerized model verification: is defined as a computer programming and executing of a conceptual model.

Operational validity: is defined as a model result behavior has enough correctness for a model intended aim over the area of system intended applicability.

Information validity: is defined as the information necessary for system construction, model assessment and testing, and guiding the system experiments to solve the difficulty is sufficient and accurate.

Numerous versions of a system are generally developed in the modeling process before to getting a satisfactory valid model. Throughout every model iteration the model validation and verification are achieved (Sargent, 1996). The diversity of validation methods are employed, which are explained in the following section. There is no algorithm and process exists to choose which methods to employ.

VALIDATION METHODS

In this section we are going to explains different validation methods and tests employed in model validation and verification. Most of the methods

Figure 1. Typical version of a system process

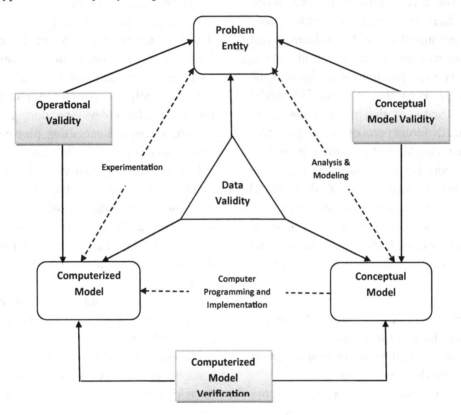

explained in this section are obtained from the literature, while certain could be explained slightly in a different way. They may be employed either subjectively or objectively. With objectively, we are employing certain kind of statistical test or mathematical method, for instance hypothesis tests and confidence period. The combination of methods is usually employed. These methods are employed for validation and verification the sub-systems and general system.

Animation: A **model operational performance** is showed graphically as a model moves from side to side time. For instance, the travels of parts through a factory during a simulation are exposed graphically. Different outputs of a simulation system being validated are compared to outputs of other valid systems. For instance:

- Straightforward cases of a simulation model could be compared to recognized outputs of investigative systems.
- A simulation model could be compared to other simulation systems that have been validated.

Degenerate Tests: A degeneracy of a system behavior is tested via suitable collection of results of an input and internal variables. For instance, does an average number in a queue of the single server remain to increase with respect to rate if an arrival rate is greater than the check time?

Event Validity: The events of occurrences of a simulation system are compared with a real model to decide if they are equal. For instance the events are deaths in a fire section simulation.

Extreme Condition Tests: The system structure and result must be reasonable for any extreme and improbable combination of levels of parts in the model; for instance when in process inventories are zero, production result must be zero.

Face Validity: Face validity is request persons knowledgeable concerning a model if a system and its performance are logical. This method could be employed in deciding when the logic in a conceptual model is accurate and when the system **input-output relationship** is sound.

Determined Values: Determined values for instance, constants are employed for different system input and internal variables. This must permit a checking of system output versus easily computed results.

Historical Information Validation: When historical information exists or if information is collected on a model for construction or testing a system, part of the information is employed to construct a system and the remaining information is employed to fix test if a system behaves as a model does. This testing is guided via making a simulation model with either example from distributions or traces (Brade, 2003).

Historical Methods: The three historical methods of validation are rationalism, empiricism, and positive economics. Rationalism supposes that each one knows if the basic assumptions of the system are factual. Logic deductions are employed from these assumptions to develop an accurate valid system. Empiricism needs each assumption and result to be empirically validated. Positive economics needs just that a system is able to expect a future and is not concerned with the system assumptions or structure connecting relationships or system.

Internal Validity: some duplication runs of a stochastic model are created to decide an amount of internal stochastic variability in the system. The high amount of variability lack of consistency could result a system outcomes to be uncertain and when characteristic of a problem entity, might question a suitability of a policy or model is examined.

Multistage Validation: As (Wang and Lehmann, 2008) suggested joining the three historical techniques of **rationalism**, **empiricism**, and **positive economics** into a multistage procedure of validation. This validation technique embraces of:

- Developing the system assumptions on theory, remarks, common knowledge, and role.
- Validating the system assumptions where likely via empirically assessment them.
- Comparing testing an input-output relationship of a system to an actual one.

Operational Graphics: Results of different performance measures. For instance number in queue and proportion of servers busy, are displayed graphically as a system moves during time. For instance the dynamic behaviors of execution indicators are visually shown as a simulation model moves during time.

Parameter Variability Sensitivity Analysis: This method embraces of changing the values of an input and internal variables of the system to decide the effect in the model behavior and its result. The same relationships must happen in a model as in the actual one. Those variables are sensitive, for instance cause important changes in a model performance and must be create sufficiently correct before to employing the system. This can need iterations in system development.

Predictive Validation: A system is employed to predict forecast a model performance, and then comparisons are concluded between the model performance and a system forecast to decide when they are equal. The data can come from an operational model or from experiments achieved on the model. For instance field checks.

Traces: The behavior of various sorts of particular entities in the system is traced followed during a system to decide when the model logic is accurate and when a necessary correctness is got.

Turing Tests: Individuals who are well-informed regarding the operations of the model are asked when they can differentiate between model and system result (Wang and Lehmann, 2008) include statistical tests for employ with Turing tests.

INFORMATION VALIDITY

Although information validity is in fact not considered as a component of model validation, we will argue it since it is generally hard, time consuming, and costly to got enough, correct, and suitable information, and is often the cause that tries to validate the model fail. Information is required for three reasons: for construction the conceptual model, for validating a model, and for achieving experiments with a validated system. In model validation we are worried just with the first two sorts of information.

To construct the conceptual model we should have sufficient information on the problem entity to develop models that can be employed to construct the system, to develop the logical and mathematical relationships in a model that will permit it to sufficiently indicate the problem identity for its intended aim, and to check a system underlying assumptions. Also, behavioral information is required on a problem entity to be employed in the operational validity step of comparing the problem entity performance with the model activities. Generally, this information is model input/output. When this information is not available, high model confidence typically cannot be got, since sufficient operational validity cannot be accomplished.

The concern with information is that suitable, correct, and adequate information is available, and

when any information transformations are done, such as disaggregation, they are suitably achieved. Unfortunately, there is not much that can be made to ensure that the information is accurate. The best that could be performed is to develop beneficial measures for gathering and upholding it, check the gathered information employing methods for example internal consistency tests, and display for outliers and deciding when they are accurate. When an amount of information is big, a data base must be developed and kept.

CONCEPTUAL MODEL VALIDATION

Validity of conceptual model is deciding by:

- The concepts and assumptions that essential for a conceptual model are accurate.
- The model illustration of a problem entity and the system structure, logic, and arithmetical are sound for the intended aim of a system.

The concepts and assumptions constructing a model must be checked employing arithmetical analysis and statistical techniques on problem entity information. Cases of concepts and assumptions are fixed, linearity, independence and Poisson arrivals. Cases of applicable statistical techniques are appropriate distributions to information, guessing variables values from the information and plotting the information to decide when they are fixed. Also, all concepts employed must be evaluated to guarantee they were affected suitably; for instance, when a Markov chain is employed, is a model have a Markov characteristic.

However, every sub-model and the entire model should be assessed to decide when they are practical and accurate for the intended aim of the system. This must include deciding when the correct detail and aggregate relationships have been employed for the model intended aim, and when the suitable structure, logic, and arithmetical and relationships have been employed. The main validation methods employed for these assessments are face validation and traces. Face validation has experts on the problem entity evaluate a conceptual model to decide when it is accurate and practical for its aim. This generally needs checking the flowchart or graphical chart, or the collection of model formulas.

The use of traces is the tracking of entities during every sub-model and the entire model to decide when the logic is accurate and when the necessary correctness is preserved. When faults are found in a conceptual model, it should be adjusted and conceptual model validation done once more.

VERIFICATION OF THE MODEL

The model verification guarantees that a computer completion of a conceptual model is accurate. The main part effecting verification is when the simulation language for example Java is employed. The use of a special-purpose simulation language will cause in containing fewer faults than when the general-purpose simulation language is employed. The use of a simulation language generally decreases the timing required in programming, but it is inflexibility. If the simulation language is used, verification is mainly concerned with guaranteeing that a fault free simulation language has been employed, a simulation language has been correctly executed on a machine, that a tested for accuracy pseudo random number generator has been correctly executed, and that the system has been encoded properly in a **simulation language**. The main methods employed to decide that a model has been encoded properly are structured well and trace.

When the higher level language has been employed, then a **machine program** must have been designed, and implemented employing methods established in software engineering. These contain such methods as **object-oriented** **design** and **program modularity**. In this case verification is mainly concerned with deciding that the simulation tasks for example a pseudo random number generator, time-flow mechanism and the computer system have been encoded and executed properly.

There are two essential methods for **testing simulation program**: **static testing** line and **dynamic testing** line. In static testing line the machine program is analyzed to decide when it is accurate via employing such methods as well-structured accuracy, proofs, and testing the structure characteristics of a program. In dynamic testing line a machine program is implemented under various conditions and the results got including those created throughout an implementation, are employed to decide when computer software and its executions are accurate. The methods usually employed in dynamic testing line are traces, investigations of input-output relations employing various validation methods, internal consistency tests, and encoded serious parts to decide when the same values are got. When there are a large number of parameters, one might combine a few of the parameters to decrease the number of checks required or employ some kinds of design of experiments. It is essential to be conscious while testing the accuracy of the machine program and its execution that faults is caused via the information, a conceptual model, the computer software, or a computer execution.

INFORMATION MODELING PROCESS

Information modeling process in simulation model is of major significance for handling a simulation study (Banks, Caeson, Nelson and Nicol, 2005) and usually consists of the following steps.

1. Information analysis
2. Information gathering

3. Information transformation
4. Results analysis and understanding.

Information Analysis

This step is to manage **information identification** needed for model development and simulation tests from the model to be considered. Both **qualitative** and **quantitative information** which may be employed as dimensions to depict the model of interest must be studies. Along with the given restrictions in the original simulation review, for instance, cost and time restrictions, examination will be prepared to demonstrate from which resources the preferred information adaptation of verification and validation processes. Finally, the contributions of the chapter the future work is considered. Wang and Lehmann arises, which techniques must be employed, and what timetable must be followed, in order the information to be gathered more accurately and efficiently.

Information came from a diversity of sources, are employed for various aspects regarding simulation model. Mainly, there are three types of information (Sargat, 2000) for model input:

- Information for identifying the model
- Information for test
- Information for performing simulation experiments.

Based on the provided information the probability distributions must be fixed, which is employed to identify the behavior of the arbitrary processes driving the model under consideration. Basically there are two alternatives in determining probability distributions:

- Employ the real sample information to denote the probability distributions.
- Fixed a theoretical probability distribution corresponding to the information gathered.

There are many statistical methods available (Law and Kelton, 1991) that may be implemented for distribution choosing in different circumstances. As soon as this job has been entirely done, arbitrary samples employed as input to the simulation model and created from the specific distribution task.

Information Gathering

According to the result of analysis, **information gathering** must be processed in a systematic model. For certain circumstances information gathering is a simple examination and measurement of the quality of interest appears enough for the current information requirements, but from time to time, documents should be employed. Documents employed for information modeling are typically in a form of figures, reports, tables and so on. But, the present documentations do not automatically imply accessibility for information modeling. One of the main difficulties concerning the documents is the correct result in documents in a simulation study which may be wealthy in statistics, nevertheless poor in contents in fact requisite for the examination aim. In addition, the documents can be available in parts. As a result, the aptitude to determine and clarify the right information hold in documents is of particular significance.

Information Transformation

Equally **qualitative** and **quantitative** information require to be **transformed** into a computer process form during model processing. Certain information are employed to identify the model being constructed, and verification and validation of simulation models ultimately, become integrated into the model constructed; while the other information that are employed to compare with the simulation result, usually require to be handled independently from the model under analysis. So, it is necessary for information transformation not just to format information properly in format, and in type that are necessary via certain software applications employed but, also to set up an idea which facilitates a dependable information storing and information retrieving, and also the efficient information transfer between a simulation program and its cooperating information depository.

Results Analysis and Understanding

Results are created as outputs of **simulation experiments** determined via providing input. Thus, because arbitrary samples resulting from a known probability distribution tasks are normally employed, the model result is influenced via arbitrary factors consequently. When the result are not analyzed sufficiently, they can easily be misunderstanding, thus that false conclusions concerning the model of interest are depicted, despite how well the model has been really constructed. For analyzing results, it is significant to make sure when the model being modeled and come to an end or not, further to differentiate between a steady case and a temporary no steady case since different statistical methods must be employed for every case.

SETTING UP CREDIBLE INFORMATION MODELS

Collecting High-Quality Information

Getting suitable information from the model of interest is a vital ground to accomplish a valid simulation model. The process for gathering information is frequently subjective to a large number of subject and object issues. The topics describe below address the tackle of the difficulties that encountered in information gathering.

1. Gathering Information Manually or Automatically

Normally, information is manually collected by direct observation and measurement. But, because the individual recording information can easily be disturbed via the model to be measured, and in the same way, the model behavior itself can also be affected via the attendance of an observer. It is unworkable for an observer to gather information just exactly and orderly as preferred and intended. To tackle the difficulties derived from the manual environment, techniques to use automatic information gathering must be implemented.

Some new models for automatic information gathering and information integration in simulation models (Balci, 1998) have been used, by which an information interface between a simulation model and a commercial business model is developed, which gathers, stores and retrieves information, and also provides information employed for simulation test completely automatically. Since of the high practical requirements but, these methods could be implementing in a restricted number of services, for instance, in modeling production industry.

Unfortunately, there are certain circumstances where it is impractical to collect information. For instance, when the model under consideration does not continue in an actual form or if it is too complex and time consuming to collect information from an existing model. This problem can also happen via collection information only in certain processes of the model. In such situations, expert opinion and knowledge of the model and its behavior are crucial to make assumptions concerning the model for the purposes by which a simulation model is proposed. Furthermore, where appropriate, information collected from different, but similar models could also be measured.

2. Applying Historical Information

Historical information from the model being examined could be employed for a point of model validation, by which results of the actual model and the model are compared via employing the identical historical information (Robertson and Perera, 2001). But, the comparison in this way is practical, when the real situation of the model can be measured to be equal to the situation of the model, from which the historical information occurred. The same information variables cannot ensure the model and the model are driven precisely on the identical situation, since the historical information normally employed for model validation cover only a restricted range of influencing elements on the original model.

3. Gathering information via interviewing

There is no hesitation that interviews are important for information collecting. With the assist of interviews the expert knowledge not however documented in certain real form can be therefore communicated to another. In the example studies above, where information is not available from the present model, interviews can be the only method to get some data about the model to be modeled. It must be observed that interviewing is a process of getting both objective and subjective data. (Wang and Lehmann, 2008) reported that it is always verification and validation of simulation model significant to differentiate between facts and opinions; together are essential and valuable but should be processed in a different way.

Integrating Information Verification and Validation

While certain part of activities in information collecting and information analyzing may be performed concurrently with model development, information modeling in general is via no way an individual process, but intimately coupled within the original simulation study and so, must be considered as an integral part of the general simulation model. Simply like the type of model construction, conducting information model develops also in a modular and iterative mode.

As illustrated in Figure 2 which is introduced in a form following the literature (Spieckermann, Lehmann and Rabe, 2004), the results of every information model in phase give further knowledge concerning the model of interest to make the model progress, while the model under construction returns the feedbacks which prompt more information modeling attempt or a another iteration. Finally, the simulation conclusion is reached at the final intersection of the both processes. Information verification and validation is intended to disclose any quality lacks that included in every intermediate result of information model being conducted from information requirements analysis to result analysis and interpretation. Information verification is defined to ensure that information are changed during the modeling process precisely in form and content; while information validation is involve with determining if the employed of information model sufficiently satisfies the intended reason of the simulation goals. As (Spieckermann, Lehmann and Rabe, 2004) reported, information verification and validation must be done in accordance with model verification and validation throughout the whole development process of a simulation model.

Improved **verification and validation process**, which is extended via involving an exact consideration of information modeling, consists of two closely associated elements of **verification and validation activities**: verification and validation model and verification and validation information. The major stress in this section is placed on explaining information verification and validation and the relationship between the two elements. More details regarding the fundamental principle of the verification and validation triangle may be obtained in. In verification and validation model, every well defined intermediate result generated during model development from structured problem description to model results is input to verification and validation phase. Every verification and validation phase is again split into more sub-phases, with a defined sub goal to

Figure 2. Information simulation modeling

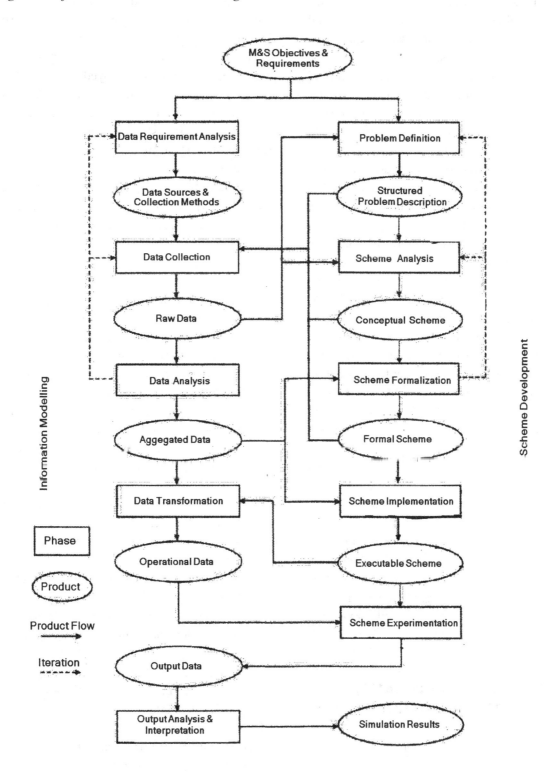

discover the internal faults or alteration faults. In the sub phases the absence of result internal faults in every particular intermediate result must be confirmed. For instance, in sub phase must be make sure that the problem description is free of error and inconsistence, and in another sub phase a syntax check may be implemented to the formal model comparison of the selected formalism. In any other sub phases, the pair wise comparison between the present intermediate result and every preceding intermediate result may be created to validate the absence of alteration mistakes. For example in some sub phases the formal model may be compared with the theoretical model, the structured problem description, and the sponsor requirements one by one through repeating the comparison versus an intermediate result. In this way more strength of verification and validation activities is reached, and then the credibility set up so far may also be strengthen accordingly. Wang and Lehmann with respect to information flow, every verification and validation phase is then extended via extra verification and validation activities of information derived from the resultant information modeling process. Two kinds of information in the information flow during model development must be distinguished: **unprocessed information** and processed information. Unprocessed information is found directly from various resources, and usually unformed information. While the **empirical information**, which are inherited from preceding simulation applications and typically given at the start of the analysis, may be available in a well-formed and input ready fashion.

THE EXTENDED VERIFICATION AND VALIDATION TRIANGLE

They are in this respect also unprocessed information, since it is via any means necessary to the use of such information to ensure when they are in fact reasonable for the present context. Processed information is generated via editing, the gather unprocessed information by modeling process. So, information verification and validation involves credibility review of unprocessed information and processed information employed for generating every intermediate result. It must be observed that unprocessed information are typically only relevant for getting structured problem description and theoretical model, may not be directly appropriate for generating formal model and other later intermediate results. Throughout verification and validation of unprocessed information related to every intermediate result, the following matters must be ensured:

- Verification and validation of processed information concentrate on ensuring that all information employed for every intermediate result are correct and accurate in their transformed from throughout the model development, with the following standard matters.
- Information resources are reasonable for the intended reason of the model.
- It is significant when the information is derived from a different model.
- To assess the assumptions of self government and homogeneity made on the collected information sets.
- To control that information have been transformed in essential structure and form.
- To make certain the probability distribution employed and the associated parameters are practical for the information gathering, for instance, via employing a goodness-of-fit test
- To make certain that sufficient independent simulation runs have been performed for a stochastic model.

Both **quantitative and qualitative information** must be measured adequately, and the amount of information collected is sufficient for the more study. Verification and **validation of simulation**

model for **documentation** aims, the contents of information verification and validation in the single phases are inserted to the verification and validation proposal and **verification and validation report**, according to the well defined document structures.

MULTISTAGE TAILORING

As mentioned above, executing verification and validation activities in verification and validation sub phases redundantly, for example comparing the formal model independently with the conceptual model, the structured problem description and the sponsor wants, takes further point of view of model evaluation into consideration. So the concluded verification and validation results in this manner are more dependable. However, for many simulation models in practice it is not possible to completely perform all verification and validation activities recommended in the verification and validation triangle because of time and budge restrictions. In such examples, a slim set of verification and validation activities, which performs the credibility evaluation still in a particular acceptable level despite the restrictions, must be tailored.

Relied on the detailed documentation requirements of verification and validation (Lehmann, Saad, Best, Kster, Pohl, Qian, Walder, Wang and Xu, 2005), in which project restrictions, intermediate results and their dependencies, verification and validation acceptance criteria, verification and validation activities, and project role is well defined and specified, a multistage tailoring process is suggested not only for model development, but also for conducting verification and validation, including the following stages:

1. **Tailoring at the process level**
2. **Tailoring at the result level**
3. **Tailoring at the role level**

At the start of a simulation model, **tailoring** of the model development process employed in the simulation study is of prime significance for preparing simulation and verification and validation project. According to the determinations of the simulation model restrictions, project-specific results and the associated verification and validation activities can be identified, and the irrelevant results are so ignored. For instance, when it is determined that the formal model is not necessary for the present plan, the related results of the formal model and its defined verification and validation activities remain therefore out of consideration. By considering the specified result dependencies, the plan adaptation to the result level is conducted. This is the cause that during the model development further results to be developed can be chosen, while the results present in the simulation project can be removed since the obligations between the results are identified. Moreover, tailoring is conducted at the role level. It means every plan Wang and Lehmann role has only the access according to its authority issued in the **simulation project**. Based on this concept, a supporting tool, so-called **simulation tailoring assistant**, is prototypically implemented.

DOCUMENTATION

Verification and validation system **documentation** is generally critical in persuasive individuals of the precision of a system and its outcome, and must be involved in the **simulation model documentation**. For a common discussion on documentation of **computer-based models** (Gass, 1999). Both detailed and outline documentation are preferred. The detailed documentation must embrace specifics on the analysis, assessment, data, and the outputs.

REMARKS ON SYSTEM VALIDATION

Researchers notice that the following steps should be made in system validation:

1. An agreement created before developing the system between a system development group and a system sponsors and if possible the individuals, identifies the basic validation method and a minimum selection of specific **validation mechanisms** is employed in the validation process.
2. Identify the amount of precision needed of system output variables of interest for the system intended application before to beginning the development of a system or each early in a system development process.
3. Analysis if possible an assumptions and hypothesizes underlying a system.
4. In certain system iteration, achieve at least face validity on the conceptual model.
5. In certain system iteration, at least discover the model behavior employing the computerized system.
6. In the last system iteration, accomplish comparisons, between the system and system behavior output for numerous selections of experimental cases.
7. Develop **validation documentation** for addition in the **simulation system documentation**.
8. When the system is employed over certain of time, develop an agenda for **cyclic evaluation** of the system validity.

The systems rarely are developed to be employed more than one time. The process for evaluating the validity of these systems over their life cycles requires to be developed, as indicated in step eight. No common process can be provided, as every state is dissimilar. For instance, when no information is available on a model and a model was initially developed and validated; then revalidation of the system must happen before to every process of a system when new information or model understanding has happened because its final validation.

CONCLUSION

On the basis of the model verification and validation idea, we introduce in this chapter an improved model for development and conducting verification and validation models and simulation results. By integrating the further information verification and validation activities for every **verification** and **validation phase**, this idea extends the consideration range of the verification and validation triangle and refines the associated documentation requirements of intermediate results and verification and validation results consistently. Within the scope of model planning, a multistage tailoring concept for the purpose of plan specific adaptation is presented. By arranging the tailoring efforts respectively at the levels of process, result and role, this generic tailoring idea offers a high degree of flexibility and feasibility for conducting simulation and verification and validation under different restrictions.

The system validation and verification is important in a development of the simulation model. Unfortunately, there is no collection of certain tests that could easily be used to deciding an accuracy of a model. In addition, no algorithm exists to decide what methods or processes to employ. Each new simulation plan introduces a new and unique idea.

FUTURE WORK

More studies can concentrate on:

- Implementing ideas of verification and validation and tailoring process in an actual simulation project in training.
- Extending the tool support for performing

verification and validation tasks, for instance, identifying the internal output dependency when developing inter- mediate output conceptual model.

The Verification and Validation of simulation models is developing a verification and validation tool to maintain choosing and implementing suitable verification and validation techniques in various **verification** and **validation milieu**.

REFERENCES

Balci, O. (1998). Verification, Validation and Testing. In J. Banks (Ed.) *Handbook of Simulation*. Hoboken, NJ: John Wiley & Sons

Banks, J., Carson, J., II, Nelson, B., & Nicol, D. (2005). *Discrete-Event System Simulation*, (4th Ed.). Upper Saddle River: Pearson Education International.

Banks, J., Gerstein, D., & Searles, S. P. (1998). Modeling Processes, Validation, and Verification of Complex Simulations: A Survey. *Methodology and Validation . Simulation Series*, *19*(1), 13–18.

Brade, D. (2003). *A Generalized Process for the Verification and Validation of Models and Simulation Results*. Dissertation, Universitöt der Bundeswehr München, Germany.

Brade, D., & Lehmann, A. (2002). Model Validation and Verification. In *Modeling and Simulation Environment for Satellite and Terrestrial Communication Networks– Proceedings of the European COST Telecommunication Symposium*. Boston: Kluwer Academic Publishers.

Gass, S. I. (1999). Decision-Aiding Models: Validation, Assessment, and Related Issues for Policy Analysis. *Operations Research*, *31*(4), 601–663.

Law, A. M., & Kelton, W. D. (2002). *Simulation Modeling and Analysis*, (3rd Ed.). New York: McGraw-Hill.

Lehmann, A., Saad, S., Best, M., Kster, A., Pohl, S., Qian, J., Walder, C., Wang, Z., & Xu, Z., (2005). *Leitfaden für Modelldokumen-tation, Abschlussbericht* (in German). ITIS **e.V.**

Robertson, N., & Perera, T. (2001). Feasibility for Automatic Data Collection. In *Proceedings of the 2001 Winter Simulation Conference*.

Sargent, R. (2000). Verification, Validation, and Accreditation of Simulation Models. In Z. Wang, A. Lehmann (Eds.) *Proceeding of the Winter Simulation Conference* (p. 240).

Sargent, R. G. (1996). Some Subjective Validation Methods Using Graphical Displays of Data. *Proc. of 1996 Winter Simulation Conf.*, (pp. 345–351).

Sargent, R. G. (1996). Verifying and Validating Simulation Models. *Proc. of 1996 Winter Simulation Conf.*, (pp. 55–64).

Sargent, R. G. (1999). Verification and Validation of Simulation Models. *Proc. of 1998 Winter Simulation Conf.*, (pp. 121–130).

Simulations, D. O. D. *Improved Assessment Procedures Would Increase the Credibility of Results*, (1987). Washington, DC: U. S. General Accounting Office, PEMD-88-3.

Spieckermann, A., Lehmann, A., & Rabe, M. (2004). Verifikation und Validierung: berlegungen zu einer integrierten Vorgehensweise. In K. Mertins, & M. Rabe, (Hrsg), *Experiences from the Future Fraunhofer IRB, Stuttgart*, (pp. 263-274). Stuttgart, Germany.

Wang, Z., & Lehmann, A. (2008). *Verification and Validation of Simulation Models and Applications*. Hershey, PA: IGI Global.

KEY TERMS AND DEFINITIONS

Verification and Validation: to measure the accuracy and validity of every intermediate result separately.

Data Modeling: is a lengthy and difficult work to accomplish, and some study stated that up to 33% of the complete time used in a simulation analysis can be used on data modeling

Model Validation: is generally defined corroboration that a computerized model with its area of applicability possesses an acceptable range of accuracy reliable with the planned use of a model and is a definition employed.

The Conceptual Model: is the arithmetical or logical statement imitated of the problem entity developed for the specific report. The conceptual model is developed during an analysis and prototype phase.

The Computerized System: is the conceptual model executed on the machine. The computerized system is developed during a computer programming and executing phase, and inferences regarding the problem entity are got via guiding machine experiments on a computerized system in an experimentation phase.

Operational Validity: is defined as a model result behavior has enough correctness for a model intended aim over the area of system intended applicability.

Information Validity: is defined as the information necessary for system construction, model assessment and testing, and guiding the system experiments to solve the difficulty is sufficient and accurate.

Animation: A model operational performance is showed graphically as a model moves from side to side time. For instance, the travels of parts through a factory during a simulation are exposed graphically.

Static Testing Line: In static testing line the machine program is analyzed to decide when it is accurate via employing such methods as well-structured accuracy, proofs, and testing the structure characteristics of a program.

Dynamic Testing Line: In dynamic testing line a machine program is implemented under various conditions and the results got including those created throughout an implementation, are employed to decide when computer software and its executions are accurate.

Chapter 5
DEVS–Based Simulation Interoperability

Thomas Wutzler
Max Planck Institute for Biogeochemistry, Germany

Hessam Sarjoughian
Arizona Center for Integrative Modeling and Simulation, USA

ABSTRACT

This chapter introduces the usage of DEVS for the purpose of implementing interoperability across heterogeneous simulation models. It shows that the DEVS framework provides a simple, yet effective conceptual basis for handling simulation interoperability. It discusses the various useful properties of the DEVS framework, describes the Shared Abstract Model (SAM) approach for interoperating simulation models, and compares it to other approaches. The DEVS approach enables formal model specification with component models implemented in multiple programming languages. The simplicity of the integration of component models designed in the DEVS, DTSS, and DESS simulation formalisms and implemented in the programming languages Java and C++ is demonstrated by a basic educational example and by a real world forest carbon accounting model. The authors hope, that readers will appreciate the combination of generalness and simplicity and that readers will consider using the DEVS approach for simulation interoperability in their own projects.

INTRODUCTION

Interoperability among simulators continues to be of key interest within the simulation community. A chief reason for this interest is the existence of heterogeneous legacy simulations which are developed using a variety of programming practices and software engineering approaches. For many studied

DOI: 10.4018/978-1-60566-774-4.ch005

problems there exist already simulations models. Much work has been dedicated to develop the models, estimate parameters, verify the simulations and validate the model assumptions by comparing model results to observations. Hence, it is desirable to reuse such existing models for additional tasks and to integrate parts of several existing models into a common framework. However, this integration is hampered by the fact that the existing models have been developed in different programming languages, with different software and different software engineering approaches. There exist already several approaches to implement a joint execution and some of them are summarized in the background section. In this book chapter we suggest an additional approach to realize interoperability among disparate simulators that utilizes the Discrete Event System Specification (DEVS). We argue that this approach yields several benefits. One of the most important benefits is the reduced complexity for adapting heterogeneous legacy models.

The interoperability issue will be exemplified with a typical problem which we encountered in our work. The task was to construct a forest ecosystem carbon tracking model. With such a model the exchange of carbon between the forest ecosystem and the atmosphere can be studied. One can then implement and test several scenarios of forest management and simulate how these influence the exchange of carbon dioxide with the atmosphere to explore how these management strategies influence atmosphere carbon concentrations and global warming. There already existed a model for the stand growth, i.e. the growth of trees within a plot, which was based on extensive measurement of tree properties within the study region (Appendix A). It accounted for competition among different trees and incorporated knowledge of many species. Hence, the source code was quite extensive. There already existed also a model for the soil carbon balance that have been used and validated by many research groups (Appendix B). Only the management strategies had to be implemented as a new component model.

However, the stand growth model was specified as discrete-time model (DTSS) and implemented in JAVA and the soil carbon balance model was specified as continuous (differential equations) model (DESS) and implemented in C++ (see Figure 1). So how could we couple the heterogeneous models and perform a joint and integrated simulation?

The purpose of this chapter is to discuss the benefits of DEVS concept compared to several commonly applied alternatives of tackling the problem of simulation interoperability. To this end we introduce the Shared Abstract Model (SAM) interoperability approach (Wutzler & Sarjoughian, 2007). We will exemplify its application first by a simple educational example model. This simple example provides the basis to compare the SAM approach to other DEVS-based approaches. Finally we present a setup using SAM that we used to solve the problem posed in Figure 1. Next, we start with a discussion of several commonly used alternatives of tackling the problem of simulation interoperability.

BACKGROUND

There exist several alternative approaches to construct a model from the component models such as the one described in the Introduction section (refer to Figure 1). One solution to the interoperability task is to develop all models using a single programming language. We could have reimplemented the soil model in JAVA as a time-stepped model. The reimplementation alternative, however, impedes independent development of the component models by different research groups. This disadvantage combined with weak support for simulation model verification and validation results makes reimplementation unattractive and generally impractical. In particular, there is a growing need for alternative simulation interoperability approaches in the domain of environmental modeling and simulation (Papajorgji et al., 2004; Filippi & Bisgambiglia, 2004; Roxburgh & Davies, 2006).

A second alternative is to use the High Level Architecture (HLA) simulation middleware (IEEE, 2000). It supports interoperation among simulated and physical software/systems. The HLA standard is widely used and considered more powerful in terms of supporting different kinds

Figure 1. Motivation example: Simulating a coupled forest ecosystem carbon budget model which is composed of component models that have been specified in simulation formalisms and programming languages

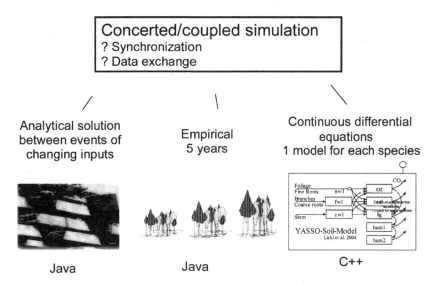

of simulations (e.g., conservative and optimistic (Fujimoto, 2000)) that can be mapped into HLA Object Model Template. The HLA Object Model Template (HLA/OMT) plays a key role in building interoperable simulations. Its primary role is to specify HLA-relevant information about federates that collectively form one or more federations. To simulate a federation of models (referred to as federates), Federation Object Model (FOM) and Simulation Object Model (SOM) must be developed. FOM is used as a specification for exchange of data and general coordination among members of a federation. SOM is used as a standardized mechanism for federates to interact. The FOM and SOM are specified in terms of object-oriented concepts and methods (Unified Modeling Language). Important model specifications are object and interaction classes which define data types and exchanges among federates. Another part of HLA/OMT is routing spaces which helps to support efficient data distribution among federates.

The HLA standard rules and interface specifications together with HLA/OMT provide a general basis for developing interoperable simulated and non-simulated federates. The standard rules are divided into federation and federate rules where each set of rules specify the constraint under which federates and federations and interface specification work with one another. The federation rules are primarily concerned with execution and therefore with HLA Runtime Infrastructure (RTI). The specification of the HLA rules are defined such that in a federation execution, all data exchanges must be in accordance with FOM data, and each SOM can be owned by at most one federate. The interoperation of simulations must be defined in terms of a set of services including time, data, and ownership management services. Hence, given the HLA's intended level of generality, developing interoperable simulations in general remains demanding despite availability of tools. Furthermore, it is difficult to ensure simulation correctness with HLA (Lake et al. 2000).

A third alternative is to use DEVS concept to realize simulation interoperability. We prefer this alternative because of several benefits. First, the DEVS framework is based on formal syntax and semantics that can ensure simulation correctness among heterogeneous DEVS-based simulations (Sarjoughian & Zeigler, 2000). The model and simulator are separated from one another, which greatly helps the verification and validation of the simulator and the model respectively (Zeigler & Sarjoughian, 2002). Second, there exist freely available DEVS simulation environments for most common programming languages. Hence, the coverage of existing models that can potentially take part in coupled simulations is high. Third, we will show, that the interfaces required for interoperations are not complex. This helps to keep the necessary effort to overcome heterogeneity in programming languages and simulation engines on a feasible level. And fourth, common modeling formalisms can be represented in the DEVS paradigm. This includes all event driven formalisms (Zeigler et al., 2000b), time-stepped systems (DTSS), and continuous systems (DESS) by quantization (Cellier & Kofman, 2005). In summary, the properties of DEVS combined with advances in object-oriented software design methods make it feasible to adapt existing code with heterogeneities in programming languages, simulation engines, and simulation formalisms to take part in interoperable simulations.

There already exist several other approaches in order to interoperate several DEVS environments. Efforts are underway to standardize interfaces of several DEVS environments (DEVS-Standardization-Group, 2008). In this book chapter we will first describe the SAM approach (Wutzler & Sarjoughian, 2007), which is based solely on the description of an abstract atomic model. Alternative DEVS based approaches will be discussed and compared after the description of the SAM approach.

THE SAM APPROACH OF TACKLING SIMULATION INTEROPERABILITY

In the ecological modeling example one component model is implemented in JAVA and another one is implemented in C++ (see Figure 1). Fortunately, there exist several DEVS simulation engine implementations for both programming languages. We chose DEVSJAVA (ACIMS, 2003) to simulate component models that have been implemented in JAVA and Adevs (Nutaro, 2005) to simulate component models that have been implemented in C++.

Both simulation engines share the same formal specification and the abstract parallel DEVS simulation protocol. However, their realizations are quite different. For example, the communication between a coordinator and its child coordinators is implemented very differently in DevsJava and in ADevs. So how could we set up a simulation in which Adevs and DEVSJAVA models can be coupled together? One strategy was to support interoperability at the modeling level. For example one could allow Adevs simulator B to execute a DEVSJAVA component model A. This strategy, which is taken by the SAM approach, is depicted in Figure 2. The level of independence from implementation details is achieved by standardizing the basic interface of the atomic model and its invocation by an atomic simulator. As shown in Figures 2 and 3, the Abstract Model Interface is defined using the meta-language OMG-idl (Vinoski, 1997).

The Abstract Model Interface corresponds to the mathematical representation in the DEVS specification (Zeigler et al., 2000a). It only slightly differs from the DEVS atomic simulation protocol by making the various transition functions (δ_{ext}, δ_{int}, δ_{conf}) already returning the result of the time advance function (λ). This modification has been introduced to save computing time during interprocess communications.

The disparity between a particular simulation engine (e.g., Adevs) and a model implementation

Figure 2. SAM interoperability approach. All the DEVS simulation engines share the same simulation protocol. This allows to specifify this in a meta language and allow the simulator in one programming language to execute models that have been written in other languages

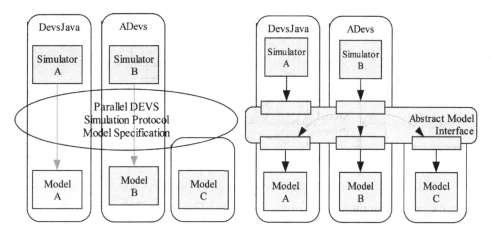

(e.g., DEVSJAVA) is handled with the Model Proxy and Model Adapter as shown in Figure 4. For each simulator, which should execute a model within a different simulation engine, a model proxy is created. This proxy translates the engine specific method invocations of the atomic model into method invocations of the abstract model interface.

On the other side, a model adapter translates the invocations of the abstract model interface into engine specific invocations of the atomic model. For an atomic component model the implementation of the adapter is straightforward.

Coupled models are mapped into this schema by a special model adapter. In this approach the nature of coupled component model is transparent. The simulator only sees an atomic model. This is possible because of the DEVS closure under coupling property. This means, that every coupled model can be treated as an atomic model

Figure 3. The interface of the atomic DEVS model specified in the meta-language OMG-idl

```
interface DEVS {// OMG-idl (Corba)
    // begin of simulation
    double doInitialize()

    // time of next internal transition without inputs
    // value also returned by doInitialize and State functions.
    double timeAdvance()

    // produce outputs for current time
    // is not allowed to change the state of the model
    Message outputFunction()

    // state transition
    double internalTransition()

    // transition with input event before timeAdvance
    double externalTransition(in double e, in Message msg)

    // input event at time of internal transition
    double confluentTransition(in Message msg)
};
Message: bag { inputPort -> value }
```

Figure 4. Software architecture of the SAM approach. Proxy and Adapter which are based on the DEVS interface together with a middleware allow inter process and inter DEVS-simulation engine communication

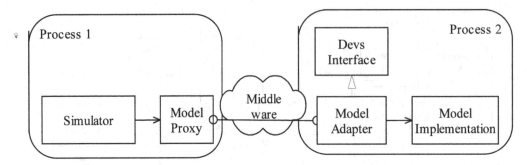

AN SIMPLE EXAMPLE OF USING THE SAM APPROACH

We will illustrate the usage of the SAM approach of tackling simulation interoperability by a simple model that consists of three component models that are coupled in a hierarchical manner.

The Experimental-Frame Processor Model

The experimental-frame processor (ef-p) model is a simple coupled model of three atomic models

with respect to its external inputs and outputs. At the implementation level, this is achieved by modeling the invocation of a coordinator of a coupled model, i.e. how parent coordinators call the coordinator, as an atomic model. The invocation of the coordinator usually happens in a DEVS engine specific way. However, by modeling it as an atomic model, the coupled case is mapped to the already solved atomic case. For details and the description of the example implementations of the proxies and adapters in DEVSJAVA and Adevs (C++) we refer the reader to (Wutzler & Sarjoughian, 2007). The way of how the SAM approach works, is best illustrated with an example using a very simple model.

(see Figure 5). The atomic and coupled models are shown as blocks and couplings between them are shown as unidirectional arrows with input and output port names attached to them. The generator atomic model generates job-messages at fixed time intervals and sends them via the Out port. The transducer atomic model accepts job-messages from the generator at its Arrived port and remembers their arrival time instances. It also accepts job-messages at the Solved port. When a message arrives at the Solved port, the transducer matches this job with the previous job that had arrived on the Arrived port earlier and calculates their time difference. Together, these two atomic models form an experimental frame coupled model. The experimental frame (ef) model sends the generators job messages on the Out port and forwards the messages received on its In port to the transducers Solved-port. The transducer observes the response (in this case the turnaround time) of messages that are injected into an observed system. The observed system in this case is the processor atomic model. A processor accepts jobs at its In port and sends them via Out port again after some finite, but non-zero time period. If the processor is busy when a new job arrives, the processor discards it.

In order to demonstrate the SAM approach, we partitioned the component models into two different simulation engines. The coupled experimental

Figure 5. Experimental frame (ef)-processor (p) model

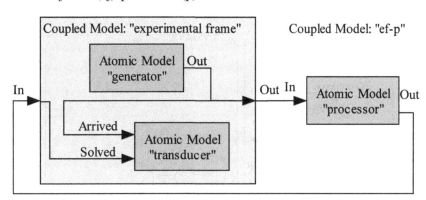

frame model was implemented in DEVSJAVA while the processor atomic model and the overall simulation were implemented in Adevs.

This setup is depicted by Figure 6. Rounded boxes (Adevs, DEVSJAVA, and Middleware) represent operating system processes; white angled boxes represent simulators, dark gray boxes represent models, light grey shapes represent interoperation components, and arrows represent interactions.

The model the model proxies and the model adapters for the atomic and coupled models in the DEVSJAVA and Adevs simulation engines were developed beforehand. They need to be developed only once for each simulation engine. The experimental frame coupled model, a message translator, and the model adapter were constructed and started in a DEVSJAVA server process (Figure 7(a)). Further the CORBA-Object of the model adapter was constructed and published using the SUN Object Request Broker (ORB) and naming service which is part of the JDK 1.5 (SUN, 2006). The CORBA-stub of this adapter was then obtained in the C++/Adevs client process using the ACE/TAO ORB version 1.5 (Schmidt, 2006). Together with a message translator the model proxy was constructed (Figure 7(b)). The message translator had been introduced into the SAM approach to handle the transfer of message contents between different programming languages that are more complex than stings or numbers. Finally, the

model proxy was used as any other Adevs atomic model within the Adevs simulation (Figure 7(c)). The example was developed and run on personal computers running the operating system Windows XP. It has been tested on a single machine and in addition also with running the component models on different machines.

COMPARISON OF DEVS INTEROPERABILITY APPROACHES

After having introduced and demonstrated the SAM approach, we can now compare it to other approaches. There exist alternative approaches of using DEVS to implement interoperability between simulation models written in different programming languages.

The first DEVS based approach for building interoperable simulations is called DEVS-Bus (Kim et al., 2003). The DEVS-Bus, which was originally introduced to support distributed execution, uses HLA (Dahmann et al., 1999; Fujimoto, 1998) and ACE-TAO ORB in logical and (near) real-time (ACIMS, 2000; Cho et al., 2003). The DEVS-Bus framework conceptually consists of three layers: the model layer, the DEVS layer, and the HLA (High Level Architecture) layer. The DEVS layer provides a common framework, called the DEVS-Bus, so that such simulation models can communicate with each other. Finally,

Figure 6. Distributed setup of the ef-p model

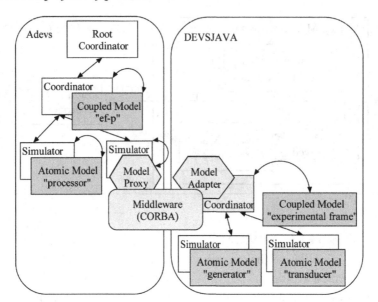

the HLA layer is employed as a communication infrastructure, which supports several important features for distributed simulation. In both the SAM and DEVS-Bus approaches generic adapters for each simulation engine are used for conformity to the DEVS. If this adapter is developed once, all models designed for the given simulation engine can take part in heterogeneous simulation. The major difference between the approaches is that the DEVS-Bus defines a new simple protocol. Contrary, the SAM approach is specified entirely within the DEVS specification. The DEVS-Bus controls the communication between several models and the participating models or simulators are aware of the distributed setup. In contrast, in the SAM approach a model proxy is used and by this, the heterogeneous models become transparent to the root coordinator. The DEVS-Bus can result in a performance bottleneck on simulations with many component models (Kim et al., 2003). The SAM approach shows good scaling properties (Wutzler & Sarjoughian, 2007).

A second approach for simulation interoperability is to execute DEVS simulations using Service

Figure 7. Constructing and using the remote experimental frame sub-model

```
(a)  digraph ef = new Ef();
     MessageTranslator trans = new StringMessageTranslator();
     DEVS efAdapter = new DevsDigraph( ef, trans );

(b)  MessageTranslator *trans = new StringMsgTranslator();
     atomicDevs *efProxy = new atomicDevs(efAdapterStub._retn(),trans);

(c)  staticDigraph *coupledModel = new staticDigraph();
     coupledModel->add(proc);
     coupledModel->add(efProxy);
     coupledModel->couple(proc,proc->outPort("out"),
        efProxy, efProxy->inPort("in"));
     coupledModel->couple(efProxy,efProxy->outPort("out"),
        proc, proc->inPort("in"));
     devssim sim(coupledModel);
     sim.run(100);
```

Oriented Architecture (SOA) technology (Mittal & Risco-Martin, 2007). It is based on the SOA (Erl, 2005) and the specification of participating models within the XML-based language DEVSML (Mittal & Risco-Martin, 2007). Upon execution initialization, the syntax of the DEVSML models is translated to the syntax of the DEVSJAVA or DEVS-C++ models. The translation requires all the models to be specified in the DEVSML syntax. A key implication is that the behaviors of the target DEVSJAVA and DEVS-C++ models must be represented within the DEVSML which is significantly restricted as compared with those of the Java and C++ programming languages. The high-level DEVSML abstraction is well suited for coupled models, but imposes fundamental restrictions on specifying atomic models. Therefore, the SOA approach cannot address interoperating existing models that are developed by different teams in different programming languages.

A third approach for interoperable DEVS-based simulators was suggested by Lombardi et al. (2006). It uses adapters for the simulators instead of adapters for the models. The advantage is that this approach allows transforming hierarchical models to flat models where only leaf node models exchange messages. In the SAM approach the hierarchical model structure is preserved and messages need to be passed up and down the hierarchy. However, we argue that simulators must communicate at each instance of time when events occur. In contrast, models must communicate only at the time instances when the model is imminent, i.e. it undergoes internal or external transitions. Hence, in the SAM approach there are fewer inter-process communications required (Wutzler & Sarjoughian, 2007) and we expect that this will outweigh the overhead of passing messages down the hierarchy within one simulation engine.

In summary we argue that for the purpose of integrating heterogeneous submodels, the SAM approach is best suitable from all the discussed approaches. However, in order to demonstrate

its suitability we go one step further and apply it to the real world application example that was introduced in the beginning.

A MORE COMPLEX EXAMPLE OF USING THE SAM APPROACH

In order to demonstrate the applicability of the SAM approach to more complex real world situations of model interoperability we describe a setup of the solution to problem in Figure 1 and the introduction. In order to let the heterogeneous component models take part in the joint simulation a few adaptations were necessary.

Adaptation of the Component Models

In the ecological example shown in Figure 1, the product model is event-driven and belongs to the class of discrete-event models. The stand growth component model, however, runs in time steps of five years (DTSS) and the soil carbon balance model is a continuous time model (DESS). We used general adapters that were developed together with the SAM approach to interoperate these models. The general adapter for the time stepped models collected all input events during one period, executed the transition function at the time steps and generated output events at these time steps. In order to use the DESS model in the coupled simulation, the computation of the derivatives was encapsulated into a single function. This derivative function was then evaluated using the quantization approach, which was already a part of the Adevs simulation engine. Hence, after the non-trivial development of the general adapters, the adjustments to the component models were quite simple and straightforward. So we could proceed with the setup of the simulations.

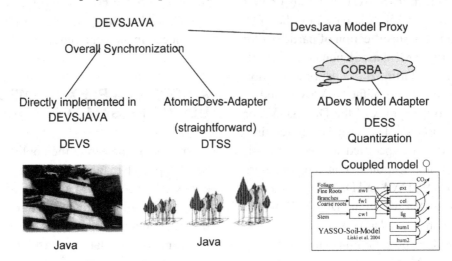

Figure 8. Distributed setup of the interoperability solution of the motivation example

Setup of the Simulation

The setup was almost as straightforward as in the simple example (Figure 7). The adapter of the coupled model of soil carbon dynamics was specified in Adevs. The adapter was started in a separate server process. This process registered the Abstract model interface of the model adapter with the CORBA Naming service. In a second DEVSJAVA process the model proxy then could connect to this interface and invoke the operations of the soil model adapter via the CORBA middleware. The product model as well as the model adapter for the stand growth model were directly specified in DEVSJAVA. Hence it was now straightforward to construct a coupled simulation of all three heterogeneous component models (see Figure 8).

The major difference to the simple example was that the data exchanged between the component models were more complex than simple strings. A major part of the implementation effort was devoted to developing the idl-specification of the structured data that was exchanged, i.e. the message contents. In addition to the general model adapter and model proxies, message translator components had to be developed, that converted the data structures from implementation specific formats to the idl-specifications.

The second major difference to the simple example was that the submodels required a quite complex parameterization and initialization. In order to handle the parameterization in a centralized manner, i.e. not scattered across the component model operating system processes, we implemented initialization and parameterization of the component model hierarchy by sending xml-formatted strings to the initialization functions of the component models. By this way the interface of the abstract model was extended by only one two methods (Listing 2a). Further, extensions involved by getting names of the component models and its ports and setting or getting the state for interruption and continuation of the model execution.

The coupled model was used in research in natural sciences and results can be found for example in (Wutzler, 2008). The component models will be further developed independently by different research groups and the incorporation of future versions will require solely a minimum effort of recoding in the model adapters and the parts responsible for parameterization and initialization.

Figure 9. Constructing and using the remote experimental frame sub-model

```
(a)    interface XMLParamInitModel {
           void setModelParameters(in string xml)
             raises (DevsBridgeException);
           string getParameters();
       };

(b)    interface NamedModel {
            string getModelName(); //  for distinguishing submodels
            void setModelName(in string name);
       };

       interface PortNames {
         stringSequence inPorts();
         stringSequence outPorts();
       };

(c)    interface XMLStateInitModel {
           void initializeState(in string xml) raises (DevsBridgeException);
           string getState(in string scenario);
       };
```

CONCLUSION

Based on the comparison of DEVS based approaches with other approaches of implementing interoperability across simulation models we conclude that DEVS based approaches are applicable and very suitable for this task. There exist several DEVS based approaches which were designed for different goals and therefore have different advantages and disadvantages. With the goal of designing a general approach that supports verification of coupled models and at the same time fosters a relatively uncomplicated adaptation of existing simulation models implemented in different programming languages, we conclude that the SAM approach is best suitable and has great potentials. This conclusion was supported by demonstrating the usage of the SAM approach by both a very simple and a more complex real world application. Further development and standardization is required for other simulation services such as formats of data exchange between component models and component model parameterization. The DEVS-based SAM interoperability approach made it possible to overcome heterogeneity in programming languages while allowing models specified in different modeling formalisms to seamlessly communicate with one another while keeping the adaptation of existing programming code uncomplicated.

ACKNOWLEDGMENT

Due to courtesy of SCS, the Society for Modeling and Simulation International, this book chapter partly reproduces contents of the article: Wutzler, T. & Sarjoughian, H. S. 2007: Interoperability among parallel DEVS simulators and models implemented in multiple programming languages. Simulation Transactions, 83, 473-490.

REFERENCES

ACIMS. (2000). *DEVS/HLA software*. Retrieved September 1st, 2008, from http://www.acims.arizona.edu/SOFTWARE/software.shtml. Arizona Center for Integrative Modelling and Simulation.

ACIMS. (2003). *DEVSJAVA modeling & simulation tool*. Retrieved September 1st, 2008, from http://www.acims.arizona.edu/SOFTWARE/ software.shtml. Arizona Center for Integrative Modeling and Simulation.

Cellier, F., & Kofman, E. (2005). *Continuous system simulation*. Berlin: Springer.

Cho, Y. K., Hu, X. L., & Zeigler, B. P. (2003). The RTDEVS/CORBA environment for simulation-based design of distributed real-time systems. *Simulation Transactions*, *79*(4), 197–210. doi:10.1177/0037549703038880

Dahmann, J., Salisbury, M., Turrel, C., Barry, P., & Blemberg, P. (1999). *HLA and beyond: Interoperability challenges*. Paper no. 99F-SIW-073 presented at the Fall Simulation Interoperability Workshop Orlando, FL, USA.

DEVS-Standardization-Group. (2008). *General Info*. Retrieved September 1st, 2008, from http:// cell-devs.sce.carleton.ca/devsgroup/.

Erl, T. (2005). *Service-Oriented Architecture Concepts, Technology and Design*. Upper Saddle River, NJ: Prentice Hall.

Filippi, J. B., & Bisgambiglia, P. (2004). JDEVS: an implementation of a DEVS based formal framework for environmental modelling. *Environmental Modelling & Software*, *19*(3), 261–274. doi:10.1016/j.envsoft.2003.08.016

Fujimoto, R. (1998). Time management in the High-Level Architecture. *Simulation: Transactions of the Society for Modeling and Simulation International*, *71*(6), 388–400. doi:10.1177/003754979807100604

Fujimoto, R. (2000). *Parallel and distributed simulation systems*. Mahwah, NJ: John Wiley and Sons, Inc.

Hasenauer, H. (2006). *Sustainable forest management: growth models for europe*. Berlin: Springer.

IEEE. (2000). *HLA Framework and Rules* (Version IEEE 1516-2000). Washington, DC: IEEE Press.

Kaipainen, T., Liski, J., Pussinen, A., & Karjalainen, T. (2004). Managing carbon sinks by changing rotation length in European forests. *Environmental Science & Policy*, *7*(3), 205–219. doi:10.1016/j.envsci.2004.03.001

Kim, Y. J., Kim, J. H., & Kim, T. G. (2003). Heterogeneous Simulation Framework Using DEVS BUS. *Simulation Transactions*, *79*, 3–18. doi:10.1177/0037549703253543

Lake, T., Zeigler, B., Sarjoughian, H., & Nutaro, J. (2000). *DEVS Simulation and HLA Lookahead*, (Paper no. 00S-SIW-160). Presented at Spring Simulation Interoperability Workshop Orlando, FL, USA.

Liski, J., Palosuo, T., Peltoniemi, M., & Sievanen, R. (2005). Carbon and decomposition model Yasso for forest soils. *Ecological Modelling*, *189*(1-2), 168–182. doi:10.1016/j.ecolmodel.2005.03.005

Lombardi, S., Wainer, G. A., & Zeigler, B. P. (2006). *An experiment on interoperability of DEVS implementations* (Paper no. 06S-SIW-131). Presented at the Spring Simulation Interoperability Workshop Huntsville, AL, USA.

Mittal, S., & Risco-Martin, J. L. (2007). DEVSML: Automating DEVS Execution over SOA Towards Transparent Simulators Special Session on DEVS Collaborative Execution and Systems Modeling over SOA. In *Proceedings of the DEVS Integrative M&S Symposium, Spring Simulation Multiconference, Norfork, Virginia, USA*, (pp. 287–295). Washington, DC: IEEE Press.

Mund, M., Profft, I., Wutzler, T., Schulze, E.D., Weber, G., & Weller, E. (2005). Vorbereitung für eine laufende Fortschreibung der Kohlenstoffvorräte in den Wäldern Thüringens. Abschlussbericht zur 2. *Phase dem BMBF-Projektes "Modelluntersuchungen zur Umsetzung des Kyoto-Protokolls".* (Tech. rep., TLWJF, Gotha).

Nabuurs, G. J., Pussinen, A., Karjalainen, T., Erhard, M., & Kramer, K. (2002). Stemwood volume increment changes in European forests due to climate change-a simulation study with the EFISCEN model. *Global Change Biology, 8*(4), 304–316. doi:10.1046/j.1354-1013.2001.00470.x

Nagel, J. (2003). *TreeGrOSS: Tree Growth Open Source Software - a tree growth model component.*

Nagel, J., Albert, M., & Schmidt, M. (2002). Das waldbauliche Prognose- und Entscheidungsmodell BWINPro 6.1. *Forst und Holz, 57*(15/16), 486–493.

Nutaro, J. J. (2005). *Adevs.* Retrieved Jan 15, 2006, from http://www.ece.arizona.edu/ nutaro/

Palosuo, T., Liski, J., Trofymow, J. A., & Titus, B. D. (2005). Litter decomposition affected by climate and litter quality - Testing the Yasso model with litterbag data from the Canadian intersite decomposition experiment. *Ecological Modelling, 189*(1-2), 183–198. doi:10.1016/j.ecolmodel.2005.03.006

Papajorgji, P., Beck, H. W., & Braga, J. L. (2004). An architecture for developing service-oriented and component-based environmental models. *Ecological Modelling, 179*(1), 61–76. doi:10.1016/j.ecolmodel.2004.05.013

Peltoniemi, M., Mäkipää, R., Liski, J., & Tamminen, P. (2004). Changes in soil carbon with stand age - an evaluation of a modelling method with empirical data. *Global Change Biology, 10*(12), 2078–2091. doi:10.1111/j.1365-2486.2004.00881.x

Porté, A., & Bartelink, H. H. (2002). Modelling mixed forest growth: a review of models for forest management. *Ecological Modelling, 150,* 141–188. doi:10.1016/S0304-3800(01)00476-8

Roxburgh, S. H., & Davies, I. D. (2006). COINS: an integrative modelling shell for carbon accounting and general ecological analysis. *Environmental Modelling & Software, 21*(3), 359–374. doi:10.1016/j.envsoft.2004.11.006

Sarjoughian, H., & Zeigler, B. (2000). DEVS and HLA: Complementary paradigms for modeling and simulation? *Simulation Transactions, 17*(4), 187–197.

Schmidt, D. C. (2006). *Real-time CORBA with TAO.* Retrieved September 5th, 2008, from http://www.cse.wustl.edu/ schmidt/TAO.html.

SUN. (2006). *JDK-ORB.* Retrieved September 1st, 2008, from http://java.sun.com/j2se/1.5.0/docs/guide/idl/

Vinoski, S. (1997). CORBA - Integrating diverse applications within distributed heterogeneous environments. *IEEE Communications Magazine, 35*(2), 46–55. doi:10.1109/35.565655

Wutzler, T. (2008). Effect of the Aggregation of Multi-Cohort Mixed Stands on Modeling Forest Ecosystem Carbon Stocks. *Silva Fennica, 42*(4), 535–553.

Wutzler, T., & Mund, M. (2007). Modelling mean above and below ground litter production based on yield tables. *Silva Fennica, 41*(3), 559–574.

Wutzler, T., & Reichstein, M. (2007). Soils apart from equilibrium – consequences for soil carbon balance modelling. *Biogeosciences, 4,* 125–136.

Wutzler, T., & Sarjoughian, H. S. (2007). Interoperability among parallel DEVS simulators and models implemented in multiple programming languages. *Simulation Transactions, 83*(6), 473–490. doi:10.1177/0037549707084490

Zeigler, B. P., Praehofer, H., & Kim, T. G. (2000). *Theory of modeling and simulation 2nd Edition.* New York: Academic Press.

Zeigler, B. P., & Sarjoughian, H. S. (2002). Implications of M&S Foundations for the V&V of Large Scale Complex Simulation Models, Invited Paper. In *Verification & Validation Foundations Workshop Laurel, Maryland, VA.*, (pp. 1–51). Society for Computer Simulation. Retrieved from https://www.dmso.mil/public/transition/vva/foundations

Zeigler, B. P., Sarjoughian, H. S., & Praehofer, H. (2000). Theory of quantized systems: DEVS simulation of perceiving agents. *Cybernetics and Systems, 31*(6), 611–647. doi:10.1080/01969720050143175

KEY TERMS AND DEFINITIONS

Simulation Interoperability: ability to build a heterogeneous simulator from two or more different simulators. Models can belong to distinct formalisms and simulation engines can be implemented in multiple programming languages.

DEVS Model Specification: the specification of atomic and coupled models as mathematical structures.

DEVS Abstract Atomic Model Interface: specification of the operations of the atomic DEVS model in a meta programming language.

Simulator and Coordinator: realizations of the DEVS atomic and coupled simulation protocols to execute atomic and coupled models, respectively.

SAM Approach: approach for implementing simulation interoperability based on the DEVS model specification and the DEVS atomic model interface.

Model Adapter: software component of a DEVS simulation engine that maps the DEVS abstract atomic model interface to the implementation specific atomic model interface and the direction and execution of a coordinator of a coupled model.

Model Proxy: software component of a DEVS simulation engine that maps the implementation specific atomic model interface to the DEVS abstract atomic model interface.

APPENDIX A: THE TREEGROSS STAND GROWTH MODEL

The TreeGrOSS (Tree Growth Open Source Software) model (Nagel, 2003) is a public domain variant of the BWinPro model (Nagel et al., 2002). According to the classification of Porté and Bartelink (2002) it belongs to the class of non-gap distance-independent tree models. The empirical model is based on data of a growth and yield experiments of about 3500 plots in northern Germany. It uses the potential growth concept (Hasenauer, 2006), which reduces species and site dependent potential relative height growth of a top height tree $i_{hrelPot}$ by the single trees competition situation (Eq. A1).

$$i_{hrel} = i_{hrelPot} + p_1 (h_{100} / h)^{p_2} \qquad\qquad (A1)$$

Where p_i are species specific constants, h_{100} is the topheight of the stand, i.e. the average height of the highest 100 trees, and h the height of the considered specific tree. The basal area growth of a tree is estimated by Eq. A2.

$$\ln(\mathrm{D}a_{Basal}) = p_0 + p_1 \ln(c_S) + p_2 \ln(age) + p_3 c_{66} + p_4 c_{66c} + p_5 \ln(\mathrm{D}t) \qquad\qquad (A2)$$

Where p_i are species specific constants, c_S is the crown surface area calculated from diameter, height of the tree, and the topheight of the stand, age is the tree age, $\mathrm{D}t$ is the time period of usually 5 years, c_{66} is the competition index (Figure 10) and c_{66c} is an index that increases when the competition situation is relieved, i.e. neighbouring trees are thinned.

Further, the model was extended by thinning routines based only on information of the sum of basal area and mean quadratic diameter of thinned trees. These routines selected trees randomly from a probability distribution of tree diameters. Eventually, one side of a Gaussian distribution with a mean of the cohorts minimum or maximum diameter was used, respectively to thinning from below or above, and a standard deviation chosen in a way, so that the expected quadratic mean diameter of thinned trees was equal to the specified one.

The model and the extensions were validated against plot data of permanent sampling inventories of three monospecific stands and two multi-cohort stands within the study region. An example is shown in Figure 11. The TreeGrOSS model performed at least as good as local yield tables with significant improvements for co-dominant and suppressed cohorts.

The complete time series, which at several stands covered more than 100 years, were kindly provided by the Eberswalde forestry research institute and the chair of Forest Growth and Timber Mensuration at TU-Dresden and preprocessed by Mund et al. (2005).

Figure 10. Calculation of the competition index in TreeGrOSS (Nagel 2003, used with permission). At a height of 2/3 (or 66%) of the crown length all crowns are cut, if they reach that height. If the crown base is above the height then cross sectional area of that tree will be taken. The sum of the cross sectional area is divided by the stand area

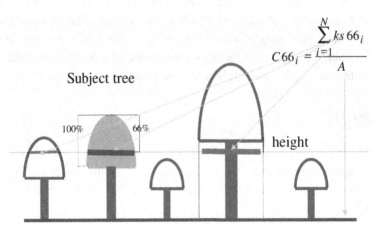

APPENDIX B: THE YASSO SOIL MODEL

The soil carbon model Yasso was designed by Liski et al. (2005) in order to model soil carbon stocks of mineral soils in managed forests. Figure 12 displays the model structure and the flow of carbon.

The colonization part (Figure 12 (a)) describes a delay before decomposers can attack the parts of the woody litter compartments and additionally describes the composition of the different litter types of compartments that correspond to the kinetically defined pools. The decomposition part (Figure 12 (b))

Figure 11. Comparison of inventoried timber volume from a suppressed beech cohort of the permanent inventory plot Leinefelde 245 to model predictions by a yield table (Dittmar et al. 1986) and predictions of the TreeGrOSS model

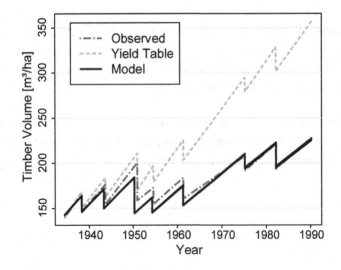

Figure 12. Flow chart of the Yasso model. a) species dependent part of litter colonization and separation of litter into chemical compounds b) species independent part of decomposition of chemical compounds

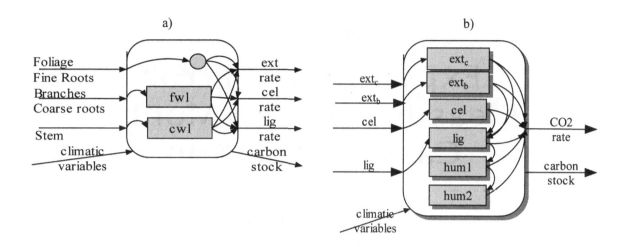

describes the decomposition of the chemical compounds. The fwl-pool can be roughly associated with undecomposed litter, the cwl-pool with dead wood, and all the other parts with organic matter in soil including the organic layer. The decay rates are dependent on mean annual temperature (or alternatively effective temperature sum) and a drought index (difference between precipitation and potential evapo-transpiration during the period from Mai to September). In the standard parameterization the decay rates of the slower pools are less sensitive to temperature increase than the fast pools (humus one: 60%, humus two: 36% of sensitivity of fast pools). The model has been tested and successfully applied to boreal forest (Peltoniemi et al., 2004), litter bag studies in Canada (Palosuo et al., 2005), and as part of the CO2FIX model all over Europe (Nabuurs et al., 2002; Kaipainen et al., 2004). In order to simulate multi-species stands the colonization part was duplicated and parameterized for each tree cohort and coupled all the duplicates to the single species independent decomposition part.

The soil pools were initialized by spin-up runs with repeated climate data of the last century and average soil carbon inputs. The average soil carbon inputs were derived for each species by simulating the stand growth model over an entire rotation cycle including final harvest (Wutzler & Mund, 2007). Soil carbon inputs for cohorts, i.e. tree groups, in multi-cohort stands were decreased by the proportion of tree groups basal area to stands basal area. In order to account for soil degradation in the past, the slowest pool was reset after the spin-up run so that the sum of pools match the carbon stocks that were obtained by spatial extrapolation of observed carbon stocks using the dominating tree species and site conditions (Wutzler & Reichstein, 2007).

Chapter 6
Experimental Error Measurement in Monte Carlo Simulation

Lucia Cassettari
University of Genoa, Italy

Roberto Mosca
University of Genoa, Italy

Roberto Revetria
University of Genoa, Italy

ABSTRACT

This chapter describes the set up step series, developed by the Genoa Research Group on Production System Simulation at the beginning of the '80s, as a sequence, through which it is possible at first statistically validate the simulator, then estimate the variables which effectively affect the different target functions, then obtain, through the regression meta-models, the relations linking the independent variables to the dependent ones (target functions) and, finally, proceed to the detection of the optimal functioning conditions. The authors pay great attention to the treatment, the evaluation and control of the Experimental Error, under the form of Mean Square Pure Error (MS_{PE}), a measurement which is always culpably neglected in the traditional experimentation on the simulation models but, that potentially can consistently invalidate with its magnitude the value of the results obtained from the model.

INTRODUCTION

The canonical modelling type of many disciplines and, particularly, for that concerned by this chapter, of many engineering studies is that allowing to supply representations of the phenomenal reality through mathematical propositions whose elaboration gives quantitative data making possible evaluation of the target system deriving from the formulated target function (see Figure 1).

Therefore, when the reality is excessively complex, the attempt to close it inside a rigid formalism of an equation series is practically impossible, then, the going on this way can mean the changing of its real characteristics due to the introduction of

DOI: 10.4018/978-1-60566-774-4.ch006

conceptual simplifications necessary, in any case, to achieve the model making up.

The fact that, with this formulation one of the modelling fundamental principles stating that "it is the model which should adapt to the target reality and not the reality which must be simplified to be put down in a model" is failed, has a great importance since, under these conditions, the value of the achievable results, afterward, will result from not much significant to distorted with a serious prejudice for their usability for system correct analysis purposes, as, unfortunately, often takes place for numerous models of complex systems acting in the discrete in presence of stochastic character.

In these cases, the simulating tool able to avoid the purely analytic model typical rigidities exploiting the logic proposition flexibility, with which compensate the descriptive impossibilities of the mathematic type ones, is the only tool able to allow the investigated system effective and efficient representation.

The remarkable power, in terms of adherence to the target reality, of discrete and stochastic simulation models is, therefore, frequently dissipated in the traditional experimentation phase that, as it is carried out, is, indeed, strongly self-limiting and never able to make completely emerging that developed inside the model. The what if analysis, indeed, making varying in in-

put, at each experimental act, one or at most few input variables, produces, in output, partial and inhomogeneous among them scenarios, since related to punctual single situations and not resulting from an univocal matrix of experimental responses (see Figure 2). Therefore such a gap can be conveniently overcome using some planned test techniques (see Figure 3) borrowed from the Design of Experiments and the Response Surface Methodology, through which translate the experimental responses, resulting from suitable solicitations imposed to the model through values assigned to the independent variables according to pre-organized schemes, in real state equations valid inside a pre-established domain of the target system operating field.

In the following pages the set up step series (see Figure 4), developed by the Genoa Research Group on the production system simulation at the beginning of the '80s are shown as a sequence, through which it is possible at first statistically validate the simulator, then estimate the variables which effectively affect the different target functions, then obtain, through the regression meta-models, the relations linking the independent variables to the dependent ones (target functions) and, finally, proceed to the detection of the optimal functioning conditions (Mosca and Giribone, 1982).

DETERMINATION OF THE SIMULATION RUN

Introduction

After the model construction and analogical validation (that is after having shown the model ability to faithfully describe the investigated reality) it is necessary to achieve the statistic validation. With this acceptation it is intended to make clear the confirmation of a suitable model ability to treat the stochastic character transferred in it by the target system. To understand the determinant importance of this aspect it is sufficient to observe how, in a

Figure 1.

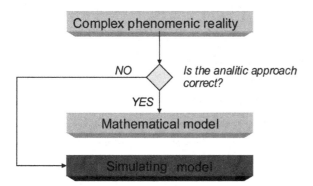

Figure 2.

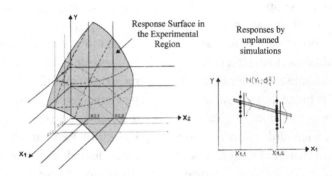

simulation model, there is always an accumulation of frequency distributions, whose in progress effects intersect and/or superpose by conditioning the experimental response amount.

A great part of simulation model builders and/or users of the same, therefore, were, and are still today, missing of the conceptual perception of the problems connected with a correct duration of the simulation run, a duration, among others, deeply connected with the stochastic character treatment and to its effect invalidating the responses

of the built models, even with a great adherence and reproductive ability of the target reality. And in spite of it many "modelling and simulation" texts whose length became classics warn about the connected risks and suggested some useful methodologies for the concerned problem solving, whose schematisation can be so summarized: downward of the analogical validation and before the experimental campaign beginning, it is necessary to verify that the two essential conditions, called of stabilisation, related respectively to the

Figure 3.

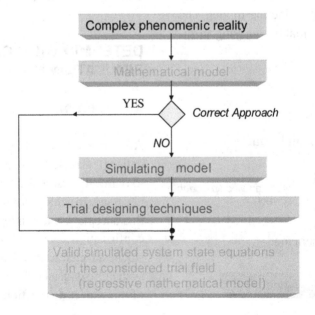

Figure 4.

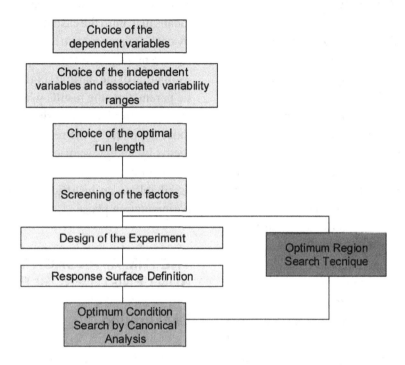

beginning transitory and the presence, just, of stochastic character, are met.

Duration of the Beginning Transitory or Warm-Up Period

The warm-up period is that run beginning phase allowing inside the model in its evolution phase, that the simulated system come from its beginning zero state, of first operating starting, to the regime operation condition. During this simulated period, which is not representative of the model normal operation condition, the accounting neither of the target function, nor of the statistically significant parameters obviously, is not carried out since the data supplied by the model can be assimilated to situations which, in the system life, take place at its start-up and, at the most, few other times after particular events (ex. Important maintenances, revamping).

This experimental phase is totally analogous to that which we observed in the life of a new system built at the time of the passage from the begin-

ning quiet state (for the production systems for example: empty warehouses, stopped machines, resting operators, non active transportation systems etc.) to that of the same system starting with the resulting unbalances characteristics of each transitory condition.

The time where the transitory condition ends, is normally estimated by the expert experimenters on their sensations according to the global behaviour which can be deduced from a given model or other similar ones on which they have already operated.

Moreover there are also scientific methodologies with which achieve the evaluation of the warm up period; this is done putting under control pre-determined point of interest of the modelled system, the so called regeneration points (warehouse stock levels, queue entity before the machines etc.); from the study of their behaviour it is possible to evaluate, just, with a good approximation, the time of the passage, in the simulated system, from the transitory to the regime condition.

Simulation Run Length

This is the second essential problem that, still today, after more than forty years of common use of the simulation tool, or it has not been perceived by the most (it is sufficient read many of the published articles on specialized reviews or attend the main international event concerning this field), or by those who faced it, it has been unsatisfactorily solved through approaches based on the experience and/or on punctual methodologies, in any case, very expensive in terms of time-machine and such, really, to bring to conclusions not different from those empirically detected by the already mentioned skilled experimenters.

Among the three mentioned cases the first is necessarily the most dangerous in terms of possible negative impact on the investigated target functions, while the other two limit their effect to expensive, though almost causal, extension of the experimentation activity.

All the before stated, now then see where the need to correctly determinate a simulation run length evaluation raises. The presence in the model of frequency distributions taken from the target reality in order to describe it at the best, as mentioned in the paragraph 1, is one of the qualifying arguments of the simulation existence justification as excellent modelling: indeed the simulation allows to face a stochastic reality with an equally and identically stochastic model.

The essential distinction between the two situations (reality vs model) is represented by the fact that, while the real system sees conditioned the targets assigned to it by the background noise through which the different stochastic sources express in it, the model is affected, in the output results by a double uncertainty source represented by the superposition of that naturally existing in the real system (not simple but composite stochastic character deriving both from endogen and exogenous causes) with which related to the Monte Carlo Method exploitation, allowing the metabolism of the real system stochastic character

by the simulation model. Explicitly speaking this means that, until the casual extractions carried out by each frequency distribution is not sufficiently high to make possible the supply of not distorted estimation of the starting single distribution statistic parameters, the results which can be obtained from the simulation run shall not be in line with those supplied by the real system, being just affected by an extra-noise, which is characteristic of each investigated target function, completely ascribable to an insufficient duration of the experimentation phase.

THE ITIM APPROACH TO THE RUN LENGTH PROBLEM

Background

The ITIM approach to the run length problem starts from a fundamental remark shared by all those that in their study, research, work activity deal with the DOE and RSM methodologies by suitably interiorizing the meaning and the analytic and descriptive power of these techniques. Following, exactly, the DOE approach philosophy, the system concerned by the experimentation can, as a first approximation and given as expected the following deepening, be considered as a black box subjected to the imposition of precise experimental solicitations. Under the effect of the impact of these solicitations we want to understand what of the same system, measured by means of a size called total variability, can be ascribed to the effect, on the target function, of each independent variable, having an effective conditioning ability on the response, and what, on the contrary, not resulting as referable singularly or in combination to one of them, represents the ignorance rate or non knowledge of the experimenter of the target system behaviours. The ignorance measuring is committed to a quantitative term called Experimental Error, commonly expressed through a statistic size called Sum Squares Error (SS_E) or, equally, through the Mean Squares Error (MS_E) of the previous directly derived. Evidently, as in any experimental situation, the higher is the SS_E percentage compared to the SS_T total variation, the higher is the misunderstanding level of the investigated system behaviours, which can be appreciated through the modus agendi of the independent variables. The above said expressed in other words means, by extremising, that made 100 the SS_T value, if the SS_E is zero, the detected independent variables, with their behaviours, explicated by the relevant SS_{EFF}, would allow to completely explain also the studied target function. In the opposite case, that is in the case that the SS_E value would be 100, the detected independent, whose SS_{EFF} would result all null, should not have any incident ability on the target, in the field of the surrounding conditions considered for the investigated system and the results obtained would represent nothing if not the background noise echo. The Experimental Error is, then, in all the trials, the simulation ones included, a fundamental comprehension element for which its knowledge and for as possible, its control, represent the distinctive element of a valid experimentation plan compared to a plan that is not only insufficient but also potentially dangerous for the lack of result transparency and reliability which, from the same error, will result strongly affected.

At the end of the '70s, because of the above mentioned reasons, Mosca and Giribone of the ITIM required to quantify the error affecting the responses of some big iron and steel plant simulation models on which they were carrying out experimentation campaigns with the Operating Researchers of Italimpianti, one of the most important companies at the international level, of big production or infrastructure plant design and realisation. Contingently the problem passed over the simple scientific speculation and was economically important for the Company since the result masking by the Experimental Error, which could affect the responses of the simulators used by the Offer Engineering to detect the most advantageous plant configurations, would have been translated into cost variations shown in the economic offers quantified in millions of dollars.

In a parallel way the first applications of DOE and RSM, carried out on the already mentioned models, had pointed out the need to make use of run lengths, then estimated by Italimpianti in 2.880' for the warming up and 1.000.000' for the standard run, incompatible with the experimental campaign period (averagely 1.000 runs for each campaign with a run length of 50' machine for each run) necessary to verify the design solutions detected by the Engineering.

By contextually studying the two problems, they advanced that they could represent the two sides of the same medal: the Experimental Error variable side, linked to the dimension of the same samples resulting from the extractions of the frequency distributions in the model, could not increase with the rise, in the simulated time, of the same sample dimension under the effect of the resulting improvement of the statistic inference, until to annul themselves for a simulation t time tending to the infinite, that is sufficiently high, with stabilisation of the background noise according to the value linked to the sole endogen stochastic character to the modelling target reality (with each target function having its characteristic noise).

Therefore a methodology through which it was possible to point out the evolution in the simulated time of the Experimental Error would have allowed, at each run time, to know the entity of the whole noise afflicting the experimental results for which, complying with the elimination impossibility of the real system intrinsic stochastic character once achieved an error level considered adequate for the single investigated target function, The run would have been interrupted at the corresponding time and the punctual value of the searched response, extrapolated or interpolated at the detection time provided by the design. To make an example, always making reference to the already mentioned simulations of iron and steel plants, the application of the new methodology brought, besides to the knowledge of the MS_{PE} evolution curve in the simulated time, to determinate a run length, calculated on the mostly unfavoured target function, equal to a fourth of that normally used in the previous simulations according to precautionary estimations carried out by the same model builders.

The ITIM Methodology

The reference scheme for the simulation optimal run length detection can be articulated as follows (Mosca and Giribone, 1986):

1. Choice of a t time, of attempt, of the sufficiently wide simulation run length. To merely exemplifying, for cascade production systems, we can think to a t equal to 12-24 month of operation of the real system
2. Simulation program predisposition with:
   ○ assignation to the independent variable of the variability field central value of each of them
   ○ trigging seed replacement, at each following run, of the random numbers ruling the casual extractions
   ○ simulation trial replication for n_0 times, as many as are the central test provided by the relevant CCD.

After having established, then, N detection moments in the dependent variable value simulated time, all equidistant each others by an identical Δt, so that $t_1 = t_0 + \Delta t$; $t_2 = t_1 + \Delta t \ldots$, for each of the n_0 run it is predisposed a file containing the N detections relevant to each of the target functions that you intend to investigate. This procedure scheme is equivalent, under the conceptual profile, to the N run with a t_i duration, with i=1…N, replicated for n0 times

3. to the N detection moments having a t_i, duration for each i, we calculate the two statistic

sizes called Sum Squares and Mean Squares of the pure Experimental Error through the relations:

$$SS_{PE}(t_i) = \sum_{j=1}^{N} (y_j(t_i) - \overline{y}_j(t_i))^2$$

$$MS_{PE}(t_i) = \frac{\sum_{j=1}^{N} (y_j(t_i) - \overline{y}_j(t_i))^2}{n_0 - 1}$$

for each $1 \leq i \leq N$ being:

- SSpe(ti) the Sum Squares of the Experimental Error of the N simulation having a ti duration
- MS_{PE} (ti) the corresponding Mean Squares
- Yi (ti) the response of the j-th target function observed in a ti duration run
- $\overline{y}_j$ (ti) the average of the responses observed in the same ti time in the n0 simulation run carried out in parallel.

It should be noticed that

- since the Experimental Error, by its nature, in a complex system simulation model depends on a higher and higher number of independent causes is distributed according to the central limit theorem as NID $(0,\sigma2)$
- complying with the Cochran's Theorem the expected MS_{PE} value is just the σ^2 variance of the Pure Experimental Error

In other words the Experimental Error, for each target function, if the number of central test n_0 is sufficiently high, assumes, complying with the central limit theorem, a Gaussian distribution of which we calculate the average value $\overline{y}_j$ (t_i) and the σ^2 *variance (t)* under the form of MS_{PE} (t_i) for which the MS_{PE} (t_i) gives a representation of the Experimental Error evolution in the simulated period. Graphical representation of the N values of the $MS_{PE}(t_i)$ and interpretation by the experi-

Figure 5.

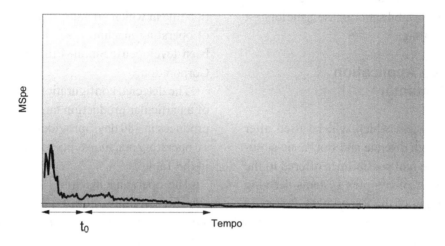

menter of an interpolating curve which trend is classically like that of a knee curve (see Figure 5): for little values of t_i, indeed, the number of extractions from the single frequency distributions results reduced then the re-sampled extracted data allow approximate interferences and, as such, very different from run to run, with an obvious effect on the investigated target function which, at t_i parity supplies, in each of the n_0 runs, values also extremely misaligned.

With the t_i growing the samples become richer in width and, as result, the target functions values, at instant t_i parity tend in the n_0 runs to more marked value homogeneity, being still intended the dependence of the single MS_{PE} on the investigated target function type as well as on the stochastic character entity in the real system. After having detected the different areas of stability which are normally in a MS_{PE} evolution curve in the time on temporal width Δt_1, Δt_2 etc which the experimenter can evaluate through the application of a Fisher test on the variances, the run stop moment can be assumed according to, at condition that it complies with the characteristic background noise of the investigated real system, the acceptable considered Experimental Error level on the final result and expressed through the:

$$e_i = \pm 3 \sqrt{\sigma^2(t_i)}$$

then, in the following runs it will be know, afterward, the fact that the responses punctually obtained by the simulator shall be interpreted, really, inside a variability field defined through e_i. By wanting exemplify if, under particular operating conditions, $y_1(t_1) = 1000$ and $\sigma^2 = 100$ the real target function value shall not 1000 but $y_1^*(t_i) = 1000 \pm 3\sqrt{100}$ that is under the effect of the Pure Experimental Error $970 \pounds y_1^*(t_i) \pounds 1030$

4. in the case of additional target functions in the time, such as the production, to maintain the classic knee trend of the MS_{PE}, trend which can be well and easily visually interpreted, it is necessary to carry out a normalisation operation of each response by dividing their value, at each of the N t_i detection moments for the same t_i time according to the $y_N(t_i) = \dfrac{y(t_i)}{t_i}$

5. in the case of the investigation simultaneously carried out on different target functions the optimal run length complying with the remarks of which at the previous paragraph

4, will result to be that of the target function attaining the stabilisation phase in the longest simulated time.

Methodology Application to a Test Simulator

The physical system which will be used after modelling through discrete and stochastic simulator to show the real possibilities offered to the designer/manager of complex systems deriving by the application of the Experiment Theory to the planning of the simulation experimentation campaigns, consists of a computer-based production line in which operate 10 different typologies of operating machines (see Figure 6) and it has been developed in Simul8 Professional by Simul8 Corporation.

The detected configuration for the attainment of a particular production target, 180.000 pieces produces in 380 days, provides, totally, the use of 10 operating machine typology divided as shown in the Table 1.

The operating machines do not undergo to significant failures during the production phase since they are daily maintained in the moments

Figure 6.

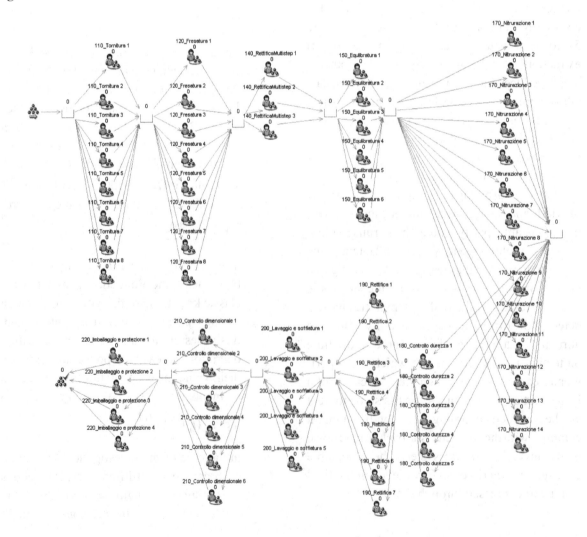

of line-stop. The working times, by piece, for each machine, are expressed under the form of frequency distributions characterised as shown in the table.

The law of the raw material arrival is a negative exponential with an average of 8 minutes.

On the contrary there are not limits to the productions resulting from the output warehouse dimension.

For the run curve building, after having observed that the decisional freedom degrees are represented by the sole 4 typologies of machines shown with the letters A,B,C,D, we consider as opportune to assume a positioning of the 4 decisional variable at the central level of the relevant variability ranges, that is:

A = 8 ; B = 5 ; C = 14 ; D = 7

While the remaining typologies results to be automatically defined, just, by the lack of freedom degrees deriving from the choices already done.

By fixing in 5 the number n_0 of central replications we can obtain, if we would decide to carry out the following investigations on the screening and the RSM exploiting factorial designs or central composed designs, even the possibility of their re-use to carry out the screening or the so

called Pure Quadratic Curvature test, allowing to evaluate the eventual curving in a model of the 1st order or to not launch the center points in case of re-use of a central composed design, which is used for the research of a 2nd order link among the independent and dependent variables.

As explained in the previous phase of the theory organisation, which is the base of the simulation run optimal period, the steps to carry out on the model are the following ones:

1. fix:
   a. the number of tests to carry out: 5
   b. the run length: 780 working days of 8 hours each
   c. the detection path Δt: 1 day
   d. the total number of r detection time moments: 780
2. provide to the production function normalisation, step by step, obtained by dividing the cumulated production in the t_i time by the number of t_i days:

The output obtained from the 5 simulation runs, by changing at each new run the random number triggering seeds, are transferred inside the Microsoft EXCEL tables organized as shown hereunder (see Figure 8).

Table 1.

Code	Typology	Min N°	Max N°	Freq Distrib working period	Charact stat Parameters
A	Milling machines	7	9	Uniform	3-5
B	Multistep grinding machines	4	6	Normal	$\mu=3,8; \sigma=1,5$
C	Nitriding machines	13	15	Normal	$\mu= 4,5; \sigma=1$
D	Dimensional check	6	8	Normal	$\mu=6,8; \sigma= 1,5$
E	Lathes	8	8	Triangular	3-4-5
F	Balancing machines	6	6	Uniform	1-2
G	Hardness check	5	5	Triangular	1-2-3
H	Washing	5	5	Fixed	2,5
I	Packaging	4	4	Uniform	1-2
L	Grinding Machines	7	7	Normal	$\mu=2,4; \sigma=0,5$

Clearly, particularized to the concerned case, the MS_{PE} formula will be so structured:

$$MS_{PE}(t_i) = \sum_{i=1}^{780} \frac{(y(t_i) - \bar{y}(t_i))^2}{4}$$

where $y(t_i)$ represents the 5 simulator responses in the 5 runs in the moments t_i e $\bar{y}(t_i)$ the average of these responses.

The example shown hereunder describes the necessary steps to calculate the $MS_{PE}(t_i)$ (see Figure 8). In the $MS_{PE}(t_i)$ column it is possible to see the values, just, of the Mean Squares and Pure Experimental Error which, for the Cochran's Theorem, represents the best variance estimator σ^2 of the experimental error distributed, just, as a NID($0, \sigma^2$). The $MSPE(t_i)$ evolution is shown in Figure 7.

The $\sqrt{MSPE(t_i)}$ supplies, therefore, at each t_i the error quadratic average difference.

Being the responses under each t_i at their turn distributed as a Gauss ($\bar{y}(t_i), \sigma^2$) we can deduce that, once selected the run optimal duration having a σ^2 variance, the simulator response, under a given

target function, $y^*(t_0)$ really shall be read as one of the possible values included in an interval

$$y_{MED}{}^* - 3\sqrt{MSPE} \; \pounds \; y^*(t_o) \; \pounds \; y_{MED}{}^* + 3\sqrt{MSPE}$$

In correspondence of 380 simulated days the MS_{PE} on the normalized value of the production is of the order of $5 \cdot 10^{-2}$ then:

$$\sigma = \sqrt{5 \cdot 10^{-2}} = 0{,}23 \, pz$$

and, then,

$$\pm 3\sigma \approx \pm 0{,}7 \; pz$$

value with a negligible impact on a daily average production of about 494 pieces. The graphic exam reveals a good curve arrangement already starting from 160/170 simulated days in correspondence of whom the MS_{PE} value is of the $9 \cdot 10^{-2}$ order then

$$\sigma = \sqrt{9 \cdot 10^{-2}} = 0{,}3 \, pz$$

$$\pm 3\sigma \approx \pm 0{,}9 \; pz$$

Figure 7.

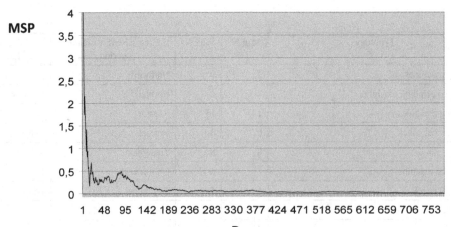

from which we can evict that by doubling the simulation run we have a paltry gain in terms of benefice on the normalized production date masking.

In a purely speculative optic, we can observe by opportunely magnifying the scale on the y axe, as shown in the Figure 9, a slow descending trend of the MS_{PE} with adjustment, probably definitive, around a value of $9 \cdot 10^{-3}$ to which correspond a σ of 0,1 pz. The choice to stop the run at 380 days depends exclusively on the opportunity to have not to make adding runs to attain the cumulated production whose value, said in passing, in all five launches carried out on the central values widely overcome the required 180.000 pz (included the experimental error).

Methodology Critical Analysis

What described above gives rise at least to two questions, which can spring out doubts about the generalisation possibility of the methodology (Mosca e Giribone, 1982). They are:

1. Is there the possibility that the random number sets chosen for the n_0 runs can in some way condition, as it is obvious, the "stories" that the simulator tells, make varying the trend of the MS_{PE} curve and, as result, differently place the instant corresponding to the optimal period?

2. Can the auto-correlation, which, undoubtedly, exists among the following responses in the ti time of each of the n_0 run condition the methodology validity?

Figure 8.

Days	Cumulata vi(t) / ti					E[yi(t)]	{vi(t) - E[vi(t)]}^2					SSPE(ti)	MSPE(ti)
	Run 1	Run 2	Run 3	Run 4	Run 5	Mean	Run 1	Run 2	Run 3	Run 4	Run 5		
1	444	445	440	434	448	442,2	3,24	7,84	4,84	67,24	33,64	116,8	29,2
2	469	468	468,5	461,5	471	467,6	1,96	0,16	0,81	37,21	11,50	51,7	12,925
3	476,3333	478,3333	477,3333	473,6667	479,3333	477	0,444444	1,777778	0,111111	11,11111	5,444444	18,88880	4,722222
4	481,25	482,5	482,25	478	481,75	481,15	0,01	1,8225	1,21	9,9225	0,36	13,325	3,33125
5	484,8	485,2	483,8	481,8	483,6	483,84	0,9216	1,8496	0,0016	4,1616	0,0576	6,992	1,748
6	486,1667	486	485,8333	482,6667	484,6667	485,0667	1,21	0,871111	0,587778	5,76	0,16	8,588889	2,147222
7	487	488,2857	487,2857	484,7143	487,1429	486,8857	0,013061	1,96	0,16	4,715102	0,066122	6,914286	1,728571
8	488,5	489,125	488,875	486,125	488,25	488,175	0,105625	0,9025	0,49	4,2025	0,005625	5,70625	1,426563
9	488,4444	489,7778	489,8889	487,5556	488,8889	488,9111	0,217778	0,751111	0,956049	1,837531	0,000494	3,762963	0,940741
10	489,8	490,8	490,2	487,8	488,8	489,48	0,1024	1,7424	0,5184	2,8224	0,4624	5,648	1,412
11	490,2727	491,0909	490,7273	488,8182	489,6364	490,1091	0,026777	0,963967	0,382149	1,666446	0,223471	3,26281	0,815702
12	490,75	491,5833	491,25	489,0833	490,4167	490,6167	0,017778	0,934444	0,401111	2,351111	0,04	3,744444	0,936111
13	491	491,8462	491,6154	490	490,6154	491,0154	0,000237	0,690178	0,36	1,031006	0,16	2,24142	0,560355
14	490,8571	491,9286	491,1429	489,7857	490,8571	490,9143	0,003265	1,028776	0,052245	1,273673	0,003265	2,361224	0,590306
15	490,8	491,5333	490,9333	490,1333	490,6	490,8	0	0,537778	0,017778	0,444444	0,04	1,04	0,26
16	491,3125	491,6875	490,75	490,75	490,875	491,075	0,056406	0,375156	0,105625	0,105625	0,04	0,682813	0,170703
17	491,7647	492,2941	490,7647	490,7647	491,0588	491,3294	0,189481	0,930657	0,318893	0,318893	0,073218	1,831142	0,457785
18	491,6667	492,5556	491,0556	490,9444	491,1667	491,4778	0,035679	1,161605	0,178272	0,284444	0,09679	1,75679	0,439198
19	491,7895	492,9474	491,0526	491,0526	491,4737	491,6632	0,015956	1,649197	0,372742	0,372742	0,0359	2,446537	0,611634
20	491,85	493,15	491,2	491,1	492,15	491,89	0,0016	1,5876	0,4761	0,6241	0,0676	2,757	0,68925
21	491,619	492,8571	491,1905	491,5714	492,2857	491,9048	0,081633	0,907029	0,510204	0,111111	0,145125	1,755102	0,438776
22	491,8636	493,3182	491,7273	491,7273	492,5	492,2273	0,132231	1,190083	0,25	0,25	0,07438	1,896694	0,474174
23	492,1304	493,2609	491,3913	491,9565	492,4783	492,2435	0,012779	1,035085	0,7262	0,082344	0,055123	1,911531	0,477883
24	492,375	493,2917	491,7917	492,25	492,5833	492,4583	0,006944	0,694444	0,444444	0,043403	0,015625	1,204861	0,301215
25	492,52	493,32	491,8	492,08	492,76	492,496	0,000576	0,678976	0,484416	0,173056	0,069696	1,40672	0,35168

Figure 9.

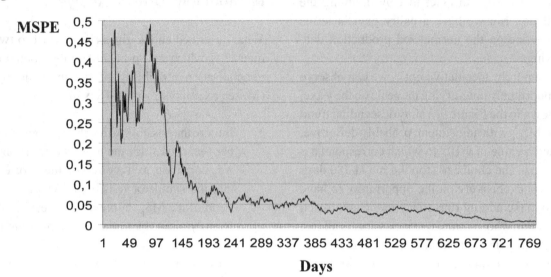

In both cases to show the groundlessness of the questions proposed instead of going on the way of difficult and almost undoubtedly non-exhaustive theoretical dissertations we preferred to base ourselves on experimental analysis and the interpretative simplicity and solidity of their immediateness. Therefore, with reference to the possible dependence of the MS_{PE} evolution curve on the random numbers ruling the extractions from the frequency distributions in the module according to the Monte Carlo technique, with reference to the first of the two remarks we will show that, through the application to a real case, which is sufficient to run k set of n_0 central test being each $k \geq 5$ and operating for each set the total changing of the trigging seed of the random number generators ruling the extraction from the frequency distribution in the model and, therefore, of all the random numbers which are used in each simulation run. Such an operations causes that the simulator tells stories, at least initially, different the ones from the others. As we can remark in the Figure 10, just, relevant to 5 series of tests for each target function carried out on the already described model and used as guide test case for the whole chapter:

• the 5 MS_{PE} evolution curves of each target function tends to stabilize at the same instant t_{ott}

• the MS_{PE}, and then the variances of the Pure Experimental Error, as we can see from the curve trend, are, for low values of ti strongly conditioned by the effect of the random numbers and give rise to different Gaussian k distributions for each ti. With the simulated time passing the Gaussian k tend to superpose up to create a single normal distribution with a $\sigma 2$ variance. From this assertion results the consequent confirmation of the t_{ott} independence from the random number generators since the behaviour differences in the Experimental Error curve exist only in the beginning temporal moments and not in the following in which the k set of simulation test generate curves of the MS_{PE} which can be absolutely superposed.

For as concern, on the contrary, the possible response autocorrelation effect on the MS_{PE} evolution curve, in output from the model at the following time t_i, we can show that it results

Figure 10.

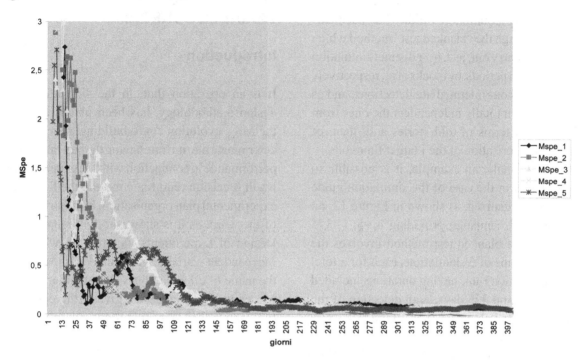

non influent. The problem in it is, conceptually, consistent since each story told by a simulator is such that the value of each of the j target functions under exam in the same instant ti is, undoubtedly, affected from that occurred in the previous times, from t_0 to t_{i-1}, and affects the entity of the responses in the following times from t_{i+1} to t_r: just to exemplify we can observe as a very low occurrence probability extraordinary event, which could be in a production system an unusual failure of a fundamental machine or the combined effect of simultaneous failures on more machines with significant periods of machine stop superposition, not only would strongly condition the story of that precise run but it could generate a distorting effect on the average value estimation and, then, of the punctual values of SS_{PE} and MS_{PE} in each of the following detections. The set up methodology for the study of the MS_{PE} evolution presupposes, on the contrary, that the remarks in each of the $r \cdot n_0$ fictitious simulations, through which we calculate at each time t_i the MS_{PE} values, are independent

then the eventual correlation among the responses of the following blocks would irremediably invalidate the results. In the methodology conceptualization we had therefore thought to eliminate such a risk through the choice of an interval Δt width between two following detections of the target functions values, sufficiently wide, so as to make that only the first "few" events of the sub-th run would result correlated with the last events of the sub-(i-1)th run for which, by direct consequence, $\overline{y}_j(t_i)$ e $\overline{y}_j(t_{i-1})$ are affected by autocorrelation almost not influent. In other terms the base idea was that to damp, until to annul it almost completely, the unavoidable correlation existing among the following instants of one same run through the horizontal "cut" of the n_0 simulations, carried out at the temporal instants t_i at which the target function detections are carried out. By the effect of this procedure is as the experimenter would carry out n_0 simulations with a t_1 period, n_0 simulations with a t_2 period,....n_0 simulation with a t_r period.

All that before stated, the totally experimental check of this assumption validity has been carried out through the "blanked test" method which provides to carry out, just, $n_0 \cdot r$ distinct simulation launches with periods, by blocks of n_0, respectively $t_1, t_2, \ldots t_r$ without intermediate detections, and as result, as such totally independent the ones from the other in terms of told stories and, then, of punctual valorisation of the j target functions.

Only to make an example, it is possible to observe that in the case of the simulation guide model we organized, as shown in Figure 12, an experimental campaign providing $n_0=5$; $t_r=375$ days; $r=9$ the blanked test method involves the run of 9 groups of 5 simulations each for a total of 45 simulation runs, having durations included between 35 and 375 days, with detection of the target function values and, then, of the MS_{PE} only at the end of each run.

Easy to verify as the MS_{PE} resulting curve obtained with the above described technique, does not show starting from the conditions of first stabilisation, differences statistically remarkable compared to those obtained with the proposed methodology (see Figure 11).

THE INDEPENDENT VARIABLE SCREENING

Introduction

It is an operation that, in the simulation trial design methodology, has been placed between the MS_{PE} evolution curve building, necessary to determinate the run time having the best ratio price/ performance in connection with the experimenter result precision requirements, and the following experimental plan organisation, in the strict sense of the word, as it is shown in the Figure 4. The Design of Experiments literature, in which the independent variable screening is shown with the name of effect analysis (Montgomery, 2005; Mosca and Giribone 1982), gives to this operation two targets, one conceptual and one utilitarian, with a certain importance:

- Conceptual target→ when we face the study of a complex system, an error which cannot be never committed, since it is so serious to prejudge the validity of the whole modelling, is that to not take into consideration one or more independent variables able to

Figure 11.

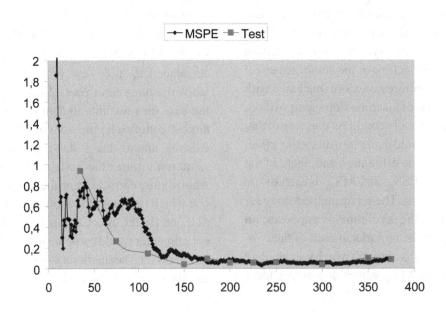

affect, with their behaviour, at least one of the target functions concerned by the experimenter study. As result, in the choice of the independent variable set which will be taken into consideration, it is necessary to pay great attention not only to include those that, by experience or knowledge of the system, shall affect the j target functions but also those that, for any reason, it could be assumed that can have some conditioning effect on the dependent variables.

The need to avoid this risk brings, as result, in the experimentation organisation phase, to make growing, sometimes also significantly, the number of independent variables which are taken into consideration. Since, therefore, the number of simulation runs provided by the following application of the Response Surface Methodology increases, at least, with exponential law (laws designs of the 2k series) each additional variable, compared to those really incident on the target function, generates a devastating multiplicative effect on the run number which should be carried out (Myers and Montgomery, 1995). All that before stated, it should result clear how a technique, just that of screening, allowing at the experimental plan organisation bottom to know the possibilities of each k independent variable to affect each of the j target functions and to make, as result, in a

comparison among the same variable, a classification by importance, target by target, this technique represents a cognitive tool, on the behaviours of the target system, of absolute importance for the experimenter and the designer/manager.

- Utilitarian target → the detection of the independent variable with a low effect on a target function allows, as we will see in the guide example and according to theorisation of the Design of Experiments, to "kill" the variability of those independent variables, resulted after the screening operation as non significant, by assigning them constant values, chosen in the field of the beginning variability range, in the following experimentation, the utilitarian effect of this approach on the number of tests to carry out is evident when the total number of the tests necessary to carry out a central composite design is explained, a design for the description of the statistical characteristics for which see the following paragraph 4, which are:

$$N - 2^t + n_c \mid 2 \cdot K$$

being k, as already before shown, the number of independent variables detected by the experimenter for the design achievement.

Figure 12.

Days	Run 1	Run 2	Run 3	Run 4	Run 5	Mean	SSPE(ti)	Mspe
35	493,285714	490,914286	493,228571	492,285714	492,142857	492,371429	3,75346939	0,938367
75	493,773333	493,306667	493,506667	493,293333	493	493,376	0,32796444	0,262667
110	493,909091	494,009091	493,245455	493,409091	493,190909	493,552727	0,58122314	0,145306
150	493,633333	493,56	493,4	493,94	493,493333	493,605333	0,16954667	0,042387
175	493,405714	493,605714	493,908571	493,2	493,165714	493,457143	0,37955918	0,09489
250	493,848	493,916	493,84	493,308	493,628	493,708	0,246688	0,061672
300	493,9	494,153333	493,88	493,72	493,633333	493,857333	0,15898667	0,039747
350	494,562857	494,354286	493,757143	494,017143	494,017143	494,141714	0,40147918	0,10037
375	494,312	493,656	494,376	493,914667	494,018667	494,055467	0,34930347	0,087326

All the before stated it result, obviously, the display of that we have defined as utilitarian target of the screening operation and which can so summarized: for each of the afterward selected independent variables and resulted as non significant at the screening, the number of necessary test for a complete description of a given target function is halved compared to that initially assumed.

It is well, therefore, specify that, when we face problems in which it is necessary to study simultaneously the behaviour of several dependent variables, the offered advantage by the "conceptual target" of the screening technique continues to fully express as in the case of single dependent problems, since, dependent by dependent, we continue to make clear and clear the role that, on it, have the single independent variables. "The utilitarian target", on the contrary, is often more difficult to achieve since an independent variable which would result not much significant for the j-th target function can, on the contrary, express a remarkable importance on the dependent variable (j+1)-th. if that is how things are any independent variable, if the situation would be extended to all the k variable, shall not be eliminated from the experimental plan then the number of simulation launches to carry out would be that corresponding to the N test of the full central composite design(eventually reduced, if too onerous, through the application of a suitable DOE methodology called "factorial fractioning").

Experimental Statistics References

The concept of an independent variable importance (or "factor" in the DOE terminology) is not an absolute concept but relevant to the value range that the same variable can assume in the field of pre-fixed variability for it by the experimenter of the system manager and by the considered target function.

The manpower resource in a not fully computer-based manufacturing system can be affirmed afterward, is undoubtedly an independent variable able to condition the production target function.

Therefore, in the choosing of the employed number to assign to a particular group of machines of that system, the plant manager has detected in the time and with the experience a variability field such for which inside it he manages to achieve the production fixed targets, after a screening on the production target function almost certainly the "employed number" independent variable will result not much or no significant, while it could be for the "useful" target function. This is why, we repeat it, the range and importance concepts are indissolubly connected. To realize it, it is sufficient to place in the simulation model the number of employed in a contiguous range, levelled downwards, and, immediately the position of the variable in the relative importance classification will change (Mosca and Giribone, 1983).

A remarkably important second notice concerning the screening is related to the methodology ability, whose exhaustive description is in the DOE texts listed in the bibliography, to analyse not only the capacity of the independent variables, as single, to affect the target functions, but, also, the so called and already mentioned interaction effects of the second, third ….k-th order that is the independent variables to affect the target functions or in combination between two or more of them.

Obviously, at the purposes of the two methodological targets proposed for the screening, the fact that a variable affects a dependent in single or combined action is not important: in a case or in the other, it will result able to affect a target function and, as such, important and non eliminable. The experience acquired in the production and service complex system study through the construction of more than three hundred different reality models allowed to the authors to focus some remarks from those derive some empiric rules, which, even if in the fields of non exhaustive generalisation with which it is necessary to see these typologies of assumptions can represent a useful warning for the experimenter who starts the study of the screening methodology:

- Besides to all or part of the effects of the first order, generally, some effects of the second order can result significant, rarely enough those of the third order, practically never those from the fourth order on
- Two independent variables A and B giving rise to significant effects of the first order do not generate, necessarily, a significant interaction effect
- On the contrary two independent variables giving rise to non significant effects have more times generated significant effects of interaction. This concretely means that in the field of the assumed variability ranges the two variables are not, as single, able to affect the dependent while their combined effect can result, in any case, important.

Stated that, as we have already mentioned before, for an exhaustive treatment of the theoretical experimental statistics assumptions read the DOE literature mentioned in the bibliography, for an adequate comprehension of the screening methodology is necessary to remind at least some definitions.

After having remembered that in the factorial designs of the 2^k series each independent variable can assume, in the case of quantitative names, one of the values included between the specified ends of the same range, it is defined as main effect of an independent variable the production variation entity for a given target function, between the average of the values assumed by the dependent variable in correspondence of the high level of A and the average of the values calculated in correspondence of the low level of A (Montgomery, 2005).

This said in other terms, the main effect is only the capacity measure of an independent variable to affect a given dependent when the independent goes from the range low level to the high one.

Since at the high/low level of an independent variable, A for ex, are linked the low levels, the high ones and the relevant combinations of high and low of the other concerned factors that is that the physical interpretation of a factor with the sole exception of the case of two sole independent variables is all except elementary for the experimenter it is determinant, in a relative comparison optic, the knowledge of the sole effect magnitude, since it will be this to reveal if an effect is important and how it is in percentage, compared to the other effects, really important. (In the same reading key there is the effect algebraic sign of the effect to which, as result, it is not possible attribute any information content).

Only to make an example in the case of a 2^2 design the 4 experiment responses can be obtained with:

- A1 (at the first level) and B at the two levels B1 and B2 (then A1→B1 and A1→B2)
- A2 (at the second level) and B at the two levels B1 and B2 (then A2→B1 and A2→B2)

For which, by representing the effect of A the produced variation between the response average under A_2 and the average under A_1, can be easily understood as the intelligibility of the same cannot go further, for the experimenter the "easy" interpretation of its magnitude. This is, in any case, more than sufficient for the purposes assigned to the screening operation and summarized in the two targets enumerated above

The interaction effect between two or more independent variables, much more complex to define, expresses the ability of two or more independent variables to affect a given dependent through a combined action of the average responses at the simultaneously high, low and mixed levels (for their theoretical deepening see Montgomery, 2005; Box and Draper, 1987).

Under the strictly methodological profile the knowledge of the EFFECT size allows to make, case by case, a relative importance classification of the independent variables, singularly or by multiple combinations, to affect the dependent ones.

Clearly if the effect of A is 1000, the effect of B is 1 and the AB interaction effect is 0,5 it is possible to affirm that:

- A is undoubtedly more important than B in the carried out trial field, of the analyzed target function and of the variable ranges assigned to the two independent variables
- With as much reasonable certainty it should be possible to affirm the negligibility of B in affecting, directly or in combination with A, the target function for which the B independent variable can be transformed in constant, by assigning to it one of the pre-assigned values of the variability range.

If, on the contrary, the B effect would be 10 and the AB interaction would be 5 it could arise some doubts about the real negligibility of B.

For these situations is possible to obtain a statistically reliable analysis to carry out through a suitable table of the Variance Analysis built through the concept of "contrast; the contrast allows, indeed, to obtain the suitable amounts and then averages of the squares through which make a statistic summary $F_o = \dfrac{MS_{EFF}}{MS_e}$ to compare with an F of tabled Fisher and which can be detected, on the relevant tables, through the chosen α reliability level and the freedom degrees $\upsilon_1 = 1$ always for MS_{EFF} and υ_2 for the pure experimental error.

The Pure Experimental Error

In order to understand the part of the ANOVA test and the operations which should be carried out to organise the experimental plan, to achieve it, it is sufficient to recall the basis relation of the whole DOE philosophy:

$$SS_T = SS_{TRAT} + SS_E$$

that is the total statistic variability of all the remarks of a given experimental plan it is possible to divide it in the two main components:

a) $SS_{TRAT} = \sum SS_{EFF}$ of the $1°, 2°, ..., K°$ order or Sum Squares of the Effects through which it is possible to express the experimenter capacity to understand how the total statistic variability can be attributed to the independent variable behaviour

b) SS_E Sum Square of the experimental error, which is only the experimenter ignorance level face to a multitude of causes intervening to condition the experiment (including its eventual interpretation model), without that he manages to explain them in a statistically consistent way. The casual effects are joined in it as non systematic measure errors, having endogen and/or exogenic interference effects affecting the dependent variables without that the experimenter manages to detect neither the triggering causes or to singularly measure the results. After having estimated the SS_E, the higher is SS_E the less the independent variables manage to explain the behaviour of the analysed dependent variable. When the trial is translated into a meta-model SS_E can be divided into two components, one relevant to the SS_{PE} experimental phase and one relevant to the SS_{LOF} model. All that before stated for as is competence of the screening methodology, the possibility to carry out an exhaustive investigation which contemplates besides to the effect pure analysis also the contraction of the ANOVA table, requires to attain to the trial MS_E knowledge.

Screening Suitable Experimental Designs

The screening operation can be carried out in different ways according to the desired precision level and the test number that you want to achieve on the simulation model:

1. Daniel method: it is used in the case of mono-replicated factorial trials. It makes reference to a normal probability diagram showing in the abscissa the factor effects and in the ordinate the pk. The effects resulting reasonably aligned on a straight line are non significant effects while the misaligned are significant, the first are, as result, distributed as a NID(0,σ2) then, calculating the SS of these effects and adding them, Daniel obtains the Sum Squares of the pure error, whose freedom degrees are equal to the sum of the non significant effect number.
2. Replication of the full factorial design: with usual formulas we can calculate the SS_T, SS_{EFF}, SS_E and the ANOVA. obviously, for both cases 1 and 2, if it is made reference to a factorial design and the effect analysis would give as such clear indications on the relevant positions and the role of the different independent variables taken singularly or in interaction, the same effect analysis could be considered exhaustive at the screening operation purposes, without making reference to the interpretation through the ANOVA.
3. Center points addition: as from theory, these trials, which are replicated in correspondence of the design centre allow, beside to the achievement of the test about the pure curving, the measure of the experimental pure error SS_{PE} and then of the MS_{PE} necessary to obtain the F_0 summaries for the Fisher test.
4. High level fractioning factorial designs: it is advised to make use of them when the concerned independent variable number is high, the high simulation experimentation costs/times, exists the reasonable certainty that some of the independent variables will result non significant, the experimenter is willing to pay a contribution, growing with the reduction of the test number, in terms of effect "confusion". This last statement means that the experimenter will not able to isolate the single effects, then the effect representative number of a particular factor will contain not only that but also other factors (Montgomery, 2005).

By making use of minimal aberration and maximal resolution concepts it will be possible to obtain, fractioning by fractioning, the minimal perturbation on the evaluations.

Through a further trial replication with generators which are copies in negative of the first, it will be possible, moreover, the separation of the effects considered most significant and then, for as possible, isolate or confuse with high order interaction the main effects and the interactions of the second order which are, generally, those greatly representative of the system behaviour.

Methodology Application to the Guide Model

For the achievement of the screening operation on the simulation model used as test-case we remember that the independent variables affecting the production under the designer and/or the line manager control are represented by the four machine typologies:

1. A = milling machines range: 7-9 machines
2. B = multistep grinding machine range: 4-6 machines
3. C = nitriding machines range: 13-15 machines
4. D = dimensional control range: 6-8 machines

The question that in this trial management phase is necessary to make is then: are all the four machine typologies, classified with the letters A,B,C,D, in the field of the variability ranges planned for them by the decision-maker, really able to generate variation on the production realized by the plan in a particular period of time?

The expected operative answer is no/yes and in the affirmative case is necessary to know which typologies result really influent.

Of the four possible investigation methods listed before, see the low number of the concerned independent variables we consider three of them:

5. Mono-replicated factorial design with the Daniel Methodology application
6. Factorial design with replication
7. Factorial design with the addiction of 5 center points

After having remembered that the factor effect calculation can be normally carried out using the so called sign table from which not only the "contrasts" are deduced but also it is possible to easily take both the factor effects and their Sum Squares through:

$$EFF = \frac{2 \cdot (contrast)}{2^k \cdot n} = \frac{1}{2^{k-1}}(contrast)$$

$$SS_{EFF} = \frac{(contrast)^2}{n \cdot 2^k}$$

being n the number of replicated tests to use in the formulas when the target function is expressed under each experimental level, through the addiction of the obtained responses.

In the case of a 3 independent variable factorial design replicated twice the effect of A and its Sum Squares result to be so configured:

$$A = \frac{1}{2 \cdot 2^{3-1}}(a + ab + ac + abc - (1) - b - c - bc)$$

$$SS_A = \frac{1}{2 \cdot 2^3}(a + ab + ac + abc - (1) - b - c - bc)^2$$

where the capital letters between parentheses represent, just, the sum of the two results obtained from each single experimental response.

The small letter shows that the corresponding variable entered in the trial at its high variability range level while the lack of reading means that the variable is entered at its low level. Then:

8. a is the value which is obtained by adding the two responses obtained by soliciting the target system with the factor (independent variable) A placed at the high range level with B and C placed at their low levels
9. (1) is the value which is obtained with A,B and C all at the lower level
10. abc is the value which is obtained with A,B and C all at the higher level

In the case of a 4 variable factorial design the contrast consists of 16 terms corresponding to the 16 A,B,C,D experimental level combinations and the relevant calculations, if achieved without the help of a PC (it would be better if it was equipped with an experimental statistic software), result expensive in terms of necessary time and generate frequent calculation errors.

Make, then, reference in the applicative example to the Design-Expert 6.0.10, the tool of the Stat-Ease, Inc.

In the Factorial section chose the 4 factor "2 level factorial" design with a single replication for a total of $2^4=16$ trials.

The levels for the four variables are those previously shown that is:

$7 \leq A \leq 9$

$4 \leq B \leq 6$

$13 \leq C \leq 15$

$6 \leq D \leq 8$

The software directly proposes the experimental plan that is the levels at which the 4 factors must be placed in the 16 simulation runs which shall be carried out.

Each run, obviously, shall have duration equal to the time selected after the previous research analysis of the optimal run length. The 16 responses are placed in the "Response 1" column (Figure 13).

Then under "Evaluation" all the 15 first, second, third and fourth order effects are selected. In the "Response" screen under Effects→ View→Effects List it is possible to see, for each effect, both the value and its Sum Squares, as well as the effect contribution % on the total and, under View→ Half Normal Graph, an easy interpretable graphic representation of a Gauss plan showing in the abscissa the factor effects (see Figure 14

and Figure 15). As it is possible to observe in the Figure 15, 12 effects on 15, that is all the effects excepting B, D and BD (having values respectively of 5047, 18929 and 5064, with contribution percentages of 6,22%, 87,51% and 6,26%), result placed along a straight line.

This means that, as theorised by Daniel (1959), these effects are negligible and distributed as a NID $(0, \sigma^2)$ while the significant ones are out of the same having an average $\neq 0$.

Now, by adding up the *SS* of the non significant effects we are able to calculate the Experimental Error and use it for the construction of an ANOVA table in B,D and BD for a 4 time replicated 2^2 factorial design, whose experimental plan is shown in the Figure 16.

Stat-Ease allows to carry out this operation, which is substantially equivalent to the 4 factor beginning design projections in 2 factor, B and D, 4 factorial designs simply by acting under Ef-

Figure 13.

Std	Run	Block	Factor 1 A:A	Factor 2 B:B	Factor 3 C:C	Factor 4 D:D	Response 1 Response 1
1	7	Block 1	7.00	4.00	13.00	6.00	160057
2	2	Block 1	9.00	4.00	13.00	6.00	160872
3	15	Block 1	7.00	6.00	13.00	6.00	160833
4	3	Block 1	9.00	6.00	13.00	6.00	160917
5	6	Block 1	7.00	4.00	15.00	6.00	160829
6	14	Block 1	9.00	4.00	15.00	6.00	160912
7	9	Block 1	7.00	6.00	15.00	6.00	160849
8	5	Block 1	9.00	6.00	15.00	6.00	160892
9	4	Block 1	7.00	4.00	13.00	8.00	191546
10	1	Block 1	9.00	4.00	13.00	8.00	191670
11	13	Block 1	7.00	6.00	13.00	8.00	214546
12	12	Block 1	9.00	6.00	13.00	8.00	214641
13	11	Block 1	7.00	4.00	15.00	8.00	192157
14	10	Block 1	9.00	4.00	15.00	8.00	191850
15	8	Block 1	7.00	6.00	15.00	8.00	214544
16	16	Block 1	9.00	6.00	15.00	8.00	214285

Figure 14.

	Term	Stdized Effects	Sum of Squares	% Contribution
	Intercept			
[M]	A	-15.25	930.25	1.137E-005
[M]	B	11351.75	5.154E+008	6.30
[M]	C	54.50	11881.00	1.452E-004
[M]	D	42284.75	7.152E+009	87.40
[M]	AB	6.00	144.00	1.760E-006
[M]	AC	-94.75	35910.25	4.389E-004
[M]	AD	-71.50	20449.00	2.499E-004
[M]	BC	-146.25	85556.25	1.046E-003
[M]	BD	11346.50	5.150E+008	6.29
[M]	CD	53.75	11556.25	1.412E-004
[M]	ABC	-4.00	64.00	7.821E-007
[M]	ABD	-1.25	6.25	7.638E-008
[M]	ACD	-101.50	41209.00	5.036E-004
[M]	BCD	-141.00	79524.00	9.719E-004
[M]	ABCD	23.25	2162.25	2.642E-005
	Lenth's ME	208.70		
	Lenth's SME	423.69		

Figure 15.

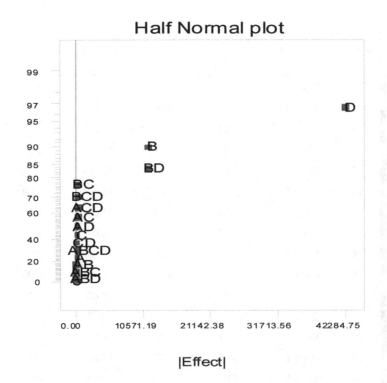

fects→ View→ Effects List and clicking on the M column, in correspondence of each non significant effect, so as to transform the "M" in "e".

Coming back under ANOVA the relevant variance analysis table is displayed (Figure 17) in which the freedom degrees are:

11. for SS_T → being 16 the total number of observation 16-1=15
12. for the Model SS → consisting of the 3 terms relevant to B,D and BD, each with 1 freedom degree then for 3 freedom degrees in total
13. for the SS of the global Error →15-3 =12

The ANOVA table confirms, then, the significant character of the B, D and BD variables with respect of the production target function and the non influence of the remaining on the

same function for which they shall be, therefore, fixed at any value of their range, particularly, at the central one.

The production target function results, therefore, in the analysed production design in the shown variability ranges, as affected at first, and in a preponderant way, by the variable D, number of machines for the dimensional check, but also, even if in a less important way, of the variable B, number of multistep grinding machine and, in the same way, by the combined effect of B and D. It is interesting to note how, complying with what said above, in spite of D has a very remarkable importance, its interaction effect with B is greatly less important in affecting the production.

The second screening method which is analysed is that of the factorial trial replication, which for its activation requires the execution of further 16 simulation trials, one for each of the factor

Figure 16.

Std	Run	Block	Factor 1 A:B	Factor 2 B:D	Response 1 Response 1
1	13	Block 1	4.00	6.00	71934
2	2	Block 1	4.00	6.00	71990
3	16	Block 1	4.00	6.00	71957
4	5	Block 1	4.00	6.00	71832
5	10	Block 1	6.00	6.00	71911
6	8	Block 1	6.00	6.00	71872
7	1	Block 1	6.00	6.00	71966
8	3	Block 1	6.00	6.00	71985
9	6	Block 1	4.00	8.00	85752
10	11	Block 1	4.00	8.00	85828
11	12	Block 1	4.00	8.00	85851
12	7	Block 1	4.00	8.00	85741
13	9	Block 1	6.00	8.00	95897
14	14	Block 1	6.00	8.00	95899
15	4	Block 1	6.00	8.00	95884
16	15	Block 1	6.00	8.00	95937

Figure 17.

	Transform	Effects	ANOVA	Diagnostics	Model Graphs

Use your mouse to right click on individual cells for definitions.

Response: Response 1

ANOVA for Selected Factorial Model

Analysis of variance table [Partial sum of squares]

Source		Sum of Squares	DF	Mean Square	F Value	Prob > F	
Model		8.182E+009	3	2.727E+009	1.131E+005	< 0.0001	significant
	B	5.154E+008	1	5.154E+008	21373.69	< 0.0001	
	D	7.152E+009	1	7.152E+009	2.966E+005	< 0.0001	
	BD	5.150E+008	1	5.150E+008	21353.93	< 0.0001	
Residual		2.894E+005	12	24116.04			
Cor Total		8.183E+009	15				

combinations detected in the previous design(see Figure 18).

After having carried out the additional runs and obtained the relevant responses it is necessary to provide to their input in Stat-Ease with identical procedure compared to what described at the previous case and with the sole difference to specify, in the first window, 2 replications instead of 1.

After having re-selected all the 15 effects under Evaluation go on under Response→Effects→Effects List to obtain the effect magnitude reading, which results about superposable to the previous and, in any case, with such variation which do not modify their importance classification (the SS_{EFF} are obviously bigger than the previous), and the signal effect contribution percentage (see Figure 19).

Under ANOVA, it is possible to observe that the trial replication allows to dispose also of the freedom degrees for the Experimental Pure Error evaluation. From the organised ANOVA table of the experimental plan results still the importance on the production target function of the independent variables B,D and BD (see Figure 20).

Said passing, the freedom degrees are now:

14. for $SS_T = 32-1 = 31$
15. for $SS_{MODEL} = 15$
16. for $SS_E = 31-15 = 16$ which can all be attributed to the experimental Pure Error

By deselecting from effect "M" to error "e", under Effects, the non significant effects, it is possible to obtain a new ANOVA table in B,D and BD, exploiting the 32 carried out tests.

The table confirms, obviously, the importance of the two variables and of the 3 effects and

proposes a regression meta-model, interpreting the production target function which we will analyze in detail in the following paragraph, for which also the freedom degrees are available and necessary to carry out the Lack of Fit Fisher test (see Figure 21).

The last of the 3 selected methods to carry out the screening operation is, undoubtedly, to consider highly profitable in the relationship price/performance since with only 21 points, those of the first design, with the addition of 5 central replications (see Figure 22), obtains:

1. the same effects and Sum Squares of the Daniel Method

Figure 18.

Std	Run	Block	Factor 1 A:A	Factor 2 B:B	Factor 3 C:C	Factor 4 D:D	Response 1 Response 1
1	10	Block 1	7.00	4.00	13.00	6.00	71934
2	11	Block 1	7.00	4.00	13.00	6.00	71988
3	5	Block 1	9.00	4.00	13.00	6.00	71990
4	7	Block 1	9.00	4.00	13.00	6.00	71972
5	29	Block 1	7.00	6.00	13.00	6.00	71911
6	22	Block 1	7.00	6.00	13.00	6.00	71874
7	20	Block 1	9.00	6.00	13.00	6.00	71872
8	3	Block 1	9.00	6.00	13.00	6.00	71957
9	32	Block 1	7.00	4.00	15.00	6.00	71957
10	21	Block 1	7.00	4.00	15.00	6.00	71977
11	17	Block 1	9.00	4.00	15.00	6.00	71832
12	25	Block 1	9.00	4.00	15.00	6.00	71873
13	15	Block 1	7.00	6.00	15.00	6.00	71966
14	14	Block 1	7.00	6.00	15.00	6.00	71998
15	6	Block 1	9.00	6.00	15.00	6.00	71895
16	13	Block 1	9.00	6.00	15.00	6.00	71914
17	26	Block 1	7.00	4.00	13.00	8.00	85752
18	23	Block 1	7.00	4.00	13.00	8.00	85724
19	24	Block 1	9.00	4.00	13.00	8.00	85828
20	19	Block 1	9.00	4.00	13.00	8.00	85754
21	16	Block 1	7.00	6.00	13.00	8.00	95897
22	27	Block 1	7.00	6.00	13.00	8.00	95872
23	8	Block 1	9.00	6.00	13.00	8.00	95899
24	30	Block 1	9.00	6.00	13.00	8.00	95993
25	31	Block 1	7.00	4.00	15.00	8.00	85851
26	12	Block 1	7.00	4.00	15.00	8.00	85653
27	28	Block 1	9.00	4.00	15.00	8.00	85741
28	4	Block 1	9.00	4.00	15.00	8.00	85750
29	9	Block 1	7.00	6.00	15.00	8.00	95884
30	18	Block 1	7.00	6.00	15.00	8.00	95998
31	1	Block 1	9.00	6.00	15.00	8.00	95937
32	2	Block 1	9.00	6.00	15.00	8.00	95929

2. a measure of the Pure Experimental Error
3. the Pure Quadratic Curvature Test, allowing to verify if the 1st order model is adequate to describe the situation, after the decline of error non significant factors and dispose of the freedom degrees for the I and II Fisher test, respectively concerning the regressive approach validity and the model suitability lack.

We remember at this concern that the freedom degrees are respectively:

Figure 19.

	Term	Stdized Effects	Sum of Squares	% Contribution
	Intercept			
M	A	-6.25	312.50	9.544E-006
M	B	5076.25	2.061E+008	6.30
M	C	-3.87	120.13	3.669E-006
M	D	18909.50	2.861E+009	87.36
M	AB	5.75	264.50	8.078E-006
M	AC	-45.38	16471.13	5.030E-004
M	AD	31.25	7812.50	2.386E-004
M	BC	34.62	9591.13	2.929E-004
M	BD	5093.25	2.075E+008	6.34
M	CD	6.87	378.12	1.155E-005
M	ABC	3.13	78.13	2.386E-006
M	ABD	-4.00	128.00	3.909E-006
M	ACD	13.13	1378.13	4.209E-005
M	BCD	-15.87	2016.12	6.157E-005
M	ABCD	-5.63	253.13	7.731E-006
e	Lack Of Fit		0.000	0.000
e	Pure Error		41683.00	1.273E-003
	Lenth's ME	34.25		
	Lenth's SME	54.34		

Figure 20.

Use your mouse to right click on individual cells for definitions.

Response: Response 1

ANOVA for Selected Factorial Model

Analysis of variance table [Partial sum of squares]

Source	Sum of Squares	DF	Mean Square	F Value	Prob > F	
Model	3.274E+009	15	2.183E+008	83788.43	< 0.0001	significant
A	312.50	1	312.50	0.12	0.7336	
B	2.061E+008	1	2.061E+008	79129.24	< 0.0001	
C	120.13	1	120.13	0.046	0.8327	
D	2.861E+009	1	2.861E+009	1.098E+006	< 0.0001	
AB	264.50	1	264.50	0.10	0.7541	
AC	16471.13	1	16471.13	6.32	0.0230	
AD	7812.50	1	7812.50	3.00	0.1026	
BC	9591.13	1	9591.13	3.68	0.0730	
BD	2.075E+008	1	2.075E+008	79660.13	< 0.0001	
CD	378.13	1	378.13	0.15	0.7082	
ABC	78.13	1	78.13	0.030	0.8647	
ABD	128.00	1	128.00	0.049	0.8274	
ACD	1378.13	1	1378.13	0.53	0.4775	
BCD	2016.13	1	2016.13	0.77	0.3920	
ABCD	253.13	1	253.13	0.097	0.7593	
Pure Error	41683.00	16	2605.19			
Cor Total	3.274E+009	31				

Figure 21.

Transform	Effects	ANOVA	Diagnostics	Model Graphs

Use your mouse to right click on individual cells for definitions.

Response: Response 1

ANOVA for Selected Factorial Model

Analysis of variance table [Partial sum of squares]

Source		Sum of Squares	DF	Mean Square	F Value	Prob > F	
Model		3.274E+009	3	1.091E+009	3.797E+005	< 0.0001	significant
	B	2.061E+008	1	2.061E+008	71715.16	< 0.0001	
	D	2.861E+009	1	2.861E+009	9.951E+005	< 0.0001	
	BD	2.075E+008	1	2.075E+008	72196.30	< 0.0001	
Residual		80486.50	28	2874.52			
Lack of Fit		38803.50	12	3233.63	1.24	0.3370	not significant
Pure Error		41683.00	16	2605.19			
Cor Total		3.274E+009	31				

Figure 22.

Std	Run	Block	Factor 1 A:A	Factor 2 B:B	Factor 3 C:C	Factor 4 D:D	Response 1 Response 1
1	7	Block 1	7.00	4.00	13.00	6.00	160857
2	5	Block 1	9.00	4.00	13.00	6.00	160872
3	3	Block 1	7.00	6.00	13.00	6.00	160833
4	18	Block 1	9.00	6.00	13.00	6.00	160917
5	4	Block 1	7.00	4.00	15.00	6.00	160829
6	16	Block 1	9.00	4.00	15.00	6.00	160912
7	13	Block 1	7.00	6.00	15.00	6.00	160849
8	9	Block 1	9.00	6.00	15.00	6.00	160892
9	2	Block 1	7.00	4.00	13.00	8.00	191546
10	6	Block 1	9.00	4.00	13.00	8.00	191670
11	12	Block 1	7.00	6.00	13.00	8.00	214546
12	19	Block 1	9.00	6.00	13.00	8.00	214641
13	20	Block 1	7.00	4.00	15.00	8.00	192157
14	10	Block 1	9.00	4.00	15.00	8.00	191850
15	11	Block 1	7.00	6.00	15.00	8.00	214544
16	21	Block 1	9.00	6.00	15.00	8.00	214285
17	15	Block 1	8.00	5.00	14.00	7.00	187840
18	14	Block 1	8.00	5.00	14.00	7.00	187858
19	17	Block 1	8.00	5.00	14.00	7.00	187609
20	8	Block 1	8.00	5.00	14.00	7.00	187849
21	1	Block 1	8.00	5.00	14.00	7.00	187681

- $SS_T = 21\text{-}1 = 20$
- $SS_{EFF} = 15$
- $SS_{PC} = 1$
- $SS_{ERR} = 20\text{-}15\text{-}1 = 4$

For the case of the 4 factor complete design(see Figure 23), while for the two factor design, after screening (see Figure 24):

- $SS_T = 20 SS_{EFF} = 3$
- $SS_{ERR} = 20\text{-}3 = 17$ of which ($SS_{PE} = n_c\text{-}1 = 5\text{-}1 = 4$; $SS_{LoF} = 17\text{-}4 = 13$)

RESPONSE SURFACE CONSTRUCTION AND OPTIMAL DESIGN CHOICE

Theoretical Fundamentals

The worry of the Experimental Statisticians concerning the need to detect designs allowing to obtain regression models with which approximate the real response surface (or natural connection among the independent and dependent variables) whose variance is in the same time the smallest possible but also the most steady along the investigated field (Myers and Montgomery, 1995). The expression of the Prediction Variance $Var(\hat{y}(x))$ of the regression model is pointed out:

$$Var(\hat{y}(x)) = x^{(m)'} \cdot (X'X)^{-1} \cdot x^{(m)} \cdot \sigma^2$$

Figure 23.

Transform	Effects	ANOVA	Diagnostics	Model Graphs						

Use your mouse to right click on individual cells for definitions.

Response: Response 1

ANOVA for Selected Factorial Model

Analysis of variance table [Partial sum of squares]

Source		Sum of Squares	DF	Mean Square	F Value	Prob > F	
Model		8.183E+009	15	5.455E+008	41410.58	< 0.0001	significant
	A	930.25	1	930.25	0.071	0.8036	
	B	5.154E+008	1	5.154E+008	39128.31	< 0.0001	
	C	11881.00	1	11881.00	0.90	0.3960	
	D	7.152E+009	1	7.152E+009	5.429E+005	< 0.0001	
	AB	144.00	1	144.00	0.011	0.9218	
	AC	35910.25	1	35910.25	2.73	0.1741	
	AD	20449.00	1	20449.00	1.55	0.2808	
	BC	85556.25	1	85556.25	6.49	0.0634	
	BD	5.150E+008	1	5.150E+008	39092.12	< 0.0001	
	CD	11556.25	1	11556.25	0.88	0.4020	
	ABC	64.00	1	64.00	4.858E-003	0.9478	
	ABD	6.25	1	6.25	4.744E-004	0.9837	
	ACD	41209.00	1	41209.00	3.13	0.1517	
	BCD	79524.00	1	79524.00	6.04	0.0699	
	ABCD	2162.25	1	2162.25	0.16	0.7061	
Curvature		1.262E+008	1	1.262E+008	9577.49	< 0.0001	significant
Pure Error		52693.20	4	13173.30			
Cor Total		8.309E+009	20				

from which it can be just evicted that it depends on:

1. The investigated point field position, through the positional vector x(m)
2. On the experimental design adopted through the (X'X)-1 matrix being X a particular matrix, expressed in Coded variable terms, a -1; +1 corresponding to the low/high level, which consider the experimental design type adopted and the presence of higher order effects and interaction
3. On the regression model with which the real response surface is approximated, through the variance of the σ^2 error, a variance containing both the component which can be attributed to the pure experimental error and that which can be attributed to the lack of adaptation.

The way to face the problem underwent in the second half of the XXI century significant evolutions. For the first order models, whose regression equation is expressed through: $\hat{y} = Xb$ being $b = (X'X)^{-1} \cdot X'y$, starting from the consideration that if it would possible to reduce the single b_i variance of the regression equation, it would be possible, as result, also to reduce the whole $\hat{y}$ model, it has been levered on two concepts of optimal variance and orthogonal character.

We remember, in passing, that a model is an optimal variance when the variances of all the b_i (i=1...k) are all equal among them and equal to the variance of $b_0 = \dfrac{\sigma^2}{N}$, being N the number of experimental levels eventually replicated appearing in the X matrix and which, a I order design is defined orthogonal when X'X is a diagonal matrix and, still, an optimal variance design is, always, orthogonal while an orthogonal design could not be at optimal variance since the X matrix, read for example the case of the central test addiction example can respect the vector orthogonal character condition, a column expressed by the product:

$$x_i' \cdot x_j = 0$$

even if not all the terms contained in X placed at value ±1.

For the II order designs, to the concept of the regression equation variance minimization has been placed before the concept of masking rate achievement by the error on the responses supplied

Figure 24.

Transform	Effects	ANOVA	Diagnostics	Model Graphs				

Use your mouse to right click on individual cells for definitions.

Response: Response 1

ANOVA for Selected Factorial Model

Analysis of variance table [Partial sum of squares]

Source	Sum of Squares	DF	Mean Square	F Value	Prob > F	
Model	8.182E+009	3	2.727E+009	366.51	< 0.0001	significant
B	5.154E+008	1	5.154E+008	69.26	< 0.0001	
D	7.152E+009	1	7.152E+009	961.07	< 0.0001	
BD	5.150E+008	1	5.150E+008	69.20	< 0.0001	
Residual	1.265E+008	17	7.442E+006			
Lack of Fit	1.265E+008	13	9.727E+006	738.42	< 0.0001	significant
Pure Error	52693.20	4	13173.30			
Cor Total	8.309E+009	20				

by the model used as predictor, which is the steadiest possible on the whole detected area. Box and Hunter developed at this purpose the concept of rotation possibility which they intended to impose to the Scaled Prediction Variance V_x:

$$V_x = \frac{N \cdot Var\left[\hat{y}(x)\right]}{\sigma^2}$$

the maintenance of its value at a constant level at least on each of the infinite spheres having a radius equal to the distance between a domain point and the design centre. In the obvious impossibility to obtain a constant V_x on the whole field, Box and Hunter try to detect experimental designs allowing to have an equal value of the V_x for all the field points placed at the same distance from the design centre, as well as trends of the same V_x as most uniform as possible. It can be immediately observed how the V_x, being sterilized compared to $Var(\hat{y}(x))$ of the σ^2 variance, depends only on the adopted design type, on the investigated experimental domain point and a penalisation N coefficient making growing it at the increasing of the carried out test number. It results, then, useful in the phase of the choice of the experimental design to adopt to evaluate which is the most suitable design, even in compared to the previously exposed characteristics and the requirements of the same experimenter. Obviously, once chosen the design, it will be the σ^2 variance to play a non secondary role in the final model quality. All the before stated, it result how the knowledge of the properties shown before could be a valid guide for the choice of the factorial designs, fundamental class for the target reality adaptation to the first order models and of the spherical/cubic central composed designs for the adaptation with second order models, each time more convenient in relation with the expected reliability type and the maximal number of available tests. We want add also that:

- Factorial designs of the 2k series or eventually 2k-pfractionary, for which it is possible to obtain the optimal variance and/ or the orthogonal character, allow to operate on independent variables acting in a continuous or discrete way in the field of ranges characterised by a quantitative or qualitative high/low level (on/off), having a link with the target function which can be expressed through a regression model of the first order defined linear simple or multiple in relation to the presence of one or more independent variables

$$\hat{y} = \hat{b}_0 + \hat{b}_1 x_1 + \hat{b}_2 x_2 + \hat{b}_{12} x_1 x_2$$

link which, translated in geometric terms, expresses itself in the space a k dimensions under the form of hyper-planes which, in case of mixed terms or interactions become of the twister type. Each xi is normally Coded in -1;+1. The number of points necessary for a single design is equal to:

$$2^k \cdot n$$

being k the number of independent variables and n the number of replications which generally will result ≥ 2, eventually integrated with a suitable number of tests carried out at the design centre in relation with the protection of particular characteristics of the same design.

- Central composite design for which is possible, by suitably acting, guarantee the rotation possibility. It allows, for two level variable having the same characteristics of the analysed ones for the factorial design, to make clear the link among the independents and the dependents which can be expressed through second order regression models as:

$$\hat{y} = \hat{b}_0 + \hat{b}_1 x_1 + \hat{b}_2 x_2 + \hat{b}_{12} x_1 x_2 + \hat{b}_{11} x_1^2 + \hat{b}_{22} x_2^2$$

with a required test number equal to

$$N = 2^k + n_c + 2 \cdot k$$

being:

- 2^k the factorial core test number
- n_c the added center points through which is possible to obtain the experimental error
- $2 \cdot k$ the so called adding axial points necessary to obtain all the second order model b
  - The experimental error normality checks, which must be distributed as a NID(0, σ2) and on the σ² variance constant character, must be always carried out downstream of the model construction
  - The experimental error measure under the MS_E form and the same scission in its two MS_{PE} (Pure Error) and MS_{LOF} (Lack of Fit) components and it is indispensable to carry out the two cascade Fisher tests on the regression and built, as seen, the MS_{PE} evolution curve. A DOE/RSM software, as the already mentioned Design Expert, makes possible a helped choice of the whole experimental path and an almost null duration for the execution of an absolutely insignificant computational mass, graphics included.

In starting up the screening operation we wanted explore 3 different designs:

1. the mono-replicated factorial in A,B,C,D for which we have carried out 2^4 simulation tests and which, seeing the screening results, has been projected in four 2^2 factorial designs (that is one 2^2 in B and D replicated 4 times effect of the constant degradation through the placement of the two not influent variables on

the response, A and C, at the central values of the relevant variability ranges

2. the 2^4 factorial, in A,B,C,D, replicated twice which, as for the previous paragraph 1), it is projected in a 2^2 factorial design replicated 8 times

3. the 2^4 factorial, in A,B,C,D, mono-replicated with the addiction of 5 center points giving raise to a 4 time replicated 2^2 factorial design with the addiction of 5 center points

A zero cost fourth design can be added to the above-mentioned ones for a performance comparison:

4. 2^2 factorial with 5 center points

Now we want to analyze the quality of the mathematical relation which can be obtained from the four experimental designs in a cost vs advantage optic that is the number of tests carried out related to the response "bounty", by meaning with this word both the check test type and the response quality in the investigated field in terms of orthogonal character, optimal variance and rotation possibility as well as, finally, the Confidence Interval width in the average response.

1st design: 2^4 factorial in A,B,C,D, mono-replicated, which after the screening transform itself into a factorial 2^2 in B and D replicated 4 times.

The tests carried out on the model have been 16 in total according to the scheme of which at the Figure 13.

The analysis which can be carried out on the $\sqrt{\dfrac{\hat{V}\left[y(x)\right]}{\sigma^2}}$ that is on the standard deviation standardized by the predicted response means values included between a minimum of 0,25 and a maximum of 0,50. This is an index of the selected experimental design quality and it gives an idea of how, in the experimental field, the error will afflict the answer by amplifying itself from the centre, where it is minimal, towards the range ends where it is the maximum.

By observing the graphic which can be obtained from Design Expert (see Figure 25) under Evaluation→graph→view→ standard error/contour we can notice how the iso-error curve tracks are not perfectly circular.

This since, being the regression model assumed of the 1st order with a mixed term $x_1 x_2$, the rotation possibility property is, at least partially, lost for which $\hat{V}\left[\hat{y}\left(x\right)\right]$ is function of the distanced from the centre also in the investigation direction. On the contrary the optimal variance condition and the orthogonal character one maintain, as it is possible to confirm from the matrix $\left(X'X\right)^{-1}$ exam which result to be diagonal and from which is obtained $Var(\hat{\beta}_0) = Var(\hat{\beta}i) = Var(\hat{\beta}ij) = \dfrac{\sigma^2}{16}$ (see Figure 26).

After having carried out the processing on the design (see Response at Design Expert section) under Response/Anova we notice from the ANOVA table that:

- the MS_E value is 14144,92

- the regressive approach validity test is passed
- it is not possible, being absent the central test, have information about the presence of the Pure Quadratic Curvature in the design centre
- it is not possible to carry out the test on the lack of adaptation since we have not the necessary freedom degrees. The design is then of the SATURATED type.

It result that, relatively to the regression equation, which is proposed by the software in Coded variable, under the form

$$\hat{y} = 1,820E+0,05+5715,62B+21127,63D+5740,38BD$$

it can be represented with the twister surface which can be obtained under Response→ Graphs→ View→ Response→ 3D but nothing can be added about the adapted model type for which some doubts could remain.

It is possible, on the contrary, calculate the standard error on the average response that is

Figure 25.

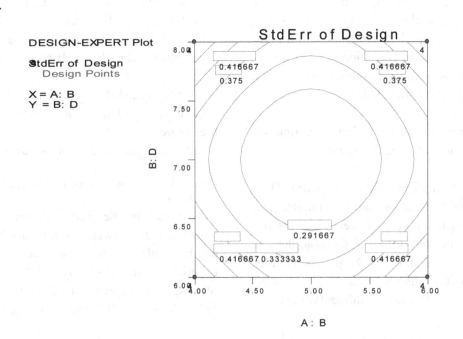

the square root of the $V\left[\hat{y}\left(x\right)\right]$, error which, as the Stat-Ease shown under Response→ Graphs and View→ Standard Error/3D, fluctuates in the investigated field between a minimum of 29,73 and a maximum of 59,46.

The Figure 28 displays the confidence interval on the average response calculated through

$$\hat{y}(x_0) \pm t_{\frac{\alpha}{2},N-p-1}\sqrt{MSEx_0{}'(X'X)^{-1}x_0}$$

The Figure 29 displays the confidence interval (see Figure 30).

2nd design: 2^2 replicated 4 times with the addition of 5 center points.

Figure 26.

X			
b0	**B**	**D**	**BD**
1	-1	-1	1
1	-1	-1	1
1	-1	-1	1
1	-1	-1	1
1	1	-1	-1
1	1	-1	-1
1	1	-1	-1
1	1	-1	-1
1	-1	1	-1
1	-1	1	-1
1	-1	1	-1
1	-1	1	-1
1	1	1	1
1	1	1	1
1	1	1	1
1	1	1	1

X' X			
b0	**B**	**D**	**BD**
16	0	0	0
0	16	0	0
0	0	16	0
0	0	0	16

(X' X)^ -1			
b0	**B**	**D**	**BD**
1/16	0	0	0
0	1/16	0	0
0	0	1/16	0
0	0	0	1/16

Figure 27.

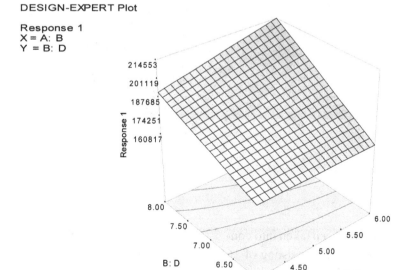

DESIGN-EXPERT Plot

Response 1
X = A: B
Y = B: D

Figure 28.

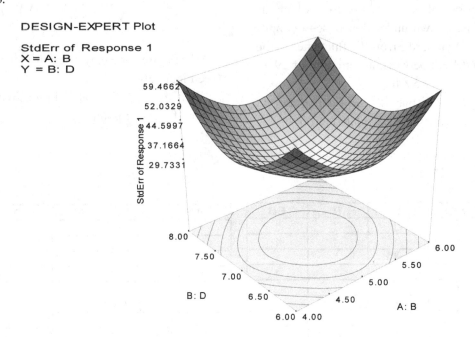

Figure 29.

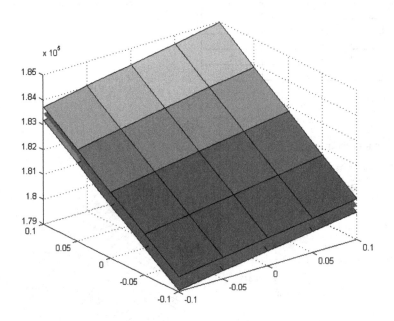

The test which they have been taken into consideration in total, now, are 21, consisting of 16 of the previous design and 5 suitably replicated in correspondence of the design centre. We can then notice that:

Figure 30.

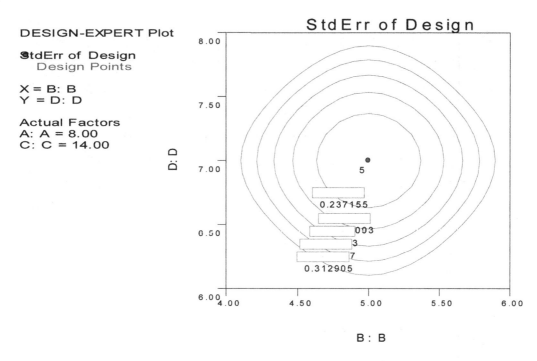

* standardized standard deviation $\sqrt{\dfrac{V\left[\hat{y}\left(x\right)\right]}{\sigma^2}}$

  has a minimum of 0,2182 at the design centre and a maximum of 0,4848 in the factorial design range extreme points (see Figure 30)
* as in the case of the 1° design the iso-error lines show the rotation possibility loss
* the matrix $\left(X'X\right)^{-1}$ analysis (see Figure 31) shows the orthogonal character maintenance but we have, as effect of the central test presence, the optimal variance loss since

$$Var(\hat{\beta}_0) = \frac{\sigma^2}{21} \quad Var(\hat{\beta}_i) = Var(\hat{\beta}_{ij}) = \frac{\sigma^2}{16}$$

* the MS_{PE} value is 13173,3 while, by disposing now of the freedom degrees, it is possible to calculate also the MS_{LOF}, which is 21856,04, and carry out the relevant test

showing a non significant adaptation lack of the chosen model
* the central curving test show, on the other end, a modest significant character, the result of the $x_1 x_2$ term presence inducing a faintly distortive effect in the prevailing plane trend the $\hat{y} = f(x_1, x_2)$, as preannounced by the contribution percentage of 1,5 percent of the curving effect on the effect totality
* the regression equation in coded variability confirms a twister plane (see Figure 32), now wholly validated by the Lack of Fit and Pure Quadratic Curvature tests, through the equation:

$$\hat{y} = 1{,}820 \cdot 105 + 5667{,}75B + 21128D + 5658{,}87BD$$

equation which, from the analysis of the single terms, results extremely near to the previous one

* the standard error on the average response (see Figure 33) has a minimum at the design

Figure 31.

X

b0	B	D	BD
1	-1	-1	1
1	-1	-1	1
1	-1	-1	1
1	-1	-1	1
1	1	-1	-1
1	1	-1	-1
1	1	-1	-1
1	1	-1	-1
1	-1	1	-1
1	-1	1	-1
1	-1	1	-1
1	-1	1	-1
1	1	1	1
1	1	1	1
1	1	1	1
1	1	1	1
1	0	0	0
1	0	0	0
1	0	0	0
1	0	0	0
1	0	0	0

X' X

b0	B	D	BD
21	0	0	0
0	16	0	0
0	0	16	0
0	0	0	16

(X' X)^ -1

b0	B	D	BD
1/21	0	0	0
0	1/16	0	0
0	0	1/16	0
0	0	0	1/16

Figure 32.

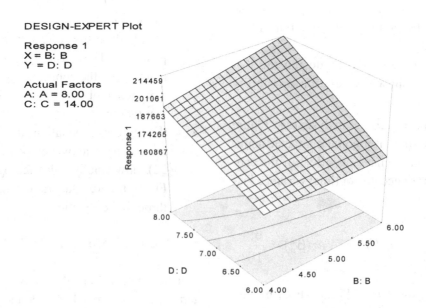

DESIGN-EXPERT Plot

Response 1
X = B: B
Y = D: D

Actual Factors
A: A = 8.00
C: C = 14.00

Figure 33.

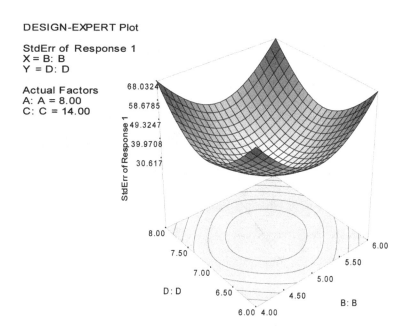

Figure 34.

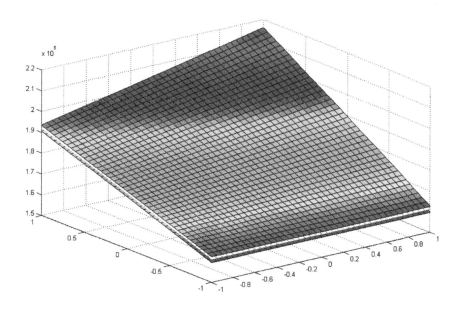

centre of 25,04 and a maximum in correspondence of the range ends of 55,65.

The confidence intervals are shown in Figure 34 and their magnifications are shown in Figure 35, Figure 36 and Figure 37 in which the blue line represents the mean response, the red one represents the upper bound and the yellow one the lower bound.

3rd design: it descends from the 2^4 replicated twice originating a 2^2, in B and D, replicated 8 times.

Figure 35.

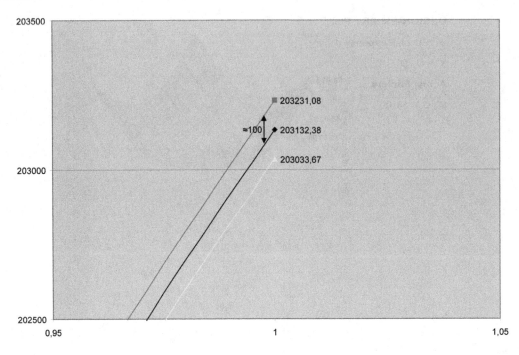

Figure 36.

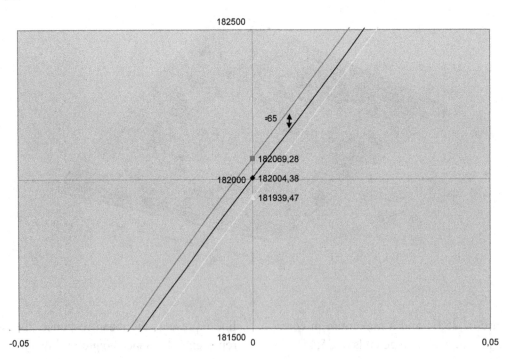

Figure 37.

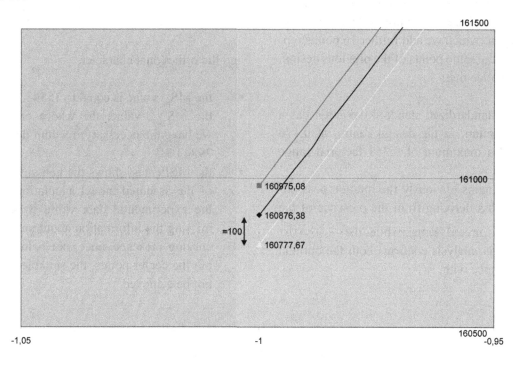

Figure 38.

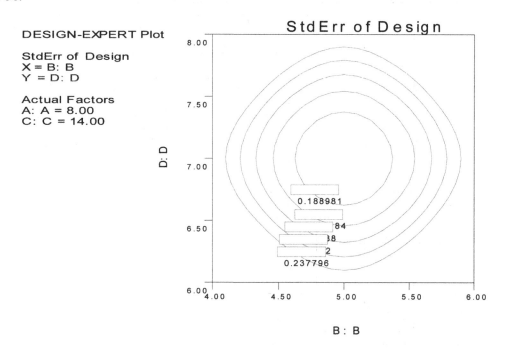

The test which have been taken into consideration in total are 32 and precisely the 16 of the 1° design to which we add further 16 points replicated in the same points of the previous design. We can notice that:

- the standardized standard deviation has a minimum, in the design centre, of 0,176 and a maximum of 0,353 factorial range ends
- it remains obviously the rotation possibility loss deriving from the presence of the $x_1 x_2$ mixed term, while the $(X'X)^{-1}$ matrix analysis confirms both the optimal variance with

$$Var(\hat{\beta}_0) = Var(\hat{\beta}_i) = Var(\hat{\beta}_{ij}) = \frac{\sigma^2}{32}$$

and the orthogonal character.

- the MS_{PE} value is equal to 15543,81
- the MS_{LOF}, value, the whose calculation we have the necessary freedom degrees, is 29843,81
- the MSPE test shows the non significance of the assumed model adaptation lack to the experimental data while it is totally missing the information about an eventual curving presence since, not being carried out the center points, the suitable test cannot be achieved

Figure 39.

X			
b0	B	D	BD
1	-1	-1	1
1	-1	-1	1
1	-1	-1	1
1	-1	-1	1
1	-1	-1	1
1	-1	-1	1
1	-1	-1	1
1	-1	-1	1
1	1	-1	-1
1	1	-1	-1
1	1	-1	-1
1	1	-1	-1
1	1	-1	-1
1	1	-1	-1
1	1	-1	-1
1	1	-1	-1
1	-1	1	-1
1	-1	1	-1
1	-1	1	-1
1	-1	1	-1
1	-1	1	-1
1	-1	1	-1
1	-1	1	-1
1	-1	1	-1
1	1	1	1
1	1	1	1
1	1	1	1
1	1	1	1
1	1	1	1
1	1	1	1
1	1	1	1
1	1	1	1

X' X			
b0	B	D	BD
32	0	0	0
0	32	0	0
0	0	32	0
0	0	0	32

(X' X)^ -1			
b0	B	D	BD
1/32	0	0	0
0	1/32	0	0
0	0	1/32	0
0	0	0	1/32

- the detected regression equation (see Figure 40) is, again, almost superimposable to the previous and it has the form

$$\hat{y} = 1,820E+0,05+5674,75B+21129,75D+5666,19BD$$

- the standard error on the estimated response, expressed as $V\left[\hat{y}\left(x\right)\right]$, has a minimum at the design centre equal to 26,02, and a maximum in correspondence of the range ends equal to 52,04 (see Figure 41)

4th design: We decided to test, finally, the significant character margin of a high value design of the test number ratio vs obtained responses quality and we choose a 2^2 factorial design in B and D, mono-replicated with 5 replications carried out at the design centre.

The required tests are, in total, 9 and they are, in this case, obtained from those already used for the first three designs and, then, with a zero cost.

We can notice that:

- the standardised standard deviation has a minimum in 0,33 at the design centre and a maximum of 0,92 in the range extreme point of the factorial design (see Figure 42)

- as for all the other designs, the rotation possibility fails, even if moderately

- the $\left(X'X\right)^{-1}$ matrix analysis shows the orthogonal character presence but also the loss of the optimal variance caused by the central test presence (see Figure 43)

- the MS_E value is 13173,3 which, being calculated on the same central test of the 2nd design, has the same value. On the contrary, the freedom degrees are missing to study MS_{LOF} while the Pure Quadratic Curvature test shows how not much significant because of the presence of the x_1x_2 interaction as well as of the consequent modification generated on the plane configuration of the $\hat{y} = f\left(x_1x_2\right)$ without mixed terms.

- The impossibility to carry out the Lack of Fit test would leave, now, some doubts

Figure 40.

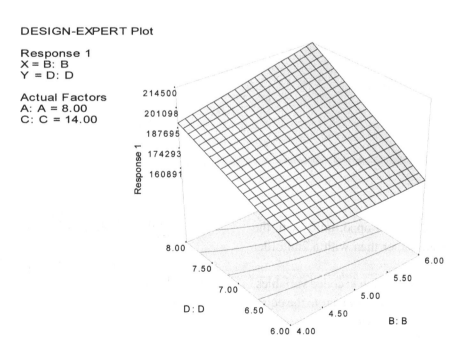

DESIGN-EXPERT Plot

Response 1
X = B: B
Y = D: D

Actual Factors
A: A = 8.00
C: C = 14.00

Figure 41.

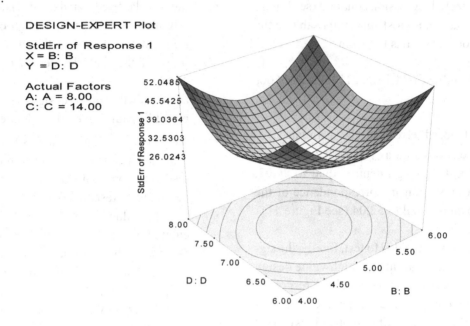

Figure 42.

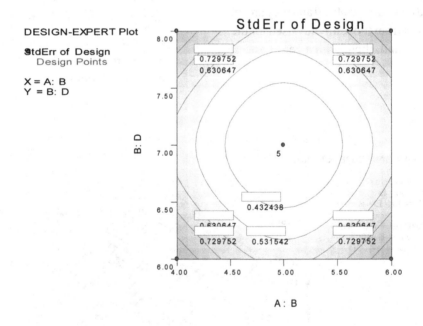

about the adaptation opportunity with the twister plane rather than with a 2nd order surface

- The regression equation in coded variables, shows, still, $\hat{b}_i$ values very near to the equations obtained for previous design

$$\hat{y} = 1{,}819\text{E}0{,}05 + 5743{,}5B + 21100D + 5755{,}5BD$$

relation representing in a three dimension way the usual twister plan (see Figure 44)

Figure 43.

	X		
b0	B	D	BD
1	-1	-1	1
1	1	-1	-1
1	-1	1	-1
1	1	1	1
1	0	0	0
1	0	0	0
1	0	0	0
1	0	0	0
1	0	0	0

	X' X		
b0	B	D	BD
9	0	0	0
0	4	0	0
0	0	4	0
0	0	0	4

	(X' X)^ -1		
b0	B	D	BD
1/9	0	0	0
0	1/4	0	0
0	0	1/4	0
0	0	0	1/4

Figure 44.

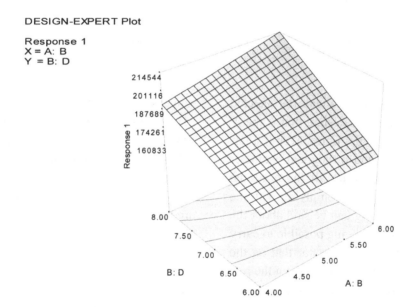

DESIGN-EXPERT Plot

Response 1
X = A: B
Y = B: D

- The standard error on the average response, intended as $\sqrt{V\left[\hat{y}\left(x\right)\right]}$, shows a minimum at the centre equal to 38,25 and a maximum corresponding to the range ends equal to 106,507 (see Figure 45).

The Confidence Interval is about 3 times wider compared to the second design(22 replicated 4 times with 5 center points), as it was logic provide from the experimental error entity.

A reduced number of tests is paid in accuracy on the final result.

Comparison Among the Four Design Alternatives

Stated that all the four analysed designs managed to detect relations among the dependent variable and the two independent ones, almost superimposable, very different from design to design, results the global information content at

Figure 45.

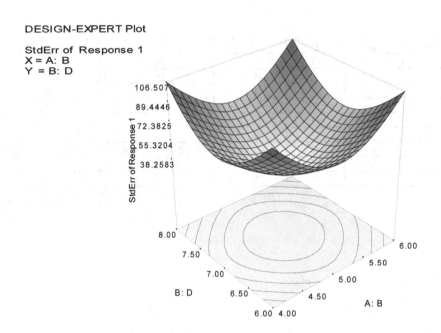

DESIGN-EXPERT Plot

StdErr of Response 1
X = A: B
Y = B: D

the experimenter disposal to validate the detected regression model. The 3rd design, that is the 2^2 factorial design replicated 4 times, even if it has the optimal character and orthogonal character variance properties, showing all the $\hat{b}_i$ of the minimal variance equation, complying with the used test number, nothing can be said about the adopted model order not being possible to carry put neither the Lack of Fit test nor that on the Pure Curvature; then some doubts about the real validity of the 1st order model with interaction would be totally justified.

By maintaining the same experimental approach type, that is that of the factorial design also in presence of a whole replications of the n_0 original tests then projected in a 2^2 design replicated 8 times after screening, is not possible to obtain a fully explanation of all the doubts concerning the detected $\hat{y}(n)$ adherence to the real response surface. The 3rd design, indeed, even if it uses 32 simulation tests, being orthogonal and with optimal variance and allowing also the execution Lack of Fit test, has the conceptual defect to use as investigation points the sole extreme variability

range points for which or you are sure beforehand of a really 1st order link, still twister, or, not having at your disposal information inside the extreme limits, you risk to consider as correctly adaptable to the real response surface a model which really is not. Under this profile of undoubted interest there are two designs (2nd and 4th) using the replication at the design centre. If it is true, indeed, that the center points causes the loss of the variance optimal character, it is also true that the orthogonal character is safeguarded and that already with nine experimental tests we can obtain the information on the curving presence and the eventual need of additional supplementary tests for a complete analysis in the exposed test case.

The 21 tests of the 2° designs allows, on the contrary, an exhaustive analysis since they supply also the freedom degrees to evaluate the eventual lack of the first order model adaptation to an experimental plan, enriched by the information about the investigated reality behaviour in correspondence of the design centre. In this case it is explained the reason for which a first order model, obviously modified by the presence of the $x_1 x_2$

Figure 46.

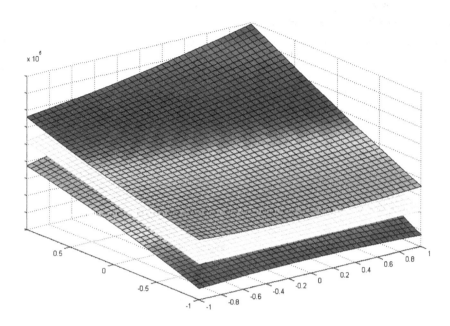

mixed term, can be considered valid in presence of a modest entity central curvature, such as just the deformation compared to the pure flat trend, which is typical of the so called twister plans. To confirm this assertion it is sufficient to observe the ANOVA table which could be obtain by imaging to adapt with a model including the sole main effects, the reality described through the 2nd design(16 factorial points and 5 central).

It is possible to evict from it that the model is not, now, able to adapt the experimental data and also considerably seen the F_0 summary average value and, then, the investigated reality (see Figure 47).

It should be noted, still, how the MS_E global error entity, in which contribution of the BD effect Mean Square by enriching it, mask also the even if modest curving in realities present in the correct model, just expressed by the 2nd design by the effect of the $x_1 x_2$ term (see Figure 46).

FINAL CONSIDERATIONS

The integration between Simulation Model, Experimental Design and Response Surface Methodology allows to the designer, plant manager, to draw the following operating conclusions:

*   of the 4 typologies of operating machines, on which number we could intervene to reach the target production set to 180.000 pieces, the milling machines (typology A) and the nitriding machines (typology B) has a non significant incident capacity for which, if no further considerations linked to the system operation would not intervene, we can consider correct chose for them an intermediate number between the assumed maximum and minimum that is $A = 8$ and $B = 14$ (the eventual additional machine for each typology can act as reserve in case of accidental and not foreseeable failures which we have not considered).

Figure 47.

Transform | Effects | ANOVA | Diagnostics | Model Graphs

Use your mouse to right click on individual cells for definitions.

Response: Response 1

ANOVA for Selected Factorial Model

Analysis of variance table [Partial sum of squares]

Source	Sum of Squares	DF	Mean Square	F Value	Prob > F	
Model	7.656E+009	2	3.828E+009	126.94	< 0.0001	significant
B	*5.140E+008*	*1*	*5.140E+008*	*17.04*	*0.0007*	
D	*7.142E+009*	*1*	*7.142E+009*	*236.83*	*< 0.0001*	
Curvature	1.265E+008	1	1.265E+008	4.20	0.0563	not significant
Residual	5.127E+008	17	3.016E+007			
Lack of Fit	*5.126E+008*	*13*	*3.943E+007*	*2993.40*	*< 0.0001*	*significant*
Pure Error	*52693.20*	*4*	*13173.30*			
Cor Total	8.295E+009	20				

Figure 48.

Transform | Effects | ANOVA | Diagnostics | Model Graphs

Use your mouse to right click on individual cells for definitions.

Response: Response 1

ANOVA for Selected Factorial Model

Analysis of variance table [Partial sum of squares]

Source	Sum of Squares	DF	Mean Square	F Value	Prob > F	
Model	8.182E+009	3	2.727E+009	366.51	< 0.0001	significant
B	*5.154E+008*	*1*	*5.154E+008*	*69.26*	*< 0.0001*	
D	*7.152E+009*	*1*	*7.152E+009*	*961.07*	*< 0.0001*	
BD	*5.150E+008*	*1*	*5.150E+008*	*69.20*	*< 0.0001*	
Residual	1.265E+008	17	7.442E+006			
Lack of Fit	*1.265E+008*	*13*	*9.727E+006*	*738.42*	*< 0.0001*	*significant*
Pure Error	*52693.20*	*4*	*13173.30*			
Cor Total	8.309E+009	20				

- of the other two categories of operating machines, the machines for the dimensional check (type D) result to be important compared to those of the B type, absolutely prominent for the target achievement, which is overcome, with a little safety margin, 182.000 vs 180.000, in the $B = 5$ e $D = 7$ configuration (see Figure 49). Opportunity reasons, therefore, can address the designer/ manager to change this

Figure 49.

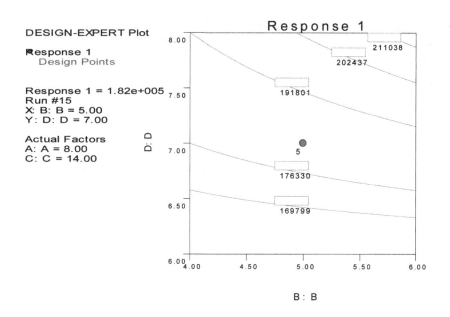

Figure 50.

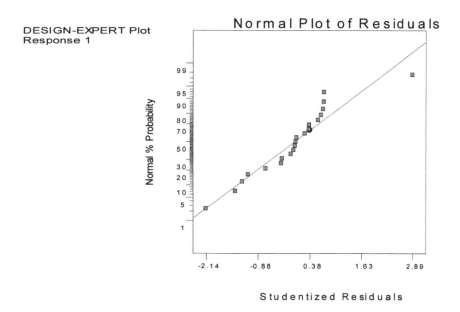

mix in $B = 4$ e $D = 8$ with a production in the period increased up to about 192.000 or consider the $B = 5$ e $D = 8$ configuration with a production of about 202.500 pieces.

These data, taken from the graphics obtained from the detected regression equation, must, still consider the error term influence and, then, be evaluated in the field of the Confidence Interval.

We remember therefore how, form the analysis carried out to determinate the run length, the experimental pure error put into evidence, through the $\sqrt{MSPE}$, values so obtained to make acceptable already the configuration $B = 5$ and $D = 7$. The graphics hereunder attest the normality condition satisfaction of the error and off the σ^2 variance constant character (see Figure 50, Figure 51 and Figure 52)

Figure 51.

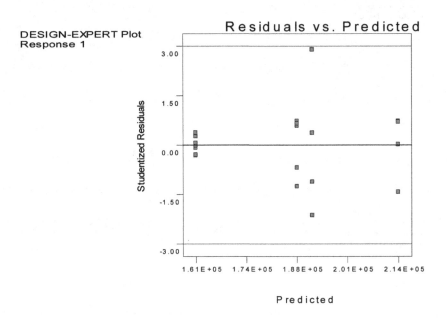

Figure 52.

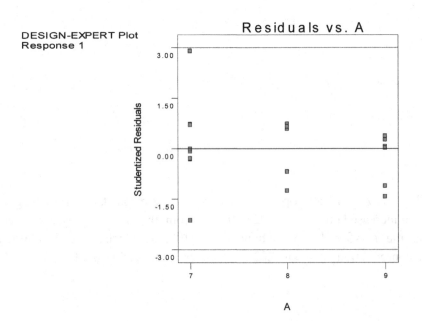

ACKNOWLEDGMENT

The authors want to thank the PhD student Carlo Caligaris for the generation of some response surfaces of this chapter by using the software MatLab v.14.

REFERENCES

For a better understanding of the theoretical requirements of Experiment Theory and Response Surface Methodology it is advised the study of the following books:

Box, G. E. P., & Draper, N. R. (Eds.). (1987). *Empirical Model- Building and Response Surfaces*. New York, NY: John Wiley & Sons.

Montgomery, D. C. (Ed.). (2005). *Design and Analysis of Experiments*. New York: John Wiley & Sons.

Mosca, R., & Giribone, P. (1982).Optimal length in o.r. simulation experiments of large scale production system. In M.H. Hamza (Ed.), *IASTED International Symposium on Modelling, Identification and Control* (pp. 78-82). Calgary, Canada: ACTA Press.

Mosca, R., & Giribone, P. (1982). An interactive code for the design of the o.r. simulation experiment of complex industrial plants. In M.H. Hamza (Ed.), *IASTED International Symposium on Applied Modelling and Simulation* (pp. 200-203). Calgary, Canada: ACTA Press.

Mosca, R., & Giribone, P. (1982). An application of the interactive code for design of o.r. simulation experiment to a slabbing-mill system. In M.H. Hamza (Ed.), *IASTED International Symposium on Applied Modelling and Simulation* (pp. 195-199). Calgary, Canada: ACTA Press.

Mosca, R., & Giribone, P. (1983). O.r. muliple-objective simulation: experimental analysis of the independent varibales ranges. In M.H. Hamza (Ed.), *IASTED International Symposium on Applied Modelling and Simulation* (pp. 68-73). Calgary, Canada: ACTA Press.

Mosca, R., & Giribone, P. (1986). FMS: construction of the simulation model and its statistical validation. In M.H. Hamza (Ed.), *IASTED International Symposium on Modelling, Identification and Control* (pp. 107-113). Calgary, Canada: ACTA Press.

Mosca, R., & Giribone, P. (1986). Flexible manufacturing system: a simulated comparison between discrete and continuous material handling. In M.H. Hamza (Ed.), *IASTED International Symposium on Modelling, Identification and Control* (pp. 100-106). Calgary, Canada: ACTA Press.

Mosca, R., & Giribone, P. (1988). Evaluation of stochastic discrete event simulators of F.M.S. In P. Breedveld et al. (Ed.), *IMACS Transactions on Scientific Computing*: *Modelling and Simulation of Systems* (Vol. 3, pp. 396-402). Switzerland: Baltzer AG.

Mosca, R., & Giribone, P. (1993). Critical analysis of a bottling line using simulation techniques. In M.H. Hamza (Ed.), *IASTED International Symposium on Modelling, Identification and Control* (pp. 135-140). Calgary, Canada: ACTA Press.

Myers, R. H., & Montgomery, D. C. (Eds.). (1995). *Response Surface Methodology*. New York: John Wiley & Sons.

Sincich, T. (Ed.). (1994). *A Course in Modern Business Statistics.* New York: Macmillan College Publishing Company. For a wider vision of the relationship between simulation and experiment design applied to complex industrial systems it is possible to make reference o the following articles and/author memories: Mosca, R., & Giribone, P. (1982).A mathematical method for evaluating the importance of the input variables in simulation experiments. In M.H. Hamza (Ed.), *IASTED International Symposium on Modelling, Identification and Control* (pp. 54-58). Calgary, Canada: ACTA Press.

KEY TERMS AND DEFINITIONS

Design of Experiments (DOE): refers to the process of planning the experiment so that appropriate data that can be analysed by statistical methods will be collected, resulting in valid and objective conclusions (Montgomery, 2005).

Factorial Experiment: is an experimental strategy in which factors are varied together, instead of one at a time (Montgomery, 2005).

Experimental Error: is the noise that afflict the experimental results. It arises from variation that is uncontrolled and generally unavoidable. It is distributed as a NID $(0, \sigma^2)$ and its unbiased estimator is $E(MS_E)$.

Response Surface Methodology (RSM): is a collection of statistical and mathematical tecniques useful for developing, improving and optimazing processes (Myers and Montgomery, 1995).

Regression Analysis: the statistical tecniques used to investigate the relationships among a group of variables and to create models able to describe them.

Central Composite Design (CCD): is the best design to obtain second order regression metamodels.

Confidence Interval for a Parameter: is an interval of numbers within which we expect the true value of the population parameter to be contained at a specified confidence level. The endpoints of the interval are computed based on sample information (Sincich, 1994).

Mean Square Pure Error (MS_{PE}): is an intrinsic characteristic of each experiment and also of each simulation model and is strictly connected to the investigated reality, since it is directly dependent on the overall stochasticity of which this reality is affected.

Chapter 7
Efficient Discrete Simulation of Coded Wireless Communication Systems

Pedro J. A. Sebastião
Instituto de Telecomunicações, Portugal

Francisco A. B. Cercas
Instituto de Telecomunicações, Portugal

Adolfo V. T. Cartaxo
Instituto de Telecomunicações, Portugal

ABSTRACT

Simulation can be a valuable tool for wireless communication system's (WCS) designers to assess the performance of its radio interface. It is common to use the Monte Carlo simulation method (MCSM), although this is quite time inefficient, especially when it involves forward error correction (FEC) with very low bit error ratio (BER). New techniques were developed to efficiently evaluate the performance of the new class of TCH (Tomlinson, Cercas, Hughes) codes in an additive white Gaussian noise (AWGN) channel, due to their potential range of applications. These techniques were previously applied using a satellite channel model developed by Lutz with very good results. In this chapter, we present a simulation method, named accelerated simulation method (ASM), that provides a high degree of efficiency and accuracy, namely for lower BER, where the application of methods like the MCSM is prohibitive, due to high computational and time requirements. The present work generalizes the application of the ASM to a WCS modelled as a stochastic discrete channel model, considering a real channel, where there are several random effects that result in random energy fluctuations of the received symbols. The performance of the coded WCS is assessed efficiently, with soft-decision (SD) and hard-decision (HD) decoding. We show that this new method already achieves a time efficiency of two or three orders of magnitude for SD and HD, considering a $\mathrm{BER} = 1 \times 10^{-4}$, when compared to MCSM. The presented performance results are compared with the MCSM, to check its accuracy.

DOI: 10.4018/978-1-60566-774-4.ch007

EFFICIENT DISCRETE SIMULATION OF CODED WIRELESS COMMUNICATION SYSTEMS

Modern communications are already part of everyone's life. Technologies such as wireless fidelity (Wi-Fi), universal mobile telecommunications system (UMTS) and its developing long term evolution (LTE), and worldwide interoperability for microwave access (WiMAX) are already familiar. For regions of the globe where these technologies are not yet implemented, new interface radio systems are being deployed using satellites, so as to allow the use of common wireless systems anywhere and anytime, that is, a global communications system.

Whatever the radio systems may be, they all have one aspect in common: prior to implementation, several studies must be done to assess the performance of its radio interface. It is common to use the Monte Carlo simulation method (MCSM) to evaluate the system's performance including some or all of its radio interface components, such as scrambling, coding, modulation, filtering, channel effects and all of its counterparts at the receiver. Depending on the required accuracy, this is usually quite a time consuming task, even when high computational systems are used. This situation gets even worse when systems involve forward error correction (FEC) with very low bit error ratios (BER), typically less than 10^{-6}.

As an alternative to MCSM, there are several techniques described in the literature which can help to shorten this time consuming task. One of the most efficient techniques is the importance sampling (IS) technique; however this has the disadvantage that it is only applicable to some particular cases, and cannot be generalized for a wider range of applications (Jeruchim, Balaban & Shanmugan, 2000, pp. 710-737). An important contribution to solve this problem has been given by (Bian, Poplewell & O'Reilly 1994) who optimised some simulation techniques in order to evaluate the performance of coded communication

systems at low BER in an additive white Gaussian noise (AWGN) channel. Based on that work, new techniques were developed to evaluate the performance of block codes in an AWGN channel, in a very efficient way (Cercas, Cartaxo & Sebastião, 1999) They were also applied to a satellite channel model developed by Lutz, Cygan, Dippold, Dolainsky & Papke, (1991) obtaining very good agreement with the foreseen upper bounds of some FEC schemes performance (Sebastião, Cercas & Cartaxo, 2002).

In this chapter, we present a new simulation method named accelerated simulation method (ASM) since it can provide a high degree of efficiency when compared with the MCSM, which increases for very low BER, while maintaining very good accuracy.

This method can be applied to communication systems with hard-decision (HD) and soft-decision (SD) decoding, in a more realistic channel model.

In this chapter, the ASM was applied to compute the performance of the new class of Tomlinson, Cercas, Hughes (TCH) codes. These codes are a class of non-linear block codes that were devised for a wide range of applications, including FEC. These codes exhibit good performance and undertake maximum likelihood soft-decision decoding with a very simple decoder structure, using digital signal processing techniques and correlation in the frequency domain. Furthermore, they can be used simultaneously in code division multiple access (CDMA), channel estimation and synchronization of the receiver, due to the very good correlation properties of its code words (Cercas, Tomlinson & Albuquerque, 1993).

The main contribution of this chapter is the generalization of the ASM method to a more realistic channel model. Real channels are far more complex than AWGN ones, as the signal is also affected by other effects such as multipath components with different delays and other interference phenomena that result in random energy fluctuations of the received symbols, that is, the signal is affected by fading that can be described by a given statistical model. In this chapter, we consider channels with slow fading (the fading is at least constant over the duration of a symbol) (Simon & Alouini, 2000) and non-selective in frequency (all frequency components of the received signal are affected in a similar way). This assumption is commonly used even for modern wideband systems using orthogonal frequency-division multiplexing (OFDM). With these assumptions, this model can be applied to typical personal and mobile communications systems, taking into account, for example, fading for non-selective channels in frequency with shadowing, as well as any type of modulation and coding. This process will be exemplified for a wireless communication system (WCS), with a Rayleigh channel and TCH codes.

Following this introductory section, the remaining text is organized as follows: Section "Simulation of Coded Wireless Communication Systems" describes the role of simulation in the evaluation of the performance of coded WCS and introduces the ASM. Section "Discrete Channel Model" describes the discrete channel model (DCM) for a WCS. Section "Accelerated Simulation Method Description" describes the ASM to be used with SD and HD decoding in WCS. Section "Simulation Results" presents some results to validate the proposed simulation method and section "Conclusions" summarises the main conclusions. Seven appendixes add more detail to some subjects presented along the chapter.

SIMULATION OF CODED WIRELESS COMMUNICATION SYSTEMS

A key issue in the development of new communication systems, prior to its implementation, is the assessment of its performance in a given environment where, supposedly, it will operate. In WCS with FEC, the main parameter characterizing performance is its BER. Its knowledge for

SD and HD decoding is very important to design communication systems. Modern communication systems are so complex that the evaluation of their performance can only be assessed by simulation and not by analytical formulation. A classic and widely used simulation method to evaluate the performance of a communication system is the MCSM (Jeruchim, Balaban & Shanmugan, 2000). However, this method requires that all information data is processed throughout all blocks of a system, which may result in a long simulation time, especially for low BER values.

In this case, we are interested in the probability of occurrence of rare events, that is, the occurrence of an error in a very large number of transmitted symbols. In the case of MCSM, all transmitted symbols are simulated, using large computational resources during a long time, without any real advantage. To validate the simulation results with a good acceptable accuracy, it is necessary to wait until a relevant number of these rare events happen, that is errors. For example, assume that $BER = 1 \times 10^{-6}$, i.e., in average, we have a single received bit in error for every million transmitted bits. To achieve an acceptable accuracy we need to simulate 10 to 100 bits received in error, so the MCSM must simulate 10 to 100 million transmitted bits, which must be processed through the entire transmission system, composed by a series of different blocks.

In order to mitigate the simulation time needed to obtain the BER of a WCS, especially for lower error ratios, a general simulation method is presented, called ASM. The main objectives of this method are time efficiency and accuracy of the obtained results.

Generally, we can say that the ASM consists on generating a sequence of symbols, with the length necessary for all simulation, in which each symbol can be predicted to be, or not, in error, after being transmitted through the channel, according to its known statistics. Then, this method will only simulate the symbols, or groups of symbols such

Figure 1. WCS model with a DCM

as code words that can result in received errors, ignoring all others.

Assuming that we are simulating a coded system that uses block codes (this can easily be generalised to convolutional codes), the generated sequence of symbols containing the positions of the expected errors in the channel is divided in blocks with the length of a code word. Since in a coded system we cannot process individual bits but complete received code words at the decoder, this simple procedure allows us to check if the number of expected errors in a given code word exceeds, or not, the error correcting capacity of the code being used. In the ASM, only those code words with a number of erroneous bits exceeding the error correcting capacity of the code will be simulated, provided all others will certainly be corrected, and therefore they don't need to be processed.

For those code words requiring simulation, an information word is generated and coded, according to the rules of the code being used. Then, its bits are changed in accordance with the positions of errors and non errors, in the previously generated sequence of symbols.

This processing can be more or less simple according to the decoding method used. For HD decoding it is only needed to invert the bits (assuming that these symbols are binary) for each position of the code word, that was indicated by the previously generated error sequence as an erroneous bit. This modified code word is decoded and the resulting estimated information word is compared with the original information word, to obtain the effective number of bits in error.

If SD decoding is used, the simulation time is longer, once all amplitudes for each bit in a code word need to be generated. Depending on the channel statistics, amplitude samples are generated for the bit positions in error or non error. Similarly to HD decoding, this modified code word is decoded and the resulting estimated information word is compared with the original, to obtain the number of bits in error.

The mentioned objectives of efficiency and accuracy in ASM are achieved as follows. The efficiency in ASM is due to three factors: only events in error are simulated, which are rare events for low BER; only code words with a number of erroneous bits exceeding the code's error capacity are simulated and the description of the WCS is concentrated in the DCM, that is a single system block, as described in the next section. The accuracy of the method also depends on the referred DCM, which must be as close as possible to the real environment.

The characterization of the DCM is then crucial for the ASM and is presented in the following section.

DISCRETE CHANNEL MODEL

The DCM used in the ASM includes all blocks of a transmission chain and it accounts for all physical phenomena of a WCS. In Figure 1 we can see the DCM which is located between the coding and decoding blocks, in the transmitter and receiver, respectively. **a** denotes a generated information word (message), **b** is a transmitted code word corresponding to that information word, R contains the demodulated signal and **â** is a estimated information word.

Figure 2. Discrete channel model used in the ASM

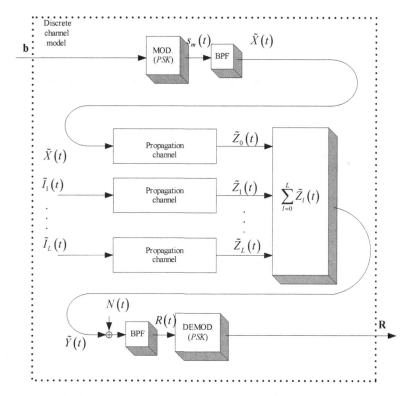

The main objective of the DCM characterization in a WCS is to allow the study and analysis of digital communication systems, namely its coding blocks, interleavers and all its components that help to reduce the number of received information errors. With the DCM it is possible to get the error distribution in the channel for a given propagation model, the amplitude distribution of the received signal including antenna characteristics, thermal noise (modelled as AWGN), interfering sources and the type of modulation used.

Figure 2 represents a generic DCM including all these factors, in which the signal is represented by its low-pass equivalent.

As it can be observed in Figure 2, the blocks of the DCM are: modulator (MOD.), demodulator (DEMOD.), band-pass filters (BPF) and a general representation of the propagation channel which may include a combination of different random effects to better fit the random physical phenomena involved, including a three-dimensional description of the signal.

The meaning of variables shown in the DCM is as follows: $s_m(t)$ is the mth symbol at instant t, corresponding to the modulated vector b (set of information bits or information word), $\tilde{X}(t)$ is a sample of the transmitted signal after band-pass filtering, $\tilde{I}_L(t)$ is the Lth interfering signal, $\tilde{Z}_L(t)$ is the Lth received signal affected by the propagation channel, $\tilde{Y}(t)$ is a sample of the random signal at the input of the receiver, including signal plus interference, $N(t)$ is a sample of thermal noise with Gaussian distribution and $R(t)$ is a sample of the actual signal received by the demodulator. Interfering signals can be originated in systems operating in the same frequency band (co-channel interference) (Yacoub, 2000), in which case the use of high order filters helps to mitigate it, or in adjacent frequency bands (adjacent-channel interference) (Ha, 1990).

Figure 3. General model for the propagation channel of a WCS including the effects of transmitting and receiving antennas

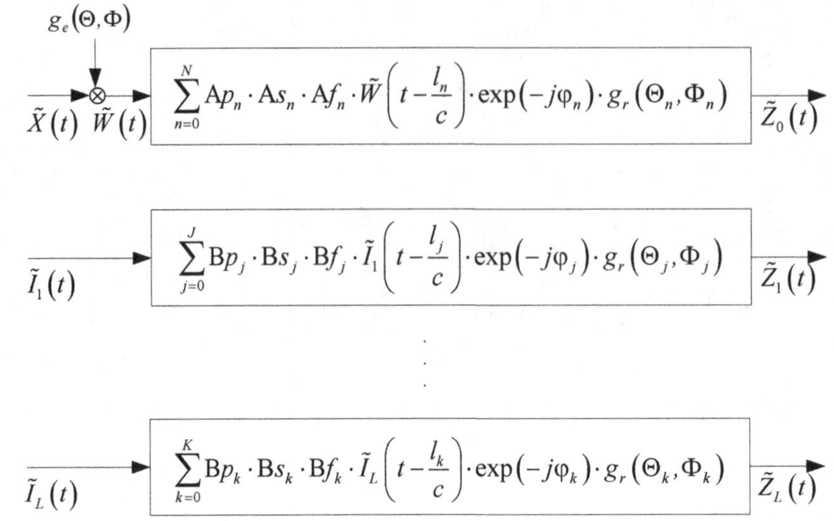

Figure 3 represents the propagation channel, including the effects of transmitting and receiving antennas.

The propagation channel accounts for all the physical random phenomena happening in the physical medium, where electromagnetic waves travel from emitter till the receiver. It is common to assume the mobile radio channel as linear, but time-variant, due to the possible relative random movement of the receiver terminal to the emitter or even of surrounding objects in a WCS. In the propagation channel the transmitted signal can reach the receiver directly, indirectly or in both ways. Indirectly received signals are due to reflection, diffraction or dispersion of the transmitted signal in surrounding objects such as buildings, trees or even the orography. The received signal is then a summation of all these contributions, each one having its own attenuation, delay and phase shift. Furthermore, each replica of the received signal can also be affected by the movement of a terminal (emitter or receiver) or the movement of surrounding objects, which translates to a Doppler shift.

As shown in Figure 3, we define the parameters that affect the transmitted signal in the propagation channel as the random variables (RV), Ap, As and Af^1, that are the free space attenuation, attenuation due to shadowing and fading, respectively. In a similar way, interfering signals are affected by parameters Bp, Bs and Bf^2. The first two types of attenuation exhibit a large scale variation in the time domain[3], while the last one exhibits a small scale variation[4] (Rappaport, 2002, pp. 205-210).

Free space attenuation is assumed deterministic and there are many empirical models used to evaluate it in WCS environments, *e.g.*, (Walfish & Bertoni, 1988; Hata, 1990; Rappaport, 2002, pp. 145-167; Ikegami, Yoshida, Takeuchi & Umehira, 1984; Bertoni, Honcharenko, Macel & Xia, 1994; Parsons, 1992, pp. 90-93; Lee, 1989, Chapter 3;ITU-R, P341-5, 1999; Feuerstein, Blackard, Rappaport, Seidel & Xia, 1994; Alexander, 1982; Hashemi, 1993b; Molkdar, 1991) amongst others. In appendix A, we present an expression to characterize the free space attenuation.

Attenuation due to shadowing has a stochastic behaviour since, for a fixed transmission distance and carrier frequency, the received signal has a random behaviour due to the movement of surrounding objects and other effects (Su-

Figure 4. PSK modulator and signals

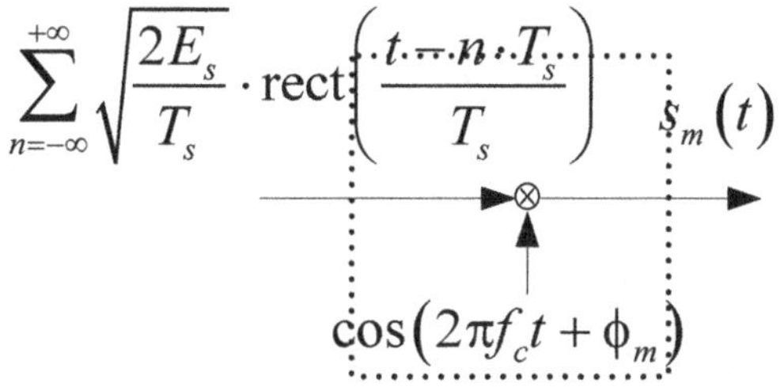

$$\sum_{n=-\infty}^{+\infty} \sqrt{\frac{2E_s}{T_s}} \cdot \mathrm{rect}\left(\frac{t - n \cdot T_s}{T_s}\right) \cdots \quad s_m(t)$$

$$\cos\left(2\pi f_c t + \phi_m\right)$$

zuki, 1977; Hashemi, 1979; Rappaport, Seidel & Takamizawa, 1991; Yegani & McGillem, 1991; Hashemi, 1993a). In appendix B we present two expressions to characterize the probability density function (PDF) of power and amplitude for this phenomenon.

Attenuation due to fading is derives from the existence of multipath components and it has a stochastic behaviour, however its variation in the time domain is fast, when compared to attenuation due to shadowing. Variables l_n and φ_n define the length and phase of the nth received multipath component, both for signal and interference. Variables Θ and Φ define azimuth and elevation angles for the transmitting and receiving antennas. The speed of light in vacuum is represented, as usually, by c. Appendix C presents some insight on this subject together with the derivation of analytical expressions for the propagation channel.

The three types of attenuation just mentioned act on the signal in the propagation channel and are responsible for its random behaviour.

The modulator transforms the baseband signal in a bandpass signal centred on a carrier that can easily propagate in the mentioned propagation channel of the WCS. Only digital modulation is considered since it presents considerable advantages over analogue modulation such as improved immunity to noise and fading, ease of multiplexing input data, improved security and the possibility to implement FEC and digital signal processing (DSP) techniques for most of the process. DSP techniques can actually implement the overall process in the emitter and receiver, including modulator, demodulator, filtering, and remaining blocks by the simple use of software.

The most popular modulation techniques used in WCS are linear. In linear modulation the transmitted signal $s_m(t)$ changes linearly with the modulating signal. These techniques are spectrally efficient, which is an important property, since the electromagnetic spectrum is already saturated.

A very popular linear digital modulation technique used in WCS is the phase shift keying (PSK). In this technique the amplitude remains constant but the phase changes according to the transmitted symbol. Figure 4 shows the basic operations of a PSK modulator and corresponding signals.

The modulated signal at the output of this modulator can be written as:

$$s_m(t) = \Re\left[b(t) \cdot \exp\left(j2\pi f_c t\right)\right] \tag{1}$$

where

$$b(t) = \sum_{n=-\infty}^{+\infty} b_n \cdot \mathrm{rect}\left(\frac{t - nT_s}{T_s}\right) \tag{2}$$

and

$$b_n = \sqrt{\frac{2E_s}{T_s}} \cdot \exp\left(j\phi_m\right),$$

$$\phi_m = \frac{2\pi}{M}(m-1), \quad (m = 1, ..., M) \tag{3}$$

E_s is the symbol energy, T_s is the symbol time and ϕ_m is the phase associated with symbol m. We also assume that during a symbol interval T_s the number of cycles of the carrier is an integer.

In the receiver, the demodulator is used to recover the basedband signal sent on a carrier through the propagation channel, using the inverse operation. Assuming that the PSK demodulator is coherent and is synchronized, then it has infor-

Figure 5. PSK demodulator

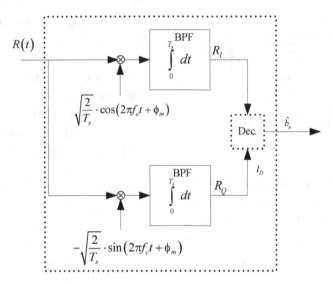

mation about carrier frequency and phase of the received signal. Figure 5 shows the schematic of a PSK demodulator using base functions, correlators and a decision circuit (Proakis, 2001, pp. 232-236).

Each correlator in the PSK demodulator compares the received signal $R(t)$ with each base function $f_1(t)$ and $f_2(t)$ (Proakis, 2001, pp. 172) by multiplication followed by integration in a symbol period T_s, so as to recover the baseband transmitted symbol. After detection, the signal amplitude of each symbol is compared with a threshold value l_D so as to estimate the set of information bits $\hat{b}_n$ of vector b. This type of decision is known as hard decision (HD). Systems that have a SD decoder following the demodulator don't need to make hard decisions since the complex signal at the output of the demodulator can be directly fed to it.

Equation (4) characterizes the signal at the output of the DCM. It is deduced in appendix D and assumes PSK modulation, emitting and receiving antennas gain, AWGN noise, interfering signals with a given distribution and the three types of attenuation mentioned: free space attenuation, shadowing and fading.

$$R = \int_0^{T_s} \left\{ \left[\begin{array}{c} g_e(\Theta,\Phi) \sum_{n=0}^{N} \Re \left[\begin{array}{c} Ap_n \cdot As_n \cdot Af_n \cdot b(t) \cdot \exp j \left[2\pi f_c \left(t - \frac{l_n}{c} \right) \right] \cdot \\ \cdot \exp(-j\varphi_n) \cdot \exp(j2\pi \cdot D_n \cdot t) \end{array} \right] \cdot \\ \cdot g_r(\Theta_n,\Phi_n) + \sum_{i=1}^{L} \sum_{k=0}^{K} \Re \left[\begin{array}{c} Bp_k \cdot Bs_k \cdot \tilde{B}f_k \cdot \tilde{I}_i \left(t - \frac{l_k}{c} \right) \exp(j2\pi \cdot D_k \cdot t) \cdot \\ \cdot g_r(\Theta_k,\Phi_k) \end{array} \right] \\ \cdot \left[\sqrt{\frac{2}{T_s}} \cdot \cos(2\pi f_c t) - \sqrt{\frac{2}{T_s}} \cdot \sin(2\pi f_c t) \right] \end{array} \right\} dt + N$$

(4)

As shown in appendix D, this can be simplified so as to write the vector of the received signal amplitudes as:

$$R = \sqrt{E_s} \cdot As \cdot Af \cdot \left[R_a \quad R_b \right] + N$$

(5)

where R_a and R_b depend on the base functions used in correlators. Appendix D also presents a simplified and useful expression for a typical case using binary phase shift keying (BPSK) modulation.

ACCELERATED SIMULATION METHOD DESCRIPTION

In the previous sections the role of simulation to obtain the performance of coded WCS was shown, as well as how to characterize a general

Figure 6. Algorithm for implementing the ASM method in a WCS, applied in the evaluation of the performance of block codes for both HD or SD decoding

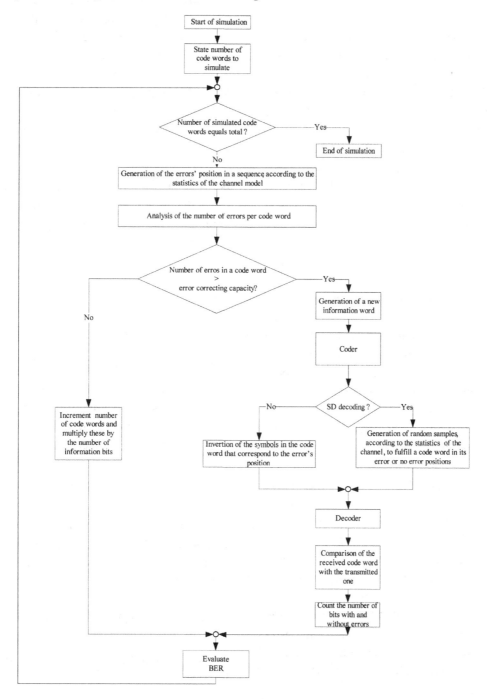

DCM, which can be adapted and simplified for a particular case study, to be efficiently used in simulation.

Based on the general principles, it is now possible to present a very efficient algorithm for assessing the performance of any coding scheme in any real environment.

The algorithm for implementing the ASM

method, as shown in the flowchart of Figure 6, can be summarized as follows:

1) Define the number of erroneous words to be processed for each E_b/N_0 value, within the considered range. As in the Monte Carlo method this is related to the required precision and defines the end of the simulation cycle.

2) Generate the sequence of intervals between consecutive errors $L_1, L_2, L_3, \ldots$, according to the method described in Appendix E so as to define the position of erroneous symbols in the channel for the coding, modulation and channel conditions desired.

3) If the block of n symbols corresponding to the code word being processed contains more errors e than the error-correcting capacity of the code ecc, i.e., $e > ecc$, then a new information word length k is generated, based on a uniform distribution. This word is coded following the rules of the considered code, resulting in a code word length n, which is then modulated.

4) If SD decoding is used, the generated code word is replaced by a set of n amplitude samples, Rne or Re, according to the information provided by the L values, noise and fading distributions. The expressions to obtain those amplitude samples are presented in Appendix F.

5) If HD decoding is used, the generated set of n coded and modulated symbols, sometimes also referred to as code word, for simplicity, have their amplitudes inverted or not, according to the information of the corresponding L stream. This amplitude inversion corresponds to exchange "-1" with "+1" and vice-versa.

6) In both cases, the resulting code word is then sent to the decoding block.

7) The output of the decoding block estimates the transmitted information word, which, is compared with the generated one. If they differ, the counter for erroneous words is incremented, as well as the counter for erroneous bits, depending on the number of different bits detected. The counter for the total number of information words (or bits) processed is also incremented.

8) This process is repeated until the desired number of erroneous information words, or bits, is reached.

This algorithm is suitable for evaluating the performance of different families of error correcting codes in any desired environment, since all parameters can be specified.

The estimated bit error ratio, $B\hat{E}R$, is then evaluated by:

$$B\hat{E}R = \frac{NIB_e}{NIB_{TOTAL}} \tag{6}$$

where NIB_e is the number of information bits in error. The total number of information bits, NIB_{TOTAL}, is the number of information bits in each word of length k multiplied by the total number of coded words, NCW, and can be expressed as:

$$NIB_{TOTAL} = k \cdot NCW = NIB_{ne} + NIB_e \tag{7}$$

where NIB_{ne} is the number of information bits without errors, found within information words without errors ($IWne$) or within information words with errors (IWe):

$$NIB_{ne} = NIB_{ne}\left(IWne\right) + NIB_{ne}\left(IWe\right) \tag{8}$$

The total number of code words NCW can also be expressed as:

$$NCW = NCW_{e=0} + NCW_{0<e\leq ecc} + NCW_{e>ecc} \tag{9}$$

where $NCW_{e=0}$ is the number of code words without errors, $NCW_{0<e\leq ecc}$ is the number of code words with a number of errors equal or smaller then the error-correcting capacity of the code, and $NCW_{e>ecc}$ is the number of code words with a number of errors exceeding the error-correcting capacity of the code. This allows us to define the processing advantage (PA). This is defined as the time required, to accomplish simulation using the ASM relative to the MCSM and can have a significant impact on the simulation time and computational resources needed:

$$PA = \frac{NCW}{NCW_{e>ecc}} \qquad (10)$$

As already mentioned, this processing advantage increases for high signal-to-noise ratios or very low fading conditions, allowing us to easily evaluate performance results where the application of other methods, like Monte Carlo, would be prohibitive.

As an illustrative example, we consider BPSK modulation, so the binary symbols "0" or "1" will be replaced by the corresponding amplitudes and respectively. Figure 7 and Figure 8 depict the ASM algorithms used to evaluate the performance of a given coded system with SD and HD decoding, respectively. Here we assume that a block code length n with k information bits and an error-correcting capacity of ecc bits is used, so all the basic processing is done in blocks length n. The upper stream of zeros and ones, divided in blocks length n of a code word is the generated stream containing the error's occurrence position, according to the method described in Appendix E. Therefore, the presence of a "0" means that the corresponding symbol in the channel was not mistaken by the channel effects considered (noise, fading, etc.) and the presence of a "1" means that the corresponding symbol in the channel is wrong. The distance values L between two consecutive ones was generated by that method, using the appropriate random variables.

In Figure 7 we can also see a major block named "*Re* and *Rne* generator". Its function is to generate the simulated amplitude samples for a coded and modulated block of n symbols in the channel, according to the procedure explained in Appendix F. As can be seen, it generates an *Re* or *Rne* sample, depending if the corresponding symbol position in the code word being processed was in error ("1" in upper stream) or not ("0" in upper stream), respectively. As shown, the generation of these samples is based on the generation of a coded and modulated block of n symbols affected by the considered levels of noise and fading, as well as the previous information.

It is important to note that this procedure is only used for soft-decision decoding. When HD decoding is used, as shown in Figure 8, this is a lot simpler and quicker. In this case, the lower generated symbol stream will have its symbols inverted whenever they correspond to a "1" in the upper stream and remain unchanged otherwise, prior to be submitted to the decoding block. It is also important to note that this block is only activated in the simulation chain whenever the number of errors in a given code word exceeds the error-correcting capacity of the code. Since for high signal-to-noise ratios most of the code words will not be in error, this simulation method can achieve a significant processing time advantage relative to the MCSM, without compromising its accuracy.

In Appendix G we derive the probability of error of the channel and the cumulative probability density function (CPDF) for error and non error amplitudes, applied to the case of Rayleigh fading distribution, additive white Gaussian noise and BPSK modulation.

SIMULATION RESULTS

In this section, we illustrate the proposed simulation method for estimating the performance of the TCH family of codes. The obtained results are

Figure 7. ASM algorithm to evaluate the performance of a TCH code with SD decoding

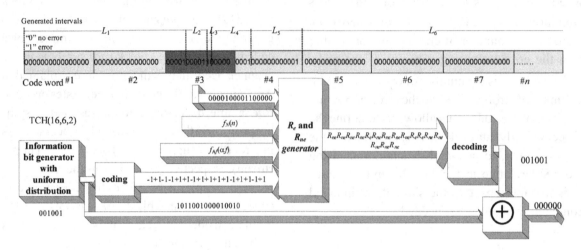

compared with the MCSM. BPSK modulation is assumed, as well as a non-selective Rayleigh channel with different fading levels. The simulation time was measured and compared in these conditions, for both HD and SD decoding and for several values of BER.

Although different TCH codes have been tested with different channel distributions, including Rice (1958), Nakagami-*m* (Yacoub, 1999), Lognormal (Bullington, 1977; Braun & Dersch, 1991), Suzuki (which includes both Rice and Lognormal distributions) (Suzuki, 1977) and Weibull (which is frequently used for radio communication channels)

(Babich & Lombardi, 2000; Yegani & McGillem, 1991), the performance of this simulation method is illustrated using a simple TCH(16,6,2) block code in a Rayleigh environment.

The results were compared for several fading levels, ranging from a less severe, *e.g.*, rural environment, with an average fading of 0dB, to a more severe one, e.g., urban, with an average fading of -20dB. The BER values considered, range from 1×10^{-3} to 1×10^{-9} since these values are used for most practical applications such as voice, video or data (Tanenbaum, 1998). Each value plotted in the graphs was determined considering 1000

Figure 8. ASM algorithm to evaluate the performance of a TCH code with HD decoding

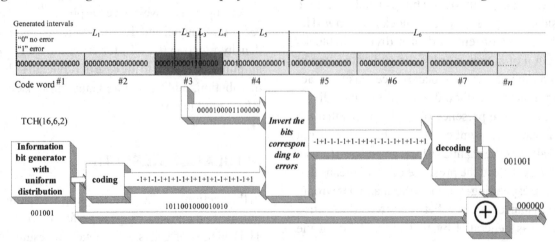

Figure 9. Performance of a TCH(16,6,2) code in a Rayleigh channel, with average fading of 0dB, using different simulation methods for both SD and HD decoding

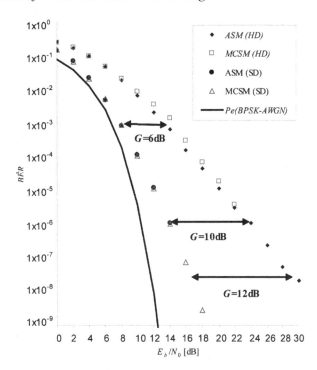

words in error, which guarantees results with high accuracy.

Figure 9 plots the performance of TCH(16,6,2) code with an average fading of 0dB (rural environment), as a function of the information bit signal to noise ratio E_b/N_0. As we can see for SD decoding, the two methods give similar performance results. For HD decoding the results are similar, with a small deviation from the MCSM. As we should expect, the advantage of SD decoding relative to HD decoding is notorious in this type of channel relative to a simple AWGN channel. For $BER \approx 1 \times 10^{-3}; 1 \times 10^{-6}$ and 3×10^{-8} the coding gain obtained by SD decoding in this Rayleigh channel is $G \approx 6\text{dB}; 10\text{dB}$ and 12dB, respectively, while in an AWGN channel the coding gain was $G \approx 2\text{dB}; 2.2\text{dB}$ and 2.5dB (Sebastião, 1998).

Figure 10 plots results for the same code in similar conditions, the only difference being that the average fading is now -20dB (urban environ-

ment). Besides the range of *BER* values is now smaller, we can verify that we can take exactly the same conclusions as in Figure 9, if we just make a shift in the x axis by 20dB. This illustrates the influence of the increased fading.

Figure 11 shows a comparison of simulation times needed by each method, for the simulations shown in Figure 9, i.e., for an average fading of 0dB

Generally, we can observe that the PA of this method is inversely proportional to *BER*, as previously predicted. That advantage is small for high values of *BER*, however it is for low values of *BER* that the ASM method is most useful.

The time advantage is significantly higher when HD decoding is used, since there is no need to generate the *Re* and *Rne* values. In this case, the time advantage, for $BER \approx 1 \times 10^{-4}$ is 1568 relative to the MCSM, while for SD decoding it is 40. This time advantage further increases for lower BER values. For example, for $BER \leq 1 \times 10^{-5}$

Figure 10. Performance of a TCH(16,6,2) code in a Rayleigh channel, with average fading of -20dB, using different simulation methods for both SD and HD decoding

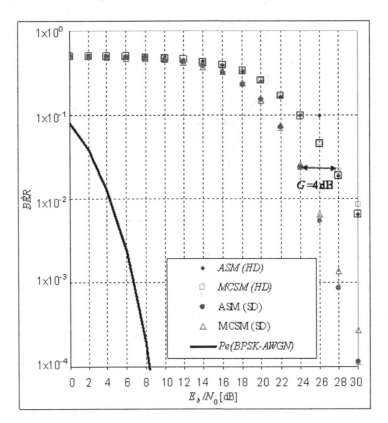

it is greater than 7000 and 350, for HD and SD decoding, respectively.

CONCLUSION

The ASM presented in this chapter provides an efficient way to evaluate the performance of wireless radio communication systems. It is clearly more efficient than the MCSM. In this chapter, the ASM was used to evaluate the performance of a coded system in a given environment, for which the modulation, noise and channel statistics were fully specified, including AWGN noise, fading, shadowing and interference.

The application of this method is based on the DCM of the system, which contains the description of all relevant parameters of the WCS, including modulation, coding and channel statistics reflecting the physical phenomena to model.

This method presents a significant time efficiency, also demonstrated by simulation results, that increases for good channel conditions and high signal-to-noise ratios, especially for very low BER values, where the application of the MCSM gets nearly prohibitive and requires huge computational resources.

Both ASM and MCSM were used to evaluate the performance of a TCH(16,6,2) code, for SD and HD decoding receivers, using BPSK modulation, AWGN noise and Rayleigh fading, although other codes and channel models have previously been tested with similar results. This new method achieves a time efficiency of two or three orders of magnitude for SD and HD, considering a $BER = 1 \times 10^{-4}$, when compared to MCSM.

Figure 11. Comparison of the simulation times needed by different methods to evaluate the performance of a TCH(16,6,2) code in a Rayleigh channel, average fading of 0dB, for both SD and HD decoding.

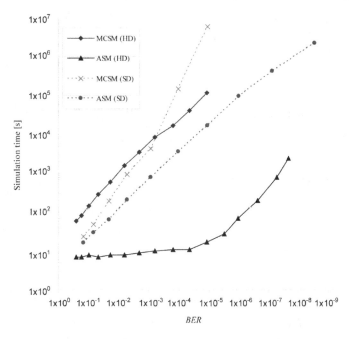

Simulation results also showed that both methods present similar performance results.

REFERENCES

Alexander, S. E. (1982). Radio propagation within buildings at 900 MHz. *IEE Electronics Letters*, *18*(21), 913–914. doi:10.1049/el:19820622

Aulin, T. (1979). A modified model for fading signal at a mobile radio channel. *IEEE Transactions on Vehicular Technology*, *28*(3), 182–203. doi:10.1109/T-VT.1979.23789

Babich, F., & Lombardi, G. (2000). Statistical analysis and characterization of the indoor propagation channel. *IEEE Transactions on Communications*, *48*(3), 455–464. doi:10.1109/26.837048

Bertoni, H. L., Honcharenko, W., Macel, L. R., & Xia, H. H. (1994). UHF propagation prediction for wireless personal communications. *IEEE Proceedings*, *82*(9), 1333–1359. doi:10.1109/5.317081

Bian, Y., Poplewell, A., & O'Reilly, J. J. (1994). Novel simulation technique for assessing coding system performance. *IEE Electronics Letters*, *30*(23), 1920–1921. doi:10.1049/el:19941297

Braun, W. R., & Dersch, U. (1991). A physical mobile radio channel model. *IEEE Transactions on Vehicular Technology*, *40*(2), 472–482. doi:10.1109/25.289429

Bullington, K. (1977). Radio propagation for vehicular communications. *IEEE Transactions on Vehicular Technology*, *26*(4), 295–308. doi:10.1109/T-VT.1977.23698

Cercas, F. A., Tomlinson, M., & Albuquerque, A. A. (1993). TCH: A new family of cyclic codes length 2m. *International Symposium on Information Theory, IEEE Proceedings*, (pp. 198-198).

Cercas, F. A. B., Cartaxo, A. V. T., & Sebastião, P. J. A. (1999). Performance of TCH codes with independent and burst errors using efficient techniques. *50th IEEE Vehicular Technology Conference*, Amsterdam, Netherlands, *(VTC99-Fall)*, (pp. 2536-2540).

Clarke, R. H. (1968). A statistical theory of mobile radio reception. *The Bell System Technical Journal*, *47*, 957–1000.

Feuerstein, M. J., Blackard, K. L., Rappaport, T. S., Seidel, S. Y., & Xia, H. H. (1994). Path loss, delay spread, and outage models as functions of antenna height for microcellular system design. *IEEE Transactions on Vehicular Technology*, *43*(3), 487–489. doi:10.1109/25.312809

French, R. C. (1979). The effect of fading and shadowing on channel reuse in mobile radio. *IEEE Transactions on Vehicular Technology*, *28*(3), 171–181. doi:10.1109/T-VT.1979.23788

Ha, T. T. (1990). *Digital satellite communications* (2nd Ed.). New York: McGraw-Hill.

Hansen, F., & Meno, F. I. (1977). Mobile fading-Rayleigh and lognormal superimposed. *IEEE Transactions on Vehicular Technology*, *26*(4), 332–335. doi:10.1109/T-VT.1977.23703

Hashemi, H. (1979). Simulation of the urban radio propagation channel. *IEEE Transactions on Vehicular Technology*, *28*(3), 213–225. doi:10.1109/T-VT.1979.23791

Hashemi, H. (1993a). Impulse response modelling of indoor radio propagation channels. *IEEE Journal on Selected Areas in Communications*, *11*(7), 967–978. doi:10.1109/49.233210

Hashemi, H. (1993b). The indoor radio propagation channel. *Proceedings of the IEEE*, *81*(7), 943–968. doi:10.1109/5.231342

Hata, M. (1990). Empirical formula for propagation loss in land mobile radio services. *IEEE Transactions on Vehicular Technology*, *29*(3), 317–325. doi:10.1109/T-VT.1980.23859

Haykin, S. (2001). *Communication systems* (4th Ed.). Chichester, UK: John Wiley & Sons, Inc.

Helstrom, C. W. (1984). *Probability and stochastic processes for engineers* (1st Ed.). New York: MacMillan.

Ikegami, F., Yoshida, S., Takeuchi, T., & Umehira, M. (1984). Propagation factors controlling mean field on urban streets. *IEEE Transactions on Antennas and Propagation*, *32*(8), 822–829. doi:10.1109/TAP.1984.1143419

ITU-R, P.341-5, (1999). *The concept of transmission loss for radio links,* [Recommendation].

Jakes, W. C. (1974). *Microwave mobile communications* (1st Ed.). Washington, DC: IEEE Press.

Jeruchim, M., Balaban, P., & Shanmugan, K. S. (2000). *Simulation of communication systems – modelling methodology and techniques* (2nd ed.). Amsterdam, The Netherlands: Kluwer Academic.

Lee, W. C. Y. (1989). *Mobile cellular telecommunications systems*. New York: McGraw-Hill.

Lutz, E., Cygan, D., Dippold, M., Dolainsky, F., & Papke, W. (1991). The land mobile satellite communication channel – recording, statistics, and channel model. *IEEE Transactions on Vehicular Technology*, *40*, 375–386. doi:10.1109/25.289418

D. Molkdar, D. (1991). Review on radio propagation into and within buildings. *IEEE Proceedings*, *138*(11), 61-73.

Papoulis, A. (1984). *Probability, random variables, and stochastic processes* (2nd Ed.). New York: McGraw-Hill, Inc.

Parsons, J. D. (1992). *The mobile radio propagation channel* (1st Ed.). Chichester, UK: John Wiley & Sons, Inc.

Proakis, J. G. (2001). *Digital communications* (4th Ed.). New York: McGraw-Hill.

Rappaport, T. S. (2002). *Wireless communications principles and practice* (2nd Ed.). Upper Saddle River, NJ: Prentice Hall.

Rappaport, T. S., Seidel, S. Y., & Takamizawa, K. (1991). Statistical channel impulse response models for factory and open plan building radio communication system design. *IEEE Transactions on Communications*, *39*(5), 794–806. doi:10.1109/26.87142

Rice, S. O. (1958). Distribution of the duration of fades in radio transmission: Gaussian noise model. *The Bell System Technical Journal*, *37*(3), 581–635.

Ross, M. S. (1987). *Introduction to probability and statistics for engineers and scientists*. Chichester, UK: John Wiley & Sons, Inc.

Sebastião, P. J. A. (1998). *Simulação eficiente do desempenho dos códigos TCH através de modelos estocásticos* [Efficient simulation to obtain the performance of TCH codes using stochastic models], (Master Thesis, Instituto Superior Técnico – Technical University of Lisbon, 1998), Lisboa, Portugal.

Sebastião, P. J. A., Cercas, F. A. B., & Cartaxo, A. V. T. (2002). Performance of TCH codes in a land mobile satellite channel. *13th IEEE International. Symposium on Personal, Indoor and Mobile Radio Communication., (PIMRC2002)*, Lisbon, Portugal, (pp. 1675-1679).

Shanmugam, K. S. (1979). *Digital and analog communication systems*. Chichester, UK: John Wiley & Sons.

Simon, M. K., & Alouini, M. (2000). *Digital communication over fading channels*. Chichester, UK: John Wiley & Sons.

Suzuki, H. (1977). A statistical model for urban radio propagation. *IEEE Transactions on Communications*, *25*(7), 673–680. doi:10.1109/TCOM.1977.1093888

Tanenbaum, A. S. (2003). *Computer networks* (4th ed.). Upper Saddle River, NJ: Prentice Hall.

Walfish, J., & Bertoni, H. L. (1988). A theoretical model of UHF propagation in urban environments. *IEEE Transactions on Antennas and Propagation*, *36*, 1788–1796. doi:10.1109/8.14401

Yacoub, M., Baptista, J. E. V., & Guedes, L. G. R. (1999). On higher order statistics of the Nakagami-m distribution. *IEEE Transactions on Vehicular Technology*, *48*(3), 790–794. doi:10.1109/25.764995

Yacoub, M. D. (2000). Fading distributions and co-channel interference in wireless systems. *IEEE Antennas & Propagation Magazine.*, *42*(1), 150–159. doi:10.1109/74.826357

Yegani, P., & McGillem, C. D. (1991). A statistical model for the factory radio channel. *IEEE Transactions on Communications*, *39*(10), 1445–1454. doi:10.1109/26.103039

KEY TERMS AND DEFINITIONS

ASM: Accelerated Simulation Method proposed to reduce the simulation time by some orders of magnitude when compared with traditional methods, like Monte Carlo, while keeping the same precision.

Coding Performance: Performance of codes, usually expressed by its bit error ratio, for a given system and environment, expressed by its channel model.

Efficient Simulation: Simulation that is less time consuming, and if possible with lower computational requirements, when compared with classic simulation methods like Monte Carlo.

FEC: Forward error correction is a method commonly used in most digital data transmission systems to enable correction of some of the data symbols received, due to noise and interference introduced by the channel that separates the emitter from the receiver. This is usually done by an error correcting code that detects and corrects some of the symbols received, without the need for retransmission. These codes always introduce some redundancy to the transmitted symbols, which are then removed at the receiver to estimate the transmitted symbols. The performance of a given error correcting code depends on its characteristics and also the channel model, so it is often evaluated by simulation.

Hard-Decision Decoding: The decoding process is said to be "hard" when the signal at the input, or output, of the decoder is binary, i.e., a signal with only two quantization levels.

The Monte Carlo Simulation Method is a classic method to simulate the performance of a system in which all the required elements and system parameters are included for all time instants. Depending on the system under test: this may result in a complex method requiring high computational requirements and a long time to get accurate results

Radio Propagation Channel: This is the environment in which the radio signal carrying the data information travels from the emitter till the receiver. The radio signal, and therefore the information that it carries, is affected by thermal noise, antenna characteristics and several other effects that depend on that environment such as fading, shadowing, reflections, and other effects. which is usually described by a channel model that approaches the physical phenomena.

Soft-Decision Decoding: The decoding process is said to be "soft" when the signal at the

input, or output, of the decoder is quantized with more than two levels or is left unquantized.

Discrete Channel Model: The discrete channel model (DCM) maps an alphabet of M input symbols at the input of the channel to N output symbols at its output (N > M), so as to be used in the simulation chain. The DCM is modelled by the probability of each symbol at the input of the channel and by the set of transition probabilities caused by errors that depend on the randomness of the physical phenomena described in the radio propagation channel.

WCS: Wireless Communication System is a system in which the transmitter and the receiver are not physically connected by wires so the transmission is made using radio waves that propagate in the radio channel and carry the desired information.

NOTATION: SYMBOLS

Lowercase Roman Letters

a – Information word vector.

$\hat{\mathbf{a}}$ – Estimated information word vector.

b – Coded word vector.

$b(t)$ - Input sequence of symbols.

b_n - Transmitted symbols.

$\hat{b}_n(t)$ - Vector of bits estimated by the demodulator.

c - Velocity of light in vacuum.

d - Distance between transmitting and receiving antennas.

d_0 – Reference distance in the far field of the antenna.

e - Error.

e_b - Energy of bit.

ecc - Error correcting capacity of the code.

f - Frequency.

$f_{Af}(\alpha f)$ - Probability density function of the random variable of the fading, Af.

$f_{As}(\alpha s)$ - Probability density function of the random variable of the shadow attenuation, As.

f_c - Transmitted carrier's frequency of the bandpass signal.

f_D - Doppler frequency.

$f_L(l)$ - Probability density function of the random variable of the interval between consecutive errors, L.

$f_N(n)$ - Probability density function of the random variable of the additive white Gaussian noise, N.

$f_R(r)$ - Probability density function of the random variable of the received signal, R.

$f_{Re}(r)$ - Probability density function of the random variable of the received signal for values in error, Re.

$f_{Rne}(r)$ - Probability density function of the random variable of the received signal for values in non error, Rne.

$f_\Gamma(\gamma)$ - Probability density function of the random variable of the shadow power variation, Γ.

$f_1(t),\ f_2(t),\ f_j(t)$ - Base functions.

g - Error correcting capacity.

$g_e(\Theta, \Phi)$ - Transmitter antenna gain.

$g_r(\Theta, \Phi)$ - Receiver antenna gain.

k - Number of bits in an information word.

l_D - Decision threshold.

l_n - Length of path n.

m - Modulation symbols.

n – Number of bits in a code word.

ne – Non error.

r – Signal amplitude.

$\mathrm{rect}[\cdot]$ - Rectangular function.

$s_m(t)$ - Symbol m, corresponding to a set of bits of coded word, according to the used modulation.

t - Time.

t_0 - Reference time.

v - Velocity of terminal station.

Uppercase Roman Letters

BER - Bit error ratio.

$B\hat{E}R$ - Estimated bit error ratio.

D_n - Doppler shift.

E_b - Information bit energy.

E_s - Symbol energy.

E[N] - Average of noise amplitudes.

E(Af) - Average of the fading.

$F_L(l)$ - Cumulative probability density function of random variable L.

$F_R(r)$ - Cumulative probability density function of random variable R.

$F_{Re}(r)$ - Cumulative probability density function of random variable Re.

$F_{Rne}(r)$ - Cumulative probability density function of random variable Rne.

G   - Gain of the coded WCS.

$\tilde{I}_L(t)$ - Interfering source.

IWe - Information words with errors.

$IWne$ - Information words without errors.

L - Interval between two consecutive errors.

M - Number of constellation symbols.

N - Vector of the noise amplitudes.

NCW - Number of code words.

$NIBe$ - Number of information bits in error.

$NIBne$ - Number of information bits without error.

NIB_{TOTAL} - Total number of information bits.

$N(t)$ - Additive white Gaussian noise samples.

N_0 - Noise spectrum density.

N_1, N_2 - Noise samples.

PA - Processing advantage for the accelerated simulation method.

P_e - Probability of error.

R_l - Amplitude reference level.

R_a - Auxiliary variable.

R_b - Auxiliary variable.

R_e - Error samples.

R_I - In phase component of the demodulated amplitude.

R_{ne} - Non error samples.

R_Q - Quadrature component of the demodulated amplitude.

$R(t)$ - Received signal at the demodulator.

R - Vector with the random amplitudes of the received signal.

R_1, R_2 - Amplitudes for binary phase shift keying.

T - Received signal time exceeding the reference level.

T_s - Symbol time.

U - Uniform random variable.

$W(t)$ - Transmitted signal.

$\tilde{W}(t)$ - Complex envelope of transmitted signal.

$\tilde{X}(t)$ - Transmitted signal.

$\tilde{Y}(t)$ - Complex envelope of received signal plus interfering sources at the demodulator.

$\tilde{Z}_L(t)$ - Complex envelope of interfering signal.

$Z_0(t)$ - Received bandpass signal.

$\tilde{Z}_0(t)$ - Complex envelope of received signal.

Lowercase Greek Letters

af – Range of values for the random variable Af.

as – Range of values for the random variable As.

β – Parameter that characterizes the environment of communication systems.

δl_n - Variation of path length.

γ – Range of values for the random variable Γ.

$\mu_{\Gamma dB}$ - Average power variation due to shadowing in dB.

λ_c - Carrier wavelength of transmitted signal.

σ - Standard deviation of filtered additive white gaussian noise.

$\sigma^2_{\Gamma dB}$ - Power variance, due to shadowing, in dB.

σ^2_N - Noise variance at the correlator's output.

$\sigma^2_{\tilde{h}}$ - Variance of complex gain.

σ^2_{Afs} - Variance of the Rayleigh probability density function.

τ_n - Signal delay of path n.

π - Constant given by the ratio between perimeter and diameter of a circumference.

ϕ_m - Phase of m symbol.

φ_n - Carrier phase shift for the nth path.

Uppercase Greek Letters

A - Fading and attenuation due to shadowing that affects the signal.

Af - Fading that affects the signal.

A$p(d_0)_{dB}$ - Free space attenuation in the reference field, in dB.

A$p(d)$ - Free space attenuation for the transmitted signal as a function of distance.

Ap - Free space attenuation for the transmitted signal.

As - Attenuation due to shadowing for the transmitted signal.

Bf - Fading for interfering signal.

Bp - Free space attenuation for interfering signal.

Bs - Attenuation due to shadowing for interfering signal.

Γ - Random variable of the signal power variation, due to shadowing.

Θ - Azimuth angle.

Φ - Elevation angle.

Other Letters

$\Re[\cdot]$ - Real part.

Notation: ACRONYMS

ASM - Accelerated simulation method.

AWGN - Additive white Gaussian noise.

BER - Bit Error Ratio.

BPF - Band-pass filters.

BPSK – Binary phase shift keying.

CDMA - Code division multiple access.

CPDF – Cumulative probability density function.

DCM - Discrete channel model.

DEMOD. – Demodulator.

DSP – Digital signal processing.

FEC - Forward Error Correction.

HD - Hard-decision.

LTE - Long term evolution.

MCSM - Monte Carlo simulation method.

MOD – Modulator.

OFDM - Orthogonal frequency-division multiplexing.

PA – Processing advantage.

PDF – Probability density function.

PSK – Phase shift keying.

RV – Random variable.

SD - Soft-decision.

TCH – Tomlinson, Cercas and Hughes family of codes.

UMTS - Universal mobile telecommunications system.

WCS - Wireless communication systems.

Wi-Fi - Wireless fidelity.

WiMAX - Worldwide interoperability for microwave access.

ENDNOTES

[1] Variables p, s, f, represent path, shadowing and fading, respectively.

[2] Variable B is used to express the interfering signal.

[3] This phenomenon is characterized by a slow variation of the received amplitude of the signal during a long period or large distances between transmitter and receiver.

[4] This is used to describe the phenomena in which the amplitude and phase of the received signal, or its multi-path components, exhibit fast variations in very short periods of time or small distances between transmitter and receiver, in the order of a few wavelengths.

APPENDICES

Free Space Attenuation

Free space attenuation Ap depends essentially on frequency and distance. Assuming that in a radio communication link the carrier frequency remains approximately constant, we can emphasize its dependency on distance d between emitter and receiver as:

$$\mathrm{A}p\left(d\right) \propto \left(\frac{d}{d_0}\right)^{\beta}$$
(A.1)

where parameter β depends on the communication channel (Rappaport, 2002, p. 139, table 4.2). Considering d_0 as a reference distance in the distant zone of the antenna, we can express the average of Ap, in dB, as:

$$\mathrm{A}p\left(d\right)_{dB} = \mathrm{A}p\left(d_0\right)_{dB} + 10 \cdot \beta \cdot \log\left(\frac{d}{d_0}\right)$$
(A.2)

where the reference value $\mathrm{A}p\left(d_0\right)_{dB}$ can be obtained by evaluation of the electromagnetic field.

Attenuation Due to Shadowing

This phenomenon occurs due to several physical propagation effects that take place when obstacles interfere in the normal path of electromagnetic waves. For example, diffraction occurs at the edges of buildings or similar objects, reflections take place in the terrain and other objects like buildings, dispersion may occur in the soil, trees, buildings, bridges, etc., refraction may occur with walls and windows and absorption may occur in green zones like forests or parks. The coexistence of all these effects may have a slow (small scale) or fast variation in time (large scale). The random nature of this phenomenon results in a variation of the received power signal, centred on its average value. (Hansen & Meno, 1977) which is the corresponding free space attenuation and is deterministic. Its stochastic behaviour can be characterized by a lognormal PDF, that is, it follows a normal PDF in which its results are expressed using logarithmic units.

The physical phenomena behind the lognormal distribution include all effects previously identified, which interfere with electromagnetic waves in a given environment. As a result, electromagnetic waves travel through different and independent paths until they reach the receiver. Considering that there is a great number of signal contributions arriving from independent paths, they converge at the receiver, where they are added, to a signal that can be characterized by a random variable with Gaussian distribution (central limit theorem) (Helstrom, 1984, pp. 223-227). This is usually represented by the power of the received signal in decibels (dB). Some authors related the PDF of the received signals with experimental results (Suzuki, 1977); French, 1979; Hansen & Meno, 1977). According to this last author, the average power of the received signal, γ, follows a lognormal distribution given by:

$$f_\Gamma\left(\gamma\right) = \frac{10}{\sqrt{2\pi} \cdot \sigma_{\gamma\text{dB}} \cdot \ln\left(10\right) \cdot \gamma} \cdot \exp\left(-\frac{\left(10 \cdot \log_{10}\left(\gamma\right) - \mu_{\gamma\text{dB}}\right)^2}{2\,\sigma_{\gamma\text{dB}}^2}\right) \cdot \text{u}\left(\gamma\right)$$

(B.1)

where $\mu_{\gamma dB}$ and $\sigma_{\gamma dB}^2$ are the average and variance, respectively, of the received signal power affected by shadowing, in dB. The step function u(γ) is used since the lognormal PDF only makes sense for nonnegative values.

Sometimes it is useful to know the amplitude of the received signal just characterized by a power variation due to shadowing γ. Based on its equation, and using some manipulation, it was possible to derive an expression for the PDF of the corresponding amplitude of the signal, A*s*, which can be expressed as:

$$f_{\text{A}s}\left(\alpha s\right) = \frac{20}{\sqrt{\pi} \cdot \sigma_{\gamma\text{dB}} \cdot \ln\left(10\right) \cdot \alpha s} \cdot \exp\left(-\frac{\left(10 \cdot \log_{10}\left(\alpha s^2/2\right) - \mu_{\gamma\text{dB}}\right)^2}{2\,\sigma_{\gamma\text{dB}}^2}\right) \cdot \text{u}\left(\alpha s\right)$$

(B.2)

Attenuation Due to Fading

The phenomenon responsible for this type of attenuation, A*f*, usually known as fading, is dispersion of the electromagnetic wave in the surrounding environment which originates multipath propagation. Fading produces a variation in the amplitude and/or phase of the received signal and can be verified in the time or frequency domain. This variation can be fast or slow depending on several factors such as the velocity of the surrounding objects, or even the receiver, number and type of objects and communication distance.

A typical radio propagation channel considers n different paths length l_n. Each of these signal replicas arrive at the receiver with delay $\tau_n = l_n/c$. Let us define A*f*$_n$ as the fading associated with the signal arriving from path n. If we assume that all objects are static, including emitter, receiver and all objects in the environment, then its effect on the channel is only delay spread with different attenuation factor and the channel is said to be time invariant. On the other hand, if the different paths vary with time, the channel is said to be time variant and therefore A*f*$_n$ and τ_n change with time.

As we can see in the general model for the propagation channel shown in Figure 3, the mathematical characterization of fading considers the transmission of a bandpass signal with a carrier frequency f_c and complex envelope $\tilde{W}\left(t\right)$. Since we want to concentrate our attention on the characterization of fading, we omit by now the attenuation due to the other effects (free space and shadowing), so the bandpass signal can be written as:

$$W\left(t\right) = \Re\left[\tilde{W}\left(t\right) \cdot \exp\left(j2\pi f_c t\right)\right]$$

(C.1)

and the received signal as:

$$Z_0(t) = \Re\left[\tilde{Z}_0(t) \cdot \exp\left(j2\pi f_c t\right)\right] \tag{C.2}$$

where $\Re[\cdot]$ is the real part operator.

In these conditions, and assuming that all objects are static, the received signal $Z_0(t)$ can be written as:

$$Z_0(t) = \sum_{n=0}^{N} Af_n \cdot W\left(t - \frac{l_n}{c}\right) = \Re\left[\sum_{n=0}^{N} Af_n \cdot \tilde{W}\left(t - \frac{l_n}{c}\right) \cdot \exp\left[j2\pi f_c\left(t - \frac{l_n}{c}\right)\right]\right] \tag{C.3}$$

The complex envelop of the lowpass equivalent of this signal, relating wavelength and carrier frequency by $\lambda_c = c/f_c$, can be written as:

$$\tilde{Z}_0(t) = \sum_{n=0}^{N} Af_n \; \tilde{W}\left(t - \frac{l_n}{c}\right) \cdot \exp\left(-j2\pi \frac{l_n}{\lambda_c}\right) \tag{C.4}$$

Equation (C.4) shows that the phase shift of the carrier from path n is $\varphi_n \equiv 2\pi\left(l_n/\lambda_c\right)$. Therefore the delay associated with the nth path τ_n is l_n/c and we can rewrite (C.4) as:

$$\tilde{Z}_0(t) = \sum_{n=0}^{N} Af_n \cdot \tilde{W}\left(t - \tau_n\right) \cdot \exp\left(-j\varphi_n\right) \tag{C.5}$$

Equation (C.5) clearly shows that the lowpass equivalent of the received signal depends on the attenuation, phase shift and delay associated with each replica of the signal arriving from path n.

A more generic mathematical model can be achieved using the modifications proposed in (Aulin, 1979) for the two dimensional model presented in (Clarke, 1968). This considers a model with the gain of transmitting or receiving antennas in which the signal can arrive from any direction defined by its azimuth Θ and elevation angle Φ. This model also considers movement, so the static restriction was removed.

Therefore, and defining the velocity of the receiver terminal as v, the length variation of path n can be written as:

$$\delta l_n = -v \cdot \left(t - t_0\right) \cdot \cos\left(\Theta_n\right) \cdot \sin\left(\Phi_n\right) \tag{C.6}$$

and the complex envelope of the received signal expressed by equation (C.5) can be written as:

$$\tilde{Z}_0(t) = \sum_{n=0}^{N} Af_n \cdot \tilde{W}\left(t - \frac{l_n + \delta l_n}{c}\right) \cdot \exp\left[-j2\pi\left(\frac{l_n + \delta l_n}{\lambda_c}\right)\right] \tag{C.7}$$

which can be expressed in the form:

$$\tilde{Z}_0\left(t\right) = \sum_{n=0}^{N} Af_n \cdot \tilde{W}\left(t - \tau_n + \frac{v \cdot \left(t - t_0\right) \cdot \cos\left(\Theta_n\right) \cdot \sin\left(\Phi_n\right)}{c}\right) \cdot$$
$$\cdot \exp\left(-j\varphi_n\right) \cdot \exp\left[j2\pi \cos\left(\Theta_n\right) \cdot \sin\left(\Phi_n\right) \cdot \left(\frac{v}{\lambda_c}\right) \cdot \left(t - t_0\right)\right]$$

(C.8)

This equation can be simplified using $\tilde{A}f_n = Af_n \cdot \exp\left(-j\varphi_n\right)$ and assuming that:

$$\frac{v \cdot \left(t - t_0\right) \cdot \cos\left(\Theta_n\right) \cdot \sin\left(\Phi_n\right)}{c} << \tau_n$$

(C.9)

By introducing the frequency shift due to movement or Doppler shift f_D, at carrier frequency $f = f_c$, (Jakes, 1974, p. 20), that is:

$$f_D = f_c \frac{v}{c}$$

(C.10)

The Doppler shift associated with the n_{th} path can be expressed as:

$$D_n = \cos\left(\Theta_n\right) \sin\left(\Phi_n\right) f_D$$

(C.11)

so we can express the complex envelop of the lowpass equivalent of the received signal as:

$$\tilde{Z}_0\left(t\right) = \sum_{n=0}^{N} \tilde{A}f_n \cdot \tilde{W}\left(t - \tau_n\right) \cdot \exp\left(j2\pi D_n t\right)$$

(C.12)

This equation defines the propagation channel, emphasizing the effects of Doppler shift and delay spread, and it is of major importance for the characterization of the DCM.

Demodulated Amplitude in a Discrete Channel Model

A general expression for the received, and demodulated, signal in a WCS using a DCM is expressed by equation (D.1). The demodulator can be represented by a bank of correlators and its associated base functions to obtain the demodulated signal $R(t)$ (Proakis, 2001, pp. 232-236). For example, in PSK modulation with a modulation index $M \geq 2$ there are two base functions.

$$R = \int_0^{T_s} \left\{ \begin{array}{l} \left[\begin{array}{l} g_e\left(\Theta,\Phi\right)\sum_{n=0}^{N}\Re\left\{ \begin{array}{l} Ap_n \cdot As_n \cdot Af_n \cdot b\left(t\right)\cdot\exp\text{j}\left(2\pi f_c\left(t-\dfrac{l_n}{c}\right)\right)\cdot \\ \cdot\exp\left(-\text{j}\varphi_n\right)\cdot\exp\left(\text{j}2\pi\cdot D_n\cdot t\right) \end{array} \right\}\cdot \\ \cdot g_r\left(\Theta_n,\Phi_n\right)+\sum_{l=1}^{L}\sum_{k=0}^{K}\left\{ \begin{array}{l} \Re\left\{ Bp_k \cdot Bs_k \cdot \tilde{B}f_k \cdot \tilde{I}_l\left(t-\dfrac{l_k}{c}\right)\exp\left(\text{j}2\pi\cdot D_k\cdot t\right)\right\}\cdot \\ \cdot g_r\left(\Theta_k,\Phi_k\right) \end{array} \right\} \\ \cdot\left[\sqrt{\dfrac{2}{T_s}}\cdot\cos\left(2\pi f_c t\right)-\sqrt{\dfrac{2}{T_s}}\cdot\sin\left(2\pi f_c t\right)\right] \end{array} \right] \end{array} \right\}dt + N$$

(D.1)

In this expression we have:

$$b\left(t\right) = \sum_{n=-\infty}^{+\infty} b_n \cdot \text{rect}\left(\frac{t-nT_s}{T_s}\right)$$

(D.2)

and

$$b_n = \sqrt{\frac{2E_s}{T_s}}\cdot\exp\left(j\phi_m\right), \qquad \phi_m = \frac{2\pi}{M}\left(m-1\right), \quad \left(m=1,...,M\right)$$

(D.3)

where M is the modulation index, $\sqrt{2E_s/T_s}$ is the carrier amplitude, E_s is the symbol energy and T_s is the symbol time. The energy of an information bit E_b is related to E_s by $E_b = E_s/\log_2\left(M\right)$. N is a vector containing the random amplitudes of noise at the output of the demodulator after low-pass filtering. Since the noise that entered this filter, assumed linear, is Gaussian, then the noise at its output is also Gaussian, (Haykin, 2001, pp. 56, *property* 1) and (Proakis, 2001, pp. 234), with $E\left[N\right]=0$ and $\sigma_N^2 = N_0/2$, where $N_0/2$ is the power spectral density of noise $N(t)$ (Haykin, 2001, pp. 318-322).

The complex envelope for the received signal with the DCM shown in Figure 2, will now be deduced with a few assumptions. First of all we assume PSK modulation, so a PSK will be used. We also assume non-selective fading in the frequency domain, *i.e.*, $1_n/c \ll T_s$, we assume that this fading is slow, *i.e.* $T_s \ll 1/f_D$ and therefore it remains constant for at least a symbol duration. We also assume that the antenna presents a constant gain for all multipath signals involved, we do not consider interfering signals and the attenuation due to shadowing follows a lognormal PDF.

We also define the amplitude attenuation that affects a given symbol, due to fading and shadowing, with random variables Af and As, respectively. Fading also produces a random variation in the signal phase. In the analysis of communication systems, it is often assumed that random changes in the signal phase are not relevant and can be corrected in the receiver, namely if we use an ideal coherent receiver. On the other hand, if the modulation does not require a coherent receiver, then its random change does not affect the receiver performance (Simon, 2000, pp. 15-16) and so it can be neglected. Therefore we can simplify equation (D.1) to:

$$R = \int_0^{T_s} \left\{ \left[As \cdot Af \cdot \sqrt{\frac{2E_s}{T_s}} \cdot \cos\left(2\pi f_c t + \phi_m\right) \right] \cdot \left[\sqrt{\frac{2}{T_s}} \cos\left(2\pi f_c t\right) - \sqrt{\frac{2}{T_s}} \sin\left(2\pi f_c t\right) \right] \right\} dt + N$$

(D.4)

which can be written in the simple form:

$$R = \sqrt{E_s} \cdot As \cdot Af \cdot \begin{bmatrix} R_a & R_b \end{bmatrix} + N$$

(D.5)

where

$$R_a = \cos\left(\phi_m\right) - \frac{1}{4\pi f_c}\left(\sin\left(\phi_m\right)\right) + \sin\left(\phi_m + 4\pi f_c T_s\right)$$

(D.6)

and

$$R_b = \sin\left(\phi_m\right) - \frac{1}{4\pi f_c}\left(\cos\left(\phi_m\right)\right) + \cos\left(\phi_m + 4\pi f_c T_s\right)$$

(D.7)

Assuming that $T_s = N_c / f_c$, where N_c is an integer, and assuming BPSK modulation, we can further simplify equation (D.5) to:

$$\begin{bmatrix} R_1 \\ R_2 \end{bmatrix} = \begin{bmatrix} \sqrt{E_s} \cdot As \cdot Af \\ -\sqrt{E_s} \cdot As \cdot Af \end{bmatrix} + \begin{bmatrix} N_1 \\ N_2 \end{bmatrix}$$

(D.8)

where R_1 e R_2 are demodulated amplitudes corresponding to transmitted symbols s_1 and s_2, respectively. N_1 and N_2 are random variables with Gaussian distribution with $E[N] = 0$ and $\sigma_N^2 = N_0/2$.

Error's Occurrence Position

The occurrence of errors in the channel is directly related to the power, or amplitude, of the received signal. In the analysis of positions where errors in the DCM are more likely to occur, we assume that they correspond to periods for which the amplitude of the received signal r is below a given reference threshold level R_l and that these periods have a geometric distribution. For this model we sample the received amplitude of the signal every symbol period, that is, at the symbol frequency, as shown in Figure 12. Defining T as an independent random variable that accounts for the time in which the signal

Figure 12. Sampling process of the received signal amplitude affected by fading.

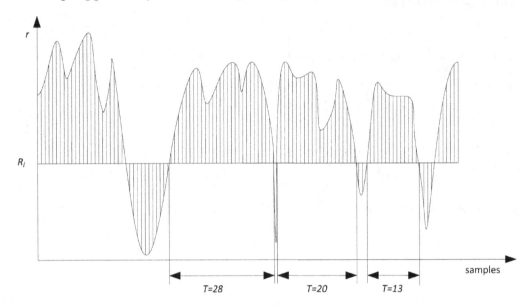

is above R_p that is a number of n integer symbol periods in which that condition is verified, then we can express its probability of occurrence as:

$$\Pr\left(T = n\right) = \left[\Pr\left(r \geq R_l\right)\right]^n \cdot \Pr\left(r < R_l\right)$$

(E.1)

which is a geometric distribution (Ross, 1987).

As shown in Figure 12, the amplitude of the received signal is sampled every T_s and the number of symbols not affected by fading in each interval, i.e. when $r > R_p$, is given by $T = nT_s$. Therefore, the number of symbols considered, it depends both on the symbol rate and reference level R_l. For the example depicted in the Figure 12, we show a sequence for n=28, 20 and 13 consecutive symbol periods not affected by fading.

Then, the probability of transmitting a sequence of $l-1 = n$ sequential symbols in the channel without error, for example a sequence corresponding to l transmitted zeros, is given by the geometric PDF:

$$f_L\left(l\right) = \left(1 - P_e\right)^{l-1} \cdot P_e, \quad l = 1, 2, \ldots$$

(E.2)

where L is the RV defining the interval between errors and Pe is the channel probability of error, sometimes referred to as transition probability. The corresponding CPDF is given by:

$$F_L\left(l\right) = \sum_{i=1}^{n} \left(1 - P_e\right)^{i-1} P_e$$

(E.3)

So

$$F_L\left(l\right) = \sum_{i=1}^{n}\left(1-P_e\right)^{i-1} P_e \qquad (E.4)$$

which can be simplified to:

$$F_L\left(l\right) = 1-\left(1-P_e\right)^l, \quad P_e \neq 0 \qquad (E.5)$$

and using the analytical transformation method referred in (Jeruchim, Balaban & Shanmugan, 2001, pp. 377-378), we have

$$\left(1-P_e\right)^l = 1-U \qquad (E.6)$$

where U is an uniform RV. After some manipulation we can write:

$$L = \frac{\log(1-U)}{\log(1-P_e)} \qquad (E.7)$$

Considering that both (1-U) and U are RVs with the same uniform distribution and L only takes integer values, equation (E.7) can be expressed as:

$$L = \frac{\log(U)}{\log(1-P_e)} \qquad (E.8)$$

in which $\lceil \; \rceil$ denotes the "integer greater or equal to" operator.

Amplitude Samples for the Received Signal

Once the positions of the erroneous symbols in the transmitted sequence in the channel are known, we need to generate R samples with amplitudes in accordance with that condition, that is, samples that are likely to cause errors (*Re*), as well as samples that do not cause errors (*Rne*), for the remaining positions. These samples are generated according to the corresponding PDF of $A = Af \cdot As$ that models the amplitudes of the digital channel.

For simplicity, and assuming that $s_1(t) = +1$, the PDFs of the generated samples are given by:

$$f_{Re}\left(r\right) = \Pr\left(A \cdot s_1\left(t\right) + N < 0\right) = \frac{f_R\left(r\right)}{F_R\left(0\right)} \cdot u\left(-r\right) \qquad (F.1)$$

and

$$f_{Rne}\left(r\right) = \Pr\left(A \cdot s_1\left(t\right) + N > 0\right) = \frac{f_R\left(r\right)}{1 - F_R\left(0\right)} \cdot u\left(r\right)$$

(F.2)

where $u(r)$ is the step function.

Assuming that Af and As are statistically independent, its PDF is given by (Helstrom, 1984, pp. 139-147):

$$f_A\left(\alpha\right) = \int\limits_{-\infty}^{\infty} \frac{1}{\left|\alpha s\right|} \cdot f_{As}\left(\frac{\alpha}{\alpha s}\right) \cdot f_{Af}\left(\alpha s\right) d\alpha s$$

(F.3)

Since A and N are independent RVs, the PDF of the received signal amplitudes R, $f_R(r)$, can be obtained using the convolution of their PDFs, which can be easily evaluated using their characteristic function (Papoulis, 1984, pp. 155-158).

The probability of error when $s_1(t) = +1$ can be achieved by:

$$F_{Re}\left(0\right) = \int\limits_{-\infty}^{a} f_R\left(r\right) dr$$

(F.4)

The CPDFs of *Re* and *Rne* are given, respectively, by:

$$F_{Re}\left(a\right) = \int\limits_{-\infty}^{a} f_{Re}\left(r\right) dr$$

(F.5)

and

$$F_{Rne}\left(a\right) = \int\limits_{0}^{a} f_{Rne}\left(r\right) dr$$

(F.6)

Finally, the desired samples are evaluated by $Re = F_{Re}^{-1}\left(U\right)$ and $Rne = F_{Rne}^{-1}\left(U\right)$ using the transformation method (analytical or empirical) described in [Jeruchim, Balaban & Shanmugan, 2000, pp. 377-380]. When sending the other symbol, i.e., $s_2(t) = -1$, the generation of these *Re* and *Rne* samples follows exactly the same procedure, except that they are multiplied by -1 at the end.

Application Example for Fading with Rayleigh Distribution and Additive White Gaussian Noise

Let us consider that the amplitude A = Af follows a Rayleigh distribution described by its PDF:

$$f_{Af}\left(\alpha f\right) = \frac{\alpha f}{\sigma_{\tilde{h}}^{2}} \cdot \exp\left(-\frac{\alpha f^{2}}{2 \cdot \sigma_{\tilde{h}}^{2}}\right) \cdot u\left(\alpha f\right)$$

(G.1)

where σ_h is the standard deviation of the propagation channel and u(αf), denotes the step function, in which αf is the range of values for the RV Af.

Similarly, consider that noise samples follow a Gaussian PDF:

$$f_{N}\left(n\right) = \frac{1}{\sqrt{2\pi}\sigma} \cdot \exp\left(-\frac{n^{2}}{2\sigma^{2}}\right)$$

(G.2)

where σ is the standard deviation of the filtered AWGN and n is the range of values for RV N.

Since the performance of a given WCS is usually expressed by its BER and this one can be written as a function of the ratio between the received energy per information bit E_b and the power spectral density of noise N_0, E_b/N_0, it is useful to express the RVs as a function of it. By doing so, and considering the normalization $e_b = 1$ $[E_b = 10\log_{10}(e_b)]$, its standard deviation σ can be expressed as:

$$\sigma = \frac{1}{\sqrt{2 \cdot 10^{\left(E_b/N_0\right)/10}}}$$

(G.3)

It is useful to express the fading samples as a function of the average fading, E(Af):

$$E\left(Af\right) = \int_{0}^{\infty} \alpha f \cdot f_{Af}\left(\alpha f\right) d\alpha f = \sigma_{\tilde{h}} \cdot \sqrt{\frac{\pi}{2}}$$

(G.4)

that can also be written as

$$\sigma_{\tilde{h}} = \frac{10^{\left(\frac{E\left(Af\right)_{dB}}{10}\right)}}{\sqrt{\frac{\pi}{2}}}$$

(G.5)

where $E\left(Af\right)_{dB} = 10 \cdot \log_{10}\left(E\left(Af\right)\right)$. The variance of the Rayleigh PDF is then given by:

$$\sigma_{Af}^{2} = \sigma_{\tilde{h}}^{2} \cdot \left(\frac{4-\pi}{2}\right)$$

(G.6)

We can now express $f_R(r)$ as a function of these variances:

$$f_R(r) = \frac{\exp\left(-\frac{r^2}{2\sigma^2}\right) \cdot \begin{bmatrix} 2\sigma^2\sqrt{\frac{1}{\sigma^2} + \frac{1}{\sigma_{\tilde{h}}^2}} + \exp\left(\frac{\sigma_{\tilde{h}}^2\, r^2}{2\sigma^4 + 2\sigma^2\sigma_{\tilde{h}}^2}\right)\sqrt{2\pi}\cdot r + \\ + \exp\left(\frac{\sigma_{\tilde{h}}^2\, r^2}{2\sigma^4 + 2\sigma^2\sigma_{\tilde{h}}^2}\right)\sqrt{2\pi}\cdot r\cdot \mathrm{erf}\left(\frac{\sigma_{\tilde{h}}^2\cdot\sqrt{\frac{1}{\sigma^2}+\frac{1}{\sigma_{\tilde{h}}^2}}\cdot r}{\sqrt{2}\cdot\left(\sigma^2+\sigma_{\tilde{h}}^2\right)}\right) \end{bmatrix}}{\left(2\sigma\cdot\sqrt{\frac{1}{\sigma^2}+\frac{1}{\sigma_{\tilde{h}}^2}}\cdot\left(\sigma^2+\sigma_{\tilde{h}}^2\right)\cdot\sqrt{2\pi}\right)}\cdot u(-r)$$

(G.7)

For BPSK modulation, matrix s has two terms: $s_1(t) = +1$ and $s_2(t) = +1$, for information bits "0" and "1", respectively. Considering that these symbols are equiprobable, and the decision threshold is assumed to be zero, the probability of error in the channel is obtained from the CPDF of the received signal R, i.e., $P_e = F_R(0)$. Substituting equation (G.7) in (F.4) and after some mathematical manipulation, we can express the probability of error as:

$$F_R(0) = \frac{1}{2}\left(1 - \frac{\sigma_h}{\sqrt{\sigma^2 + \sigma_h^2}}\right)$$

(G.8)

which agrees with the results presented in (Proakis, 2001, pp. 155-158).

The derivation of the CPDFs for *Re* and *Rne* using a Rayleigh distribution can be obtained from equation (G.9). After some algebraic manipulation:

Figure 13. CPDF $F_{Re}(r)$ for $E_b / N_0 = 10dB$ and three fading values

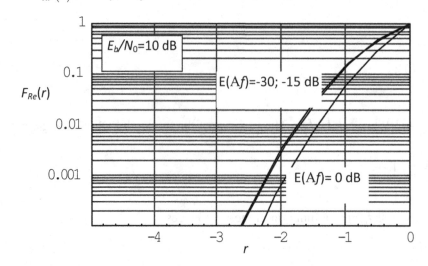

$$F_{Re}\left(r\right) = \frac{\left[\begin{array}{l}\left\{\dfrac{\sigma_{\tilde{h}}^2}{\sigma^2+\sigma_{\tilde{h}}^2}\left[1-\exp\left(-\dfrac{r^2}{2\left(\sigma^2+\sigma_{\tilde{h}}^2\right)}\right)\cdot\left(1+\operatorname{erf}\left(\dfrac{\sigma_{\tilde{h}}^2\cdot r}{\sqrt{2}\cdot\left(\sigma^2+\sigma_{\tilde{h}}^2\right)}\right)\right)\right]\right\}+ \\ +\dfrac{\sigma^2}{\sigma^2+\sigma_{\tilde{h}}^2}+\operatorname{erf}\left(\dfrac{r}{\sqrt{2}\sigma}\right)\end{array}\right]}{2\cdot F_R\left(0\right)}\cdot u\left(-r\right)$$

(G.9)

Similarly, and using equation (G.9), the CPDF for *Rne* gives:

$$F_{Rne}\left(r\right) = \frac{\left\{\left\{\dfrac{\sigma_{\tilde{h}}}{\left(\sigma^2+\sigma_{\tilde{h}}^2\right)}\left[1-\exp\left(-\dfrac{r^2}{2\left(\sigma^2+\sigma_{\tilde{h}}^2\right)}\right)\cdot\left(1+\operatorname{erf}\left(\dfrac{\sigma_{\tilde{h}}\cdot r}{2\cdot\sigma\cdot\left(\sigma^2+\sigma_{\tilde{h}}^2\right)}\right)\right)\right]\right\}+\operatorname{erf}\left(\dfrac{r}{\sqrt{2}\sigma}\right)\right\}}{2\cdot\left(1-F_R\left(0\right)\right)}\cdot u\left(r\right)$$

(G.10)

The expressions for RVs *Re* and *Rne*, are simply obtained by inverting the previous equations.

Figure 13 and Figure 14 plot the analytical expressions derived for the CPDF of *Re*, considering $E_b/N_0 = 10\text{dB}$ and $E_b/N_0 = 30\text{dB}$, respectively. Figure 13 shows that 99% of the *Re* samples have amplitudes greater than −1.4 and -1.7 for $\mathrm{E}\left(Af\right) = 0\text{dB}$ and $\mathrm{E}\left(Af\right) = -15\text{dB}$; -30dB, respectively. In a similar way, Figure 15 and Figure 16 show the PDF of *Rne* samples considering $\mathrm{E}\left(Af\right) = 0\text{dB}$ and $\mathrm{E}\left(Af\right) = -20\text{dB}$, respectively. Figure 15 shows that 50% of the *Rne* samples have amplitudes greater than 1.0 and 2.0 for $E_b/N_0 = 15\text{dB}$; 30dB and $E_b/N_0 = 0\text{dB}$, respectively. About 90% of the samples are lower than 2.0 and 4.0 for $E_b/N_0 = 15\text{dB}$; 30dB e 0dB, respectively. The probability of having more samples with small amplitude is then greater. Namely, we can observe that 90% of the

Figure 14. CPDF $F_{Re}\left(r\right)$ for $E_b / N_0 = 30dB$ and three fading values

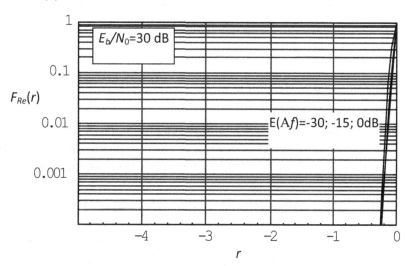

Figure 15. CPDF $F_{Rne}(r)$ *for* $E(Afs) = 0\text{dB}$ *and three* E_b / N_0 *values*

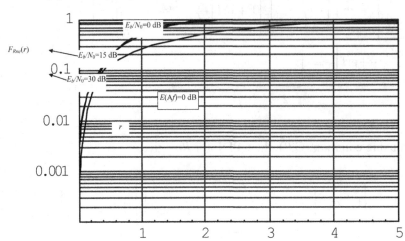

Figure 16. CPDF $F_{Rne}(r)$ *for* $\mathrm{E}(Afs) = -20\text{dB}$ *and three* E_b / N_0 *values*

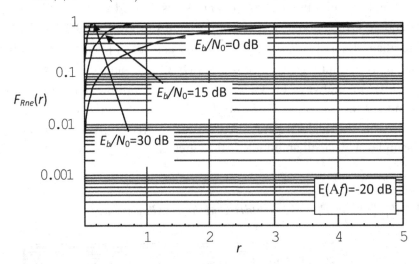

Rne samples are smaller than +0.2, +0.6, +3.8, for $E_b/N_0 = 30\text{dB}$; 15dB and 0dB, respectively. At low E_b/N_0 values these samples are more diverse.

From these results we conclude that *Re* samples depend more on E_b/N_0 while *Rne* samples depend more on the average fading E(A*f*). This fact can be easily explained since the Gaussian PDF has a greater contribution to samples that are able to produce errors (*Re*) and the Rayleigh PDF on those who don't (*Rne*).

The evaluation of the distribution functions for RVs *Re* and *Rne* is a fundamental task using the ASM for estimating the performance of block codes with SD decoding. Once they are obtained, it is an easy task to generate the amplitude samples corresponding to the potential cases of error or non-error as described. Since the generated *Re* and *Rne* samples play a crucial role in the presented ASM method and its

Figure 17. Theoretical and simulated distribution of the Rne random variable, considering several average fading values

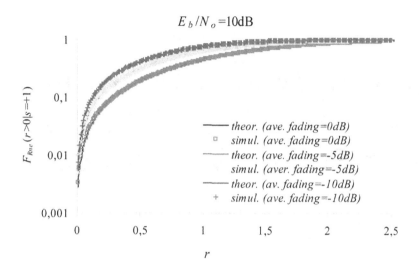

Figure 18. Theoretical and simulated distribution of the Re random variable, considering several average fading values

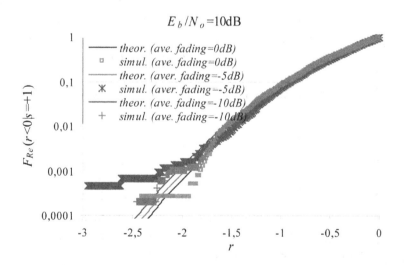

precision, Figure 17 and Figure 18 show their distribution, using some deduced theoretical expressions and simulated results. As we can observe, the match is nearly perfect, which is an important indication for the validation of the simulation results obtainable with this simulation method.

Chapter 8
Teaching Principles of Petri Nets in Hardware Courses and Students Projects

Hana Kubátová
Czech Technical University in Prague, Czech Republic

ABSTRACT

The paper presents the principles of using Petri Net formalism in hardware design courses, especially in the course "Architecture of peripheral devices". Several models and results obtained by student individual or group projects are mentioned. First the using of formalism as a modeling tool is presented consecutively from Place/Transition nets to Coloured Petri nets. Then the possible Petri Nets using as a hardware specification for direct hardware implementation (synthesized VHDL for FPGA) is described. Implementation and simulation results of three directly implemented models are presented.

INTRODUCTION

Petri nets (PN) are a well established mechanism for system modeling. They are a mathematically defined formal model, and can be subjected to a large variety of systems. PN based models have been widely used due to their ease of understanding, declarative, logic based and modular modeling principles, and finally because they can be represented graphically. Since Petri nets began to be exploited in the 1960s, many different types of models have been introduced and used. The most popular models are presented in this paper, their main advantages are shown and the dif-

ferences between them are mentioned. Everything is described according the teaching of formal methods used in digital systems design especially during the design of peripheral devices of computers, where some asynchronous and parallel actions without any coupling to internal clock frequency have to be designed and modeled.

This basic knowledge and method of the model construction is enlarged and exploited in student group projects. Petri net based models have been used e.g. in the design of a processor or a control system architecture with special properties, e.g. fault-tolerant or fault-secure, hardware-software co-design, computer networks architecture, etc. This has led to the development of PN models in

DOI: 10.4018/978-1-60566-774-4.ch008

some Petri net design tools and then the analysis and simulation of models using these tools. After this high-level design has been developed and validated it becomes possible, through automatic translation to a Hardware Description Language obviously used in digital hardware design (VHDL or Verilog design languages), to employ proper implementation in a programmable hardware (FPGA – field programmable gate array or CPLD – complex programmable logic device).

Our students have been teaching and making many experiments based on the massive using of FPGA or CPLD development kit. They have practical skills from the 3rd semester of bachelor studies (Kubátová, 2005; Bečvář, 2006). It enables a custom device to be rapidly prototyped and tested (however the ASIC implementation is also possible). An FPGA version of a digital circuit is likely to be slower than the equivalent ASIC version, due to the regularly structured FPGA wiring channels compared to the ASIC custom logic. However, the easier custom design changes, the possibility of easy FPGA reconfiguration, and relatively easy manipulation make FPGAs very good final implementation bases for our experiments. This is most important due to strict time schedule of these student group projects – everything must be finished during one semester.

Most models used in the hardware design process are equivalent to the Finite State Machine (FSM), (Adamski, 2001; Erhard, 2001; Gomes, 2001; Uzam, 2001). It is said that the resulting hardware must be deterministic, but we have found real models that are not equivalent to an FSM. Therefore we have concentrated on those models with really concurrent actions, with various types of dependencies (mutual exclusion, parallel, scheduled), and have studied their hardware implementation.

Petri nets are a good platform and tool in the "multiple-level" design process. They can serve as a specification language on all levels of specifications, and as a formal verification tool throughout these specification and architectural

description levels. The first problem to be solved during the design process is the construction of a good model, which will enable the specification and further handling and verification of the different levels of this design. Therefore this paper presents such model constructions on the basis of a number of simple examples. These experiments can use the automatic translation process from PNML language to the synthesized VHDL description that can be easily implemented in FPGA. We have used universal VHDL description divided into several blocks. The blocks can be easily modified.

The paper is organized as follows. The brief description of used hardware and software tools is in section 2. Section 3 contains the concrete example and construction of its models by Petri nets of several types. The brief description of experiments for the dinning philosophers' problem, the producer-consumer PN model and a railway critical rail are described in section 4. Section 5 concludes the paper.

TECHNOLOGY AND DESIGN TOOLS

Xilinx and Altera are two most significant companies in the market of programmable devices. Their products, including circuits, design kits and development systems, are comparable. As Xilinx provides better university support, we have decided to use Xilinx products. ISE 7.1i is the development system in which students design their circuits. Our students have practical skills with the design kits Digilent XCRP (Digilent, 2009), equipped with CPLD Xilinx CoolRunner XCR3064 (Xilinx, 2009) and FPGA Xilinx Spartan2E.

ModelSim simulator is used for simulation. In introductory and intermediate course students simulate designs created in Xilinx ISE. In advanced course designs are created in HDL Designer and then again simulated in ModelSim.

Figure 1. The Petri net model of two printers working in parallel

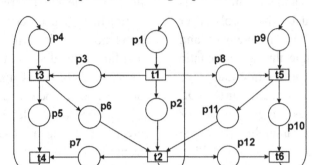

Petri net models construction, analysis and simulations are performed by the Petri net software tools Design/CPN, (CPN Tools, 2009), JARP, (Jarp Petri Nets Analyzer Home Page, (2009), CPN Tools, (Coloured Petri Nets at the University of Aarhus, (2009). The MICROSOFT based or UNIX based platforms is allowed.

PETRI NET DEFINITIONS AND EXAMPLES USED IN COURSES

Petri nets can be introduced in many ways, according to their numerous features and various applications (Girault, 2003). Many attempts have been made to define the principles of basic types of Petri nets. The way chosen here involves a brief introduction to the basic principles and to the hierarchical construction of the most complicated and widely used Petri net based models used in professional software tools. The example is chosen to explain to our students the necessity of some formalism in hardware design.

Example and its Model

The essential features of Petri nets are the principles of duality, locality, concurrency, graphical and algebraic representation (Girault, 2003). These notions will be presented on a simple model of a handshake used by printers communicating with a control unit that transmits data according to

the handshake scheme. The control unit uses the control signal STROBE to signal "data valid" to the target units – printers, receivers. The printer's signal "data is printing" to the control unit by ACK signals. After the falling edge of a STROBE signal, all printers must react by the falling edges of ACK signals to obtain the next portion of data (e.g., a byte). Our Petri net will model cooperation between only two printers A, and B, with one control unit C, see Figure 1.

Following essential conditions and actions have been identified:

- List of conditions:
  - p1: control unit C has a byte prepared for printing
  - p2: control unit C is waiting for signals ACK
  - p3: control unit C is sending a byte and a STROBE signal to printer A
  - p4: printer A is ready to print
  - p5: printer A is printing a byte
  - p6: printer A sends ACK signal
  - p7: control unit C sends STROBE = 0 to A
  - p8: control unit C is sending a byte and a STROBE signal to printer B
  - p9: printer B is ready to print
  - p10: printer B is printing a byte
  - p11: printer A sends ACK signal
  - p12: control unit C sends STROBE = 0 to B

Figure 2. Initial state of the Petri net from figure

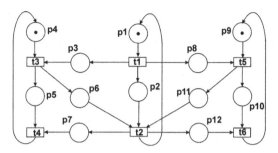

- • List of actions:
  - ○ t1: control unit C sends STROBE = 1
  - ○ t2: control unit C sends STROBE = 0
  - ○ t3: printer A sends ACK = 1
  - ○ t4: printer A sends ACK = 0
  - ○ t5: printer B sends ACK = 1
  - ○ t1: printer B sends ACK = 0

Separating or identifying passive elements (such as conditions) from active elements (such as actions) is a very important step in the design of systems. This duality is strongly supported by Petri nets. Whether an object is seen as active or passive may depend on the context or the point of view of the system. The following principles belong to the essential features of Petri nets that express locality and concurrency:

- • The principle of *duality* for Petri nets: there are two disjoint sets of elements: *P-element*s (*places*) and *T-elements* (*transitions*). Entities of the real world, interpreted as passive elements, are represented by P-elements (conditions, places, resources, waiting pools, channels etc.). Entities of the real world, interpreted as active elements, are represented by T-elements (events, transitions, actions, executions of statements, transmissions of messages etc.).
- • The principle of *locality* for Petri nets: the behavior of a transition depends exclusively on its locality, which is defined as

the totality of its input and output objects (pre- and post- conditions, input and output places, ...) together with the element itself.

- • The principle of *concurrency* for Petri nets: transitions having a disjoint locality occur independently (concurrently).
- • The principle of *graphical representation* for Petri nets: P-elements are represented by rounded graphical elements (circles, ellipses, ...), T-elements are represented by edged graphical symbols (rectangles, bars, ...). Arcs connect each T-element with its locality, which is a set of P-elements. Additionally, there may be inscriptions such as names, tokens, expressions, guards.
- • The principle of *algebraic representation* for Petri nets: For each graphical representation there is an algebraic representation containing equivalent information. It contains the set of places, transitions and arcs, and additional information such as inscriptions.

In contrast to concurrency, there is the notion of conflict. Some transitions can fire independently (e.g. t4 and t6 in Figure 2, only tokens must be inside the input places), but there can be Petri nets that model mutual exclusion, see Figure 3. Concurrent transitions behave independently and should not have any impact on each other. Sometimes this can depend on the state of the net – these transitions can behave independently.

Figure 3. Concurrency of t3 and t5 transitions a) after t1 firing both t3 and t5 are enabled, b) after t3 firing t5 still remains enabled

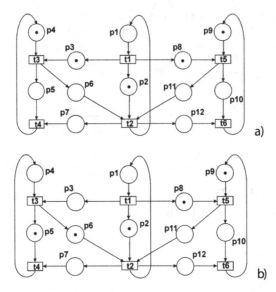

a)

b)

Definition 1. A net is a triple N = (P, T, F) where

- P is a set of places
- T is a set of transitions, disjoint from P, and
- F is a flow relation F **Í** (P x T) **Ç** (T x P) for the set of arcs.

If P and T are finite, the net is said to be finite.

The state of the net is represented by tokens in places. The tokens distributions in places are called markings. The holding of a condition (which is represented by a place) is represented by a token in the corresponding place. In our example, in the initial state control system C is prepared to send data (a token in place p1), printers A and B are ready to print (token s in places p4 and p9), see Figure 3. A state change or marking change can be performed by firing a transition. A transition "may occur" or "is activated" or "is enabled" or "can fire" if all its input places are marked by a token. Transition firing (the occurrence of a transition) means that all tokens are removed from the

input places and are added to the output places. The transitions can fire concurrently (simultaneously – independently, e.g. t3 and t5 in Figure 3a, or in conflict, see Figure 4).

Place/Transition Net, Arc-Constant Coloured Petri Net

According Definition 1 the arc can be only simple – only one token can be transmitted (removed or added) from or to places by firing of a transition. Place/transition nets are nets in the sense of Definition 1 together with a definition of arc weights. This can be seen as an abstraction obtained from more powerful coloured Petri nets by removing the individuality of the tokens. The example derived from the Petri net from Figure 1 is shown in Figure 5. Here more (two) printers are expressed only by two tokens in one place p4. The condition "all printers are ready" expressed by two tokens in place p4 and fulfilled by multiply edge from place p6 to transition t2.

Definition 2. A place/transition net (P/T net) is defined as a tuple N^{PT} =<P, T, **Pre, Post**> where:

Figure 4. Mutual exclusion of places p5 and p10, transition t3 and t5 in conflict, a) initial state where t3 and t5 are both enabled, b) the state after t3 firing, where t5 is not enabled

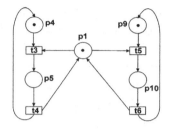 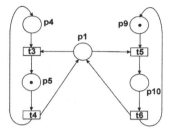

- P is a finite set (the set of places of N^{PT})
- T is a finite set (the set of transitions of N^{PT}), disjoint from P, and
- **Pre**, **Post** $\hat{I}$ $N^{|P|\times|T|}$ are matrices (the backward and forward incidence matrices of N^{PT}). **C** = **Pre** – **Post** is called the incidence matrix of N^{PT}

The set of these arcs is $F:=\{(p,t) \hat{I} P \times T | \mathbf{Pre}[p,t] > 0\}$ Ç $\{(t,p) \hat{I} T \times P | \mathbf{Post}[p,t] > 0\}$. This interpretation leads to the alternative definition, which is closer to the graphical representation.

Definition 3. A place/transition net (P/T net) is defined as a tuple N^{PT} =<P, T, F, W>, where:

- (P, T, F) is a net (see Definition 1) with finite sets P and T, and
- W: F $\rightarrow$ **N** \ {0} is a function (weight function)

N^{PT} together with an initial marking (m_0) is called a P/T net system $S = < N^{PT}, m_0>$ or $S =$

$<P, T, F, W, m_0>$. For a net system $S = < N^{PT}, m_0>$ the set $RS(S):= \{m \mid \$ w \hat{I} T^*, m_0 \rightarrow^w m\}$, where T^* is the sequence of transitions and $w \hat{I} T^*$ and $t \hat{I} T$, is the reachability set. $FS(S):= \{w \hat{I} T^* \mid \$ m, m_0 \rightarrow^w m \}$ is a set of occurrence-transition sequences (or a firing-sequence set) of S. It is sometimes convenient to define the set $Occ(S)$ of occurrence sequences to be the set of all sequences of the form

$$m_0, t_0, m_1, t_1, m_2, t_2, \ldots, t_{n-1}, m_n (n \geq 1)$$

such that

$$m_i \rightarrow^{ti} m_{i+1} \text{ for } i \hat{I} \{0, \ldots, n-1\}.$$

The tokens in Figures 2, 3, 4 and 5 are not distinguished from each other. The tokens representing printers A and B are distinguished by their places p4 and p9. A more compact and more natural way is to represent them in one place p4&p9 by individual tokens A and B. Distinguishable tokens are said to be coloured. Colours can be thought of as data types. For each place p, colour set $cd(p)$ is defined. In our case $cd(p4\&p9) = \{A, B\}$. For a coloured net we have to specify the colours, and for all places and transitions, particular colour sets (color domains). Since arc inscriptions may contain different elements or multiple copies of an element, multisets (bags) are used, 'bg'. The bag over a non-empty set A is a function $bg: A \rightarrow N$, sometimes denoted as a formal sum $\sum_{a|A} bg(a)'a$. Extending set operations *sum* and *difference* to Bag(A) are defined (Girault, 2003).

Figure 5. Place/transition net

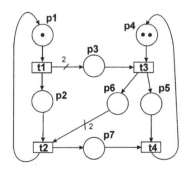

Definition 4. An arc-constant coloured Petri net (ac-CPN) is defined as a tuple

$$N^{aC} = <P, T, \textbf{Pre}, \textbf{Post}, C, cd>$$

where

- P is a finite set (the set of places of N^{aC}),
- T is a finite set (the set of transitions of N^{aC}), disjoint from P,
- C is the set of colour classes,
- cd: P→C is the colour domain mapping, and
- **Pre, Post** Î $\textbf{B}^{|P|\times|T|}$ are matrices (the backward and forward incidence matrices of N^{aC}) such that **Pre**[p,t] Î Bag(cd(p)) and **Post**[p,t] Î Bag(cd(p)) for each (p,t) Î P x T. **C = Post - Pre** is called incidence matrix of N^{aC}.

In this definition **B** is taken as the set Bag(*A*), where *A* is the union of all colour sets from *C*. The difference operator in *C* = Post – Pre is a formal one here, i.e. the difference is not computed as a value. A marking is a vector m such that *m[p]* Î Bag*(cd(p))* for each *p* Î *P*. The reachability set, firing sequence, net system and occurrence have the same meaning as for P/T nets.

Coloured Petri Net

The example for constructing Coloured Petri nets (CPN) is discussed in several following examples and figures derived from our original model of parallel printers. Arc-constant CPN in Figure 7 is simply derived from the initial example, with the same meaning of all places and transitions. Places p4 and p9 (and p5 and p10) originally used for distinguishing two printers are connected ("folded") to one place here named p4&p9 (p5&p10). For a transition *t*, it is necessary to indicate which of the individual tokens should be removed (with respect to its input places). This is done by the inscriptions on the corresponding arcs in Figure

7. Transition t3 can fire if there is an object A in place p4&p9 (and an indistinguishable token in the place p3). When it fires, token A is removed from place p4&p9 and is added to place p5&p10, and an (indistinguishable) token is added to p6. Places p4&p9 and p5&p10 have the colour domain printers = {A, B} denoting printer A and printer B. The control process is modelled by tokens (STROBE). Colour domains are represented by lower case italics near the place symbols in Figure 6. Places p3, p6, p7, p8, p11 and p12 are assumed to hold an indistinguishable token and therefore have the colour domain token = {•}, which is assumed to hold by default. The net from Figure 2 (ordinary or black-and-white PN) and the net from Figure 6 (coloured PN) contain the same information and have similar behavior. Only two places are "safe". This CPN is called arc-constant, since the inscriptions on the arcs are constants and not variables.

Colour sets:

- control = {s}
- printers = {A, B}
- constants: *s, A,*

The next step will be to simplify the graph structure of ac-CPN. We will represent the messages "STROBE signal sent to printer A" (stA) and "STROBE signal sent to printer B" (stB), ACK signal sent from printer A (ackA) and ACK signal sent from printer B (ackB). We can connect places p3 and p8, p6 and p11, p7 and p12, in Figure 7 they are named by the first name of the connected places. The behaviour of the net is the same. As a new feature of this net, transition t2 has to remove both signals ackA and ackB from place p6. The expression ackA + ackB denotes the set {ackA, ackB}. Transition t3 is enabled if both ackA and ackB are in place p4 and by t3 firing both tokens are removed. Therefore in the general case, bags (multisets) will be used instead of sets. The transition firing rule for arc-constant CPN can be expressed as: all input places must contain at

Figure 6. Arc-constant CPN

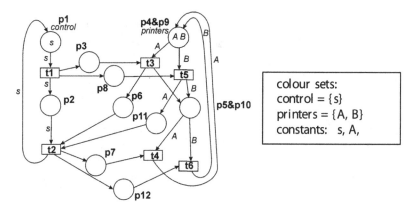

least as many individual tokens as specified by the corresponding arcs. The transition firing means that these tokens are removed and added to the output places as indicated by arc inscriptions.

The firing rule for ac-CPN is sketched in Figure 8.

Colour sets:

- control = {s}
- printers = {A, B}
- ack = {ackA, ackB}
- strobe = {stA, stB}
- **constants**:s, A, B, ackA,
- ackB, stA, stB

Figure 7. Arc-constant CPN without three places

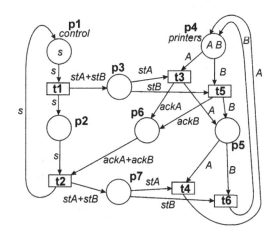

colour sets:
  control = {s}
  printers = {A, B}
  ack = {ackA, ackB}
  strobe = {stA, stB}
  constants:s, A, B, ackA,
    ackB, stA, stB

Figure 8. Firing rule for ac-CPN

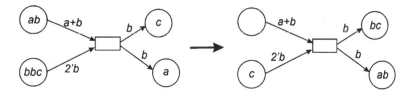

Figure 9. Firing rule for CPN

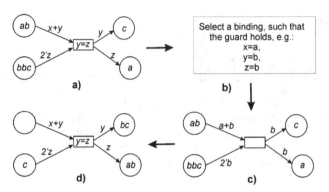

In a coloured Petri net the incidence matrices cannot be defined over **B** = Bag(*A*) as for arc-constant CPNs. The different modes or bindings of a transition have to be represented. These are called colours, and are denoted by *cd(t)*. Therefore the colour domain mapping cd is extended from *P* to *P Ç T*. In the entries of the incidence matrices for each transition colour, a multiset has to be specified. This is formalized by a mapping from *cd(t)* into the bags of colour sets over *cd(p)* for each *(p,t) Î P x T*.

Our example expressed by CPN is shown in Figure 10. The number of places and transitions corresponds to the P/T net in Figure 5, but the expression power is greater. For each transition a finite set of variables is defined which is strictly local to this transition. These variables have types or colour domains which are usually the colours of the places connected to the transition. In Figure 10 the set of variables of transition t3 is {x, y}. The types of x and y are dom(x) = printers and dom(y) = ack, respectively. An assignment of values to variables is called a binding. Not all possible bindings can be allowed for a correctly behaving net. The appropriate restriction is defined by a predicate at the transition, which is called a guard. Now the occurrence (firing) rule is as follows, see Figure 9, where all places have the colour set cd(p) = objects = {a, b, c}, and the colour domain of all variables is also objects:

1. Select a binding such that the guard holds (associate with each variable a value of its colour), Figure 9b)
2. Temporarily replace variables by associated constants, 9c)
3. Apply the firing rule from ac-CPN from Figure 8 as shown in 9d) (remove all appropriate tokens from input and add to output places according the arc inscriptions).

The firing rule should be understood as a single step from 9a) to d). If the binding x=a, y=b, z=c is selected, then the transition is not enabled in this binding, since the guard is not satisfied. The selection of a binding is local to a transition.

Definition 5. A coloured Petri net (CPN) is defined by a tuple

$$N^{CPN} = <P, T, \textbf{Pre}, \textbf{Post}, C, cd> \text{ where}$$

- P is a finite set (the set of places of N^{CPN}),
- T is a finite set (the set of transitions of N^{CPN}), disjoint from P,
- C is the set of colour classes,
- cd: P Ç T → C is the colour domain mapping, and

Pre, Post Î $\textbf{B}^{|P|x|T|}$ are matrices (the backward and forward incidence matrices of N^{CPN}) such that **Pre**[p,t]: cd(t) → Bag(cd(p)) and **Post**[p,t]: cd(t) → Bag(cd(p)) are mappings for each pair (p,t) Î P x T.

Figure 10. CPN model of printers

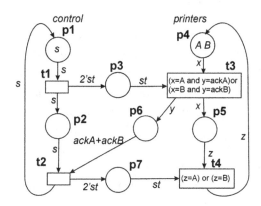

colour sets:
control = {s}
printers = {A, B}
ack = {ackA, ackB}
strobe = {st}
variables: x, y, z, st
constants: ackA, ackB, stA, stB

Figure 11. The dining philosophers PN model

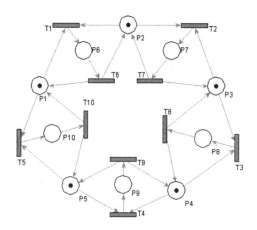

B can be taken as the set of mappings of the form f: cd(t) → Bag(cd(p)). **C = Post - Pre** is called incidence matrix.

The mapping **Pre***[p,t]*: *cd(t) → Bag(cd(p))* defines for each transition the colour (occurrence mode) *β* Î *cd(t)* of *t* a bag **Pre***[p,t] (β)* Î Bag*(cd(p))* denoting the token bag to be removed from *p* when *t* occurs (fires) in colour *β*. In a similar way, **Post***[p,t] (β)* specifies the bag to be added to *p* when *t* occurs (fires) in colour *β*. The overall effect of the action performed on the transition firing is given by a tuple corresponding to the arcs connected with *t*.

The colours of the transition can be seen as particular subsets of tuples *cd(t)* Î Bag*(cd(p1))* x … x Bag*(cd(p|P|))*, i.e., vectors having an entry for each place. But this can be an arbitrary set as well. Effective representations of this set are necessary. The mappings Pre*[p,t]* and Post*[p,t]* can be denoted by vectors, projections, functions and terms with functions and variables (see Figure 10).

PETRI NET APPLICATIONS IN STUDENTS PROJECTS

We performed several experiments with direct implementation of the Petri nets model in hardware (FPGA). The results were presented in (Kubátová, 2004; Kubátová, 2003, June; Kubátová, 2003, September).These models are briefly described here. They were constructed in software tools (Design/CPN or JARP editor) and from these tools their unified description in PNML language (Kindler, 2004). was directly transformed (by our *pnml2vhdl* compiler) to synthesized VHDL and then into the FPGA bitstream. The non-deterministic selection of one from more enabled transitions was implemented by the hardware aids (the linear feedback shift register - LFSR and the counter with preset), (Kubátová, 2003).

We have modeled 5 philosophers, who are dining together, Figure 11. The philosophers each have two forks next to them, both of which they need in order to eat. As there are only five forks it is not possible for all 5 philosophers to be eating at the same time. The Petri net shown here models a philosopher who takes both forks simultaneously, thus preventing the situation where some philosophers may have only one fork but are not able to pick up the second fork as their neighbors have already done so. The token in the fork place (places P1, P2, ..., P5) means that this fork is free. The token in the eat place (places P6, P7, ..., P10) means that this philosopher is eating.

We also performed experiments with a "producer-consumer" system, Figure 12. Our FPGA implementation used 59 CLB blocks, 47 flip-flops with maximum working frequency 24.4 MHz. (The relatively great number of flip-flops is consumed mainly for the hardware random choice of a transition to be fired.) The maximum input capacity parameter for places (the size of the counter) was set to the value 3. The average occupation of a place called "buffer" (average number of tokens) during 120 cycles (transition firings) was 1.43, (Kubátová, 2004).

Our real application experiment models a railway with one common critical part – a rail, see Figure 13. The PN model, Figure 14, has the initial marking where tokens are in places "1T" and "3T" (two trains are on rails 1 and 3, respectively), "4F" (a critical rail is free) and 2F (rail 2 is free). This model has eight places, two places T (train) and F (free) for each rail: a token in the first place means that the train is in this rail (T-places), and the second means that this rail is free (F-places). This was described and simulated in the Design/CPN system and then it was implemented in the real FPGA design kit ProMoX, (Kubátová, 2003 June).

CONCLUSION

This paper describes our practical use of Petri nets in digital hardware design courses. Different levels and types, practical and concrete styles of modeling are presented on the basis of the simple and clear examples which are understandable to our students from 8th semester. The example presented here in which parallel printers are served by a controlling process, was chosen due its practical presentation and practical iterative construction during the teaching process at the Department of Computer Science and Engineering (DSCE) of the Czech Technical University in Prague.

Our recent and future effort has involve the practical and direct implementation of Petri net based models into FPGA based design kits involving some visible inputs and outputs and with respect to quantitative properties: space, time, power and reliability.

ACKNOWLEDGMENT

This research was in part supported by the MSM6840770014 research program.

Figure 12. Producer – consumer model

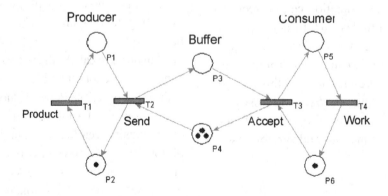

Figure 13. Railway semaphore model

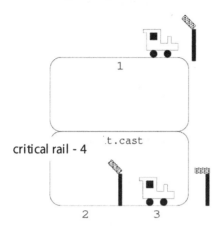

Figure 14. The PN model of 4 rails

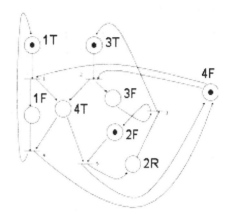

REFERENCES

Adamski, M. (2001). A Rigorous Design Methodology for Reprogrammable Logic Controllers. In *Proc. DESDes'01*, (pp. 53 – 60), Zielona Gora, Poland.

Bečvář, M., Kubátová, H., & Novotný, M. (2006). Massive Digital Design Education for large amount of undergraduate students. [Royal Institute of Technology, Stockholm.]. *Proceedings of EWME, 2006,* 108–111.

Coloured Petri Nets at the University of Aarhus (2009). Retrieved from http://www.daimi.au.dk/CPnets/

Digilent, (2009). Retrieved from http://www.digilentinc.com

Erhard, W., Reinsch, A., & Schober, T. (2001). Modeling and Verification of Sequential Control Path Using Petri Nets. In *Proc. DESDes'01,* (pp. 41 – 46) Zielona Gora, Poland.

Girault, C., & Valk, R. (2003). *Petri Nets for Systems Engineering*. Berlin: Springer-Verlag.

Gomes, L., & Barros, J.-P. (2001). Using Hierarchical Structuring Mechanism with Petri Nets for PLD Based System Design. In *Proc. DESDes'01* (pp. 47 – 52), Zielona Gora, Poland.

JarpPetri Nets Analyzer Home Page (2009). Retrieved from http://jarp.sourceforge.net/

Kindler, E. (Ed.). (2004). Definition, Implementation and Application of a Standard Interchange Format for Petri Nets. In *Proceedings of the Workshop of the satellite event of the 25th International Conf. on Application and Theory of Petri Nets*, Bologna, Italy.

Kubátová, H. (2003, June). Petri Net Models in Hardware. [Technical University, Liberec, Czech Republic.]. *ECMS, 2003,* 158–162.

Kubátová, H. (2003, September). Direct Hardware Implementation of Petri Net based Models. [Linz, Austria: J. Kepler University – FAW.]. *Proceedings of the Work in Progress Session of EUROMICRO, 2003,* 56–57.

Kubátová, H. (2004). Direct Implementation of Petri Net Based model in FPGA. In *Proceedings of the International Workshop on Discrete-Event System Design - DESDes'04*. Zielona Gora: University of Zielona Gora, (pp. 31-36).

Kubátová, H., & Novotný, M. (2005). Contemporary Methods of Digital Design Education. *Electronic Circuits and Systems Conference*, (pp. 115-118), Bratislava FEI, Slovak University of Technology.

Tools, C. P. N. (2009). Retrieved from http://wiki. daimi.au.dk/cpntools/cpntools.wiki

Uzam, M., Avci, M., & Kürsat, M. (2001). Digital Hardware Implementation of Petri Nets Based Specification: Direct Translation from Safe Automation Petri Nets to Circuit Elements. In *Proc. DESDes'01*, (pp. 25 – 33), Zielona Gora, Poland.

Xilinx, (2009). Retrieved from http://www.xilinx. com/f

Chapter 9
An Introduction to Reflective Petri Nets

Lorenzo Capra
Università degli Studi di Milano, Italy

Walter Cazzola
Università degli Studi di Milano, Italy

ABSTRACT

Most discrete-event systems are subject to evolution during lifecycle. Evolution often implies the development of new features, and their integration in deployed systems. Taking evolution into account since the design phase therefore is mandatory. A common approach consists of hard-coding the foreseeable evolutions at the design level. Neglecting the obvious difficulties of this approach, we also get system's design polluted by details not concerning functionality, which hamper analysis, reuse and maintenance. Petri Nets, as a central formalism for discrete-event systems, are not exempt from pollution when facing evolution. Embedding evolution in Petri nets requires expertise, other than early knowledge of evolution. The complexity of resulting models is likely to affect the consolidated analysis algorithms for Petri nets. We introduce Reflective Petri nets, a formalism for dynamic discrete-event systems. Based on a reflective layout, in which functional aspects are separated from evolution, this model preserves the description effectiveness and the analysis capabilities of Petri nets. Reflective Petri nets are provided with timed state-transition semantics.

INTRODUCTION

Evolution is becoming a very hot topic in discrete-event system engineering. Most systems are subject to evolution during lifecycle. Think e.g. of mobile ad-hoc networks, adaptable software, business processes, and so on. Such systems need to be updated, or extended with new features, during lifecycle. Evolution can often imply a complete system redesign, the development of new features and their integration in deployed systems.

It is widely recognized that taking evolution into account since the system design phase should be considered mandatory, not only a good practice. The design of dynamic/adaptable discrete-event systems calls for adequate modeling formalisms and tools.

DOI: 10.4018/978-1-60566-774-4.ch009

Unfortunately, the known well-established formalisms for discrete-event systems lack features for naturally expressing possible run-time changes to system's structure.

System's evolution is almost always emulated by directly enriching original design information with aspects concerning possible evolutions. This approach has several drawbacks:

- all possible evolutions are not always foreseeable;
- functional design is polluted by details related to evolutionary design: formal models turn out to be confused and ambiguous since they do not represent a snapshot of the current system only;
- evolution is not really modeled, it is specified as a part of the behavior of the whole system, rather than an extension that *could* be used in different contexts;
- pollution hinders system's maintenance and reduces possibility of reuse.

Petri nets, for their static layout, suffer from these drawbacks as well when used to model adaptable discrete-event systems. The common modeling approach consists of merging the Petri net specifying the base structure of a dynamic system with information on its foreseeable evolutions. A similar approach pollutes the Petri net model with details not pertinent to the system's current configuration. Pollution not only makes Petri net models complex, hard to read and to manage, it also affects the powerful analysis techniques/tools that classical Petri nets are provided with.

System evolution is an aspect orthogonal to system behavior, that crosscuts both system deployment and design; hence it could be subject to separation of concerns (Hürsch & Videira Lopes, 1995), a concept traditionally developed in software engineering. Separating evolution from the rest of a system is worthwhile, because evolution is made independent of the evolving system and the above mentioned problems are overcome. Separation of concerns could be applied to a Petri net-based modeling approach as well. Design information (in our case, a Petri net modeling the system) will not be polluted by non pertinent details and will exclusively represent current system functionality without patches. This leads to simpler and cleaner models that can be analyzed without discriminating between what is and what could be system structure and behavior. Reflection (Maes, 1987) is one of the mechanisms that easily permits the separation of concerns.

Reflection is defined as the activity, both *introspection* and *intercession*, performed by an agent when doing computations about itself (Maes, 1987). A reflective system is layered in two or more levels (base-, meta-, meta-meta-level and so on) constituting a *reflective tower*; each layer is unaware of the above one(s). Base-level entities perform computations on the application domain entities whereas entities on the meta-level perform computations on the entities residing on the lower levels. Computational flow passes from a lower level (e.g., the base-level) to the adjacent level (e.g., the meta-level) by intercepting some events and specific computations (*shift-up action*) and backs when meta-computation has finished (*shift-down action*). All meta-computations are carried out on a representative of lower-level(s), called *reification*, which is kept *causally connected* to the original level. For details look at Cazzola, 1998.

Similarly to what is done in Cazzola, Ghoneim, & Saake, 2004, the meta-level can be programmed to evolve the base-level structure and behavior when necessary, without polluting it with extra information. In Capra & Cazzola, 2007 we apply the same idea to the Petri nets domain, defining a reflective Petri net model (hereafter referred to as Reflective Petri nets) that separates the Petri net describing a system from the high-level Petri net (Jensen & Rozenberg, 1991) that describes how this system evolves upon occurrence of some events/conditions. In this chapter we introduce Reflective Petri nets, and we propose a simple state-transition semantics as a first step toward the implementation of a (performance-oriented) discrete-event simulation engine. With respect to other proposals recently appeared with similar goals (Cabac, Duvignau, Moldt, & Rölke, 2005; Hoffmann, Ehrig, & Mossakowski, 2005), Reflective Petri nets do not define a new Petri net paradigm, rather they rely upon a combination of consolidated classes of Petri nets and reflection concepts. What gives the possibility of using existing tools and analysis techniques in a fully orthogonal fashion. The short-time perspective is to integrate the GreatSPN graphical simulation environment (Chiola, Franceschinis, Gaeta, & Ribaudo, 1995) to directly support Reflective Petri nets.

In the rest of the chapter, we briefly present the (stochastic) Petri net classes used for the two levels of the reflective model; then we introduce Reflective Petri nets and the associated terminology, focusing on the (high-level) Petri net component (called *framework*) realizing the causal connection between the logical levels of the reflective layout; at last we provide a stochastic state-transition semantics for Reflective Petri nets; finally we present some related work and draw our conclusions and perspectives. An application of Reflective Petri nets to dynamic workflow design will be presented in the companion chapter (Capra & Cazzola, 2009).

SWN AND GSPN BASICS

Colored Petri nets (CPN) (Jensen & Rozenberg, 1991) are a major Petri net extension belonging to the high-level Petri nets category. For the *meta-level* of Reflective Petri nets we have chosen Well-formed Nets (WN) (Chiola, Dutheillet, Franceschinis, & Haddad, 1990), a CPN flavor (enriched with priorities and inhibitor arcs) retaining expressive power, characterized by a structured syntax. For performance analysis purposes, we are considering *Stochastic* Well-formed nets (SWN)

(Chiola, Dutheillet, Franceschinis, & Haddad, 1993). SWN are the high-level counterpart of Generalized Stochastic Petri nets (GSPN) (Ajmone Marsan, Conte, & Balbo, 1984), the Petri net class used for the *base-level*. In other words, the unfolding of a SWN is defined in terms of a GSPN.

This section introduces SWN semi-formally, by an example. The GSPN definition is in large part derived. Figure 1 shows the portion of the evolutionary framework (Figure 3) that removes a given node from the base-level PN modeling the system (reified as a WN marking). The removal of a node provokes as side-effect the withdrawal of any arcs connected to the node itself. Trying to remove a marked place or a not-existing node cause a restart action. We assume hereafter that the reader has some familiarity with ordinary Petri nets.

A SWN is a 11-tuple $(T, P, \{C_1, \ldots, C_n\}, \mathcal{C}, W^+, W^-, H, \mathrm{F}, \mathrm{P}, \mathbf{M}_0, \lambda)$ where P is the finite set of *places*, T is the finite set of *transitions*, $P \cap T = \varnothing$. With respect to ordinary Petri nets, places may contain "colored" tokens of different identity. $C_1, \ldots, C_n$ are finite basic color classes. In the example there are only two classes C_1, and C_2, denoting the base-level nodes, and the different kinds of connections between them, respectively. A basic color class may be partitioned in turn into static sub-classes, $C_i = \bigcup_k C_{i,k}$.

C assigns to each $s \in P \cup T$ a color domain, defined as Cartesian product of basic color classes: e.g. tokens staying at place BLreif|Arcs are triplets $\langle n_1, n_2, k_1 \rangle \in C_1 \times C_1 \times C_2$. A CPN transition actually folds together many elementary ones, so one speaks of instances of a colored transition. In Figure 1 $\mathcal{C}(t) = C_1$, for t ¹ delAFromToN ; $\mathcal{C}(\text{delAFromToN}) = C_1 \times C_1 \times C_1 \times C_2$. An instance of delAFromToN is thus a 4-tuple $\langle n_1, n_2, n_3, k_1 \rangle$.

A SWN marking $\mathbf{M}$ maps each place p to an element of $Bag(\mathcal{C}(p))$. $\mathbf{M}_0$ denotes the initial

Figure 1. A Well-Formed Net

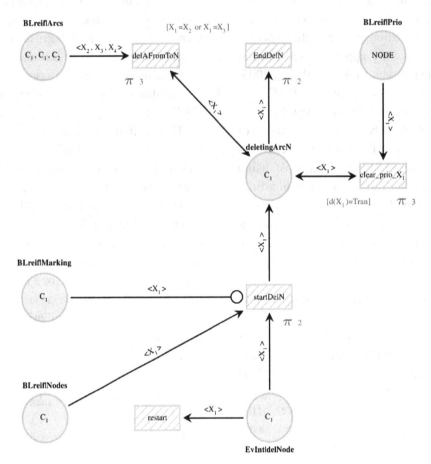

marking.

W^-, W^+ and H assign each pair $(t, p) \in T \times P$ an (input, output and inhibitor, respectively) arc function $C(t) \to Bag(\mathcal{C}(p))$. Any arc function is formally expressed as a (linear combination of) *function-tuple(s)* $\langle f_1, \ldots, f_n \rangle$, tuple components are called *class-functions*. Each f_i is a function, $C(t) \to Bag(C_j)$, C_j being the color class on i-th position in $\mathcal{C}(p)$, and is called class-j function. Letting $F : \langle f_1, \ldots, f_n \rangle$ and $t_c : \langle c_1, \ldots, c_m \rangle \in \mathcal{C}(t)$, then $F(t_c) = f_1(t_c) \times \ldots f_n(t_c)$, where operator $\times$ denotes the multi-set Cartesian product. Each f_i is expressed in terms of *elementary* functions: the only ones appearing in this chapter are the projection X_k ($k \le m$), defined as $X_k(t_c) = c_k$, and the constants S and $S_{j,k}$, mapping any t_c to C_j and $C_{j,k}$, respectively.

$\langle X_2, X_3, X_4 \rangle$ in Figure 1 (surrounding transition delAFromToN) is a function-tuple whose 1st and 2nd components are class-1 functions, while the 3rd one is a class-2 function: $\langle X_2, X_3, X_4 \rangle(\langle n_1, n_2, n_3, k_1 \rangle) = 1 \cdot n_2 \times 1 \cdot n_3 \times 1 \cdot k_1$, that is, $1 \cdot \langle n_2, n_3, k_1 \rangle$.

Φ associates a guard $[g] : \mathcal{C}(t) \to \{true, false\}$ to each transition t. A guard is built upon a set of basic predicates testing equality between projection applications, and membership to a given static subclass. As an example, $[X_1 = X_2 \vee X_1 = X_3](\langle n_1, n_2, n_1, k_1 \rangle) = true$.

A transition color instance $t_c \in \mathcal{C}(t)$ *has concession* in **M** if and only if, for each place p:

(i) $W^-(t, p)(t_c) \le \mathbf{M}(p)$,

(ii) $H(t, p)(t_c) > \mathbf{M}(p)$,

(iii) $\Phi(t)(t_c) = true$

(the operators $>, £, +, -$ are here implicitly extended to multisets). $\Pi : T \to \mathbb{N}$ assigns a priority level to each transition. Level 0 is for *timed* transitions, while greater priorities are for *immediate* transitions, which fire in zero time.

t_c is *enabled* in $\mathbf{M}$ if it has concession, and no higher priority transition's instances have concession in $\mathbf{M}$. It can fire, leading to $\mathbf{M'}$:

$$\forall p \in P \; \mathbf{M'}(p) = \mathbf{M}(p) + W^+(t, p)(t_c) - W^-(t, p)(t_c)$$

Finally, $\lambda : T \to \mathbb{R}^+$ assigns a rate, characterizing an exponential firing delay, to each timed transition, and a weight to each immediate transition. Weights are used to probabilistically solve conflicts between immediate transitions with equal priority.

The behavior of a SWN model is formally described by a state-transition graph (or reachability-graph), which is built starting from $\mathbf{M}_0$. As a result of the SWN time representation, the SWN reduced reachability graph, which is obtained by suitably removing those markings (called vanishing) enabling some immediate transitions, is isomorphic to a Continuous Time Markov Chain (CTMC) (Chiola, Dutheillet, Franceschinis, & Haddad, 1993).

Special *restart transitions*, denoted by prefix *rest*, are used in our models once again for modeling convenience (we might always trace it back to the standard SWN definition). While the enabling rule of restart transitions doesn't change, their firing leads a SWN model back to the initial marking.

The class of Petri nets used for the *base-level* correspond to the unfolded (uncolored) version of SWN, that is, GSPN (Ajmone Marsan, Conte, & Balbo, 1984). A GSPN is formally a 8-tuple $(T, P, W^+, W^-, H, \Pi, \mathbf{m}_0, \lambda)$.

With respect to SWN definition, W^+, W^-, H are functions $T \times P \to \mathbb{N}$. Analogously, a marking $\mathbf{m}$ is a mapping $P \to \mathbb{N}$. The definitions of concession, enabling, firing given before are still valid (guards have disappeared), but for replacing $F(t, p)(t_c)$ by $F(t, p)$, and interpreting the operators in the usual way.

SWN Symbolic Marking Notion

The particular syntax of SWN color annotations allows system symmetries to be implicitly embedded into SWN models. This way efficient algorithms can be applied, e.g., to build a compact Symbolic Reachability Graph (SRG) (Chiola, Dutheillet, Franceschinis, & Haddad, 1997), with an associated *lumped* CTMC, or to launch symbolic discrete-event simulation runs. These algorithms rely upon the notion of *Symbolic Marking* (SM).

A SM provides a *syntactical* equivalence relation on ordinary SWN colored markings: two markings belong to the same SM if and only if they can be obtained from one another by means of *permutations* on color classes that preserve static subclasses.

Formally, a SM $\hat{\mathbf{M}}$ comprises two parts specifying the so called dynamic subclasses and the distribution of colored symbolic tokens (tuples built of dynamic subclasses) over places, respectively. Dynamic subclasses define a *parametric partition* of color classes preserving static subclasses: let $\hat{C}_i$ and s_i denote the set of dynamic subclass of C_i (in a given $\hat{\mathbf{M}}$), and the number of static subclasses of C_i. The j-th dynamic subclass $Z_j^i \in \hat{C}_i$ refers to a static subclass, denoted $d(Z_j^i)$, $1 \le d(Z_j^i) \le s_i$, and has an associated cardinality $|Z_j^i|$, i.e., it represents a parametric set of colors (we shall consider cardinality one dynamic subclasses). It must hold:

$$\forall k : 1 \dots s_i \quad \sum_{j : d(Z_j^i) = k} |Z_j^i| = |C_{i,k}|.$$

The token distribution in $\hat{\mathbf{M}}$ is defined by a function mapping each place p to a multiset on the *symbolic* color domain of p, $\hat{\mathcal{C}}(p)$, obtained replacing C_i with $\hat{C}_i$ in $\mathcal{C}(p)$.

Among several, possible equivalent forms, the SM canonical representative (Chiola, Dutheillet, Franceschinis, & Haddad, 1997) provides a univocal representation for SM, based on a lexicographic ordering of dynamic subclass distribution over places.

REFLECTIVE PETRI NETS

The *Reflective Petri nets* approach (Capra & Cazzola, 2007) quite strictly adheres to the classical reflective paradigm (Cazzola, 1998). It permits anyone having a basic knowledge of ordinary Petri nets to model a system and *separately* its

possible evolutions, and to dynamically adapt system's model when evolution occurs.

The adopted reflective architecture (sketched in Figure 2) is structured in two logical layers. The first layer, called *base-level PN*, is represented by the GSPN specifying the system prone to evolve; whereas the second layer, called *meta-level* is represented by the *evolutionary meta-program*; in our case the meta-program is a SWN composed by the *evolutionary strategies*, which might drive the evolution of the base-level PN. More precisely, in the description below we will refer to the (untimed) carriers of SWN (i.e., WN nets) and GSPN, respectively, according to (Capra & Cazzola, 2007). Considering also the stochastic extension is straightforward, as discussed at the end of the next sub-section.

We realistically assume that several strategies

Figure 2. A Snapshot of the Reflective Layout

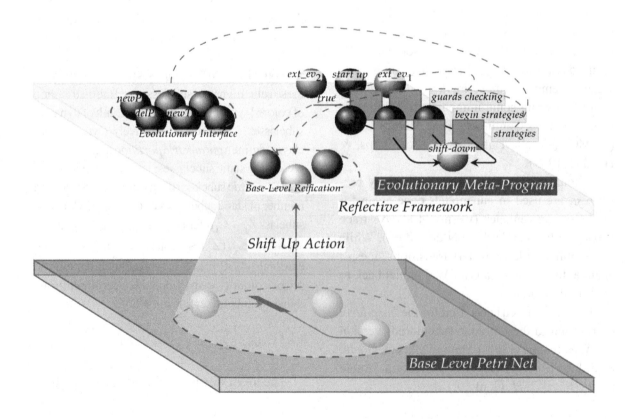

Figure 3. A Detailed View of the Framework Implementing the Evolutionary Interface

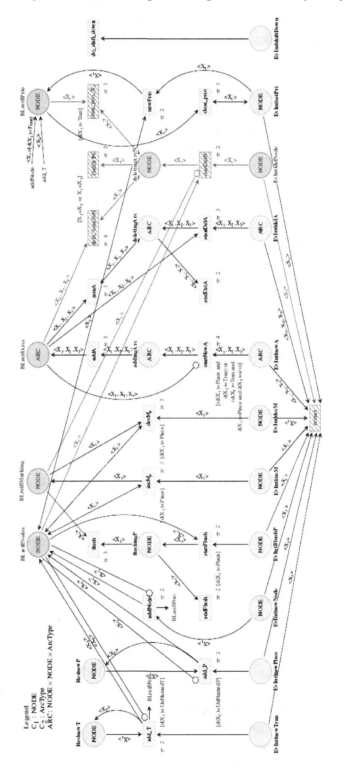

are possible at a given instant: in such a case one is selected in non-deterministic way (default policy). Evolutionary strategies have a *transactional* semantics: either they succeed, or leave the base-level PN unchanged.

The *reflective framework*, realized by a WN as well, is responsible for really carrying out the evolution of the base-level PN. It reifies the base-level PN into the meta-level as colored *marking* of a subset of places, called *base-level reification*, with some analogy to what is proposed in Valk, 1998. The base-level reification is updated every time the base-level PN enters a new state, and is used by the evolutionary meta-program to observe (*introspection*) and manipulate (*intercession*) the base-level PN. Each change to the reification will be reflected on the base-level PN at the end of a meta-program iteration, i.e., the base-level PN and its reification are *causally connected* and the reflective framework is responsible for maintaining this connection.

According to the reflective paradigm, the base-level PN runs irrespective of the evolutionary meta-program. The evolutionary meta-program is activated (*shift-up action*), i.e., a suiTable strategy is put into action, under two conditions non mutually exclusive: i) when triggered by an external event, and/or ii) when the base-level PN model reaches a given configuration.

Intercession on the base-level PN is carried out in terms of basic operations on the base-level reification suggested by the evolutionary strategy, called *evolutionary interface*, which permit any kind of evolution regarding both the structure and the current state (marking) of the base-level PN.

Each evolutionary strategy works on a specific area of the base-level PN, called *area of influence*. A conflict could raise when the changes induced by the selected strategy are reflected back (*shift-down action*) on the base-level, since influence area's local state could vary, irrespective of meta-program execution. To avoid possible inconsistency, the strategy must explicitly preserve the state (marking) of this area during its execution. To this aim the base-level execution is *temporary* suspended (using priority levels) until the reflective framework has inhibited any changes to the influence area of the selected evolutionary strategy. The base-level PN afterward resumes. This approach would favor concurrency between levels, and in perspective, between evolutionary strategies as well.

The whole reflective architecture is characterized by a fixed part (the reflective framework WN), and by a part varying from time to time (the base-level PN and the WN representing the meta-program). The framework hides evolutionary aspects to the base-level PN. This approach permits a clean separation between evolutionary model and evolving system model (look at the companion chapter (Capra & Cazzola, 2009) for seeing the benefits), which is updated only when necessary. So analysis/validation can be carried out separately on either models, without any pollution.

Reflective Framework

The framework formalization in terms of (S)WN allows us to specify complex evolutionary patterns for the base-level PN in a simple, unambiguous way.

The reflective framework (Figure 3) driven on the content of the evolutionary interface performs a sort of concurrent-rewriting on the base-level PN, suitably reified as a WN marking.

Places with prefix "BLreif"[1] belong to the base-level reification (*BLreif*), while those having prefix "EvInt" belong to the evolutionary interface (*EvInt*). Both categories of places represent interfaces to the evolutionary strategy sub-model.

While topology and annotations (color domains, arc functions, and guards) of the framework are fixed and generic, the structure of basic color classes and the initial marking need to be instantiated for setting a link between meta-level and base-level. In some sense they are similar to formal parameters, which are bound to a given base-level PN.

Let $\mathbf{BL}_0 : (P_0, T_0, W_0^+, W_0^-, H_0, \Pi_0, \mathbf{m}_0)$ be the base-level PN at system start-up. The framework basic color classes are $C_1 : NODE, C_2 : ArcType$. We have **Definition 1**, where $P_0 \subseteq Place, T_0 \subseteq Tran$.

Class *ArcType* identifies two types of WN arcs, input/output and inhibitor. Class *NODE* collects the potential nodes of any base-level PN evolutions, therefore it should be set large enough to be considered as a logically unbounded repository. The above partitioning of *NODE* into singleton static subclasses may be considered as a default choice, which might be further adapted, depending on modeling/analysis needs. Symbols $p_i(t_j)$ denote base-level places (transitions) that can be explicitly referred to in a given evolutionary strategy. Instead symbols $x_i(y_j)$ denote anonymous places (transitions) added from time to time to the base-level without being explicitly named. To make it possible the automatic updating of the base-level reification (as explained in the sequel), also these elements can be referred to, but only at the net level, by means of WN constant functions.

Base-Level Reification

The color domains for the base-level PN reification are given below.

Definition 2 (Reification Color Domains)

$$\mathcal{C}(p) \qquad : \quad NODE \quad \forall p \in BLreif \setminus \{BLreif \mid Arcs\}$$
$$\mathcal{C}(BLreif \mid Arcs) \quad : \quad ARC = NODE \times NODE \times ArcType$$

The reification of the base-level into the framework, i.e., its encoding as a WN marking, takes place at system start-up (initialization of the reification), and just after the firing of any base-level transition, when the current reification is updated.

Definition 3 (reification marking) *The reification of Petri net* $\mathbf{BL} : (P, T, W^+, W^-, H, \Pi, \mathbf{m}_0)$, *reif* $(\mathbf{BL})$, *is the marking:*

$$\mathbf{M}(BLreif \mid Nodes) \quad = \quad \sum_{n \in P \cup T} 1 \cdot n$$

$$\mathbf{M}(BLreif \mid Prio) \quad = \quad \sum_{t \in T} (\Pi(t) + 1) \cdot t$$

$$\mathbf{M}(BLreif \mid Marking) \quad = \quad \sum_{p \in P} \mathbf{m}_0(p) \cdot p$$

$$\forall p \in P, t \in T \begin{cases} \mathbf{M}(BLreif \mid Arcs)(\langle p, t, i/o \rangle) & = & W^-(p,t) \\ \mathbf{M}(BLreif \mid Arcs)(\langle t, p, i/o \rangle) & = & W^+(p,t) \\ \mathbf{M}(BLreif \mid Arcs)(\langle p, t, h \rangle) & = & H(p,t) \\ \mathbf{M}(BLreif \mid Arcs)(\langle t, p, h \rangle) & = & 0 \end{cases}$$

The evolutionary framework's colored initial marking ($\mathbf{M}_0$) is the reification of base-level PN at system start-up (*reif* $(\mathbf{BL}_0)$). Place BLreif|Nodes holds the set of base-level nodes; the marking of place BLreif|Arcs encodes the connections between them: the term $2\langle t_2, p_1, i/o \rangle$ corresponds to an output arc of weight 2 from transition t_2 to place p_1.

Transition priorities are defined by the marking of BLreif|Prio: if t_2 is associated to priority level k, there will be the term $(k+1) \cdot \langle t_2 \rangle$ in BLreif|Prio. The above three places represent the base-level topology: any change operated by the

Definition 1. (Basic Color Classes)

$$ArcType \quad = \quad i/o \cup h$$

$$NODE \quad = \quad \underbrace{\overbrace{p_1 \cup p_2 \ldots}^{Named_p} \cup \overbrace{x_1 \cup x_2 \ldots}^{Unnamed_p}}_{Place} \bigcup \underbrace{\overbrace{t_1 \cup t_2 \ldots}^{Named_t} \cup \overbrace{y_1 \cup y_2 \ldots}^{Unnamed_t}}_{Tran} \cup \quad null$$

evolutionary strategy to their marking causes a change to the base-level PN structure that will be reflected at any shift-down from the meta-level to the base-level.

The marking of place BLreif|Marking defines the base-level (current) state: the multiset $2\langle p_1 \rangle + 3\langle p_2 \rangle$ represents a base-level marking where places p_1 and p_2 hold two and three tokens, respectively. At the beginning BLreif|Marking holds the base-level initial state.

The marking of BLreif|Marking can be modified by the evolutionary strategy itself, causing a real change to the base-level current state immediately after the shift-down action.

Conflicts and inconsistencies due to the concurrent execution of several strategies are avoided by defining an influence area for each strategy; such an influence area delimits a critical region that can be accessed only by one strategy at a time. More details on the influence areas are in the section about the model semantics.

The meaning of each element of the *BLreif* interface is summarized in Table 1. Let us only remark that some places of the interface (e.g. BLreif|Arcs) hold multisets, while other (e.g. BLreif|Nodes) logically hold only sets (in such a case the reflective framework is in charge of eliminating duplicates).

As subject to change, the base-level reification needs to preserve a kind of well-defineness over the time. Let $\overline{m}$ be the support of multiset m, i.e., the set of elements occurring on m.

Definition 4 (well-defined marking) *Let* n_1, n_2: *NODE*, k: *ArcType*. $\mathbf{M}$ *is well-defined if and only if*

- $\overline{\mathbf{M}(\mathrm{BLreif} \mid \mathrm{Marking})} \subseteq Place \cap \overline{\mathbf{M}(\mathrm{BLreif} \mid \mathrm{Nodes})}$
- $\overline{\mathbf{M}(\mathrm{BLreif} \mid \mathrm{Prio})} \equiv Tran \cap \overline{\mathbf{M}(\mathrm{BLreif} \mid \mathrm{Nodes})}$
- if n_1 occur on $\overline{\mathbf{M}(\mathrm{BLreif} \mid \mathrm{Arcs})}$ then $n_1 \in \overline{\mathbf{M}(\mathrm{BLreif} \mid \mathrm{Nodes})}$
- $\langle n_1, n_2, k \rangle \in \overline{\mathbf{M}(\mathrm{BLreif} \mid \mathrm{Arcs})} \Rightarrow$
  $\langle n_1, n_2 \rangle \in Place \times Tran \vee$
  $\langle n_1, n_2 \rangle \in Tran \times Place \wedge k = i / o$

The other way round, a well-defined WN marking provides a univocal representation for the base-level PN.

Definition 5 (base-level mapping) *The* $GSPN$ $bl(\mathbf{M})$: $(P, T, W^+, W^-, H, \Pi, \mathbf{m}_0)$, associated to a well-defined $\mathbf{M}$, is such that: $P = Place \cap \overline{\mathbf{M}(\mathrm{BLreif} \mid \mathrm{Nodes})}$, $T = Tran \cap \overline{\mathbf{M}(\mathrm{BLreif} \mid \mathrm{Nodes})}$, $\forall p \in P$ $\mathbf{m}_0(p) = \mathbf{M}(\mathrm{BLreif} \mid \mathrm{Marking})(p)$, $\forall t \in T$ $\Pi(t) = \mathbf{M}(\mathrm{BLreif} \mid \mathrm{Prio})(t) - 1$, finally W^-, W^+, H are set as in Definition 3 (reading equations from right to left).

From definitions above it directly follows $bl(reif(\mathbf{BL})) = \mathbf{BL}$. By the way $\mathbf{M}_0$ is assumed well-defined. Through the algebraic structural calculus for WN introduced in Capra, De Pierro, & Franceschinis, 2005 it has been verified that well-definiteness is an invariant of the evolutionary framework (Figure 3), and consequently of the whole reflective model. The proof, involving a lot of technicalities, is omitted.

Including the time information of GSPN and SWN in the reflective model is immediate, once we restrict to integer values for transition rate/weights (as if λ where a mapping $T \to \mathbb{N}^+$). The encoding of transition parameters then would be analogous to transition priorities. The *BLreif* interface (and of course also *EvInt*) would include an additional place BLreif|Param (EvInt| Param), with domain *NODE*. A base-level transition t_1 with firing rate k would be reified by a token $k \cdot \langle t_1 \rangle$ on place BLreif|Param.

Evolutionary Framework Behavior

The evolutionary framework WN model implements a set of basic transformations (rewritings) on the base-level PN reification. Its structure is modular, being formed by independent subnets (easily recognizable) sharing interface *BLreif*, each implementing a basic transformation.

The behavior associated to the evolutionary framework is intuitive. Every place labeled by the EvInt prefix holds a (set of) basic transformation

Table 1. The Evolutionary Interface API and the Base-Level Reification Data Structure

Evolutionary Interface (the asterisk means that the marking is a set)	
EvInt| newTran* adds an anonymous transition to the base-level reification.	EvInt| newPlace* adds an anonymous place to the base-level reification.
EvInt| newNode* adds a given new node in the base-level reification.	EvInt| FlushP* flushes out the current marking of a place in the base-level reification.
EvInt| IncM increments the marking of a place in the base-level.	EvInt| decM decrements the marking of a place in the base-level.
EvInt| newA adds a new arc between a place and a transition in the base-level reification.	EvInt| delA deletes an arc between a place and a transition in the base-level reification.
EvInt| delNode* deletes a given node in the base-level reification (places must be empty).	EvInt| setPrio changes the priority to a node in the base-level reification.
EvInt| shiftDown* instructs the framework to reflect the changes on the base-level.	
Reification (the asterisk means that the marking is a set)	
BLreif| Nodes* the content of this place represents the nodes of the base-level PN.	BLreif| Marking the content of this place represents the current marking of the base-level PN.
BLreif| Arcs the content of this place represents the arcs of the base-level PN.	BLreif|Prio the content of this place represents the transition priorities of the base-level PN.

command(s) issued by the evolutionary strategy sub-model. Every time a (multiset of) token(s) is put on one of these places, a sequence of immediate transitions implementing the corresponding command(s) is triggered. A succeeding command results in changing the base-level reification, that is, the marking of *BLreif* places.

The implemented basic transformations are: adding/removing given nodes (EvInt|newNode, EvInt|delNode), adding anonymous nodes (EvInt|newPlace, EvInt|newTran), adding/removing given arcs (EvInt|newA, EvInt|delA), increasing/decreasing the marking of given places (EvInt|incM, EvInt|decM), flushing tokens out from places (EvInt|FlushP), finally, setting the priority of transitions (EvInt|setPrio). The color domain of each place (either *NODE* or *ARC*) corresponds to the type of command argument, except for EvInt|newPlace, EvInt|newTran, which are uncolored places.

Term $2\langle p_1 \rangle$ occurring on place EvInt|incM is interpreted as "increase the current marking of place p_1 of two units"'. Many commands of the same kind can be issued simultaneously, e.g. $2\langle p_1 \rangle + 1\langle p_3 \rangle$ on EvInt|incM. Depending on their meaning, some commands are encoded by multisets (as in the last examples), while other are encoded by sets. Interface *EvInt* is described on Table 1 and is implemented by the net on Figure 3.

In some cases command execution result must be returned back: places whose prefix is Res hold command execution results, e.g., places Res|newP and Res|newT record references to the last nodes that have been added to the base-level reification anonymously. Initially they hold a *null* reference. As interface places, they can be acceded by the evolutionary strategy sub-model.

Single commands are carried out in *consistent* and *atomic* way, and they may have side effects.

Let us consider for instance deletion of an existing node, which is implemented by the subnet depicted (in isolation) in Figure 1. Assume that a token n_1 is put in place EvInt|delNode. First the membership of n_1 to the set of nodes currently reified as not marked is checked (transition startDelN). In case of positive check the node is removed, then all surrounding arcs are removed (transition delAfromToN), last (if n_1 is a transition) its priority is cleared (transition clearPrio$_{x1}$). Otherwise the command aborts and the whole meta-model composed by the reflective framework and the evolutionary strategy is restarted, ensuring a transactional execution of the evolutionary strategy. A unique restart transition appears in Figure 3, with input arcs having an "OR" semantics.

Different priority levels are used to guarantee the correct firing sequence, also in case of many deletion requests (tokens) present in EvInt|delNode simultaneously. Boundedness is guaranteed by the fact that each token put on this place is eventually consumed.

The other basic commands are implemented in a similar way. Let us only remark that newly introduced base-level transitions are associated to the default priority 0 (encoded as 1).

Priority levels in Figure 3 are *relative*: after composing the evolutionary framework WN model to the evolutionary strategy WN model, the minimum priority in the evolutionary framework is set greater than the maximum priority level used in the evolutionary strategy.

Any kind of transformation can be defined as a combination of basic commands: for example "replacing the input arc connecting nodes p and t by an inhibitor arc of cardinality three" corresponds to put the token $\langle p,t,i\,/\,o \rangle$ on EvInt|delA and the term $3\langle p,t,h \rangle$ on place EvInt|newA. Who designs a strategy (the meta-programmer) is responsible for specifying consistent sequences of basic commands, e.g., he/she must take care of flushing the contents of a given place before removing it.

Base-level Introspection. The evolutionary framework includes basic introspection commands. Observation and manipulation of base-level PN reification are performed passing through the framework evolutionary interface; what enhances safeness and robustness of evolutionary programming. Figure 4 shows (from left to right) the subnets implementing the computation of the cardinality (thereupon the kind) of a given arc, the preset of a given base-level node, and the current marking of a given place (subnets computing transition priorities, post-sets, inhibitor-sets, and checking existence of nodes, have a similar structure).

As for the basic transformation commands, each subnet has a single entry-place belonging to the evolutionary interface *EvInt* and performs atomically. Introspection result is recorded on places having the Res| prefix, accessible by the evolutionary strategy: regarding e.g., preset computation, a possible result (after a token p_1 has been put in place EvInt|PreSet) is $\langle p_1,t_2 \rangle + \langle p_1,t_3 \rangle$, meaning the preset of p_1 is $\{t_2,t_3\}$ (other results are encoded as multisets). Since base-level reification could be changed in the meanwhile, every time a new command is issued any previously recorded result about command's argument is cleared (transitions prefixed by string "flush").

The Evolutionary Strategy

The adopted model of evolutionary strategy (only highlighted in Figure 2) specifies a set of arbitrarily complex, alternative transformation patterns on the base-level (each denoted hereafter as *i*-th strategy or st_i), which can be fired when some conditions (checked on the base-level PN reification by introspection) hold and/or some external events occur.

Since a strategy designer is usually unaware of the details about the WN formalism, we have provided him/her with a tiny language that allows everyone to specify his own strategy in a simple and formal way. As concerns control structures the lan-

Figure 4. Basic introspection functions

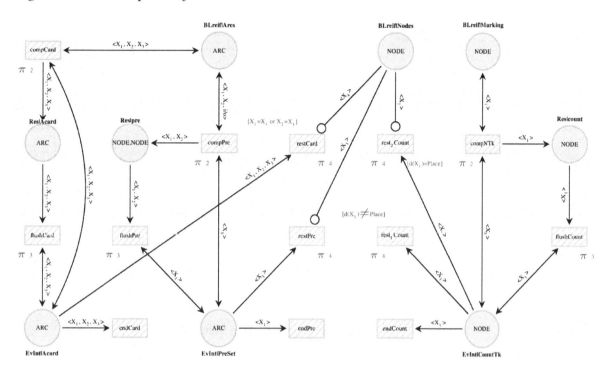

guage syntax is inspired by Hoare's CSP (Hoare, 1985), enriched with a few specific notations. As concerns data types, a basic set of built-in's and constructors is provided for easy manipulation of nets. The use of a CSP-like language to specify a strategy allows its automatic translation into a corresponding WN model. We will provide some examples of mapping from pieces of textual strategy descriptions into corresponding WN models. In Petri nets literature there are lot of examples of formal mappings from CSP-like formalisms (e.g. process algebras) to (HL)Petri nets models (e.g. Best, 1986 and more recently Kavi, Sheldon, Shirazi, & Hurson, 1995), from which we have been inspired.

The evolutionary meta-program scheme corresponds to the CSP pseudo-code[2] in Figure 6. The evolutionary strategy as a whole is cyclically activated upon a shift-up, here modeled as an input command. A non-deterministic selection of guarded commands then takes place. Each guard is evaluated on base-level reification by using "ad-

hoc" language notations described in the sequel. Guard *true* means the corresponding strategy may be always activated at every shift-up. A guard optionally ends with an input command simulating the occurrence of some external events.

A more detailed view of this general schema in terms of Petri nets is given in Figure 5. Figure 5(a) shows the non-deterministic selection, whereas Figure 5(b) shows the structure of i-th strategy. Color domain definitions are inherited from the evolutionary framework WN. An additional basic color class ($STRAT = st_1 \cup \dots st_n$) represents possible alternative evolutions

Focusing on Figure 5(a), we can observe that any shift-up is signaled by a token in the homonym place, and guards (the boxes on the picture, which represent the only not fixed parts of the net) are evaluated concurrently, accordingly to the semantics of CSP alternative command. After the evaluation process has been completed one branch (i.e., a particular strategy) is chosen (transition chooseStrat) among those whose guard

Figure 5. Meta-Program Generic Schema

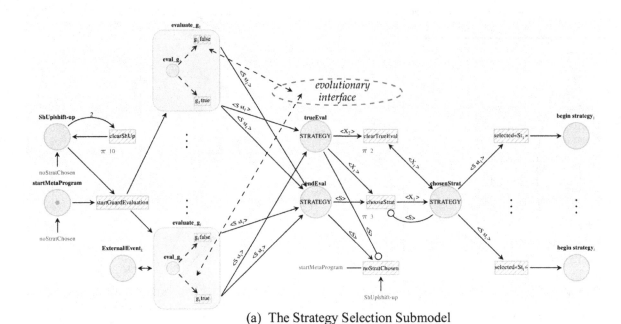

(a) The Strategy Selection Submodel

(b) The Strategy Structure

was successfully evaluated (place trueEval). By the way, introspection has to be performed with priority over base-level activities, so the lowest priority in Figure 5(a) is set higher than any base-level PN transition, when the whole model is built. In case every guard is valued false the selection command is restarted just after a new shift-up occurrence transition noStratChoosen), avoiding any possible *livelock*. Occurrence of external events is modeled by putting tokens in particular "open" places (e.g. External|event$_k$ in Figure 5(a). The idea is that such places should be shared with other sub-models simulating the external event occurrence. If one is simply interested in interactively simulating the reflective model, he/she might think of such places as a sort of buttons to be pushed by request.

(a)   The Strategy Selection Submodel
(b)   The Strategy Structure

Figure 6. CSP code for the meta-program scheme

```
*[shift-up ? sh-up-occurred →
    [
        guard_1; event_1 ? event_1-occurred → strategy_1()
        □
        guard_2 → strategy_2()
        □
        true → strategy_3()
        □
        ...
    ]
]
```

The ith Strategy. The structure of the WN model implementing a particular evolutionary strategy is illustrated in Figure 5(b). It is composed of fixed and programmable (variable) parts, which may be easily recognized in the picture. It realizes a sort of *two-phases* approach: during the first phase (subnet freeze(«pattern_i»)) the meta-program sets the local influence area of the strategy, a portion of the base-level Petri Net reification potentially subject to changes. This area is expressed as a language's "pattern", that is, a parametric set of base-level nodes defined through the language notations, denoted by a colored homonym place in Figure 5(b). The pattern contents are flushed at any strategy activation. A simple isolation algorithm is then executed, which freezes the strategy influence area reification, followed by a shift-down action as a result of which freezing materializes at the base-level PN. The idea is that all transitions belonging to the pattern, and/or able to change the marking of places belonging to it, are temporary inhibited from firing, until the strategy execution has terminated (the place pattern* holds a wider pattern image after this computation).

```
*[shift-up ? sh-up-occurred →
[
guard_1; event_1 ? event_1-occurred →
```

```
strategy_1()
    □
    guard_2 → strategy_2()
    □
    true → strategy_3()
    □
    ...
    ]
]
```

During the freezing phase the base-level model is "suspended" to avoid otherwise possible inconsistencies and conflicts: this is achieved by forcing transitions of freeze(«pattern_i») subnet to have a higher priority than base-level PN transitions. The freeze(«pattern_i») sub-model is decomposed in turn in two sub-models that implement the influence area identification and isolation, respectively. While the latter has a fixed structure, the former might be either fixed or programmable, depending on designer needs (e.g. it might be automatically derived from the associated guard).

After the freezing procedure terminates the evolutionary algorithm starts (box labeled by dostrategy_i in Figure 5(b)), and the base-level resumes from the "suspended" state: what is implicitly accomplished by setting no dependence between the priority of dostrategy_i subnet transitions (arbitrarily assigned by the meta-programmer) and the priority of base-level PN transitions (in practice: setting the base-level PN lowest priority equal to the priority level, assumed constant, of dostrategy$_i$ subnet). The only forced constraint is that dostrategy$_i$ submodel can *exclusively* manipulate (by means of framework's evolutionary interface) the nodes of base-level reification belonging to the pattern previously computed (this constraint is graphically expressed in Figure 5(b) by an arc between dostrategy$_i$ box and place «pattern$_i$»). As soon as the base-level PN enters a new state (marking), the newly entered base-level state is instantaneously reified into the meta-level. This reification does not involve the base-level area touched by the evolutionary strategy, which can continue operating without inconsistency. Before activating the final shift-down (which ends the strategy and actually operates the base-level evolution planned by the strategy) the temporary isolated influence area is unfrozen in a very simple way.

The described approach is more flexible than a brute-force blocking one (where the base-level is suspended for the whole duration of the strategy) while guaranteeing a sound and consistent system evolution. It better adheres to the semantics and the behavior of most real systems (think e.g. of a traffic control system), which cannot be completely suspended while their evolution is being planned.

Casually Connecting the Base-Level and the Meta-Program

The base-level and the meta-program are (reciprocally) causally connected via the reflective framework.

Shift-up action. The shift-up action is realized for the first time at system start-up. The idea (illustrated in Figure 7) is to connect in transparent, fully automatic way the base-level PN to the evolutionary framework interface by means of colored input/output arcs drawn from any base-level PN transition to place *BLreif| Marking* of base-level

reification. Any change of state at base-level PN provoked by transition firing is instantaneously reproduced on the reification, conceptually maintaining base-level unawareness about the meta-program. The firing of base-level transition t_1 results in withdrawing one and two tokens from places p_1 and x_1, respectively, and in putting one in p_2. While token consumption is emulated by a suitable input arc function ($\langle S p_1 \rangle + 2 \cdot \langle S x_1 \rangle$), token production is emulated by an output arc function ($\langle S p_2 \rangle$). The complete splitting of class *NODE* allows anonymous places introduced into the base-level (x_1) to be referred to by means of SWN constant functions. The occurrence of transition t_1 is signaled to the meta-program by putting one token in the uncolored boundary-place ShUp| shift-up (Figure 5(a)).

Shift-down action. The shift-down action is the only operation that cannot be directly emulated at Petri nets (WN) level, but that should be managed by the environment supporting the reflective architecture simulation. This is not surprising, rather is a consequence of the adopted choice of a traditional Petri nets paradigm to model an evolutionary architecture. The shift-down action takes place when the homonym uncolored (meta-) transition of the framework (Figure 3) is enabled. This transition has the highest priority within the whole reflective model, its occurrence replaces the current base-level PN with the Petri net described by the current reification, according to Definition 5. After a shift-down the base-level restarts from the (new) base-level initial marking, while the meta-program continues executing from the state preceding the shift-down.

Putting all together. The behavior of the whole reflective model (composed of the base-level PN, the evolutionary framework interface and the meta-program) between consecutive shift-downs can be represented using a uniform, Petri net-based approach. We are planning to extend the GreatSPN tool (Chiola, Franceschinis, Gaeta, & Ribaudo, 1995), which supports the GSPN and SWN formalisms, to be used as editing/simula-

Figure 7. Reification implemented at Petri net level

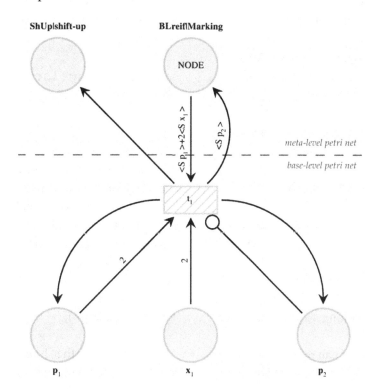

tion environment of Reflective Petri nets. For that purpose it should be integrated with a module implementing the causal-connection between base-level and meta-program.

The reflective framework, the evolutionary meta-program, and the base-level are separated sub-models, sharing three disjoint sets of boundary places: the base-level reification, the evolutionary interface, and the places holding basic command results. Their interaction is simply achieved through *superposition* of homonym places. This operation is supported by the Algebra module (Bernardi, Donatelli, & Horvàth, 2001) of GreatSPN.

Following the model composition, absolute priority levels must be set, respecting the reciprocal constraints between components earlier discussed (e.g. framework's lowest priority must be grater than meta-program's highest priority). Finally, the whole model's initial marking is set according to Definition 3 as concerns base-level reification,

putting token *null* in both places Res|newP and Res|newT (Figure 4), and one uncolored token in place startMetaProgram (Figure 5(a)).

Meta-Language Basic Elements

The meta-programming language disposes of four built-in types NAT, BOOL, NODE, ArcType and the **Set** and *Cartesian product* ($\times$) constructors. The arc (ARC: NODE $\times$ NODE $\times$ ArcType), arc with multiplicity (ArcM: ARC $\times$ NAT), and marking (Mark: NODE $\times$ NAT) types are thus introduced, this way a multi-set can be represented as a set. Place, Tran and static subclass names can be used to denote subtypes or constants (in case of singletons), and new types can be defined on-the-fly by using set operators.

Each strategy is defined in terms of basic actions, corresponding to the basic commands previously described. Their signatures are:

- newNode(Set(NODE)), newPlace(), newTran(), remNode(Set(NODE));
- flush(Set(Place))
- addArc(Set(ArcM)), remArc(Set(Arc));
- incMark(Set(Mark)), decMark(Set(Mark))
- setPrio(Set(Tran))

A particular version of repetitive command can be used. Letting E_i be a *set* (Grammar 1):

*(e_1 in E_1, ..., e_n in E_n)[«command»]

makes the instruction «command» be executed iteratively for each $e_1 \in E_1$,.., $e_n \in E_n$; at each iteration, variables e_1,.., e_n are bound to particular elements of E_1,.., E_n, respectively. If E_1 is a color (sub-)class, then we implicitly refer to its elements that belong to the base-level reification.

The meta-programmer can refer to base-level elements either explicitly, by means of constants, or implicitly, by means of *variables*.

By means of the assignments p=newPlace(), t=newTran(), it is also possible to add unspecified nodes to the base-level, afterwards referred to by variables p,t.

Base-level introspection is carried out by means of simple net-expressions allowing the meta-programmer to specify patterns, i.e., parametric base-level portions meeting some requirements on base-level's structure/marking.

The syntax for patterns and guards is shown in Grammar 1. The symbols: pre(n), post(n), inh(n), #p, card(a) denote the pre/post-sets of a base-level PN node n, the set of elements connected to n via inhibitor arcs, the current marking of place p, and the multiplicity of an arc a, respectively. They are translated into introspection commands (Figure 4). A pattern example is:

```
{p:Place|#p > #p1 and isempty
(pre(p)∩inh(p))},
```

where p1 is a constant, and p is a variable.

Below is an example of guard is (in the current version of the language quantifiers cannot be nested):

```
exists t:Tran|isempty (pre(t) ∪
inh(t)).
```

Having at our disposal a simple meta-programming language, it becomes easier specifying (even complex) parametric base-level evolutions, such as "for each marked place p belonging to the preset of t, if there is no inhibitor arc connecting p and t, add one with cardinality equal to the marking of p'', which becomes:

*(p in pre(t)) [#p>0 and card(<p,t,h>)==0 → addArc(<p,t,h,#p>)]

The code of the freezing algorithm acting on a precomputed influence area (box isolate(«$pattern_i$») in Figure 5(b)), which is one of the fixed parts of the meta-program, is given in Figure 8. all base-level transitions that belong to the pattern, or that can change its local marking (state), are temporarily prevented from firing by adding a new (marked) place to the base-level reification, to which pattern transitions are connected via inhibitor arcs. A shift-down action is then activated to freeze the base-level PN. Unfreezing is simply achieved by removing the artificially introduced inhibitor place at the end of the evolutionary strategy (Figure 5(b)).

```
[
```
isempty(pattern) → **skip**
□
not(**isempty**(pattern)) →
pattern* = {};
isolating_pattern = **newPlace**();
incMark(<isolating_pattern,1>);
*(p **in** Pattern ∩ **Place**)
[**true** → pattern* ∪ = **pre**(p) ∪ **post**(p)];
*(t **in** pattern* ∩ **Tran**)

Figure 8. CSP Code for the Isolating-Pattern Subnet (Language's Keywords are in Bold)

```
[
  isempty(pattern) → skip
    □
  not(isempty(pattern)) →
    pattern* = {};
    isolating_pattern = newPlace();
    incMark(<isolating_pattern,1>);
    *(p in Pattern □ Place)
       [true → pattern* □ = pre(p) □ post(p)];
    *(t in pattern* □ Tran)
       [true →newArc(<isolating_pattern,t,h,1>)];
    shiftDown;
]
```

[**true →newArc**(<isolating_pattern,t,h,1>)];
shiftDown;

]

A MARKOV-PROCESS FOR REFLECTIVE PETRI NETS

The adoption of GSPN (Ajmone Marsan, Conte, & Balbo, 1984) and SWN (Chiola, Dutheillet, Franceschinis, & Haddad, 1993) for the base- and meta- levels of the reflective layout, respectively, has revealed a convenient choice for two reasons: first, the timed semantics of Reflective Petri nets is in large part inherited from GSPN (SWN); secondly, the symbolic marking representation the SWN formalism is provided with can be exploited to efficiently handle the intriguing question related to how identifying equivalences during a Reflective Petri net model evolution.

On the light of the connection set between base- and meta- levels, the behavior of a Reflective Petri net model between any meta-level activation and the consequent shift-down is fully described in terms of a SWN model, the meta-level PN, including (better, suitably connected to) an uncolored part (the base-level PN). This model will be hereafter denoted *base-meta PN*. Hence,

we can naturally set the following notion of state for Reflective Petri nets:

Definition 6 (state). *A state of a Reflective Petri net is a marking* $\mathbf{M}_i$ *of the base-meta PN obtained by suitably composing the base-level PN (a GSPN) and the meta-level PN (a SWN).*

Then, letting $t \neq$ shiftdown be any transition (color instance) enabled in $\mathbf{M}_i$, according to the SWN (GSPN) firing rule, and $\mathbf{M}_j$ be the marking reached upon its firing, we have the labeled state-transition

$$\mathbf{M}_i \overset{\lambda(t)}{\to} \mathbf{M}_j,$$

where $\lambda(t)$ denotes a weight, or an exponential rate, associated with t, depending on whether t is timed or immediate.

There is nothing to do but consider the case where $\mathbf{M}_f$ is a vanishing marking enabling the pseudo-transition *shift-down*: then,

$$\mathbf{M}_f \overset{w=1}{\to} \mathbf{M}'_0,$$

$\mathbf{M}'_0$ being the marking of the base-meta PN obtained by first replacing the (current) base-level PN with the GSPN isomorphic to the reification marking (once it has been suitably connected to

Table 2.

Grammar 1 BNF for language expressions.		
Element	::=	NODE | Arc†
NODE	::=	«*variable*» | «*constant*» | **singleton** (NodeSet)
Arc	::=	< NODE , NODE , «*arc_type*» >
Expression	::=	«*digit*» | BasicExpr
BasicExpr	::=	# «*place*»‡ | **card**(Set) | **card** (Arc) | **prio** («*transition*»)
Predicate	::=	BasicExpr RelOp Expression | **kind** (Arc) EqOp «*arc_type*» | NODE InExpr | NODE **is connected to** NODE | **isempty** (Set)
RelOp	::=	< | > | =
EqOp	::=	=\= | =
Set	::=	{ } | { ArcList } | NodeSet | «*static_subclass*» | «*color_class*» | Element | Set SetOp Set
SetOp	::=	$\cap$ | $\cup$ | \
ArcList	::=	Arc | ArcList **,** Arc
NodeSet	::=	{ } | { NodeList } | Pattern | AlgOp (NodeSet) | NODE
NodeList	::=	NODE | NodeList **,** NODE
AlgOp	::=	**pre** | **post** | **inh**
Pattern	::=	{ «*variable*» InExpr | Guard }
Guard	::=	Predicate | LogOp «*variable*» InExpr Predicate | **not** (Guard)
InExpr	::=	$\in$ | **in** «*place*» | **in** NodeSet
LogOp	::=	**exists** | **foreach**
BoolOp	::=	**and** | **or**

† Terminals are in bold font, non-terminals are in normal font. ‡ Terms in «» represent elements whose meaning can be inferred from the model.

the meta-level PN), then firing *shift-down* as it were a normal immediate transition.

Using the same technique for eliminating vanishing states as it is employed in the *reduced reachability graph algorithm* (Ajmone Marsan, Conte, & Balbo, 1984), it is possible to build a CTMC for the Reflective Petri net model.

Recognizing Equivalent Evolutions

The state-transition graph semantics just introduced precisely defines the (timed) behavior of a Reflective Petri net model, but suffers from two evident drawbacks. First, it is highly inefficient: the state description is exceedingly redundant, comprising a large part concerning the meta-level

PN, which is unnecessary to describe the evolving system. The second concern is even more critical, and indirectly affects efficiency: there is no way of recognizing whether the modeled system, during its dynamics/evolution, reaches equivalent states. The ability of deciding about a system's state-transition graph finiteness and strongly-connectedness, of course strictly related to the ability of recognizing equivalent states, is in fact mandatory for performance analysis: we know that the most important sufficient condition for a finite CTMC to have stationary solution (steady-state) is to include one maximal strongly connected component.

More generally, most techniques based on state-space inspection rely on the ability above.

Recognizing equivalent evolutions is a tricky question. For example, it may happen that (apparently) different strategies cause in truth equivalent transformations to the base-level PN (the evolving system), which cannot be identified by Definition 6. Yet, the combined effect of different sequences of evolutionary strategies might produce the same effects. Even more likely, the internal dynamics of the evolving system might lead to reach equivalent configurations. The above question, which falls into a graph isomorphism sub-problem, as well as the global efficiency of the approach, are tackled by resorting to the peculiar characteristic of SWN: the symbolic marking notion (Chiola, Dutheillet, Franceschinis, & Haddad, 1997).

For that purpose, we refer to the following static partition of class *NODE*:

$$NODE = \underbrace{\overbrace{p_1 \cup \ldots p_k}^{Named_p} \cup Unnamed_p}_{Place} \cup \underbrace{\overbrace{t_1 \cup \ldots t_n}^{Named_t} \cup Unnamed_t}_{Tran}.$$

Symbols p_i, t_j denote singleton static subclasses. Conversely, $Unnamed_p$ and $Unnamed_t$ are static subclasses collecting all anonymous (i.e., indistinguishable) places/transitions. Behind there is a simple intuition: while some ("named") nodes, for the particular role they play, preserve the identity during base-level evolution, and may be explicitly referred to during base-level manipulation, others ("unnamed") are indistinguishable from one another. In other words any pair of "unnamed" places (transitions) might be freely exchanged on the base-level PN, without altering the model's semantics. There are two extreme cases: $Named_p$ ($Named_t$) = $\varnothing$ and, opposite, $Unnamed_p$ ($Unnamed_t$) = $\varnothing$. The former meaning all places/transitions can be permuted, the latter instead all nodes are distinct.

It is remarkable that the static partition of class *NODE* actually used for the base-meta PN is different from the previous one, given that any places of base-level PN must be explicitly referred to when connecting the base-level PN to the meta-level PN (Figure 7).

The technique we use to recognize equivalent base-level evolutions relies on the base-level reification and the adoption of a symbolic state representation for the base-meta PN that, we recall, results from composing in transparent way the base-level PN and the meta-level PN.

We only have to set as initial state of the Reflective Petri net model a symbolic marking ($\hat{\mathbf{M}}_0$) of the base-meta PN, instead of an ordinary one: any dynamic subclass of $Unnamed_p$ ($Unnamed_t$) will represent an arbitrary "unnamed" place (transition) of the base-level PN.

Because of the simultaneous update mechanism of the reification, and the consequent one-to-one correspondence along the time between the current base-level PN and the reification at the meta-level, we can state the following:

Definition 7 (equivalence relation) *Let* $\hat{\mathbf{M}}_i$, $\hat{\mathbf{M}}_j$ be two symbolic states of the Reflective Petri net model. $\hat{\mathbf{M}}_i \equiv \hat{\mathbf{M}}_j$ if and only if their restrictions on the reification set of places have the same canonical representative.

Lemma 1. *Let* $\hat{\mathbf{M}}_i \equiv \hat{\mathbf{M}}_j$. Then the base-level PNs at states $\hat{\mathbf{M}}_i$ and $\hat{\mathbf{M}}_j$ are isomorphic.

Consider the very simple example in Figure 9, which depicts three base-level PN configurations, at different time instants. The hypothesis is that while symbol t_2 denotes a "named" transition, symbols x_i and y_j denote "unnamed" places and transitions, respectively. Since there are no inhibitor arcs we assume that arcs are reified as tokens (2-tuples) belonging to *NODE* × *NODE*. We assume that all transitions have the same priority level, so we disregard the reification of priorities.

We can observe that the Petri nets on the left and on the middle are nearly the same, but for their current marking: we can imagine that they represent a possible (internal) dynamics of the base-level PN. Conversely, we might think of the right-most Petri net as an (apparent) evolution of the base-level PN on the left, in which transition y_2 has been replaced by the (new) transition y_3, new connections are set, and a new marking is defined.

Figure 9. Equivalent Base-Level Petri Net Evolutions

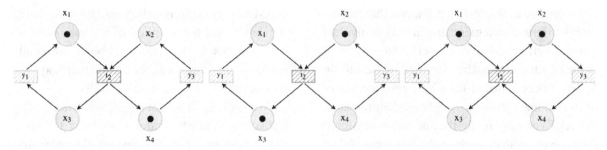

Nevertheless, the three base-level configurations are equivalent, according to Definition 7. It is sufficient to take a look at their respective reifications, which are encoded as symbolic markings (multisets are expressed as formal sums): consider for instance the base-level PN on the left and on the middle of Figure 9, whose reification are:

$$\hat{\mathbf{M}}(\text{BLreif} \mid \text{Nodes}) = y_1 + y_2 + t_2 + x_1 + x_2 + x_3 + x_4,$$

$$\hat{\mathbf{M}}(\text{BLreif} \mid \text{Marking}) = x_1 + x_4,$$

$$\hat{\mathbf{M}}(\text{BLreif} \mid \text{Arcs}) = \langle x_1,t_2 \rangle + \langle t_2,x_3 \rangle + \langle x_3,y_1 \rangle + \langle y_1,x_1 \rangle + \langle x_2,t_2 \rangle +$$

$$\langle t_2,x_4 \rangle + \langle x_4,y_2 \rangle + \langle y_2,x_2 \rangle$$

and

$$\hat{\mathbf{M}}'(\text{BLreif} \mid \text{Nodes}) = y_1 + y_2 + t_2 + x_1 + x_2 + x_3 + x_4,$$

$$\hat{\mathbf{M}}'(\text{BLreif} \mid \text{Marking}) = x_3 + x_2,$$

$$\hat{\mathbf{M}}'(\text{BLreif} \mid \text{Arcs}) = \langle x_1,t_2 \rangle + \langle t_2,x_3 \rangle + \langle x_3,y_1 \rangle + \langle y_1,x_1 \rangle +$$

$$\langle x_2,t_2 \rangle + \langle t_2,x_4 \rangle + \langle x_4,y_2 \rangle + \langle y_2,x_2 \rangle$$

respectively. They can be obtained from one another by the following permutation of "unnamed" places and transitions (we denote by $a \leftrightarrow b$ the bidirectional mapping: $a \rightarrow b, b \rightarrow a$):

$$\{x_1 \leftrightarrow x_2, x_3 \leftrightarrow x_4, y_1 \leftrightarrow y_2\},$$

thus, they are equivalent.

With similar arguments, the left-most and the right-most Petri nets of Figure 9 are shown to be equivalent. The left-most Petri net's reification is:

$$\hat{\mathbf{M}}''(\text{BLreif} \mid \text{Nodes}) = y_1 + y_3 + t_2 + x_1 + x_2 + x_3 + x_4,$$

$$\hat{\mathbf{M}}''(\text{BLreif} \mid \text{Marking}) = x_1 + x_2,$$

$$\hat{\mathbf{M}}''(\text{BLreif} \mid \text{Arcs}) = \langle x_1,t_2 \rangle + \langle t_2,x_3 \rangle + \langle x_3,y_1 \rangle + \langle y_1,x_1 \rangle +$$

$$\langle x_2,y_3 \rangle + \langle y_3,x_4 \rangle + \langle x_4,t_2 \rangle + \langle t_2,x_2 \rangle$$

$\hat{\mathbf{M}}$ and $\hat{\mathbf{M}}''$ can be obtained from one another through the following permutation:

$$\{x_2 \leftrightarrow x_4, y_3 \leftrightarrow y_2\},$$

The canonical representative for these equivalent base-level PN's reifications (i.e., states of the Reflective Petri net model), computed according to the corresponding SWN algorithm, turns out to be $\hat{\mathbf{M}}$.

RELATED WORKS

Although many other models of concurrent and distributed systems have been developed, Petri Nets are still considered a central model for concurrent systems with respect to both the theory and the applications due to the natural way they allow to represent reasoning on concurrent active objects which share resources and their changing states. Despite their modeling power (Petri nets with inhibitor arcs are Turing-equivalent) however, classical Petri nets are often considered unsuiTable to model real systems. For that reason, several high-level Petri nets paradigms (Colored Petri nets, Predicate/Transition Nets, Algebraic Petri nets) have been proposed in the literature (Jensen & Rozenberg, 1991) over the last two decades to provide modelers with a more flexible and parametric formalism able to exploit the symmetric structure of most artificial discrete-event systems.

Modern information systems are more and more characterized by a dynamic/reconfigurable (distributed) topology and they are often conceived as self-evolving structures, able to adapt their behavior and their functionality to environmental changes and new user needs. Evolutionary design is now a diffuse practice, and there is a growing demand for modeling/simulation tools that can better support the design phase. Both Petri nets and HLPN are characterized by a fixed structure (topology), so many research efforts have been devoted, especially in the last two decades, in trying to extend Petri nets with dynamical features. Follows a non-exhaustive list of proposals appeared in the literature.

In Valk, 1978, the author is proposing his pioneering work, *self-modifying* nets. Valk's self-modifying nets introduce dynamism via self modification. More precisely the flow relation between a place and a transition is a linear function of the place marking. Techniques of linear algebra used in the study of the structural properties of Petri nets can be adapted in this extended framework. Only simple evolution patterns can be represented using this formalism. Another major contribution of Valk is the so-called *nets-within-nets* paradigm (Valk, 1998), a multi-layer approach, where tokens flowing through a net are in turn nets. In his work, Valk takes an object as a token in a unary elementary Petri net system,

whereas the object itself is an elementary net system. So, an object can migrate across a net system. This bears some resemblance with logical agent mobility. Even if in the original Valk's proposal no dynamic changes are possible, many dynamic architectures introduced afterward (including in some sense also the approach proposed in this chapter) rely upon his paradigm.

Some quite recent proposals have extended Valk's original ideas. Badouel & Darondeau, 1997 introduces a subclass of self-modifying nets. The considered nets appear as stratified sums of ordinary nets and they arise as a counterpart to cascade products of automata via the duality between automata and nets. Nets in this class, called *stratified nets*, cannot exhibit circular dependences between places: inscription on flow arcs attached to a given place depends at most on the content of places in the lower layers. As an attempt to add modeling flexibility, Badouel & Oliver, 1998 defines a class of high-level Petri nets, called *reconfigurable nets*, that can dynamically modify their own structure by rewriting some of their components. Boundedness of a reconfigurable net can be decided by calculating its covering tree. Moreover such a net can be simulated by a self-modifying Petri net. The class of reconfigurable nets thus provides a subclass of self-modifying Petri nets for which boundedness can be decided.

Modeling mobility, both physical and logical, is another active subject of ongoing research. Mobile and dynamic Petri nets (Asperti & Busi, 1996) integrate Petri nets with RCHAM (Reflective Chemical Abstract Machine) based process algebra. In dynamic nets tokens are names for places, an input token of a transition can be used in its postset to specify a destination, and moreover the creation of new nets during the firing of a transition is also possible. Mobile Petri nets handle mobility expressing the configuration changing of communication channels among processes.

Tokens in Petri nets, even in self-modifying, mobile/dynamic and reconfigurable nets, are passive, whereas agents are active. To bridge the gap between tokens and agents, or active objects, many authors have proposed variations on the theme of *nets-within-nets*. In Farwer & Moldt, 2005, objects are studied as higher-level net tokens having an individual dynamical behavior. Object nets behave like tokens, i.e., they are lying in places and are moved by transitions. In contrast to ordinary tokens, however, they may change their state. By this approach an interesting two-level system modeling technique is introduced. Xu, Yin, Deng, & Ding, 2003 proposes a two-layers approach. From the perspective of system's architecture, it presents an approach to modeling logical agent mobility by using Predicate Transition nets as formal basis for the dynamic framework. Reference nets proposed in Kummer, 1998 are another formalism based on Valk's work. Reference nets are a special high level Petri net formalism that provide dynamic creation of net instances, references to other reference nets as tokens, and communication via synchronous channels (Java is used as inscription language).

Some recent proposals have some similarity with the work we are presenting in this chapter or, at least, are inspired by similar aims. In Cabac et al., 2005 the authors present the basic concepts for a dynamic architecture modeling (using nets-within-nets) that allows active elements to be nested in arbitrary and dynamically changeable hierarchies and enables the design of systems at different levels of abstractions by using refinements of net models. The conceptual modeling of such architecture is applied to specify a software system that is divided into a plug-in management system and plug-ins that provide functionality to the users. By combining plug-ins, the system can be dynamically adapted to the users needs. In Hoffmann et al., 2005 the authors introduce the new paradigm of *nets and rules as tokens*, where in addition to nets as tokens also rules as tokens are considered. The rules can be used to change the net structure and behavior. This leads to the new concept of high-level net and rule systems, which allows to integrate the token game with

rule-based transformations of P/T-systems. The new concept is based on algebraic nets and graph transformation systems. Finally, in Odersky, 2000 the author introduces functional nets, which combine key ideas of functional programming and Petri nets to yield a simple and general programming notation. They have their theoretical foundation in join calculus. Over the last decade an operational view of program execution based on rewriting has become widespread. In this view, a program is seen as a term in some calculus, and program execution is modeled by stepwise rewriting of the term according to the rules of the calculus.

All these formalisms, however, set up new hybrid (high-level) Petri net-based paradigms. While the expressive power has increased, the cognitive simplicity, which is the most important advantage of Petri nets, has decreased as well. In Badouel, 1998 the authors argued that the intricacy of these models leaves little hope to obtain significant mathematical results and/or automated verification tools in a close future. The approach we are presenting differs from the previous ones mainly because it achieves a satisfactory compromise between expressive power and analysis capability, through a quite rigorous application of classical reflection concepts in a consolidated (high-level) Petri net framework.

CONCLUSION AND FUTURE WORK

Most discrete-event systems are subject to evolution, and need to be updated or extended with new characteristics during lifecycle. Covering the evolutionary aspects of systems since the design phase has been widely recognized as a crucial challenge. A good evolution has to pass through the evolution of the design information of the system itself. Petri nets are a central formalism for the modeling of discrete-event systems. Unfortunately classical Petri nets have a static structure, so Petri net modelers are forced to hard-code all the foreseeable evolutions of a system at the design level.

This common practice not only requires modeling expertise, it also makes system's design be polluted by lot of details that do not regard the (current) system functionality, and affect the consolidated Petri nets analysis techniques.

We have faced the problem through the definition of a Petri net-based reflective architecture, called Reflective Petri Nets, structured in two logical levels: the base-level, specifying the evolving system, and the evolutionary meta-program (the meta-level). The meta-program is in charge of observing in transparent way, then (if necessary) transforming, the base-level PN. With this approach the model of the system and the model of the evolution are kept separated, granting, therefore, the opportunity of analyzing the model without useless details. The evolutionary aspects are orthogonal to the functional aspects of the system.

In this chapter we have introduced Reflective Petri nets, and we propose an effective timed state-transition semantics (in terms of a Markov process) as a first step toward the implementation of a (performance-oriented) discrete-event simulation engine for Reflective Petri nets. Ongoing research is in different directions. We are planning to extend the GreatSPN tool to directly support Reflective Petri nets, both in the editing and in the analysis/simulation steps. We are investigating other possible semantic characterizations (in terms of different stochastic processes), on the perspective of improving the analysis capability. We are currently using two different formalisms for the base- and meta- levels (ordinary and colored stochastic Petri nets). It might be convenient to adopt the same formalism for both levels, what would give origin to the reflective tower allowing the designer to model also the possible evolution of the evolutionary strategies.

REFERENCES

Asperti, A., & Busi, N. (1996, May). *Mobile Petri Nets* (Tech. Rep. No. UBLCS-96-10). Bologna, Italy: Università degli Studi di Bologna.

Badouel, E., & Darondeau, P. (1997, September). Stratified Petri Nets. In B. S. Chlebus & L. Czaja (Eds.), *Proceedings of the 11th International Symposium on Fundamentals of Computation Theory (FCT'97)* (p. 117-128). Kraków, Poland: Springer.

Badouel, E., & Oliver, J. (1998, January). *Reconfigurable Nets, a Class of High Level Petri Nets Supporting Dynamic Changes within Workflow Systems* (IRISA Research Report No. PI-1163). IRISA.

Bernardi, S., Donatelli, S., & Horvàth, A. (2001, September). Implementing Compositionality for Stochastic Petri Nets. *Journal of Software Tools for Technology Transfer, 3*(4), 417–430.

Best, E. (1986, September). COSY: Its Relation to Nets and CSP. In W. Brauer, W. Reisig, & G. Rozenberg (Eds.), *Petri Nets: Central Models and Their Properties, Advances in Petri Nets (Part II)* (p. 416-440). Bad Honnef, Germany: Springer.

Cabac, L., Duvignau, M., Moldt, D., & Rölke, H. (2005, June). Modeling Dynamic Architectures Using Nets-Within-Nets. In G. Ciardo & P. Darondeau (Eds.), *Proceedings of the 26th International Conference on Applications and Theory of Petri Nets (ICATPN 2005)* (p. 148-167). Miami, FL: Springer.

Capra, L., & Cazzola, W. (2007, December). Self-Evolving Petri Nets. *Journal of Universal Computer Science, 13*(13), 2002–2034.

Capra, L., & Cazzola, W. (2009). Trying out Reflective Petri Nets on a Dynamic Workflow Case. In E. M. O. Abu-Atieh (Ed.), *Handbook of Research on Discrete Event Simulation Environments Technologies and Applications*. Hershey, PA: IGI Global.

Capra, L., De Pierro, M., & Franceschinis, G. (2005, June). A High Level Language for Structural Relations in Well-Formed Nets. In G. Ciardo & P. Darondeau (Eds.), *Proceeding of the 26th international conference on application and theory of Petri nets* (p. 168-187). Miami, FL: Springer.

Cazzola, W. (1998, July 20th-24th). Evaluation of Object-Oriented Reflective Models. In *Proceedings of ecoop workshop on reflective object-oriented programming and systems (ewroops'98)*. Brussels, Belgium.

Cazzola, W., Ghoneim, A., & Saake, G. (2004, July). Software Evolution through Dynamic Adaptation of Its OO Design. In H.-D. Ehrich, J.-J. Meyer, & M. D. Ryan (Eds.), *Objects, Agents and Features: Structuring Mechanisms for Contemporary Software* (pp. 69-84). Heidelberg, Germany: Springer-Verlag.

Chiola, G., Dutheillet, C., Franceschinis, G., & Haddad, S. (1990, June). On Well-Formed Coloured Nets and Their Symbolic Reachability Graph. In *Proceedings of the 11th international conference on application and theory of Petri nets*, (p. 387-410). Paris, France.

Chiola, G., Dutheillet, C., Franceschinis, G., & Haddad, S. (1993, November). Stochastic Well-Formed Coloured Nets for Symmetric Modeling Applications. *IEEE Transactions on Computers*, *42*(11), 1343–1360. doi:10.1109/12.247838

Chiola, G., Franceschinis, G., Gaeta, R., & Ribaudo, M. (1995, November). GreatSPN 1.7: Graphical Editor and Analyzer for Timed and Stochastic Petri Nets. *Performance Evaluation*, *24*(1-2), 47–68. doi:10.1016/0166-5316(95)00008-L

Farwer, B., & Moldt, D. (Eds.). (2005, August). *Object Petri Nets, Process, and Object Calculi*. Hamburg, Germany: Universität Hamburg, Fachbereich Informatik.

Hoare, C. A. R. (1985). *Communicating Sequential Processes*. Upper Saddle River, NJ: Prentice Hall.

Hoffmann, K., Ehrig, H., & Mossakowski, T. (2005, June). High-Level Nets with Nets and Rules as Tokens. In G. Ciardo & P. Darondeau (Eds.), *Proceedings of the 26th International Conference on Applications and Theory of Petri Nets* (p. 268-288). Miami, FL: Springer

Hürsch, W., & Videira Lopes, C. (1995, February). *Separation of Concerns* (Tech. Rep. No. NUCCS-95-03). Northeastern University, Boston.

Jensen, K., & Rozenberg, G. (Eds.). (1991). *High-Level Petri Nets: Theory and Applications*. Berlin: Springer-Verlag.

Kavi, K. M., Sheldon, F. T., Shirazi, B., & Hurson, A. R. (1995, January). Reliability Analysis of CSP Specifications Using Petri Nets and Markov Processes. In *Proceedings of the 28th Annual Hawaii International Conference on System Sciences (HICSS-28)* (p. 516-524). Kihei, Maui, HI: IEEE Computer Society.

Kummer, O. (1998, October). Simulating Synchronous Channels and Net Instances. In J. Desel, P. Kemper, E. Kindler, & A. Oberweis (Eds.), *Proceedings of the Workshop Algorithmen und Werkzeuge für Petrinetze* (Vol. 694, pp. 73-78). Dortmund, Germany: Universität Dortmund, Fachbereich Informatik.

Maes, P. (1987, October). Concepts and Experiments in Computational Reflection. In N. K. Meyrowitz (Ed.), *Proceedings of the 2nd conference on object-oriented programming systems, languages, and applications (OOPSLA'87)* (Vol. 22, p. 147-156), Orlando, FL.

Odersky, M. (2000, March). Functional Nets. In G. Smolka (Ed.), *Proceedings of the 9th European Symposium on Programming (ESOP 2000)* (p. 1-25). Berlin, Germany: Springer.

Valk, R. (1978, July). Self-Modifying Nets, a Natural Extension of Petri Nets. In G. Ausiello & C. Böhm (Eds.), *Proceedings of the Fifth Colloquium on Automata, Languages and Programming (ICALP'78),* (p. 464-476). Udine, Italy: Springer.

Valk, R. (1998, June). Petri Nets as Token Objects: An Introduction to Elementary Object Nets. In J. Desel & M. Silva (Eds.), *Proceedings of the 19th International Conference on Applications and Theory of Petri Nets (ICATPN 1998)* (p. 1-25). Lisbon, Portugal: Springer.

Xu, D., Yin, J., Deng, Y., & Ding, J. (2003, January). A Formal Architectural Model for Logical Agent Mobility. *IEEE Transactions on Software Engineering, 29*(1), 31–45. doi:10.1109/TSE.2003.1166587

KEY TERMS AND DEFINITIONS

Evolution: Attitude of systems to change layout/functionality.

Dynamic Systems: Discrete-event systems subject to evolution.

Petri Nets: Graphical formalism for discrete-event systems.

Reflection: Activity performed by an agent when doing computations about itself.

Base-Level: Logical level of a reflective model representing the system prone to evolve.

Meta-Level: Logical level of a reflective model representing the evolutionary strategy.

State-Transition Graph: Graph describing the behavior of a system in terms of states and transitions between them.

ENDNOTES

[1] Labels taking the form place_name | postfix denote *boundary-places*

[2] Recall that: i) CSP is based on *guarded-commands*; ii) structured commands are included between square brackets; and iii) symbols ?, *, and □ denote input, *repetition* and *alternative* commands, respectively.

Chapter 10
Trying Out Reflective Petri Nets on a Dynamic Workflow Case

Lorenzo Capra
Università degli Studi di Milano, Italy

Walter Cazzola
Università degli Studi di Milano, Italy

ABSTRACT

Industrial/business processes are an evident example of discrete-event systems which are subject to evolution during life-cycle. The design and management of dynamic workflows need adequate formal models and support tools to handle in sound way possible changes occurring during workflow operation. The known, well-established workflow's models, among which Petri nets play a central role, are lacking in features for representing evolution. We propose a recent Petri net-based reflective layout, called Reflective Petri nets, as a formal model for dynamic workflows. A localized open problem is considered: how to determine what tasks should be redone and which ones do not when transferring a workflow instance from an old to a new template. The problem is efficiently but rather empirically addressed in a workflow management system. Our approach is formal, may be generalized, and is based on the preservation of classical Petri nets structural properties, which permit an efficient characterization of workflow's soundness.

INTRODUCTION

Business processes are frequently subject to change due to two main reasons (Aalst & Jablonski, 2000): i) at design time the workflow specification is incomplete due to lack of knowledge, ii) errors or exceptional situations can occur during the workflow execution; these are usually tackled on by deviating

DOI: 10.4018/978-1-60566-774-4.ch010

from the static schema, and may cause breakdowns, reduced quality of services, and inconsistencies.

Workflow management facilitates creating and executing business processes. Most of existing Workflow Management Systems, WMS in the sequel (e.g., IBM Domino, iPlanet, Fujisu iFlow, Team-Center), are designed to cope with static processes. The commonly adopted policy is that, once process changes occur, new workflow templates are defined and workflow instances are initiated accordingly from scratch. This over-simplified approach forces tasks that were completed on the old instance to be executed again, also when not necessary. If the workflow is complex and/or involves a lot of external collaborators, a substantial business cost will be incurred.

Dynamic workflow management might be brought in as a solution. Formal techniques and analysis tools can support the development of WMS able to handle undesired results introduced by dynamic change. Evolutionary workflow design is a challenge on which lot of research efforts are currently devoted. A good evolution is carried out through the evolution of workflow's design information, and then by propagating these changes to the implementation. This approach should be the most natural and intuitive to use (because it adopts the same mechanisms adopted during the development phase) and it should produce the best results (because each evolutionary step is planned and documented before its application).

At the moment evolution is emulated by directly enriching original design information with properties and characteristics concerning possible evolutions. This approach has two main drawbacks: i) all possible evolutions are not always foreseeable; ii) design information is polluted by details related to the design of the evolved system.

In the research on dynamic workflows, the prevalent opinion is that models should be based on a formal theory and be as simple as possible. In Agostini & De Michelis, 2000 process templates are provided as 'resources for action' rather than strict blueprints of work practices. May be the most famous dynamic workflow formalization, the ADEPTflex system (Reichert & Dadam, 1998), is designed to support dynamic change at runtime, making at our disposal a complete and minimal set of change operations. The correctness properties defined by ADEPTflex are used to determine whether a specific change can be applied to a given workflow instance or not.

Petri nets play a central role in workflow modeling (Salimifard & Wright, 2001), due to their description efficacy, formal essence, and the availability of consolidated analysis techniques. Classical Petri nets (Reisig, 1985) have a fixed topology, so they are well suited to model workflows matching a static paradigm, i.e., processes that are finished or aborted once they are initiated. Conversely, any concerns related to dynamism/evolution must be hard-wired in classical Petri nets and bypassed when not in use. That requires some expertise in Petri nets modeling, and might result in incorrect or partial descriptions of workflow behavior. Even worst, analysis would be polluted by a great deal of details concerning evolution.

Separating evolution from (current) system functionality is worthwhile. This concept has been recently applied to a Petri net-based model (Capra & Cazzola, 2007b), called Reflective Petri nets, using reflection (Maes, 1987) as mechanisms that easily permits separation of concerns. A layout formed by two causally connected levels (base-, and meta-) is used. the base-level (an ordinary Petri net) is unaware of the *meta-level* (a high-level Petri net).

Base-level entities perform computations on the entities of the application domain whereas entities in the meta-level perform computations on the entities residing on the lower level. The computational flow passes from the base-level to the meta-level by intercepting some events and specific computations (*shift-up* action) and backs when the meta-computation has finished (*shift-down* action). Meta-level computations are carried out on a representative of the lower-level, called *reification*, which is kept causally connected to the original level.

With respect to other dynamic Petri net extensions (Cabac, Duvignau, Moldt, & Rölke, 2005; Hoffmann, Ehrig, & Mossakowski, 2005; Badouel & Oliver, 1998; Ellis & Keddara, 2000; Hicheur, Barkaoui, & Boudiaf, 2006), Reflective Petri nets (Capra & Cazzola, 2007b) are not a new Petri net class, rather they rely upon classical Petri nets. That gives the possibility of using available tools and consolidated analysis techniques.

We propose Reflective Petri nets as formal model supporting the design of sound dynamic workflows. A structural characterization of sound dynamic workflows is adopted, based on Petri net's free-choiceness preservation. The approach is applied to a localized open problem: how to determine what tasks should be redone and which ones do not when transferring a workflow instance from an old to a new template. The problem is efficiently but rather empirically addressed in Qiu & Wong, 2007, according to a template-based schema relying on the concept of *bypassable* task. Conforming to the same concept we propose an alternative, that allows evolutionary steps to be soundly formalized, and basic workflow properties to be efficiently verified.

As widely agreed (Agostini & De Michelis, 2000), the workflow model is kept as simple as possible. Our approach has some resemblance with Reichert & Dadam, 1998, sharing some completeness/smallness criteria, even if it considerably differs in management of changes: it neither provides exception handling nor undoing mechanism of temporary changes; rather it relies upon a sort of "on-the-fly" validation.

The balance of the chapter is as follows: first we give a few basic notions around Petri nets and workflows; then we sketch a template-based dynamic workflow approach (Qiu & Wong, 2007) adopted by an industrial WMS; finally, we present our alternative based on Reflective Petri nets, using the same application case as in Qiu & Wong, 2007; we conclude drawing conclusions and perspectives. We refer to the companion chapter (Capra & Cazzola, 2009) for a complete, up-to-date introduction on Reflective Petri nets.

WORKFLOW PETRI NETS

This section introduces the base-level Petri net subclass used in the sequel, with related notations, and properties. We refer to Reisig, 1985; Aalst, 1996 for more elaborate introductions.

Definition 1 (Petri net). *A Petri net is a triple* $(P;T;F)$, *in which:*

- P is a finite set of places,
- T is a finite set of transitions $(P \cap T = \varnothing$;$)$,
- $F \subseteq (P \times T) \cup (T \times P)$ is a set of arcs (flow relation)

In accordance with the simplicity assumption (Agostini & De Michelis, 2000), we are considering a restriction of base-level Petri nets used in Capra & Cazzola, 2009. In the workflow context, it makes no sense to have weighted arcs, because tokens in places correspond to conditions. Consequently, in a well-defined workflow a marking **m** is a set of places, i.e., $\mathbf{m} \in Set(P)$. In general a marking is a mapping, $\mathbf{m} : P \rightarrow \mathbb{N}$. Inhibitor arcs and priorities are unnecessary to model the routing of cases in a workflow Petri net.

$^\bullet x, x^\bullet$ denote the pre- and post- sets of $x \in P \cup T$, respectively (the set-extensions $^\bullet A, A^\bullet A \subseteq P \cup T$, will be also used). Transitions change the state of the net according to the following rule:

- t is enabled in **m** if and only if each place $p \in {}^\bullet t$ contains at least one token.
  - if t is enabled in **m** the it *can* fire, consuming one token from each $p \in {}^\bullet t$ and producing one token for each $p \in {}^\bullet t$

Let $PN = (P;T;F)$, $t_i \in T$, $n_i \in T \cup P$, $\sigma = t_1, t_2, \ldots t_{k-1}$ (possibly $\sigma = \varepsilon$).

BASIC NOTIONS/NOTATIONS

$\mathbf{m}_1 \overset{t_1}{\to} \mathbf{m}_2$ if and only if t_1 is enabled in $\mathbf{m}_1$ and its firing results in $\mathbf{m}_2$

- $\mathbf{m}_1 \overset{\sigma}{\to} \mathbf{m}_k$ if and only if $\mathbf{m}_1 \overset{t_1}{\to} \mathbf{m}_2 \overset{t_2}{\to} \ldots, \mathbf{m}_{k-1} \overset{t_{k-1}}{\to} \mathbf{m}_k$.
- $\mathbf{m}_k$ is *reachable* from $\mathbf{m}_1$ if and only if $\exists \sigma, \mathbf{m}_1 \overset{\sigma}{\to} \mathbf{m}_k$.
- $(PN; \mathbf{m}_0)$ is a Petri net with an initial state $\mathbf{m}_0$.
- Given $(PN; \mathbf{m}_0)$, $\mathbf{m}'$ is said reachable if and only if it is reachable from $\mathbf{m}_0$.

Behavioral Properties

(Live). $(PN; \mathbf{m}_0)$ is live if and only if, for every reachable state $\mathbf{m}'$ and every transition t there exists $\mathbf{m}''$ reachable from $\mathbf{m}'$ which enables t.

(Bounded, safe). $(PN; \mathbf{m}_0)$ is bounded if and only if for each place p there exists $b \in \mathbb{N}$ such that for every reachable state $\mathbf{m}, \mathbf{m}(p) \leq b$. A bounded net is safe if and only if $b = 1$. A marking of a safe Petri net is denoted by a set of places.

Structural Properties

(Path). A path from n_1 to n_k is a sequence $n_1, n_2, \ldots, n_k$ such that $(n_i, n_{i+1}) \in F$, $\forall i$ $1 \leq i \leq k-1$

(Conflict). t_1 and t_2 are in conflict if and only if $^\bullet t_1 \cap {}^\bullet t_2 \neq \varnothing$.

(Free-choice). PN is free-choice if and only if $\forall t_1, t_2 \; {}^\bullet t_1 \cap {}^\bullet t_2 \neq \varnothing \Rightarrow {}^\bullet t_1 = {}^\bullet t_2$.

(Causal connection - CC). t_1 is causally connected to t_2 if and only if $(t_1{}^\bullet \setminus {}^\bullet t_1) \cap {}^\bullet t_2 \neq \varnothing$.

Sound Workflow-Nets and Free-Choiceness

A Petri net can be used to specify the control flow of a workflow. Tasks are modeled by transitions, places correspond to task's pre/post-conditions. Causal dependencies between tasks are modeled by arcs (and places).

Definition 2 (Workflow-net). *A Petri net PN* $= (P;T;F)$ *is a Workflow-net (hereafter WF-net) if and only if:*

- There is one source place i such that $^\bullet i = \varnothing$.
- There is one sink place o such that $o^\bullet = \varnothing$.
- Every $x \in P \cup T$ is on a path from i to o.

A WF-net specifies the life-cycle of a case, so it has exactly one input place (i) and one output place (o). The third requirement in definition 2 avoids dangling tasks and/or conditions, i.e., tasks and conditions which do not contribute to the processing of cases.

If we add to a WF-net PN a transition $t*$ such that $^\bullet(t*) = \{o\}$ and $(t*)^\bullet = \{i\}$, then the resulting Petri net $\overline{PN}$ (called the *short-circuited* net of PN) is strongly connected.

The requirements stated in definition 2 only relate to the structure of a Petri net. However, there is another requirement that should be satisfied:

Definition 3 (soundness). *A WF-net PN* $= (P;T;F)$ *is sound if and only if:*

- for every $\mathbf{m}$ reachable from state $\{i\}$, there exists σ, $\mathbf{m} \overset{\sigma}{\to} \{o\}$
- $\{o\}$ is the only marking reachable from $\{i\}$ with at least one token in place o
- there are no dead transitions i)n $(PN;\{i\})$, i.e., $\forall t \in T$ there exists a reachable $\mathbf{m}$, $\mathbf{m} \overset{t}{\to} \mathbf{m}'$

In other words: for any cases, the procedure will terminate eventually[1], when the procedure terminates there is a token in place o with all the other places empty (that is referred to as *proper termination*), moreover, it should be possible to execute any tasks by following the appropriate route through the WF-net.

The soundness property relates to the dynamics of a WF-net, and may be considered as a basic requirement for any process. It is shown in Aalst, 1996 that a WF-net PN is sound if and only if $(\overline{PN}; \{i\})$ is *live and bounded*. Despite that helpful characterization, deciding about soundness of arbitrary WF-nets may be intractable: liveness and boundedness are decidable, but also EXPSPACE-hard.

Therefore, structural characterizations of sound WF-nets were investigated (Aalst, 1996). Free-choice Petri nets seem to be a good compromise between expressive power and analysis capability. They are the widest class of Petri nets for which strong theoretical results and efficient analysis techniques do exist (Desel & Esparza, 1995). In particular (Aalst, 1996), soundness of a free-choice WF-net (as well as many other problems) can be decided in *polynomial* time. Moreover, a sound free-choice WF-net (PN; $\{i\}$) is guaranteed to be *safe*, according to the interpretation of places as conditions.

Another good reason to restrict our attention to workflow models specified by free-choice WF-nets is that the routing of a case should be independent of the order in which tasks are executed. If non free-choice Petri nets were admitted, then the solution of conflicts could be influenced by the order in which tasks are executed. In literature the term confusion is often used to refer to a situation where free-choiceness is violated by a badly mixture of parallelism and conflict. Free-choiceness is a desirable property for workflows. If a process can be modeled as free-choice WF-net, one should do so. Most of existing WMS support free-choice processes only. We will admit as base-level Petri nets free-choice WF-nets.

Even though free-choice WF-nets are a satisfactory characterization of well-defined workflow procedures, for which soundness can be efficiently checked, there are WF-nets non free-choice which correspond to sensible processes. S-coverability (Aalst, 1996) is a generalization of free-choiceness: a sound free-choice WF-net is in fact S-coverable. In general, it is impossible to verify soundness of an arbitrary S-coverable WF-net in polynomial time, that problem being PSPACE-complete. In many practical cases, however, this theoretical complexity significantly lowers, so that S-coverability could be considered as an interesting alternative to free-choiceness.

A TEMPLATE-BASED APPROACH TO DYNAMIC WORKFLOWS

An interesting solution to facilitate an efficient management of dynamic workflows is proposed in Qiu & Wong, 2007. WMS supporting dynamic workflow change can either directly modify the affected instance, or restart it on a new workflow template. The first method is instance based while the second is template based. The approach we are considering, in accordance with a consolidated practice, falls in the second category, and is implemented in Dassault Systèmes SmarTeam (ENOVIA, 2007), a PLM (Product Lifecycle Management) system including a WMS module. In Qiu & Wong, 2007 workflows are formally specified by Directed Network Graphs (DNG), which can be easily translated into PN.

The idea consists of identifying all *bypassable* tasks, i.e., all tasks in the new workflow instance that satisfy the following conditions: i) they are unchanged, ii) they have finished in the old workflow instance, and iii) they need not be re-executed.

A task (transition, in Petri nets) is said *unchanged*, before and after a transformation of the workflow template, if and only if it represents the same activity (what will be always assumed true), and preserves input/output connections. To determine if a task is *bypassable* when the instance is transferred to a new template, an additional constraint is needed: all tasks from which there is a path (i.e, are causally connected) to the task itself, must be bypassable in turn. A smart algorithm permits the identification of bypassable tasks: starting from the initial task, which is bypassable by default, only successors of bypassable tasks are considered.

This solution has been implemented in SmarTeam system, that includes a workflow manager and a messaging subsystem, but no built-in mechanisms to face dynamic workflow's change. A set of API enables detaching and attaching operations between processes and workflow templates. A process is redone entirely if its template is changed. Workflow's change is implemented by an application-server, which executes the following steps:

1. Obtain a process instance;
2. Obtain the old and new workflow templates;
3. Attach the new workflow template to the process;
4. Identify and mark the tasks that can be bypassed in the new workflow instance;
5. Initiate the new workflow without redoing the marked tasks.

What appears completely unspecified in Qiu & Wong, 2007 is how to safely operate steps 4 and 5: some heuristics appear to be adopted, rather than a well defined methodology. No formal tests are carried out to verify the soundness of a workflow instance transferred to the modified template.

AN ALTERNATIVE BASED ON REFLECTIVE PETRI NETS

We propose an alternative to Qiu & Wong, 2007, based on Reflective Petri nets, which allows a full formalization of the evolutionary steps, as well as a validation of changes proposed for the workflow template, by means of a simple Petri nets structural analysis. Validation is accomplished "on-the-fly", i.e., by operating on the workflow reification while change is in progress. Changes are not reflected to the base-level in case of a negative check. With respect to a preliminary version (Capra & Cazzola, 2007a), the evolutionary strategy, as concerns in particular the validation part, is redesigned and some bugs are fixed.

We consider the same application case presented in Qiu & Wong, 2007. A company has several regional branches. To enhance operation consistence, the company headquarter (HQ) standardizes business processes in all branches. A workflow template is defined to handle customer problems. When the staff in a branch encounters a problem, a workflow instance is initiated from the template and executed until completion.

The Petri net specification of the initial template is given in Figure 1. A problem goes through two stages: problem solving and on-site realization. Problem solving involves several tasks, included in a dashed box. When opening a case, the staff reports the case to HQ. When closing the case, it archives the related documents. The HQ manages all instances related to the problem handling process.

In response to business needs, HQ may decide to change the problem handling template. The new template (Figure 2) differs from the original one in two points: a) "reporting" and "problem solving" become independent activities; b) "on site realization" can fail, in that case procedure "problem solving" restarts.

At Petri net level, we can observe that transition Report is causally-connected to ProductChange in Figure 1, while it is not in Figure 2, and that a new transition has been added in Figure 2 (RealizationRejected) which is in free-choice conflict with OnSiteRealization.

When using Reflective Petri nets, the evolutionary schema has to be redesigned. The new workflow template is not passed as input to the staff of the company branches, but it results from

Figure 1. An instance of a workflow template (begin, end are used instead of i and o)

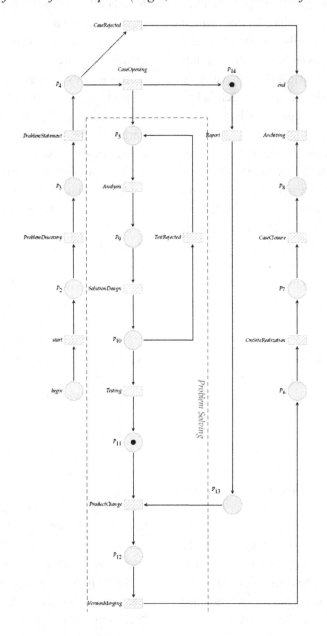

applying an evolutionary strategy to a workflow instance belonging to the current template. The initial base-level Petri nets is assumed a *free-choice WF-net*. No details about the workflow dynamics are hard-wired in the base-level net. Evolution is delegated to the meta-program, that acts on the WF-net reification.

The meta-program is activated when an evolutionary signal is sent in by HQ, or some anomaly

(e.g., a deadlock) is revealed by introspection. (Late) introspection is also used to discriminate whether evolutionary commands have been safely applied to the current workflow instance, or they have to be discarded.

Figure 1 depicts the following situation: a workflow instance running on the initial template has received a message from HQ. At the current state (marking) SolutionDesign, a sub-task of

Figure 2. Workflow's evolution

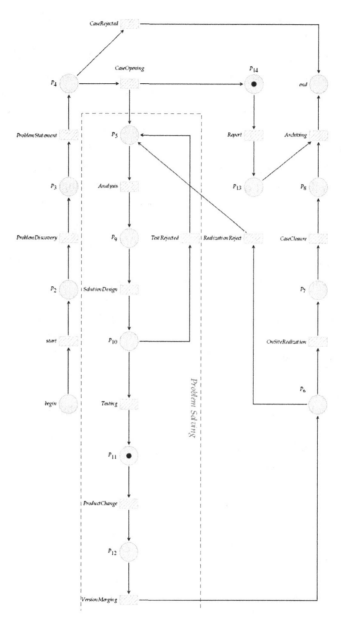

ProblemSolving, and Report are pending tasks, whereas a number of tasks (e.g., Analysis and CaseOpening) have been completed. The meta-program in that case successfully operates a change on the old template's instance, once verified that all paths to any pending tasks arc only composed of bypassable tasks.

The workflow instance transferred to the new template is illustrated in Figure 2.

One might think of this approach as instance-based, rather than template-based. In truth it covers both: if the evolutionary commands are in fact broadcasted to workflow's instances we fall in the latter scheme.

The evolutionary strategy relies upon the notion of *adjacency preserving* task, which is more general than the *unchanged* task used in Qiu & Wong, 2007. It is inspired by van der Aalst's concept that any workflow change must preserve the inheritance relationship between old and new templates (Aalst & Basten, 2002). Let us introduce some notations used in the sequel.

Let $PN = (Old\_P; Old\_T; Old\_A)$, be a base-level WF-net (better, its reification at the meta-level), $PN' = (P'; T'; A')$ be the resulting Petri net after some modifications[2], $Old\_N = Old\_P \cup Old\_T$, $N' = P' \cup T'$.

Symbols x and $\bar{x}$ refer to a node "preserved" by change, considered in the context of PN and PN', respectively.

Sets $Del\_N = Del\_P \cup Del\_T$, $New\_N = New\_P \cup New\_T$, and New_A, Del_A, denote the base level nodes/arcs added to and removed from PN, respectively.

We assume that $New\_A \cap Del\_A = \varnothing$. No other assumptions are made: for example "moving" a given node across the base-level Petri net might be simulated by first deleting the node, then putting it again setting new connections.

As explained in (Capra & Cazzola, 2009), the evolutionary framework (a transparent meta-level's component) being in charge of carrying out evolution rejects a proposed change if not consistent with respect to the current base-level's reification.

Finally, *NO_ADJ, NO_BYPS* denote the tasks not preserving adjacency and the non-bypassable tasks, respectively (of course, $NO\_ADJ \subseteq NO\_BYPS$). Some of the symbols just introduced will be used as names for the evolutionary strategy parameters.

Definition 4 (adjacent set). *Let t be a transition. The set of adjacent transitions A_t is:*

$$^{\bullet}(^{\bullet}t \cup t^{\bullet}) \cup (^{\bullet}t \cup t^{\bullet})^{\bullet} \setminus \{t\}.$$

Definition 5 (adjacency preserving task). *Let $t \in Old\_T$, $\bar{t} \in T'$. Task t is adjacency preserving if and only if $\forall x \in Old\_T, \bar{x} \in A_{\bar{t}} \Leftrightarrow x \in A_t$ and there exist a bijection $\phi : ^{\bullet}t \cup t^{\bullet} \to ^{\bullet}\bar{t} \cup \bar{t}^{\bullet}$ such that*

$\forall x \in A_t \forall y \in ^{\bullet}t \cup t^{\bullet}, y \in ^{\bullet}x \Leftrightarrow \phi(y) \in ^{\bullet}\bar{x}$ and $y \in x^{\bullet} \Leftrightarrow \phi(y) \in \bar{x}^{\bullet}$

If t is adjacency preserving then all its causality/conflict relationships to adjacent tasks are maintained. A case where Definition 5 holds, and another one where it does not, are illustrated in Figure 3 (the black bar denotes a new task, t' is used instead of $\bar{t}$). In case (b) the original input connections of t are maintained (output connections are unchanged): if the occurrence of t is made possible by the occurrence of some preceding tasks it, the same may happen in the new situation. That is not true in case (c): the occurrence of the new task represents in fact an additional precondition for any subsequent occurrence of t.

Checking definition 5 is computationally very expensive. However, if useless changes are forbidden, e.g., "deleting a given place p, then adding p' inheriting from p all connections", or "adding an arc $\langle p, t \rangle$, then deleting p or t", check's complexity can be greatly reduced.

Lemma 1 states some rules for identifying a *superset* of tasks N_a not preserving adjacency. It can be easily translated to an efficient meta-program's routine. Almost always it comes to be $N_a \equiv NO\_ADJ$.

Lemma 1. *Consider set N_a, built as follows*

$p \in Del\_P \Rightarrow ^{\bullet}p \cup p^{\bullet} \subseteq N_a$

$t \in Del\_T \Rightarrow ^{\bullet}(^{\bullet}t) \cup (t^{\bullet})^{\bullet} \subseteq N_a$

$\langle p, t \rangle \in Del\_A \vee \langle t, p \rangle \in Del\_A \Rightarrow ^{\bullet}p \cup p^{\bullet} \subseteq N_a$

$\langle p, t \rangle \in New\_A \wedge t \in Old\_N \Rightarrow \{t\} \cup D \subseteq N_a$

where $D = ^{\bullet}p \cup p^{\bullet}$ if $p \in Old\_N$, else $D = \varnothing$

Then $NO\_ADJ \subseteq N_a$.

The evolutionary meta-program if formalized in Figure 4. The use of a CSP-like syntax (Hoare, 1985; Capra & Cazzola, 2009) makes it possible its automatic translation to a high-level Petri net

Figure 3. Definition 5 Illustrated

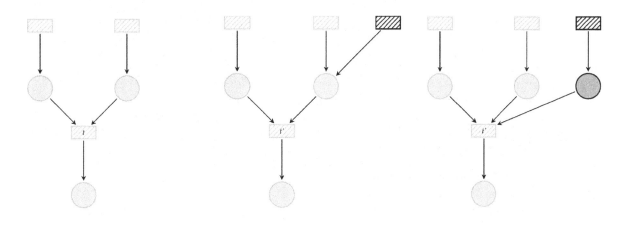

(a) initial situation   (b) change adjacency preserving   (c) change not preserving adj.

(the logical meta-level of the Reflective Petri nets layout). The meta-program is activated at any transition of state on the current workflow instance (shift-up), reacting to three different types of events. In the case of deadlock, a signal is sent to HQ, represented by a CSP process identifier. If the current instance has finished, and a "new instance" message is received, the workflow is activated. Instead if there is an incoming evolutionary message from HQ, the evolutionary strategy starts running.

```
*[
  VAR p, t, n: NODE;
  VAR New_P,New_T,Old_N,Del_N, NO_BYPS:
SET(NODE);
  VAR New_A,Del_A: SET(ARC);
  //receiving an evolutionary signal
  HQ ? change-msg() -> [
  //receiving the evolutionary commands
  HQ ? New_P; HQ ? New_T; HQ ? New_A; HQ
? Del_A; HQ ? Del_N;
  //getting the WF-net reification
  Old_N = ReifiedNodes();
  //computing the non-bypassable tasks
  NO_BYPS = ccTo(notAdjPres());
```

```
//changing the current reification
  newNode(New_P ∪ New_T);newArc(New_A);
deleteArc(Del_A); delNode(Del_N);
  //checking the (new) WF-net's well-def-
initeness
  checkWfNet(); checkFc();
  /*there might be a deadlock, or a non-
bypassable task is causally
  Connected  to a pending one ...*/
  !exists t in Tran, enab(t) or (exists t
in Tran ∩ Old_N, enab(t) and
  !isEmpty(ccBy(t) ∩ NO_BYPS)) -> [re-
start()] //rejecting changeshiftDown() //
reflecting change
  ]
[]
  #end=0 and !exists t in Tran, enab(t)
-> [HQ ! notify-deadlock()]
[]
  #end=1; HQ ? newInstance-msg() ->
[flush(end); incMark(begin)]
]
```

Just after an evolutionary signal, HQ communicates the workflow nodes/connections to

Figure 4. Workflow's evolutionary strategy

```
*[
  VAR p, t, n : NODE;
  VAR New_P,New_T,Old_N,Del_N, NO_BYPS : SET(NODE);
  VAR New_A,Del_A: SET(ARC);
  //receiving an evolutionary signal
  HQ ? change-msg() -> [
  //receiving the evolutionary commands
  HQ ? New_P; HQ ? New_T; HQ ? New_A; HQ ? Del_A; HQ ? Del_N;
  //getting the WF-net reification
  Old_N = ReifiedNodes();
  //computing the non-bypassable tasks
  NO_BYPS = ccTo(notAdjPres());
  //changing the current reification
  newNode(New_P∪New_T);newArc(New_A);              deleteArc(Del_A);
delNode(Del_N);
  //checking the (new) WF-net's well-definiteness
  checkWfNet(); checkFc();
  /*there might be a deadlock, or a non-bypassable task is causally
  Connected  to a pending one ...*/
  !exists t in Tran, enab(t) or (exists t in Tran∩Old_N, enab(t) and
  !isEmpty(ccBy(t) ∩ NO_BYPS)) -> [restart()] //rejecting change
  shiftDown() //reflecting change
  ]
[]
  #end=0 and !exists t in Tran, enab(t) -> [HQ ! notify-deadlock()]
[]
  #end=1; HQ ? newInstance-msg() -> [flush(end); incMark(begin)]
]
```

be removed/added. For the sake of simplicity we assume that change can only involve workflow's topology. The (super)set of non-bypassable tasks is then computed.

After operating the evolutionary commands on the current workflow reification, definition 2 and free-choiceness are tested on the newly changed reification. Following, the strategy checks by reification introspection whether the suggested workflow change might cause a deadlock, or there might be any non-bypassable tasks causally-connected to an old task which is currently pending. In either case, a restart procedure takes the workflow reification back to the state before strategy's activation. Otherwise, change is reflected to the base-level (shift-down). The

scheme just described might be adopted for a wide class of evolutionary patterns.

Language's keywords and routine calls are in bold. We recall (Capra & Cazzola, 2009) that type **NODE** represents a (logically unbounded) recipient of base-level nodes, and is partitioned into **Place** and **Tran** subtypes . The **exists** quantifier is used to check whether a net element is currently reified. The built-in routine **ReifNodes** computes the nodes belonging to the current base-level reification. The routine **notAdjPres** initializes the set of non-bypassable tasks to N_a according to lemma 1. The routines **ccTo** and **ccBy** compute the set of nodes the argument is causally connected to, and that are causally connected to routine's argument, respectively.

On-the-Fly Structural Check

The structural changes proposed from time to time to a dynamic workflow can be validated by means of classical Petri nets analysis techniques. Validation is accomplished on the workflow reification "on-the-fly", i.e., while the evolutionary strategy is in progress. Thanks to a restart mechanism, potentially dangerous changes are discarded before they are reflected to the base-level, at the end of a meta-computation.

Routines **checkWfNet**, **checkFc** test the preservation of base-level Petri nets well-definiteness (definition 2) and free-choiceness, respectively. Their calls are located in the meta-program just after the evolutionary commands, which operate on the base-level workflow reification.

```
[
VAR t,tx: Tran;
VAR p: Place;
*(<p,t> in New_A ∪ Del_A)
  [
    exists(p) and exists(t) ->
      [
        *(tx in post(pre(t))/{t})
          [pre(t) <> pre(tx) -> restart();]
      ]
  ]
]
```

Free-choiceness preservation, in particular, may be checked in a simple, efficient way. Figure 5 expands the corresponding routine. It works under the following assumptions and principles:

- the initial base-level Petri net is a free-choice WF-net (conservative hypothesis)
- variables New_A, Del_A record *all* the arcs which are added/deleted to/from the base-level reification during the evolutionary strategy's execution; they are cleared at any meta-program activation;

- the only operations affecting free-choiceness, under a conservative hypothesis, are the addition/removal of an input arc $\langle p,t \rangle$ (the removal of a node produces as a side-effect the withdrawal of all adjacent arcs, so it is fair, with respect to free-choiceness)
- for each arc $\langle p,t \rangle$ which has been added/removed we only have to check the free-choiceness between t and every transition sharing with t some input places.

Putting the Strategy to the Test

Let us explain how the strategy works, considering again Figures 1-2, upon receiving the evolutionary commands:

New_P={}
New_T={ RealizationRejected}
Del_A={ $\langle p13$, ProductChange$\rangle$ }
Del_N={}
New_A={$\langle p6$, Realization Rejected$\rangle$, $\langle p13$, Archiving$\rangle$, $\langle$Realization Rejected, $p5 \rangle$}.

The non-bypassable tasks come to be: {Report, Archiving, ProductChange, OnSiteRealization, CaseClosure}. In the workflow instance running on the modified template (Figure 2) tasks (transitions) Report and ProductChange are pending (enabled) in the current state (marking) $\mathbf{m}$:{p_{11}, p_{14}}. All preexisting completed tasks that are causally connected to one of them can be bypassed, so the new workflow has not to be restarted from scratch, saving a lot of work.

The approach just described ensures a dependable evolution of workflows, while being enough flexible. We have not intended to propose a general solution to the particular problem addressed in Qiu & Wong, 2007. Better policies do probably exist. Rather, we have tried to show that an approach merging consolidated reflection concepts to classical Petri nets techniques can suitably address the criticisms of dynamic workflow change.

Figure 5. Meta-program's routine checking free-choiceness

```
[
  VAR t,tx: Tran;
  VAR p: Place;
  *(<p,t> in New_A∪Del_A)
    [
      exists(p) and exists(t) ->
        [
         *(tx in post(pre(t))/{t})
           [pre(t) <> pre(tx) -> restart();]
        ]
    ]
]
```

Structural Base-Level Analysis. The base-level is guaranteed to be a free-choice WF-net all over its evolution: that makes is possible to use polynomial algorithms to check workflow's soundness. In particular techniques based on the calculus of flows (invariants) are elegant and very efficient. In general they are highly affected by the base-level Petri net complexity. The separation between evolutionary and functional aspects encourages their usage.

For instance, by operating the structural algorithms of GreatSPN tool (Chiola, Franceschinis, Gaeta, & Ribaudo, 1995), it is possible to discover that both nets depicted in Figures 1-2 are covered by *place-invariants*. A lot of interesting properties thereby descend: in particular boundedness and liveness, i.e., workflow soundness.

Counter Example

Assume that evolution occurs when the only pending task is OnSiteRealization, i.e., consider as current marking of the net in Figure 1 $\mathbf{m}'$: $\{p_6\}$. That means, among the other things, tasks ProductChange, VersionMerging and Report have been completed: change in that case is discarded after having verified that there are some non-bypassable tasks which are causally connected to the pending one. If the suggested change were really carried out (reflected) on the base-level, without doing any consistency control, a deadlock would be eventually entered (state $\{p_8\}$) after the workflow instance continues its run on the modified template. The problem is that $\mathbf{m}'$ is not a reachable state of (PN'; $\{begin\}$), but reachability is NP-complete also in live and safe free-choice Petri nets, so it would make no sense checking reachability directly at meta-program level.

Current Limitations

The proposed reflective model for dynamic workflows suffers from a major conceptual limitation: only the control-flow perspective is considered. Let us shortly discuss this choice. We abstract from the resource perspective because in most workflow management systems it is not possible to specify that several (human) resources are collaborating in executing a task. Even if multiple persons are executing a task, only one is allocated to it from the WMS perspective: who selected the work item from the in-basket. In contrast to other application domains such as flexible manufacturing systems, anomalies resulting from locking problems are not possible (it is reasonable to assume that each task will be eventually executed by the person having in charge it). Therefore, from the viewpoint of workflow verification, we can abstract from resources. However, if collaborative features will be explicitly supported by WMS (through a tight integration of groupware and workflow technology), then the resource perspective should be taken into account. We partly abstract from the data perspective. Production data can be changed at any time without notifying the WMS. Their existence does not even depend upon the workflow application and they may be shared among different workflows. The control data used to route cases are managed by the WMS. Some of these data are set or updated by humans or applications. Clearly, some abstraction is needed to incorporate the data perspective when verifying a given workflow. The abstraction currently used is the following. Since control data (workflow attributes such as the customer id, the registration date, etc.) are only used for the routing of a case, we model each decision as a non-deterministic choice. If we are able to prove soundness for the situation without workflow attributes, it will also hold for the situation with attributes. Abstracting from triggers and workflow attributes fits in the usage of ordinary Petri nets for the base-level of the reflective model: this is preferable because of the availability of efficient and powerful analysis tools.

CONCLUSION

Industrial/business processes are an example of discrete-event systems which are increasingly subject to evolution during life-cycle. Covering the intrinsic dynamism of modern processes has been widely recognized as a challenge by designers of workflow management systems. Petri nets are a central model of workflows, but traditionally they have a fixed structure. We have proposed and discussed the adoption of Reflective Petri nets as a formal model for sound dynamic workflows. The clean separation between (current) workflow template and evolutionary strategy on one side, and the use of classical Petri nets notions (free-choiceness) on the other side, make it possible

to efficiently check preservation of workflow's structural properties, which in turn permit soundness -a major behavioral property- to be checked in polynomial time. All is done while evolution is in progress. An algorithm is delivered to soundly transferring workflow instances from an old to a new template, redoing already completed workflow's task only when strictly necessary. The approach formalizes and improves a procedure currently implemented in an industrial workflow management system. We are studying the possibility of using even more general structural notions than free-choiceness, in particular S-coverability (Aalst, 1996), that provides in most practical cases a structural characterization of soundness.

REFERENCES

Agostini, A., & De Michelis, G. (2000, August). A Light Workflow Management System Using Simple Process Models. *Computer Supported Cooperative Work*, *9*(3-4), 335–363. doi:10.1023/A:1008703327801

Badouel, E., & Oliver, J. (1998, January). *Reconfigurable Nets, a Class of High Level Petri Nets Supporting Dynamic Changes within Workflow Systems* (IRISA Research Report No. PI-1163). IRISA.

Cabac, L., Duvignau, M., Moldt, D., & Rölke, H. (2005, June). Modeling Dynamic Architectures Using Nets-Within-Nets. In G. Ciardo & P. Darondeau (Eds.), *Proceedings of the 26th International Conference on Applications and Theory of Petri Nets (ICATPN 2005)* (p. 148-167). Miami, FL: Springer.

Capra, L., & Cazzola, W. (2007a, on 26th-29th of September). A Reflective PN-based Approach to Dynamic Workflow Change. *In Proceedings of the 9th International Symposium in Symbolic and Numeric Algorithms for Scientific Computing (SYNASC'07)* (p. 533-540). Timisoara, Romania: IEEE CS.

Capra, L., & Cazzola, W. (2007b, December). Self-Evolving Petri Nets. *Journal of Universal Computer Science*, *13*(13), 2002–2034.

Capra, L., & Cazzola, W. (2009). An Introduction to Reflective Petri Nets. In E. M. O. Abu-Atieh (Ed.), *Handbook of Research on Discrete Event Simulation Environments Technologies and Applications*. Hershey, PA: IGI Global.

Chiola, G., Franceschinis, G., Gaeta, R., & Ribaudo, M. (1995, November). GreatSPN 1.7: Graphical Editor and Analyzer for Timed and Stochastic Petri Nets. *Performance Evaluation*, *24*(1-2), 47–68. doi:10.1016/0166-5316(95)00008-L

Desel, J., & Esparza, J. (1995). *Free Choice Petri Nets* (Cambridge Tracts in Theoretical Computer Science Vol. 40). New York: Cambridge University Press.

Ellis, C., & Keddara, K. (2000, August). ML-DEWS: Modeling Language to Support Dynamic Evolution within Workflow Systems. *Computer Supported Cooperative Work*, *9*(3-4), 293–333. doi:10.1023/A:1008799125984

ENOVIA. (2007, September). *Dassault systèmes plm solutions for the mid-market* [white-paper]. Retrieved from. http://www.3ds.com/fileadmin/brands/enovia/pdf/whitepapers/CIMdata-DS_PLM_for_the_MidMarket-Program_review-Sep2007.pdf)

Hicheur, A., Barkaoui, K., & Boudiaf, N. (2006, September). Modeling Workflows with Recursive ECATNets. *In Proceedings of the Eighth International Symposium on Symbolic and Numeric Algorithms for Scientific Computing (SYNACS'06)* (p. 389-398). Timisoara, Romania: IEEE CS.

Hoare, C. A. R. (1985). *Communicating Sequential Processes*. Upper Saddle River, NJ: Prentice Hall.

Hoffmann, K., Ehrig, H., & Mossakowski, T. (2005, June). High-Level Nets with Nets and Rules as Tokens. In G. Ciardo & P. Darondeau (Eds.), *Proceedings of the 26th International Conference on Applications and Theory of Petri Nets (ICATPN 2005)* (pp. 268-288). Miami, FL: Springer.

Maes, P. (1987, October). Concepts and Experiments in Computational Reflection. In *N. K. Meyrowitz (Ed.), Proceedings of the 2nd conference on object-oriented programming systems, languages, and applications (OOPSLA'87)* (Vol. 22, pp.147-156), Orlando, FL.

Qiu, Z.-M., & Wong, Y. S. (2007, June). Dynamic Workflow Change in PDM Systems. *Computers in Industry*, *58*(5), 453–463. doi:10.1016/j.compind.2006.09.014

Reichert, M., & Dadam, P. (1998). ADEPTflex - Supporting Dynamic Changes in Workflow Management Systems without Losing Control. *Journal of Intelligent Information Systems*, *10*(2), 93–129. doi:10.1023/A:1008604709862

Reisig, W. (1985). *Petri nets: An introduction* (EATCS Monographs in Theoretical Computer Science Vol. 4). Berlin: Springer.

Salimifard, K., & Wright, M. B. (2001, November). Petri Net-Based Modeling of Workflow Systems: An Overview. *European Journal of Operational Research*, *134*(3), 664–676. doi:10.1016/S0377-2217(00)00292-7

van der Aalst, W. M. P. (1996). *Structural Characterizations of Sound Workflow Nets* (Computing Science Reports No. 96/23). Eindhoven, the Netherlands: Eindhoven University of Technology.

van der Aalst, W. M. P., & Basten, T. (2002, January). Inheritance of Workflows: An Approach to Tackling Problems Related to Change. *Theoretical Computer Science*, *270*(1-2), 125–203. doi:10.1016/S0304-3975(00)00321-2 van der Aalst, W. M. P., & Jablonski, S. (2000, September). Dealing with Workflow Change: Identification of Issues and Solutions. *International Journal of Computer Systems, Science, and Engineering*, *15*(5), 267–276.

KEY TERMS AND DEFINITIONS

Evolution: attitude of systems to change layout/functionality.

Dynamic Workflows: models of industrial/business processes subject to evolution.

Petri Nets: graphical formalism for discrete-event systems.

Reflection: activity performed by an agent when doing computations about itself.

Workflow Nets: Petri net-based workflow models.

Soundness: behavioral property of a well-defined workflow net.

Structural Properties: properties derived from the incidence matrix of Petri nets.

Free-Choiceness: typical structural property which can be efficiently tested.

ENDNOTES

1   If we assume, as it is reasonable in the workflow context, a strong notion of fairness: in every infinite firing sequence, each transition fires infinitely often.

2   We recall that in Reflective Petri nets any evolutionary strategy is defined in terms of basic operations on base-level's elements

Chapter 11
Applications of Visual Algorithm Simulation

Ari Korhonen
Helsinki University of Technology, Finland

ABSTRACT

Understanding data structures and algorithms is an integral part of software engineering and elementary computer science education. However, people usually have difficulty in understanding abstract concepts and processes such as procedural encoding of algorithms and data structures. One way to improve their understanding is to provide visualizations to make the abstract concepts more concrete. In this chapter, we represent a novel idea to promote the interaction between the user and the algorithm visualization system called visual algorithm simulation. As a proof of concept, we represent an application framework called Matrix that encapsulates the idea of visual algorithm simulation. The framework is applied by the TRAKLA2 learning environment in which algorithm simulation is employed to produce algorithm simulation exercises. Moreover, we discuss the benefits of such exercises and applications of visual algorithm simulation in general.

INTRODUCTION

Data structures and algorithms are important core issues in computer science education. They are also complex concepts, thus difficult to grasp by novice learners. Fortunately, algorithm animation, visual debugging and algorithm simulation are all suitable methods to aid the learning process. Much research has been carried out to identify the great number of issues that we must take into account while designing and creating effective visualizations and algorithm animation for teaching purposes (Baecker, 1998; Brown & Hershberger, 1992; Fleischer & Kucera, 2001; Gloor, 1998; Miller, 1993). See, for example, the techniques developed for using color and sound (Brown & Hershberger, 1992) or hand-made designs (Fleischer & Kucera, 2001) to enhance the algorithm animations. We argue, however, that these are only minor details (albeit important ones) in the learning process as a whole.

DOI: 10.4018/978-1-60566-774-4.ch011

In order to make a real difference here, we should change the point of view and look at the problem from the learner's perspective. How can we make sure the learner actually gets the picture? It is not what the learner sees but what he or she does. In addition, we argue that no matter what kind of visualizations the teacher has available, the tools cannot compete in their effectiveness with environments in which the learner must perform some actions in order to become convinced of his or her own understanding.

From the pedagogical point of view, for example, a plain tool for viewing the execution of an algorithm is not good enough (C. D. Hundhausen, Douglas, & Stasko, 2002; Naps et al., 2003). Even visual debugging cannot cope with the problem because it is always bound to the actual source code. It is still the system that does all the work and the learner only observes its behavior. At least we should ensure that a level of progress in learning has taken place. This requires an environment where we can give and obtain feedback on the student's performance.

Many ideas and systems have been introduced to enhance the interaction, assignments, mark-up facilities, and so on, including (Astrachan & Rodger, 1998; Brown & Raisamo, 1997; Grillmeyer, 1999; Hansen, Narayanan, & Schrimpsher, 2000; Mason & Woit, 1999; Reek, 1989; Stasko, 1997). On the other hand, the vast masses of students in basic computer science classes have led us into the situation in which giving individual guidance for a single student is impossible even with semi-automated systems. Thus, a kind of fully automatic instructor would be useful such as (Baker, Boilen, Goodrich, Tamassia, & Stibel, 1999; Benford, Burke, Foxley, Gutteridge, & Zin, 1993; Bridgeman, Goodrich, Kobourov, & Tamassia, 2000; English & Siviter, 2000; Higgins, Symeonidis, & Tsintsifas, 2002; Hyvönen & Malmi, 1993; Jackson & Usher, 1997; Reek, 1989; Saikkonen, Malmi, & Korhonen, 2001). However, the topics of data structures and algorithms are often introduced on more abstract

level than those of basic programming courses. We are more interested in the logic and behavior of an algorithm than its implementation details. Therefore, systems that grade programming exercises are not suitable here. The problem is to find a suitable application framework for a system that is capable of interacting with the user through canonical data structure illustrations in this logical level and giving feedback on his or her performance. The aim is to extend the concept of direct manipulation (Stasko, 1991, 1998) to support not only manipulation of a visualization but also the real underlying data structures that the visualization reflects. It is a kind of combination of direct manipulation and visual debugging in which the user can debug the data structures through graphical user interface. Our approach, however, allows the user to manipulate the data structures in two different levels. First, in low level, the data structures and the data they contain can be altered, for example, by swapping keys in an array. Second, in higher level, the framework can provide ready-made algorithms that the user can execute during the manipulation process. Thus, instead of swapping the keys, the user can sort the whole array with one command. In addition, the high level algorithms can be simulated in terms of the low level operations. Thus, the simulation process can be verified by comparing it to the execution of an actual algorithm. Quite close to this idea comes PILOT (Bridgeman et al., 2000) in which the learner solves problems related to graph algorithms and receives graphical illustration of the correctness of the solution, along with a score and an explanation of the errors made. However, the current tool covers only graph algorithms, and especially the minimum spanning tree problem. Hence, there is no underlying general purpose application framework that can be extended to other concepts and problem types such as trees, linked lists, and arrays.

In this chapter, we will introduce the concept of algorithm simulation to reach the goal set and fill the gap between visual debuggers and real-time algorithm simulation. The idea is to develop a general purpose platform for illustrating all the common data structure abstractions applied regularly to illustrate the logic and behavior of algorithms. Moreover, the platform is able to allow user interaction in terms of visual algorithm simulation. As an application, we support exercises in which automatically generated visual feedback is possible for algorithm simulation exercises. We call such a process automatic assessment of algorithm simulation exercises (Korhonen & Malmi, 2000).

Organization of this Chapter

The next sections first introduce the concept of visual algorithm simulation and the method of algorithm simulation exercises. In addition, the literature survey compares the above with work of others. After that, the Matrix algorithm simulation framework is described, and we show how to apply the application framework to come up with visual algorithm simulation exercises. Finally, we conclude our ideas and addresses some future research topics.

ALGORITHM SIMULATION

The goal of Algorithm Simulation is to further the understanding of algorithms and data structures inductively, based on observations of an algorithm in operation. In the following, we first give a vision by an example what kind of operations such a method should provide.

Consider a student studying basic search trees who can perform operations on a binary search tree (BST) by dragging new keys into the correct leaf positions in the tree, thus simulating the BST insertion algorithm. After mastering this, one can switch to work on the conceptual level and drag the keys into data structure. The keys are inserted into the tree by the pre-implemented

BST insertion routine. Now, one faces the question of balancing the tree. First, rotations can be studied on the detailed level by dragging edges into the new positions and by letting the system redraw the tree. Second, after mastering this, the available rotation commands can be invoked directly from menus. Finally, one can choose to work on AVL trees, create a new tree from the menu, and use the AVL-tree insertion routine to add new elements into the search tree. In addition, one can experiment on the behavior of AVL trees by creating an array of keys, and by dragging the whole array into the title bar quickly creating a large example tree. The system inserts the keys from the array one by one into the tree using the implemented insertion routine. Moreover, the result is not a static tree, but a sequence of states of the tree between the single insertions, which can be stepped back and forth to examine the working of the algorithm more closely similar to that in any algorithm animation system. Thus, the vision above extends the concept of algorithm animation by allowing the user to interact with the system in more comprehensive level than that of a simple animator panel can provide (step, back, forward, etc.).

Visual Algorithm Simulation

In visual algorithm simulation, we are interested in the detailed study of the dynamic behavior of data structures. Sequences of data structures are directly represented through event procedures. Each event altering any part of the data structure is completed by a GUI operation updating the corresponding visualization. This paradigm permits the representation of systems at an essentially unlimited level of detail. Simulation experiments are performed under the control of an animator entity with event process orientation. Model executions are guarded by an algorithm or by human interaction. However, an algorithm here corresponds to a code implemented by a developer – not by the

Figure 1. An overview of algorithm animation and visual algorithm simulation. Five cycles of interaction can be identified. A typical Control Interface allows (1) to customize the layout, change the speed and direction of the animation, etc. and (2) to manipulate the data structures by invoking predefined operations. Not only (3) Direct Manipulation is possible, but (4) the changes can also be delivered into the underlying data structures by means of Visual Algorithm Simulation. In addition, (5) even the underlying data structures can be passed to the algorithm as an input by utilizing Visual Algorithm Simulation functionality

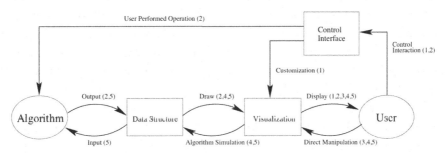

user itself. Thus, the user does not code anything while simulating algorithms. Instead, the user can execute predefined algorithms or take any other allowed action to alter the data structures by means of simple GUI operations. Actually, the code does not have to be even visible during the simulation. Thus, one can simulate algorithms that do not even exist, yet. However, in case we apply this method, for example, for algorithm simulation exercises (as we will do in the next section), there is usually a need to represent also the code that the learner is supposed to follow while solving the exercise (i.e., while simulating the corresponding algorithm in the exercise).

The manipulation process is conceptually the opposite of the algorithm animation with respect to the information flow. Where algorithm animation visually delivers the information from the system to the user, direct manipulation delivers the input from the user to the system through a graphical user interface (see (3) in Figure 1). Generally, if human interaction is allowed between the visual demonstration of an algorithm and the user in such a way that the user can directly manipulate the data structure representation, the process is called direct manipulation. However, visual algorithm simulation allows the user directly to

manipulate not only the representation but also the underlying implemented data structure (see (4) and (5) in Figure 1).

Matrix is an application framework for algorithm visualization tools that encapsulates the idea of visual algorithm simulation. The system seamlessly combines algorithm visualization, algorithm animation, and visual algorithm simulation and provides a novel approach for the user to interact with the system.

Simulation Techniques

We do not know any other system that is capable of direct manipulation in terms of visual algorithm simulation similar to Matrix. Astrachan et al. discuss simulation exercises while introducing the Lambada system (Astrachan & Rodger, 1998; Astrachan, Selby, & Unger, 1996). However, their context is completely different, because the students simulate models of practical applications, partly coded by themselves, and the system is used only for illustrating the use of primitive data structures without much interaction with the user.

On the other hand, GeoWin (Bäsken & Näher, 2001) is a visualization tool for geometric algorithms in which the user can manipulate a set of actual geometric objects (e.g. geometric attributes of points in a plane) through the interactive interface. However, the scope of the system is quite different from Matrix. While all the relations between objects in GeoWin are determined by their coordinates in some geometric space, the relations between the underlying object instances in Matrix are determined by their interconnected references.

More close to Matrix, in this sense, comes CATAI (Cattaneo, Italiano, & Ferraro-Petrillo, 2002) and JDSL Visualizer (Baker et al., 1999). They allow the user to invoke some methods on the running algorithm. In terms of method invocations it is directly possible to access the content of the data structures or to execute a piece of code encapsulated in an ordinary method call. However, Matrix also provides a user interface and an environment for this task in terms of direct manipulation. Thus, Matrix not only allows method invocations, but also the facility to simulate an algorithm in a more abstract level by drag & dropping new input data at any time to the corresponding data structure.

Moreover, Matrix is designed for students working on a higher level of abstraction than, for example, JDSLVisualizer or AlvisLive! (C. Hundhausen & Brown, 2005). In other words, both of these tools are designed for a programming course to provide interactive debugging tools for educational purposes (Program Visualization and Animation), while the representations in Matrix are intended for a data structures and algorithms course to illustrate and grasp the logic and concepts of data structures and algorithms (Algorithm Visualization and Animation). Of course, both kinds of tools are fit for use.

In Matrix, the user can directly change the underlying data structure on-the-fly through the graphical user interface. Also, for example, Animal (Rößling, Schüler, & Freisleben, 2000) and Dance (Stasko, 1991, 1998) both have the look and feel of building an algorithm anima-

tion by demonstration. In addition, the JAWAA (Pierson & Rodger, 1998) editor is capable of producing scripting language commands that can be animated. However, within these systems the user does not manipulate an actual data structure, but only a visualization of an alleged structure. The system produces the algorithm animation sequence based on the direct manipulation. However, while creating, for example, an AVL tree demonstration, it is the user's concern to maintain the tree balanced. In Matrix, several levels of interaction are possible: one can manipulate a tree as with Animal or it is also possible to invoke an actual insert method for the AVL tree that inserts an element into the appropriate position. The actual underlying structure is updated and the new state of the structure is visualized for the user. Another system that allows the user to simulate algorithms in this sense is Pilot (Bridgemanet al., 2000). However, it is targeted only to graph algorithms. Moreover, the user is only allowed to interact with some attributes of edges and vertices (e.g., change the color) and not the structure itself.

Finally, Matrix is implemented in Java, which gives more flexibility in terms of platform independence, compared to older systems such as Amethyst (Myers, Chandhok, & Sareen, 1988) and UWPI (Henry, Whaley, & Forstall, 1990). Of course, Java has its own restrictions, but Java together with WWW has given a new impetus to algorithm visualization techniques.

MATRIX SIMULATION FRAMEWORK

Two kinds of functionality are provided for interaction with the Matrix system. First, control over the visualization is required, for example, in order to adjust the amount of detail presented in the display, to navigate through large data structures, or to control the speed and direction of animations. In Figure 1, Control Interface allows this kind of functionality. A considerably

Figure 2. Arrays, lists, trees and graphs are important fundamental data types, i.e., reusable abstractions regularly used in computer science. The figure above depicts these concepts printed from the Matrix system

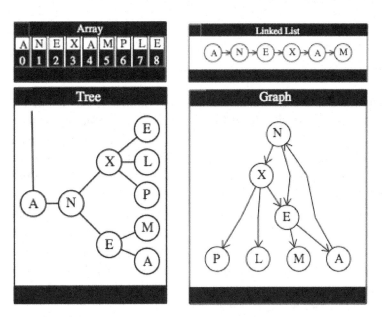

large number of systems exist providing miscellaneous sets of functionality for these purposes. For example, Dynalab (Boroni, Eneboe, Goosey, Ross, & Ross, 1996) supports the flexible animation control for executing animations forward and backward. On the other hand, Brown (1988) was the first one to introduce the support for custom input data sets.

Second, some meaningful ways to perform experiments are needed in order to explore the behavior of the underlying structure. Here, Matrix allows the user to change the state of the underlying data structure in terms of direct manipulation (see algorithm simulation in Figure 1). The manipulation events are targeted to the visualization and correspond to the changes mentioned earlier. Again, the display is automatically updated to match the current state after each change. Moreover, all the changes are recorded in order to be reversed through the control interface. Therefore, this second item is virtually our primary contribution and is the type of interaction we mean by algorithm simulation. Of course, both kinds of

functionality are needed for exploring the underlying structure.

Elements of Visualization

From the user's point of view, Matrix operates on a number of visual concepts which include arrays, linked lists, binary trees, common trees, and graphs, as depicted in Figure 2. Many of the basic layouts for these representations are based on the algorithms introduced in the literature of information visualization (see, for example, Battista, Eades, Tamassia, & Tollis, 1999). We call the corresponding real underlying data structures as Fundamental Data Types (FDT). FDT is a data structure that has no semantics, i.e., it does not commit on the data it stores, but merely ignores the type of the data.

We distinguish FDTs from Conceptual Data Types (CDT) that also have the semantics on what kind of information is stored to them. Any CDT can be composed of FDTs, however, and thus visualized by the same visual concepts as FDTs.

Figure 3. Matrix control panel

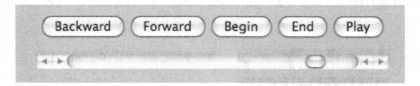

For example, a binary search tree can reuse the binary tree FDT, and thus can be visualized by the same representation.

Next, we introduce the four basic entities that all can be subjected to changes in Matrix application framework. All the visual concepts can be assembled by integrating the following parts into a whole. First, a visual container is a graphical entity that corresponds to the overall visual structure and may contain any other visual entities. Second, visual components are parts of visual containers that are connected to each other by visual references. Finally, the visual components can hold another visual container, recursively, or a visual key, which has no internal structure.

For example, in Figure 2, the Tree layout is composed of 9 visual components, each holding a visual key (denoted by letters A, N, E, X, A, M, P, L, and E). The components are connected to each other by eight visual references to form a tree like structure drawn from left to right (the default orientation, however, is top to bottom). In addition, one reference is needed to point into the root of the tree. Finally, the frame around the structure corresponds to the visual container that responds to events targeted to whole structure (for example, in a binary search tree, the user can insert new keys into the structure by drag & dropping the keys into the frame).

The user can interact with all the entities described above as far as the underlying structure allows the changes. For example, the user may insert or delete components, replace any key with another one (again, simple drag & drop of any visible key onto the target key is sufficient) or rename keys. On the other hand, the structure

can similarly be changed by setting a visual reference to point to another visual component. Finally, the visual container (whole structure) can be attached to a visual component, resulting in nested visualization of two or more concepts. This is an important feature providing new opportunities to create complex structures such as adjacency lists or B-trees. Matrix does not restrict the level of nesting. Moreover, context sensitive operations can also be invoked for such composed structures.

Control over the Visualization

Object-oriented modeling seems to offer a natural way to implement these kinds of systems. The entity descriptions encapsulate the label, the structure and its behavior into one organizational unit. The changes in the data structure can then be illustrated by a sequence of discrete states or by a continuous process. Either the algorithm or the human controlling the model can be the dominant participant. In order to integrate all of this, the animator must continually check for both the state and the control events. These are defined in the following.

The control events are trivially obtained by implementing a control panel in which the control operations are supported. The basic set of control operations are illustrated in Figure 3. The actions these operations take are obvious.

Moreover, the user has several other control operations to perform. These operations influence the layout of the visualization and are implemented by most of the modern algorithm animation systems. Thus, we only summarize these briefly. See, for example, *A Principled Taxonomy of Software Visualization* by Price, Baecker, & Small (1993) to have more details.

1. Multiple views: User can open structure or part of it in the same or a new window.
2. Multiple layouts: User can change the layout of the structure.
3. Orientation: User can change the orientation of layout (rotate, mirror horizontally, and mirror vertically).
4. Granularity and Elision control: User can minimize structure or part of it; hide unnecessary details such as title, indices of arrays, direction of references, back, forward, or cross edges in graphs, and empty subtrees.
5. Labeling: User can name or rename entities.
6. Security: User can disable or enable entities in order to allow or prevent them to respond particular events.
7. Scaling: User can change the font type or font size.

Finally, the system provides several additional features that can be used to finalize a task. First, the current implementation includes an extensive set of ready-made data structures and algorithms that can be directly summoned from the menu bar. The implemented fundamental data types are array, linked list, several tree structures, and graphs. Moreover, also included are many CDTs such as Binary Search Tree, 2-3-4-Tree, Red-Black-Tree, Digital Search Tree, Radix Search Trie, Binary Heap, AVL Tree, and Splay Tree. In addition, the prototype includes several non-empty structures that are already initialized to contain useful data for simulation purposes, for example, a set of keys in alphabetical or in random order. Second, the produced algorithm animation can be exported in several formats. For example, as a smooth SVG (Scalable Vector Graphics) animation to be embedded into a Web page or a series of still images in TeXdraw format (Kabal, 1993)

that can be embedded in a LATEX source file. Matrix also supports text formats to import and automatically create various data structures from edge lists and adjacency lists. Third, the current job can be saved into the file system and loaded back into the Matrix system. Here, the whole animation sequence, i.e., the invoked operations and states of the underlying data structure, can be stored and restored by means of Java serialization.

Actions on the Underlying Data Structures

The set of state events may vary among the models to be simulated due to the CDTs in which the conceptual model can be subjected to several operations. On the other hand, there exists only a limited set of actions in the GUI that a user may perform during the execution of a simulation. Thus, the simulation environment should be responsible for mapping these actions to particular state events. The same action might lead to a very different result depending on the model to be simulated. On the other hand, there might be a situation in which some actions are not allowed, and thus the model should be aware of this and throw an exception.

Naturally, the set of actions above could be targeted to any of the visual objects (visual container, visual component, visual reference, and visual key). Nevertheless, the functionality may differ from object to object. However, the simulation model gives a meta-level proposition for the actions as described above. We discuss this general set of actions here. Furthermore, a number of exceptions are discussed briefly.

Read and Write Operations. From the animator's point of view, the only operations we are interested in are those that in some way manipulate the data structure to be visualized. In procedural programming languages, this manipulation takes the form of assignments. An assignment is the operation that stores the value of an expression in a variable. Thus, a visual component is considered to be the expression above; the variable refers to some other visual components key attribute. Moreover, we may assign any FDT into the key because the data structure the visual component points to (represents) is by definition a fundamental data type.

A single drag on an object assigns an internal reference to point into that object. The object could be rewritten to some other place by dropping it on the target object. The object read can be a single piece of data (datum) as well as, for example, a subtree of a binary search tree. A drop on a visual data object causes the action to be delivered to the component holding the data object. This is because the target object is considered to be the value of an expression, and thus cannot possibly change or replace itself. If the component similarly cannot handle the write operation, the action is forwarded to the container holding the component with the additional information where the write operation occurred (especially if the container is an array, the array position component invokes the write operation of the array with the additional information of the actual index where the action took place). Usually, the object read is rewritten as the key of the target object. Thus, we may end up having very complex structures if, for example, we drag a binary tree and drop it to some position of an array and then again drag this array and drop it into some other tree structure.

Insert Operation. The drag-and-drop action is sometimes referred as an insert operation. This is especially true in the case of conceptual data types such as binary search trees and heaps. Thus, the insert operation is executed by dragging and dropping the object to be inserted (source) into a container (target), for example to its label top of the frame. Thus, the target must implement a special insert method that takes the source to be inserted as an argument. This method is declared in the special interface CDT that indicates that the visualized structure is a conceptual data type and capable of handling such an action. This interface declares other methods such as delete and search

as well. If the target is not a CDT, the drag & drop action is interpreted as the write action.

Pointer Manipulation. The visual references have also functionalities of their own. Especially if it is implemented for the underlying structure. However, such pointer manipulation requires a different approach because changing a reference to point into another object may lead up to the whole structure to become inconsistent. Parts of the whole structure may become unreachable for a moment until a whole set of pointer operations is performed. Thus, pointer operations are queued to be invoked only when all the corresponding operations are completed. This kind of encapsulation ensures that the user can perform any combination of pointer manipulations for the underlying data structure.

Instrumental Operations. The GUI can also provide several instrumental operations that help the user to perform several complex tasks more easily. For example, the user can turn the drag & drop facility to swap mode, in which not only is the source structure inserted into the target structure, but also vice versa. Thus, the GUI swaps the corresponding structures without any visible temporal variables. Another example is the insertion of multiple keys with only one single GUI operation by dragging & dropping the whole array of keys into the title bar of the target structure visualization. The GUI inserts the keys in the array one at a time.

Other Operations. The default behavior of the drag & drop functionality can be changed. For example, it can be interconnected to the delete operation declared in the interface CDT. In addition, such miscellaneous operations can be declared in pop-up menu attached to all visual objects. By default, the delete operation is included there. Similarly, almost any kind of additional operations could be implemented. Thus, the actual set of possible simulation operations depend heavily on those procedures allowed by the programmer of the underlying data structure. For example, the AVL tree visualization may include a special set of rotate operations to illustrate the behavior of this particular balanced search tree.

Decoration. There exist also certain predefined decoration operations in the pop-up menus attached to each entity. For example, the label (name) of a component could be enabled, disabled and set by selecting the proper operation. Note, however, that in this case the label is not necessarily a property of the actual visualized data structure but rather a property of the visualization, and thus does not appear in every visual instance of the underlying structure.

The discussion of extending simulation functionality from the visualizer's perspective is left out of this chapter.

VISUAL ALGORITHM SIMULATION EXERCISES

One of the main applications for Matrix and algorithm simulation is TRAKLA2 that is a web-based learning environment dedicated to distribute visual algorithm simulation exercises (Malmi et al., 2004) in data structures and algorithms courses. Some other significant applications for the same framework exist as well (See, e.g., MatrixPro (Karavirta, Korhonen, Malmi, & Stålnacke, 2004) or MVT (Lönnberg, Korhonen, & Malmi, 2004)). However, we have chosen to use TRAKLA2 as an example to illustrate the concept in practice for two reasons. First, this is the main application for why we have developed the framework in the first place. Second, several universities in Finland and US have already adopted the TRAKLA2 system in their courses. Thus, we have had very good results to show that the concept works also in practice.

In visual algorithm simulation exercises, the learner is supposed to drag & drop graphical entities such as keys, nodes and references to new positions on the screen to simulate the operations a real algorithm would do. Consequently, the system performs the corresponding changes on the underlying data structures, and thereafter redraws the display. An example assignment could be "Insert the keys I, P, B, T, R, Q, F, K, X, and U into an initially empty red-black tree." The task is to show how the corresponding data structure evolves during the insertions. The insertions are performed by drag & dropping the keys from a stream of keys into the target data structure (binary tree) and selecting a balancing operation, if necessary. Initially, the tree is empty and contains only one node (the root of the tree). Each insertion into an empty node alters the data structure such that the node is occupied with the corresponding inserted key and two new empty sub trees appears below the node.

The exercise appears as an applet (See Figure 4) that portrays individually tailored exercises in which each learner has different initial input data structures that he or she manipulates by means of the available functionality. Actually, an exercise is individually tailored each time the exercise is initialized. This feature has several advantages over traditional homework exercises as learners can freely collaborate without the temptation to copy answers from each other. In addition, the system is capable of recording the sequence of simulation operations, and automatically assessing the exercise by comparing it with another sequence generated by the actual implemented algorithm. Based on this, TRAKLA2 can give immediate feedback to the learner. This supports self studying at any place or time.

Figure 4 shows an example exercise in which the learner is to insert (drag and drop) the keys from the given array (initial data) one by one into the red-black tree. After completing the exercise, the learner can ask the system to grade his or her performance. The feedback received contains the number of correct steps out of the maximum number of steps, which is turned to points relative to other exercises. The final points are determined by the best points received among all the submissions for a single exercise. The learner can also view the model solution for the exercise as an algorithm animation sequence at any time. The model solution is shown as a sequence of discrete states of the data structures, which can be browsed backwards and forwards in the same way as learner's own solution.

After viewing the grading results, the learner can either submit the solution or restart the same exercise with different input data. If the model solution has been requested, grading and submission are disabled until the exercise has been reset again.

Feedback

Even though feedback to students is the most essential form of feedback, very few systems are also capable of assessing students' work and giving continuous feedback on their performance to the teacher. This is very important in improving the teaching process. Another concern is whether the student is actually doing something useful with these tools or merely playing and enjoying, for example, the animation without any actual

Figure 4. The TRAKLA2 exercise window (an applet) includes data structures and push buttons to manipulate them in addition to the GUI operations (click, drag & drop, etc.). In addition, the model answer for the exercise can be opened in a separate window

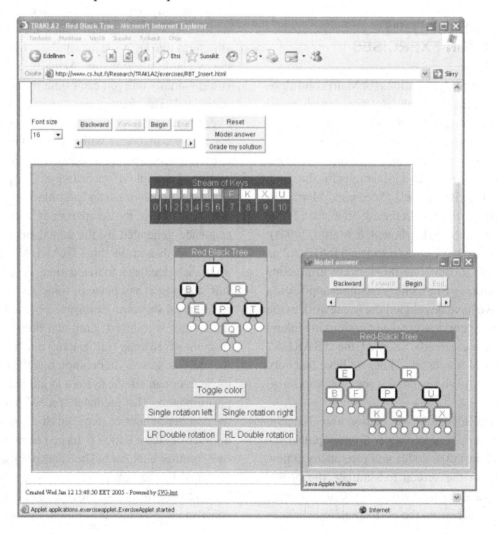

learning. As reported by Baker et al. (1999), some students have difficulties seeing the systems as complementary tools, and therefore some of them do not use them in the most effective manner.

Traditionally, grading has been based on final examination, but a variety of weekly homework assignments are also widely used. Thus, automatic assessment of these kinds of assignments has been seen to provide great value to large-scale courses. However, nowadays automatic assessment has a role to play with small student groups as well. For example, learners studying while they have a steady job can benefit a great deal from environments that can be accessed at any place or time.

Implementation of Algorithm Simulation Exercises

From the technical point of view, an exercise is a class that conforms to the particular Exercise interface. Basically, in order to implement the interface, one needs to define a couple of methods. First, one needs a method to determine all the data structures and their names for the visualization during the simulation of the exercise algorithm. These data structures are expected to be fundamental data types and ready-made visualizations for them should exist. Second, a method to solve the exercise is needed when automatic assessment takes place or the model solution is otherwise requested.

An implementation of such an exercise in actual learning environment[1] is shown in Figure 4. The binary search tree exercise requires the solve method that is equal to binary search tree insert routine. In addition, the assignment text and a couple of initiating methods (such that fills in the array with new random data) are needed as well.

The framework is capable of visualizing the exercise by showing the assignment in some text window and by illustrating the structures needed to simulate the algorithm. By invoking the solve method, it is also capable of determining the model

solution for the exercise. This model solution is then automatically compared to the submitted answer. The assessing procedure then gives some feedback to the student on his or her performance. The process of creating new exercises, however, is left out of the scope of this chapter as it is explained elsewhere (Malmi et al., 2004).

DISCUSSION

In this chapter, we have introduced a novel application framework for algorithm simulation tools. The aim is to explore the capabilities of algorithm simulation — a novel concept that fosters the interaction between the user and the visualization environments. The framework has been applied to the TRAKLA2 learning environment for data structures and algorithms courses. In addition, we have also paid attention to the process of developing new assignments in order to allow creation of new exercises by only focusing on the algorithms needed to evaluate the student's answers.

Three main concepts can be identified within the system. First, the system is based on algorithm visualization in which common reusable visualizations of all the well known fundamental data types can be attached to any underlying objects within an executable run-time environment. Second, the execution of an algorithm can be memorized in order to animate the running algorithm that manipulates these objects. Third, algorithm simulation allows the user to interact with the system and to change the content of the data structures in terms of direct manipulation.

The benefits of the Matrix framework are summarized in the next section. In addition, we discuss the educational benefits provided by algorithm simulation exercises in terms of automatic assessment. Finally, we address some future research topics that remains to be studied.

Matrix

In Matrix, the fundamental idea to enhance the human–computer interaction is to allow the user to simulate algorithms, thus he or she specifies the animation in terms of algorithm simulation. In addition, it is also possible to produce user-coded programs by reusing existing components called probes, thus the framework provides also a set of self-animating components. We summarize the properties of the framework as follows:

1. The system makes distinction between the implementation of an actual data structure and its visualizations;
2. Manual simulation is possible by interacting with the user interface;
3. One data structure can have many conceptual visualizations;
4. One conceptual visualization can be re-used for displaying many different data structures;
5. The framework provides fast prototyping of algorithm simulation applications;
6. The framework enables visualization, algorithm animation, and algorithm simulation of user-made code without restrictions concerning object-oriented design methods; and
7. Many applications already exist such as the TRAKLA2 to automatically assess exercises in web based learning environment.

Automatic Assessment

Development of learning environments requires also awareness of what is pedagogically appropriate for students and teachers. In this respect, we have conducted, for example, a research that shows that there is no significant difference in the learning results between students doing their homework exercises in a virtual learning environment and students attending a traditional classroom session (Korhonen, Malmi, Myllyselkä,

& Scheinin, 2002). In addition, commitment to the course (low attrition), is almost equal in both cases even though students working in the virtual environment seems to drop the course earlier than students working in the classroom. However, virtual learning environments can provide advantages in terms of Automatic Assessment (AA) which the traditional teaching methods cannot offer.

The principal benefit of AA, based on our experience, is that it enables one to set up enough compulsory exercises for the students and to give them feedback on their work on large scale. Our experience shows that voluntary exercises do not motivate students enough to reach the required level of skills (Malmi, Korhonen, & Saikkonen, 2002). Compulsory assignments do not provide much more unless we can monitor students' progress regularly and, more important, give them feedback on their performance. This would be possible in weekly classroom exercises, if we only had enough classrooms, time and instructors, which unfortunately is not the case. By means of AA, we can partly solve the feedback problem even though we do not argue that computerized feedback would generally match expert human feedback. In some cases, however, it does, and we have conducted surveys in which the attitude towards TRAKLA2 learning environment increases during a course (Laakso et al., 2005). Thus, in case of simulation exercises, computerized feedback is experienced to be superior to class room sessions due to the fact that the students can get the feedback immediately and try the exercise again with different input data.

The second benefit of AA is that the computer can give feedback at any time and place. Thus, it applies particularly well to virtual courses, and in fact, it has turned most of our courses partially virtual. However, we do have lectures and classroom sessions as well, but the students do most of their self-study on the Web.

The third benefit is that we can allow the students to revise their submissions freely based on the feedback (Malmi & Korhonen, 2004). By setting up the assignments in such a way that pure trial-and-error method is no option, the student is pushed to rethink his or her solution anew, and to make hypotheses about what is wrong. This is one of the conventions that constructivism (Phillips, 2000) suggests we should put into effect. Moreover, it should be noted that in classroom sessions, such a situation is rarely achieved for every student, since the teacher cannot follow and guide the work of each individual at the same time.

The fourth benefit is that we can personalize exercises, i.e., all students have different assignments, which discourages plagiarism and encourages natural co-operation while solving problems. With human teaching resources, it is practically impossible to achieve this in large courses.

Finally, AA tools save time and money. We feel, however, that they represent an extra resource that helps us to teach better. Moreover, they allow us to direct human resources to work which cannot be automated, for instance, personal guidance and feedback for more challenging exercises such as design assignments.

The Future

At the moment, we feel that all the capabilities the framework supports are only a very small subset of all those features possible to include. Many new ideas remain and are discussed very briefly here. Moreover, several open research problems are still to be solved. Thus, in the near future at least the following tasks should be studied:

1. Enhanced recording facilities for algorithm simulation. Especially, to be able to exchange algorithm animations among different animation systems is one of the future challenges.
2. Further customization of representations. The current system is aimed at small examples. However, in order to widen the applicability, e.g., to software engineering

in general, also large examples must be supported.
3. More research on program animation and simulation capabilities. The current framework does not support the program code to be executed (like in the debuggers) with the simulation or animation.
4. Easy creation of new exercises in TRAKLA2 environment. This includes exercises that can be easily created and incorporated into one's own course web pages or electronic exercise books without the intervention of developers.

The primary research topics include those aiming at completing the work needed to create the electronic exercise book and the learning environment. On the other hand, the scope and content of the new system should provide a generalized platform-independent framework that is capable of visualizing even large examples. The system should be rich enough to provide flexibility to develop the framework and its applications further. For example, elision control is essential since its value is emphasized especially in large examples. The application framework should also provide tools for developing proper user interfaces for new applications. Nevertheless, the effectiveness of such systems cannot be evaluated until an application is actually implemented. Thus, the effectiveness of the new framework has been beyond the scope of this chapter due to its subjective nature, but should be promoted in future studies. Finally, the framework itself could be developed further to provide an even more flexible environment for software visualization.

Of course, developing the visualization techniques is only a half of the whole potential for new research topics. The other side is the evaluation of the applications from the learning point of view. For example, it is an open question whether the TRAKLA2 system should limit the learner from submitting his answers as many times as one pleases. The first version of TRAKLA did limit the submissions, but the current TRAKLA2 does not. However, the preliminary results (Malmi, Karavirta, Korhonen, & Nikander, 2005) are somewhat mixed and we have considered to limit the resubmissions in the future. This, however, requires more research before we can argue which option leads to better learning.

REFERENCES

Astrachan, O., & Rodger, S. H. (1998). Animation, visualization, and interaction in CS1 assignments. In *The proceedings of the 29th SIGCSE technical symposium on computer science education* (pp. 317-321), Atlanta, GA. New York: ACM Press.

Astrachan, O., Selby, T., & Unger, J. (1996). An object-oriented, apprenticeship approach to data structures using simulation. In *Proceedings of frontiers in education* (pp. 130-134).

Baecker, R. M. (1998). Sorting out sorting: A case study of software visualization for teaching computer science. In M. Brown, J. Domingue, B. Price, & J. Stasko (Eds.), *Software visualization: Programming as a multimedia experience* (pp. 369–381). Cambridge, MA: The MIT Press.

Baker, R. S., Boilen, M., Goodrich, M. T., Tamassia, R., & Stibel, B. A. (1999). Testers and visualizers for teaching data structures. In *Proceedings of the 30th SIGCSE technical symposium on computer science education* (pp. 261-265), New Orleans, LA. New York: ACM Press.

Bäsken, M., & Näher, S. (2001). GeoWin a generic tool for interactive visualization of geometric algorithms. In S. Diehl (Ed.), *Software visualization: International seminar* (pp. 88-100). Dagstuhl, Germany: Springer.

Battista, G. D., Eades, P., Tamassia, R., & Tollis, I. (1999). *Graph drawing: Algorithms for the visualization of graphs*. Upper Saddle River, NJ: Prentice Hall.

Benford, S., Burke, E., Foxley, E., Gutteridge, N., & Zin, A. M. (1993). Ceilidh: A course administration and marking system. In *Proceedings of the 1st international conference of computer based learning,* Vienna, Austria.

Boroni, C. M., Eneboe, T. J., Goosey, F. W., Ross, J. A., & Ross, R. J. (1996). Dancing with Dynalab. In *27th SIGCSE technical symposium on computer science education* (pp. 135-139). New York: ACM Press.

Bridgeman, S., Goodrich, M. T., Kobourov, S. G., & Tamassia, R. (2000). PILOT: An interactive tool for learning and grading. In *Proceedings of the 31st SIGCSE technical symposium on computer science education* (pp. 139-143). New York: ACM Press. Retrieved from http://citeseer.ist.psu.edu/bridgeman00pilot.html

Brown, M. H. (1988). *Algorithm animation*. Cambridge, MA: MIT Press.

Brown, M. H., & Hershberger, J. (1992). Color and sound in algorithm animation. *Computer, 25*(12), 52–63. doi:10.1109/2.179117

Brown, M. H., & Raisamo, R. (1997). JCAT: Collaborative active textbooks using Java. *Computer Networks and ISDN Systems, 29*(14), 1577–1586. doi:10.1016/S0169-7552(97)00090-1

Cattaneo, G., Italiano, G. F., & Ferraro-Petrillo, U. (2002, August). CATAI: Concurrent algorithms and data types animation over the internet. *Journal of Visual Languages and Computing, 13*(4), 391–419. doi:10.1006/jvlc.2002.0230

English, J., & Siviter, P. (2000). Experience with an automatically assessed course. In *Proceedings of the 5th annual SIGCSE/sigcue conference on innovation and technology in computer science education, iticse'00* (pp. 168-171), Helsinki, Finland. New York: ACM Press.

Fleischer, R., & Kucera, L. (2001). Algorithm animation for teaching. In S. Diehl (Ed.), *Software visualization: International seminar* (pp. 113-128). Dagstuhl, Germany: Springer.

Gloor, P. A. (1998). User interface issues for algorithm animation. In M. Brown, J. Domingue, B. Price, & J. Stasko (Eds.), *Software visualization: Programming as a multimedia experience* (pp. 145–152). Cambridge, MA: The MIT Press.

Grillmeyer, O. (1999). An interactive multimedia textbook for introductory computer science. In *The proceedings of the thirtieth SIGCSE technical symposium on computer science education* (pp. 286–290). New York: ACM Press.

Hansen, S. R., Narayanan, N. H., & Schrimpsher, D. (2000, May). Helping learners visualize and comprehend algorithms. *Interactive Multimedia Electronic Journal of Computer-Enhanced Learning, 2*(1).

Henry, R. R., Whaley, K. M., & Forstall, B. (1990). The University of Washington illustrating compiler. In *Proceedings of the ACM SIGPLAN'90 conference on programming language design and implementation* (pp. 223-233).

Higgins, C., Symeonidis, P., & Tsintsifas, A. (2002). The marking system for CourseMaster. In *Proceedings of the 7th annual conference on innovation and technology in computer science education* (pp. 46–50). New York: ACM Press.

Hundhausen, C., & Brown, J. (2005). What you see is what you code: A "radically-dynamic" algorithm visualization development model for novice learners. In *Proceedings IEEE 2005 symposium on visual languages and human-centric computing.*

Hundhausen, C. D., Douglas, S. A., & Stasko, J. T. (2002, June). A meta-study of algorithm visualization effectiveness. *Journal of Visual Languages and Computing, 13*(3), 259–290. doi:10.1006/jvlc.2002.0237

Hyvönen, J., & Malmi, L. (1993). TRAKLA – a system for teaching algorithms using email and a graphical editor. In *Proceedings of hypermedia in Vaasa* (pp. 141-147).

Jackson, D., & Usher, M. (1997). Grading student programs using ASSYST. In *Proceedings of 28th ACM SIGCSE symposium on computer science education* (pp. 335-339).

Kabal, P. (1993). *TEXdraw – PostScript drawings from TEX*. Retrieved from http://www.tau.ac.il/cc/pages/docs/tex-3.1415/ texdraw_toc.html

Karavirta, V., Korhonen, A., Malmi, L., & Stålnacke, K. (2004, July). MatrixPro – A tool for on-the-fly demonstration of data structures and algorithms. In *Proceedings of the third program visualization workshop* (pp. 26–33). Warwick, UK: Department of Computer Science, University of Warwick, UK.

Korhonen, A., & Malmi, L. (2000). Algorithm simulation with automatic assessment. In *Proceedings of the 5th annual SIGCSE/SIGCUE conference on innovation and technology in computer science education, ITiCSE'00* (pp. 160–163), Helsinki, Finland. New York: ACM Press.

Korhonen, A., Malmi, L., Myllyselkä, P., & Scheinin, P. (2002). Does it make a difference if students exercise on the web or in the classroom? In *Proceedings of the 7th annual SIGCSE/SIGCUE conference on innovation and technology in computer science education, ITICSE'02* (pp. 121-124), Aarhus, Denmark. New York: ACM Press.

Laakso, M.-J., Salakoski, T., Grandell, L., Qiu, X., Korhonen, A., & Malmi, L. (2005). Multi-perspective study of novice learners adopting the visual algorithm simulation exercise system TRAKLA2. *Informatics in Education, 4*(1), 49–68.

Lönnberg, J., Korhonen, A., & Malmi, L. (2004, May). MVT — a system for visual testing of software. In *Proceedings of the working conference on advanced visual interfaces* (AVI'04) (pp. 385–388).

Malmi, L., Karavirta, V., Korhonen, A., & Nikander, J. (2005, September). Experiences on automatically assessed algorithm simulation exercises with different resubmission policies. *Journal of Educational Resources in Computing*, 5(3). doi:10.1145/1163405.1163412

Malmi, L., Karavirta, V., Korhonen, A., Nikander, J., Seppälä, O., & Silvasti, P. (2004). Visual algorithm simulation exercise system with automatic assessment: TRAKLA2. *Informatics in Education*, 3(2), 267–288.

Malmi, L., & Korhonen, A. (2004). Automatic feedback and resubmissions as learning aid. In *Proceedings of 4th IEEE international conference on advanced learning technologies, ICALT'04* (pp. 186-190), Joensuu, Finland.

Malmi, L., Korhonen, A., & Saikkonen, R. (2002). Experiences in automatic assessment on mass courses and issues for designing virtual courses. In *Proceedings of the 7th annual SIGCSE/SIGCUE conference on innovation and technology in computer science education, ITiCSE'02* (pp. 55–59), Aarhus, Denmark. New York: ACM Press.

Mason, D. V., & Woit, D. M. (1999). Providing mark-up and feedback to students with online marking. In *The proceedings of the thirtieth SIGCSE technical symposium on computer science education* (pp. 3-6), New Orleans, LA. New York: ACM Press.

Miller, B. P. (1993). What to draw? When to draw? An essay on parallel program visualization. *Journal of Parallel and Distributed Computing*, 18(2), 265–269. doi:10.1006/jpdc.1993.1063

Myers, B. A., Chandhok, R., & Sareen, A. (1988, October). Automatic data visualization for novice Pascal programmers. In *IEEE workshop on visual languages* (pp. 192-198).

Naps, T. L., Rößling, G., Almstrum, V., Dann, W., Fleischer, R., & Hundhausen, C. (2003, June). Exploring the role of visualization and engagement in computer science education. *SIGCSE Bulletin*, 35(2), 131–152. doi:10.1145/782941.782998

Phillips, D. C. (2000). Constructivism in education. opinions and second opinions on controversial issues. *99th yearbook of the national society for the study of education (Part 1)*. Chicago: The University of Chicago Press.

Pierson, W., & Rodger, S. (1998). Web-based animation of data structures using JAWAA. In *Proceedings of the 29th SIGCSE technical symposium on computer science education* (pp. 267-271), Atlanta, GA. New York: ACM Press.

Price, B. A., Baecker, R. M., & Small, I. S. (1993). A principled taxonomy of software visualization. *Journal of Visual Languages and Computing*, 4(3), 211–266. doi:10.1006/jvlc.1993.1015

Reek, K. A. (1989). The TRY system or how to avoid testing student programs. In [New York: ACM Press.]. *Proceedings of SIGCSE*, 89, 112–116. doi:10.1145/65294.71198

Rößling, G., Schüler, M., & Freisleben, B. (2000). The ANIMAL algorithm animation tool. In *Proceedings of the 5th annual SIGCSE/SIGCUE conference on innovation and technology in computer science education, ITiCSE'00* (pp. 37-40), Helsinki, Finland. New York: ACM Press.

Saikkonen, R., Malmi, L., & Korhonen, A. (2001). Fully automatic assessment of programming exercises. In *Proceedings of the 6th annual SIGCSE/SIGCUE conference on innovation and technology in computer science education, ITiCSE'01* (pp. 133-136), Canterbury, UK. New York: ACM Press.

Stasko, J. T. (1991). Using direct manipulation to build algorithm animations by demonstration. In *Proceedings of conference on human factors and computing systems* (pp. 307-314), New Orleans, LA.

Stasko, J. T. (1997). Using student-built algorithm animations as learning aids. In *The proceedings of the 28th SIGCSE technical symposium on computer science education* (pp. 25-29), San Jose, CA. New York: ACM Press.

Stasko, J. T. (1998). Building software visualizations through direct manipulation and demonstration. In M. Brown, J. Domingue, B. Price, & J. Stasko (Eds.), *Software visualization: Programming as a multimedia experience* (pp. 103-118). Cambridge, MA: MIT Press.

KEY TERMS AND DEFINITIONS

Software Visualization: is an active research field in software engineering that uses graphics and animation to illustrate different aspects of software.

Algorithm Visualizations: are abstract graphical representations that provide an insight into how small sections of code (algorithms) compute.

Algorithm Animation: is the process of visualizing the behavior of an algorithm by abstracting the data, operations, and semantics of the algorithm by creating dynamic graphical views of those abstractions.

Direct Manipulation: is a human-computer interaction style, which involves continuous representation of objects of interest, and rapid, reversible, incremental actions and feedback (Wikipedia).

Visual Algorithm Simulation: is direct manipulation, which not only allows actions in the level of the representation, but also alters the real underlying implemented data structures.

Automatic Assessment: is computer-aided grading method for various types of exercises.

Algorithm Simulation Exercises: are simulation exercises solved by means of visual algorithm simulation, which are typically graded in terms of automatic assessment.

ENDNOTE

[1]   at http://svg.cs.hut.fi/TRAKLA2/

Chapter 12
Virtual Reality:
A New Era of Simulation and Modelling

Ghada Al-Hudhud
Al-Ahlyia Amman University, Amman, Jordan

ABSTRACT

The chapter introduces a modern and advanced view and implementations of Virtual reality systems. Considering the VR systems as tools that can be used in order to alter the perceived information from real world and allow perceiving the information from virtual world. Virtual Reality grounds the main concepts for interactive 3D simulations. The chapter emphasizes the use of the 3D interactive simulations through virtual reality systems in order to enable designers to operationalize the theoretical concepts for empirical studies. This emphasize takes the form of presenting most recent case studies for employing the VR systems. The first emphasizes the role of realistic 3D simulation in a virtual world for the purpose of pipelining complex systems production for engineering application. This requires highly realistic simulations, which involves both realism of object appearance and object behaviour in the virtual world. The second case emphasizes the evolution from realism of virtual reality towards additional reality. Coupling interactions between virtual and real worlds is an example of using the VR system to allow human operators to interactively communicate with real robot through a VR system. The robots and the human operators are potentially at different physical places. This allows for 3D-stereoscopic robot vision to be transmitted to any or all of the users and operators at the different sites.

VIRTUAL REALITY: OVERVIEW

Virtual reality is commonly known as a 3D projection of a seemed to be real image of the mind. This world of 3D projections is believed to alter what human senses perceive.

Virtual Reality (VR) has been known only in the past few years, but VR has a history dating back to the year 1950s. VR roots started as an idea that would improve the way people interacted with computers. Douglas Engelbart 1960s introduced the use of computers as tools for digital display. Inspired by Engelbart past experience as a radar

DOI: 10.4018/978-1-60566-774-4.ch012

engineer, he proposed that any digital information could be viewed on a screen connected to the computer; data visualisation. In addition, by the early 1960s, communications technology was intersecting with computing and graphics technology. This intersection leads to the emergence of virtual reality.

The emergence of VR served in a diversity of scientific views of VR uses. For example, it is cheaper and safer to train pilots on the ground before real flight. Flight simulators were one of the earliest applications of virtual reality and were built on motion platforms.

COMPUTER VISUALIZATION AND ANIMATION

Computer visualization is being thought of as a new way of how scientists evaluate and explore their data through an interactive human interface. Because of the V R evolution, advances in graphic display and high-end computing have made it possible to transform data into interactive, three-dimensional images. Hence, all the display and feedback devices that make this possible are termed Virtual Environments. Considering the various possible goals of the virtual environments, each provides easier way for scientists to interact with computers.

Interactivity was the mainstay for scientists, military, business, and entertainment.

Therefore, the advances in VR systems were also accompanied by computer visualization evolution to comply with the demand for interactivity. At this end, scientific visualization identified the imagery concept that is to transform the numerical data into images using computer graphics. Scientists can benefit from this conceptual view for compiling the enormous amount of data required in some scientific investigations. Examples of these scientific investigations are fluid dynamics, nuclear reactions, communication models or cosmic explosions.

By early 1980s, creating many of the special effects techniques for visualised data, scientific visualization moved into animation. Animation was a compelling testament of the value of a kind of imagery, 1990s. Meanwhile, animation had severe limitations. These limitations had addressed both cost and lack of interactivity. Once the animation completed changes in the data or conditions governing an experiment could not alter the responses in the imagery. In this context, VR manifests the experience of transforming the data into 3D images through various display devices. This implies building a computer-generated "virtual" world that possesses the following features: a) realism, b) immersion and c) presence. These features provides support for visualising, hearing or even touching objects inside this computer generated environment

Realism

The ever-increasing evolution in computer graphical technologies helped in the rapid change towards using 3D simulations in testing theoretical models. This is important because the lack of the realism factor in 2D simulation leads to the production of an incomplete view of the simulated world. Realism can be defined as geometrical realism and behavioural realism. The former describes to what extent the simulated world has a close appearance to the representation of the real world (Slater, Steed & Chrysanthou, 2002.). The more realistic, an object's representation, and the more realistic views the user gets. The later implies the existence of behavioural signs that indicate interactive responses which cannot be caused by geometric realism but because of the realistic responses and behaviour.

Realism is considered to be important in order to grasp and get a reasonable sense of dimensions, spaces, and interactions in the simulated world. Therefore, for more realistic representations for objects in theoretical models and the virtual world as well as their behaviours in the simulated world, the 3D-simulation and visualisation tools are of great importance.

Immersion

The feeling of being there, that is the common description of being immersed in a virtual reality environment. The user switches all the communication channels off with the real world and receives the information from the virtual world. This feeling varies depend on the type of the VR system.

Presence

Unlike the animated scenes in recorded movies, interactive virtual reality systems improve the overall feeling of being inside the simulated world. This is considered of great help especially for visualising system's behaviours in the cases of theoretical models. This dues to the ability of providing the user with the suitable means to fly and walk around the objects, for example to monitor what is happening behind a wall or under a table. In addition, the user can zoom into the scene when a precise local evaluation is needed or zoom out when a global view is required. Presence is one of the key outputs of the VE visualization. The reason for this is that presence in the simulated environment played a major role in designing the experiments in order to integrate all the visual outputs. Both aspects, presence and immersion, required a high level of realism in the simulation and a certain minimum level of quality for display.

WHY VR SYSTEMS

VR is a very expensive technology, and has emerged within institutional contexts: NASA, military researchers, video game manufacturers, universities, software and hardware developers, and entertainment industries. However, as VR has being seen as a medium used within physical reality, it is nowadays believed as an additional reality. VR opens up a broaden area of ideas and possibilities as VR systems supports both simulation and modelling.

The nature of virtual reality technology also brings up related issues about simulation.

Simulation as an efficient tool for analysing the properties of a theoretical model, can be practically used for realistic representation of these models.

Due to the complexity of designing these theoretical models, simulating the model in a virtual world can reduce this complexity by building and testing the system components separately. This step-by-step building strategy allows the scientists to test and evaluate individual components during the development stages.

In order to benefit most from VR simulations before creating physical implementations, the simulation must give an insight into the operational requirements. Such requirements include the size of the models and the space they move in. Therefore, visualising the simulation of the theoretical model within a virtual environment (VE) can actually be more efficient and functional than within conventional simulations. The realism of the simulation requires real time simulation tools, i.e. no pre-computations. Loscos et al (Loscos, Marchal & Meyer June 2003) described a crowd behaviour real time simulation that allowed for the rendering of the scene and the individuals as well as simulating the crowd behaviours. The system described by Locos et al is an individual-base model, i.e. it concentrates on the microscopic view to the system and at the same time it does not use AI techniques. In addition, it allows the emerging characteristics to be empirically defined, tested and explained by considering both quantitative and qualitative outputs. The performance of a model can be evaluated and assessed within different simulated environments. This implies that entities within a these theoretical models can be exposed to a variety of different tasks; performance can be tested in different virtual environments without an excessive amount of development time.

TYPES OF COMMON VR SYSTEMS

Commonly used VR systems vary according to the viewing tools (e.g. lenses, glasses) and display devices that add depth to flat images. A common aspect of the V R systems is that these systems should help the user switching off the communication channels with real world and only perceive the information received from the virtual world. Examples of these systems are described below.

Head-Mounted Display

User looks inside motor-cycle like helmet where two lenses can be seen. Movement tracking is being obtained by a device on top of the helmet to report head movements signals relative to a stationary tracking device. Datagloves and wands are the most common interface devices used with head-mounted displays. These tracking devices are attached to the glasses, lenses, and relay the viewer's position to the computer. The computer re-computes the image to reflect the viewer's new perspective. The computer, then, continually updates the simulation to reflect according to the new perspective. One disadvantage of the head-mounted displays they weigh several pounds.

The Binocular Omni Orientation Monitor (BOOM)

BOOM is a no-helmet head-mount system. The BOOM's elements are the viewing box and eye-glasses. The users place forehead against two eyeglasses in the viewing box. To change the perspective on an image, one can grab the handles on the side of the viewing box and move around the image. BOOM's control buttons on the handles usually serve as the interface as well as datagloves or other interface devices.

The CAVE

One of the newest, most "immersive" virtual environments is the CAVE. The CAV E is a 10x10x9 foot darkened room and data are projected in stereoscopic images onto the walls and floor of the CAV E so that they fill the room. The CAV E provides a greater sense of being immersed in the data. CAV E possesses two advantages over other V R systems. The first advantage, CAV E is that no helmets or viewing boxes are needed. Only pair of glasses and a wand is required. The second advantage of the CAV E is its large field of view.

Presagis

Presagis, previously known as (MultiGen Paradigm) is most recently recognised as advanced VR system for simulation and modelling. Presagis offers Creator, API and VegaPrime in addition to other products. Creator is specifically designed for real-time 3D simulation by producing OpenFlight models, see figure 1. Creator rapids the modelling process and increases productivity by enabling easily and effectively creating highly detailed 3D models and digital terrains. Vega Prime, with its cross-platform, scalable environment, is the most productive toolkit for real-time 3D application development and deployment. The Vega Prime provides the only framework one need to configure, create, and deploy advanced simulation applications. And, because it allows for the easy integration of new or existing code, Vega Prime offers tremendous cost and time savings by improving re-usability.

For the stereoscopic display of the scene in a full scale VE, a distributed version of the desktop model can be produced through a cluster of 6-PC's to generate six synchronised images. These six images are projected onto an 8X2 meters, 145 degrees curved screen (giving a 3Kx1K resolution) using six different projectors. Recall that the number of views and cameras are controllable via

Figure 1. Presagis system architecture; Vega Prime System

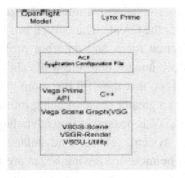

the user interface, and synchronously displayed on the screen.

HOW DOES VIRTUAL REALITY SYSTEMS PROVIDE A 3D EFFECT

To get a 3D effect, the computer projects stereoscopic images whilst controls the lenses in the viewing glasses; stereo glasses, in synchronization with the images being flashed on the screen. The VR systems are conceptually common as they are based on projecting two slightly different computer generated images on the screen: one representing the view seen through the right eye, the other, through the left eye. These two images are then fused by human brain into one stereo image. Some images are accompanied by sounds mapped to the same data driving the imagery.

A virtual roller coaster ride is so much more compelling when you can hear the sounds and air crashing on the face and riders screams. But beyond providing ambiance, sounds can reveal fine features in data not easily captured in images, such as speed and frequency. Recently, researchers in the field work on feeling the virtual world through exploration, such as the resistance of a weight whilst pulling up an incline surface. Therefore, new input devices such as stair steppers and other tactile devices will allow users to do so.

CURRENT IMPLEMENTATION OF VES

3D simulations not only need to mimic the real physical spaces and but also needs to support real time visualisation and monitoring (Teccia and Chrysanthou, 2001).This is essential for a large scale interactive virtual environment application. A recent example of an interactive virtual environment system was presented in (Cairo & Aldeco & Algorri, 2001.) where a virtual museum's assistant takes the tourists in a virtual tour and interactively answers questions.

Other examples of current utilisation of full scale 3D semi-immersive simulations include simulating an urban space environment, an interior architectural environment, and simulating the behavioural models for the training purposes. Example of recent 3D immersive environments that have been used successfully to develop group behaviour models, and perception models are: simulating the movements of crowds (Tang, Wan & Patel, 3-5 June 2003.), simulating a fire evacuation system (Li, Tang, Simpson 2004.), intelligent transportation systems (Wan and Tang, 2004), urban behaviour development (Tecchia, Loscos, Conroy & Chrysanthou, 2003.), and an intelligent vehicle model for 3D visual traffic simulation (Wan and Tang 2003). These examples have shown that the immersive 3D simulation V E supports training purposes as they feature: presence, realism, and immersion which all add value to the simulation.

Virtual prototypes and product evaluation is another application that exploits virtual environments technologies. It propagates the idea of a computer based 3D simulations of systems with a degree of functional realism. Accordingly, the virtual prototypes are used for testing and evaluation specific characteristics of the product design. This can guide the product design from idea to prototype, which helps to address the engineering design concerns of the developer, the process concerns of the manufacturer, the concerns of the maintainer, and the training and programmatic concerns of the operation. Simulations of these systems are being developed to enable the creation of a variety of realistic operational environments. Virtual prototypes can be tested in this simulated operational environment and during all the development stages. Once a virtual prototype is approved, design and manufacturing tradeoffs can be conducted on the virtual prototype to enhance productivity and reduce the time required to develop a physical prototype o even direct to the final product.

Another useful area where real time semi-immersive simulations can be useful is controlling the movements of mobile physical robots, and assessing the individual behaviour in a robotic application (Navarro-Serment, Grabowski, aredis & hosla, ecember 2002) example is presented in (Leevers, Gil, Lopes, Pereira, Castro, Gomes-Mota, Ribeiro, Gonalves, Sequeira, Wolfart, Dupourque, Santos, Butterfield, & Hogg, 1998) which provides working model of its autonomous environmental sensor for where the robot tours the inside of a building and automatically creates a 3-D telepresence map of the interior space. An example that presents how virtual reality helps in handling the connection of the various tools and the communication between the software and the hardware of the robot is presented in (Rohrmeier 1997.). Simulating such systems require real time visualisation, a high level of geometrical realism in representing the world and the moving objects, and support for the specifics of the application. For example, in order for a set of robots, representing a set of autonomous mobile robots, to build their knowledge system they need to perceive the environment. Accordingly, specifying a sensing device and sensing techniques is essential. This can not be achieved by implementing point mass objects. Alternatively, the computations need to be dependent on the sensing devices and rely on real data gathered from the world.

To summarise, the use of large scale visualisation tools in recent published work included the areas of assisting architectural design, urban planning, safety assessment, and virtual prototyping. Using a large-scale virtual environment in evaluating robotic products and applications has been used for simulating and testing the hardware whilst producing single-robot applications. Using a 3D full-scale semi-immersive environment for simulating communication and co-operation between multiple robots has not yet been fully covered.

CASE STUDY 1: REALISM OF VIRTUAL REALITY

This section presents a case study for using a V R system in producing communication model to control movements and task assignment for a set of multiple mobile robots. The proposed theoretical model is based on multi-agent systems MAS and architectures. The

MAS communication model classifies the communications for the set of robots into two levels. The first level is the local communications for interactive movement co-ordination. This communication level adopts the flocking algorithm to mimic animal intelligence. The second level tackles the interactive task assignment and ensures keeping the human operator in the loop as a global communication level. The global communication is being obtained through a virtual blackboard.

The role of VR in this study was to emphasise the human operators collaboration with a set of virtual robots through a virtual blackboard. The VR system used for modelling and simulating this model was the Presagis, installed at Virtual Reality Center at De Montfort University[1]. Inspired by Presagis available tools, the model was being built in both desktop version and full scale immersive version. For both versions, major anticipations of using 3D-simulations were:

- 3D immersive simulations can support realism in representing the simulated world

Figure 2. Rotating sensor

Realism of Simulated Agent's Virtual Vision System

Another issue that is required in a real-time 3D simulation is the ability to focus on the specifics of the simulation; e.g. simulating the agent's vision system as a laser sensor. This aims at giving a direct link to the implementation of a real life robot's sensor.

The agent's sensor is simulated as a fixed line segment at a defined angle centred at the agent's location but starting just outside of the robots' physical space, see figure 2.

The length of the line segment determines the laser sensor range. The sensor can rotate 360 degrees quantized into 18 degree intervals and therefore it detects one of 20 different locations at each time interval (τ).

Figure 3 shows that at each location, the sensor detects only one object. In this case, the sensor will only detect the first one hit (that is object A in figure 3).

The range of the agent's sensor is characterised by the length of this horizontal line segment. The visualisation whether on a desktop or using the semi-immersive projection, has helped enormously in adjusting the sensor range during the very early development stages. This is aided by visually showing the sensor with colour coding.

This horizontal sensor fired from the agent towards the environment returns the distance and the intersection point of any detected object.

In the 3D-simulation, a user can adjust the influence of the local communications with nearby robots by controlling the characteristics of the sensor in the simulation. Previous implementations of the flocking algorithms in a VE often lacked the tools to simulate the sensor that mimics real world sensors. Therefore, a goal at the very early stages of evaluation involved adjusting the range within which an agent needs to be aware of the surrounding by setting a sensible sensor range, see section 8.4.3. In order to adjust the sensor range, it is important to consider the effect of detecting

in order to sense the dimensions and spaces, these terms are referred to as geometrical realism.

- 3D immersive simulations can support the specifics of the simulations for example simulating the sensors.
- Allows the user interaction with the simulated world at interactive rates, referred to as behavioural presence.
- 3D immersive simulations must allow for real time visualisation of a large number of robots displayed simultaneously in real time, referred to as scalability.

The realism of this simulation is critical in ensuring that the implemented algorithm during the simulation can be feasibly transferred to a real robotic application. Simulating a MAS model, as a geometrical physical model implies that we have to represent the environment and the robots with geometrical shapes, which is termed geometrical realism. At the same time, it is believed realism is important to gain an increased intuitive understanding of the robots behaviours inside the VE. Therefore, great attention is paid to the behavioural representation, which is termed a behavioural realism.

Figure 3. The sensor renders green once it hits an object, Object A is detected but B is not

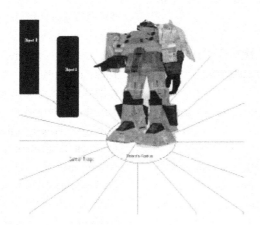

a relatively high number of robots during each sensor sweep and visualising the influence of the interaction rules on the agent's progress.

Realism of Robots' Interactions: Behavioural Realism

Behavioural realism involves visualising believable behaviours that imitate real life reactions between robots, as a result of the interaction between their cognition units (an agent's beliefs and intentions. However, recent research hypothesised that behaviour realism within a simulation is important to aid believability (Technical Report, 2004), (Chrysanthou, Tecchia, Loscos & Conroy 2004).

The creation of a believable representation of robots together with believable behaviours results in a more realistic simulation. Therefore, the main concern was to produce a behaviour model consistent with the physical appearance of the virtual robots in order to believe that the virtual robot could be seen in a manner as it would operate in the real world. The proposal aimed at implementing the three different behavioural models, section 8.4, and the main goal of this stage was to quickly evaluate each model cutting down the time required to change parameters for

optimisation purposes and as an illustration to future users.

The evaluation involved running the different models on both the desktop and on the semi-immersive VR system. The feedback from the observers was of great importance, for example, when the one of the models was demonstrated to groups of students, they expressed their views that robots do not all communicate all the time, which meets our expectation for this model. Moreover, groups of students were able to describe the actions as if they were describing real actions. For example, the virtual robots do feel the objects in the environment, as virtual robots do not go through the walls, or through each other. This is because of the virtual perception system was modelled properly that allows objects to feel the other objects; walls and robots. In addition, when running the students expressed their feeling; as they believed the human operator (me) could speak to the robots and can ask them to go somewhere very specific within the environment. They expressed an impression that the robots-user interaction demonstrates a 'real time response'.

This section has shown that realism does not only mean designing and building physically believable virtual models, but, also embodying them with believable and realistic behaviours.

This helps the user to believe or disbelieve actions and provide suitable tools to interact with the robots.

User's Interaction with the Robots in a VE: Behavioural Presence

Using Presagis, and for both the desktop and the full scale VEs the user can:

1. Interactively choose a path to move and fly around any object in the environment.
2. Choose different starting points when issuing commands.
3. Initiate new tasks or simply define new targets and monitor, closely, the robots' reactions and changing behaviours.
4. Issue a new command for a new team; initialised by, for example, grouping two existing teams together.
5. Interactively monitor the robots' responses. This improves the user's impression of being immersed in what is seen.

Unlike the animated scenes in recorded movies, these interactive aspects improve the overall feeling of being inside the simulated world. This implies providing the user with the ability to fly and walk around the objects, for example to monitor what is happening behind a wall or under a table. In addition, the user can zoom into the scene when a precise local evaluation is needed or zoom out when a global view is required, Figures 6 and 7.

Presence is one of the key outputs of the VE visualization. The reason for this is that presence in the simulated environment played a major role in designing the experiments described below. A key aspect in the experimentation process is to assess robots' behaviour by integrating all the visual outputs. Both aspects, presence and immersion, required a high level of realism in the simulation and a certain minimum level of quality for display.

The VE as a Testbed

The 3D simulation tools, introduced above, have been implemented at two versions; a desktop VE and a semi-immersive projection VE. The former implies displaying the 3D simulation at a desktop size whereas the later implies that the simulated world is displayed on a big screen. In addition, when running the visual simulation, all numerical information to be exchanged between robots and between robots and human operator are recorded. These numerical values represent the paths followed by all robots, x and y positions, the heading angle, the new heading, as well as all the interaction weights.

The Desktop VE Version

The desktop display is used for verifying the built components during most of the design stages. The software environment used for the real-time visual simulations includes: a user interface and the programming environment. This simulation interface provides the user with the ability to manage the set up, e.g. the appearance of the complete scene including the number of view points needed and the level of details required. There is also complete flexibility of the viewing location and the direction being monitored and the view of any action possible with multiple views. The interface enables the user to: a) control the dimensions of the environment, i.e. the sizes of the rooms and corridors, and b) define and test, interactively, the size of the target and the target model.

The Immersive Full Scale VE Version

This large scale visualization allows for robots' movements and interaction inside the virtual world to be projected ion a big screen enabling multiple users to visualize and assess the simulation at once. Figure 5 shows an abstract version of the VEC at De Montfort University. The space in front of the screen can host up to 20 users at once and allows

Figure 4. A screenshot, photograph taken while running the large scale VR system to a group of students for evaluation

for collaborative analysis to take place between experts from various fields to monitor, discuss and control a simulation. This has been used for group analysis, and for information presentations in the form of demonstration, see figure 4. The demonstrations aimed at displaying different models and versions have been used to obtain feedback from non-experts, i.e. undergraduate students from different disciplines.

Advantages of Immersive Large Scale Simulation

Because of the additional features that can be obtained using semi-immersive full-scale environment V E, the big advantage over a pure simulation is the building of an environment that mimics, admittedly to a different quality level, the real physical space, see Figure 8. This full-scale visualisation enables us to test different situations with different scales and dimensions and can enhances the sense of the dimension and sizes of

Figure 5. Virtual laboratory with different starting points and target positions marked

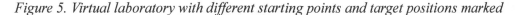
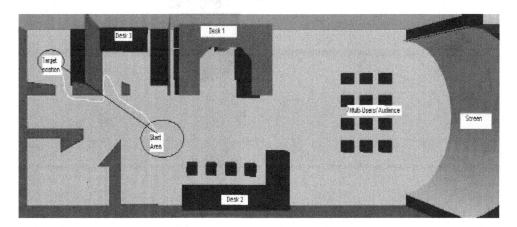

Figure 6. Viewing robots' interaction; zoom in

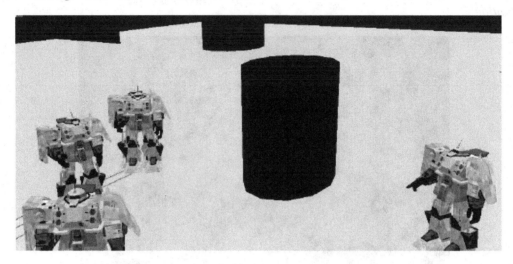

objects inside the environment see figure 9.

The large-scale display also offers the opportunity to visualise multiple views at once, see figure 10. This allowed for a quick visual, individual and group, analysis for the quality of the robots' actions in the virtual world for this large number of robots by allowing us to move closely to the individual robots in different situations.

Another issue that is considered as an advantage of using the 3D simulation within VEs is the ability of increasing the appearance of scene complexity whilst reducing the time-cost of always rendering the highest details. Since the object representation inside the world does not necessarily imply representing all the details all the time, the simulation in a VE allows the system to render different level of details according to the distance from the viewpoint. The higher detail geometry is rendered when objects are close to the eye point and only lower detail geometry is rendered when objects are further away. It also allows for multiple levels of detail, where there

Figure 7. Team members split into two groups; zoom out

Figure 8. The large-scale simulation supports real physical sizes and spaces

would otherwise be abrupt changes.

Visual Evaluation of the Emergent Behaviours

Significant benefits of using interactive 3D-simulations only occur if the VE assists the user in achieving objectives more efficiently than other simulations would. The simulation tools used in this work allow the human vision system to assess an agent's behaviour by running the system on a desktop or projecting the scenes onto a large screen in order to improve the ability to investigate many more design alternatives using different micro structures that implies testing different agent's architectures. Therefore, the evaluation process focuses on visually assessing the quality of the robots' actions and tests different behavioural models to see whether they meet the user's expectations. Visualising different levels of behaviour under different conditions allows us to define 'what-if' situations, to discuss times when the system fails, limitations on the number of robots, and sensor range modifications, etc. It provides us with a way to explain the cases that are considered as bottlenecks. This improves the performance by evaluating the emergent behaviour at the system level not just at the individual level

Figure 9. Different scales give different representation of the same spaces

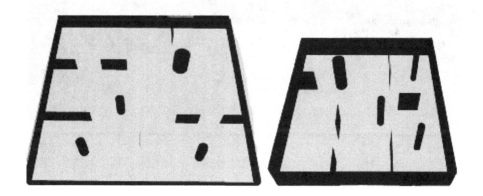

Figure 10. Leicester Reality Centre, De Montfort University, displaying multiple views simultaneously

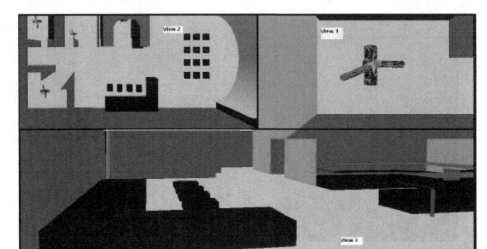

over a number of iterations.

In this respect, the visual assessment considers two main issues. First, to what extent the robots' actions are consistent with their knowledge; where rationality is considered as a measure of the consistency. This is carried out by comparing the numerical and written messages sent by these robots with the observable actions of these robots. For example, a message of content:

I am agent Ai at position x, y and can see agent Aj 18 degrees to the right within the avoidance zone.

The user expects this agent when appropriate to move 18 degrees to the left in order to avoid the detected agent. Second, the quality of the performed actions and the decision made are feasible of being performed in real-time; that is they are guaranteed to behave within a certain time.

Figure 11. Viewing a large number of robots, photograph taken while running the large-scale system

The experiments are being run for testing four levels of communication: a) Local communications for movement coordination using the flocking algorithm described in (Al Hudhud and Ayesh 2008), b) Global Communication for interactive task assignment by the human operator based on Blackboard technique (Al-Hudhud, 2006), and c) A combined local and global communications. These levels of communications are coded into four layers. These layers encode the different levels of behaviour and agent's architectures within different models: Local communication Model, (LC −Model), Global Communication Model (GC −Model), Local-Global Communication Model (LGC − Model), and Follow Wall Model (FW −Model).

Local Communication
Model LC −Model

The LC −Model represents an initial case where robots are expected to only communicate with nearby robots to coordinate movements. Therefore the only inputs for the robots in this model are the received information via the agent's sensor and they are not assigned any tasks. The expected behaviour from this model is to obtain the natural behaviour of a flock. The robots are expected to show this reactive behaviour that represents animal intelligence in avoiding each other and moving in a group (see Figure 12).

Running this model results in a lower level of behaviour and allows for the reactive components of the robots to be active. This model allows us to test the system's micro structure; i.e. the reactive component of the agent's architecture (see Figure 13).

The tests show a high level of co-ordination as robots were able to move in groups with signs of natural behaviours. For example, the flock can split up into two smaller flocks to go around both sides of an obstacle and then rejoin once past the obstacle. In addition, a dynamic leadership is also achieved as any front agent can lead. So, if the leader should get trapped between other robots, any front agent will take over the leadership and the nearest agent will follow. Figure 14 shows a set of robots represented as 3D-robots. They move randomly following the first three rules of the algorithm.

Global Communication
Model GC −Model

For the GC − Model the ground based controller (human) broadcasts messages, via the keyboard, to all registered robots within the system. These messages include explicit instructions to allocate tasks for a set of robots. When these robots read the message, they are grouped into a team; the concept of team forming. In terms of the flocking rules, each agent only considers the collision avoidance rule. In this context, an agent's internal system sets the weights that control the strength of both alignment and cohesion force to zero. The effect of applying global communication in this way is equivalent to the effect of applying a global alignment force, i.e. all robots will align their velocity in the direction of the target position.

According to this model, an agent is expected to activate only the cognitive component of its architecture. This component allows an agent to possess a cognitive knowledge structure and in this case each agent of the group is supposed to possess a joint mental state that leads to a joint intention; i.e. performing the common goal.

This model is tested by running the system with a specified number of robots, (five robots for the first trial), and allowing the GBC to interactively issue a message to the robots using the keyboard as an input device. The robots inside the virtual world receive the message and interpret the contents of the message. The robots first issued messages to the GBC to report their status at each time interval. For example, an agent is happy to perform the task if $(T <= C)^2$, also it is a little bit "Tired" if $(T − C <= 20)^3$.

Figure 12. A set of robots are moving within a team and influenced by the cohesion force and the alignment force

Local-Global Communication Model (LGC –Model)

According to this model, robots are expected to be able to communicate with each other as well as with the ground based controller GBC; i.e. all the communication levels are implemented. All robots are supposed to be grouped in teams as a consequence of issuing a group command by the GBC. So this model exploits agent's reactive and cognitive components represented by the Hybrid Belief Desire Intention integrated with the Black-Board in one architecture.

The test considered the scenario where a set of robots are assigned a task, e.g. they are given a target location, in the upper left in figure 5. By assigning the virtual task, each of the robots in the group is expected to: a) compute the expected distance to the task, b) estimate the time to finish the task, and, c) issue messages to the GBC reporting these information as a status 'HAPPY'. Each agent is expected to report its status depending upon

Figure 13. A team of robots moving forward, the team members split into two teams as they encountered the wall

Figure 14. Viewing robots' interaction in a large scaled model

its dynamically changing beliefs. The reported status is a result of activating the deliberative component of the agent's architecture together with the reactive component.

In other words, an agent uses all the information available, not only those related to the local reactions but also those related to the GBC's commands. On arrival, robots are to circle around the target and continuously modify their weight for the blackboard negotiation rule, in order to avoid getting too close to the target.

Running this model has shown interesting results across the micro and macro levels.

Regarding the micro structure, the agent's

actions have met the expectations where the deliberative component in the agent's architecture works synchronously with the reactive component. This test allows us to compare the different behaviours based on different knowledge structures. The emergent behaviour depends on the cognition intelligence as a prerequisite for the deliberation, see GC −Model. Regarding the macro level structure, the visual tests assists in building the new model that reflects the features of both models into one, namely the LGC −Model.

The visual tests played a major role in evaluating the group communication as it allows for interactively monitoring the robots' actions in real

Figure 15. Viewing robots' interaction in small-scaled model

Figure 16. Team members are circling around a target position

time. The four layers of communication (three layers for the flocking algorithm plus one layer for the blackboard rule) are all implemented.

In addition to the visual outputs, the numerical outputs can also be analysed, for example, the interaction weights and positions. This information together with the visual experiments allowed us to identify the effect of the cohesion force as a binding force that affects the robots' progress, see section 8.4.1 where the user is able to numerically analyse the weights. This has been significantly useful when the visual test showed slow responses in the agent's progress when combining the flocking rules with the blackboard.

The results of running this model show that the user is able to get comprehensive information from robots in the form of actions and written messages. The user can determine the conditions that increase the chance of completing the task despite difficulties that may arise, for example, when any agent fails to perform the specified task and other team members will then continue to perform the task. Practically, this has been implemented in the same manner as described in section 8.4.2.

Oscillate State Detection and Follow Wall Mode: FW −Model

The FW − Model resolves the conflict that can arise when an agent needs to reach a specified point that lies behind a barrier or a wall. The 'Wall' problem implies that an agent would turn to avoid the wall then turn back heading toward the target so leading to oscillation. This can also happen, for example, when an agent's sensor reads three consecutive similar values for the identity of the detected object within the perception zone of the collision avoidance rule.

The basic idea behind the FW − Model is to let a meta-level component run the world model faster than real time to make predictions of future states. When the metalevel component detects that the system has specified an undesired action, it modifies the decision made to produce a new actual action in order to avoid reaching this state. This model enables the agent to detect the oscillation state and then allows the agent to switch between two modes. The first is the standard LGC − Model, whilst the second is the Follow Wall Mode or FW − Mode. The FW − Mode is used as a recovery mode and allows the agent to move smoothly alongside the wall until it can turn again toward the target. Once an agent has passed the oscillation state, it switches back to the standard LGC −Model.

The FW −Mode is implemented as follows: Firstly, each agent performs a pre-collision detection test using its current heading. Secondly, it computes a new heading according to the communication algorithm. The agent then will use the new heading to perform a post-collision detection test before changing its current heading. An agent will not change its heading unless there is an object straight ahead. For the cases when an agent detects three different objects this model may still fail as an agent may still show oscillation whilst trying to avoid these objects.

Directed Numerical Analysis

The results obtained from the visual evaluation in the previous section are of great importance in directing the numerical analysis. Instead of blindly analysing the numerical outputs of the robots, one can numerically assess the performance of the local communication unit separately. This for example can be obtained by testing different sensor ranges, as the sensor is the only source of the information governs the flocking system. In addition, one can test the influence of the flocking weights on team progress towards the target location.

Testing the Appropriateness of Sensor Range SR

As the sensor links an agent to the environment and controls its local interactions via the flocking rules, this section aims at testing the optimum sensor range that allows robots to: a) move and act as a team, and b) minimise the number of frames to complete a specified task. The number of frames indicates the number of steps, and consequently the distance an agent moves in order to reach this target. Completing the task means being within a distance equal to double the sensor range from the

specified target. When an agent moves within a team towards a target, this implies that it activates both the local interaction rules together with the external blackboard rule. The local interaction rules require an agent to filter the sensory data according to the minimum separation distance allowed between those robots. Therefore, the separation distance S_d is also considered when adjusting the sensor range as it controls the influence of the local interactions.

Theoretically, the minimum number of frames required for an agent to reach a target is when it detects no objects during its path to the target. This can be done by setting the sensor range to zero which implies switching off the flocking system. Consequently, the number of frames times the step length an agent moves each frame exactly equals the direct distance to the target. However, the fastest route implies that robots move as a set of individuals rather than as team members. This also implies that robots do not interact locally with the surroundings in the environment; they do not align, cohere, or avoid colliding with other objects. On the other hand, using a large sensor range implies increasing the influence of the flocking system. This in turn increases the number of interactions as each agent moves towards the nearest agent to align with, as well as towards the team centroid to keep itself bound to the team. This implies that the number of frames or movements, towards the target increases and accordingly, an agent takes a slower route towards the target.

The effect of the minimum distance allowed between objects in the environment that is the separation distances S_d, is also considered in the experiment. The visual tests have shown that with S_d less than 7units 4 an agent is happy to slightly bump into things, as this distance is less than the agent's dimensions (radius, width). In reality, the separation distance must allow for an object to turn safely without hitting the detected object. In contrast, higher values for S_d increases the time for an agent to complete the task. This is partially because with a large separation distance an agent

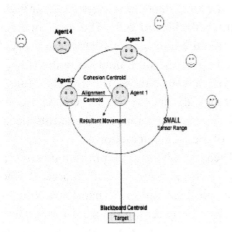

Figure 17. The smaller sensor range reduces the influence of the flocking system

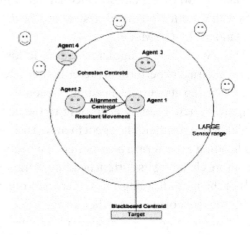

Figure 18. A larger sensor range increases the influence of the flocking system

may not be able to go through the space between two closely detected objects or squeeze tightly round a corner. For this, an experiment is designed to run the LGC −Model with 20 robots. The user interactively chooses a start point to issue the team task command by giving the position of the specified target location. The robots are to move in a team to reach this target location.

The experiment resulted in the fact that increasing the sensor range results in an increase of the perception zones for the flocking system; i.e. an agent may see more robots, and therefore, the number of interactions increases, see figure 18. This implies more steps towards the target represented by more number of frames, see figure 19.

To summarise, choosing a lower value for the sensor range leads to reducing the influence [4] of the flocking system. This in turn yields many individualists rather than team and group performance, each lives his own life for itself and does not try to co-operate with or follow others. Nevertheless, it is essential to maintain the influence of the flocking system by setting the sensor range that helps keep the essence of the group co-operation in the form of the team movements.

Controlling the Interaction Weights of the Agent's Subsystems

This section tests, with the aid of visual evaluation, how the user can adjust the interaction weights to help accelerating the robots' progress? For this purpose, controlling the interaction weights is carried out by running the Local Communication Model (LC−Model). The weights associated with the flocking rules are dynamically computed at each time interval depending on the rule's centroid and on the attitudes of each rule; these are the perception zone for this rule and the filtering strategy.

Originally, the flocking system is implemented here with the weights computed in a conventional way, see table 1. Since the collision avoidance weight is given precedence over other weights, as it is the most important interaction rule, the visual tests involved the influence of the cohesion weight $W_{Ai}^{R_\beta}$ on the progress of the robots. The visual simulation has been useful at this stage in assessing and evaluating the extent to which varying the cohesion weight allows the robots in the same team to move as a unit. According to the visual evaluation, it was found that the cohesion weight slows the robots' progress, due to the

Figure 19. The number of movements towards the target increases as a result of a higher influence of the flocking system

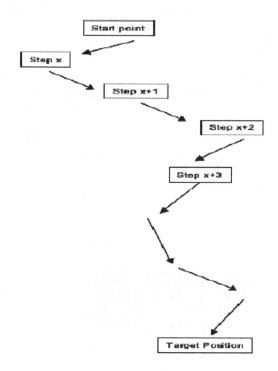

high influence of the cohesion force. In addition, it causes overcrowding in the surrounding area which is used as an indicator for examining the strength of this binding force.

Consider the situation where an agent detects a large number of nearby robots, then each of these robots modifies its velocity to move towards the cohesion centroid. If one or more of these robots detects a wall and at the same time some of the other robots within the avoidance zone, it may become trapped. In this trap situation, a neighbour of this agent (who may not detect the same objects) will be influenced by the trapped agent. In the same manner, the remaining robots will be influenced by the trapped robots as a result of a high cohesion weight. This can become worse if this set of robots is assigned a task to reach a specified target. Considering this scenario, the trapped agent continuously checks its capabilities of performing

this task using the mechanism described in GC −Model section. According to this mechanism, the trapped agent may discard his commitment regarding completing the task. The other robots who detect the trapped agent will be influenced by the trapped agent, which can still significantly slow their progress. This leads to a longer expected completion time, or even prevents the influenced robots from completing the task.

In this respect, a main goal of analysing the interaction weights then is to adjust the cohesion weight in order to avoid these impacts of a high cohesion weights without loosing the benefits of the supportive role of this weight in the team performance. Therefore, the start point was to test the conventional implementation of the weights in flocking algorithms, and the values are shown in table 1, for the alignment $w_{Ai}^{R_\alpha}$ and cohesion weight $w_{Ai}^{R_\beta}$. For this implementation, the cohesion weight is computed as the inverse of the distance to the cohesion centroid $C_{Ai}^{R_\beta}$ if the $C_{Ai}^{R_\beta}$ falls within the avoidance range, otherwise it set equal to one. This implies that the cohesion force is mostly inversely proportional to the distance to the centroid. The weight becomes bigger very quickly as the centroid position falls outside the avoidance range (S_d) whilst it does not become very small within the avoidance range.

In order to numerically assess the dominance of the cohesion weight in situations where the robots dos not detect any avoidance cases, the LC − Model was used. Accordingly, these inter-action weights are shown in figure 20. The bar graph shows the weights that control the strength of the interaction forces, according to the values shown in Table 1, on an agent over the first 200 frames of the simulation. Points of high cohesion weight, in figure 20, implies that an agent will be highly influenced by the nearby robots, and via monitoring the trap problem can be observed.

To overcome the trap problem, $W_{Ai}^{R_\beta}$ is modified in the following manner. Within the cohesion

Table 1. The values of set of interaction weights

Alignment $W_{Ai}^{R_\alpha}$		Cohesion $W_{Ai}^{R_\beta}$		Collision Avoidance $W_{Ai}^{R_\gamma}$	
$C_{Ai}^{R_\alpha} < S_d$	$C_{Ai}^{R_\alpha} > S_d$	$C_{Ai}^{R_\beta} < S_d$	$C_{Ai}^{R_\beta} > S_d$	$C_{Ai}^{R_\gamma} < S_d$	$C_{Ai}^{R_\gamma} > S_d$
$1/C_{Ai}^{R\alpha}$	1	$1/C_{Ai}^{R_\beta}$	1	1	1

Figure 20. The interaction weights over the first 200 frames. The cohesion weight dominates the interaction weights whenever the avoidance weight is zero. The unmodified cohesion weight values are shown in Table 1

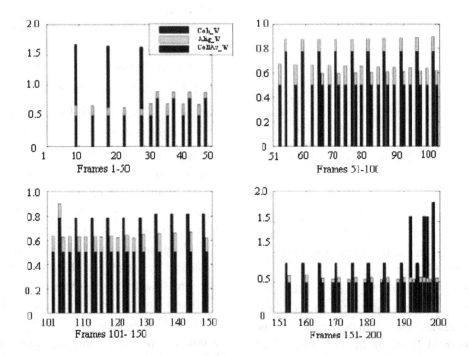

range, $W_{Ai}^{R_\beta}$ is inversely proportional to the square of the distance to $C_{Ai}^{R_\beta}$ otherwise it is inversely proportional to the distance to $C_{Ai}^{R_\beta}$ elsewhere as in table 2.

Figure 21 shows the effect of modifying the way the cohesion weight is computed in reducing the influence of the cohesion force as well as in maintaining the essence of team performance. This can reduce the expected completion time

when assigning a task to these robots. The Local Global Communication Model (LGC − Model) is used to examine the efficiency of the modified weight of the cohesion rule in terms of completion time (in frames).

Table 2. The interaction weights, modified

Alignment $W_{Ai}^{R_\alpha}$		Cohesion $W_{Ai}^{R_\beta}$		Collision Avoidance $W_{Ai}^{R_\gamma}$	
$C_{Ai}^{R_\alpha} < S_d$	$C_{Ai}^{R_\alpha} > S_d$	$C_{Ai}^{R_\beta} < S_d$	$C_{Ai}^{R_\beta} > S_d$	$C_{Ai}^{R_\gamma} < S_d$	$C_{Ai}^{R_\gamma} > S_d$
$1 / C_{Ai}^{R\alpha}$	1	$1 / (C_{Ai}^{R_\beta})^2$	$1 / C_{Ai}^{R_\beta}$	1	1

Figure 21. The interaction weights over the first 200 frames, with the cohesion weight modified according to the values shown in table 2

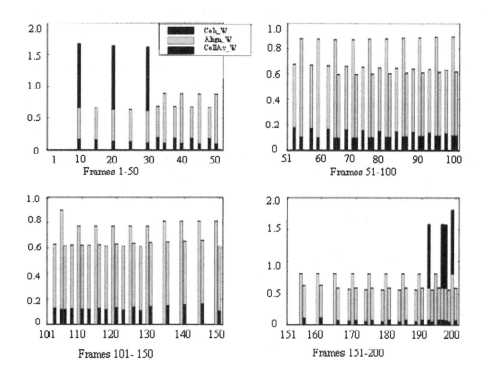

Detecting Locations of Complexity within the Environment

A novel aspect of the numerical analysis of the interaction weights was the ability by analysing the cohesion weights to extract ideas about the structure of the environment.

This implies a human operator can draw a rough idea about the locations of complexity by comparing the cohesion weights with the results of analysing teams x, y positions in terms of their means and standard deviations.

By considering that the communication model can be deployed as a communication with a higher level human controller, who could physically exist in a different location, the human controller can analyse the information sent by a set of robots so as to detect the locations of complexity in the environment. This is carried out by viewing the distribution of the cohesion weights while performing a specified task by running the LGC−Model. The experiment is designed to run the simulation by launching a set of five robots in the simulated environment from a start point, at the front of the screen, and assign them a task, to reach the target position shown in top left in the same figure. The numerical outcomes of the experiment consist of all the cohesion weights, and the (x, y) positions.

The graph shown in figure 22 shows the distribution of the cohesion weights along the frames. In this graph, low values of cohesion weight indicate a large distance to the cohesion centroid. A small cohesion weight may represent those robots, which are moving away from each other in an attempt to avoid an obstacle. This also may imply that the detected robots are not close to each other and may be splitting up, depending on their positions from the obstacle and from each other, in order to avoid one or more obstacles. On the other hand, high values of the cohesion weights imply a reduced distance to the cohesion centroid, which indicates that the detected robots are close to each other. Therefore, the graph in figure 22

can be considered as a way to extract locations of difficulties encountered in the environment.

In addition, the test showed that the x, y positions can be fruitfully analysed together with the distribution of the cohesion weights to give a more explicit structure of the environment. Therefore, the x, y positions, sent by the robots to the GBC, is used to plot the deviations from the mean positions. During each frame, the mean positions of the robots and how far individually they are from the mean are calculated.

The graph in figure 23 shows the deviation of the robots' positions from the mean, for the task used to analyse these cohesion weights above. The deviation follows five different routes and shows the times of the obstacles encountered, as high deviations, and the times of open areas as low deviations. For example, the time encountered and locations of the four rows of chairs shown in figure 5 can be extracted. This also can be useful in assessing the robots ability to autonomously organise themselves by maintaining their positions with respect to their neighbours. This implies that these robots were capable of maintaining

Figure 22. The distribution of the cohesion weights associated with the cohesion forces for each frame

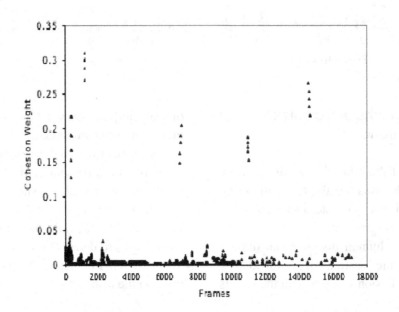

their positions during each frame in order to act as a team on their way towards the target, which supports the survivability aspect in the long-term tasks. This level of autonomy is currently a high demand in robotic applications. This example has demonstrated the following issues:

1. The set of robots are able to efficiently avoid each other as they feel complete the task within a team so as to count the collision avoidance rule and social relations represented by the alignment and cohesion forces.
2. The high level of autonomy these robots have whilst they are moving towards the target as they are capable of self-organizing and position-maintaining in order to control their motion is considered efficient in controlling a large number of robots and supports the scalability objectives.

The numerical assessment was strongly directed by the visual assessment. These numerical analysis can be deployed successfully for analyse the cohesion weights and can draw out an abstract picture of the environment by integrating the ideas from both graph 24 and graph 22, defining an explicit structure of the environment and the locations of complexity.

A comparison between the performances of the 3D simulator using the above described VR system and a set of real multiple robot system is being carried out. The set of real robots was interactively assigned the same task as assigned to the virtual robots in the above-described experiment. The x, y positions of the real robots is being plotted in Figures 25 and 26. These plots exhibit the similar behaviour of both simulated robots; Figures 23 and 24, and the real robots; Figure 25 and 26. This result emphasizes the role of the virtual environments in pipelining the complex systems production.

CASE STUDY 2: FROM REALISM TO ADDITIONAL REALITY

This case study presents the implementation of a 3D virtual environment VE as an interactive collaboration environment between a team of robots.

Figure 23. The individual deviations from the mean positions for the set of 5 robots

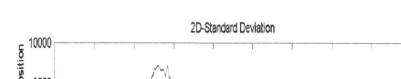

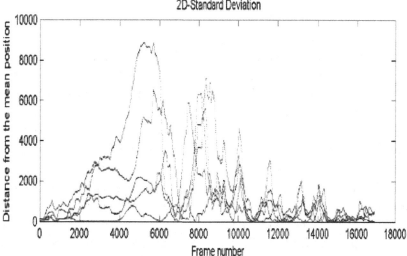

Figure 24. The average standard deviation for the same group, the set of 5 robots

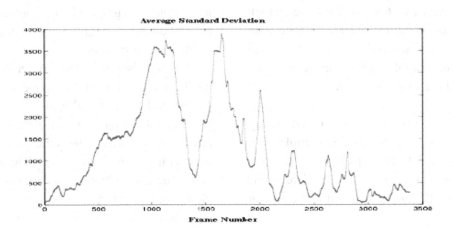

Figure 25. The deviation from the mean positions, two flocking robots

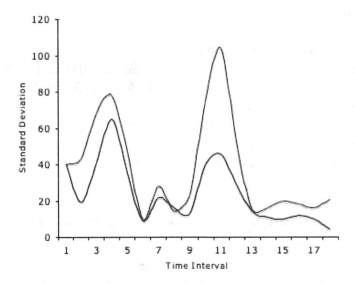

This team can include human operators and physical robots all at different physical locations. The use of VE as a virtual Blackboard and a virtual world has shown to be useful in order to allow the human operator to: a) exchange information regarding the robots environment, b) observe the emergent behaviour of the robots through a stereoscopic projection of the images sent by robots, c) allow for user interaction, real time monitoring, and d) visually assess the robots' behaviour and interactively issue a relevant decision through the virtual blackboard.

Recently, research in the area of communication and control emphasizes combining both reality and realism for controlling a set of robots physically existing in a different location (Turner, Richardson, Le Blanc, Kuchar, Ayesh, and Al Hudhud 2006). This implies a set of properties can be achieved by integrating various tools together, to create a testbed network for the next generation of robot telepresence

The above-described research aims to be able to launch a manned space craft, twice in a defined period of time, with a skeleton crew of technicians

Figure 26. The average standard deviation; two flocking robots

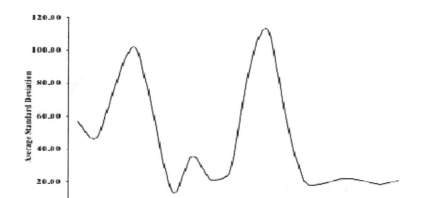

to operate it. Many current UMVs (Unmanned Vehicles) instead of requiring a small operating crew, can require a large team of operators, and be more expensive than the equivalent manned version to run, thus defeating some of the purposes of having UMVs in the first place. Also, in the last 15 years there has been a rapid growth in the study of semi-emergent behaviour when many autonomous robots operate in a closed environment. It is thus imperative if we require emergent behaviour from UMVs we are going to have to change the way telepresence operates.

RoboViz (Turner et al, 2006). is a small step in the way to consider robotic autonomous engines, as connected computational engines, that have to be steered and also have local communication modes towards each other as well as to and from command centres and operators. This way of describing heterogeneous computing elements being connected with diverse networking standards and wishing to be computationally steered by human operators, has many similarities to traditional e-Science computational steering systems. This paper highlights two main dimensions: a) First, simulation results for multi communication levels of heterogeneous agent-based system; human operators and robots, and b) Second, advanced

experimentation study for testing real implementation for multiple command centres and accordingly, describing the individual parts of the testbed being used through the CompuSteer project (Turner et al, 2006).

A Collaborative User and Robot Environment Network Testbed

This integration between the virtual and real networks feature key practical aspects.

First, an increased level of presence and immersion within the simulation helps gaining an increased level of understanding of the robots behaviour inside their environment. Second, the virtual network enables a real-time user-robots interaction by observing and monitoring the robots' actions and analysing the information sent by the robots to a human operator.

The proposed implementation of the virtual network combines the realism and reality of the robots-based communication modes and the corresponding behaviours. This can be of great importance for ability to control the real physical robots from different physical locations allowed for easy fault detecting and for real-world problems to be tested and seen in an easy and understandable

Figure 27. The robots receive the user's commands as well as messages from other robots via ethernet connection

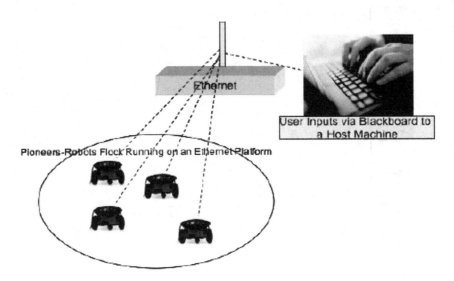

manner. The following sections presents a study for this kind of implementation including the response time for multiple connections, building a testbed for these multiple connections, and the choices for the this testbed.

Loss, Latency and Multiple Connections

The networking involved within a telepresence robotic interface has two key components; the control network predominately sending instructions from an operator to the robot, and the information network transmitting data, often predominately video (especially when considering required bandwidth), from the robot back to an operator[5]. Given reliable communication channels, and dedicated links with known, if not actually removed latency then the command-and-control system, within this telepresence, is tightly controlled and becomes an easy to understand loop.

We can now consider the time delays involved in this ideal system. Video and diagnostics information from the robot are transmitted over a time delay, δ_v, and after a response time from the operator, δ_u, an instruction is sent to the robot over a further network time delay, δ_c, and acted by the robot after interpretation with a final delay of, δ_r. This cycle repeats with trained operators controlling the robot with an extended reaction time of,

$$rt = \delta_v + \delta_u + \delta_c + \delta_r$$

A trained operator can use this kind of simple system with a high degree of efficiency, even experiencing extra input for example robotic haptic information (transmission of force/touch direct to vibration/force feedback devices) over quiet a range of latency times. As latency times increase efficiency decreases, but is in some respects a controlled degradation of service. An issue arises when extra influences occur that can make the control or robotic steering operation difficult or even impossible, which we will now list and consider.

The first influence we will describe is variable latency. It is well known that given a fixed latency, even if it is very large for example from Moon to Earth (up to 2 seconds time delay with direct visibility but raising to 10 seconds if a data relay satellite is used), over a training period, preferably off-line, an experienced operator can reliably control an on-line robot at a constant level of efficiency. This is unlikely to approach the same efficiency of an operator with direct control, but what is important is that there is a constant percentage efficiency value. Networks are not usually built like this (unless for example they are dedicated switching systems [dark light fiber]) and their latency will fluctuate over time. Now the extended reaction time is a function of time t,

$$rt(t) = \delta_v(t) + \delta_u + \delta_c(fn(t)) + \delta_r$$

These fluctuations in latency make the task an extra degree harder for the operator, potentially drastically reducing the amount of useful work achievable. A simple approximation is to model these fluctuations around Gaussians or Poisson distributions, with known mean values, but this may not take into account burst temporaral delays, as networks have non-homogenous effects. A second influence of a standard network is the probability of loss and corruption (e.g. data convolution and additive noise) within the transmitted data that is a natural occurrence. Again, for an operator this introduces uncertainty and thus reduces performance. So for each of the networks we have probabilities p of corruption or loss for a particular element of size s, which again is time dependent,

$$p_s(v(t)), p_s(c(t))$$

Although latency and loss can be modelled by a generic corruption/delay possibly in threshold filtering the convolution of the transmitted stream t with a point spread function p' and adding noise n. As networks are non-linear in (packet) data recovery this is only a crude approximation.

$$s = t \otimes p' + n$$

If s is very different from t, i.e. above some threshold T then the resulting data can be unrecoverable.

$$Fail : \{T > |s - t|\}$$

A third problem introduced is the fact that a single operator controlling only one robot is inefficient[6], and the introduction of multiple robot control is essential. This aids both efficiency, as well as allowing new joint collaborative actions to occur between the robots, that may not have been possible otherwise.

Finally we would like to add specialist expertise and guidance, for the operator, involving other users, each monitoring the progress as well as being able to act, take over control, or simply suggest alternative courses of actions. This brings together a requirement for a set of multiple command-and-control centres with multiple robots over standard networks. This brings a need for a third network to be introduced that connects command centres together creating a shared collaborative space.

Technical Choices for Building a Testbed Communication System

To consider these issues, a real robot network with a set of real telepresence operators are proposed and distributed using different packet style systems, each considering the requirements for multi-way communication, loss and latency.

UDP/IP

The network connections will consider UDP/IP to transmit continual streams with no concern for full error corrections and recovery, by inherently not allowing packet resending. In a real-time system, hearing or seeing data, which should have been transmitted some time previously, if missed, is possibly too late to be useful. As temporal latency increase for a packet, a practical solution is to introduce larger than average packet buffers at the receiving end - which will also increase the mean latency value.

There is a continual battle of trade-offs between mean latency and amount of packet loss. Increasing the mean latency, by having a large packet buffer, reduces the number of packets lost, but also increase the reaction time rt for the system. There is a difference of opinion as to whether the data stream, consisting of commands, should be error correction for missing packets, e.g. TCP/IP, or if even simple command streams can also have lossy influences that are acceptable.

Multicast transmission

Any system should be scalable, and the usual unicast (one-to-one) communication systems have an O (n2) scaling issue as the number of robots and/or the number of command centres increases. Using multicast, the aim is for a single packet to be optimally transmitted to a range of addresses, meaning along any specific connection no more than one copy will need to be transmitted. This is essential to cope with a large increase in number of robots, operators or/and command centres.

Compression Standards

All data streams that do not need to be transmitted faithfully, for example video and audio can be also lossy compressed. For a 25Mb/s connection (low average guaranteed within academia), with lets say 20-30 video streams each should aim to be well under 1Mb/s in order to accommodate the outgoing network as well as include audio and other data streams. Compression can consider all forms of quantisation; temporal (number of frames per second), spatial (x–y resolution of the image) and within the compression codec for example quantising in frequency (for example in Discrete Cosine Transforms, or Wavelet transform codecs).

Intra-Robot Communication

The language required for robot to robot requests needs to be formal in structure.

This allows for analysis prediction, and behavioural modelling. This also allows localised communication, for when two robots physically (or visually) see each other and can pass intentions, behaviours and states of being.

Semi-Autonomous Robot Behaviour

If the arrival of data transmitted cannot be guaranteed, nor guaranteed the exact response times to request, commands cannot be at the microscopic detailed level. Thus, robots need also semi-autonomous behaviour for two main reasons; one so that they can continue to operate safely (negotiate doors, walls etc.) when there is no direct assistance, and secondly so that together, by working in teams, the emergent behaviour can allow functionality that is too complex for a single operator to manipulate. The system currently used is based on flocking rules and known blackboard intents.

Steering Architecture

With this system every command centre will receive all the video streams (possibly in stereoscopic projection if required and available) from all the robots, as well as from other command centres. This gives a specified experience of latency and thus efficiency to control the robots. Each robot can be considered as a computational engine, considering its next actions based on both higher-level tasks from the command centres, as well as, low-level information from its environment.

Multiple users can try and steer the same robot, which in temporal latency issues can occur no matter how well practiced operators are. The robot needs to take a decision based on the multiple instructions, possibly contradictory, as well as of course the local environment. For example this means that two instructions, one to turn right and the other to turn left, to avoid a hole will not result in the robot carrying out the average of the two instructions. Diagnostic status information returning from the robot, indicate the current course of action, back to the operators and thus with communication across command-centres difficulties can be alerted.

The users still need protocols to operate but as the command centres are video and audio linked inter-command centre steering can be done (initially by shouting). This is not ideal but for the first generation of test-bed this has advantages of procedural optimisation as well as adding layers of computational blocking at a later stage.

Required Facilities at Command Centres

All the standard benefits from an Access Grid (Collaborative Working Environment) structure are expected within any command centre (which may not be the case in the future). This helps to increase the level of presence experienced by the users, so other command centres appear in similar co-located spaces as well as co-located with the spaces inhabited by the robots. This includes;

1. Large life-size projected screens (for full size viewing)
2. Directionless remote microphones - so there are no cables or even radio-tags required
3. Echo cancellation system – so headphones are not needed
4. Shared data sets as well as the media streams – so environments can be considered integrated

A final issue to be considered is that of stereoscopic projection, that is available on a subset of conference rooms. This allows for 3D-stereoscopic robot vision to be transmitted to any or all of the users and operators, as well as data sets - for example building schematics to be shared in 3D at different sites.

SUMMARY

This chapter presented an overview of the current virtual reality systems. It also introduced a new VR system that is Presagis. Presagis allows for interactive full scale immersive simulations without helmets and with variety of tracking devices.

This chapter introduced future implementations of the virtual reality systems. These implementations are: pipelining complex systems production and telepresence. These areas are currently highly demanded. What is being presented in this chapter are case studies for those future implementations of virtual reality systems. The results of these studies have been shown to be fruitful. In one hand, the realism of the VR simulations helps in pipelining systems production as it can cut off the time required for physical implementations. On the other hand, it can be useful for advanced applications for the purpose of gaining additional reality as seen in the case study 2, telepresence example.

REFERENCES

Al-Hudhud, G. (2006, July 10-12). Visualising the emergent behaviour of a multiagent communication model. In *Proceedings of the 6th International Conference on Recent Advances in Soft Computing*, (pp. 375–381). Canterbury, UK: University of Kent.

Al Hudhud, G., & Ayesh, A. (2008, April 1-4). Real Time Movement Cooredination Technique Based on Flocking Behaviour for Multiple Mobile Robots System. In *Proceedings of Swarming Intelligence Applications Symposium*. Aberdeen, UK.

Avatars and agents in immersive virtual environments. (2004). Technical Report, The Engineering and Physical Sciences Research Council. Retrieved from http://www.equator.ac.uk/index.php/articles/697.

Cairo, O., Aldeco, A., & Algorri, M. (2001). Virtual Museum's Assistant. In *Proceedings of 2nd Asia-Pacific Conference on Intelligent Agent Technology*. Hackensack, NJ: World Scientific Publishing Co. Pte. Ltd.

Chrysanthou, Y., Tecchia, F., Loscos, C., & Conroy, R. (2004). *Densely populated urban environments*. The Engineering and Physical Sciences Research Council. Retrieved from http://www.cs.ucl.ac.uk/research/vr/Projects/Crowds/

Leevers, D., Gil, P., Lopes, F. M., Pereira, J., Castro, J., Gomes-Mota, J., et al. (1998). An autonomous sensor for 3d reconstruction. In *3rd European Conference on Multimedia Applications, Services and Techniques (ECMAST98)*, Berlin, Germany.

Li, H., Tang, W., & Simpson, D. (2004). Behavior based motion simulation for fire evacuation procedures. In *Conference Proceedings of Theory and Practice of Computer Graphics*. Washington DC: IEEE.

Loscos, C., Marchal, D., & Meyer, A. (2003, June). Intuitive crowd behaviour in dense urban environments using local laws. In *Proceedings of the conference of Theory and Practice of Computer Graphics, TP.CG03*, University of Birmingham, Birmingham UK. Washington DC: IEEE.

Navarro-Serment, L., Grabowski, R., Paredis, C. & Khosla, P. (2002, December). Millibots. *IEEE Robotics & Automation Magazine*.

Rohrmeier, M. (1997). *Telemanipulation of robots via internet mittels VRML2.0 and Java*. Institute for Robotics and System Dynamic, Technical University of Munchen, Munich, Germany.

Slater, M., Steed, A., & Chrysanthou, Y. (2002). *Computer Graphics and Virtual Environments: from Realism to Real-Time*. Reading, MA: Addison Wesley.

Tang, W., Wan, T., & Patel, S. (2003, June 3-5). Real-time crowd movement on large scale terrains. In *Theory and Practice of Computer Graphics*. Washinton, DC: IEEE Computer Society.

Tecchia, F., Loscos, C., Conroy, R., & Chrysanthou, Y. (2003). Agent behaviour simulator (abs): A platform for urban behaviour development. In *Conference Proceedings of Theory and Practice of Computer Graphics*. Washington, DC: IEEE.

Teccia, F., & Chrysanthou, Y. (2001). *Agent behavior simulator*. Web Document, University College London, Department of Computer Science.

Turner, M. J., Richardson, R., Le Blanc, A., Kuchar, P., Ayesh, A., & Al Hudhud, G. (2006, September 14). Roboviz a collaborative user and robot. In *CompuSteer Workshop environment network testbed*. London, UK: Oxford University.

Wan, T., & Tang, W. (2004). Agent-based real time traffice control simulation for urban environment. *IEEE Transactions on Intelligent Transportation Systems*.

Wan, T. R., & Tang, W. (2003). An intelligent vehicle model for 3d visual traffic simulation. In *IEEE International Conference on Visual Information Engineering, VIE*.

KEY TERMS AND DEFINITIONS

Pipelining Software Production: for the purpose of categorising the development processes of complex software systems. There is a high demand to the use of virtual models in producing the system as part of the production pipeline.

Behavioural Realism: using the virtual reality to model theoretical models supports the realism of visualized emergent behaviours inside the virtual world. These behaviours should be observer-convenient and possess high level of realism.

Intra-Robot Communication: Robot-robot communications

Stereoscopic View: a projection of the images sent by robots through Human-Robot communications.

ENDNOTES

[1] Thanks to De Montfort University, Leicester, UK for providing the facilities and support for this study

[2] C is the expected time for task completion, while T represents the elapsed time since the agent started the task.

[3] T − C is the time elapsed since the agent started to encounter problems in performing a specified task

[4] A unit is used with respect to the environment dimensions, in other words, if the dimensions of the environment is 1700 units °— 800 units the separation distance is 7 units

[5] An operator is define here as a close connected hands-on controller (note there could be more than one), and a user is defined as any human with the ability to take control directly or indirectly.

[6] In fact many operators may be required to operate one robot

Chapter 13
Implementation of a DES Environment

Gyorgy Lipovszki
Budapest University of Technology and Economics, Hungary

Istvan Molnar
Bloomsburg University of Pennsylvania, USA

ABSTRACT

In this chapter the authors describe a program system that implements a Discrete Event Simulation (DES) development environment. The simulation environment was created using the LabVIEW graphical programming system; a National Instruments software product. In this programming environment, the user can connect different procedures and data structures with "graphical wires" to implement a simulation model, thereby creating an executable simulation program. The connected individual objects simulate a discrete event problem. The chapter describes all simulation model objects, their attributes and methods. Another important element of the discrete event simulator is the task list, which has also been created using task type objects. The simulation system uses the "next event simulation" technique and refreshes the actual state (attribute values of all model objects) at every event. The state changes are determined by the entity objects, their input, current content, and output. Every model object can access (read) all and modify (write) a selected number of object attribute values. This property of the simulation system provides the possibility to build a complex discrete event system using predefined discrete event model objects.

GENERAL INTRODUCTION OF THE DES SIMULATOR

Implementation of a DES can be realized in different ways (Kreutzer, 1986). To simplify the procedure and to avoid difficulties related to computer science subjects (language definition, syntax and semantics discussion, translation, etc.), in this chapter the authors decided to remain focused on those issues, which are closely related to the DES and the simple implementation of the DES computational model. Doing so, the authors present a DES extension of the industry standard programming system LabVIEW.

DOI: 10.4018/978-1-60566-774-4.ch013

The LabVIEW DES simulation is the numerical computation of a series of discrete events described with the help of a set of blocks with given characteristics (the framework system of simulation processes, which can be described with discrete stochastic state variables).

- With the help of the framework system, a simulation of processes can be realized. The processes are driven by several independent, parallel events, between which information exchange is possible,
- Within the framework system, the linear, parallel and feedback connection of objects is possible in optional quantity and depth.
- The framework system is designed in an object-oriented manner. Both, the blocks with different characteristics serving the process simulation and the entities carrying information are designed in the same way.
- The programs prepared with the help of the framework system can be saved as subroutines, too. These subroutines can be reused in the simulation program; an arbitrary number of times with arbitrary input parameters.

The simulation framework operates in the following structure:

Why is it Necessary to Extend the LabVIEW Program System with Discrete Event Objects (DEO)?

The LabVIEW program system was developed for measuring, analysis and display of data generated in discrete time in equidistant (time) steps. It has numerous procedures, which make the measurement of data easier by using triggering technique based on a given time or signal level. For the data analysis, there is a wide scope procedure library at disposal, which makes it possible to realize detailed signal analysis either in time or in frequency range. As it can be seen, the program system is able to execute sample processing of continuous signals with the help of digital computers. It also contains procedures, which are able to handle elements of queues (creating queue objects, placing a new element into the queue, remove an element of a queue, and finally. deleting a queue object). These procedures and a few others, which help parallel programming (Notifier and Semaphore Operations, or Occurrences), are objects and procedures, which can be used to create (put together) a discrete event simulation model.

A new research and development has been started to make LabVIEW capable to create new object types, which make it possible to generate discrete event simulation models of arbitrary complexity in an easy way.

What is Needed to Create a Discrete Event Simulator (DES)?

Realizing a DES, there are a series of basic functionalities and elements, which must be implemented to ensure a modular program structure. When the basic elements were implemented, object-oriented data structures and object related methods were used, utilizing fully the possibilities and features of the host, the LabVIEW.

Simulation time and event handling

The most important step in a DES system is to establish the event objects (**Task**) with given data, the storage of the data according to given conditions and the removal of them from the system, when given events have already taken place. The individual event objects have to be properly stored and organized according to given conditions using another object (called **TaskList**). When different DES systems are implemented, different event lists (differing both in number and in tasks) can be used. In the DES system, realized in LabVIEW, there is only one such list, which contains all the events (events' data) of the simulation model in

Figure 1. General block diagram of simulation system in LabVIEW

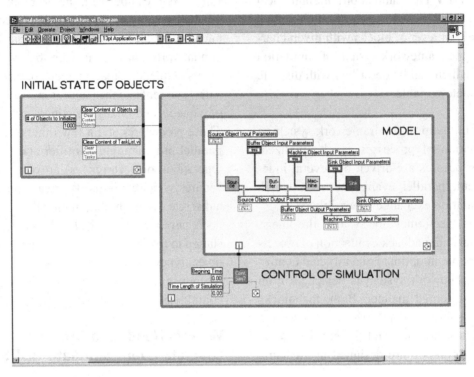

ascending order of time. Each new event is put into its proper place within the event objects list, by keeping the time in ascending order.

Random Number Generators

In the LabVIEW DES system, the operation of numerous random number generator types has to be provided to fulfill the different timing tasks in the simulation model. The operation of random number generators in LABVIEW is ensured by the

random number generator of uniform distribution between 0 and 1. This random number generator is the base of Constant, Uniform, Exponential, Normal, Triangle and User Defined random number generator types. At a call, the random number generators generate random numbers in accordance with the parameters of the given distribution type. If needed, further random number generator types can be implemented and included into the set of model elements developed previously.

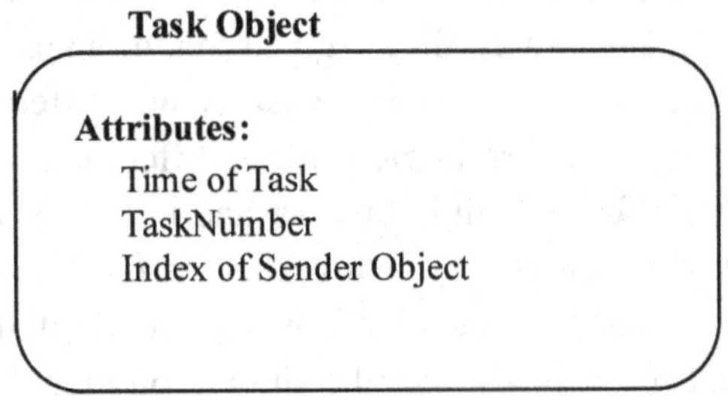

Types of Discrete Event Objects

The most important elements in a DES simulator are the base objects fulfilling different tasks. The base objects make it possible to build up different simulation models. There are five base-objects in the LabVIEW-DES simulator, which provide the foundations of more complex DES objects with complicated operations. These base objects provide the tools for generation, receiving, temporary

Figure 2. Characteristics of task object

Task Object

Attributes:
Time of Task
TaskNumber
Index of Sender Object

Figure 3. Structure of TaskList object and its characteristics

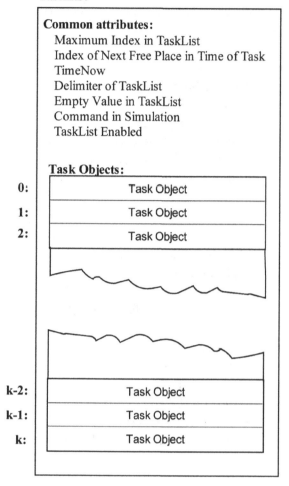

TaskList

> **Common attributes:**
> Maximum Index in TaskList
> Index of Next Free Place in Time of Task
> TimeNow
> Delimiter of TaskList
> Empty Value in TaskList
> Command in Simulation
> TaskList Enabled
>
> **Task Objects:**

0:	Task Object
1:	Task Object
2:	Task Object
k-2:	Task Object
k-1:	Task Object
k:	Task Object

storage, movement delay and the removal of Entity objects representing the movement of material and information. Besides the Entity objects ensuring the operation of the DES system, there are other objects as well, which create Entity objects according to an order given by a time distribution; these objects are called Source objects. The admittance and temporary storage of Entity objects are done by the Buffer objects, which are able to store Entities temporarily, although only with a finite storage capacity. The Machine object is able to postpone/delay the advancement of an Entity according to a given time distribution. This capability enables to

model the different time needed for operations in real systems. Those entities, which have already completed their tasks, can be (have to be) removed from the simulation model; the Entity will be passed to a Sink type object, which removes the Entity from the objects list and deletes it to avoid further tasks to be executed with it.

The object names in LabVIEW DES system are composed using two name elements. Each object has a specific, individual name; while all objects have a name parameter that shows which other objects contain it. The naming convention of Entity objects enables tracing and administration. The **Full Name** of the object is made up from the **Name** and the so-called **Container Object Name**; it shows which other object or objects contain the given Entity object. As a consequence, the base objects handling the discrete events have to possess a **Container Object Name** parameter, which receives the data from a Container object. The Container object has only one task, to ensure the value of the **Container Object Name** for the basic objects.

The objects described above are called DES Objects. The DES models in a simulation system are made up of these objects.

Connecting Discrete Event Objects

The input and output of DES model objects has to be connected according to the structure of the simulation model. This is the way to construct the network of objects, which ensure the fulfilling of a specific task with the simulation model. In the LabVIEW graphical programming system, each base object of a DES model has a single input and a single output, which can (have to) be connected with a data exchange line of "identical type" according to its data type. The framework system executing the simulation supplies each DES object of the model with an ID Number, then determines which output is connected to which input. Also, each DES basic object has one data (Entity) input and one data (Entity) output. If a data

Figure 4. Characteristics of DES object

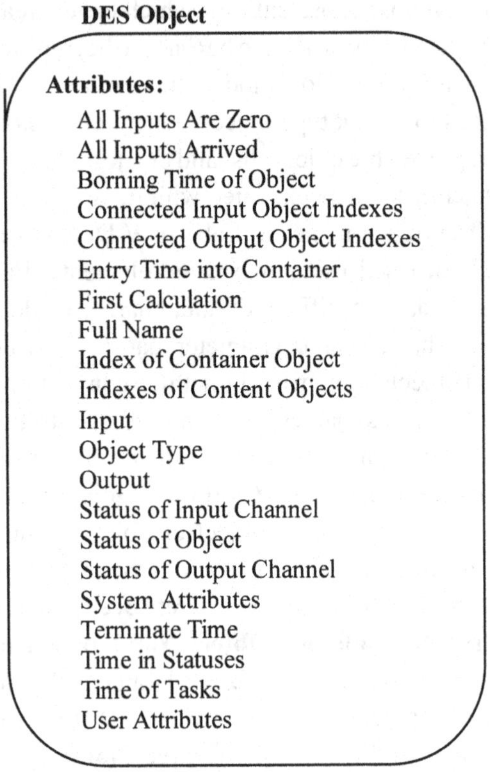

DES Object

Attributes:

All Inputs Are Zero
All Inputs Arrived
Borning Time of Object
Connected Input Object Indexes
Connected Output Object Indexes
Entry Time into Container
First Calculation
Full Name
Index of Container Object
Indexes of Content Objects
Input
Object Type
Output
Status of Input Channel
Status of Object
Status of Output Channel
System Attributes
Terminate Time
Time in Statuses
Time of Tasks
User Attributes

output channel is connected to the input channel of more than one DES object, then the state of DES objects (occupied or not occupied) determines to which input channel of the DES object the Entity will be forwarded. In case each DES object is ready to receive the incoming Entity, the (physical) order of the object definition determines to which DES object the Entity will be forwarded. Besides this "wired" connection mode, we can select with the help of supplementary objects an input channel according to an optional strategy, ensuring a flexible selection of DES objects, i.e. processing direction.

Output Statistical Data of Discrete Event Objects

Each DES base object has an input and an output parameter set (record). The input parameters define the operation of DES objects. The output param-

eters provide statistical data about the operation of the given object depending on its particular DES object type.

Data provided by Source objects (Figure 18):

- **TimeNow**
- **Time of Next Launching**
- **Time Step**
- **Index of ObjectList**
- **Content Object Index**
- **Number of Created Objects**
- **Status Time Parameter** (Duration (time) in Idle, Busy, Blocked, Failed, Paused state)
- **Status of Source** (The possible states are: Idle, Busy, Blocked, Failed, Paused)
- **Full Name**

Data provided by Buffer objects (Figure 19):

- **TimeNow**
- **Index of ObjectList**
- **Content of Buffer**
- **Indexes of Content Objects**
- **Used Buffer Capacity** (in percentage)
- **Status Time Parameters** (Duration (time) in Idle, Busy, Blocked, Failed, Paused state)
- **Status of Buffer** (The possible states are: Idle, Busy, Blocked, Failed, Paused)
- **Full Name**

Data provided by Machine objects (Figure 20):

- **TimeNow**
- **Time of Next Launching**
- **Time Step**
- **Index of ObjectList**
- **Content Object Index**
- **Utilization** (in percentage)
- **Histogram of States**
- **Pie Chart of States**

Figure 5. Structure of ObjectList object and its characteristics

ObjestList

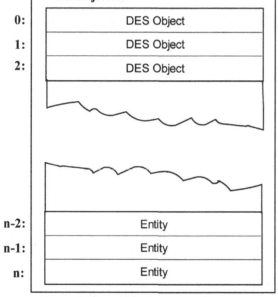

Common attributes:
Index Of Last Model Object
Maximum Index of ObjectList
Input # for Inputless Objects
Separator of Name
Delimiter of List
Identity Number
Possible Number of Objects in Model
ObjectList Enabled
# of Rows of SYSTEM Attributes
# of Columns of SYSTEM Attributes
# of Rows of USER Attributes
# of Columns of USER Attributes

DES Objects:

0:	DES Object
1:	DES Object
2:	DES Object
n-2:	Entity
n-1:	Entity
n:	Entity

- **Status Time Parameters** (Duration (time) in Idle, Busy, Blocked, Failed, Paused state)
- **Status of Buffer** (The possible states are: Idle, Busy, Blocked, Failed, Paused)
- **Full Name**

Data provided by Sink objects (Figure 21):

- **TimeNow**
- **Index of ObjectList**
- **Last Content Object List**
- **Number of Sinked Objects**
- **Status of Sink** (The possible states are: Idle, Busy, Blocked, Failed, Paused)
- **Full Name**

Each DES object possesses a two-dimensional dynamic array variable, the elements of which are string variables (**User Attribute**). Arbitrary data, belonging to specific DES objects, emerging during the execution of the simulation program can be stored in these cells and referred to by indexes as necessary. This ensures that each DES object is able to collect information as needed to define statistical data, which can be continuously evaluated during the execution of the simulation program or at the end of the simulation.

Example 1: The Model of M/M/1 System in a LabVIEW System

The M/M/1 system model in the LabVIEW DES system can be created with connecting the four basic objects. This has to be done by mapping the elements of the system model into LabVIEW objects (Figure 14, Figure 15 and Figure 16). The element ensuring the Entity generation in the system model can be represented in the LabVIEW DES as a Source object. Similarly, the queue can be represented as a Buffer object, the service operation as a Machine object, and the removal of an Entity as a Sink object. The next step, as described in the chapter Connecting Discrete Event Objects (see also Figure 16), is the creation of a running model by connecting the DES objects.

In order to complete the numerical computations, all the objects have to be provided with the record consisting of the input parameter values and with the so-called output parameter record, which ensures the display of the result (the statistical data). All this has to be done through the panel of the LabVIEW program (see also the chapter Structure and tasks Source object).

System Model Mapping

A system model, based on discrete events, can be built with objects, which fulfill the basic tasks and functionalities of a general simulation system. Such basic types are the Source type objects, which issue Entity objects necessary for the functioning of the simulator. After executing the defined task, the Entity objects are extinguished by the Sink type objects. The intermediate storage of Entity objects is realized using Buffer objects, while the delay of Entity data stream processing – which represents the working process in a model – is realized using Machine objects. The creation of simulation models depicted in Figure 14 to Figure 17, can be realized using the above four basic object types. Subsequently, the four basic object types, their characteristics and use will be discussed.

Structure and Tasks of the Source Object

The Source object issues Entity objects at intervals determined by different function types.

During its operation, the Source object sends the generated Entity objects to the object connected to its output. In case it is not ready to receive the Entity, the Source object changes its state into a **Blocked** state at the next active computational period. In a blocked state, there is a repeated attempt to send the Entity to the object connected to the Source object's output.

It is possible to connect more than one object input to a Source output. In such cases, the Source object attempts to assign the Entity object in the definition order of the connected objects. Arbitrary Entity generation strategies can be achieved with the help of the connected output Source objects' indexes. It is compulsory to define the input parameter record of the Source object.

The input and output parameters of the object are shown in Figure 6.

Structure and Tasks of the Sink Object

The Sink object extinguishes (swallows) the Entity objects.

During its operation, the Sink object determines whether the Entity received objects contain other Entity objects. Following this, the operation will be recursively continued until it does not find any more objects containing further Entity objects. It puts all the indexes of Entity objects "explored" (all the children objects) into a stack memory, and deletes them from the object list. Finally, only the Entity remains that was received through the input channel. Finally, the Sink object deletes this object also from the object list.

Deleting the object from the object list means that its name is extinguished (the name will be a text type constant of zero length).

There is no output defined for the Sink object.

It is compulsory to connect the input channel of the Sink object, as it is compulsory to define the record of its parameter record.

The input and output parameters of the object are shown in Figure 7.

Structure and Tasks of the Buffer Object

The Buffer object ensures a temporary storage of the Entity objects (Entities) until the connected object behind the Buffer object in the material or information flow is able to fulfill the predefined task.

During its operation, the Buffer object tries to send immediately the received object input to the object connected as output. If it fails, then it stores it temporarily.

It is possible to connect more than one object input to the Buffer object output. In such cases, the Buffer object attempts to assign the Entity

Figure 6. The input and output parameters of the object

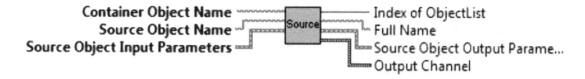

Figure 7. The input and output parameters of the Sink object

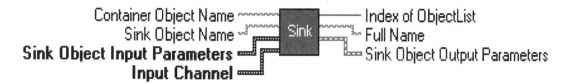

object to its output in the definition order of the connected objects.

An arbitrary strategy can be defined with the help of object indexes of those objects, which are connected to the output of the Buffer object.

It is compulsory to activate the input channel of the Buffer object, as it is compulsory to define the record of its parameter record.

The input and output parameters of the object are shown in Figure 8.

The parameter sets and their setup is demonstrated with the help of the Buffer object example (as a DES object) having both input and output channels. The base objects with similar structure as described above, are of similar set-up, except that in some cases the input data channel (Source), while in other cases the output data source (Sink) function is missing, although the channel physically is at disposal.

Buffer objects have the following input parameters (Figure 8):

- **Container Object Name:** String variable, which contains the name of the container object of the Buffer object
- **Buffer Object Name:** Contains the name of its own Buffer object

- **Buffer Object Input Parameters:** The input parameters of the Buffer object (**Capacity, Enabled Status of Buffer, Type of Queue**)
- **Input Channel:** A record of two integer type, which provides in its **Data** variable the name of that Entity object, which is waiting for the Buffer object to take it from the connected object. If the value of **Data** is zero or negative, it means that the **Input Channel** is empty, i.e., it does not contain any data. If the **Data** value is positive, it means that it is the index value of a real Entity object. The **Channel Index** variable provides the information about the channel number from which the Entity arrived.

The output parameters of the Buffer objects are as follows (Figure 8):

- **Index of ObjectList:** A positive integer type value, which provides the object index value in the ObjectList/DES Objects vector.
- **Full Name:** A String variable, which stores the name of the container object of the Buffer object as well as the own name

Figure 8. The input and output parameters of the Buffer object

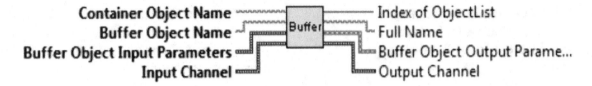

of the Buffer object.

- **Buffer Object Output Parameters:** The output parameters of the Buffer object (**TimeNow, Content of Buffer, Index of Content Objects, Status of Buffer, Command in Simulation, Full Name, Status Time Parameters, Used Buffer Capacity [in percentage]**)
- **Output Channel:** A record consisting of two integer type data, giving in its **Data** variable the index of that Entity object, which is waiting for the Buffer object to be passed over to the connected object. If the value of **Data** is zero or negative, it means that the **Input Channel** is empty, does not contain any data. If the value of **Data** is positive, it means that it marks a real Entity index.

The **Channel Index** variable provides information on the channel number through which the Entity has arrived.

The structure of base objects Source, Machine, Sink and Container are similar to the Buffer object described previously. The connections of the objects are demonstrated in Figure 16, where an object named "Source 1" realizes the creation of the Entity.

The next figures (Figure 9 to Figure 13) demonstrate the input parameter values of the M/M/1 DES Model.

The Source object generates from the starting time of the simulation (**First Creation Time**) Entities, named "Apple", with the help of an EXPONENTIAL(Mean) distribution function.

The Source object does not limit the number of Entities issued, since the value of **Maximum Batch Size** is infinite (Inf. = Infinite). The other values used as input parameters bear their input values in case of other functions. When the user of the program chooses CONSTANT(Value) distribution, **Value** can be dynamically changed during the simulation, and thus makes it possible to define arbitrary distribution functions. The **Enabled Status of Source** state selection combo box can support the selection of three possible object states (Enabled, Failed, Paused). In **Enabled** status, the DES object executes all computations. In **Failed** status, it does not execute any, since this state shows that there is an error. While in **Pause** status, the device is in an excellent condition, but it does not execute any computation, rather waits to start work to complete the task of a (parallel working) DES object, which is currently in "failed" state.

The input parameters of the Buffer Object (Figure 10) include the number of Entities that can be stored by the object (**Capacity**), as well as the type of the object, and the **Type of the Queue**, which is one of the three possible choices in the combo box form. The Buffer types that can be chosen are **First in First Out, Last in First Out and Using Entity Priority** (where the Entity leaves the storage according to the values stored in **System Attribute** parameters of the same Entity).

The **Enabled Status of Buffer** status can be chosen out of three possible object statuses (Enabled, Failed, and Paused) using a combo box. The meaning of the statuses is the same as described under Source objects.

Figure 9. Input parameters of the Source object

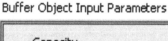

Source Object Input Parameters

Name of Produced Entity

Apple

First Creation Time   Maximum Batch Size

0,0000   Inf

Distribution

EXPONENTIAL(Mean)

Value   Maximum

0,0000   0,0000

Mean   Usual

9,0000   0,0000

Deviation   Minimum

0,0000   0,0000

Enabled Status of Source

Enabled

Figure 10. The input parameters of the Buffer Object

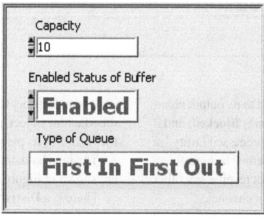

Buffer Object Input Parameters

Capacity

10

Enabled Status of Buffer

Enabled

Type of Queue

First In First Out

Structure and Tasks of the Machine Object

The Machine object executes operations of specified time duration determined by different function types on Entity objects.

During its operation, the Machine object can delay the advance of Entity objects arrived at its input with an operation time. Operation time can be defined with the help of different distribution functions. When the operation time is over, the Machine object tries to hand over the Entity object

Figure 11. The input and output parameters of the Machine object

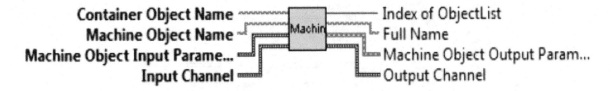

Figure 12. The input parameters of the Machine object

Machine Object Input Parameters

Distribution

EXPONENTIAL(Mean)

Value
0,0000

Maximum
0,0000

Mean
9,0000

Usual
0,0000

Deviation
0,0000

Minimum
0,0000

Enabled Status of Machine

Enabled

to the model object connected to its output channel. If it fails, the status becomes **Blocked**, and it will attempt to "get rid of the processed Entity" at each computation cycle. While the Machine object is in blocked status, it does not receive any other Entity object through its input channel.

More than one object input can be connected to the Machine object output. In such cases, the Machine object attempts to pass over the Entity object in the defined order of the connected objects.

An arbitrary output strategy can be realized with the help of the indexes of the objects connected to the Machine object's output.

It is compulsory to activate the input channel of the Machine object, as it is compulsory to define the record of its parameters.

The input and output parameters of the object are shown in Figure 11.

There is a **Distribution** parameter among the input parameters of the Machine object (Figure 12). It is a data element of combo box type, out of which values can be chosen as follows:

- **CONSTANT (Value)**
- **EXPONENTIAL (Mean)**
- **NORMAL (Mean, Deviation)**

Figure 13. Input parameters of the Sink Object

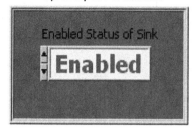

Sink Object Input Parameters

- **TRIANGLE (Minimum, Usual, Maximum)**
- **UNIFORM (Minimum, Maximum)**

It can be seen from the list above that the distributions use specific numerical values as input parameters; this way the input parameters can be adjusted easily and precisely to the given distribution types.

The **Enabled Status of Machine** combo box allows a choice out of three possible object statuses (Enabled, Failed, Paused). The meaning of the statuses is the same as described under Source objects.

The Sink object (Figure 13) has only one input parameter value, which gives the status of the object for the simulation model.

The status of DES objects in a simulation model can be dynamically changed (i.e. during the simulation run, too). This way, in case of a predefined or examined operational case, object statuses can be defined either manually or with the help of a program (see figures 14 and 15).

Figure 16 demonstrates the connections of the model elements with help of the so-called Diagram Panel, which connects the input and output data channels with the help of graphical programming. This program segment demonstrates how specific DES objects receive the input parameters, and how the connection of specific objects can be realized.

Figure 17 shows the picture of such a Front Panel, which can be easily realized using the output parameter data of specific DES objects. The output data of some objects appear in a single data structure, in a record (also called in LabVIEW "cluster"), as Figures 18-21 show.

Figure 14 shows the results of an M/M/1 model as displayed after executing it for a specified time. It can be seen on the left side of the figure that during the simulation the Source object generated 972 entities. In the square symbolizing the Sink object, there is a numeric value displayed under the sign **Produced**. This is where information is delivered to about the management and exit of 967 Entities from the simulation process. The difference between the number of the generated and terminated entities are those entities, which have stayed in some of the objects even after the simulation has ended. Information on this is shown on the numeric display seen under the display of the Sink object below the **Work in Process Objects** title.

There is also other information displayed on the Front panel. The simulated time, **Real Time (sec)** of the simulation model, as well as the simulation execution time on the given computer, furthermore

Figure 14. System Model of M/M/1

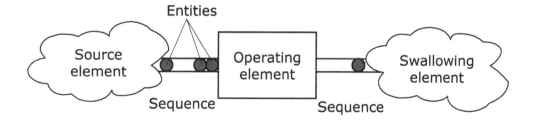

Figure 15. Block diagram of M/M/1 System

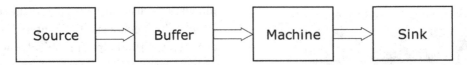

the quotient of both values, i.e. the speed factor of the simulation. This is shown in the **Simulation Time/Real Time** display.

The values of **Status of xxx** combo box variables shown in Figure 17, can be set preceding the simulation run to the values needed by operational conditions. In the case of this simulation model, the duration of the simulation model run can be manually adjusted, too. Before the simulation is started, the selected values and their parameters can also be initialized using the combo box option of **Distribution**, and with the help of **Mean Time xxx** knob. The adjustment shown in the case of both the Source and the Machine object is an EXPONENTIAL(9) distribution, which means an exponential distribution with an average value of 9.0.

The following figure shows the records of the output parameters of the objects in M/M/1 example after the end of the simulation run with predefined duration.

Figure 18 shows the output parameters of the Source object. This object initializes and, generates those Entity objects using random number generators, which pass the different objects of the simulation model and wait in those for events.

The display **TimeNow** shows that the simulation is at 9322 time unit (which was the time duration of the simulation).

The variable **Time of Next Launching** consists of the current time (given in simulation time units) when the Source object has to generate (launch) the next Entity (this will not happen since the simulation is over, already finished). The **TimeStep**

Figure 16. (M/M/1) Model Diagram Panel of Example 1

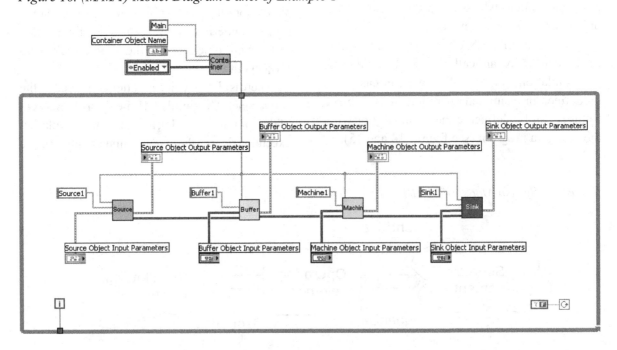

Figure 17. (M/M/1) Model Front Panel of Example 1

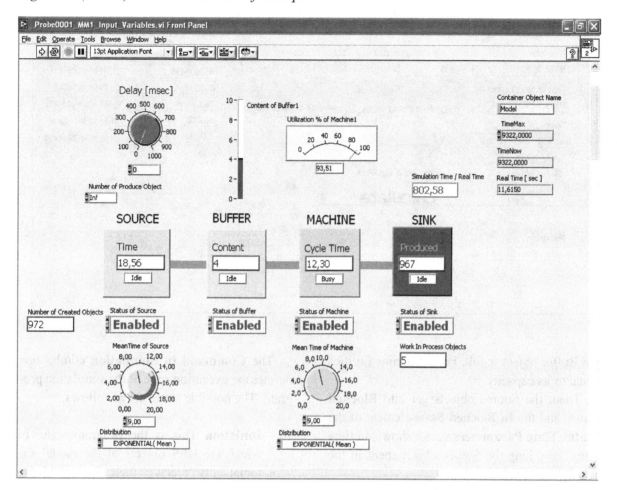

value shows, according to the selected distribution function, how big the last time step was. This also means that the last Entity was generated at that time (**Time of Next Launching – TimeStep**). The **Index of ObjectList** displays the index of the Source object in the ObjectList object, while the display **Content Object Index** right besides it shows that there is no generated object in the Source object at this time (which it could not yet passed to the input of the connected object). The switch, **Entity at Output,** would set to ON state if there were any Entity in the Source object. At this moment there is none, this is why the switch is in OFF state. The **Number of Created Objects** display shows how many Entities has been cre-

ated by the Source object until this point of time. The vector named **Status Time Parameters** can be found on the right hand side of Figure 18. The right hand side labels show the time duration value of the given vector element in its different states. It is in **Idle** state all through the operation of the Source object.

There is one exception, when the Source object is not able to pass over (within the same simulation step) the Entity generated at a previously specified time to the object connected to the data output (in our case, the Buffer object). This can only happen if the object connected to the output of the Source object is not able to receive the new Entity offered for it. In this example this can happen only when

Figure 18. Output parameters of the Source Object

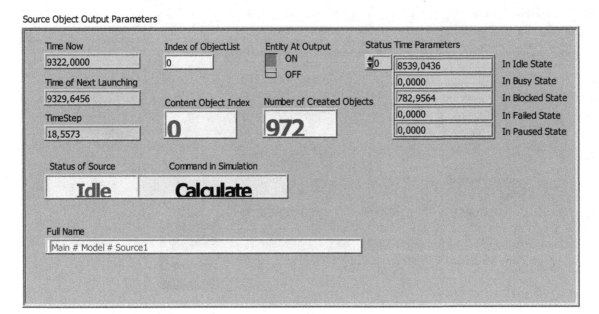

the Buffer object is full, i.e. it contains Entities equal to its capacity.

Then, the Source objects get into **Blocked** status, and the **In Blocked State** element of the **Status Time Parameters** vector shows, in time units, how long the Source object spent in the Blocked status.

The desirable state from the point of discrete simulation model view is to minimize or abolish the blocked state(s).

The Source object can never fall into **In Busy State** during the simulation model run, since the basic principle of its operation is that it does not execute any operation on Entities. The time duration of the Source object in disabled state is shown by the displayed time **In Failed State**, while the time duration in stand-by status by the **In Paused State** vector element.

The **Status of Source** combo box defines the state of the Source object in a given simulation time (**TimeNow**). The possible states of the object are as follows: **Idle, Busy, Blocked, Failed and Paused.** We have already described the meaning of each of these states.

The **Command in Simulation** combo box defines the execution state of the simulation program. The possible states are as follows:

* **Initiation** This is the program state, in which the DES objects of the model automatically receive their individual ID Numbers. The ID number will be used as identification index in the ObjectList.
* **Clear Inputs** This is the program state, in which the inputs and outputs of each DES object are filled up with zero values. At this state, the input and output of the object does not have an index marked with a positive integer number.
* **Calculate** This is the program state, in which the simulation program runs with the help of connected objects bearing identification indexes. The simulation system examines the state of each object at every event time and, if needed, executes a state change. There are a number of such state changes defined by procedures. The similarity of these different procedures

is that the change in a given object state (for example receiving a new Entity at the input channel), affects the object(s) connected to it, and thus the state of this latter has to be changed, too. In order to comfortably manage the Entity traffic, each Entity, as all other DES objects, as well, have their own state variable values. Entities are in **Idle** state when they are waiting at the output data channel of one of the DES objects to be "taken" by one of the objects connected to the output. The Entities are in **Busy** state, when one of the objects already takes them; their **Index of Container Object** will show the DES object they are in.

The field **Full Name** displays the DES object's full name. This includes the name of that Container type object to which the Source objects belongs, and the object's own name, which is also given. The variable follows the method usually used in relation with family names, i.e. each DES object has a "family name", called **Container Full Name,** and in addition to this its own name. Figure 18 demonstrates this by showing that such a Container object has been connected to the **ContainerName** input of the Source object named **Source1.** The Full Name of this Container object is **Main # Model** and its own Full Name is **Main # Model # Source1.**

Figure 19 shows the output parameters of the Buffer object. The object is able to store temporarily those Entity objects, which it receives at its input. At the time of their arrival, the Buffer object tries to send the arrived Entity objects through its output channel. If it fails, it stores them.

The display **TimeNow** also shows that the time of the simulation is 9322 simulated time units (the end of the simulation). The display **Content of Buffer** shows how many Entities are at the given moment in the Buffer object. The simulation presents in the **Index of Content Objects** in a string variable all the indexes of those Entities in the ObjectList variable, which are in the Buffer object at this point of time.

Figure 19. Output parameters of the Buffer Object

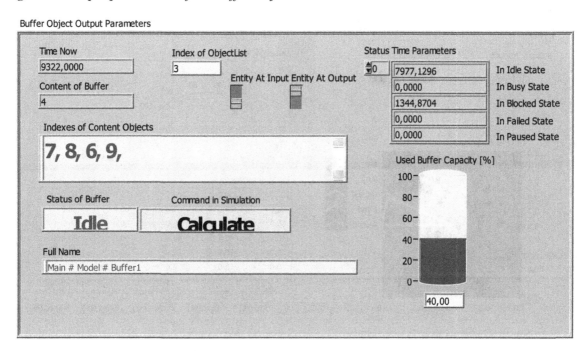

The **Status of Buffer** and the **Command in Simulation** combo boxes contain (display) identical selection values, as already described when tackling the Source objects. Their tasks are also the same, as was also described above. The **Status of Buffer** display shows the actual state of the Buffer object (**Idle, Busy, Blocked, Failed, Paused**). The **Command in Simulation** display combo box shows the current operation of the running simulation program (**Initiation, Clear Inputs, Calculate**).

The vector elements of **Status Time Parameters** show the duration of each of the states of the Buffer object (**In Idle State, In Busy State, In Blocked State, In Failed State, in Paused State**). While in operation, the Buffer object can be only in four states: **Idle, Blocked, Failed and Paused**. State **Idle** means in the case of the Buffer object, that it does not contain any Entity object. The Buffer object is in state **Blocked**, if it cannot pass over the Entity objects it contains to the DES object connected to its output. The State **Failed** means that the Buffer object is disabled, cannot receive Entities at its input, and cannot pass over Entities it contains at its output. State **Paused** means, that every unit of the Buffer object is ready for operation, it is a security standby of the simulation model. Its function is to substitute a failed Buffer object that operates parallel (connected to the same input and output).

The output parameters of the Machine object are demonstrated in Figure 20. The object does

Figure 20. Output parameters of the Machine Object

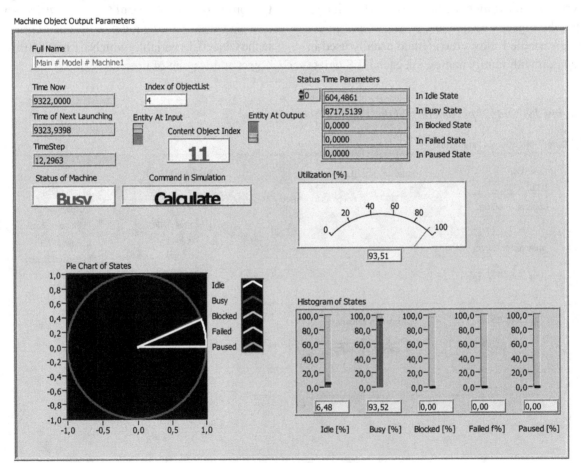

not allow that the Entity object, which it has read from its input channel, to pass for a given time (**TimeStep**).

The field **Full Name** displays the full name of the DES object. The field **TimeNow** displays that the time corresponds to time unit 9322 of the simulation (the ending time of the simulation). The time (measured in simulation time units) in the variable **Time of Next Launching** shows when the Machine Object has to release the Entity it stores. The value **TimeStep** shows the size of the last time step according to the selected distribution function. This also means that the Machine object has released the last Entity at a time equal to its value (**Time of Next Launching – TimeStep**). The **Index of ObjectList** displays the object index of the Machine object in the ObjectList object. Right besides it, the field **Content Object Index** displays that particular Entity object which is in the Machine object at this point of time.

The **Entity at Input** switch is in the on (upper) position because an Entity is waiting in the input data channel for the Machine object to be read.

The **Entity at Output** switch would be in the on (upper) position if an Entity waited in an output channel for another object linked to the Machine object to be taken over.

The **Utilization (%)** instrument indicates the magnitude of (useful) utilization of the Machine object. This numerical value will be calculated based on the time spent in Busy state divided by the full simulation time until the moment of calculation.

On the right hand side of Figure 20 is the vector with the name **Status Time Parameters,** the right hand side of which indicates the time the given vector spent in each state.

The Machine object is

- In **Idle State** if no Entity object is found in it;
- In **Busy State** if an Entity object is found in it;

- In **Blocked State** if it has finished the operation (the time duration of which is specified by the **TimeStep** parameter), but is unable to pass the Entity object on to the DES object linked to its output because the DES object is unable to receive the Entity object;
- In **Failed State**, giving the time spent by the Machine object in disabled state;
- In **Paused State**, giving the time spent in readiness state.

The **Histogram State** and the **Pie Chart State** give the same information on the vector as the **Status Time Parameter**, only in different graphical form.

The **Status of Machine** combo box indicates the state of the Machine object in the given simulation moment (**TimeNow**). The possible states of the object are: **Idle, Busy, Blocked, Failed and Paused,** as already explained. The **Command in Simulation** combo box indicator shows the actual operation performed by the simulation program (**Initiation, Clear Inputs and Calculate**).

The output parameters of the Sink Object are presented in Figure 21. This object receives and exits those Entity objects from the simulation system, with which all necessary tasks were completed and which were terminated.

In the indicator called **Full Name,** the full name of the DES object is given. The **TimeNow** indicator shows in which simulation time (moment) the execution is. The **Last Content Object Index** shows the index of that Entity object which was the last in the Sink object. The **Number of Sinked Object** shows the number of Entity objects that have exited until then.

The **Entity at Input** switch is in an off (low) position because there is no Entity waiting in the input data channel to be read by the Sink object.

The **Status of the Sink** combo box indicates the state of the Sink object in the given moment. The possible states of the object are: **Idle, Busy,**

Figure 21. Output parameters of the Sink Object

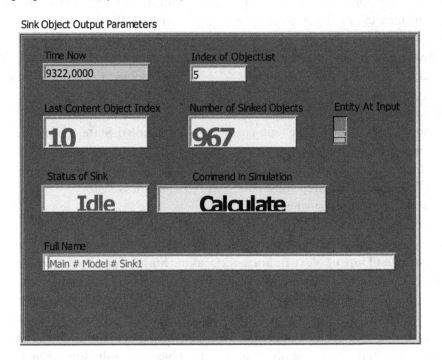

Blocked, Failed and Paused as already explained. The **Command in Simulation** combo box indicates the actual operation carried out by the simulation program (**Initiation, Clear Inputs and Calculate**).

The input parameters of the simulation program are to be set and the execution of the program completed until the given time with the help of value adjustment and selector elements as shown in Figure 17. After the completion of the simulation program, the accumulated statistical values, which were gathered during the simulation run (execution of the simulation program), are delivered. Obviously, during the execution of the program one can follow the change of simulation results and the actual values (maximum, minimum) of special interest. For this, the LabVIEW program provides numerous indicator objects, with the help of which any type of display is easily accomplished.

The Structure and Task of the Entity Object (Moving Object)

This object can be used as a freely usable task performing object. The structure of the DES object allows it to be either a model or a working object. The type of the DES object determines what type of task is performed by the given object.

In the LabVIEW DES system, only Source type objects generate Entity objects. In regard of programming technique, the programmer is able to create an Entity object independently, but the handling and the organization of its operation entails so many interlinked tasks that it is not recommended.

Entity objects can also be material goods with defined characteristics (e.g., materials in production or logistics processes) or persons with different qualifications, whose turnover or servicing have to be managed, scheduled, etc. within the given conditions.

Several other examples can be found for the appearance and role of the Entity objects in models. On the whole, this object is a simulation object that enters the simulation process at a given physical point, during its progress is obliged to wait and finally exits the simulation process at a given physical point.

The progress of the Entity through the simulation system results in numerous relations (statistical information) with those objects that it met during its progress. The Entity objects progressing through the simulation system also gather valuable unique statistical data about the system through which they pass through.

Example 2: Joining of Several Output Points (operation Join)

Example 2 presents objects, which are able to select, based on an algorithm, one Entity object out of a series of Entity objects generated by multiple sources. The characteristics and structure of the Join object will be presented next.

The Structure and Task of a Join Object

A Join object has several inputs and one output channel; moreover, it can select the input channel through which it can receive the Entity object with one of its input parameters (**Join Input Channel Index**).

The Join object possesses more than one input channel (a vector of input channels). The Join object tries to forward immediately the selected Entity object that arrived to its input channel to

the object linked to the output channel. If that is unsuccessful, it temporarily stores the Entity.

The entities leave the Join object based on the **First In First Out** strategy.

The output channel of the Join object can be linked to not only one, but several object input channels. In this case, the Join object tries to forward the Entity object in its output channel in the order in which the linked objects have been defined. Any type of output strategy can be accomplished with the help of the objects' indexes linked to the output channel of the Join object,

It is mandatory to link up the input channel of the Join object and to define the record of the input parameter.

Input and output parameters of the object are shown in Figure 22.

Example 2 presents in Figure 23 the operation of the Join object. The Entity series emitted by two identically structured lines consisting of Source, Buffer and Machine objects will be put to the input channels of the object **Join1**. The object (now) chooses with a 50-50% probability between the two possible input channels and will take the Entity object found at its channel to the operational object called **Machine3**.

Example 3: Selection between Several Input Channels Based on Given Rules (Select operation)

Example 3 further expands the list of helpful objects and introduces an object, which realizes an algorithm-based distribution of Entity objects among multiple outputs. The characteristics and

Figure 22. The input and output parameters of the Join object

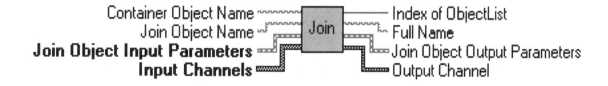

Figure 23. Example 2 of the LabVIEW DES Diagram Panel

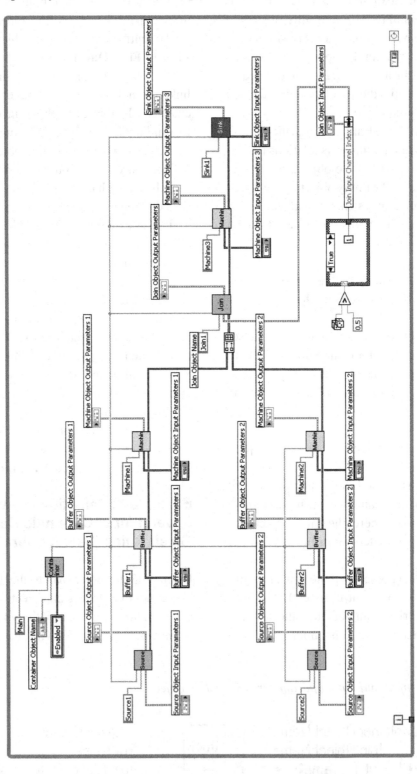

structure of the Select object will be presented next.

The Structure and Task of the Selector Object

The Selector object has more than one output channels and one input channel; moreover, it can select the output channel to which it will send the Entity object with one of its input parameters (**Selector Channel Index**).

The Selector object has more than one output channel (the vector of output channels). The Selector object tries to forward the selected Entity object that arrived to its input channel immediately to the object linked to the output channel. If that is unsuccessful, it temporarily stores the Entity.

The stored entities leave the Selector object based on the **First In First Out** strategy.

It is obligatory to link one model object to each of the output channels of the Selector object.

Any type of output strategy can be accomplished with the help of the objects' indexes linked to the output channel of the Selector object.

It is mandatory to link up the input channel of the Selector object and to define the record of the input parameter.

Input and output parameters of the object are shown in Figure 24.

Example 3 shows in Figure 25 the operation of the Selector object. The Entities outputted by the Source object situated in the input channel (left side of the figure) are forwarded by the Selector object to one of its two output channels,

defined by the index, which can be given as an input parameter.

There are two identically structured lines consisting of the Buffer, Machine and Sink objects linked to the output channel of the Selector object, in which the processing of the Entity series continues. The Selector object (now) chooses with a 50-50% probability between the two possible output channels.

Example 4: Placing More than one Entity in Another Entity (Pack Process) and Unpacking More than one Entity from Another Entity (UnPack Process)

Example 4 presents two new objects, which are able to pack Entity objects into other Entity objects using the Pack object, and later unpack it using the UnPack object at a certain point of time during the simulation. The characteristics and structure of the Pack and UnPack objects will be presented next.

The Structure and Task of the Pack Object

The Pack object has two input channels and one output channel. Through the first input channel (Channel_0) the number of objects to be packed arrives. At the same time, through the second input channel (Channel_1) the package (box) object also arrives. Packaging is done in a way that first the package (box) object has to arrive,

Figure 24. Input and output parameters of the Selector object

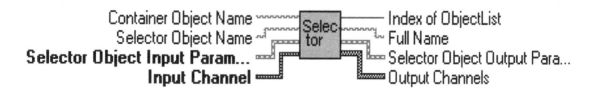

Figure 25. Example 3 of the LabVIEW DES Diagram Panel

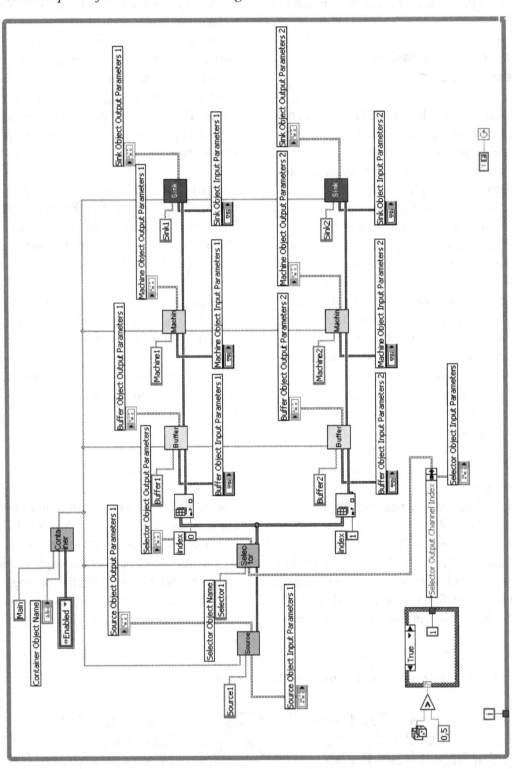

and then the object waits until the amount of Entities to be packaged arrive. The object places the Entities to be packaged into the package (box) object and then sends off the package (box) object thus modified.

The Pack object is a specially formed Join object, which has two input channels (a vector of input channels). In the object, the task of packaging is done by a sequential logic program, which manages the input and output channels of the Pack object based on the required operations. This object required the creation of switches authorizing input and output channels and therefore in this version of the LabVIEW DES program the same solution for all other model objects were also applied.

For the task of channel defining and handling of the Pack object, the following input parameter is available: **Packed Quantity Request**, which is a positive integer, defining the number of packaged Entities.

More than one object input channel can be linked to the output channel of the Pack object. In such case, the Pack object tries to forward the packaged Entity objects that are in its output channel in the order of the definition of the linked objects.

Any type of output strategy can be accomplished with the help of the objects' indexes linked to the output channel of the Pack object,.

It is mandatory to link up all the input channel of the Pack object and to define the record of the input parameter.

Input and output parameters of the object are shown in Figure 26.

Structure and Task of the UnPack Object

The UnPack object has two input channels and one output channel. Through the first channel (Channel_0) the unpackaged objects get out, while through the second channel (Channel_1) the package (box) object leaves. During unpacking, first a package (box) object has to arrive and then the object unpacks the Entities in the package object and temporarily stores them. It continually removes the unpacked entities through its first output channel (Channel_0) and when all of them have been removed, it disposes the package (box) object through its second output channel (Channel_1).

The UnPack object is a specially formed Selector object with two output channels (vector of output channels). It tries to forward the arrived packaged entities to the object linked to the selected output channel. If this is unsuccessful, it will temporarily store the unpacked Entities and the package Entity.

There are no input parameters available for the tasks of defining and handling the output channel of the UnPack object.

Entities that are stored leave the UnPack object based on the **First In First Out** strategy. To each of the input channels of the UnPack object one model object can be linked. Any type of output strategy can be accomplished with the help of the objects' indexes linked to the output channel of the UnPack object,.

It is mandatory to link up all the output channel of the UnPack object and to define the record of the output parameter.

Figure 26. Input and output parameters of the Pack object

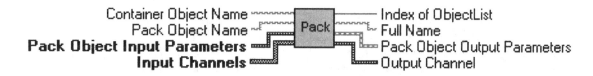

Input and output parameters of the object are shown in Figure 27.

Example 4 shows in Figure 28 the operation of Pack and UnPack objects. The Entity series inputted by the line consisting of two identically structured Source, Buffer and Machine objects will be put to the input channels of the object called **Pack1**. The Entity objects to be packed are directed to the first input channel, while the package objects to the second input channel. Packaging cannot start until a package object arrives. The input parameter of the Pack object is the number of objects to be packaged into one package.

The outputting and processing elements of the package and the Entity object to be packaged are shown on the left hand side of Figure 28. A basic programming capability of LabVIEW allows that any number of LabVIEW icons can be merged into one subroutine. Thus, the subroutine shown in the lower part of Figure 28 can fulfill the same task as the Entity handling system that is composed of various elements in the upper part.

In this simple example, the packaged objects are immediately unpacked with the help of an UnPack object then the packaged objects and the packages in which they were packaged are processed with separate Sink objects.

COMMON CHARACTERISTICS OF THE OBJECTS OF THE SIMULATION SYSTEM (GLOBAL VARIABLES)

The simulation system consists of several system variables, which must be accessed by all objects and methods. The simulation objects obtain information from these variables about the state and state changes of all objects in the system, including their own. The globally usable list elements of the **ObjectList** and **TaskList** objects and their characteristics will be presented next.

Global Variables of ObjectList

During simulation, each element of the global variable, **ObjectList** shown on Figure 5 can be reached with any of the procedures. The simulation model in fact is built in the **ObjectList** global variable in the DES Objects vector in a way that the type and input parameters of the DES object in the simulation model are given (as it has been done in the case of the Buffer object shown in Figure 8). With the help of the graphical programming capability of the LabVIEW program, the DES object link to be examined is created. By using the indicator records of LabVIEW DES or any other type of indicator provided for in the LabVIEW system, the presentation of calculated quantities is planned and realized. Then the execution of the simulation program follows where various DES objects read out information on the actual state of other (any) DES object and if specified conditions are fulfilled, change these. Consequently, the **ObjectList** global variable is a status storage system, where the state and state changes are generated by the running simulation program over the time; it represents the system behavior.

A few variables, performing administrative tasks appear among the attributes of the **ObjectList** variable (Figure 29), which provide values to each **DES Object** for their functioning. The **ObjectList** variables are the following:

Figure 27. Input and output parameters of the UnPack object

Figure 28. Example 4 Panel of LabVIEW DES Diagram

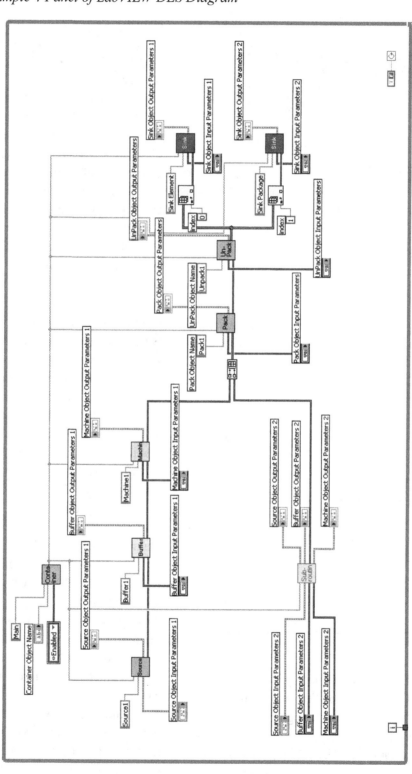

Figure 29. Values of ObjectList Global Variable after the running of M/M/1 model

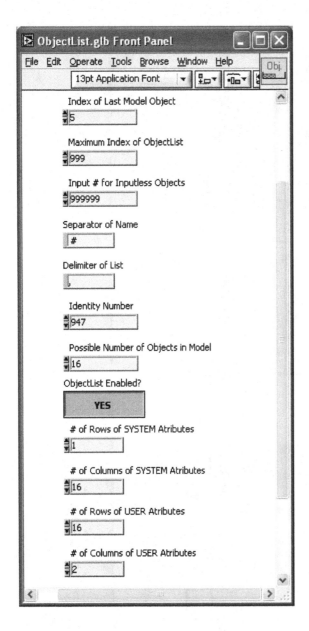

- **Index of Last Model Object** provides in the **DES Objects** vector the index value for which there is no operating (existing) Entity object.
- The **Maximum Index ObjectList** provides the maximum index number of elements that the **DES Objects** vector can still store.

(The **DES Objects** vector can dynamically change its size). This is necessary because during the simulation significant time can be saved if the **DES Objects** vector is not replaced.

- **Input # for Inputless Objects**: each of the **DES Objects** has identical structure. To differentiate the Source object type that has no input, a constant has been used.
- **Separator of Name** character, used for separating individual name components.
- **Identity Number** is an integer, which increases its value by one at the time when a new DES object is created.
- **Possible Number of Objects in Model** indicates how many **DES Objects** are used for the execution of the program at the given moment of the simulation model run. It is possible that these **DES Objects** fill the **DES Objects** vector with gaps.
- **ObjectList Enabled** logical value, if it is FALSE, it will not allow changing the values of the **DES Objects** vector.
- **# of Rows of SYSTEM Attributes,** the maximum row index of the storage elements of individual system attributes belonging to the DES Object used by the simulation system.
- **# of Columns of System Attributes,** the maximum column index of the storage elements of individual system attributes belonging to the DES Object and used by the simulation system.
- **# of Rows of USER Attributes**, the maximum row index of the storage elements of individual parameters belonging to the **DES Objects** in the simulation system and can be programmed by the user.
- **# of Columns of USER Attributes,** the maximum column index of the storage elements of individual parameters belonging to the **DES Objects** in the simulation system and can be programmed by the user.

Because of programming technique reasons, the simulation system stores the attributes of the **DES Objects** vector not in one single object, but in a vector element that can be reached globally and which corresponds to the number of attributes. The vector attributes of **DES Objects**, the maximum index number of which is given in the Maximum Index of ObjectList global variable, are the following:

- **ShiftMemory (All Inputs Are Zero).vi** is a global variable serving in the simulation system for the mapping of the linkages between individual **DES Objects** that gives a TRUE logical value if the value of all inputs is zero.
- **ShiftMemory (All Inputs Arrived).vi** is the variable serving in the simulation system for the mapping of the linkages between the individual **DES Objects**. It contains logical value that indicates that the related DES Object information arrived to the input channel of all given **DES Objects**.
- **ShiftMemory (Borning Time of Object). vi** is a floating point value which indicates at what moment in the simulation the given DES Object has been created and from which moment on it participates in the operation of the model. This parameter value of the main components of the simulation model is of 0.0 value. This parameter is used first of all to determine the age of the Entity type **DES Objects**; the time duration of the pass through and residence can be determined.
- **ShiftMemory (Connected Input Object Indexes).vi** is a string list that indicates what other objects are linked to the input channel of the given DES Object. The list stores the index of **DES Objects** linked to the input channel, where the position on the list indicates the sequential number (index of the input).

- **ShiftMemory (Connected Output Object Indexes).vi** is a string list that indicates which other objects are linked to the output channel of the given DES Object. The list stores the index of **DES Objects** linked to the output channel, where the position on the list indicates the sequential number (index of the output).
- **ShiftMemory (Entry Time into Container Object).vi** is a floating point variable indicating when the given object entered in a DES Object, which will store it or delay its progress during the simulation.
- **ShiftMemory (First Calculation).vi** is a logical variable, which indicates that during the simulation no operation has yet been performed with the given object. Its value is set to be TRUE when the first operation has been accomplished.
- **ShiftMemory (Full name).vi** is a string variable that contains the full name of the DES Object. This is used first of all during searches based on object name.
- **ShiftMemory (Index of Container Object).vi** is an integer type variable that indicates the index of the DES Object in which the DES Object (usually an Entity) is presently located.
- **ShiftMemory (Indexes of Content Objects).vi** is a string variable that indicates in an object list the index of those objects which can be found in the given object (belong to it) at that moment.
- **ShiftMemory (Input).vi** is vector type variable that indicates which Entity type **DES Objects** (identified using indices) are to be found in the given DES Object's input channel.
- **ShiftMemory (Output).vi** is a vector type variable that indicates which Entity type **DES Objects** (identified using indices) are to be found in the given DES Object's output channel.

- **Shiftmemory (Object Type).vi** is a combo box type variable, which indicates the type of the given DES Object. The following types are possible: EMPTY, CONTAINER, ENTITY, SOURCE, BUFFER, MACHINE, SINK, JOIN, SELECTOR, PACK, and UNPACK.
- **ShiftMemory (Status of Input Channel). vi** is a logic variable, which indicates whether traffic is allowed in the input channels of the DES Object. It is logically TRUE, if the channel is closed and logically FALSE, if the channel is open.
- **ShiftMemory (Status of Output Channel).vi** is a logic variable, which indicates whether traffic is allowed in the output channels of the DES Object. It is logically TRUE if the channel is closed and logically FALSE if the channel is open.
- **ShiftMemory (Status Object).vi** is a combo box type variable that indicates the state in which the DES object is in. Possible states include: IDLE, BUSY, BLOCKED, FAILED, and PAUSED.
- **ShiftMemory (System Attributes).vi** is a structure containing vector type integer variable values storing system attributes belonging to given **DES Objects**. The user of the program can freely access the system attributes and can expand them.
- **ShiftMemory (Terminate Time).vi** is a floating point variable indicating when the given DES Object completes the operation actually performed.
- **ShiftMemory (Time in Statuses).vi** is a floating point vector type variable indicating how much time the given DES Object has spent until that simulation moment in various states (Idle, Busy, Blocked, Failed, Paused).
- **ShiftMemory (Time of Tasks).vi** is a record type vector containing the values of the Time of task, TaskNumber and Index

of Sender Object that were created during the simulation run.
- **ShiftMemory (User Attributes).vi** is structure containing matrix type string variables storing user characteristics of given **DES Objects**. With the help of the user characteristics, the user of the program may link (with the help of a program) values that form the base of arbitrary statistical calculations.

Global Variables of TaskList

During simulation, all components of the **TaskList** global variable shown on Figure 3 can be reached from any process. During the simulation run, the given **DES Objects** place the **Tasks** needed for the operation of the DES Model in the components of the vector consisting of Task Objects records. To speed up the program execution, the program places a new event into the first free place of the **Task Objects** vector, then the list of executing the events in time is determined by a special program, which determines the order in a way that no data movement occurs in the **Task Objects** vector during this time.

The components of the **TaskList** global variable are the following (Figure 30):

- **Maximum Index in TaskList** indicates the maximum number of events (Tasks) that can be stored in the **Shiftmemory (Time of Tasks).vi** vector.
- **Index of Next Free Place on the Time of Tasks** is an integer type index value that indicates the index of the next free space in the **ShiftMemory (Time of Tasks).vi** vector.
- **TimeNow** is a floating point variable that indicates the actual time (moment) of the running simulation program.
- **Delimiter of TaskList** is a string type variable that indicates that string value is used in the Task list as a separator character string.

Figure 30. Values of the TaskList global variable during the run of the M/M/1 model

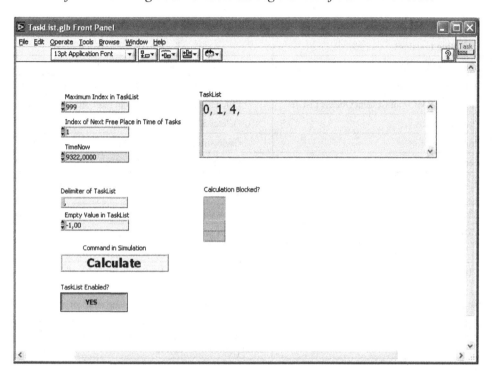

- **Empty Value in TaskList** is a floating point variable that allows to fill up time value of not yet used tasks in the **ShiftMemory (Time of Tasks).vi** vector. Values that do not occur are used (e.g., negative values).
- **Command in Simulation** is a combo box indicator that indicates the actual operation affected during the simulation program (**Initiation, Clear Inputs and Calculate**).
- **TaskList Enabled?** is a logic type variable. If it is FALSE, it does not allow to change the vector values of the **ShiftMemory (Time of Tasks)**.
- **Calculation Blocked?** Is a logic type variable, which plays the role of allowing the uninterrupted run of the simulation program.
- **TaskList** is a string type variable that ensures the chronological operation of the elements of the **ShiftMemory (Time of Tasks).vi** vector. The TaskList string itself

contains the indices of the Task in execution order.

The global variables listed here and in Table 1 can be expanded with any elements, but the processing of the information of the new variables and their (re)programming in the given DES basic components have to be accomplished.

Processes of the simulation system are shown in Table 1.

CONCLUSION AND POSSIBILITIES FOR FURTHER DEVELOPING THE SIMULATION PROGRAM

The directions, which seem essential for any future simulation application development, are discussed next. These elements were not implemented, because they were not indispensable for the models used in an educational environment.

Table 1.

Name	Comment
Object handling functions	
Clear Content of Objects.vi	Clearing the content of the ObjectList
Delete and Object by Index.vi	Deletion of an object from the ObjectList based on its index
Delete an Object Index from Content Objects List.vi	Deletes one object index from those stored in the object
Delete Packed Objects.vi	Deletes all elements of the packed Entity object
Get User Attribute.vi	Giving user attribute value
Has Object Arrived.vi	Examines if there is a DES Object in the input channel
Index of Object by Name.vi	Based on the full name, searches the index of the object in the ObjectList
Input Channel Enable.vi	Allows/disables the data flow of the given input channel
Input ChannelS Enable.vi	Allows/disables the data flow of the input channels
Insert an Object into ObjectList	Creates a new object in the ObjectList
Insert Index AS FIRST into Content Objects List by Priority.vi	Inserts a new index before the index of the objects stored in the object
Insert Index AS LAST into Content Objects List.vi	Inserts a new index after the index of the objects stored in the object
Last Index of content Objects List.vi	Gives the last index of those object indices, which are indexes of objects stored in an object.
Entity Operations	
Entity is Idle.vi	The function examines the state of the Entity object
Entity System Attribute Setting.vi	Sets the value of the system variable assigned to the Entity
Task management functions	
Clear Content of TaskList.vi	Deletes the content of the TaskList
Continue of Simulate.vi	Examination of he continuation of simulation
Delete a Task by Index.vi	Deletion of a Task from the TaskList object based on its index
Insert a Task into TaskList.vi	Insertion of a Task into the TaskList object
Task at Index.vi	Parameters of the Task appearing at the given index of the TaskList object
Distribution functions	
Exponential Distribution.vi	Exponential distribution function
Empirical Distribution.vi	Empirical distribution function
Normal Distribution.vi	Normal distribution function
Triangle Distribution.vi	Triangle distribution function
Uniform Distribution.vi	Uniform distribution function
Other processes	
Choose.vi	Selects one channel out of two with a given probability
Next Empty Place Index in ObjectsList.vi	Determining the index of the next empty space in the ObjectList
Object Parameters.vi	Provides the parameters of the object that is at the given index of the ObjectList
Piechart.vi	Draws a pie chart

continued on following page

Table 1. continued

Name	Comment
Real Output Channels Series (Selector Object).vi	Accomplishes the merging of the physical and logic channels
Set System Attribute.vi	The process of setting the values of the variables of the given object system
Set User Attribute.vi	The process of setting the user values of the given object
Status Histogram.vi	Draws a status histogram
Input Connection Control.vi	Determines the index of the object linked to the input channel
Used Objects.vi	Provides the map of the objects used in the ObjectList

When the simulation applications demand statistical calculations or new object definition during runtime, these can be achieved with the definition of new object attributes and/or with the extension of the object's functionality.

Including Further Statistical Calculations in the DES Objects

The statistical calculations built into the objects of the LabVIEW DES system, can be extended without any difficulties with further calculations. To accomplish this (e.g., any statistical analysis), it is not necessary to interfere with the objects already completed, but the most effective process is to "surround" an already existing basic object with the new requirements and with controlling the input and output channels of the Entity object's flows and with the help of the information measured and stored by the Entity objects. To improve the system, graduate students have already completed new objects with which the choice of input and output channels can be accomplished with a given distribution.

Creation of New Attributes and Incorporation of their Effects into the DES Objects

The creation of all new attributes that are present in the DES Object – the creation of a vector cor-responding to the data type of the attribute – can easily be accomplished. The user has to provide for its initialization and its tasks in the DES Object with new program code segments. Generally, the object attributes are read in the **Calculate** state of the simulation system and they are given new values in this state after certain calculations.

The attributes storing the position, speed, acceleration, etc. and the position of the axis of the Entity object's rotation are already built in into the present version of the simulation system. There was no possibility in the present version, however, to service these new features with algorithms.

Creation of New DES Objects

If the aim is to create a new DES Object for a completely new problem, it is always worthwhile to examine what type of system theoretical links can be used to create the new object by using the existing DES Object(s). In such a case, the tasks of the new DES Object have to be programmed in the three run states (Initiation, Clear Inputs, Calculate) in a way that the Entity flow and the changes in the state of the new DES Object are continually stored based on accomplished tasks in the object attributes.

If the user aims to create a fully new, previously non-existent DES object, it is worthwhile to study the previously created basic objects.

REFERENCES

Brown, P. J. (1980). *Writing Interactive Compilers and Interpreters*. Chichester, UK: John Wiley & Sons.

Hilen, D. (2000). *Taylor Enterprise Dynamics (User Manual)*. Utrecht, The Netherlands: F&H Simulations B.V.

Johnson, G. W. (1994). *LabVIEW Graphical Programming*. New York: McGraw-Hill.

Kelton, W. D., Sadowski, R. P., & Sadowski, D. A. A. (1998). *Simulation with Arena*. Boston: McGraw-Hill.

Kheir, N. A. (1988). *Systems Modeling and Computer Simulation*. Basel, Switzerland: Marcel Dekker Inc.

Kreutzer, W. (1986). *System Simulation - Programming Styles and Languages*. Reading, MA: Addison Wesley Publishers.

Law, A. M., & Kelton, W. D. (1991). *Simulation Modeling and Analysis*. San Francisco: McGraw-Hill.

Ligetvári, Zs. (2005). *New Object's Development in DES LabVIEW* (in Hungarian). Unpublished Master's thesis, Budapest University of Technology and Economics, Hungary.

Lönhárd, M. (2000). *Simulation System of Discrete Events in Delphi* (in Hungarian). Unpublished Master's thesis, Budapest University of Technology and Economics, Hungary.

NI LabVIEW Developer Team. (2007). *LabVIEW 8.5 User Manual*. Austin, TX: National Instruments.

Rohl, J. S. (1986). *An Introduction to Compiler Writing*. New York: Macdonald and Jane's.

KEY TERMS AND DEFINITIONS

Entity: The Entity objects are representing the movement of material and information in the simulation system.

Buffer: The Buffer object ensures a temporary storage of Entity objects until the connected object behind the Buffer object in the material or information flow is able to fulfill the predefined task.

Machine: The Machine object executes operations of specified time duration determined by different function types of Entity objects.

Sink: The Sink object extinguishes (swallows) the Entity objects.

Source: The Source object issues Entity objects at intervals determined by different function types.

ObjectList: The ObjectList contains the predefined discrete event model objects of the simulation model.

TaskList: The TaskList contains the list of executing events in time.

Chapter 14
Using Simulation Systems for Decision Support

Andreas Tolk
Old Dominion University, USA

ABSTRACT

This chapter describes the use of simulation systems for decision support in support of real operations, which is the most challenging application domain in the discipline of modeling and simulation. To this end, the systems must be integrated as services into the operational infrastructure. To support discovery, selection, and composition of services, they need to be annotated regarding technical, syntactic, semantic, pragmatic, dynamic, and conceptual categories. The systems themselves must be complete and validated. The data must be obtainable, preferably via common protocols shared with the operational infrastructure. Agents and automated forces must produce situation adequate behavior. If these requirements for simulation systems and their annotations are fulfilled, decision support simulation can contribute significantly to the situational awareness up to cognitive levels of the decision maker.

INTRODUCTION

Modeling and simulation (M&S) systems are applied in various domains, such as

- supporting the analysis of alternatives,
- supporting the procurement of new systems by simulating them long before first prototypes are available,
- supporting the testing and evaluation of new equipment by providing the necessary stimuli for the system being tested,
- training of new personnel working with the system, and many more.

The topic of this chapter is one of the most challenging applications for simulation systems, namely the use of simulation systems for decision support in general, and particularly in direct support of operational processes. In other words, the decision maker is directly supported by M&S applications, helping with

DOI: 10.4018/978-1-60566-774-4.ch014

- "what-if" analysis for alternatives,
- plausibility evaluation for assumptions of other party activities,
- consistency checks of plans for future operations,
- simulation of expected behavior based on the plan and trigger the real world observations for continuous comparison (are we still on track),
- manage uncertainty by simulating several runs faster than real time and display variances and connected risks,
- trend simulation to identify potentially interesting developments in the future based on current operational developments, and additional applications that support the meaningful interpretation of current data.

While current decision support systems are focused on data mining and data presentation, which is the display of snap-shot information and historical developments are captured in most cases in the form of static trend analyses and display curves (creating a common operating picture), simulation systems display the behavior of the observed system (creating a common executable model). This model can be used by the decision maker to manipulate the observed system "on the fly" and use it not only for analysis, but also to communicate the results very effectively to and with partners, customers, and supporters of his efforts. As stated by van Dam (1999) during his lecture at Stanford: *"If a picture is worth a 1000 words, a moving picture is worth a 1000 static ones, and a truly interactive, user-controlled dynamic picture is worth 1000 ones that you watch passively."* That makes simulation very interesting for managers and decision makers, encouraging the use of decision support simulation systems. Another aspect is that of complex systems: non-linearity and multiple connections. In order to understand and evaluate such system, traditional tools of operational research and mathematics have to be increasingly supported by the means of modeling and simulation. The same is true for decisions in complex environments, such as the battlefield of a military decision maker or the stock market for an international investment broker.

To this end, the simulation system must be integrated into operational systems as a decision support service. In order to be successful, not only the technical challenges of integration, discrete and other simulation technologies, into operational IT systems must be solved. It is also required that the simulation system fulfills additional operational and conceptual requirements as well. Simulation systems are more than software. Simulation systems are executable models, and models are purposeful abstractions of reality. In order to understand if a simulation system can be used for decision support, the concepts and assumptions derived to represent real world objects and effects in a simplified form must be understood. The conceptualization of the model's artifacts is as important as the implementation details of the simulation. As stated in Tolk (2006): *interoperability of systems requires composability of models!*

The author gained most of his experience in the military sector, integrating combat M&S into Command and Control (C2) systems. The development of the Levels of Conceptual Interoperability Model (LCIM) capturing the requirement for alignment on various levels to support decision support is a direct result of the experiences of integrating M&S services as web-services into service-oriented C2 systems (Tolk et al., 2006). It is directly related to the recommendations found in the North Atlantic Treaty Organization (NATO) Code of Best Practice for C2 Assessment (NATO, 2002) that was compiled by a group of international operational research experts in support of complex C2 analysis. It was also influenced by the recommendations of the National Research Council (2002, 2006), as using simulation for procurement decision or for analysis and using this analysis for decision support are closely related topics.

Furthermore, the growing discipline of agent-directed simulation (ADS) is very helpful in providing new insights and methods (Oren et al, 2000). ADS consists of three distinct yet related areas that can be grouped under two categories. First, *agent simulation* (or simulation for agents), that is simulation of systems that can be modeled by agents in engineering, human and social dynamics, military applications, and so on. Second, agents for simulation can be grouped under two sub-categories, namely *agent-based simulation*, which focuses on the use of agents for the generation of model behavior in a simulation study; and *agent-supported simulation*, which deals with the use of agents as a support facility to enable computer assistance by enhancing cognitive capabilities in problem specification and solving.

The vision of using simulation systems in general, and discrete event simulation systems in particular, for decision support is that a decision maker or manager can utilize an *orchestrated set of tools* to support his decision using reliable simulation systems implementing agreed concepts using the best currently available data. It does not matter if the decision support system is used in the finance market, where the stock market is simulated on a continuous basis, always being adjusted and calibrated by the real stock data, or if it used to support a traffic manager in guiding a convoy through a traffic jam during rush hour to the airport while constantly being updated by the recent traffic news. The technologies described here support the military commander in making decisions based on the best intelligence and surveillance data available by a sensor, as well as to the surgeon using a detailed model of the human body in preparation of a risky surgery. While the application fields are significantly different, the underlying engineering methods are not.

The section will start by presenting the relevant work, focusing on the special insights from the military domains before generalizing them for other applications. The main part is built by enumerating and motivating the requirements for simulation systems when being used for decision support, as identified by the National Science Foundation and related organizations. Finally, some examples are given and current developments are highlighted.

RELEVANT WORK

The area of related and relevant work regarding decision support systems in general and the use of simulation systems for decision support in general is huge. A book chapter can never suffice for a complete explanation. Therefore, the focus of this section is to highlight some of the most influencing works leading to formulation of the requirements for simulation systems. Additional information is contained in the section giving examples of decision support simulations in this chapter.

The need for using simulation systems in addition to traditional decision support systems is best derived from the work documented in the NATO Code of Best Practice for C2 Assessment (NATO, 2002). After having operated under more or less fixed strategic and doctrinal constraints for several decades, in which NATO and the Warsaw Pact faced each other in a perpetual lurking position, NATO suddenly faced a new operational environment for their decisions when the Warsaw Pact broke apart. While in the old order the enemy was well known – down to the equipment, strategy, and tactics – the new so-called "operations other than war" and "asymmetric operations" were characterized by uncertainty, incompleteness, and vagueness. At the same time, developments in information technology allowed the efficient distribution of computing power in the form of loosely coupled services. Consequently, the idea was to use an orchestrated set of operational tools – all implemented as services that can be loosely coupled in case of need – to support the decision maker with analysis and evaluation means in an area defined by uncertainty, incompleteness, and vagueness regarding the available information. In

Figure 1. Command and Control Improvements

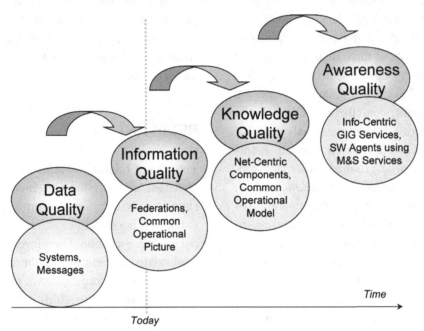

order to measure improvement in this domain, the value chain of Net Centric Warfare was introduced; see among others (Alberts and Hayes, 2003):

- *Data* is factual information. The value chain starts with *Data* Quality describing the information within the underlying C2 systems.
- *Information* is data placed into context. *Information* Quality tracks the completeness, correctness, currency, consistency, and precision of the data items and information statements available.
- *Knowledge* is procedural application of information. *Knowledge* Quality deals with procedural knowledge and information embedded in the C2 system such as templates for adversary forces, assumptions about entities such as ranges and weapons, and doctrinal assumptions, often coded as rules.
- Finally, *Awareness* Quality measures the degree of using the information and

knowledge embedded within the C2 system. Awareness is explicitly placed in the cognitive domain.

C2 quality is improved by an order of magnitude when a new level of quality is reached in this value chain. Figure 1 depicts this. C2 quality is improved by these developments as follows:

- Data quality is characterized by stand-alone developed systems exchanging data via text messages as used in most C2 systems. Having the same data available at the distributed locations was the first goal to reach.
- By the introduction of a common operational picture, data is put into context, which evolves the data into information. The collaborating systems using this common operational picture result in an order of magnitude of improvement of the Command and Control quality, as decision makers share this common information. As

stated before: a picture is worth a 1,000 words.

- The next step, which is enabled by service-oriented web-based infrastructures, is the use of simulation services for decision support. Simulation systems are the prototype for procedural knowledge, which is the basis for knowledge quality. Instead of just having a picture, an executable simulation system can be used.

- Finally, using intelligent software agents to continually observe the battle sphere, apply simulations to analyze what is going on, to monitor the execution of a plan, and to do all the tasks necessary to make the decision maker aware of what is going on, C2 systems can even support situational awareness, the level in the value chain traditionally limited to pure cognitive methods.

Traditional decision support systems enable information quality, but they need the agile component of simulation in order to support knowledge quality as well. In other words, numerical insight into the behavior of complex systems as provided by simulations is needed in order to understand them.

In order to support the integration of decision support simulations, it is necessary to provide them as services. However, this task is not limited to technical challenges of providing a web service or a grid service, but the documentation of the service and the provided functionality is essential to enable the *discovery*, *selection*, and *composition* of this service in support of an operational need. The papers (Tosic et al., 2001) and (Srivastava and Koehler, 2003) summarize the state of the art of service composition. Pullen et al. (2005) show the applicability for M&S services. Additionally, what is needed are annotations. Annotations give meaning to services by changing them into semantic web services. The reader is referred to (Agarwal et al., 2005) and (Alesso and Smith, 2005) for more information on this topic.

In order to identify what information is needed to annotate operational M&S services, the Levels of Conceptual Interoperability Model (LCIM) was developed. The closest application to the topic of this book chapter is documented by Tolk et al. (2006). The LCIM exposes layers of abstractions that are often hidden: the conceptualization layer leading to the model, the implementation layer leading to the simulation, and technical questions of the underlying network. Each layer is tightly connected with different aspects of interoperation. We are following the recommendation given by Page and colleagues (Page et al., 2004), who suggested defining composability as the realm of the model and interoperability as the realm of the software implementation of the model. Included in the technical challenge of integrating networks and protocols, the following three categories for annotations emerge:

- *Integratability* contends with the physical/technical realms of connections between systems, which include hardware and firmware, protocols, networks, etc.
- *Interoperability* contends with the software and implementation details of interoperations; this includes exchange of data elements via interfaces, the use of middleware, mapping to common information exchange models, etc.
- *Composability* contends with the alignment of issues on the modeling level. The underlying models are purposeful abstractions of reality used for the conceptualization being implemented by the resulting systems.

The LCIM increases the resolution by adding additional sub-layers of interoperation. The layer of integratability is represented by the *technical layer*, which ensures that bits and bytes can be exchanged and correctly interpreted. The *syntactic layer* allows mapping all protocols to a common structure. The *semantic layer* defines the meaning of information exchange elements. Syntax and semantics belong to the interoperability realm. In the *pragmatic layer*, the information exchange elements are grouped into business objects with a common context. Annotations on the *dynamic layer* capture the processes invoked and the system state changes taking place when business objects are exchanged between systems. Finally, the relevant constraints and assumptions are captured in the *conceptual layer*, which completes the composability realm.

The LCIM supports a structured way to annotate M&S services. Dobrev et al. (2007) show how this model can be used to support interoperation in general applications. Zeigler and Hammonds (2007) use it to compare it with their ideas on using ontological means in support of interoperation. It was furthermore applied for the Department of Defense, the Department for Homeland Security, The Department of Energy, and NATO. These annotations are necessary requirements to allow *discovery*, *selection*, and *composition* of services.

These annotations should be interpreted as a machine understandable version of the underlying conceptual model of the M&S service. Robinson (2008) defines the conceptual model as *"a non-software specific description of the simulation model that is to be developed, describing the objectives, inputs, outputs, content, assumptions, and simplifications of the model."* He furthermore points out that there is a significant need to agree on how to do develop conceptual models and capture information formally. What is needed in support of composable services is therefore to capture *objectives, inputs, outputs, content, assumptions, and simplifications* of the model in the *technical, syntactical, semantic, pragmatic, dynamic, and conceptual* category. The discipline of model-based data engineering (Tolk and Diallo, 2008) is a first step into this direction.

To understand why these annotations are so important, it is necessary to understand how machines gain understanding. Zeigler (1986) introduced a model for understanding a system within another

observing system. Figure 2 shows the three premises that need to be supported by the annotations describing the M&S services. The system – or the M&S service – is herein described by its *properties* that are grouped into propertied *concepts* (the basic simulated entities and attributes), the *processes* (the behavior of simulated entities and how their attributes change), and *constraints* (assumptions constraining the values of the attributes and the behavior of the system).

- The first premise is that the observing system has a *perception* of the system to be understood. This means that the properties and processes must be observable and perceivable by the observing system. The properties used for the perception should not significantly differ in scope and resolution from the properties exposed by the system under observation.
- The second premise is that the observing system needs to have a *meta-model* of the observed system. The meta-model is a description of properties, processes, and constraints of the expected behavior of the observed system. Without such a model of the system, understanding is not possible.
- The third premise is the *mapping* between observations resulting in the perception and meta-models explaining the observed properties, processes, and constraints.

In other words, machine understanding is the selection process of the appropriate meta-model to explain the observed properties, processes, and constraints. This corresponds to the selection of appropriate M&S services to support a decision. The properties and propertied concepts are described by syntax, semantic, and pragmatic annotations, processes by dynamic annotations, and constraints by conceptual annotations capturing objectives, inputs, outputs, content, assumptions, and simplifications in addition to implementation details and technical specifications. No matter

Figure 2. Premises for System's Understanding

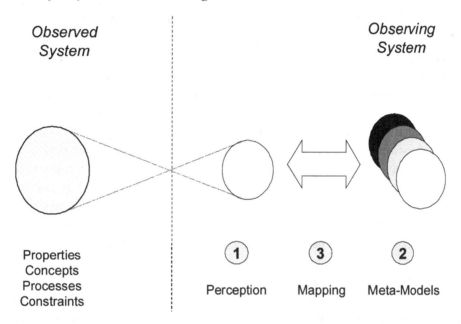

if these annotations are used to discover, select, and orchestrate M&S functionality as operational services or if they are used by intelligent agents to communicate their use, they are necessary for every application beyond the traditional system developments that are often intentionally not reused in their requirements. This section can therefore also serve as a guideline for what is needed to annotate legacy systems that shall be integrated into a net-centric and service-oriented environment to contribute to a system of systems.

Table 1 can be used as a checklist to ensure that all information is captured or obtainable

for a candidate simulation system for decision support.

All this related work sets the frame for describing M&S services to support their discovery and orchestration for integration as an orchestrated set of tools into the operational infrastructure used by the decision maker. The following section will describe the requirements for the simulation systems themselves in more detail.

Table 1. Checklist points for decision support simulation annotations

Annotation Categories	Levels of Interoperation	System Characteristics	Conceptual Model Characteristics
• Integratability	• Technical	• Properties	• Objectives
• Interoperability	• Syntactic	• Concepts	• Inputs
• Composability	• Semantic	• Processes	• Outputs
	• Pragmatic	• Constraints	• Content
	• Dynamic		• Assumptions
	• Conceptual		• Simplifications

REQUIREMENTS FOR SIMULATION SYSTEMS

This section will explain the necessary requirements for simulation systems when they are to be used as decision support systems. These requirements may not be sufficient for all application domains, so additional application domain expertise is needed for informed selection. While the focus in the last section was annotation, the focus here will be the content and completeness of the simulation system.

This section will start with general requirements for all simulation systems to be applied to decision support and will finish with additional requirements in the case a federation of simulation systems is to be applied, which is the more likely scenario. As the NATO Code of Best Practice (NATO, 2002) points out: it is highly unlikely that one tool or simulation system will be able to deal with all questions describing the sponsor's problem; the use of an orchestrated set of tools should be the rule.

This section extends and generalizes the findings documented in Tolk (1999) and referenced in NRC (2002). While the principle results are still valid, the development in the recent years, in particular in the domain of agent-based models in support of behavior modeling and of computer generated forces contributed significantly to solutions in challenging areas that need to be incorporated. The section on current developments in this chapter will focus on these developments in more detail.

Modeling of Relevant System Characteristics

Models are purposeful abstractions from reality. This means that they simplify some things, leave others out, use assumptions, etc. When using a simulation system as a decision support simulation, it is crucial that all relevant system characteristics

are captured. This includes all aspects of the system: modeled entities (properties and concepts), modeled behavior and interactions (processes), and modeled constraints. The reason is trivial: if something important is not part of the model, it cannot be considered for the analysis, nor can it be part of the recommended solution.

The artifacts used for documentation of the system (and annotation) during the conceptualization phase should capture the necessary information. As defined by Robinson (2008) in his overview work on conceptual modeling, the characteristics of a conceptual model are *objectives, inputs, outputs, content, assumptions, and simplifications*. A practical way to accomplish this task has been captured in the contributions of Brade (2000), which will be addressed in the section on verification and validation.

Example: A simulation system shall be used to support the decision of where to install additional gas stations in a town. It models the cars used in this town, the behavior of the car drivers, and the gas stations already in use within this town. The idea is to use simulation based optimization to find out how many new gas stations should be built and where.

In order to be able to use the simulation system, additional system characteristics may have to be captured, such as

- Under which circumstances are drivers willing to go to neighboring towns to buy gas to fill up their cars? (Assumption that drivers in the town will use gas stations in this town)
- How will the competition react? Will they build new stations? Will they close down stations? (Assumption that only the company conducting the study actively changes the gas supply infrastructure)
- Are there additional influences that are relevant, such as the overall driving behavior based on current average oil prices?

(Assumption that decision rules used by simulated entities follow a closed world assumption)

Even if this is not implemented, the simulation can still be used in support of analysis, but the expert must be very well aware of what the simulation systems simulates and how. In other words, an awareness of the assumptions and constraints affecting the validity of the simulation results is necessary.

In summary, it is essential that the simulation system can support the decision to be made by ensuring that all concepts, properties, processes, and constraints identified to be relevant in the problem specification process are implemented. The NATO Code of Best Practice (NATO, 2002) gives guidance for the problem specification process. The conceptual models used for the simulation development document the respective characteristics of the simulation.

Ability to Obtain All Relevant Data

Closely related is the second premise that must be fulfilled: the relevant data needed for the simulation system initialization and execution must be obtainable. Even if a simulation system is complete in describing all concepts, properties, processes, and constraints, the model can be practically useless if the necessary data to drive these models cannot be provided. The quality of the solution is driven by the quality of the model and the quality of the data.

The NATO Code of Best Practice (NATO, 2002) gives guidance with respect to obtaining data and ensuring the necessary quality of data. Among the identified factors for good data are the reliability of sources and the accuracy of data. Additional factors are the costs to obtain data, how well the data is documented, if and how the data have been modified, etc.

Another aspect that increases in importance in the area of net centricity and service- oriented

architectures is the alignment of protocols for data storage and exchange in operational systems and decision support simulation systems. The optimal case is that decision support simulation systems and the embedded operational system use the same data representation. If this is not the case, data mediation may be a possible solution to mapping the existent operationally available data to the required initialization and input data. However, it must be pointed out that data mediation requires the mapping of data is complete, unambiguous, and precise. To this extent, Model-based Data Engineering was developed and successfully applied (Tolk and Diallo, 2008).

An aspect unique to M&S services is the need that modeled data are conceptually connected to operationally available data. As models are abstractions of reality, some data may be "academic" abstractions that theoretically are constructible, but are difficult to observe or to obtain. In particular statistical measure of higher order, such as using a negative polynomial bivariate intensity probability distribution function to model the movement of entities as a fluid, often make perfectly sense when developing the model, but may be very hard to feed with real world data.

Example: A simulation system shall be used to support a decision maker with evacuation decisions during a catastrophic event (Muhdi, 2006). Most evaluation models currently used are flow-based models. The data available in a real emergency, however, is discrete, describing exit obstacles, individuals, and other data that need to be converted into this model (and potentially mapped back in support of creating elements of a plan that needs to be shared using the operational infrastructure).

In summary, it is essential that data needed by the model can be obtained and mediated. The data will be used to initialize the simulation systems and as input data during execution.

Validation and Verification of Model, Simulation, and Data

Validation and verification are processes to determine the simulation's credibility. They deal with answering questions such as "Does the simulation system satisfy its intended use? Can the simulation system be used to evaluate specific questions? How close does the simulation system come to reality?" In other words, validation and verification are the processes of determining if a simulation is correct and usable to solve a given problem.

The US Department of Defense defined validation and verification for military use in their M&S instruction (DoD, 1996). Validation is the process of determining the degree to which a model or simulation is an accurate representation of the real world from the perspective of the intended uses. Verification is the process of determining that a model or simulation implementation accurately represents the developer's conceptual description and specifications. In other words, validation determines if the right thing is coded while verification determines if the thing is coded right. Validation determines the behavioral and representational accuracy; verification determines the accuracy of transformation processes.

There are many papers available dealing with the necessity to validate and verify models and simulation before using them for decision making. The interested reader is pointed to the overview of methods and tools provided by Balci (1998) and several specific papers by Sargent (1999, 2000, 2007). The work of Brade (2000) making practical recommendations regarding artifacts was already mentioned in a previous section.

It seems to be obvious that simulation systems designed to be used as decision support simulation systems must be validated and verified. This is true for the models, the simulations, and the data. If this is not the case, the results will not be credible and reliable and as such not applicable to support decisions.

It is not trivial but is at least possible to accomplish verification and validation for physical processes and models. However, the simulated entities and processes are not limited to such physical processes. Cognitive processes and decision models need to be modeled as well. Moya and Weisel (2008) point out the resulting challenges.

Example: To show the necessity of verification and validation, two examples of simulation failures in operational environments are given that are directly applicable to decision support simulation systems as well.

Simulation in Testing: During Operation Iraqi Freedom, Patriot missiles shot down two allied aircraft & targeted another. On March 23, 2003, the pilot and co-pilot aboard a British Tornado GR4 aircraft that was shot down by a U.S. Patriot missile died. On April 2, 2003, another Patriot missile downed a U.S. Navy F/A-18C Hornet which was flying a mission over Central Iraq. The evaluation report identified one of the causes of these failures stemmed from using an invalid simulation to stimulate the Patriot's fire control system during its testing.

Simulation in Engineering: Another catastrophic event in spring 2003 was the Columbia disaster. The space shuttle had been damaged by foam debris during takeoff. NASA engineers decided, based on their professional judgment, that the damage would not endanger the shuttle when returning to earth. They were wrong and the shuttle broke apart when entering the atmosphere, killing the crew and throwing the shuttle program significantly back. What is of interest for the readers of this chapter is that the simulation available to the experts predicted the disaster, but the results were not deemed reliable and credible by the experts. Obviously they were mistaken.

In summary, it is necessary to only make use of validated and verified models and data for decision support simulation systems. It is essential that the decision maker is supported with reliable and credible information.

Creating Situation Adequate Behavior

One of the most challenging premises is to fulfill the requirement for situation adequate behavior. This premise addresses the behavior of simulated entities, which is represented by the processes of the system characteristics. The premise has a very practical side and a resulting challenge. Many simulation systems used in other application domains, in particular for training and testing, also require that the simulated entities behave as they would in the real world. If this behavior is connected with human decision making, it is quite often humans in the loop making the decision.

A typical military computer assisted exercise comprises not only the training audience, but also soldiers representing the subordinates, partners, and superior commands, as well as the opposing forces. To ensure that soldiers "train as they fight," the units are commanded by military experts. The simulation computes the movement, the attrition, the reconnaissance, and other processes that are based on physical aspects. It is more the rule than the exception that more soldiers are needed to support the simulation system than are trained in an event. The use of agents to generate the orders is mandatory for decision support; otherwise the manpower would increase to the point of no longer being practical or feasible.

Example: If training on the brigade level is conducted, approximately 800 orders have to be created in order to drive a simulation model. Taking into account that not only the orders for the brigade are needed, but also for the neighbored units and – last but not least – the orders for the enemy increases this number by the factor of four to six resulting in the number of 3,000 to 5,000 orders to be created for just one alternative. This is accomplished by a group of 500 to 600 soldiers. As this many personnel can never be supported by a brigade headquarter that wants to use the simulation for decision support, the majority of these orders must be generated by

means of behavioral representation in modeling and simulation.

In summary, intelligent software agents representing human behavior in simulation systems must ensure that the simulated entities behave correctly. Scripted and rule driven approaches are not sufficient. The conference on behavioral representation in modeling and simulation (BRIMS) is a good source of current research and proposed solutions. Yilmaz et al. (2006) are giving a good overview of such use of agents in serious games as well as in simulation systems.

Additional Issues When Using Federations of Simulation Systems

The first four premises must be fulfilled by every simulation system that will be used for decision support. However, as pointed out several times in this chapter, the application of an orchestrated set of tools in order to evaluate all relevant aspects of a model is the rule. If several simulation systems need to be used to provide the required functionality, some concerns need to be addressed that are unique to federations of simulation systems.

The main challenge is to orchestrate simulations not only regarding their execution, but also to conceptually align them to ensure that the federation delivers a consistent view to the decision maker fulfilling all requirements that have been captured. The LCIM can support this challenge. A simulation federation in itself is a complex system of systems. Current simulation interoperability standards are not sufficient to support the necessary consistency. Besides several publications by the author in this domain, this view is shared by many other experts in the field, such as Zeigler and Hammonds (2007) show in their survey. Yilmaz (2007) proposed the use of meta-level ontology relations to measure conceptual alignment.

The objective of these alignments is to harmonize the three elements essential for simulation result consistency, which are the concepts underlying the simulated entities (resolution and structure), the internal decision logic used to generate the behavior of the simulated entities, and the external measure of performance used to evaluate the accomplishment. If this is not the case, the results will be counter-intuitive at best, and inconsistent and wrong at worst. As shown in Muguira and Tolk (2006), even if all federates are validated and correct, the federation may still expose structural variances, making the result unusable for decision support.

Example: The triangle of concepts, internal decision logic, and external evaluation logic must be harmonized regarding all three aspects, or structural variance can result in non-credible results.

- *Concepts and decision logic:* Simulation *A* represents a fish swarm as a cubicle; simulation *B* uses a statistical distribution within a bowl. If the decision logic of simulation *A* is used to support a decision in simulation *B*, the decision is based on the wrong assumptions and is likely to be wrong.
- *Concepts and evaluation logic:* If the measure of merit requires inputs not exposed by the federation, or if the structure and resolution are significantly different in the federated simulation systems, the evaluation is wrong.
- *Decision and evaluation logic:* One of the most observed reasons for strange behavior in the results of federations is that the measure of merit used for the evaluation and the measure of merit used to optimize the decisions internally are not harmonized. If the decision logic targets to maximize the amount of fish captured in each event and the evaluation logic checks if the overall regeneration of fish is ensured as well, it is likely that structural variances will occur.

In summary, it must be ensured that the simulation systems are not only coupled and technically correct (based on currently available simulation interoperability standards), but that they are aligned regarding concepts, internal decision logic, and external evaluation logic as well.

Summarizing all five premises dealt with in this chapter, the following enumeration lists the questions that need to be answered to ensure that the requirements are fulfilled:

- Are all concepts having a role in solving the problem identified and simulated in the simulation?
- Are the properties used to model the propertied concepts in the necessary resolution and the necessary structure?
- Are all identified processes (entity behavior and overarching processes) modeled?
- Are the assumptions and constraints identified for the operational challenge to be decided upon reflected appropriately by the simulation system?
- Can operational data and author authoritative data sources provide all data needed for the initialization of the simulation system?
- Can operational data provide all data needed as input data during the execution of the simulation system?
- Do the operational infrastructure and the decision support simulation system share the same data model, or – if this is not the case – can model-based data engineering be applied to derive the necessary mediation functions? Are possible semantic losses resulting from the mapping acceptable?
- Is the data obtainable in the structure and resolution (and accuracy) needed, or – if this is not the case – can the data be transformed into the required format?
- Are all potential M&S services and simulation systems validated and verified?
- Are the data validated and verified?
- Is the behavior of all simulated entities situation adequate?
- In case of personnel intensive simulation systems, can the human component

be replaced with intelligent software agents to produce the required decisions (or can it be ensured that always enough persons are available to support the application)?

- Are the represented concepts (simulated entities) sufficient to produce the properties needed for the measures of merit of the decision logic and the evaluation logic?
- Are the measures of merit used for the internal decision logic aligned with the external evaluation logic?

This list builds the core of questions the developer of decision support simulation systems must be able to answer positively. Additional application specific questions are likely and need to be captured for respective development or integration projects as requirements.

EXAMPLES OF DECISION SUPPORT SIMULATION APPLICATIONS

The previous sections dealt with the necessary annotation for M&S services and the requirements for simulation systems when being used for decision support. This section gives some selected references to examples of using simulation for decision support. While these examples are neither complete nor exclusive, they do show that decision support simulation is already applied in various fields.

Kvaale (1988) describes the use of simulation systems in support of design decisions for a new generation of fast patrol boats. This application is the traditional use of simulation in support of the procurement process: alternatives are simulated and compared using a set of agreed to measures of merit. Although this application is not driving the support using operational data directly obtained from operational systems, it is one of the first journal papers describing the use of simulation systems for decision support.

Everett (2002) describes the design of a simulation model to provide decision support for the scheduling of patients waiting for elective surgery in the public hospital system. The simulation model presented in this work can be used as an operational tool to match hospital availability with patient need. To this end, patients nominated for surgery by doctors are categorized by urgency and type of operation. The model is then used to simulate necessary procedures, available resources, resulting waiting time, and other decision parameters that are displayed for further evaluation. Therefore, the model can also be used to report upon the performance of the system and as a planning tool to compare the effectiveness of alternative policies in this multi-criteria decision health-care environment.

Truong et al. (2005) present another application domain for decision supporting use of simulation: fisheries policy and management decisions in support of optimizing a harvesting plan for the fishing industry. As in many application areas, the behavior of fish and the effects of harvesting are not fully understood, but can be captured to sufficient detail to build a simulation that reflects the known facts in sufficient detail. This enables simulation-based optimization using the simulation to obtain quasi-objective function values of possible alternatives, in the example particular fishing schedules. This idea is applicable in similar environments with uncertain and imprecise data that exposes some trends that can be captured in simulations.

Power and Sharda (2007) summarized related ideas recently in their work on model-driven decision support systems. Following their definition, model-driven decision support systems use algebraic, decision analytic, financial, simulation, and optimization models to provide decision support. Like this chapter, they use optimization models, decision theory, and other means of operational analysis and research as an orchestrated set of tools in which simulation is embedded in an aligned way.

Decision support systems, as well as the use of simulation systems, have a relatively long history in the military domain. An example is given by Pohl et al. (1999) who present the results of a project sponsored by the Defense Advance Project Research Agency (DARPA). The Integrated Marine Multi-Agent Command and Control System (IMMACCS) is a multi-agent, distributed system. It is designed to provide a common tactical picture as discussed earlier in this chapter and an early adapter of the agent-based paradigm for decision support. Between 1999 and 2004, the Office for Naval Research (ONR) sponsored a series of workshops on decision support systems in the United States. Furthermore, Wilton (2001) presented an overview of decision support simulation ideas integrated with C2 devices for the training of soldiers.

Management related military applications are regularly discussed at the annual International Command and Control Research and Technology Symposia (ICCRTS), which features a special track on decision support. The work presented here is often focused on cognitive aspects of sense-making and aims more at increasing the shared situational awareness than on a common technical framework. Many principles are not limited to the military domain but are applicable to all forms of agile organizations without fixed external structures. An example is the analysis of requirements of cognitive analysis to support C2 decision support system design by Potter et al. (2006).

The books edited by Tonfoni and Jain (2002), Phillips-Wren and Jain (2005), and Phillips-Wren et al. (2008) are valuable references for examples of using means of artificial intelligence and intelligent software agents in support of decision making using simulation systems. The use of ontological means to ensure composability of models and interoperability of simulations is the topic of several additional publications.

CURRENT DEVELOPMENTS

As with the previous section of this chapter, it is extremely difficult to decide which of the current developments should be highlighted, as every development in the discipline of M&S improves the usability of resulting systems for decision support. The focus of contributions in this section is therefore relatively small. As before, the idea is not to be restrictive but to give examples.

The military community used the Simulation Interoperability Workshops to work on the development of a technical reference model (TRM) for coupling of command, control, communications, computers, intelligence, surveillance, and reconnaissance (C4ISR) with M&S systems (Griffin et al., 2002). Figure 3 shows a generalization of the model, as already recommended by Tolk et al. (2008).

The model focuses on data exchange requirements and categories. The data is categorized as:

- simulation specific management data unique to the decision support simulation system,
- operational initialization data describing the data needed for initialization of both systems describing concepts, properties, processes, and constraints,
- dynamic exchange of operational data describing information that captures the input and output data of both worlds during execution, and
- operational system specific management data unique to the IT infrastructure used by the decision maker.

Unfortunately, the standardization work on the TRM was never completed, so that besides the final report of the study group and several contributing workshop papers no standard in support of embedding decision support simulations into operational IT infrastructures exists. Work in

Figure 3. Generalization of the C4ISR Technical Reference Model

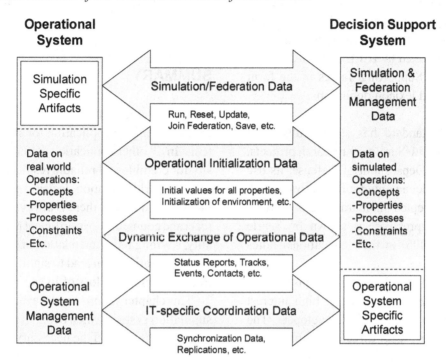

this domain would be very helpful to the M&S community.

As pointed out before, the US Department of Defense is working on a series of strategies and standards to enable net-centric operations. Another standard developed under the roof of the Simulation Interoperability Standardization Organization (SISO), the Base Object Model (BOM) Standard, is currently being evaluated to be used for the registration of M&S services. The standard is defined in two documents, the "Base Object Model (BOM) Template Standard" and the "Guide for Base Object Model (BOM) Use and Implementation" (SISO, 2006). The first document provides the essential details regarding the makeup and ontology of a BOM, the companion document gives examples and best practice guidelines for using and implementing the new standard. In summary, the BOM standard provides a standard to capture the artifacts of a conceptual model. Furthermore, it can be used to design new simulation systems as well as integrating legacy simulations. The

conceptual model elements defined by the BOM standard contain descriptions of concepts, properties, and processes. The description is not only static, but the interplay is captured in the form of state machines as well. The BOM template is divided in five categories and reuses successful ideas of the current simulation interoperability standard "High Level Architecture" (IEEE 1516) and supports:

- Model Identification by associating important metadata with the BOM. Examples include the author of the BOM, the responsible organization, security constraints, etc.
- Conceptual Model Definition by describing patterns of interplay, state machines representing the aspects of the conceptual model, entity types, and event types.
- Modeling Mapping by defining what simulated entities and processes represent what elements of the conceptual model.

- Object Model Definition by recording the necessary implementation details (objects, interactions, attributes, parameter, and data types as defined by IEEE 1516)
- Additional Supporting Tables in the form of notes and lexicon definitions.

The BOM standard has successfully been applied in several US military research projects. Outside the US Department of Defense, its use has not yet been documented sufficiently to speak of a broadly accepted standard. The potentials, however, are impressive, as shown by Searle and Brennan (2006) in their educational notes for NATO.

As mentioned at the beginning of this section, many other developments are of high interest to decision support simulation developers. The increasing use of agent-directed simulation is one aspect. The human behavior representation in M&S is another. Complex systems in knowledge-based environments (Tolk and Jain, 2008) are another domain of interest, in particular how to cope with uncertainties or how to apply ontological means in support of complex system interoperation. Enumerating all interesting fields lies beyond the scope of this chapter.

In summary, the developer of decision support simulation systems or the engineer tasked with the integration of simulation systems for operational decision support must follow developments in all levels of interoperation: from technical innovations enabling better connectivity (such as optical memories or satellite based internet communications) via improvement in the interoperability domain (such as new developments in the domain of semantic web services) to conceptual questions (including standardizing artifacts in machine understandable form). As systems developed for this domain need to be highly reliable and credible, the engineer needs not only to be highly technically competent, but also needs to follow the code of ethics of the profession, as wealth – and sometimes even survival – will depend on the work and efforts produced.

SUMMARY

Decision support of operational processes is the most challenging application for simulation systems. In all other application domains, the necessity for credible and reliable results is lower than for real world operation decision support. While in all other domains there is always the chance to react and counteract to insufficient M&S functionality, a wrong recommendation in support of real world operations can lead to significant financial trouble or even the loss of lives.

This chapter summarized the requirements for simulation systems when being used for such applications. It showed the necessary annotation to allow the discovery, selection, and orchestration of M&S systems as services in service-oriented environments. It also listed the premises for simulation system functionality, focusing on completeness of concepts, properties, processes, and constraints, obtainability of data, validation and verification, and the use of means of knowledge management. The current developments continue to close gaps so that the use of simulation in the context of operational decision support will soon enable support to even the cognitive levels of group decision making and common situational awareness.

REFERENCES

Agarwal, S., Handschuh, S., & Staab, S. (2005). Annotation, Composition and Invocation of Semantic Web Services. *Journal of Web Semantics*, 2(1), 1–24.

Alberts, D. S., & Hayes, R. E. (2003). Power to the Edge, Command and Control in the Information Age. *Department of Defense Command and Control Program; Information Age Transformation Series*. Washington, DC.

Alesso, H. P., & Smith, C. F. (2005). *Developing Semantic Web Services*. Wellesley, MA: A.K. Peters, Ltd.

Balci, O. (1998). Verification, Validation, and Testing. In J. Banks, (Ed) *Handbook of Simulation*. New York: John Wiley & Sons.

Brade, D. (2000). Enhancing M&S Accreditation by Structuring V&V Results. *Proceedings of the Winter Simulation Conference*, (pp. 840-848).

Department of Defense. (1996). *Modeling & Simulation Verification, Validation, and Accreditation* (US DoD Instruction 5000.61). Washington, DC: Author.

Dobrev, P., Kalaydjiev, O., & Angelova, G. (2007). *From Conceptual Structures to Semantic Interoperability of Content*. (LNCS Vol. 4604, pp. 192-205). Berlin: Springer-Verlag.

Everett, J. E. (2002). A decision support simulation model for the management of an elective surgery waiting system. *Journal for Health Care Management Science*, 5(2), 89–95. doi:10.1023/A:1014468613635

Family of Standards for Modeling and Simulation (M&S) High Level Architecture (HLA) – (a) IEEE 1516-2000 Framework and Rules; (b) IEEE 1516.1-2000 Federate Interface Specification; (c) IEEE 1516.2-2000 Object Model Template (OMT) Specification IEEE 1516-2000, *IEEE Press*.

Griffin, A., Lacetera, J., Sharp, R., & Tolk, A. (Eds.). (2002). *C4ISR/Sim Technical Reference Model Study Group Final Report (C4ISR/Sim TRM)*, (SISO-Reference Document 008-2002-R2). Simulation Interoperability Standards Organization, Orlando, FL.

Kvaale, H. (1988). A decision support simulation model for design of fast patrol boats. *European Journal of Operational Research*, 37(1), 92–99. doi:10.1016/0377-2217(88)90283-4

Moya, L., & Weisel, E. (2008) The Difficulties with Validating Agent Based Simulations of Social Systems. *Proceedings Spring Multi-Simulation Conference, Agent-Directed Simulation*, Ottawa, Canada.

Muguira, J. A., & Tolk, A. (2006). Applying a Methodology to Identify Structural Variances in Interoperations. *Journal for Defense Modeling and Simulation*, 3(2), 77–93. doi:10.1177/875647930600300203

Muhdi, R. A. (2006). Evaluation Modeling: Development, Characteristics and Limitations. *Proceedings of the National Occupational Research Agenda* (NORA), (pp. 87-92).

National Research Council. (2002). *Modeling and Simulation in Manufacturing and Defense Acquisition: Pathways to Success*. Washington, DC: Committee on Modeling and Simulation Enhancements for 21st Century Manufacturing and Defense Acquisition, National Academies Press.

National Research Council. (2006). *Defense Modeling, Simulation, and Analysis: Meeting the Challenge*. Washington, DC: Committee on Modeling and Simulation for Defense Transformation, National Academies Press.

North Atlantic Treaty Organization. (2002). *NATO Code of Best Practice for Command and Control Assessment*. Revised ed. Washington, DC: CCRP Press

Ören, T. I., & Numrich, S. K. S.K., Uhrmacher, A.M., Wilson, L. F., & Gelenbe, E. (2000). Agent-directed simulation: challenges to meet defense and civilian requirements. In *Proceedings of the 32nd Conference on Winter Simulation,* Orlando, Florida, December 10 – 13. San Diego, CA: Society for Computer Simulation International.

Page, E. H., Briggs, R., & Tufarolo, J. A. (2004). Toward a Family of Maturity Models for the Simulation Interconnection Problem. In *Proceedings of the Spring Simulation Interoperability Workshop*. New York: IEEE CS Press.

Phillips-Wren, G., Ichalkaranje, N., & Jain, L. C. (Eds.). (2008). *Intelligent Decision Making –An AI-Based Approach*. Berlin: Springer-Verlag.

Phillips-Wren, G., & Jain, L. C. (Eds.). (2005). *Intelligent Decision Support Systems in Agent-Mediated Environments*. The Netherlands: IOS Press.

Pohl, J. G., Wood, A. A., Pohl, K. J., & Chapman, A. J. (1999). IMMACCS: A Military Decision-Support System. *DARPA-JFACC 1999 Symposium on Advances in Enterprise Control*, San Diego, CA.

Potter, S. S., Elm, W. C., & Gualtieri, J. W. (2006). Making Sense of Sensemaking: Requirements of a Cognitive Analysis to Support C2 Decision Support System Design. *Proceedings of the Command and Control Research and Technology Symposium*. Washington, DC: CCRP Press.

Power, D. J., & Sharda, R. (2007). Model-driven decision support systems: Concepts and research directions. *Journal for Decision Support Systems*, *43*(3), 1044–1061. doi:10.1016/j.dss.2005.05.030

Pullen, J. M., Brunton, R., Brutzman, D., Drake, D., Hieb, M. R., Morse, K. L., & Tolk, A. (2005). Using Web Services to Integrate Heterogeneous Simulations in a Grid Environment. *Journal on Future Generation Computer Systems*, *21*, 97–106. doi:10.1016/j.future.2004.09.031

Robinson, S. (2008). Conceptual modelling for simulation Part I: definition and requirements. *The Journal of the Operational Research Society*, *59*, 278–290. doi:10.1057/palgrave.jors.2602368

Sargent, R. G. (1999). Validation and verification of simulation models. *Proceedings of the Winter Simulation Conference*, *1*, 39–48.

Sargent, R. G. (2000). Verification, Validation, and Accreditation of Simulation Models. *Proceedings of the Winter Simulation Conference*, (pp. 50-59).

Sargent, R. G. (2007). Verification and validation of simulation models. *Proceedings of the Winter Simulation Conference*, (pp. 124-137).

Searle, J., & Brennan, J. (2006). General Interoperability Concepts. In *Integration of Modelling and Simulation* (pp. 3-1 – 3-8), (Educational Notes RTO-EN-MSG-043). Neuilly-sur-Seine, France

Simulation Interoperability Standards Organization (SISO). (2006). *The Base Object Model Standard; SISO-STD-003-2006: Base Object Model (BOM) Template Standard; SISO-STD-003.1-2006: Guide for Base Object Model (BOM) Use and Implementation*. Orlando, FL: SISO Documents.

Srivastava, B., & Koehler, J. (2003). Web Service Composition - Current Solutions and Open Problems. *Proceedings ICAPS 2003 Workshop on Planning for Web Services*.

Tolk, A. (1999). Requirements for Simulation Systems when being used as Decision Support Systems. [), IEEE CS press]. *Proceedings Fall Simulation Interoperability Workshop*, *I*, 29–35.

Tolk, A., & Diallo, S. Y. (2008) Model-Based Data Engineering for Web Services. In Nayak R. et al. (eds) *Evolution of the Web in Artificial Intelligence Environments*, (pp. 137-161). Berlin: Springer.

Tolk, A., Diallo, S. Y., & Turnitsa, C. D. (2008). Implied Ontological Representation within the Levels of Conceptual Interoperability Model. [IDT]. *International Journal of Intelligent Decision Technologies*, *2*(1), 3–19.

Tolk, A., Diallo, S. Y., Turnitsa, C. D., & Winters, L. S. (2006). Composable M&S Web Services for Net-centric Applications. *Journal for Defense Modeling and Simulation, 3*(1), 27–44. doi:10.1177/875647930600300104

Tolk, A., & Jain, L. C. (Eds.). (2008). *Complex Systems in the Knowledge-based Environment.* Berlin: Springer Verlag.

Tonfoni, G., & Jain, L. C. (Eds.). (2003). *Innovations in Decision Support Systems.* Australia: Advanced Knowledge International.

Tosic, V., Pagurek, B., Esfandiari, B., & Patel, K. (2001). On the Management of Compositions of Web Services. In *Proceedings Object-Oriented Web Services (OOPSLA).*

Truong, T. H., Rothschild, B. J., & Azadivar, F. (2005) Decision support system for fisheries management. In *Proceedings of the 37th Conference on Winter Simulation*, (pp. 2107-2111).

van Dam, A. (1999). Education: the unfinished revolution. [CSUR]. *ACM Computing Surveys, 31*(4). doi:10.1145/345966.346038

Wilton, D. (2001). The Application Of Simulation Technology To Military Command And Control Decision Support. In *Proceedings Simulation Technology and Training Conference* (SimTecT), Canberra, Australia.

Yilmaz, L. (2007). Using meta-level ontology relations to measure conceptual alignment and interoperability of simulation models. In *Proceedings of the Winter Simulation Conference*, (pp. 1090-1099).

Yilmaz, L., Ören, T., & Aghaee, N. (2006). Intelligent agents, simulation, and gaming. *Journal for Simulation and Gaming, 37*(3), 339–349. doi:10.1177/1046878106289089

Zeigler, B. P. (1986) Toward a Simulation Methodology for Variable Structure Modeling. In Elzas, Oren, Zeigler (Eds.) *Modeling and Simulation Methodology in the Artificial Intelligence Era.*

Zeigler, B. P., & Hammonds, P. E. (2007) *Modeling & Simulation-Based Data Engineering: Introducing Pragmatics into Ontologies for Net-Centric Information Exchange.* New York: Academic Press.

KEY TERMS AND DEFINITIONS

Decision Support Systems: are information systems supporting operational (business and organizational) decision-making activities of a human decision maker. The DSS shall help decision makers to compile useful information from raw data and documents that are distributed in a potentially heterogeneous IT infrastructure, personal or educational knowledge that can be static or procedural, and business models and strategies to identify and solve problems and make decisions.

Decision Support Simulation Systems: are simulation systems supporting operational (business and organizational) decision-making activities of a human decision maker by means of modeling and simulation. They use decision support system means to obtain, display and evaluate operationally relevant data in agile contexts by executing models using operational data exploiting the full potential of M&S and producing numerical insight into the behavior of complex systems.

Integratability: contends with the physical/technical realms of connections between systems, which include hardware and firmware, protocols, networks, etc. If two systems can exchange physical data with each other in a way that the target system receives and decoded the submitted data from the sending system the two systems are *integrated.*

Interoperability: contends with the software and implementation details of interoperations; this includes exchange of data elements via interfaces, the use of middleware, and mapping to common information exchange models. If two systems are integrated and the receiving system can not only decode but understand the data in a way that is meaningful to the receiving system, the systems are *interoperable*.

Composability: contends with the alignment of issues on the modeling level. The underlying models are purposeful abstractions of reality used for the conceptualization being implemented by the resulting systems. If two systems are interoperable and share assumptions and constraints in a way that the axioms of the receiving system are not violated by the sending system, the systems are *composable*.

Conceptual Modeling: is the process of defining a non-software specific formal specification of a conceptualization building the basis for the implementation of a simulation system (or another model-based implementation) describing the objectives, inputs, outputs, content, assumptions, and simplifications of the model. The conceptual model conceptual model is a bridge between the real world observations and the high-level implementation artifacts.

Validation and Verification: are processes to determine the simulation credibility. *Validation* is the process of determining the degree to which a model or simulation is an accurate representation of the real world from the perspective of the intended uses. Validation determines the behavioral and representational accuracy. *Verification* is the process of determining that a model or simulation implementation accurately represents the developer's conceptual description and specifications. Verification determines the accuracy of transformation processes.

Model-Based Data Engineering: is the process of applying documented and repeatable engineering methods for *data administration* – i.e. managing the information exchange needs including source, format, context of validity, fidelity, and credibility –, *data management* – i.e. planning, organizing and managing of data, including defining and standardizing the meaning of data and of their relations -, *data alignment* – i.e. ensuring that data to be exchanged exist in all participating systems, focusing a data provider /data consumer relations -, and *data transformation* – i.e. the technical process of mapping different representations of the same data elements to each other – supported by a common reference model.

Chapter 15
The Simulation of Spiking Neural Networks

David Gamez
Imperial College, UK

ABSTRACT

This chapter is an overview of the simulation of spiking neural networks that relates discrete event simulation to other approaches and includes a case study of recent work. The chapter starts with an introduction to the key components of the brain and sets out three neuron models that are commonly used in simulation work. After explaining discrete event, continuous and hybrid simulation, the performance of each method is evaluated and recent research is discussed. To illustrate the issues surrounding this work, the second half of this chapter presents a case study of the SpikeStream neural simulator that covers the architecture, performance and typical applications of this software along with some recent experiments. The last part of the chapter suggests some future trends for work in this area.

INTRODUCTION

In recent years there has been a great deal of interest in the simulation of neural networks to test our theories about the brain, and these models are also being used in a wide variety of applications ranging from data mining to machine vision and robot control. In the past the majority of these simulations were based on the neurons' average firing rate and there is now a growing interest in the development of more biologically realistic spiking models, which

present their own challenges and are well suited to discrete event simulation.

This chapter starts with some background information about the operation of neurons and synapses in the brain and sets out some of the reasons why simulation plays an important role in neuroscience research. Next, some common neural models are examined and the chapter moves on to look at the differences between continuous simulation, discrete event simulation and the emerging hybrid approach. The issues in this area are then illustrated with a more detailed look at the SpikeStream neural simulator that covers its architecture, performance, typical

DOI: 10.4018/978-1-60566-774-4.ch015

Figure 1. Two connected neurons

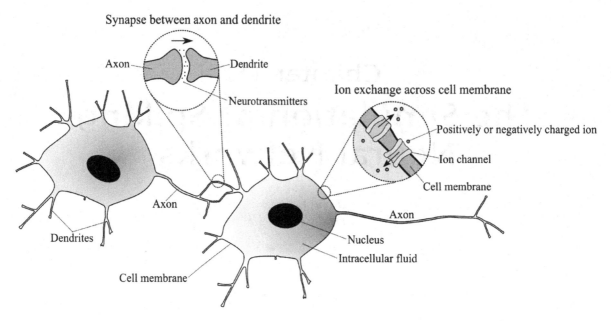

applications and recent experiments. Finally, the chapter concludes with some likely future directions for work in this area.

NEURAL SIMULATION

Neurons and the Brain

The main information-processing elements in the human brain are 80 billion cells called neurons that are organized into a highly complex structure of nuclei and layers that process different types of information.[1] Neurons send signals to each other along fibres known as axons, which connect to the dendrites of other neurons at junctions called synapses, as shown in Figure 1.

The body of each neuron is surrounded by a cell membrane that separates the nucleus and intracellular fluid from the extracellular fluid outside the cell. The cell membrane is crossed by porous channels that allow ions, such as sodium and potassium, to be exchanged with the extracellular fluid. Since these ions have a positive or negative charge, their movement through the

cell membrane alters the voltage across it and neurons actively manage this voltage by pumping ions across the cell membrane so that the voltage remains at around -70 millivolts – a value known as the resting potential.

Neurons communicate by sending pulses of electrical energy along their axons that are known as spikes. When a spike reaches the dendrite of another neuron it increases that neuron's voltage, and if the voltage passes a threshold of about -50 millivolts, then the neuron 'fires' and emits a pulse or spike of electrical activity that is transmitted to other neurons. Since axons and dendrites have different lengths, these spikes take different amounts of time to propagate between neurons, and once a neuron has fired there is a period know as the refractory period in which it is unresponsive or less responsive to incoming spikes (see Figure 2). In the human brain each neuron fires at around 1-5 Hz and sends spikes to between 3,000 and 13,000 other neurons (Binzegger, Douglas and Martin, 2004), leading to approximately 10^{22} spike events per second.

The axon of one neuron connects to the dendrite of another at a junction known as a synapse. When

Figure 2. Change in the voltage across a neuron's cell membrane over time

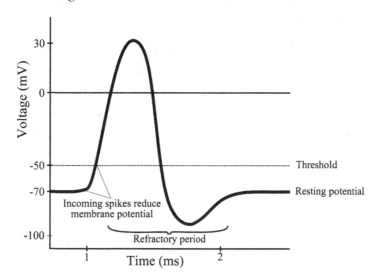

a spike reaches a synapse, the change in voltage causes a chemical called a neurotransmitter to be released, which crosses the synaptic junction and changes the voltage of the receiving neuron. Depending on the amount and type of neurotransmitter, the spike from one neuron can have a large or small effect on another, and in many neuron models this is expressed by saying that each synapse has a particular *weight*. Although there are a number of different learning mechanisms in the brain, most research on neural networks focuses on models that use changes in the synapses' weights to store information. One of the most widely used methods for learning weights in spiking networks is called spike time dependent plasticity (STDP). This algorithm increases the weight of a synapse when a spike arrives just before the firing of a neuron, because it is assumed that the spike has contributed to the neuron's firing. When a spike arrives just after the neuron has fired the weight is decreased because the synapse has not contributed to the neuron's activity.

A comprehensive theory about how the brain works should be able to explain how the interac-

tions between billions of neurons produce human behaviour. As part of the research on this area a lot of anatomical work has been carried out on humans and animals in order to understand the large scale connections in the brain, and studies of brain-damaged patients have revealed a great deal about the specialized processing of different brain areas. The detailed behaviour of individual neurons has also been measured using in vitro neuron preparations, and electrodes have been implanted into the brains of living animals and humans to record from individual neurons as they interact with their environment. However, whilst electrodes have good spatial and temporal resolution, it is only possible to use a few hundred at a time, which severely limits the amount of information that can be gathered by this method.

In recent years, a great deal of progress has been made with the development of non-invasive scanning systems, such as PET or fMRI, that provide an almost real time picture of brain activity. These technologies have helped us to understand the specializations and interactions of different brain areas, but they are limited by the fact that their maximum spatial resolution is about $1\,mm^3$, which represents the average activity of approximately 50,000 neurons, and their maximum temporal resolution is of the order of 1 second.

This limited access to neurons in the brain has led many researchers to work on large scale neural simulations and in the longer term it is hoped that this type of model will be able to predict the behaviour of neural tissue and greatly increase our understanding of the brain's functions. Many neural simulations have also been carried out in engineering and computer science as part of work on machine learning, computer vision and robotics.

Neuron and Synapse Models

In the past the majority of neural simulations modelled neurons' average firing rates and propagated these firing rates from neuron to neuron at each time step. Although this type of model is not particularly biologically realistic, it can be used for brain-inspired models of populations of neurons - see, for example, Krichmar, Nitz, Gally and Edelman, (2005) – and it has been used extensively in machine learning and robotics. More recently, an increase in computer power and the recognition that spike timing plays an important part in the neural code (Mass and Bishop, 1999) have motivated more researchers to simulate spiking neurons.

The most detailed spiking neural models are typically based on an approach put forward by Hodgkin and Huxley (1952), who treated the cell membrane as a capacitor and interpreted the movement of ions through the channels as different currents. In the standard Hodgkin-Huxley model there is a sodium channel, Na^+, a potassium channel, K^+, and an unspecific leakage channel that has resistance R. The rate of change of the voltage, V, across a neuron's membrane is given by equation (1):

$$C\frac{dV}{dt} = -\sum_k I_k(t) + I(t) \tag{1}$$

where C is the capacitance, $I(t)$ is the applied current at time t, and $\sum_k I_k$ is the sum of the ionic currents across the cell membrane. Since the resistance of the leakage channel is independent of the voltage, its conductance, g_L, can be expressed as the inverse of the resistance (2):

$$g_L = \frac{1}{R} \tag{2}$$

The conductance of the other channels depends on the voltage, V, and changes over time. When all the channels are open they transmit with maximum conductance g_{Na} or g_K. However, some of the channels are usually blocked and the probability that a channel is open is described by the variables m, n and h, where m and h control the Na^+ channels and n controls the K^+ channels. The behaviour of the variables m, n, and h is specified by equations (3), (4) and (5):

$$\frac{dm}{dt} = \alpha_m(V)(1-m) - \beta_m(V)m \tag{3}$$

$$\frac{dn}{dt} = \alpha_n(V)(1-n) - \beta_n(V)n \tag{4}$$

$$\frac{dh}{dt} = \alpha_h(V)(1-h) - \beta_h(V)h \tag{5}$$

where α and β are empirical functions of the voltage that were adjusted by Hodgkin and Huxley to fit their measurements of the squid's giant axon (see Table 1). Putting all of this together, the sum of the three current components is expressed in equation (6):

$$\sum_k I_k = g_{Na}m^3h(V - E_{Na}) + g_K n^4(V - E_K) + g_L(V - E_L) \tag{6}$$

Table 1. Parameters of the Hodgkin-Huxley equations (adapted from Gerstner and Kistler, 2002, p. 36)

Parameter	Value
α_m	$(2.5 - 0.1V) / [\exp(2.5 - 0.1V) - 1]$
α_n	$(0.1 - 0.01V) / [\exp(1 - 0.1V) - 1]$
α_h	$0.07 \exp(-V/20)$
β_m	$4 \exp(-V/18)$
β_n	$0.125 \exp(-V/80)$
β_h	$1 / [\exp(3 - 0.1V) + 1]$
E_{Na}	115 mV
E_K	-12 mV
E_L	10.6 mV
g_{Na}	120 mS/cm²
g_K	36 mS/cm²
g_L	0.3 mS/cm²
C	1 μF/cm²

where E_{Na}, E_K and E_L are parameters based on the empirical data and given in Table 1. The complex morphology of neurons' axons and dendrites is modelled by treating them as a series of interconnected compartments whose electrical properties are calculated at each time step, and more recent models include a number of different types and distributions of ion channels and the details of individual synapses. This type of modelling is very computationally expensive and it can only be carried out for a small number of neurons on a single computer, or using supercomputers for larger simulations.

A less accurate, but more computationally efficient approach is to treat each neuron as a point and use internal variables to represent the membrane potential and other attributes. One common point neuron model is the Spike Response Model (Gerstner and Kistler, 2002; Marian, 2003), which has three components: a leaky integrate and fire of the weights of incoming spikes, an absolute refractory period in which the neuron ignores incoming spikes, and a relative refractory period in which it is harder for spikes to push the neuron beyond its threshold potential. The resting poten-

tial of the neuron is zero and when it exceeds the threshold the neuron fires and the contributions from previous spikes are reset to zero. The voltage V_i at time t for a neuron i that last fired at $\hat{t}$ is given by equation (7):

$$V_i(t) = \sum_j \sum_f w_{ij} e^{-\frac{(t-t_j^{(f)})}{\tau_m}} - e^{n-(t-i_i)^m} H'(t - \hat{t}_i) \tag{7}$$

where ω_{ij} is the synaptic weight between i and j, τ_m is the membrane time constant, f is the last firing time of neuron j, m and n are parameters controlling the relative refractory period, and H' is given by equation (8):

$$H'(t - \hat{t}_i) = \begin{cases} \infty, & if\ 0 \le (t-\hat{t}_i) < \rho \\ 1, & otherwise \end{cases} \tag{8}$$

in which ρ is the absolute refractory period. The Spike Response Model is particularly good for event-based simulation because its equations can be used to calculate the voltage across the cell membrane retrospectively after a spike has been received.

A second widely used point neuron model was put forward by Izhikevich (2003). In this model the voltage V of a neuron at time t with a time step ts is given by equations (9), (10) and (11):

$$V_{t+ts} = V_t + ts(0.04V_t^2 + 5V_t + 140 - u_t + I) \quad (9)$$

$$u_{t+ts} = u_t + a(bV_{t+ts} - u_t) \quad (10)$$

if($V_t >= 30$ mV); then

$$V_t = c$$

$$u = u + d \quad (11)$$

where u is a membrane recovery variable representing the sodium and potassium currents, and a, b, c and d are parameters that are used to tune the behaviour of the neuron. Izhikevich claims that this model can reproduce the behaviour of a number of different types of neuron, but it has the disadvantage that it is more complicated to use with discrete event simulation. Both the Spike Response Model and Izhikevich's model are typically used in conjunction with basic synapses that pass on their weight to the neuron when they receive a spike, possibly with some learning behaviour.

Continuous Simulation of Spiking Neural Networks

Continuous simulation is also known as time-driven or synchronous simulation and its defining feature is that updates to the model are driven by the advance of a simulation clock.[2] At each time step the states of all the neurons and synapses are calculated, spikes are transmitted to other neurons, the time step is advanced and then the process is repeated again. These steps in a continuous simulation are summarized below:

- Initialize each component of the model.
- Advance the time step by a fixed amount. Time steps of 0.1 ms or 1 ms are typically used with spiking neural networks.

- Propagate spikes generated in the previous time step to the appropriate synapses and neurons, possibly with a delay.
- Update the states of all the neurons and synapses.
- Return to step 2 or terminate simulation if the maximum amount of time has been reached.

One of the main computational costs of continuous simulation is the update of all the neurons and synapses at each time step, which scales linearly with the number of updates and depends on the complexity of the models. In continuous simulation the propagation of spikes with different delays can be handled using a circular buffer[3] that requires a store and retrieve operation in memory for each spike, and this has a cost that scales linearly with the number of spikes. For a network of N neurons firing F times per second with an average connectivity per neuron P, the cost per second of simulated time is given in equation (12):[4]

$$\frac{C_N \times N}{ts} + \frac{C_S \times N \times P}{ts} + C_P \times F \times N \times P \quad (12)$$

where C_N is the cost of updating a neuron, C_S is the cost of updating a synapse, C_P is the cost of propagating a single delayed spike, and ts is the time step duration in seconds. The first part of (12) is the cost of updating all of the neurons at each time step, which is likely to be high for complex neuron models. The central part is the cost of updating all of the synapses at each time step and although synapse models are generally much less complex than neuron models, these synapse updates can incur a considerable cost because there can be up to 10,000 synapses per neuron in a biologically realistic simulation. The last part of (12) is the cost of propagating the spikes and passing the synapses' weights to the neurons. The cost of propagation, C_P, will be low if a circular buffer is used for the delays and the spikes' weights are simply added to the neurons' voltages. However, if the network activity or connectivity is high, then there will be a large number of spike events to process each second, and the rate of propagating the spikes will be limited by the speed of the computer network if the simulation is distributed across several machines.

One of the main advantages of continuous simulation is that it is generally easier to implement than discrete event simulation - especially when working in parallel across multiple machines - and it is good for neural models that generate spontaneous activity, such as the Hodgkin-Huxley and Izhikevich models discussed earlier. Continuous simulation can also be equally or more efficient than discrete event simulation when there are a large number of events, although it is often much less efficient when events are sparse or the neuron model is complicated, because of the updates to all the neurons and synapses at each time step.

The main disadvantage of the continuous approach is that the resolution of the time step limits the performance and accuracy of the simulation. Continuous simulations with a large time step will model a given amount of time faster than simulations with a small time step, but larger time steps can substantially alter the behaviour of the network by changing whether spikes arrive inside or outside the neurons' refractory periods.[5] Furthermore, the simultaneous transmission of spikes at each time step leads to an unnatural clustering at low time step resolutions that affects the learning behaviour.[6] Against these problems, Brette et al. (2007) argue that since neurons have no effect on each other within the minimum spike transmission delay, it should be possible to produce accurate simulations by setting the time step to this value. However, to make this work without loss of accuracy, the spikes within each time step have to be sorted and dealt with in an event-based manner.

The continuous approach is often used to simulate spiking neural networks based on

Hodgkin-Huxley models that would be difficult to handle using discrete event simulation. A good example of this type of work is the Blue Brain project (Markram, 2006), which is attempting to produce a biologically accurate model of a single cortical column of 10,000 neurons interconnected with 30 million synapses. This project is simulating these neurons on an IBM Blue Gene supercomputer containing 8192 processors and 2 TB of RAM – a total of 22 x 1012 teraflops processing power. The first simulation of a rat's cortical column was carried out in 2006 and it is currently running at about two orders of magnitude slower than real time. The main objective of this project is to reproduce the behaviour of in vitro rat tissue, and so the stimulation is not connected to sensory input and it has not been used to control the behaviour of a real or virtual robot. Continuous simulation has also been used by Izhikevich and Edelman (2008) to create an anatomically realistic neural network based on Izhikevich's model with one million neurons and half a billion synapses. This simulation ran sixty times slower than real time and was carried out on a Beowulf cluster with 60 3GHz processors and a total of 90 GB RAM.

Discrete Event Simulation of Spiking Neural Networks

The characteristic feature of discrete event simulation is that updates to the model are event-driven instead of clock-driven, and this type of simulation typically works by maintaining a queue of events that are sorted by the time at which they are scheduled to occur. The simulation engine reads the next event, advances the clock to the time specified by the event, updates the model, and then adds new events to the queue at the correct position. Discrete event simulation is considerably easier when spontaneous neural activity is not required – for example, when using the Spike Response Model – and in this case the only events that need to be handled are the arrival of spikes at neurons, with a typical simulation following the steps outlined below.

1. Add initial spike events to the event queue sorted by the time at which they are scheduled to occur.
2. Extract the spike event with the lowest time from the front of the event queue.
3. Advance the simulation clock to the time specified by the event.
4. Update the states of the neurons and synapses that are affected by the spike.
5. If any of the updated neurons fire, insert appropriate spike events into the queue.
6. Return to step 2 or terminate simulation if the queue is empty or if the maximum time has elapsed.

With neuron models that generate spontaneous activity, such as Izhikevich (2003), neuron firing can happen independently of incoming spikes and the simulation engine has to predict when each neuron will fire and handle these predictions as separate events. Whilst spike arrivals are events that definitely happen once they have been added to the event queue, predictions about neurons' firing times are uncertain because spike arrivals can advance or retard the predicted times. These uncertain events are typically handled by adding them to a second event queue and events in this second queue are made certain when no earlier spike events are scheduled to occur. This approach is similar to three phase activity scanning (Banks, Carson II, Nelson and Nicol, 2005) and the algorithm is given below.[7]

1. Add initial spike events to the spike event queue.
2. Predict the times at which the neurons will spontaneously fire and add these events to the second event queue.
3. If the next spike event is scheduled to occur earlier than the next neuron firing event.

4. Extract the spike event with the lowest timing from the front of the spike event queue.
5. Advance the simulation clock to the time specified by the event.
6. Update the states of the neurons and synapses that are affected by the spike.
7. Update the predicted firing times of the neurons that are affected by the spike.
8. Return to step 3 or terminate simulation if the maximum time has elapsed or there are no events left to process in both queues.
9. Else if no spike events are scheduled to occur earlier than the next neuron firing event.
10. Extract the neuron firing event with the lowest timing from the front of the second queue.
11. Add spikes generated by this event to the spike event list.
12. Update the predicted firing time of the neuron.
13. Return to step 3 or terminate simulation if the maximum time has elapsed or there are no events left to process in both queues.

If each neuron fires at rate F and connects on average to another P neurons, then the firing of a neuron generates $P \times F$ spike events that have to be inserted into the first queue in the correct order with a cost C_{Q1} for each event. When the spikes from a neuron are processed, the predicted firing times of all neurons connected to the firing neuron have to be revised in the second queue, with each access and update to the neurons in the second queue having a cost C_{Q2}. The processing of each spike event also triggers the updates of the associated synapse and neuron, which incurs costs C_S and C_N. Putting this together, the total cost of discrete event simulation of N neurons for one second of simulated time is given by equation (13):[8]

$$F \times N \times P \times (C_N + C_S + C_{Q1} + C_{Q2}) \qquad (13)$$

Since the time resolution of the events can be specified precisely without incurring a performance penalty, discrete event simulation avoids many of the accuracy problems that are associated with the continuous approach. When there are sparse events (i.e. N and/or P are low) discrete event simulation can be very efficient, but when event rates are high, the management of the event queues can become a major performance bottleneck - for example, a simulation of a network of 10,000 neurons firing at 5 Hz with 10,000 connections per neuron has to handle a billion events per simulated second. Although there are data structures in which the enqueue and dequeue operations take constant average time (Brown, 1988; Claverol, Brown and Chad, 2002), the cost of each operation in these types of queue can be high, and with simpler queue implementations, such as binary heaps, the cost of the enqueue and dequeue operations varies with the logarithm of the number of events. Event-based simulation has the further disadvantage that it can be difficult to distribute the event queues over multiple computers.

One of the better known event-based spiking simulators is MVASpike, which is a simulation library written in C++ that comes with a number of different neuron models and STDP learning. This simulator can be controlled using a high level scripting language, such as Python, and it was used by Tonnelier, Belmabrouk and Martinez (2007) to model a network with 1000 neurons and 10^6 connections. A second discrete event simulator is SpikeSNNS, which is based around a single event queue and was used by Marian (2003) to model the development of eye-hand coordination in a network with several hundred neurons. Other work in this area has been carried out by Mattia and Del Guidice (2000), who developed an efficient event-driven algorithm based around a discrete set of ordered delays and demonstrated it on a network of 15,000 neurons that ran approximately 150 times slower than real time. There is also the research of Reutimann, Giugliano and Fusi (2003), who

extended the event-driven strategy to efficiently handle the noisy background activity that is typically found in biological networks.

Hybrid Strategies

Over the last few years a number of simulators have emerged that are based on a hybrid approach, which combines some of the benefits of continuous and discrete event simulation and avoids many of their limitations. The most common hybrid strategy is to make the update of the synapses and possibly the neurons event driven, and to maintain a continuous simulation clock that delays the spikes and avoids the inefficiencies of event queues. The algorithm for this type of hybrid strategy is as follows.

1. Initialize each component of the model.
2. Advance the time step by a fixed amount. Time steps of 0.1 ms or 1 ms are typically used with spiking neural networks.
3. Propagate spikes generated in the previous time step, possibly with a delay.
4. Update the states of the neurons and synapses that are affected by the spikes.
5. Return to step 2 or terminate simulation if the maximum amount of time has been reached.

Hybrid strategies often work by dividing the network into a number of neuron groups that can be distributed across several machines, and the synchronization between the different groups is achieved through the exchange of spike lists at each time step.

The computational cost of the hybrid strategy consists of the cost of updating each neuron and synapse that receives a spike, C_N and C_S, and the cost of propagating each delayed spike C_P. For a network of N neurons firing F times per second with an average connectivity per neuron P, the update cost per second of simulated time is given by equation (14):

$$F \times N \times P(C_N + C_S + C_P) + \frac{C_{ts}}{ts} \qquad (14)$$

where C_{ts} is the cost of advancing the time step and ts is the time step resolution in seconds. The advance of the time step has a very small cost and on a single computer the cost of spike propagation is also reasonably low since the delays in spike transmission can be efficiently managed using a circular buffer. However, when the network is distributed across several machines the exchange of spike lists can consume a large amount of processing power and network bandwidth, especially when there are multiple delays. This problem can be reduced by managing the delays of incoming spikes locally on each machine and spike list buffering can also be used to improve the efficiency of message exchange.[9]

When the connectivity and/or neuron firing rate is low the event-driven update of the neurons leads to substantial performance gains, but with biological firing rates and levels of connectivity, the neurons become updated at the same rate as they would in a continuous simulation, or even at a greater rate. Event-driven neuron updates are also not possible with neuron models that generate spontaneous activity, such as those of Hodgkin-Huxley and Izhikevich. Since synapses receive events at a much lower rate than neurons, it is generally always advantageous to make the update of the synapses event driven, which can reduce the simulation cost by several orders of magnitude. The hybrid approach still suffers from the accuracy problems of continuous simulation, but since hybrid simulation is more efficient, the time step can be set to a high resolution without incurring a major performance penalty, and it is also possible to use an event-based approach within each time step to deliver events with a higher precision than the time step resolution.[10]

SpikeNET was one of the first hybrid neural simulators to be developed and it could simulate 400,000 neurons and 19 million connections in real time with a time step resolution of 1 ms and a firing rate of 1 Hz (Delorme and Thorpe, 2003). Whilst the SpikeNET architecture was influential, the free version was not widely used because of a number of critical limitations, such as a lack of spike delay and a poor user interface.[11] A second well-known hybrid simulator is NEST, which has been under development for a number of years and has been used for biologically inspired simulations by a number of researchers. Simulation runs are set up in NEST using a proprietary scripting language and it can simulate a network of 100,000 neurons and 1 billion connections with an average firing rate of 2.5 Hz at approximately 400 times real time using 8 processors (Morrison et al., 2005). A third example of a hybrid simulator is SpikeStream, which works along broadly similar lines to SpikeNET and NEST and will now be covered in more detail.

THE SPIKESTREAM NEURAL SIMULATOR

Introduction

SpikeStream is a hybrid neural simulator that was developed as part of the CRONOS project to build a conscious robot. It has good performance and a considerable amount of effort was put into the development of a good graphical interface that enables users to view the neuron activity as the simulation runs and fine tune the parameters of the model. SpikeStream was designed for robotic work and it can exchange streams of spikes with external devices over a network. The key features of SpikeStream are as follows:

- Written in C++ using Qt for the graphical user interface.
- Database storage.
- Parallel distributed operation.
- Sophisticated visualisation, editing and monitoring tools.
- Modular architecture.

- Variable delays.
- Dynamic synapses.
- Dynamic class loading.
- Live operation.
- Spike exchange with external devices over a network.

This overview of SpikeStream starts with its architecture and graphical interface and then moves on to its performance and communication with external devices. Some application areas and recent experiments are also covered along with some information about the SpikeStream release under the terms of the GPL license.

Architecture

SpikeStream is built with a modular architecture that enables it to operate across an arbitrary number of machines and allows third party applications to make use of its editing, archiving and simulation functions. The main components of the architecture are a number of databases, the graphical SpikeStream Application, programs to carry out simulation and archiving functions, and dynamically loaded neuron and synapse classes.

Databases

SpikeStream is organized around a number of databases that hold information about the network model, patterns and devices. This makes it easy to launch simulations across a variable number of machines and provides a great deal of flexibility in the creation of connection patterns. The SpikeStream databases are as follows:

- *Neural Network*. Each neuron has a unique ID and connections between neurons are stored as a combination of the presynaptic and postsynaptic neuron IDs. The available neuron and synapse types along with their parameters are also held in this database.

- *Patterns*. Holds spatiotemporal patterns that can be applied to the network for training or testing.
- *Neural Archive*. Stores archived neuron firing patterns. Each archive contains an XML description of the network and data in XML format.
- *Devices*. The devices that SpikeStream can exchange spikes with over a network.

These databases are edited by SpikeStream Application and used to set up the simulation run. They can also be edited by third party applications – for example, to create custom connection patterns or neuron arrangements - without affecting SpikeStream's ability to visualize and simulate the network.

Graphical User Interface

An intuitive graphical user interface has been written for SpikeStream with the following features (see Figure 3):

- *Editing*. Neuron and connection groups can be created and deleted.
- *3D Visualisation*. Neuron and connection groups are rendered in 3D using OpenGL and they can be rotated, selectively hidden or shown, and their individual details displayed. The user can drill down to information about a single synapse or view all of the connections simultaneously.
- *Simulation*. The simulation tab has controls to start and stop simulations and vary the speed at which they run. Neuron and synapse parameters can be set, patterns and external devices connected and noise injected into the system.
- *Monitoring*. Firing and spiking patterns can be monitored and variables, such as a neuron's voltage, graphically displayed.
- *Archiving*. Archived simulation runs can be loaded and played back.

Figure 3. SpikeStream graphical user interface. The numbers indicate the following features: (1) Dialog for monitoring the firing of neurons in a layer, (2) Dialog for monitoring variables inside the neurons, such as the calcium concentration and voltage, (3) 3D network view, (4) Simulation controls, (5) Dialog for viewing and setting the noise in the network, (6) Dialog for viewing and setting neuron parameters.

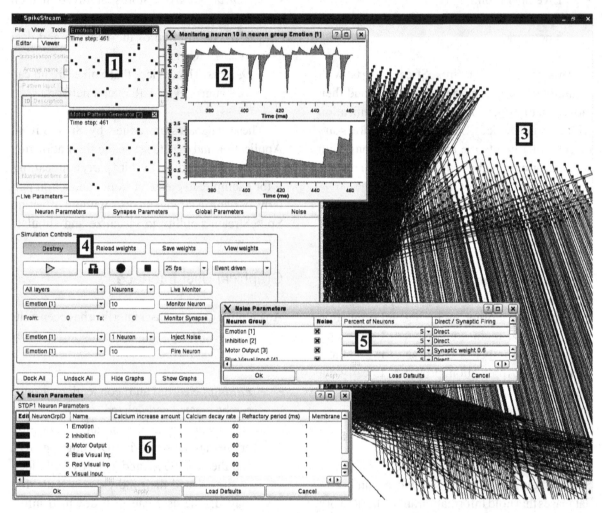

Much more information about the graphical features of SpikeStream can be found in the manual that is included with the release.

Simulation Engine

The SpikeStream simulator is based on the SpikeNET architecture and it consists of a number of processes that are launched and coordinated using PVM, with each process modelling a group of neurons using the hybrid approach. The spikes exchanged between neurons are a compressed version of the presynaptic and postsynaptic neuron IDs, which enables each spike to be uniquely routed to a class simulating an individual synapse, and variable delays are created using a circular buffer.

Unlike the majority of neural simulation tools, SpikeStream can operate in a live mode in which the neuron models are calculated using real time instead of simulation time. This enables SpikeStream to control robots that are interacting

Table 2. Test networks

	Small network	Medium network	Large network
Neurons	4,000	10,000	19,880
Connections	321,985	1,999,360	19,760,878

with the real world and to process input from live data sources, such as cameras and microphones. Although SpikeStream is primarily a hybrid simulator, it can update all of the neurons and/or synapses at each time step to accommodate neuron models that generate spontaneous activity.

Archiver

During a simulation run, the firing patterns of the network can be recorded by SpikeStream Archiver, which stores lists of spikes or firing neurons in XML format along with a simple version of the network model.

Neuron and Synapse Classes

Neuron and synapse classes are implemented as dynamically loaded libraries, which makes it easy to experiment with different neuron and synapse models without recompiling the whole application. Each dynamically loadable class is associated with a parameter table in the database, which makes it easy to change parameters during a simulation run. The current distribution of SpikeStream includes neuron and synapse classes implementing the Spike Response Model and Brader, Senn and Fusi's (2007) STDP learning rule.

Performance

The performance of SpikeStream was measured using three test networks put forward by Brette et al. (2007). These networks contained 4,000, 10,000 and 20,000 neurons that were randomly interconnected with a 2% probability (see Table 2), and they were divided into four layers to enable

them to be distributed across multiple machines. The Spike Response Model was used in these tests along with a basic synapse model.

At the beginning of each simulation run the networks were driven by random external current until their activity became self sustaining and then their performance was measured over repeated runs of 300 seconds. The first two networks were tested on one and two Pentium IV 3.2 GHz machines connected using a megabit switch with time step values of 0.1 and 1.0 ms. The third network could only be tested on two machines because its memory requirements exceeded that available on a single machine. All of the tests were run without any learning, monitoring or archiving.[12]

The results from these tests are plotted in Figure 4, which shows the amount of time taken to simulate one second of biological time for each test network. In this graph the performance difference between 0.1 and 1.0 ms time step resolution is partly due to the fact that ten times more time steps were processed at 0.1 ms resolution, but since SpikeStream is a hybrid simulator, the processing of a time step is not a particularly expensive operation. The performance difference between 0.1 and 1.0 ms time step resolution was mainly caused by changes in the networks' dynamics that were brought about by the lower time step resolution, which reduced the average firing frequency of the networks by the amounts given in Table 3.

The differences in average firing frequency shown in Table 3 suggest that the relationship between real and biological time needs to be combined with other performance measures for event-based simulators. To address this issue, the number of spikes processed in each second of real

Figure 4. Time taken to compute one second of biological time for one and two machines using time step resolutions of 0.1 and 1 ms

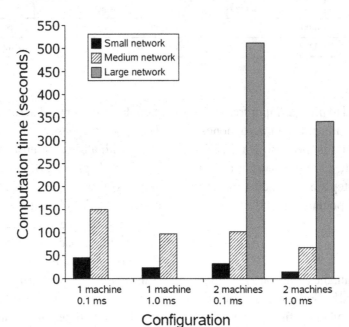

time was also measured and plotted in Figure 5. This graph shows that SpikeStream can handle between 800,000 and 1.2 million spike events per second on a single machine and between 1.2 million and 1.8 million spike events per second on two machines for the networks that were tested. Figure 4 and Figure 5 both show that the performance increased when the processing load was distributed over multiple machines, but with network speed as a key limiting factor, multiple cores are likely to work better than multiple networked machines.

Most of the performance measurements for other simulators that are cited by Brette et al. (2007) are for different neuron and synapse models, and so they cannot be meaningfully compared with

the SpikeStream results. The only results that are directly comparable are those for NEST, which are given by Brette et al. (2007, Figure 10B) for two machines. On the 4,000 neuron network NEST takes 1 second to compute 1 second of biological time when the synapse delay is 1 ms and 7.5 seconds to compute 1 second of biological time when the synapse delay is 0.125 ms. Compared with this, SpikeStream takes either 14 or 30 seconds to simulate 1 second of biological time, depending on whether the time step resolution is 1.0 or 0.1 ms, and these SpikeStream results are independent of the amount of delay.

A second point of comparison for the performance of SpikeStream is SpikeNET. The lack of a common benchmark makes comparison diffi-

Table 3. Average firing frequencies in simulation time at different time step resolutions

Time step resolution	Small network	Medium network	Large network
0.1 ms	109 Hz	72 Hz	40 Hz
1.0 ms	79 Hz	58 Hz	30 Hz

Figure 5. Number of spikes processed per second of real time for one and two machines using time step resolutions of 0.1 and 1 ms

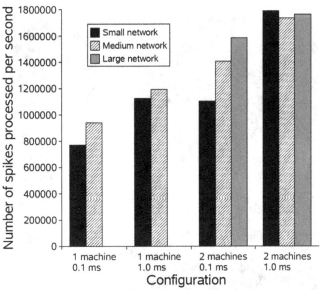

cult, but Delorme and Thorpe (2003) claim that SpikeNET can simulate approximately 19.6 million spike events per second, whereas SpikeStream can handle a maximum of 1.2 million spike events per second on a single PC for the networks tested (see Figure 5). This measurement for SpikeNET was obtained using a substantially slower machine, and its performance would probably be at least 40 million spike events per second today.

External Devices

One of the unique features of SpikeStream is that it can pass spikes over a network to and from external devices, such as cameras and real and virtual robots, in a number of different ways:

- *Synchronized TCP*. Spikes are exchanged with the device at each time step. SpikeStream and the external device only move forward when they have both completed their processing for the time step.

- *Loosely synchronized UDP*. Spikes are sent and received continuously to and from the external device with the rate of the simulation determined by the rate of arrival of the spike messages.

- *Unsynchronized UDP*. Spikes are sent and received continuously from the external device. This option is designed for live work with robots.

The main external device that has been used and tested with SpikeStream is the SIMNOS virtual robot (see Figure 6), which is simulated in soft real time using NVIDIA PhysX and has an internal structure based on the human musculoskeletal system (Gamez, Newcombe, Holland and Knight, 2006).[13] Visual data, muscle lengths and joint angles are encoded by SIMNOS into spikes that are sent across a computer network to SpikeStream, where they are used to directly fire neurons or change their voltage. SIMNOS also receives muscle length data from SpikeStream in the form of spiking neural events, which are used

Figure 6. SIMNOS virtual robot. The lines are the virtual muscles whose lengths are sent as spikes to SpikeStream. The outlines of spheres with arrows are the joint angles, which are also sent as spikes to SpikeStream

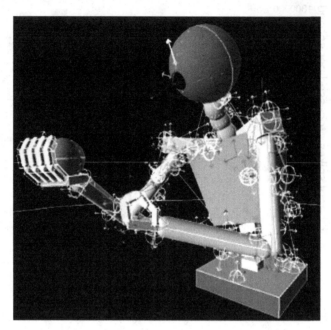

to control the virtual robot. Together SIMNOS and SpikeStream provide an extremely powerful way of exploring sensory and motor processing and integration.

Applications

SpikeStream's performance and flexibility make it suitable for a number of applications:

- *Biologically-inspired robotics*. Spiking neural networks developed in SpikeStream can be used to process sensory data from real or virtual robots and generate motor patterns. A good example of this type of work is that carried out by Krichmar et al. (2005) on the Darwin series of robots.
- *Genetic algorithms*. The openness of SpikeStream's architecture makes it easy to write genetic algorithms that edit the database to create new neural networks and automatically run simulations to identify

which network is best at performing a specific task.

- *Models of consciousness and cognition*. Dehaene and Changeux (2005) and Shanahan (2008) have built models of consciousness and cognition based on the brain that could be implemented in SpikeStream. A comprehensive review of this type of work can be found in Gamez (2008a).
- *Neuromorphic engineering*. SpikeStream's dynamic class loading architecture makes it easy to test neuron and synapse models prior to their implementation in silicon. Initial work has already been done on enabling SpikeStream to read and write address event representation (AER) events, which would enable it to be integrated into AER chains, such as those developed by the CAVIAR Project.
- *Teaching*. Once installed SpikeStream is well documented and easy to use, which makes it a good tool for teaching students

Figure 7. Experimental setup with the eye of SIMNOS in front of a red and blue cube. Spikes sent from the network control the pan and tilt of SIMNOS's eye and spikes containing red or blue visual information are received from SIMNOS and used to stimulate neurons corresponding to the location of the red or blue data in the visual field

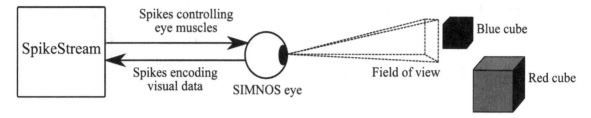

about biologically structured neural networks and robotics.

In a recent set of experiments carried out by Gamez (2008b) SpikeStream was used to simulate a network with 17,544 neurons and 698,625 connections that controlled the eye movements of the SIMNOS virtual robot. The experimental setup is shown in Figure 7.

The network was organized into ten layers whose overall purpose was to direct SIMNOS's eye towards 'positive' red features of its environment and away from 'negative' blue objects. To carry out this task it included an 'emotion' layer that responded differently to red and blue stimuli and neurons that learnt the association between motor actions and visual input. These neurons were used to 'imagine' different eye movements and select the ones that were predicted to result in a positive visual stimulus. The connections between the layers are shown in Figure 8.

The first part of the experiments was a training phase in which the network learnt the association between motor output and visual input. During this training phase spontaneous activity in Motor Cortex changed the position of SIMNOS's eye, copies of the motor signals were sent from Motor Integration to Red/ Blue Sensorimotor, and the synapse classes on these connections used Brader et al.'s (2007) rule to learn the association between an eye movement and red and blue visual input.

After training, Motor Cortex moved SIMNOS's eye around at random until a blue object appeared in its visual field. This switched the network into its offline 'imagination' mode, in which it generated motor patterns and 'imagined' the red or blue visual input that was associated with these potential eye movements. This process continued until it 'imagined' a red visual stimulus that positively stimulated Emotion. This removed the inhibition, and SIMNOS's eye was moved to look at the red stimulus. Full details about the experiments are given in Gamez (2008b).

This work was inspired by other simulations of the neural correlates of consciousness, such as Dehaene and Changeux (2005) and Shanahan (2008), and it shows how spiking neural networks can model cognitive characteristics, such as imagination and emotion, and control eye movements in an 'intelligent' way. In the future more sophisticated versions of this network might be able to teach themselves new behaviours by 'imagining' different motor actions and choosing to execute the one that has the most positive effect on their emotion systems.

Release

SpikeStream is available for free download under the terms of the GPL license. The current (0.1) release has 25,000 source lines of code,[14] full source code documentation, a mailing list for SpikeStream users, and a comprehensive 80

Figure 8. Neural network with SIMNOS eye. Arrows indicate connections within layers, between layers or between the neural network and SIMNOS

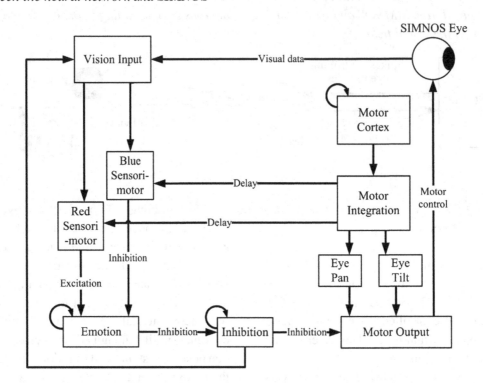

page manual. SpikeStream is also available pre-installed on a virtual machine, which works on all operating systems supported by VMware and can be run using the free VMware Player. More information about the release is available at the SpikeStream website.

FUTURE TRENDS

The measurement of living neurons is likely to be a problem for many years to come, and so neural simulations will continue to play an important role in neuroscience, where they provide a valuable way of testing theories about the brain. As computer power increases it should be possible to simulate networks with millions of neurons based on Hodgkin-Huxley models, and this type of work is likely to be carried out using the continuous approach. Although point neurons are less biologically realistic than Hodgkin-Huxley models, they are much easier to simulate and understand, and over the next few years there is likely to be much more research that models millions and possibly billions of point neurons using the hybrid approach.

Large simulations are rarely needed in less biologically inspired applications, such as machine learning and robotics, where relatively small numbers of neurons can be used to identify patterns or control a robot arm - for example, see Tani (2008). For this type of research there will be an increasing need for more user-friendly simulators, such as SpikeStream, that can exchange data with external devices and allow the user to adjust the behaviour of the network as it runs.

Over the next few years there is likely to be significant progress with the development of large scale neural models in silicon. One example of this type of work is the Neurogrid system, which uses analogue silicon circuits to emulate neurons' ion-channels and routes the spikes digitally.[15] Neurogrid is still under development and it should eventually be able to model a million neurons and six billion synapses (Silver, Boahen, Grillner, Kopell and Olsen, 2007). Another significant hardware project is SpiNNaker, which is attempting to simulate a billion spiking neurons in real time using a large array of power-efficient processors (Furber, Temple and Brown, 2006).

In the longer term it is hoped that it will become possible to validate biologically inspired neural models using data from real brains. The low spatial and/or temporal resolution of our current measurement techniques makes this almost impossible to carry out at present, although it is possible to ground simulation work using data recorded from in vitro neuron preparations. One of the major problems with the validation of brain-inspired neural systems is that the activity of even the most basic natural neural network is driven by stimulation from the environment and used to control the behaviour of an organism. This will make the use of real or virtual robots an important part of the testing of neural models in the future.

CONCLUSION

This chapter has explained why simulation plays an important role in neuroscience research and outlined some of the applications of artificial neural networks in computer science and engineering. Although the continuous simulation approach has accuracy and performance limitations, the nature and complexity of the Hodgkin-Huxley equations make continuous simulation the best choice for this type of model. Discrete event simulation can be an efficient and accurate way of simulating point neurons, but it can be complicated to implement and suffers from performance issues when there are a large number of events. Whilst the hybrid approach also suffers from inaccuracies, there

are a number of ways in which this issue can be substantially overcome, and a new generation of simulators are emerging that can model large numbers of neurons and synapses using the hybrid approach.

ACKNOWLEDGMENT

Many thanks to Owen Holland for feedback, support and advice about this work. The interface between SIMNOS and SpikeStream was developed in collaboration with Richard Newcombe, who designed the spike conversion methods, and I would also like to thank Renzo De Nardi and Hugo Gravato Marques for many useful suggestions and discussions. This research was funded by the Engineering and Physical Science Research Council Adventure Fund (GR/S47946/01).

REFERENCES

Banks, J., Carson, J. S., II, Nelson, B. L., & Nicol, D. M. (2005). *Discrete event simulation* (4th Ed.). Upper Saddle River, NJ: Pearson Prentice Hall.

Binzegger, T., Douglas, R. J., & Martin, K. A. C. (2004). A quantitative map of the circuit of cat primary visual cortex. *The Journal of Neuroscience, 24*(39), 8441–8453. doi:10.1523/JNEUROSCI.1400-04.2004

Brader, J. M., Senn, W., & Fusi, S. (2007). Learning real-world stimuli in a neural network with spike-driven synaptic dynamics. *Neural Computation, 19*(11), 2881–2912. doi:10.1162/neco.2007.19.11.2881

Brette, R., Rudolph, M., Carnevale, T., Hines, M., & Beeman, D., Bower et al. (2007). Simulation of networks of spiking neurons: A review of tools and strategies. *Journal of Computational Neuroscience, 23*, 349–398. doi:10.1007/s10827-007-0038-6

Brown, R. (1988). Calendar queues: A fast 0(1) priority queue implementation for the simulation event set problem. *Journal of Communication ACM, 31*(10), 1220–1227. doi:10.1145/63039.63045

CAVIAR project website (n.d.). Available at http://www.imse.cnm.es/caviar/.

Claverol, E., Brown, A., & Chad, J. (2002). Discrete simulation of large aggregates of neurons. *Neurocomputing, 47*, 277–297. doi:10.1016/S0925-2312(01)00629-4

CRONOS project website (n.d.). Available at www.cronosproject.net.

Dehaene, S., & Changeux, J.-P. (2005). Ongoing spontaneous activity controls access to consciousness: A neuronal model for inattentional blindness. *Public Library of Science Biology, 3*(5), 910–927.

Delorme, A., & Thorpe, S. J. (2003). SpikeNET: An event-driven simulation package for modeling large networks of spiking neurons. *Network: Computational in Neural Systems, 14*, 613–627. doi:10.1088/0954-898X/14/4/301

Diesmann, M., & Gewaltig, M.-O. (2002). NEST: An environment for neural systems simulations. In V. Macho (Ed.), *Forschung und wissenschaftliches rechnen.* Heinz-Billing-Preis, GWDG-Bericht.

Furber, S. B., Temple, S., & Brown, A. D. (2006). High-performance computing for systems of spiking neurons. In *Proceedings of the AISB'06 Workshop on GC5: Architecture of Brain and Mind,* (Vol. 2, pp 29-36). Bristol: AISB.

Gamez, D. (2007). SpikeStream: A fast and flexible simulator of spiking neural networks. In J. M. de Sá, L. A. Alexandre, W. Duch & D. P. Mandic (Eds.) *Proceedings of ICANN 2007,* (Vol. 4668, pp. 370-79). Berlin: Springer Verlag.

Gamez, D. (2008a). Progress in machine consciousness. *Consciousness and Cognition, 17*(3), 887–910. doi:10.1016/j.concog.2007.04.005

Gamez, D. (2008b). *The Development and analysis of conscious machines.* Unpublished doctoral dissertation. University of Essex, UK. Available at http://www.davidgamez.eu/mc-thesis/

Gamez, D., Newcombe, R., Holland, O., & Knight, R. (2006). Two simulation tools for biologically inspired virtual robotics. *Proceedings of the IEEE 5th Chapter Conference on Advances in Cybernetic Systems* (pp. 85-90). Sheffield, UK: IEEE.

Gerstner, W., & Kistler, W. (2002). *Spiking neuron models.* Cambridge, UK: Cambridge University Press.

Haydon, P. (2000). Neuroglial networks: Neurons and glia talk to each other. *Current Biology, 10*(19), 712–714. doi:10.1016/S0960-9822(00)00708-9

Hodgkin, A. L., & Huxley, A. F. (1952). A quantitative description of membrane current and its application to conduction and excitation in nerve. *The Journal of Physiology, 117*, 500–544.

Izhikevich, E. M. (2003). Simple model of spiking neurons. *IEEE Transactions on Neural Networks, 14*, 1569–1572. doi:10.1109/TNN.2003.820440

Izhikevich, E. M., & Edelman, G. M. (2008). Large-scale model of mammalian thalamocortical systems. *Proceedings of the National Academy of Sciences of the United States of America, 105*, 3593–3598. doi:10.1073/pnas.0712231105

Krichmar, J. L., Nitz, D. A., Gally, J. A., & Edelman, G. M. (2005). Characterizing functional hippocampal pathways in a brain-based device as it solves a spatial memory task. *Proceedings of the National Academy of Sciences of the United States of America, 102*(6), 2111–2116. doi:10.1073/pnas.0409792102

Maas, W., & Bishop, C. M. (Eds.). (1999). *Pulsed neural networks*. Cambridge, MA: The MIT Press.

Marian, I. (2003). *A biologically inspired computational model of motor control development*. Unpublished MSc Thesis, University College Dublin, Ireland.

Markram, H. (2006). The Blue Brain project. *Nature Reviews. Neuroscience, 7*, 153–160. doi:10.1038/nrn1848

Mattia, M., & Del Guidice, P. (2000). Efficient event-driven simulation of large networks of spiking neurons and dynamical synapses. *Neural Computation, 12*, 2305–2329. doi:10.1162/089976600300014953

Morrison, A., Mehring, C., Geisel, T., Aertsen, A., & Diesmann, M. (2005). Advancing the boundaries of high-connectivity network simulation with distributed computing. *Neural Computation, 17*, 1776–1801. doi:10.1162/0899766054026648

MVASpike [computer software] (n.d.). Available from http://mvaspike.gforge.inria.fr/.

NEST [computer software] (n.d.). Available from http://www.nest-initiative.org.

Newcombe, R. (2007). *SIMNOS virtual robot* [computer software]. More information available from www.cronosproject.net.

NVIDIA PhysX [computer software] (n.d.). Available from http://www.nvidia.com/object/nvidia_physx.html.

Reutimann, J., Giugliano, M., & Fusi, S. (2003). Event-driven simulation of spiking neurons with stochastic dynamics. *Neural Computation, 15*, 811–830. doi:10.1162/08997660360581912

Shanahan, M. P. (2008). A spiking neuron model of cortical broadcast and competition. *Consciousness and Cognition, 17*(1), 288–303. doi:10.1016/j.concog.2006.12.005

Silver, R., Boahen, K., Grillner, S., Kopell, N., & Olsen, K. L. (2007). Neurotech for neuroscience: Unifying concepts, organizing principles, and emerging tools. *The Journal of Neuroscience, 27*(44), 11807–11819. doi:10.1523/JNEUROSCI.3575-07.2007

SpikeSNNS [computer software] (n.d.). Available from http://cortex.cs.may.ie/tools/spikeNNS/index.html.

SpikeStream [computer software] (n.d.). Available from http://spikestream.sf.net.

Tani, J., Nishimoto, R., & Paine, R. W. (2008). Achieving "organic compositionality" through self-organization: Reviews on brain-inspired robotics experiments. *Neural Networks, 21*(4), 584–603. doi:10.1016/j.neunet.2008.03.008

Tonnelier, A., Belmabrouk, H., & Martinez, D. (2007). Event-driven simulations of nonlinear integrate-and-fire neurons. *Neural Computation, 19*, 3226–3238. doi:10.1162/neco.2007.19.12.3226

VMware Player [computer software] (n.d.). Available from http://www.vmware.com/products/player/.

Wheeler, D. A. (n.d.). *SLOCCount* [computer software]. Available from http://www.dwheeler.com/sloc/.

KEY TERMS AND DEFINITIONS

Axon: When a neuron fires it sends a voltage spike along a fibre known as an axon, which connects to the dendrites of other neurons at a junction called a synapse.

Continuous Simulation: An approach to simulation in which updates to the model are driven by the advance of a simulation clock.

Dendrite: Each neuron has a large number of fibres called dendrites that receive spikes from other neurons. The axon of one neuron connects to the dendrite of another at a junction called a synapse.

Discrete Event Simulation: An approach to simulation in which updates to the model are event-driven instead of clock-driven. This type of simulation typically works by maintaining a queue of events that are sorted by the time at which they are scheduled to occur.

Hybrid Simulation: An approach to simulation in which a continuous simulation clock is maintained and updates to the model are event-driven.

Neuron: A cell in the brain that carries out information processing. There are approximately 80 billion neurons in the human brain.

Spike: A pulse of electrical voltage sent from one neuron to another to communicate information.

SpikeStream: Software for the hybrid simulation of spiking neural networks.

STDP (Spike Time Dependent Plasticity): A learning rule in which the weight of a synapse is increased if a spike arrives prior to the firing of a neuron, and decreased if the spike arrives after the firing of a neuron.

Synapse: A junction between the axon of one neuron and the dendrite of another.

ENDNOTES

[1] The brain also contains 100 billion cells called glia, which have traditionally been thought to play a supporting role. However some people, such as Haydon (2000), have suggested that glia might contribute to the brain's information processing.

[2] Although true continuous simulation can only be carried out on an analogue system, the term "continuous simulation" is commonly used to refer to the approximation of a continuous system using a digital computer and an arbitrarily small time step.

[3] A circular buffer is commonly implemented as an array combined with an index that advances at each time step and returns to zero when it reaches the end of the array. At each time step all of the spikes at the current index position are applied to the network and new spikes are delayed by inserting them at a position in the array that is an appropriate number of steps ahead of the current index.

[4] This calculation is based on Brette et al. (2007).

[5] The effect of the time step resolution on network behavior can be seen in Table 3.

[6] The clustering of spikes at time steps affects STDP learning because it can be ambiguous which spikes come before or after the firing of a neuron when several arrive at the same time step.

[7] See Mattia and Del Guidice (2000) for a more detailed discussion of this approach.

[8] This calculation is based on Brette et al. (2007).

[9] These strategies are used by the NEST hybrid simulator - see Morrison, Mehring, Geisel, Aertsen and Diesmann (2005).

[10] See Morrison et al. (2005) for more on this approach.

[11] However, SpikeNET was developed into a commercial image recognition product.

[12] Full details can be found in Gamez (2007).

[13] SIMNOS was developed by Newcombe (2007).

[14] This was calculated using Wheeler's SLOC-Count software.

[15] This makes Neurogrid a true continuous simulation since the properties of the transistors in the silicon are used to emulate the behaviour of neurons' ion channels without the need for variables that are stored in digital format and advanced in discrete time steps.

Chapter 16
An Integrated Data Mining and Simulation Solution

Mouhib Alnoukari
Arab Academy for Banking and Financial Sciences, Syria

Asim El Sheikh
Arab Academy for Banking and Financial Sciences, Jordan

Zaidoun Alzoabi
Arab Academy for Banking and Financial Sciences, Syria

ABSTRACT

Simulation and data mining can provide managers with decision support tools. However, the heart of data mining is knowledge discovery; as it enables skilled practitioners with the power to discover relevant objects and the relationships that exist between these objects, while simulation provides a vehicle to represent those objects and their relationships. In this chapter, the authors will propose an intelligent DSS framework based on data mining and simulation integration. The main output of this framework is the increase of knowledge. Two case studies will be presented, the first one on car market demand simulation. The simulation model was built using neural networks to get the first set of prediction results. Data mining methodology used named ANFIS (Adaptive Neuro-Fuzzy Inference System). The second case study will demonstrate how applying data mining and simulation in assuring quality in higher education.

INTRODUCTION

Data mining techniques provide people with new power to research and manipulate the existing large volume of data. A data mining process discovers interesting information from the hidden data that can either be used for future prediction and/or intelligently summarizing the details of the data (Mei, and Thole, 2008).

On the other hand, Simulation is a powerful technique for systems representations; because it provides a concise way for knowledge encapsulation. Simulation can be used effectively supporting managers in decision making, especially in situations characterized by uncertainty. Simulation can provide realistic models for testing real-world decision making scenarios (what-if scenarios), and comparing alternative decisions in order to choose the best solution affecting company's success, by

DOI: 10.4018/978-1-60566-774-4.ch016

enhancing profitability, market share, and customer satisfaction.

Simulation methodologies, such as what-if analysis, can provide the engine to analyze company's policy changes. For example, adding new tellers to a bank, or adding new airline route, or changing the number of machines in a job shop (Better, Glover, and Laguna, 2007).

Using data mining can help recalibrating system simulation models in many real world applications, as it provides the insights gleaned from the hidden and interesting data patterns.

This chapter will be divided as the following: the next section will present the data mining and business intelligence techniques used in conjunction with simulation, different experiences on the integration of simulation and data mining will be presented, then we will propose an intelligent DSS framework based on data mining and simulation integration, finally the proposed framework will be validated using a two case studies on car market demand simulation, and applying data mining in assuring quality in higher education.

Introduction to Data Mining and Business Intelligence

It is noted that the number of databases keeps growing rapidly because of the availability of powerful and affordable database systems. Millions of databases have been used in business management, government administration, scientific and engineering data management, and many other applications. This explosive growth in data and databases has generated an urgent need for new techniques and tools that can intelligently and automatically transform the processed data into useful information and knowledge, which provide enterprises with a competitive advantage, working asset that delivers new revenue, and to enable them to better service and retain their customers (Stolba, and Tjoa, 2006).

In 1996, the Organization for Economic Cooperation and Development (OECD) redefined "knowledge-based economies" as "economies which are directly based on the production, distribution and use of knowledge and information" (Weiss, Buckley, Kapoor, and Damgaard, 2003). According to the definition, Data Mining and Knowledge Management, and more generally Business Intelligence, should be foundations for building the knowledge economy. Business Intelligence is an umbrella term that combines architectures, tools, data bases, applications, practices, and methodologies (Turban, Aronson, Liang, and Sharda, 2007; Cody, Kreulen, Krishna, and Spangler, 2002). Weiss et al. 2003 defined Business Intelligence as the "combination of data mining, data warehousing, knowledge management, and traditional decision support systems".

Business Intelligence is becoming vital for many organizations, especially those which have extremely large amount of data (Shariat, and Hightower, 2007; Kerdprasop, and Kerdpraso, 2007). Organizations such as Continental Airlines have seen investment in Business Intelligence generate increases in revenue and cost saving equivalent to 1000% return on investment (ROI) (Zack, Rainer, and Marshall, 2007). The measure of any business intelligence solution is its ability to derive knowledge from data. The challenge is met with the ability to identify patterns, trends, rules, and relationships from volumes of information which is too large to be processed by human analysis alone.

Decision makers depend on detailed and accurate information when they have to make decisions. Business Intelligence can provide decision makers with such accurate information, and with the appropriate tools for data analysis (Jermol, Lavrac, and Urbanci, 2003; Negash 2004; Lau, Lee, Ho, and Lam, 2004]. It is the process of transforming various types of business data into meaningful information that can help, decision makers at all levels, getting deeper insight of business (Power, 2007; Girija, and Srivatsa 2006; Gartner Group, 1996).

Any Business Intelligence application can be divided into the following three layers:

1. **Data layer** responsible for storing structured and unstructured data for decision support purposes. Structured data is usually stored in Operational Data Stores (ODS), Data Warehouses (DW), and Data Marts (DM) (Alnoukari, and Alhussan 2008). Unstructured data are handled by using Content and Document Management Systems (Baars, and Kemper 2007). Data are extracted from operational data sources, e.g. SCM, ERP, CRM, or from external data sources, e.g. market research data. Data are extracted from data sources that are transformed and loaded into DW by ETL (Extract, Transform and Load) tools.
2. **Logic layer** provides functionality to analyze data and provide knowledge. This includes OLAP (OnLine Analytical Processing), and data mining.
3. **Access layer**, realized by some sort of software portals (Business Intelligence portal).

According to Wikid Hierarchy (Steele, 2002), Intelligence is defined as "knowledge that has been evaluated and relevant insights and understandings extracted". In this context, intelligence process is "about making informed assessments of what will happen, when and how", so it relies on how to manage knowledge.

Knowledge can be created and consumed through various types of activities such as: conversation with one another, searching of information in huge databases, just-in time learning, and continuous education (Girija, and Srivatsa, 2006).

Business Intelligence is a good environment in which 'marrying' business knowledge with data mining could provide better results.

Knowledge can enrich data by making it "intelligent", thus more manageable by data mining (Graco, Semenova, and Dubossarsky, 2007). It considers expert knowledge as an asset that can provide data mining with the guidance to the discovery process. Thus, it says in a simple word, "data mining cannot work without knowledge".

Knowledge management system must address the following three elements: people, business rules, and technology (Girija, and Srivatsa, 2006). Business intelligence is an important technology that can help decision makers taking precious decisions quickly. Business intelligence includes automated tools for analyzing and mining huge amount of data (Knowledge Discovery in Databases), thus transforming data into knowledgeable information (Weiss, Buckley, Kapoor, and Damgaard, 2003; Anand, Bell, and Hughes, 1995).

Data mining is the search for relationships and distinct patterns that exist in datasets but they are "hidden" among the vast amount of data (Turban, Aronson, Liang, and Sharda, 2007; Jermol, Lavrac, and Urbanci, 2003). Data mining can be effectively applied to many areas (Alnoukari, and Alhussan 2008; Watson, Wixom, Hoffer, Lehman, and Reynolds, 2006], including marketing (direct mail, cross-selling, customer acquisition and retention), fraud detection, financial services (Srivastava, and Cooley, 2003), inventory control, fault diagnosis, credit scoring (Shi, Peng, Kou, and Chen, 2005), network management, scheduling, medical diagnosis and prognosis. There are two main sets of tools used for data mining (Corbitt, 2003): discovery tools (Chung, Chen, and Nunamaker, 2005; Wixom, 2004), and verification tools (Grigori, Casati, Castellanos, Sayal, and Shan, 2004). Discovery tools include data visualization, neural networks, cluster analysis and factor analysis. Verification tools include regression analysis, correlations, and predictions.

Data mining application are characterized by the ability to deal with the explosion of business data and accelerated market changes, these characteristics help providing powerful tools for decision makers, such tools can be used by business users (not only statisticians) for analyzing huge amount of data for patterns and trends.

Consequently, data mining has become a research area with increasing importance and it involved in determining useful patterns from collected data or determining a model that fits best on the collected data (Fayyad, Shapiro, and Smyth, 1996; Mannila, 1997; Okuhara, Ishii, and Uchida, 2005). Different classification schemes can be used to categorize data mining methods and systems based on the kinds of databases to be studied, the kinds of knowledge to be discovered, and the kinds of techniques to be utilized (Lange, 2006; Smith, 2005).

A data mining task includes pre-processing, the actual data mining process and post-processing. During the pre-processing stage, the data mining problem and all sources of data are identified, and a subset of data generated from the accumulated data. To ensure quality the data set is processed to remove noise, handle missing information and transformed it to an appropriate format (Nayak, and Qiu, 2005). A data mining technique or a combination of techniques appropriate for the type of knowledge to be discovered is applied to the derived data set. The last stage is post-processing in which the discovered knowledge is evaluated and interpreted.

Data mining techniques is a way to extract patterns (knowledge) from data (Alnoukari, Alzoabi, and Hanna, 2008; Morbitzer, Strachan, and Simpson, 2004). We are using the terms knowledge and pattern interchangeably as patterns inside the huge databases reflect what-so-called "organizational tacit knowledge". Knowledge could be one of two states: explicit or tacit (Nonaka, Toyama, and Konno, 2000). Explicit knowledge is objective, explicitly stated, easy to transfer, communicate, and codify. On the other hand tacit knowledge is subjective, implicit in human's minds, and difficult to transfer, communicate and codify. The patterns that are discovered in the databases using data mining -or any other methodology- reflect organization-wide processes, procedures, and behaviors that are not easy to explain or be figured out. Data mining can't extract all available

knowledge that is embodied in a data set, as it may discover a lot of patterns that are irrelevant for the analyzer. Refinement and variable changes would be necessary for mining that runs to acquire the required knowledge.

Data mining process contains different steps including: data cleansing, data integration (into data warehouse), data mining, pattern evaluation, and pattern presentation (Alnoukari, and Alhussan, 2008).

Data mining can use two types of data (Painter, Erraguntla, Hogg, and Beachkofski, 2006): continuous data, and categorical (discrete) data.

Data mining algorithms are separated into two main classes (Garcia, Roman, Penalvo, and Bonilla, 2008; Morbitzer, Strachan, and Simpson, 2004):

1. Supervised algorithms, or the predictive algorithms, where the object is to detect pattern in present data using a learning stage. Prediction target is a special attribute (named label). The prediction model is based on encoding the relationship between the label and the other attributes, in order to predict new, unlabeled attribute. If the label is discrete, the algorithm is named classification. If it's continuous, the algorithm is named regression.
2. Unsupervised algorithms, or the descriptive algorithm, where the object is to detect pattern in present data using a learning stage. These algorithms belong to knowledge discovery modeling. Example of such algorithms is association rules.

Different data mining techniques are used in conjunction with simulation data analysis (Morbitzer, Strachan, and Simpson, 2004; Painter, Erraguntla, Hogg, and Beachkofski, 2006):

•   Association analysis discovers association rules that occur together in a given data set. Association mining provides the techniques needed for "basket analysis", where the customer is provided with a set of correlated items that she/he may purchase or set of services she/he would like to have.

- Classification analysis discovers the rules that are relevant to one particular variable. Classification methods include Bayesian Networks (BN), Artificial Neural Networks (ANN), Decision Trees for Classifications (CARD, CHAID), and Multiple Discriminate Analysis (MDA).

- Clustering analysis is the most suitable data mining technique that is used for the analysis of simulation results. It attempts to discover the set of groups in a data set in a way that maximizes the similarity between items in the same group, and minimizes the similarity between items in any two different groups (Mei, and Thole, 2008). It differs from classification in the way that no assumptions are made about the number of groups (classes), or any other structure. Clustering methods include hierarchical clustering, and neural net-based methods.

Classical data mining considers the existence of data in a repository (such as data bases). Once data is generated, it will be considered as a static set that can be analyzed. This means that data will not be updated or modified.

Dynamic data mining features solve the static issues of classical data mining application by analyzing the processes in action (Better, Glover, and Laguna, 2007). These features provide capabilities of handling uncertainty, and find solutions to complex problems.

DATA MINING AND SIMULATION: PREVIOUS WORKS

Combining data mining and simulation techniques was applied on different area: car crash (Kuhlmann, Vetter, Lubbing, and Thole, 2005; Mei, and Thole, 2008), software project management (Garcia et al., 2008), life cycle cost (Painter, Erraguntla, Hogg, and Beachkofski, 2006), and others.

CAE-Bench is one of the most famous simulation management tools (it is currently used at BMW crash department) which applies the data mining methods on the data resultant from car crash simulation (Kuhlmann, Vetter, Lubbing, and Thole, 2005).

CAE-Bench stores data about models as complete vehicles. Such models are processed as finite element models (FE models) made up by about 500.000 independent nodes and elements (called input deck). Each input deck (a car composed of about 1200 parts) is disassembled in order to analyze the geometry of its parts. Data about parts and their geometry analysis are then provided into a data mining working environment (named SCAI-DM). Data preparation is the essential step for data mining as it costs about 80-90% of the total efforts. The data need to be processed, cleaned, checked for consistency, and combined in order to be processed by the data mining tool (Figure 1).

After completing data preparation step, similarity analysis and data reduction are conducted in order to provide the main attribute for data mining. Attribute selection method was used in order to reduce the vast amount of geometrical modifications to a small number of similar ones. Decision tree method was also employed in order to demonstrate the influence of design modification on a range of values, and leading to meaningful results.

The last step was deployment of data mining reports, and importing them into CAE-Bench simulation system in order to let them accessible to other users.

Mei and Thole (2008) described the use of data mining algorithms (especially clustering algorithm) to measure the scatter of parallel simulation results to explain the instability na-

Figure 1. CAE-Bench simulation tool. SCAI-DM working environment is taking its input from disassembled parts data and geometry based meta data of the engineer's working environment adapted from (Kuhlmann, Vetter, Lubbing, and Thole, 2005)

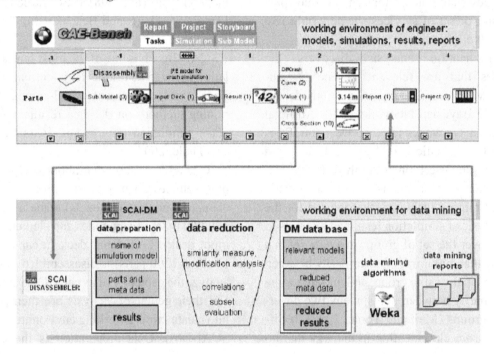

ture of parallel crash simulation, and measure the amount of the scatter results. The use of data mining algorithms was chosen to avoid the time consuming task of numerical crash simulation, as the simulation results are changing from one run to another, although the simulation parameters were identical. They also proposed solutions for direct clustering algorithms difficulties, especially the non deterministic nature of the clustering assignment, the huge amount of simulation data, and the huge number of data object comparisons needed for time dependency analysis.

Painter et at. (2006) combined simulation, data mining, and knowledge-based techniques in order to support decisions related to aircraft engine maintenance in the US Department of Defense. They developed a methodology for Life-Cycle Cost combining discrete event simulation with data mining techniques to develop and maintain cost estimation parameters. Simulation output is used as an input for data mining analysis to understand system behavior, especially sub-systems interactions, and factors affecting life-cycle metrics. The process involves simulating the fleet of engines for a set of planned operational scenarios, to collect maintenance decisions, and their cost implications over the overall service life. Multiple simulation runs are conducted to account the stochastic nature of maintenance events and decisions. Simulation outputs, and cost history data are then mined in order to find relationships that best characterize the Life-Cycle Cost implication of each maintenance decision. Such parameters relationships need periodic refinement (Learning phase) in order to characterize environments changes, maintenance practices, reliability of engine components, and other factors.

Simulation can provide results that cannot be done through any maintenance history data collection system. Once data is generated, data mining techniques is used to provide the key pattern, and parameters relationships. This can be used to define models, from which Life-Cycle Cost can be determined parametrically, in order to provide more accurate decisions. The main objective of data mining module is to determine the drivers affecting Life-Cycle Cost. The data mining techniques used for such objectives are regression, classification, and clustering.

Data mining methods (especially association rules) was also applied on software project simulation (Garcia et al., 2008). Software project management is affected by different factors. Main factors are quality, effort, duration and cost. These are affecting managers' decisions about a project.

The main issue when managers have to take decisions about a project is that they have to consider great number of variables, and relations between them.

Simulation of software project by using dynamic models provides a good tool to recognize the impact of these software project management variables, and relations between them.

Software Project Simulator (SPS) provides managers with a powerful tool that enable them to try different policies, and take decisions according to results obtained. Different type of analysis can be done using SPS at different stages (a priori analysis, project monitoring, and post-mortem analysis).

SPS based on dynamic models enables managers to set simulation environment parameters and functions. Dynamic models provide the ability to express restrictions among variables that change over time. These restrictions are the baseline for relationship analysis among different project factors.

Although SPS based on dynamic models is able to manage the large number of projects parameters, it may not be able to find the best parameters combinations for a specified situation, as the number of possible combinations is huge.

The use of data mining techniques such as association rules, machine learning, and evolutionary algorithms could help analyzing the influence of some management policy factors on some project attributes. The number of generated pattern is as high as the number of possible parameters combinations, but we only concentrate on patterns with high confidence rule. These patterns are effectively affecting decision making. Garcia et al. (2008) proposed a refinement method, based on discretisation of the continuous attributes, for obtaining stronger rules that has been successfully applied in the early software size estimation. The association rules were applied between several project management factors and attributes, such as software quality, project duration, and costs.

Data mining methods were also applied to enhance simulation optimization methods (Better, Glover, and Laguna, 2007; Huyet, 2006; Fang, Sheng, Gao, and Iyer, 2006). Such methodology can produce knowledge on system behavior (especially the high performance behaviors), and analyze efficient solutions. Such approach is also effective for the search of optimal values of input parameters in complex and uncertain situations, and avoids the "black box" effect of many optimization methods.

The methodology proposed by Huyet (2006) consists of collecting the solutions generated by optimization and evaluated by simulation. Then the learning method is applied to the generated data set. Finally the optimization method is used to generate new parameter combinations in order to constitute more efficient solution.

The approach proposed by Better et al. (2007) is based on dynamic data mining module which provides the inputs to the simulation module and optimization engine. Inputs data are relevant variables, attributes, and rules that govern the simulation module, which itself interacts with optimization engine to evaluate different scenarios in order to choose the optimal one. Optimization engine provide the means for dynamic data mining module to produce classification, clustering, and feature selection. The objective of optimization engine is to maximize the performance of the firm according to pre-specified measures; such as market share, profit, sales revenue, etc. The objective can be expressed as a single performance measure, calculated as a combinations of more than one measure.

Most of the previous researches were focused on the use of data mining methods, on huge data produced by simulation tools. Few researches discussed the reciprocal case where we can demonstrate the use of simulation in grey related analysis for data mining purposes. Grey related analysis is a decision-making technique that can be used to deal with uncertainty in forms of fuzzy data (Wu, Olson, and Dong, 2006). Wu et al. 2006 used Monte Carlo simulation to measure the impact of fuzzy decision tree models (using categorical data), compared to those based on continuous data. Monte Carlo simulation is useful to provide experiments needed to verify data mining algorithms. It can be used as a way to present the output of data mining model. Monte Carlo simulation can present the overall picture of the dispersion of the results obtained, and provide the probabilities explanations for decision makers.

A Proposed Intelligent DSS Framework Integrating Simulation and Data Mining

Detailed Simulation can result in large data sets. Exploring such data sets is difficult for users using traditional techniques. Data mining techniques can help extracting patterns, associations, and anomalies from large data sets.

Integrating simulation and data mining can provide decision makers with a more powerful tools that can support them in situations characterized by uncertainty, and provide them with the power to find hidden patterns (organizational tacit knowledge) that can either be used for future prediction and/or intelligently summarizing the data. The main output of such integration is the increase of knowledge.

Our proposed DSS framework is based on the integration of simulation and data mining (Figure 2). Simulation data output is transferred into an enterprise data warehouse using the ETL (Extract, Transform, and Load) steps. Data warehouse can produce different data marts, or multidirectional cubes, or simple aggregated data. Data mining techniques can be applied intelligently on these different data sets to facilitate the extraction of meaningful information and knowledge from such huge amount of data sets.

Most of the previous works were applying data mining techniques on traditional data bases. Such step can take a considerable time, especially of these data bases which contain many object relationships.

Our proposed model is based on the creation of enterprise data warehouse in order to facilitate the transition into OLAP applications. This can help producing more intelligent system where data mining method can be applied effectively.

The creation of the enterprise data warehouse is mainly based on the simulation data preparation. Data preparation is usually an important step, and can cost a considerable part of the total efforts. The data need to be processed, cleaned, checked for consistency, and combined in order to be processed by data mining tool.

Data mining stage can help recalibrating system simulation models in many real world applications, as it provides the insights gleaned from the hidden and interesting data patterns.

Data mining can produce a huge amount of data patterns, and patterns relationships. Patterns evaluation will provide the system the ability to analyze all these patterns and relationships, and produce only meaningful patterns, and pattern relationships. This step will produce more knowledge and enhance the overall company's knowledge.

Figure 2. A proposed intelligent framework based on the integration of simulation and data mining

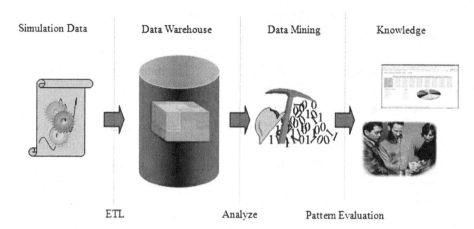

CASE STUDY I: CAR MARKET DEMAND SIMULATION

Automotive manufacturing are markets where the manufacturer does not interact with the consumer directly, yet a fundamental understanding of the market, the trends, the moods, and the changing consumer tastes and preferences are fundamental to competitiveness.

The information gathered in order to produce car market demand's simulation are the following (Alnoukari, and Alhussan, 2008):

- Supply chain process (sales, inventory, orders, production plan).
- Manufacturing information (car configurations/packages/options codes and description).
- Marketing information (dealers, business centers… etc).
- Customers' trends information (websites web-activities).

An enterprise data warehouse was built to hold web data, inventory data, car demand data and sales data to better analyzing and predicting car sales, managing car inventory and planning car production. Sales and marketing managers are interested in better leveraging data in support of the

enterprise goals and objectives. Managers envision an analytical environment that will improve their ability to support planning and inventory management, incentives management, and ultimately production planning, in addition to enable them to meet the expectations of their decision-making process which is supported by appropriate data and trends. Regardless of functional boundaries and type of analysis needed, their requirements focus on improving access to detailed data, more consistent and more integrated information.

Having a data warehouse that combines online and offline behavioral data for decision-making purposes is a strategic tool which business users can leverage to improve sales demand forecasting, improve model/trim level mix planning, adjust body model/trim level mix with inventory data, and reduce days on lot.

The main goal for the data mining phase was to get some initial positive results on prediction and to measure the prediction score of different data sources using findings of correlation studies.

The data mining solution starts by processing Stock/Sale/Order data, web data, dealer data and GAQ (Get a Quote) data and store them in a data warehouse named "Vehicle Demand Data Warehouse". The data warehouse was designed in order to support analysis that aim to use web data, inventory data, car demand data and sales data to better analyzing and predicting car sales, managing car inventory and planning car production. Inventory managers, brand managers and sales managers are demanding more metrics for analyzing the past (i.e. inventory) and predicting the future (i.e. vehicle sales, mix and launches). These metrics need to be delivered seamlessly with high quality and in a timely fashion. This will get managers closer to better understanding consumer demands and better managing the customer relationship.

The main steps for providing the Slow Turn Simulation/Launch Simulation/Prediction (we will use the term STS/LS/Prediction) are the following (Figure 3):

- Receiving and validating the data sources.
- ETL the data sources to the data warehouse.
- Processing the data warehouse to generate the required data marts.
- Building the required data marts and OLAP cubes.
- Generating the reports.
- Delivering the analysis in the form of Excel workbooks, and PowerPoint slides.

The data sources used for this solution are the followings:

- "Stock/Sales/Orders" data sources are snapshots at the (exact) date of data.
- "Production Plan" data source is a list of models quantities that are planned to be produced for a specific period.
- "TOPs" data source is a structured data which is used to map all car configurations under production.
- "SPOT" data source is used to list dealers, in addition to their rating and their geographic information.
- "Web Activity" data source is used to track all user web hits/requests on customer's websites.

The ETL was designed for transforming heterogeneous data sources formats into flat file format in order to load it as bulk insert, to gain higher performance.

The data warehouse maintains the following dimensions:

- TOPs dimension used to map all car configurations under production. This dimension is used to map vehicles "Franchise/Year/Model/Package/Option" to their "Codes/Descriptions/OptionTypes/DefaultOptions".
- Geographic dimension is used to map "ZipCode" to "Zone/Business Center/State".
- Dealer dimension is used to map dealers.

The data warehouse maintains also the following fact tables: "CarConfig" is used to store "Build and Price" configurations made on the company's web-sites. "Stock/Sales/Order" are used to store orders, sales and stock made on the company's vehicles. "Production Plan" is used to store production of the company's plans intending to achieve.

Data in a warehouse is typically updated only at certain points in time (Weekly/Monthly/Yearly in our case). In this way, there is a tradeoff exists between the correctness of data and the substantial effort required to bring the data into the warehouse. Data warehouses also provide a great deal of opportunities for performing data mining tasks such as classification and summarization. Typically, updates are collected and applied to the data warehouse periodically in a batch mode, (e.g., during the night). Then, all patterns derived from the warehouse by some data mining algorithm have to be updated as well.

Processing is the stage where data is processed, summarized and aggregated in order to create the required reporting data marts.

The processing stages are:

Figure 3. Slow Turn Simulation/Launch Simulation/Prediction Pipeline

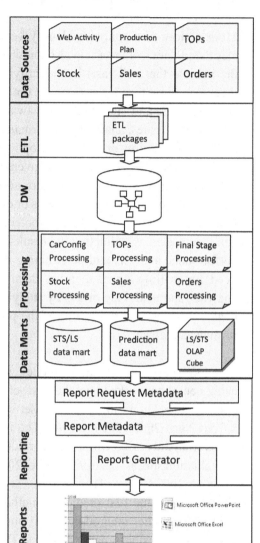

customers trends on web "Build and Price" activities).

- Inventory stage: generates the reporting inventory data mart. The inventory data is a snapshot of the inventory stock on the cutoff date.
- Order stage: generates the reporting order data mart. The order data is a snapshot of the dealer orders on the cutoff date.
- Sale stage: generates the reporting sale data mart that covers the studied period.
- Final stage: generates the final reporting data mart that combines all the data marts created previously in order to serve the Slow Turn Simulation/Launch Simulation/Prediction reporting needs.

As a result of the processing pipeline, number of data marts created to cover the reporting needs over time. Data marts are data stores which are subordinated to the data warehouse (Fong, Li, and Huang, 2003; Jukic, 2006; Sen, and Sinha, 2005, Vaduva, and Vetterli, 2001). The main data marts created are: Slow Turn Simulation/Launch Simulation data marts, and Prediction data mart. Slow turn simulation is not performed against the data marts directly; instead it is performed against OLAP cubes built above Slow Turn data mart, such OLAP cubes provide analytics with aggregations, drilldowns, and slicing/dicing of data (Youzhi, Jie, 2004).

The last stage in our solution pipeline is the reporting stage. It uses the data stored in the STS/LS/Prediction data marts, and OLAP cubes created for slow turning simulation in order to finally arrive to a strategic data reporting solution, which supports the entire organization needs of information at the highest possible degrees of flexibility and customizability that allows addressing changeful reporting needs such as STS/LS/Prediction analysis and other types of analysis.

Powerful business intelligence and reporting solution should have the capabilities to handle the complexities and diversity of data informa-

- TOPs stage: generates the reporting version of the TOPs, in order to have a centralized mapping schema that provides the latest version on the TOPs.
- CarConfig stage: generates the reporting CarConfig data mart (this data mart serves number of reports for launch analysis, where the study is only for

tion in the data warehouse and data marts (Ester, Kriegel, Sander, Wimmer, and Xu, 1998; Fong, Li, and Huang, 2003).

The approach is focusing on being able to deliver a big number of multi-dimensional pivot reports in a short time frames based on the incremental STS/LS/Prediction data marts. The core engine for delivering the STS/LS/Prediction multi-dimensional pivot reports is the report generator. It's designed to be able to read from multiple data warehouse schemas (a simple Ad-Hoc query, a data mart and OLAP cubes). The reporting layer contains a report metadata which is an XML-based metadata used to store the reports templates, and a report request metadata which is an XML-based metadata used to store the reporting parameters for each report request made by the customer (report name, start date, end date, franchise, family, etc.).

A report metadata object library is used to encapsulate the reporting metadata repository and present the interface to read/manipulate it. The launch simulation report generator is the core reporting automation engine. It drives all reporting process, coordinates the internal and underlying components jobs and delivers the final reports. This component is primarily made to automate generating a huge number of reports requested on a regular basis (daily/weekly/monthly/yearly). This component encapsulates the pivot reporting component, PowerPoint generating component, and workflow component.

The reports deployed cover a wide range of STS/LS. Such reports include:

- Models web car configurations through business centers, early indications of the customers' interest in newly launched vehicles through business centers.
- Models web car configurations, open dealer orders, production plan, K-stock and sales comparison, gives a comparison analysis between "what the customer wants" (web car configuration) and "what supply chain is providing" by comparing inventory, order, sale and production plan with the model web car configurations.
- Models slow turn analysis: identify vehicles that do not sell fast (help also knowing the vehicle that sell fast) by: identifying inventory slow-turning options or option combinations, and studying dealer awareness of such issues, analyzing performance by determining slow or fast turning options or option combinations, analyzing inventory by validating the results of performance analysis and determining the options or option combinations having stock problems, analyzing sales by validating the results of performance analysis and determining the need for drilling down to more detailed analysis, and analyzing orders by studying dealer awareness of the results of the performance analysis.

Car market demand simulation model was built using neural networks to get the first set of prediction results. The training data subset was gotten from April 2002 till June 2003. The test subset was from July 2003 till September 2003, and the evaluation subset was from October 2003 till November 2003 (Figure 4).

After evaluating the first prediction method, we tried to use another method based on linear regression without using separated weeks. This method provided more accurate results for the first week, but the next weeks predictions are inacceptable.

New car market demand simulation model was built using data mining methodology named ANFIS (Adaptive Neuro-Fuzzy Inference System), which is a combination of fuzzy logic & neural networks by clustering values in fuzzy sets, membership functions are estimated during training, and using neural networks to estimate weights. The results obtained were more accurate and this method was adapted in our solution as the MAPE errors don't exceed 10%.

Figure 4. Car marker demand simulation results using neural networks

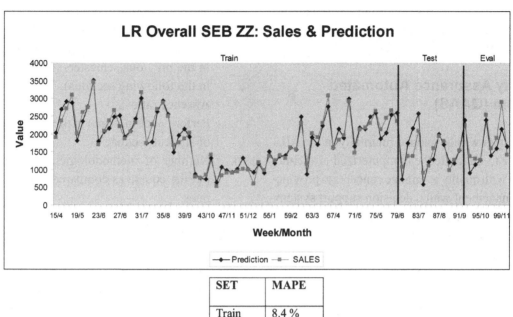

SET	MAPE
Train	8.4 %
Test	18.6 %
Eval	15.5 %

CASE STUDY II: APPLYING DATA MINING AND SIMULATION IN ASSURING QUALITY IN HIGHER EDUCATION

Quality assurance has the focus of all higher education institutes since one decade. This has been forced by different forces such as growing awareness of the need of quality assurance systems in different disciplines, pressure from government entities towards standardization, customer demand for better performance, and the need for more organizational efficiency and excellence (Gatfield, Barker, and Graham, 1999).

This has been emphasized through international recognition of the importance of assuring quality in higher education systems in order to facilitate student and instructor mobility, the need for joint and dual degree programs, and cross cultural programs. In addition, this has been forced by the need of universities to emphasize strategic planning in order to stay competitive in a highly turbulent and fast improving industry.

The emergence of business intelligence, data mining and simulation is providing this type of industry with great opportunity to invest in the huge data and information universities accumulate through their life time to discover opportunities and potential risks and to act immediately in order to act progressively to assure quality in their products and hence to stay competitive.

Sources of Data in the Arab International University (AIU)

The university has a couple of information systems that help in gathering data from different sources and all combined in the data warehouse. A data mining system empowered with simulation power will then represent the data in a way that can help visualize all strengths, weaknesses and possibly threats and opportunities. In the following, we summarize all information systems used in AIU:

Quality Assurance Automated System (QAAS)

The system was developed internally in the AIU in order to integrate the computerized academic system with quality assurance concepts to provide the management with a decision support system that helps in the effectiveness and efficiency of the decision making process.

The system allows teachers to do the following:

1. Enter the study plan of a specific course with every chapter to be covered in every week or class.
2. Enter the text book used throughout the course.
3. Enter all references- including electronic- used for every chapter or topic to be covered in every chapter.
4. Enter the methodologies that will be used for every chapter.
5. Specify the outcomes of the course.
6. Connect chapters (topics) with every outcome.

In every class, the system allows the instructor to enter the following:

1. Attendance
2. Chapter(s) to be covered in every class.
3. Methodology used: lecture, seminar, team work, field study etc.

The system then provides the management with many reports such as:

1. Plan completion (how many chapters covered divided by the chapters planned).

2. Punctuality of teachers (the time the attendance is taken is recorded).
3. Performance of the students in the subject as compared to their general performance in the previous semesters (to be explained in the following sections).
4. Absence ratios.
5. Performance indicator of the teacher in terms of student feedback.
6. Number of methodologies used throughout the course as compared to the planned ones.

Academic System

The academic systems is meant to record all academic movements of students throughout their academic lifecycle, such as admission, registration, financial management, examinations, library activities etc. in addition, the system contains invaluable demographic, geographic, and past educational history of the students . The system was supplied by an external provider.

Human Resource System

This system was developed internally in AIU, to provide management with data about academic and administrative staff: demographic, financial, historical, etc.

Examples of reports generated by the data mining system based on the previous information systems: Combining data from all systems can provide the university senior management with reports such as:

1. Number of Credit selected by students in every semester: this can help predicting the graduation year of the student along with the projected GPA. Moreover, these reports help in combining information about the students' level of English (teaching language in the university) with the current AGPA and number of credit hours given to the student

to check the effectiveness of the academic advising of the university.

2. Correlation of student's performance in different subjects: this can help in the design of the curriculum as well as in the academic advising. For example, the correlation of marks between two subjects from the business (Organizational Behavior and Business Ethics), which are not prerequisite for the other was 0.4 showing that students that have chosen OB before BE are performing better in OB. This helps the academic advisors as well as students to select subjects accordingly.

3. The relation between instructor's performance and the universities they graduated from: this report helps in the recruitment process of new instructors.

4. Correlation between instructor's performance and level of payment, incentives and rewards they get: the correlation between instructors performance taken from QAAS and their financial statuses help to achieve the payment-for-performance the university has as one of its mottos in dealing with its employees.

5. Categorizing subjects according to the student's marks: this report helps in tailoring the internship target for a student with his/her academic background so that he/she is assigned the right supervisor as well as the right industry to conduct the internship.

6. Correlation between student overall performance in different subjects and the feedback from industry in which he/she conducted the internship: this helps all faculties to review the so-called competency based learning so that all curricula are tailored to the market need.

7. Correlation of students' level of English and overall performance. This report helped a lot in evaluating the current system used in the English Language Center in the university and resulted in major changes in the system.

Figure 5 shows the correlation between students's accumulative GPA and their credit hours. It shows that students with higher accumulative hours are getting higher accumulative GPA. On the other hand it was very clear that there is strong correlation between students' level of English and accumulative GPA as shown in Figure 6.

CONCLUSION

In this chapter, we proposed an intelligent DSS framework based on data mining and simulation integration. This framework is based on different previous works tried to combine simulation with data mining, and knowledge discovery. However, most of these works applied data mining methods on the simulation data sets stored in traditional data bases. The main contribution of our work was the use of data warehousing in order to move into OLAP solution, and provide more intelligent results.

Simulation data output is transferred into an enterprise data warehouse using the ETL steps. Data warehouse can produce different data marts, or multidirectional cubes, or simple aggregated data. Data mining techniques can be applied intelligently on these different data sets to facilitate the extraction of meaningful information and knowledge from such huge amount of data sets. The main output of such framework is the increase of knowledge.

Our intelligent DSS framework has been validated by using two case studies, the first one on car market demand simulation. The simulation model was built using neural networks to get the first set of prediction results. Data mining methodology used named ANFIS (Adaptive Neuro-Fuzzy Inference System), which is a combination of fuzzy logic & neural networks by clustering values in fuzzy sets, membership functions are estimated during training, and using neural networks to estimate weights. The second case study was built in order

Figure 5. Business Administration Students clustered according to their accumulative GPA & their credit hours

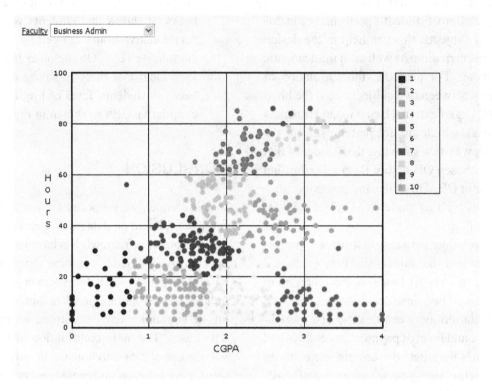

Figure 6. Relationship between accumulative GPA & English level of Business Administration Student. clustered according to their

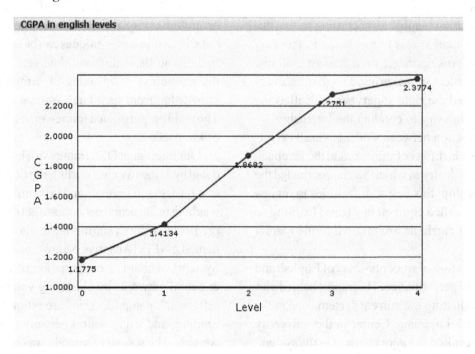

to apply data mining and simulation in assuring quality in higher education.

REFERENCES

Alnoukari, M., & Alhussan, W. (2008). Using data mining techniques for predicting future car market demand. *International Conference on Information & Communication Technologies: From Theory to Applications, IEEE Conference*, Syria.

Alnoukari, M., Alzoabi, Z., & Hanna, S. (2008). Using applying adaptive software development (ASD) agile modeling on predictive data mining applications: ASD-DM methodology. *International Symposium on Information Technology*, Malaysia.

Anand, S. S., Bell, D. A., & Hughes, J. G. (1995). The Role of Domain Knowledge in Data Mining. *CIKM'95*, Baltimore, MD, (pp. 37–43).

Baars, H., & Kemper, H. G. (2007). Management Support with Structured and Unstructured Data-An Integrated Business Intelligence Framework. *Information Systems Management, 25*, 132–148. doi:10.1080/10580530801941058

Better, M., Glover, F., & Laguna, M. (2007). Advances in analytics: Integrating dynamic data mining with simulation optimization. *IBM . Journal of Research and Development (Srinagar), 51*(3/4).

Chung, W., Chen, H., & Nunamaker, J. F. Jr. (2005). A Visual Framework for Knowledge Discover on the web: An Empirical Study of Business Intelligence Exploration. *Journal of Management Information Systems, 21*(4), 57–84.

Cody, F., Kreulen, J. T., Krishna, V., & Spangler, W. S. (2002). The Integration of Business Intelligence and Knowledge Management. *Systems Journal, 41*(4), 697–713.

Corbitt T. (2003). Business Intelligence and Data Mining. *Management Services Magazine*, November 2003.

Ester, M., Kriegel, H. P., Sander, J., Wimmer, M., & Xu, X. (1998). Incremental clustering for mining in a data warehousing environment. *Proceedings Of The 24th Vldb Conference*, New York.

Fang, X., Sheng, O. R. L., Gao, W., & Iyer, B. R. (2006). A data-mining-based prefetching approach to caching for network storage systems. *INFORMS Journal on Computing, 18*(2), 267–282. doi:10.1287/ijoc.1050.0142

Fayyad, U., Piatetsky-Shapiro, G., & Smyth, P. (1996). From data mining to knowledge discovery in databases, American Association for Artificial Intelligence. *AI Magazine*, 37–54.

Fong, J., Li, Q., & Huang, S. (2003). Universal data warehousing based on a meta-data modeling approach. *International Journal of Cooperative Information Systems, 12*(3), 318–325. doi:10.1142/S0218843003000772

Garcia, M. N. M., Roman, I. R., Penalvo, F. J. G., & Bonilla, M. T. (2008). An association rule mining method for estimating the impact of project management policies on software quality, development time and effort . *Expert Systems with Applications, 34*, 522–529. doi:10.1016/j.eswa.2006.09.022

Gartner Group. (1996, September). Retrieved November 12, 2005, from http://www.innerworx. co.za/products.htm.

Gatfield, T., Barker, M., & Graham, P. (1999). Measuring Student Quality Variables and the Implications for Management Practices in Higher Education Institutions: an Australian and International Student Perspective. *Journal of Higher Education Policy and Management, 21*(2). doi:10.1080/1360080990210210

Girija, N., & Srivatsa, S. K. (2006). A Research Study- Using Data Mining in Knowledge Base Business Strategies. *Information Technology Journal*, 5(3), 590–600. doi:10.3923/itj.2006.590.600

Graco, W., Semenova, T., & Dubossarsky, E. (2007). Toward Knowledge-Driven Data Mining. *ACM SIGKDD Workshop on Domain Driven Data Mining (DDDM2007)*, (pp. 49-54).

Grigori, D., Casati, F., Castellanos, M., Sayal, U. M., & Shan, M. C. (2004). Business Process Intelligence. *Computers in Industry*, 53, 321–343. doi:10.1016/j.compind.2003.10.007

Huang, Y. (2002). *Infrastructure, query optimization, data warehousing and data mining for scientific simulation*. A thesis, University of Notre Dame, Notre Dame, IN.

Huyet, A. L. (2006). Optimization and analysis aid via data-mining for simulated production systems. *European Journal of Operational Research*, 173, 827–838. doi:10.1016/j.ejor.2005.07.026

Jermol, M., Lavrac, N., & Urbanci, T. (2003). Managing business intelligence in a virtual enterprise: A case study and knowledge management lessons learned. *Journal of Intelligent & Fuzzy Systems*, 14, 121–136.

Jukic, N. (2006). Modeling strategies and alternatives for data warehousing projects. *Communications of the ACM*, 49(4), 83–88. doi:10.1145/1121949.1121952

Kerdprasop, N., & Kerdpraso, K. (2007). Moving data mining tools toward a business intelligence system. *Enformatika*, 19, 117–122.

Kuhlmann, A., Vetter, R. M., Lubbing, C., & Thole, C. A. (2005). Data mining on crash simulation data. *Proceedings Conference MLDM 2005, Leipzig/Germany*.

Lange, K. (2006). Differences between statistics and data mining. *DM Review*, 16(12), 32–33.

Lau, K. N., Lee, K. H., Ho, Y., & Lam, P. Y. (2004). Mining the web for business intelligence: Homepage analysis in the internet era. *Database Marketing & Customer Strategy Management*, 12, 32–54. doi:10.1057/palgrave.dbm.3240241

Mannila, H. (1997). Methods and problems in data mining. *Proceedings of International Conference on Database Theory*, Delphi, Greece.

Mei, L., & Thole, C. A. (2008). Data analysis for parallel car-crash simulation results and model optimization. *Simulation Modelling Practice and Theory*, 16, 329–337. doi:10.1016/j.simpat.2007.11.018

Morbitzer, C., Strachan, P., & Simpson, C. (2004). Data mining analysis of building simulation performance data. *Building Services Engineers Res. Technologies*, 25(3), 253–267.

Nayak, R., & Qiu, T. (2005). A data mining application: analysis of problems occurring during a software project development process. *International Journal of Software Engineering and Knowledge Engineering*, 15(4), 647–663. doi:10.1142/S0218194005002476

Nigash, S. (2004). Business Intelligence. *Communications of the Association for Information Systems*, 13, 177–195.

Nonaka, I., Toyama, R., & Konno, N. (2000). SECI, Ba and aeadership: a unified model of dynamic knowledge creation. *Long Range Planning*, 33, 5–34. doi:10.1016/S0024-6301(99)00115-6

Okuhara, K., Ishii, H., & Uchida, M. (2005). Support of decision making by data mining using neural system. *Systems and Computers in Japan*, 36(11), 102–110. doi:10.1002/scj.10577

Painter, M. K., Erraguntla, M., Hogg, G. L., & Beachkofski, B. (2006). Using simulation, data mining, and knowledge discovery techniques for optimized aircraft engine fleet management. *Proceedings of the 2006 Winter Simulation Conference*, 1253-1260.

Power, D. J. (2007). A Brief History of Decision Support Systems. *DSSResources.com*. Retrieved from http://DSSResources.COM/history/dsshistory.html, version 4.0.

Remondino, M., & Correndo, G. (2005). Data mining applied to agent based simulation. *Proceedings 19th European Conference on Modelling and Simulation*.

Sen, A., & Sinha, A. P. (2005). A comparison of data warehousing methodologies. *Communications of the ACM, 48*(3), 79–84. doi:10.1145/1047671.1047673

Shariat, M., & Hightower, R. Jr. (2007). Conceptualizing Business Intelligence Architecture. *Marketing Management Journal, 17*(2), 40–46.

Shi, Y., Peng, Y., Kou, G., & Chen, Z. (2005). Classifying Credit Card Accounts For Business Intelligence And Decision Making: A Multiple-Criteria Quadratic Programming Approach. *International Journal of Information Technology & Decision Making, 4*(4), 581–599. doi:10.1142/S0219622005001775

Smith, W. (2005). Applying data mining to scheduling courses at a university. *Communications Of AIs, 16*, 463–474.

Srivastava, J., & Cooley, R. (2003). Web Business Intelligence: Mining the Web for Actionable Knowledge. *INFORMS Journal on Computing, 15*(2), 191–207. doi:10.1287/ijoc.15.2.191.14447

Steele, R. D. (2002). *The New Craft of Intelligence: Personal, Public and Political*. VA: OSS International Press.

Stolba, N., & Tjoa, A. M. (2006). The relevance of data warehousing and data mining in the field of evidence-based medicine to support healthcare decision making. *Enformatika, 11*, 12–17.

Turban, E., Aronson, J. E., Liang, T. P., & Sharda, R. (2007). *Decision Support and Business Intelligence Systems*, (8th Ed.). Upper Saddle River, NJ: Pearson Prentice Hall.

Vaduva, A., & Vetterli, T. (2001). Metadata management for data warehousing: an overview. *International Journal of Cooperative Information Systems, 10*(3), 273. doi:10.1142/S0218843001000357

Watson H. J., Wixom B. H., Hoffer J. A., Lehman R. A., & Reynolds A. M. (2006). Real-Time Business Intelligence: Best Practices at Continental Airlines. *Journal of Information Systems Management*, 7–18.

Weiss, S. M., Buckley, S. J., Kapoor, S., & Damgaard, S. (2003). Knowledge-Based Data Mining. [Washington, DC.]. *SIGKDD, 03*, 456–461.

Wixom, B. H. (2004). Business Intelligence Software for the Classroom: Microstrategy Resources on the Teradata University Network. *Communications of the Association for Information Systems, 14*, 234–246.

Wu, D., Olson, D. L., & Dong, Z. Y. (2006). Data mining and simulation: a grey relationship demonstration. *International Journal of Systems Science, 37*(13), 981–986. doi:10.1080/00207720600891521

Youzhi, X., & Jie S. (2004). The agent-based model on real-time data warehousing. *Journal of Systems Science & Information, 2*(2), 381–388.

Zack, J., Rainer, R. K., & Marshall, T. E. (2007). Business Intelligence: An Analysis of the Literature. *Information Systems Management, 25*, 121–131.

KEY TERMS AND DEFINITIONS

Data Mining (DM): Is the process of discovering interesting information from the hidden data that can either be used for future prediction and/or intelligently summarizing the details of the data (Mei, and Thole, 2008).

Business Intelligence (BI): Is an umbrella term that combines architectures, tools, data bases, applications, practices, and methodologies (Turban, Aronson, Liang, and Sharda, 2007). It is the process of transforming various types of business data into meaningful information that can help, decision makers at all levels, getting deeper insight of business.

Data Warehouse (DW): Is a physical repository where relational data are specially organized to provide enterprise-wide, cleansed data in a standardized format (Turban, Aronson, Liang, and Sharda, 2007).

Knowledge Management (KM): Is the acquisition, storage, retrieval, application, generation, and review of the knowledge assets of an organization in a controlled way.

Decision Support System (DSS): Is an approach (or methodology) for supporting making. It uses an interactive, flexible, adaptable computer-based information system especially developed for supporting the solution to a specific nonstructured management problem(Turban, Aronson, Liang, and Sharda, 2007).

Adaptive Neuro-Fuzzy Inference System (ANFIS): Is a data mining methodology based on a combination of fuzzy logic & neural networks by clustering values in fuzzy sets, membership functions are estimated during training, and using neural networks to estimate weights (Alnoukari, Alzoabi, and Hanna, 2008).

Quality Assurance (QA): Is all those planned and systematic actions necessary to provide adequate confidence that a product or service will satisfy given requirements for quality.

Chapter 17
Modeling and Simulation of IEEE 802.11g using OMNeT++

Nurul I. Sarkar
AUT University, Auckland, New Zealand

Richard Membarth
University of Erlangen-Nuremberg, Erlangen, Germany

ABSTRACT

Due to the complex nature of computer and telecommunication networks, it is often difficult to predict the impact of different parameters on system performance especially when deploying wireless networks. Computer simulation has become a popular methodology for performance study of computer and telecommunication networks. This popularity results from the availability of various sophisticated and powerful simulation software packages, and also because of the flexibility in model construction and validation offered by simulation. While various network simulators exist for building a variety of network models, choosing a good network simulator is very important in modeling and performance analysis of wireless networks. A good simulator is one that is easy to use; more flexible in model development, modification and validation; and incorporates appropriate analysis of simulation output data, pseudorandom number generators, and statistical accuracy of the simulation results. OMNeT++ is becoming one of the most popular network simulators because it has all the features of a good simulator. This chapter aims to provide a tutorial on OMNeT++ focusing on modeling and performance study of the IEEE 802.11g wireless network.

INTRODUCTION

The use of discrete event simulation packages as an aid to modeling and performance evaluation of computer and telecommunication networks, including wireless networks has grown in recent years

(Bianchi, 2000; Fantacci, Pecorella, & Habib, 2004; Tickoo & Sikdar, 2003). This popularity is due to the availability of sophisticated simulation packages and low-cost powerful personal computers (PCs), but also because of the flexibility in rapid model construction and validation offered by simulation. A detailed discussion of simulation methodology, in general, can be found in (Carson II, 2004; Law

DOI: 10.4018/978-1-60566-774-4.ch017

& Kelton, 2000). More specifically, Pawlikowski (1990) in a comprehensive survey of problems and solutions suited for steady-state simulation mentioned the relevance of simulation techniques for modeling telecommunication networks. While various network simulators (both open source and commercial) exist for building a variety of network models, selecting an appropriate network simulation package for a particular application is not an easy task. For selecting an appropriate network simulator, it is important to have knowledge of the simulator tools available along with their strengths and weaknesses. It is also important to ensure that the results generated by the simulators are valid and credible. Sarkar and Halim (2008) classified and compared various network simulators to aid researchers and developers in selecting the most appropriate simulation tool.

We have looked at a number of widely used network simulators, including ns-2 (*Network simulator 2*, 2008) and OPNET Modeler (*OPNET Technologies*). Ns-2 is a popular network simulator among the network research community which is available for download at no costs. However, ns-2 is difficult to use and has a steep learning curve. A tutorial contributed by Marc Greis (www.isi.edu/nsnam/ns/tutorial/index.html) and the continuing evolution of the ns documentation have improved the situation, but ns-2's split-programming model remains a barrier to many developers. OPNET is a commercial package which has a comprehensive model library, user-friendly graphical user interface (GUI), and customizable presentation of simulation results. However, OPNET is a very expensive package even though the package is offered under University academic programs. However, OPNET IT Guru is available at no costs for educational use but it has very limited functionality. The motivation of using OMNeT++ (*OMNeT++*, 2008) as a network simulator in our study is that it offers the combined advantages of ns-2 and OPNET.

The remainder of this chapter is organized as follows. A review of literature including strengths and weaknesses of OMNeT++ is presented first. We then outline the system requirements and installation procedure. A brief overview of the INET Framework (a framework for OMNeT++ containing models for several Internet protocols) is presented next. A tutorial on OMNeT++ focusing on developing, configuring and running simulation models is presented. The network performance and test results are presented followed by brief conclusions.

STRENGTHS AND WEAKNESSES OF OMNET++

The strengths and weaknesses of OMNeT++ are highlighted below.

Strengths: The main strengths of OMNeT++ are the GUI, object inspectors for zooming into component level and to display the state of each component during simulation, the modular architecture, as well as a configurable and detailed implementation of modules and protocols. OMNeT ++ is an open source software package allowing users to change the source code to suit their needs. It supports a variety of operating systems (OSs) such as Linux and MS Windows. Another advantage of OMNeT++ is that it can be integrated with other programs. For example, it is possible to embed OMNeT++ in an application which creates a network model, simulates it and produces results automatically. OMNeT++ builds on small modules that can be reused and combined to more complex modules. Thus a hierarchy could be generated and different levels of abstraction can be realized. Object inspection is a useful feature offered by OMNeT++. For example, the current state of each module, parameters, and statistics can be viewed at any time during simulation experiments. This feature allows us to observe the data flow and node communications. OMNeT++ can store simulation results in a file that can be analyzed later using various tools supported by OMNeT++.

Weaknesses: OMNeT++ is slow due to its long simulation run times and high memory consumption. Developing a model using OMNeT++ requires more than just drag and drop components on a workspace. The simulation model needs to be developed in two different applications and configured in a text file. This can be inconvenient, in particular for inexperienced users.

OMNET++: A REVIEW OF LITERATURE

OMNeT++ is an object-oriented discrete event simulator written in C++ (Varga, 1999, 2001). It is a non-commercial, open source software package developed by Andras Varga at the Technical University of Budapest in 1992. It is primarily designed for simulation tasks especially for performance modeling of computer and data communication networks. It is relatively easy to integrate new modules or alter current implementations of modules within its object-oriented architecture. More details about OMNeT++ can be found at the OMNeT++ homepage (www.hit.bme.hu/phd/varga/omnetpp.htm).

Examples of commonly used open source network simulators are ns-2, GloMoSim (GloMoSim, 2001), and AKAROA (Ewing, Pawlikowski, & McNickle, 1999; Pawlikowski, Yau, & McNickle, 1994); and commercial network simulators include OPNET (www.opnet.com), QualNet Developer (Scalable Network Technologies, 2007), and NetSim (Tetcos, 2007). A brief overview of various popular network simulators with their relative strengths and weaknesses can be found in (N.I. Sarkar & Halim, 2008; N. I. Sarkar & Petrova, 2005).

While commercial network simulators support a wide range of protocols, those simulators released under open source are more specialised on one specific protocol (e.g., ns-2 supports TCP/IP). However, OMNeT++ uses a different approach, offers a dual licensing. The source code is released as open source which is available for download at no costs whereas the commercial version called OMNEST (*OMNEST*, 2007) requires a license for using it. As mentioned earlier, OMNeT++ has a GUI with its unique object inspectors for zooming into components and to display the current state of each component at any time during the simulation. Other simulators such as OPNET provide a GUI to set up and control simulation only and ns-2 has no GUI at all (Varga, 2001). Furthermore, OMNeT++ provides detailed protocol level description which is particularly useful for teaching, research and development (Varga, 1999). As OPNET, OMNeT++ can also be used for performance evaluation of larger enterprise networks as it has a modular architecture allowing module reuse at different levels of abstraction. This modular architecture allows extending the functionality of OMNeT++ without changing it. Another advantage of OMNeT++ is the automatic generation of scenarios as no proprietary binary formats are used to store models. However, one has to be aware when using network simulators. Cavin et al. (2002) demonstrate that the same model can produce different results (both quantitative and qualitative) when run under different network simulators. Thus, the simulator characteristics need to be looked at and match with the model to be simulated. The effect of detailed simulation also plays an important role in network performance evaluation. Heidemann et al. (2001) argue that a trade-off between detailed but slow simulations and those lacking details and possibly leading to incorrect results need to be considered. Protocols can be modeled in OMNeT++ at a high level of details, but it requires extensive resources. However, OMNeT++ supports parallel and distributed simulations, running not only on a multiprocessor system, but also in a network of distributed hosts. Hence, OMNeT++ can be used as an alternative tool for network modeling and performance evaluation.

SYSTEM REQUIREMENTS AND SETUP

OMNeT++ supports commonly used OSs such as MS Windows, Linux, UNIX and Macintosh. For most UNIX systems, the GNU development tools (gcc, g++) are available for system implementation. For Mac OS X, the development tools are normally shipped on a CD with the main distribution. When install on Mac OS X, it is important to install Apple's X11 in order to run graphical Linux/UNIX programs. For Linux and other UNIX systems, the development tools need to be installed. For MS Windows, various development tools such as Cygwin, MinGW and Microsoft Visual C++ can be used to build the system.

OMNeT++ relies on programs such as perl that need to be installed before installing OMNeT++. In particular, software for the GUI (tcl/tk, btl), XML support (libxslt), documentation generation (doxygen) and image processing (ghostscript, ImageMagick, graphviz, and giftrans) need to be installed separately. For Mac OS X, package management tools such as Fink (http://www.fink-project.org/) or MacPorts (http://www.macports.org/) can be used therefore. We used MacPorts for downloading, building and installing most of the packages automatically. However, only giftrans was not in the repository and therefore it was built manually and put in a directory where it could be found by OMNeT++. This is done by using the following commands:

```
bash # sudo port install tcl tk blt
libxslt doxygen ghostscript  ImageMagick
graphviz
bash# gcc -O2 -g -Wall -o giftrans
giftrans.c
bash# mv giftrans /opt/local/bin/
```

OMNeT++ is available for download at no costs under MS Windows, which includes all required third party tools and no further software is required. The package is also available to download for various Linux distributions like Debian, and it is possible to install OMNeT++ with a single command. The OMNeT++ installation procedure is outlined next.

INSTALLATION

Once all the required software packages are installed on a system, OMNeT++ can then be installed. Since OMNeT++ is an open source software package, the main distribution form is a tarball of its source code. OMNeT++ was compiled after downloading and unpacking the tarball. We specify the correct path to the libraries installed by MacPorts (which is /opt/local/...) and for Mac OS X we have also to inform the compiler that the libraries are compiled and loaded dynamically. The following lines were added in configure.user.

```
# File: configure.user
CFLAGS="-Wno-long-double -I/usr/include/
malloc -fPIC"   # other options
like -g and -O2 can be added
LDFLAGS="-bind_at_load"
SHLIB_LD="g++ -dynamiclib -undefined dy-
namic_lookup"
SO_LIB_SUFFIX=".dylib"
TK_CFLAGS="-I/opt/local/include -fwrit-
able-strings"
TK_LIBS="-L/opt/local/lib -ltk8.4
-ltcl8.4"
BLT_LIBS="-L/opt/local/lib -lBLT"
```

Next we extend the environment variables to include libraries required by OMNeT++. This is done by editing the .bashrc file in the user's home directory by replacing /path/to/omnetpp/ with the actual directory containing OMNeT++:

```
export PATH=$PATH:/path/to/omnetpp/bin
export LD_LIBRARY_PATH=/path/to/omnetpp/
lib:/path/to/omnetpp/INET/bin
export TCL_LIBRARY=/opt/local/lib/tcl8.4
```

```
export DYLD_LIBRARY_PATH=$DYLD_LIBRARY_
PATH:/path/to/omnetpp/lib
```

These changes take effect for command lines started after the file has been modified. So, either open a new command line or enter source ~/.*bashrc* in the command line to get the new environment variables.

OMNeT++ was compiled using the ./*configure* and *make* commands. This can be done inside of Apple's X11 environment or from a normal command line while X11 runs and the DISPLAY environment variable is set correctly (e.g. export DISPLAY=":0.0"):

```
bash# export MACOSX_DEPLOYMENT_TAR-
GET=10.4
bash# ./configure
bash# make
```

The ./configure checks whether all requirements for OMNeT++ are fulfilled and displays messages if anything is missing as follows.

```
WARNING: The configuration script could
not detect the following packages:
MPI (optional) Akaroa (optional)
 ...
Your PATH contains /path/to/omnetpp/bin.
Good!
Your LD_LIBRARY_PATH is set. Good!
TCL_LIBRARY is set. Good!
```

We can see from the above warning message that two packages (MPI and Akaroa) have not been found by the configuration script which are optional packages for parallel simulation. More details about Akaroa can be found at www.cosc.canterbury.ac.nz/research/RG/net_sim/simulation_group/akaroa/.

INET FRAMEWORK

OMNeT++ provides a simulation kernel and some basic utilities for queues, random number generators, and simulation output statistics only. It does not provide network components or modules for simulations. However, the INET Framework (user community) and Mobility Framework (specialised on mobile nodes and protocols) provide various modules that can be used for developing simulation models. The INET framework can be downloaded from the OMNeT++ homepage (www.hit.bme.hu/phd/varga/omnetpp.htm), and installed on a machine easily. In the inetconfig the ROOT parameter is adjusted to the directory of the framework before one can build it using the ./makemake and make commands. The INET Framework is used for modeling and simulation of IEEE 802.11g networks.

MODELING THE NETWORK

OMNeT++ Architecture

In OMNeT++, the most important elements beside events are modules. There are two different types of modules: (1) simple modules; and (2) compound modules. Simple modules are implemented in C++ and represent the active components of OMNeT++ where events occur and model behaviours are defined. Compound modules are a composition of other simple or compound modules, and are used as containers to structure a model. An example of a compound module is an 802.11 network interface card (NIC) represented in OMNeT++ as Ieee80211Nic (Figure 1). The Ieee80211Nic consists of three simple modules namely, Ieee80211Mac, Ieee80211Mgmt, and Ieee80211Radio.

Unlike simple modules, compound modules are not written in C++. However, they use NEtwork Description (NED), a simple language to describe the topology of the simulation model.

Figure 1. Compound module Ieee80211Nic

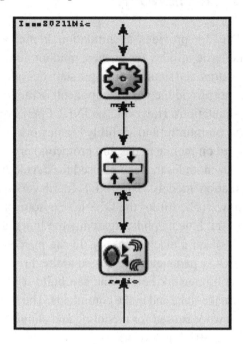

The .ned file(s) can either be loaded dynamically or compiled static into binary of the INET framework. The actual simulation model in OMNeT++ is called 'network' which is a compound module. To configure a network one can either specify the parameters for modules in .ned files or in the omnet.ini configuration file. The advantage of using the configuration file is to define simulation runs with various parameter values. This is particularly useful when we run simulations from a script or batch file.

OMNeT++ provides two types of simulation data outputs: scalar and vector. A scalar has one single value of the simulation output (e.g., the number of packets received). However, vectors store series of time-value pairs over a certain period such as response times during the simulation. One can add a new statistic by modifying simple modules to log the data of interest and recompile

Figure 2. Description of an ad hoc network in OMNeT++

```
import
    "MobileHost",
    "ChannelControl",
    "FlatNetworkConfigurator";

module Adhoc80211
    parameters:
        numHosts: numeric const,
        playgroundSizeX: numeric const,
        playgroundSizeY: numeric const;

    submodules:
        host: MobileHost[numHosts];
            display: "i=device/wifilaptop_s;r=,,#707070";
        channelcontrol: ChannelControl;
            parameters:
                playgroundSizeX = playgroundSizeX,
                playgroundSizeY = playgroundSizeY;
            display: "p=60,50;i=misc/sun";
        configurator: FlatNetworkConfigurator;
            parameters:
                moduleTypes = "MobileHost",
                nonIPModuleTypes = "", networkAddress = "145.236.0.0",
                netmask = "255.255.0.0";
            display: "p=140,50;i=block/cogwheel_s";
    connections nocheck:
endmodule

network adhoc80211 : Adhoc80211
endnetwork
```

the framework. These statistics are stored in files at the end of simulation and can be analysed later using plove and scalar programs provided by OMNeT++ or other statistical tools such as R (http://www.r-project.org/), Octave (http://www.octave.org/) or MATLAB.

Developing a Simulation Model

We develop simulation models (using INET Framework) for IEEE 802.11g networks. The following INET Framework modules are used: 'MobileHost' for an ad hoc network, 'Channel-Control' for keeping track of the station position and to provide an area for station movement, and 'FlatNetwork Configurator' for configuration of IP addresses and routing tables for simple networks. Each of the modules that we use in the simulation was imported from a .ned file. The list of modules that the INET Framework supports can be found in "documentation/index.html". We also develop a compound module called Adhoc80211 contain-

ing the following four elements described below. The complete description of an ad hoc network is shown in Figure 2.

1) **Parameters:** Module variables which are used to configure submodules.

2) **Submodules:** Instances of other modules. One can assign values to the parameters of submodules. We define a number of instances of the MobileHost which are stored in an array called host. The number of instances is determined by a module parameter which allows us to develop simulation model with several stations by changing the numHosts parameter. We also define a variable called display for the modules to display in the GUI. More details about module configuration can be found in the OMNeT++ user manual (doc/manual/usman.html).

3) **Gates:** Connection points of a module.

4) **Connections:** Define a connection between two gates or submodules. For example, two

Figure 3. AdhocSimple.ned loaded in gned

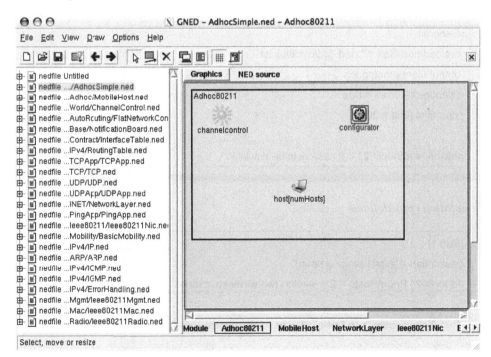

wireless stations are connected through a NIC. OMNeT++ checks whether all gates are connected properly to the network.

OMNeT++ also provides a graphical tool to build compound modules, called gned. Figure 3 shows our ad hoc network module loaded in gned. However, as the syntax of .ned is straight forward it is faster to model it directly in a text editor.

Configuring a Simulation Model

The simulation model is configured and parameter values are assigned to the network (adhoc80211) and submodules before running simulations. Figure 4 shows the network configuration file (omnet.ini). It sets the general configurations for OMNeT++ and loads all .ned files in the current directory. The network for the simulation is adhoc80211.

Next we define a couple of simulation runs as shown in Figure 5. These runs are mainly used for executing simulation experiments with differ-

ent parameters. For example, in Run 1 we assign numHosts to 2, to create two wireless stations at the start of the simulation. In Run 2, no values are assigned so that a user can enter the desired number of stations at the system prompt.

OMNeT++ provides two environments for simulations: Tkenv (GUI) and Cmdenv (non GUI). Tkenv is used for developing a model or demonstration purposes, and Cmdenv is used for fast simulation. The behaviour of the environments can be specified as follows:

```
[Cmdenv]
express-mode = no
[Tkenv]
;default-run=1
```

Figure 6 shows the detailed simulation parameter setting for an 802.11 ad hoc network. Wildcards are used to assign values to one variable of different instances. While one asterisk matches only one instance in the hierarchy (e.g. *.playground-SizeX matches adhoc80211.

Figure 4. Configuration file (omnet.ini)

```
[General]
 preload-ned-files = *.ned @../nedfiles.lst
 output-file=omnetpp.log
 ; debug-on-errors = true
 ; cpu-time-limit = 30


 network = adhoc80211  # network to be simulated
```

Figure 5. Simulation runs defined

```
[Run 1]
description = "host1 pinging host0"
adhoc80211.numHosts = 2 #  assign two wireless stations


[Run 2] description = "n hosts"  # user need to enter numHosts
```

Figure 6. Simulation parameter setting

```
[Parameters]                                    # ip settings
*.playgroundSizeX = 600                         **.routingFile=""
*.playgroundSizeY = 400                         **.ip.procDelay=10us
**.debug = true                                 **.IPForward=false
**.coreDebug = 0
**.host*.**.channelNumber = 0                   # ARP configuration
                                                **.arp.retryTimeout = 1
# channel physical parameters                   **.arp.retryCount = 3
*.channelcontrol.carrierFrequency = 2.4e+9      **.arp.cacheTimeout = 100
*.channelcontrol.pMax = 2.0 ;[mW]               **.networkLayer.proxyARP = true #
*.channelcontrol.sat = -110                     Host's is hardwired "false"
*.channelcontrol.alpha = 2
*.channelcontrol.numChannels = 1                # nic settings
                                                **.wlan.mgmt.frameCapacity = 10
# mobility                                       **.wlan.mac.address = "auto"
**.host*.mobility.x = -1                          **.wlan.mac.maxQueueSize = 14
**.host*.mobility.y = -1                         **.wlan.mac.rtsThresholdBytes = 3000
                                                  **.wlan.mac.bitrate = 2e6 # 2Mbps
**.host*.mobilityType = "MassMobility"          **.wlan.mac.retryLimit = 7
**.host*.mobility.changeInterval = truncnormal(2, 0.5)   **.wlan.mac.cwMinData = 7
**.host*.mobility.changeAngleBy = normal(0, 30)  **.wlan.mac.cwMinBroadcast = 31
**.host*.mobility.speed = truncnormal(20, 8)
**.host*.mobility.updateInterval = 0.1          **.wlan.radio.bitrate=2E+6 ;2Mbps
                                                **.wlan.radio.transmitterPower=2.0
# udp apps (off)                                ;[mW]
**.numUdpApps=0                                 **.wlan.radio.carrierFrequency=2.4E+9
**.udpAppType="UDPBasicApp"                     **.wlan.radio.thermalNoise=-110
                                                **.wlan.radio.sensitivity=-85
# tcp apps (off)                                **.wlan.radio.pathLossAlpha=2
**.numTcpApps=0                                 **.wlan.radio.snirThreshold = 4 # in dB
**.tcpAppType="TelnetApp"

# ping app (host[0] pinged by others)
*.host[0].pingApp.destAddr=""
*.host[*].pingApp.destAddr="host[0]"
**.pingApp.srcAddr=""
**.pingApp.packetSize=56
**.pingApp.interval=0.1 **.pingApp.hopLimit=32
**.pingApp.count=200
**.pingApp.startTime=uniform(1,5)
**.pingApp.stopTime=0
**.pingApp.printPing=true

# tcp settings
**.tcp.mss = 1024
**.tcp.advertisedWindow = 14336 # 14*mss
**.tcp.sendQueueClass="TCPMsgBasedSendQueue"
**.tcp.receiveQueueClass="TCPMsgBasedRcvQueue"
**.tcp.tcpAlgorithmClass="TCPReno"
**.tcp.recordStats=true
```

playgroundSizeX, but not adhoc80211.test.play-groundSizeX), two asterisks match all variables in the hierarchy. For example, **.debug matches every debug variable in each module and its sub modules. The parameters that need to be set can be found in the documentation of each module where all unassigned module parameters and its submodules are listed.

The parameters for wireless local area network (WLAN), ARP, IP, TCP, and station mobility are set. Stations are moved within the defined playground and all stations send ping messages to station [0] for an infinite time (i.e. simulation will never stop) as events will never run out. Simulation time can be defined to stop simulation. For example, sim-time-limit (elapsed time in the simulation) or cpu-time-limit (elapsed real time) can be defined in the general section of the configuration file to stop simulations. The last section of the configuration file is for output vectors which can be enabled or disabled. By default all output vectors (time-value pairs) are enabled and stored in memory. This consumes a lot of memory and slows down simulations. Thus, it is recommended to disable all output vectors except the ones that we are interested in. This can be achieved by enabling all output vectors of the pingApp in station 1 and all other vectors disabled. Instead of setting output vectors globally, it is also possible to set them up in each of the individually.

```
[OutVectors]
 **.host[1].pingApp.**.enabled = yes
**.enabled = no
```

Running a Simulation Model

Figure 7 shows a simple framework in which we develop and execute various simulation models under OMNeT++ to study WLAN performance. The INET Framework provides wireless modules for developing simulation models to be compiled and executed in OMNeT++.

While the simulation model defines the network to be simulated, the model is configured by a configuration file which is also loaded at the start of the simulator. Finally, the simulation results are stored in output files for later analysis.

A simulation model can be run by calling the INET binary from the configuration folder. However, it is more convenient to run simulations by calling the following script and make it executable (e.g., chmod +x file):

```
../bin/INET $*
```

After executing the script, one of the runs defined in Figure 5 can be selected. After selecting Run 1 two windows are opened: The main window of OMNeT++ and another window containing our

Figure 7. A framework for developing and executing simulation models in OMNeT++

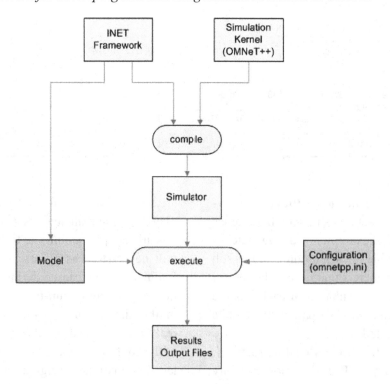

simulated network. As shown in Figure 8, the tool bar has buttons for running and stopping simulation. The simulation speed can also be adjusted using the 'slider' button (next to 'stop' button). Instead of running a simulation one can also step through the simulation, from event to event using the 'step' button. Two wireless stations are communicating by sending ping messages (Figure 8). The details of host[0] in Figure 8 can be found by double clicking on it (Figure 9).

Figure 10 shows the main window of OM-NeT++, which can be used to controlled simulations. For example, three lines between the toolbar and the timeline displaying simulation statistics such as the number of events and events per second. The main window contains the simulation log (message, event and debugging information). On the left of the window is a tree displaying the simulation events. This is very useful information if one observes the internal state of each module. While all log messages are displayed in the log window, the output of the ping command is displayed on the console and the summary is stored to files (Figure 11).

When Run 2 (Figure 5) is selected, a simulated network with N = 10 wireless stations as shown in Figure 12 is opened. The host[2] sends a ping packet to other nine hosts including host[0].

ANALYSIS OF RESULTS

For evaluation and interpretation of experimental results, it is useful to compare results obtained from more than one set of simulation outputs with different parameters. We used the same amount of events in each output vector by limiting the number of pings to 50 and have two runs by changing the packet length from 56 to 112 bytes. We set **.pingApp.count variable to 50 and change the packet length between the runs. This was achieved by defining extra simulation runs in the omnetpp.

Figure 8. Adhoc80211 network simulation with 2 stations pinging each other

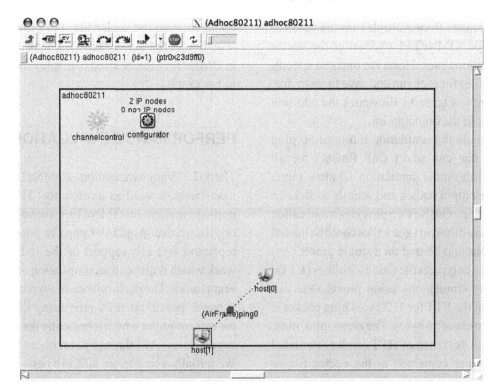

Figure 9. Details of host[0] submodule

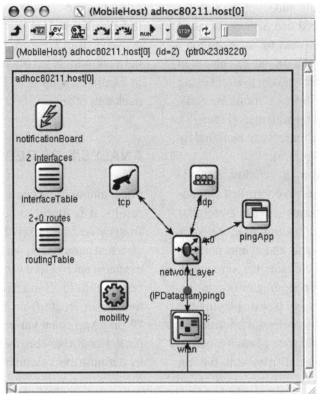

ini. While scalars from multiple runs are saved to the same file, OMNeT++ overwrites the vector files of previous runs. However one can specify the output files for each run and save them to disk independently. Figure 13 illustrates the addition of two runs in the omnetpp.ini.

To continue the simulation run until 50 ping messages, one can select Call finish() for all modules in the main simulation window menu to write the output scalars and vectors to disk. To plot vector files, OMNeT++ provides a tool called 'plove' where different vector files could be loaded simultaneous and plotted on a single graph.

Figure 14 compares the round trip times (RTTs) of two ping simulations using plove. One can observe that the RTT for 112 bytes ping packet is longer than that of 56 bytes. The mean, min, max, and standard deviation of RTT can be calculated from all values contained in the vector file or

obtained from the scalar file. For graphical presentation of the above statistics, scalars included in OMNeT++ can be used to display the statistics in bar graphs.

PERFORMANCE EVALUATION

The 802.11b implementation of OMNeT++'s INET Framework is used as a reference. The 802.11g implementation in OMNeT++ (www.omnetpp. org/listarchive/msg08494.php) is adapted here, replacing 802.11b support of the INET Framework which requires a recompilation of the INET Framework. The performance of a typical 802.11g network is evaluated by measuring the network mean throughput which is basically the same as an access point (AP) throughput without RTS/CTS. We initially consider an 802.11b network with N

Figure 10. Main window of OMNeT++ illustrating simulation runs

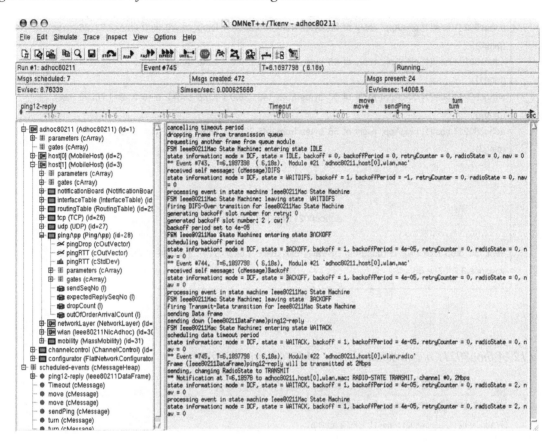

= 1 station sending a large volume of data to an AP. We then observe the network throughput by increasing the number of wireless stations (i.e., increased traffic). Figure 15 shows an 802.11b network with seven stations and an AP where all stations are sending data to the AP. Likewise, the impact of increasing the number of stations on an 802.11g throughput was investigated.

To simulate 802.11g, we made some changes to the omnetpp.ini by adding parameters as shown in Figure 16.

Each simulation experiment was run for five minutes of simulation time (up to 20 minutes in real time depending on number of stations). The experimental results for the throughput performance of 802.11b and 802.11g are summarized in Table 1. We observe that the maximum throughput is not achieved with N= 1 wireless station, but

with a few stations. The maximum throughput is achieved with N = 5 stations and N = 7 to 10 stations for 802.11b and 802.11g, respectively. The lower backoff times as a result of concurrent access to the wireless channel contributing to less wastage of channel bandwidth and hence achieving higher throughput for N >1 user. The number of collisions increases and the collisions take over the positive backoff effect leading to throughput decline at N > 5 stations for 802.11b and N > 10 stations for 802.11g networks. Our simulation results are in accordance with the work of other network researchers (Choi, Park, & Kim, 2005).

Another observation is that the achieved network throughputs are a lot lower compared to the data rate. As shown in Table 1, the maximum achieved efficiencies are 51% and 47% for 802.11b

Figure 11. Output of ping message

adhoc80211.host[1].pingApp: reply of 56 bytes from 145.236.0.1 icmp_seq=0 ttl=0 time=3.03186 msec
(ping0)

adhoc80211.host[1].pingApp: reply of 56 bytes from 145.236.0.1 icmp_seq=1 ttl=0 time=1.66294 msec
(ping1)

adhoc80211.host[1].pingApp: reply of 56 bytes from 145.236.0.1 icmp_seq=2 ttl=0 time=1.78296 msec
(ping2)

adhoc80211.host[1].pingApp: reply of 56 bytes from 145.236.0.1 icmp_seq=3 ttl=0 time=1.78298 msec
(ping3)

...

adhoc80211.host[1].pingApp

sent: 50 drop rate (%): 0 round-trip min/avg/max (ms): 1.643/1.7378/3.03186 stddev (ms): 0.192634
variance:3.71078e-08

Figure 12. Adhoc80211 network simulation with 10 stations (hosts)

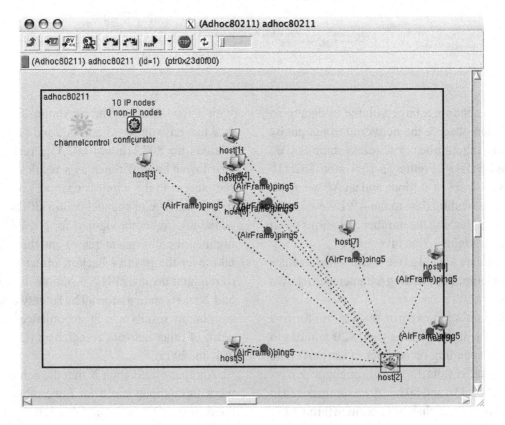

Figure 13. Run 3 and 4 are added in the omnetpp.ini

```
[Run 3]
description = "host1 pinging host0; 56 bytes packet size"
adhoc80211.numHosts = 2
output-vector-file = omnetpp_56.vec
**.pingApp.count=50
**.pingApp.packetSize=56

[Run 4]
description = "host1 pinging host0; 112 bytes packet size"
 adhoc80211.numHosts = 2
output-vector-file = omnetpp_112.vec
 **.pingApp.count=50
**.pingApp.packetSize=112
```

Figure 14. Comparison of RTT from two ping messages

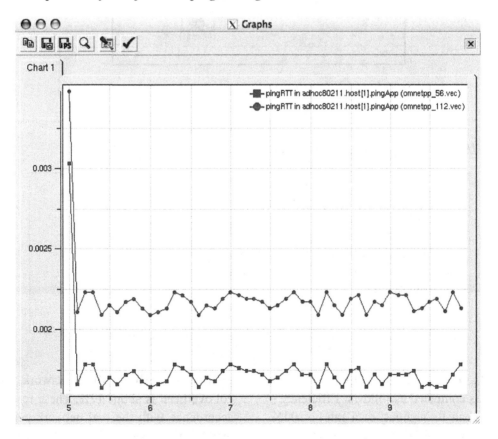

Figure 15. IEEE 802.11b network with an AP and seven wireless stations

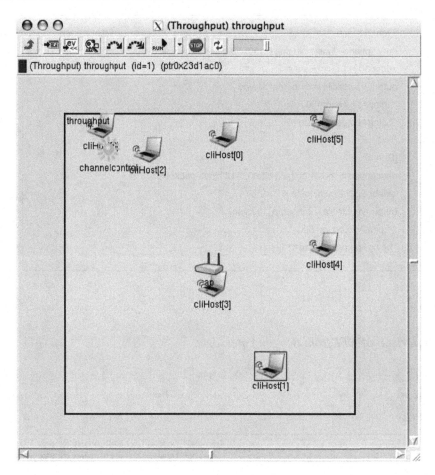

Figure 16. IEEE 802.11g parameters in the omnetpp.ini

```
**.wlan.mac.basicBitrate = 54e6    # 54Mbps
**.wlan.mac.slotTime = 9us         # slot duration
**.wlan.mac.AIFSN = 2              # DIFS
**.wlan.radio.phyOpMode = 'g'      # b/g 802.11b/802.11g-only
**.wlan.radio.channelModel = 'r'   # r/a Rayleigh/awgn
**.mac.opMode = 'g'
**.mac.bitrate = 54e6              # 54Mbps
```

and 802.11g, respectively. The network (channel) efficiency is computed as follows: Efficiency = (network mean throughput/ data rate) ×100%. Our simulation results show that more than 50% is protocol overhead for 802.11g networks. For an IEEE 802.11b (11 Mbps) network, the protocol overhead is about 49%. These results are in accordance with the real network performance measurement reported in (Broadcom, 2003).

Table 1. Impact of increasing the number of stations on the 802.11b (11 Mbps) and 802.11g (54 Mbps) network throughput

Number of nodes	IEEE 802.11b		IEEE 802.11g	
	Throughput (Mbps)	Efficiency (%)	Throughput (Mbps)	Efficiency (%)
1	5.11	46.45	20.26	37.52
3	5.39	49.00	23.67	43.83
5	5.61	51.00	25.52	47.26
7	5.53	50.27	25.56	47.33
10	5.35	48.64	25.56	47.33
20	4.94	44.91	24.9	46.11
30	4.46	40.55	22.89	42.39
40	4.12	37.45	21.27	39.39

CONCLUSION AND FUTURE WORK

Stochastic discrete event simulation has become popular as a network modeling and performance analysis tool. This chapter provided a walk-through tutorial on OMNeT++, a discrete-event network simulator that can be used for modeling and performance evaluation of computer and tele-communication networks. The tutorial focused on installation of OMNeT++, modelling the network, running simulations, and analysing results. The performance test results of a typical IEEE 802.11g network are also presented. The models built under OMNeT++ were validated using empirical measurements from wireless laptops and access points for IEEE 802.11g. A good match between simulation and measurement results for N = 1 to 3 stations validates the OMNeT++ simulation models (N. I. Sarkar & Lo, 2008).

In summary, we want to stress the importance of using a good simulator for modeling and performance analysis of wireless communication networks. The OMNeT++ offers more flexibility in model construction and validation, and incorporates appropriate analysis of simulation output data.

There are several possibilities that one can contribute in the emerging area of network simulation and modelling. The following research problems have been suggested as an extension to the work presented in this chapter: (1) to investigate the impact of backoff mechanisms on throughput of 802.11g; and (2) to run simulations in multiple replications in parallel (MRIP). This can be achieved by developing network models using OMNeT++ and interfacing them with Akaroa II (Ewing et al., 1999).

REFERENCES

Bianchi, G. (2000). Performance analysis of the IEEE 802.11 distributed coordination function. *IEEE Journal on Selected Areas in Communications, 18*(3), 535–547. doi:10.1109/49.840210

Broadcom. (2003). *IEEE 802.11g: the new mainstream wireless LAN standard*. Retrieved May 23 2007, from http://www.54g.org/pdf/802.11g-WP104-RDS1

Carson, J. S., II. (2004, December). *Introduction to Modeling and Simulation*. Paper presented at 2004 Winter Simulation Conference (pp. 1283-1289).

Choi, S., Park, K., & Kim, C. (2005). *On the performance characteristics of WLANs: revisited.* Paper presented at the 2005 ACM SIGMETRICS international conference on Measurement and modeling of computer systems (pp. 97–108).

Ewing, G., Pawlikowski, K., & McNickle, D. (1999, June). *Akaroa 2: exploiting network computing by distributed stochastic simulation.* Paper presented at European Simulation Multiconference (ESM'99), Warsaw, Poland, (pp. 175-181).

Fantacci, R., Pecorella, T., & Habib, I. (2004). Proposal and performance evaluation of an efficient multiple-access protocol for LEO satellite packet networks. *IEEE Journal on Selected Areas in Communications, 22*(3), 538–545. doi:10.1109/JSAC.2004.823437

GloMoSim. (2007). *GloMoSim Manual.* Retrieved April 20, 2007, from http://pcl.cs.ucla.edu/projects/glomosim/GloMoSimManual.html

Law, A. M., & Kelton, W. D. (2000). *Simulation modelling and analysis* (3rd ed.). New York: McGraw-Hill.

Network Simulator 2 (2008). Retrieved September 15, 2008, from www.isi.edu/nsnam/ns/

OMNEST (2007). Retrieved September 15, 2007, from www.omnest.com

OMNeT++ (2008). Retrieved September 15, 2008, from http://www.omnetpp.org/

Pawlikowski, K. (1990). Steady-state simulation of queuing processes: a survey of problems and solutions. *ACM Computing Surveys, 1*(2), 123–170. doi:10.1145/78919.78921

Pawlikowski, K., Yau, V. W. C., & McNickle, D. (1994). *Distributed stochastic discrete event simulation in parallel time streams.* Paper presented at the Winter Simulation Conference. pp. 723-730.

Sarkar, N. I., & Halim, S. A. (2008, June 23-26). *Simulation of computer networks: simulators, methodologies and recommendations.* Paper presented at the 5th IEEE International Conference on Information Technology and Applications (ICITA'08), Cairns, Queensland, Australia (pp. 420-425).

Sarkar, N. I., & Lo, E. (2008, December 7-10). *Indoor propagation measurements for performance evaluation of IEEE 802.11g.* Paper presented at the IEEE Australasian Telecommunications Networks and Applications Conference (ATNAC'08), Adelaide, Australia (pp. 163-168).

Sarkar, N. I., & Petrova, K. (2005, June 27-30). *WebLan-Designer: a web-based system for interactive teaching and learning LAN design.* Paper presented at the 3rd IEEE International Conference on Information Technology Research and Education, Hsinchu, Taiwan (pp. 328-332).

Scalable Network Technologies. (2007). *QualNet Developer.* Retrieved 20 April, 2007, from http://www.qualnet.com/products/developer.php

Technologies, O. P. N. E. T. (2009). Retrieved January 20, 2009, from www.opnet.com

Tetcos. (2007). *Products.* Retrieved 20 April, 2007, from http://www.tetcos.com/software.html

Tickoo, O., & Sikdar, B. (2003). On the impact of IEEE 802.11 MAC on traffic characteristics. *IEEE Journal on Selected Areas in Communications, 21*(2), 189–203. doi:10.1109/JSAC.2002.807346

Varga, A. (1999). Using the OMNeT++ discrete event simulation system in education. *IEEE Transactions on Education, 42*(4), 1–11. doi:10.1109/13.804564

Varga, A. (2001, June 6-9). *The OMNeT++ discrete evenet simulation system.* Paper presented at the European Simulation Multiconference (ESM'01), Prague, Czech Republic.f

KEY TERMS AND DEFINITIONS

IEEE 802.11g: The IEEE 802.11g is the high-speed wireless LAN with a maximum data rate of 54 Mbps operating at 2.4 GHz. The IEEE 802.11g is backward compatible with the IEEE 802.11b.

OMNeT++: OMNeT++ is an object-oriented discrete event network simulator. It is an open source software package primarily designed for simulation and performance modeling of computer and data communication networks.

Computer Simulation: Computer simulation is a methodology that can be used for performance study of computer and telecommunication networks. It allows greater flexibility in model construction and validation offered by simulation.

INET Framework: The INET Framework (specialised on mobile nodes and protocols) provides various modules for developing simulation models. The INET framework can be downloaded from www.hit.bme.hu/phd/varga/omnetpp.htm.

Chapter 18
Performance Modeling of IEEE 802.11 WLAN using OPNET:
A Tutorial

Nurul I. Sarkar
AUT University, New Zealand

ABSTRACT

Computer simulation is becoming increasingly popular among computer network researchers for performance modeling and evaluation of computer and telecommunication networks. This popularity is due to the availability of various sophisticated and powerful simulators, and also because of the flexibility in model construction and validation offered by simulation. While various network simulators (both open source and commercial) exist for modeling and performance evaluation of communication networks, OPNET is becoming popular network simulator as the package is available to academic institutions at no cost, especially OPNET IT Guru. This chapter aims to provide a tutorial on OPNET focusing on the simulation and performance modeling of IEEE 802.11 wireless local area networks (WLANs). Results obtained show that OPNET provides credible simulation results close to a real system.

INTRODUCTION

The IEEE 802.11 is one of the most popular WLAN technologies in use today worldwide. This popularity results from the simplicity in operation, low-cost, high-speed, and user mobility offered by the technology. Computer simulation is becoming one of the most important tools for performance modeling and evaluation of telecommunication networks. It is often used to verify analytical models and generalization of propagation measurement results. Although a real network testbed allows maximum integrity for performance testing and prediction, it is however, more economical to use simulation for performance evaluation purposes. Moreover, simulation can be performed in a very early stage of the system design and can therefore be very helpful in the design process. However, simulation can never be as accurate as a real system and there are intrinsic drawbacks that network researchers/developers need to be aware of when using network simulators.

DOI: 10.4018/978-1-60566-774-4.ch018

There are several issues that need to be considered when selecting a network simulation package for simulation studies. For example, use of reliable pseudo-random number generators, an appropriate method for analysis of simulation output data, and statistical accuracy of the simulation results (i.e., desired relative precision of errors and confidence interval). These aspects of credible simulation studies are recommended by leading network researchers (Law & Kelton, 2000; Pawlikowski, Jeong, & Lee, 2002; N.I. Sarkar & Halim, 2008; Schmeiser, 2004).

OPNET (*OPNET Technologies*, 2008) is becoming one of the most popular network simulators as the package is available to academic institutions at no cost under OPNET academic program. It contains numerous models of commercially available network elements, and has various real-life network configuration capabilities. This makes the simulation of a real-life network environment close to reality. However, network researchers are often reluctant to use this package because they may not aware of the potential strengths of this package and also because of the lack of good tutorial on wireless network simulation using OPNET. To overcome this problem we provide a walk-through tutorial on OPNET focusing on the modeling and performance evaluation of IEEE 802.11 WLANs. This tutorial may be useful to both undergraduate and postgraduate students or professionals who are interested in using a credible network simulator for wireless network simulations.

The remainder of this document is organized as follows. We first provide a review of literature on network simulations, including OPNET. We then highlight strengths and weaknesses of OPNET. A tutorial on modelling and simulation of 802.11 WLAN using OPNET is provided. The simulation results are presented for a realistic network scenario. Finally the chapter concludes with a brief summary and direction for future work.

LITERATURE REVIEW

Computer network design and implementation involves interaction of various networking devices including Servers, network interface cards (NICs), switches, routers, and firewalls. In most cases it is ineffective with respect to time, money, and effort to test the performance of a live network. Computer network simulators are often used to evaluate the system performance without building a real network. However, the operation of a network simulator relies on various stochastic processes, including random number generators. Therefore the accuracy of simulation results and model validation is an important issue. A main concern in wireless network simulations or any simulation efforts is to ensure a model is credible and represents reality. If this can't be guaranteed, the model has no real value and can't be used to answer desired questions (McHaney, 1991; Sargent, 2004). For selecting an appropriate network simulator for a particular application, it is important to have good knowledge of the simulator tools available, along with their strengths and weaknesses.

However, selecting the right level of detail for the simulation is a non-trivial task (Heidemann et al., 2001). For example, if simulating a large company intranet the elements in the network are so complex that it would be a large overhead to simulate each single instruction that is being executed on a node. This, however, may be necessary if simulating a wireless sensor network where energy consumption is one of the main concerns for the system developer (Shnayder, Hempstead, Chen, Allen, & Welsh, 2004).

While some simulation tools are multi-protocol and can be use for multi-purposes, another class of simulation tools can be highly specialized and use for specific purposes. This is why research groups of different network (cellular networks, ad-hoc networks, sensor networks, IP networks) have developed simulators to meet specific requirements with respect to the level of detail. But even within one area of network research the level of detail can make a significant difference in terms of simulation speed and memory consumption (N.I. Sarkar & Halim, 2008).

Modeling simulation of wireless networks can be challenging and a network developer must be aware of the inaccuracy of the results a simulation tool can produce. According to Takai et al. (2001) the physical layer is usually the least detailed modelled layer in network simulations. Since the wireless physical layer is more complex than that of wired physical layer and may affect the simulation results drastically. Physical layer parameters such as received signal strength, path loss, fading, interference and noise computation, and preamble length greatly influence WLAN performance. Therefore, simulation results may differ from real testbed evaluation both qualitatively and quantitatively (Kurkowski, Camp, & Colagrosso, 2005). Although Lucio et al. (2008) did not find the differences in their evaluation between OPNET and ns-2 (Fall & Varadhan, 2008) most of the other authors could observe that changing the network simulator can result in completely different conclusions. Some recommendations are being proposed to run a hybrid simulation/emulation based network evaluation which simulate the physical layer and execute more abstract layers of the protocol stack. However, this would add a huge amount of complexity and could lead to scalability problems when dealing with large number of wireless nodes.

Although drawing a conclusion from simulation run has to be done very carefully, network developers are rarely independent from using simulators. Network simulation packages offer a rich environment for the rapid development, performance evaluation and deployment of networks. Perhaps simulation results between two competing architectures or protocols are more important than quantitative results. Since the latter is not necessarily the case and the use of different simulators might be appropriate (Haq & Kunz, 2005; Takai et al., 2001). If a major design decision has to be made and different simulators suggest different conclusions, implementing a real testbed would be appropriate.

To avoid misleading simulation results it is important to select an appropriate level of detail for the simulation runs. Depending on the networking area and the layer for which new algorithms or protocols are developed, the selection of the appropriate simulator is also viable. Therefore network researchers and developers should use an appropriate simulation package for their simulation tasks.

STRENGTH AND WEAKNESSES OF OPNET

OPNET has easy to use GUI and therefore it is easier to develop a network model for simulations. A skilled user can develop a complex model containing many different hierarchical layers within a short period of time especially interoperability of wide area networks (WANs) and LANs can be modelled efficiently. Although OPNET IT Guru has limited functionality, but it supports various servers, routers and other networking devices with different manufacturer specifications which is adequate for developing models (small scale) of real-world network scenarios. It is easier to evaluate the scalability of enterprise networks and the effects of changing server capacities and switching to a different network equipment provider. Other features of OPNET include GUI interface, comprehensive library of network protocols and models, source code for all models, and graphical presentation of simulation results. More importantly, OPNET has gained considerable popularity in academia as it is being offered free of charge to academic institutions. That has given OPNET an edge over ns-2 in both marketplace and academia.

OPNET supports huge amount of low level details (CPU speed of servers, number of cores, CPU utilisation, etc.) but the effect of these remains uncertain. Even the effect of changes made to the protocol behaviour (e.g. QoS scheduling) are difficult to observe in the simulation. Modeling the effect of low level protocol modification is generally very difficult to achieve. Whereas other OPNET products are likely to allow the development of own network nodes and protocol specification the academic version of IT Guru does not. Therefore, OPNET appears to be more suitable for high level network simulations (e.g. evaluating the scalability of a network architecture) and less suitable for low level protocol performance evaluation. The main weakness lies in the abstraction from the real world. Choosing the appropriate level of detail is vital for the accuracy of network simulations.

TUTORIAL

This section provides a walk-through tutorial on performance modeling of IEEE 802.11 WLANs using OPNET IT Guru. Although OPNET Modeler has more functionality than that of IT Guru, the process of developing models is very similar in both cases. This tutorial covers how to create a new model from scratch, a scenario, setting up simulation parameters, running simulations and getting simulation results.

The Workbench and the Workflow

Figure 1 shows an empty workbench for a new project. A infrastructure can easily be developed by dragging networking devices and components on the workbench from object palette.

Figure 2 lists the eight toolbar objects and their brief description/function. These objects allow

Figure 1. An empty workbench

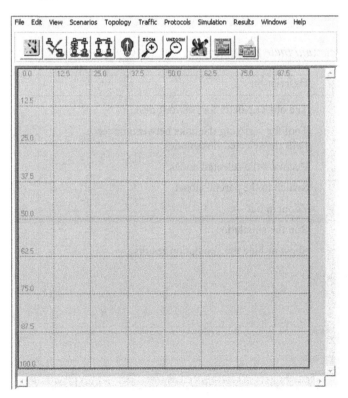

verification of links between nodes. Hierarchical networks can be developed using subnets.

In OPNET simulation models, both the 'application configuration' and 'profile configuration' are often used. The application configuration is used to define all the services offered by the network. Examples of services are FTP, database, and HTTP. These services can be assigned to network nodes and/or servers, thus defining which elements are acting as service providers. The profile configuration is used to define the kind of services/applications a network node is using. Assigning a profile to a network node allows specific node to act as client of that services.

Once the client and server roles are defined to the network nodes one has to select the properties of the network of interest. Examples of node specific properties are response time and active connections. Global properties such as global throughput or delay can also be selected. After creating the network topology, assigning server and client roles, and selecting the network parameters of interest we can run the simulation.

Figure 3 shows a framework in which OPNET models can be developed and run. OPNET supports protocol modification at various levels as shown in Figure 3. The main components of the framework are described next.

Creating a Model

After executing OPNET one can either create a new model or open an existing model. A new project can be created by selecting 'new' from file menu. After entering a project name and scenario name one can choose network topology by selecting "Create Empty Scenario". Next, we choose the scale of the model where nodes can easily be placed. In this tutorial we describe how to develop an office network. The pre-selected size of an office is 100m x 100m. We select the network technology such as wireless_lan and wireless_lan_adv for wireless network modeling. Figure 4 shows a screen shoot of the startup wizard review.

Figure 2. Tool bar objects and their function

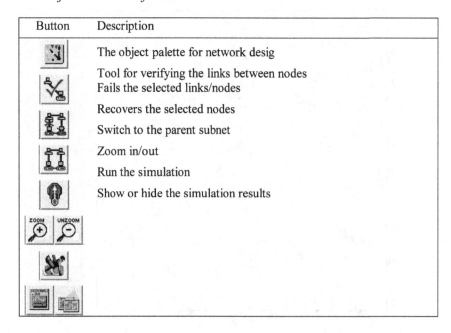

Button	Description
	The object palette for network desig
	Tool for verifying the links between nodes
	Fails the selected links/nodes
	Recovers the selected nodes
	Switch to the parent subnet
	Zoom in/out
	Run the simulation
	Show or hide the simulation results

Figure 3. A framework for developing a model using OPNET

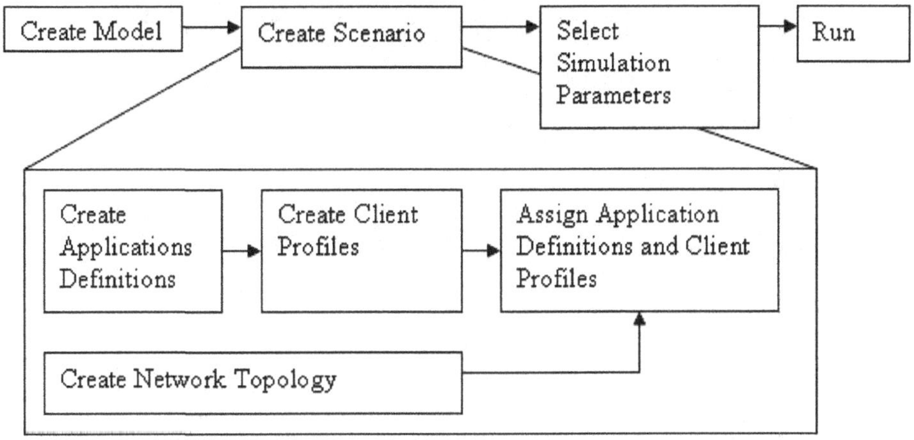

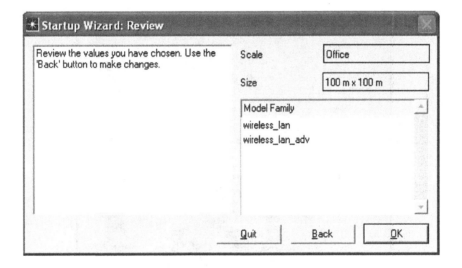

Figure 4. The review screen of the Startup Wizard

Creating the First Scenario

OPNET allows modeling a network with multiple scenarios. This is particularly useful for comparing different network behaviour under different network topologies. Therefore it makes sense to create a new scenario for each network topology for a particular project. After creating a new model the first (empty) scenario ("Scenario 1") is created implicitly and nodes are added in Scenario 1. By selecting "wireless_lan_adv" palette, nodes are added into workbench by drag and drop.

Similarly, Server is added into the workbench by selecting wlan_server_adv (fix). One can easily assign custom name to each component on the workbench by right clicking on it and selecting the 'Set Name' option from the context menu.

The mobile nodes can easily be added to Scenario 1 using rapid configuration tool. For example, by selecting Topology from Rapid Configuration menu and creating an "unconnected net". Figure 5 shows a screen shoot of mobile nodes rapid configuration. In this example, node model is "wlan_wkstn_adv" and node type is

Figure 5. Mobile nodes rapid configuration

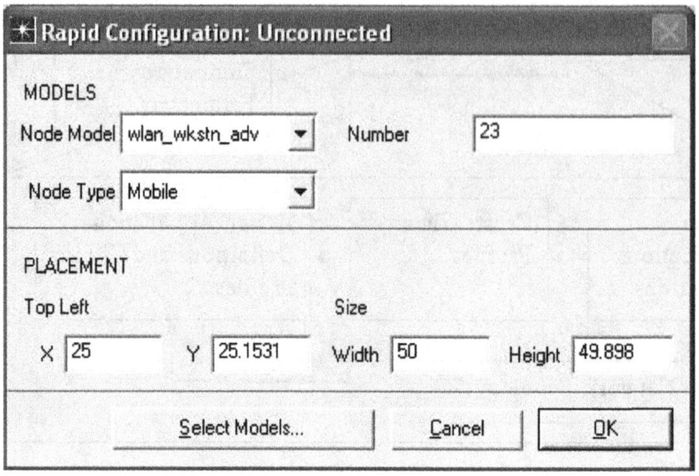

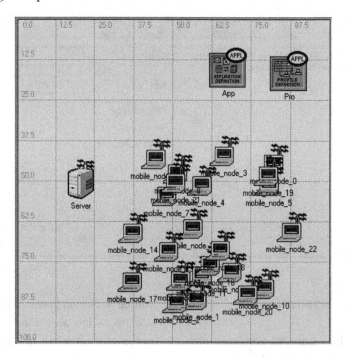

Figure 6. Developing a simple wireless network model

"mobile". In the number field one can enter the desired number of nodes for rapid configuration (in this case is 23). The placement and size of the network can remain with their default values. The network topology (after rapid configuration) is shown in Figure 6.

Because of WLAN modeling, there is no need to define a connection between the nodes. Both Application and Profile Configuration objects are included in the model to make network active and to run applications (Figure 6). After setting up the attributes of Application Configuration (Figure 7), the value of "Application definitions" attribute is then set up as shown Figure 8.

As shown in Figure. 8, various services (applications) can be selected to run on the network

Figure 7. Application Configuration attributes menu

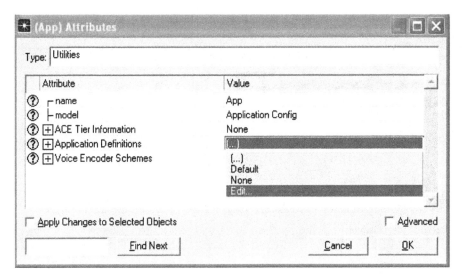

Figure 8. Assigning a service behaviour

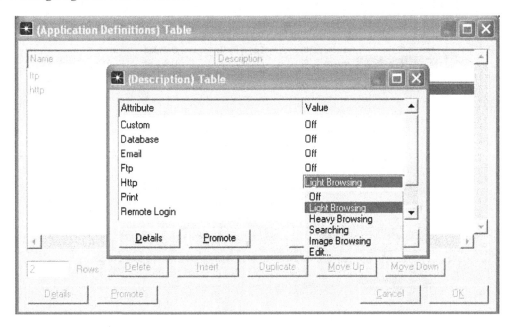

for performance evaluation. For example, http (a light web browsing) and heavy ftp services are selected to study the impact of these services on network performance. By creating two new rows in "Application Definitions" table and assigning them to ftp and http, we now have two network services available to the nodes. We then set up

Server attributes and assign services to the Server (Figure 9).

Next, we configure a Profile object so that network users (clients) can access these services. More detail about configuring a Profile object can be found in OPNET manual (www.opnet.com). We only need one Profile definition because all

Figure 9. Assigning services to the Server

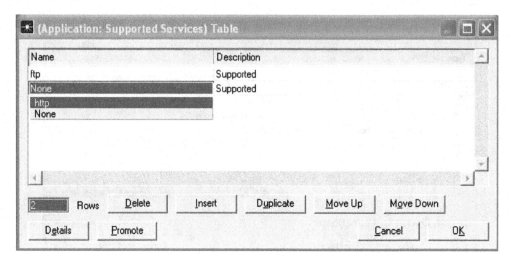

Figure 10. Setting up client profile

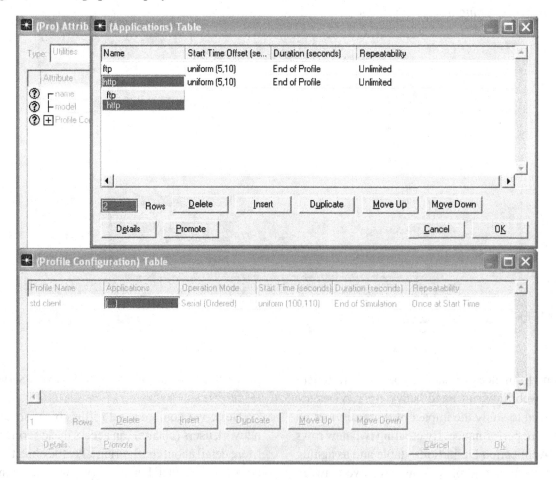

Figure 11. Assigning a client profile to multiple nodes

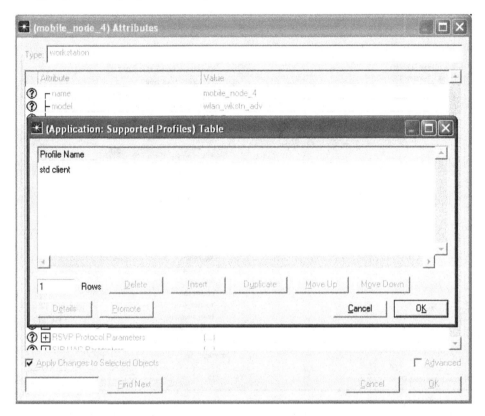

Figure 12. Selecting network performance metrics

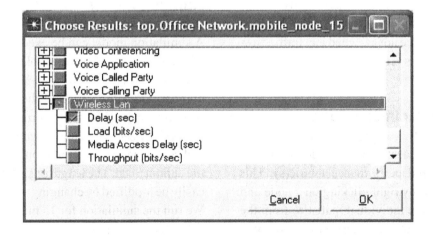

clients in the network will behave the same way. The Profile Configuration is shown in Figure 10. By editing profile attributes two rows are created in the applications table for ftp and http services.

Figure 11 illustrates the process of assigning a client profile to multiple nodes. This is achieved by right clicking on a node (client) and selecting "Similar Nodes".

Figure 13. Setting up simulation statistics

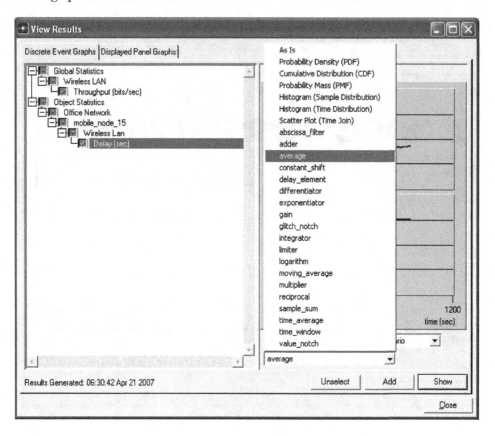

We have now created the first network Scenario 1 and configured both the server and clients. Notice that we have not assigned any traffic flow between two nodes yet. This is handled implicitly by OPNET.

Simulation Parameter Setup

Before executing a simulation model one has to select the desired performance metric(s). This can be achieved by right clicking on a node and selecting "Choose Individual Statistic" from the menu. It is likely to take longer simulation time to produce results if you choose to obtain more performance metrics. We are more interested to obtain the overall network throughput and packet delay that a node experiences. Figure 12 shows a screenshoot for the selection of network performance metrics.

Running the Simulation

A simulation model can be executed by clicking on the Run button from the tool bar. At this stage one can also specify the Seed-Value for random number generations used in the simulator. This is particularly useful for experimenting with the impact of Seed on random number generations and consequently on simulation results. We used the default Seed. The length of simulation run can easily be modified by changing the duration field. We run the simulation for 15 minutes simulation time to obtain results in steady-state. After the completion of simulation runs, results can be viewed by clicking on view graphs and tables of the collected statistics button from the toolbar.

Figure 13 shows a screen shoot of setting up simulation statistics. One can access the statistics by selecting them from the tree (left hand side). By selecting "average" from the drop down menu at the bottom of the screen one can obtain the average network throughput and packet delay.

Figure 14 shows the simulation results. The graph on the top represents the network throughput (bps) whereas the bottom graph represents packet delay for node 15.

Adding a Second Scenario and Making Changes to the Protocol

After simulating a network model for a particular scenario, it is useful to observe the network performance with another scenario. In OPNET, an existing scenario can easily be duplicated and altered to create a new network scenario. One can easily switch between scenarios by pressing CTRL+ n, where n is the number of the scenario. We created a second scenario called Scenario 2 and change the data rate from 1 Mbps to 11 Mbps.

We run Scenario 2 and compare the result with that of Scenario 1. Figure 15 compares the results obtain from Scenarios 1 and 2. The graph on the top represents Scenario 1 whereas the bottom graph represents Scenario 2. It is observed that the packet delay for Scenario 2 is slightly lower than that of Scenario 1. This is because the network under Scenario 2 operates at 11 Mbps whereas Scenario 1 operates at Mbps.

RESULTS AND ANALYSIS

Study 1: Effect of Increasing the Number of Nodes on IEEE 802.11 MAC delay

To study the impact of nodes on IEEE 802.11 media access control (MAC) delay, we simulated seven scenarios with varying number of

Figure 14. Graphical presentation of simulation results

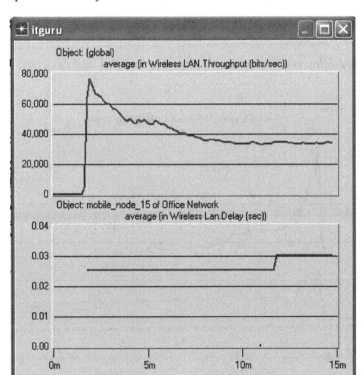

nodes. The summary of results is shown in Figure 16.

As shown in Figure 16, generally the network experiences high MAC delay when a large number of nodes contending for accessing the wireless channel. After a start-up phase the MAC delay is in the range of 10-20 ms depending on the number of nodes on the network. It is observed that the MAC delay with N=2 nodes is slightly higher than the network with N = 3 nodes. Also, the network with 5 nodes outperforms 2-node network as far as MAC delay is concerned. The lower backoff times for concurrent access to the wireless channel contributing to less wastage of channel bandwidth and hence achieving lower MAC delay for small number of nodes. The long-term averages of this value are roughly the same for the scenarios with 2 nodes and 10 nodes. However, networks with more than 10 nodes have an increased MAC delay that is proportional to the number of nods.

The network behaviour (Figure 16) can be explained further with respect to the backoff time of CSMA/CA algorithm that is used in the IEEE 802.11 protocol. The backoff time is a random number that a wireless node waits after an unsuccessful transmission attempt as well as after sending a packet. This random value changes depending on the number of nodes that are currently active in the network (Cali, Conti, & Gregori, 2000). If there are only few (less than 6) nodes in the wireless network the backoff time is lower than the same scenario with less nodes. Choi et al. (2005) observed similar results when measuring the behaviour of the throughput of wireless LANs.

Study 2: Impact of Increasing Wireless Node Density on IEEE 802.11g Throughput

In this study we focus on the throughput performance of IEEE 802.11g infrastructure network. In the simulation model an office network of 35m×15m area is used. Figure 17 shows a snapshot of the OPNET wireless network model with one AP and 30 wireless stations. A generic wireless station was configured as an IEEE 802.11g AP as well as wireless stations.

Figure 15. Mean packet delay versus simulation time (Scenarios 1 and 2)

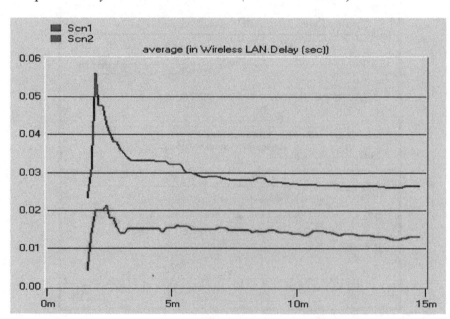

Figure 16. IEEE 802.11 MAC delay versus simulation time

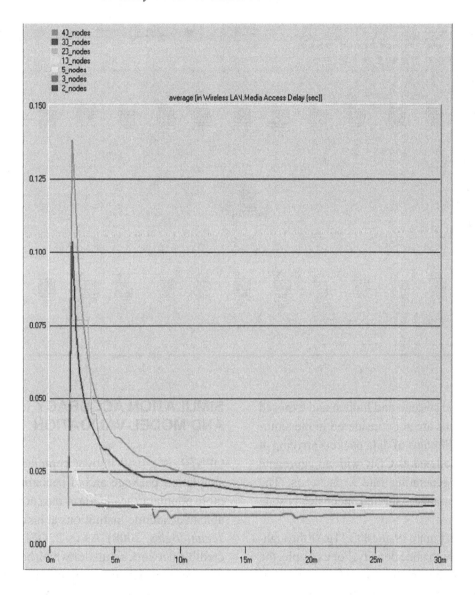

Figure 18 shows a screenshot of AP configuration and simulation parameter setting. The transmit power of the AP was set to 32 mw which is close to the D-Link (DWL-2100) AP. Another important parameter is the packet reception power threshold (same as RSS), it was set to -88 dBm. This allows the wireless AP to communicate with wireless stations even when signals are weak; a common scenario in an obstructed office environment. Other parameters such as data rate, channel setting, and the frequency spectrum were set to the default values for 802.11g. The packet length threshold was set to 2,346 bytes (a realistic figure for wireless Ethernet networks).

The data rate, Tx power, RSS threshold, packet length threshold, and segmentation threshold are the same for the AP. All wireless stations communicate using identical half-duplex wireless radio based on the 802.11g AP. The capture effects, transmission errors due to interference

Figure 17. OPNET representation of fully connected network with one AP and 30 wireless stations

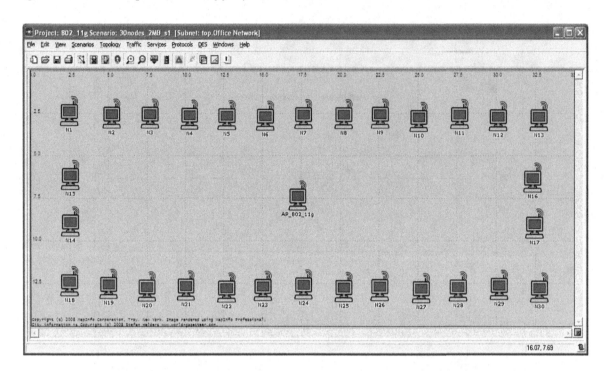

and noise in the system, and hidden and exposed station problems are not considered in the simulation model. Streams of data packets arriving at stations are modeled as CBR with an aggregate mean packet generating rate λ packets/s. The WLAN performance is studied under steady state conditions.

As shown in Figure 19, the 802.11g AP throughput decreases with node density. For example, the network mean throughputs are 8.6, 3.2, 2.0, 1.3, 0.9, and 0.7 Mbps for N = 2, 10, 15, 20, 25 and 30, respectively. Because of the higher contention delays and backoff the amount of data being transmitted by a source station to a particular destination decreases as N increases, consequently network mean throughput decreases. The main conclusion is that the number of active nodes (i.e., station density) has a significant effect on throughput of an IEEE 802.11g infrastructure network.

SIMULATION ACCURACY AND MODEL VALIDATION

OPNET is a well known commercial network simulation package and is becoming more and more popular in academia as the package is available to academic institutions at no cost (*OPNET Technologies*, 2008). As ns-2, OPNET is also a credible network simulator which has been tested by numerous network engineers and researchers worldwide (Banitsas, Song, & Owens, 2004; Chang, 1999; Chow, 1999; Green & Obaidat, 2003; Salah & Alkhoraidly, 2006; Zhu, Wang, Aweya, Oullette, & Montuno, 2002).

Lucio et al. (Lucio et al., 2008) have tested the accuracy of network simulation and modelling using both the OPNET Modeler and ns-2 by comparing the simulation results with the experimental results obtained from a live network. Based on the modelling of CBR and FTP sessions, the authors concluded that both the ns-2

Figure 18. IEEE 802.11g AP configuration

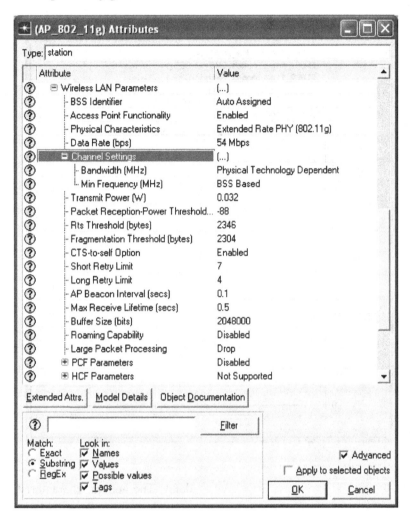

and OPNET Modeler perform well and provide very similar results.

Before evaluating the system performance it was necessary to verify that the simulation models represent reality. First, OPNET models were validated through indoor propagation measurements from wireless laptops and access points for IEEE 802.11b and 802.11g networks. A good match between simulation and real measurement results for N = 2 to 4 stations validates the simulation models (N. I. Sarkar & Lo, 2008; N.I. Sarkar & Sowerby, 2006; Siringoringo & Sarkar, 2009). Second, the function of individual network components and their interactions was checked. Third, OPNET

results were compared with the results obtained from ns-2 (Fall & Varadhan, 2008) and a good match between two sets of results validated our models (N. I. Sarkar & Lo, 2008; N. I. Sarkar & Sowerby, 2009). The simulation results presented in this chapter were also compared with the work of other network researchers to ensure the correctness of the simulation model (Heusse, Rousseau, Berger-Sabbatel, & Duda, 2003; Ng & Liew, 2007; Nicopoliditis, 2003; Schafer, Maurer, & Wiesbeck, 2002).

Figure 19. IEEE 802.11g throughput versus simulation time

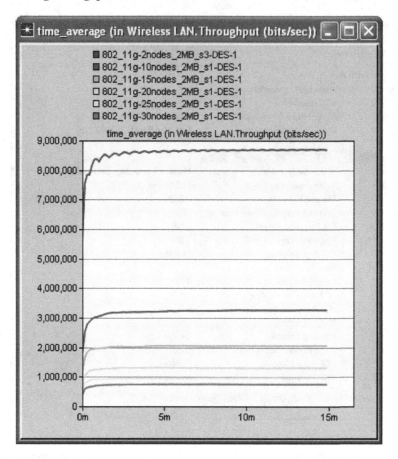

CONCLUSION

This chapter provided a tutorial on modeling and simulation of IEEE 802.11 networks using OPNET. The tutorial covers how to create a new model from scratch; creating the first scenario, setting up simulation parameters, running simulations and obtaining results. The level of detailed simulation offered by OPNET IT Guru suggests that this particular simulator is suitable for performance modeling of both wired and wireless networks. The chapter provided a review of literature on simulation in general and OPNET in particular focusing on the strengths and weaknesses of OPNET.

The chapter demonstrated the performance modeling of IEEE 802.11 by measuring MAC

delay. The general characteristic of the protocol is evident from the simulation results, i.e. the MAC delay increases with larger number of nodes. The models built using OPNET simulator were validated using propagation measurements from wireless laptops and access points for an IEEE 802.11b/g WLAN. A good match between OPNET simulation results and real measurements were reported.

The chapter stresses the importance of using a good simulator for the performance modeling of wireless networks. The OPNET offers more flexibility in model construction and validation, and incorporates appropriate analysis of simulation output data and statistical accuracy of the simulation results. Without these features, a simulation model would be useless since it will produce invalid results. An implementation of a new MAC protocol for wireless multimedia applications is suggested as an extension to the work reported in this chapter.

ACKNOWLEDGMENT

We would like to thank Christoph Lauer for setting up and conducting simulation experiments.

REFERENCES

Banitsas, K. A., Song, Y. H., & Owens, T. J. (2004). OFDM over IEEE 802.11b hardware for telemedical applications. *International Journal of Mobile Communications, 2*(3), 310–327.

Cali, F., Conti, M., & Gregori, E. (2000). IEEE 802.11 protocol: design and performance evaluation of an adaptive backoff mechanism. *IEEE Journal on Selected Areas in Communications, 18*(9), 1774–1786. doi:10.1109/49.872963

Chang, X. (1999). *Network simulation with opnet.* Paper presented at 1999 winter simulation conference, Phoenix, AZ, (pp. 307-314).

Choi, S., Park, K., & Kim, C. (2005). *On the performance characteristics of WLANs: revisited.* Paper presented at the 2005 ACM SIGMETRICS international conference on Measurement and modeling of computer systems (pp. 97–108).

Chow, J. (1999). Development of channel models for simulation of wireless systems in OPNET. *Transactions of the Society for Computer Simulation International, 16*(3), 86–92.

Fall, K., & Varadhan, K. (2008). *The ns manual. The VINT project.* Retrieved February 10, 2008, from http://www.isi.edu/nsnam/ns/doc/

Green, D. B., & Obaidat, M. S. (2003). Modeling and simulation of IEEE 802.11 WLAN mobile ad hoc networks using topology broadcast reverse-path forwarding (TBRPF). *Computer Communications, 26*(15), 1741–1746. doi:10.1016/S0140-3664(03)00043-4

Haq, F., & Kunz, T. (2005). *Simulation vs. emulation: Evaluating mobile adhoc network routing protocols.* Paper presented at the International Workshop on Wireless Ad-hoc Networks (IWWAN 2005).

Heidemann, J., Bulusu, N., Elson, J., Intanagonwiwat, C., Lan, K., & Xu, Y. (2001). *Effects of detail in wireless network simulation.* Paper presented at the SCS Multiconference on Distributed Simulation (pp. 3–11).

Heusse, M., Rousseau, F., Berger-Sabbatel, G., & Duda, A. (2003, March 30-April 3). *Performance anomaly of 802.11b.* Paper presented at the IEEE INFOCOM'03 (pp. 836-843).

Kurkowski, S., Camp, T., & Colagrosso, M. (2005). MANET simulation studies: the incredibles. *ACM SIGMOBILE Mobile Computing and Communications Review, 9*(4), 50–61. doi:10.1145/1096166.1096174

Law, A. M., & Kelton, W. D. (2000). *Simulation modelling and analysis* (3rd Ed.). New York: McGraw-Hill.

Lucio, G. F., Paredes-Farrera, M., Jammeh, E., Fleury, M., & Reed, M. J. (2008). *OPNET Modeler and Ns-2: comparing the accuracy of network simulators for packet-level analysis using a network testbed.* Retrieved June 15, from http://privatewww.essex.ac.uk/~gflore/

McHaney, R. (1991). *Computer simulation: a practical perspective.* San Diego, CA: Academic Press.

Ng, P. C., & Liew, S. C. (2007). Throughput analysis of IEEE 802.11 multi-hop ad hoc networks. *IEEE/ACM Transactions on Networking, 15*(2), 309-322.

Nicopoliditis, P., Papadimitriou, G. I., & Pomportsis, A. S. (2003). *Wireless Networks*. Hoboken, NJ: Wiley, Jonn Wiley & Sons Ltd.

OPNET Technologies. (2008). Retrieved September 15, 2008, from www.opnet.com

Pawlikowski, K., Jeong, H.-D. J., & Lee, J.-S. R. (2002). On credibility of simulation studies of telecommunication networks. *IEEE Communications Magazine, 40*(1), 132–139. doi:10.1109/35.978060

Salah, K., & Alkhoraidly, A. (2006). An OPNET-based simulation approach for deploying VoIP. *International Journal of Network Management, 16*, 159–183. doi:10.1002/nem.591

Sargent, R. G. (2004, December). *Validation and verification of Simulation Models*. Paper presented at 2004 Winter Simulation Conference, (pp. 17-28).

Sarkar, N. I., & Halim, S. A. (2008, June 23-26). *Simulation of computer networks: simulators, methodologies and recommendations*. Paper presented at the 5th IEEE International Conference on Information Technology and Applications (ICITA'08), Cairns, Queensland, Australia, (pp. 420-425).

Sarkar, N. I., & Lo, E. (2008, December 7-10). *Indoor propagation measurements for performance evaluation of IEEE 802.11g*. Paper presented at the IEEE Australasian Telecommunications Networks and Applications Conference (ATNAC'08), Adelaide, Australia, (pp. 163-168).

Sarkar, N. I., & Sowerby, K. W. (2006, November 27-30). *Wi-Fi performance measurements in the crowded office environment: a case study*. Paper presented at the 10th IEEE International Conference on Communication Technology (ICCT), Guilin, China (pp. 37-40).

Sarkar, N. I., & Sowerby, K. W. (2009, April 4-8). *The combined effect of signal strength and traffic type on WLAN performance*. Paper presented at the IEEE Wireless Communication and Networking Conference (WCNC'09), Budapest, Hungary.

Schafer, T. M., Maurer, J., & Wiesbeck, W. (2002, September 24-28). *Measurement and simulation of radio wave propagation in hospitals*. Paper presented at IEEE 56th Vehicular Technology Conference (VTC2002-Fall), (pp. 792-796).

Schmeiser, B. (2004, December). *Simulation output analysis: A tutorial based on one research thread*. Paper presented at 2004 Winter Simulation Conference, (pp. 162-170).

Shnayder, V., Hempstead, M., Chen, B., Allen, G., & Welsh, M. (2004). *Simulating the power consumption of large-scale sensor network applications*. Paper presented at the 2nd international conference on Embedded networked sensor systems, (pp. 188-200).

Siringoringo, W., & Sarkar, N. I. (2009). Teaching and learning Wi-Fi networking fundamentals using limited resources. In J. Gutierrez (Ed.), *Selected Readings on Telecommunications and Networking* (pp. 22-40). Hershey, PA: IGI Global.

Takai, M., Martin, J., & Bagrodia, R. (2001, October). *Effects of wireless physical layer modeling in mobile ad hoc networks*. Paper presented at MobiHOC, Long Beach, CA, (pp. 87-94).

Zhu, C., Wang, O. W. W., Aweya, J., Oullette, M., & Montuno, D. Y. (2002). A comparison of active queue management algorithms using the OPNET Modeler. *IEEE Communications Magazine, 40*(6), 158–167. doi:10.1109/MCOM.2002.1007422

KEY TERMS AND DEFINITIONS

IEEE 802.11: A family of wireless local area network (LAN) standards. The IEEE 802.11b is the wireless LAN standard with a maximum data rate of 11 Mbps operating at 2.4 GHz. The IEEE 802.11a is the high-speed wireless LAN with a maximum data rate of 54 Mbps operating at 5 GHz. The IEEE 802.11g is backward compatible with the IEEE 802.11b, with a maximum data rate of 54 Mbps operating at 2.4 GHz.

NIC: NIC stands for Network Interface Card which is the hardware interface that provides the physical link between a computer and a network.

GUI: GUI stands for Graphical User Interface. Most of the modern operating systems provide a GUI, which enables a user to use a pointing device, such as a computer mouse, to provide the computer with information about the user's intentions.

OPNET IT GURU: OPNET is a discrete event, object-oriented, general purpose network simulator (commercial simulation package). OPNET IT GURU is a smaller version of OPNET Modeler which is available at no costs under OPNET academic program.

Chapter 19

On the Use of Discrete-Event Simulation in Computer Networks Analysis and Design

Hussein Al-Bahadili

The Arab Academy for Banking & Financial Sciences, Jordan

ABSTRACT

This chapter presents a description of a newly developed research-level computer network simulator, which can be used to evaluate the performance of a number of flooding algorithms in ideal and realistic mobile ad hoc network (MANET) environments. It is referred to as MANSim. The simulator is written in C++ programming language and it consists of four main modules: network, mobility, computational, and algorithm modules. This chapter describes the philosophy behind the simulator and explains its internal structure. The new simulator can be characterized as: a process-oriented discrete-event simulator using terminating simulation approach and stochastic input-traffic pattern. In order to demonstrate the effectiveness and flexibility of MANSim, it was used to study the performance of five flooding algorithms, these as: pure flooding, probabilistic flooding, LAR-1, LAR-1P, and OMPR. The simulator demonstrates an excellent accuracy, reliability, and flexibility to be used as a cost-effective tool in analyzing and designing wireless computer networks in comparison with analytical modeling and experimental tests. It can be learned quickly and it is sufficiently powerful, comprehensive, and extensible to allow investigation of a considerable range of problems of complicated geometrical configuration, mobility patterns, probability density functions, and flooding algorithms.

INTRODUCTION

System designers use performance evaluation as an integral component of the design effort. Figure 1 describes the general role of simulation in design.

DOI: 10.4018/978-1-60566-774-4.ch019

The designer relies on the simulation model to provide guidance in choosing among alternative design choices, to detect bottlenecks in system performance, or to support cost-effective analysis. As part of this process, the designer may use the simulation output to modify the system abstraction, model, or implementation as opposed to the

Figure 1. The role of simulation in validating a design model

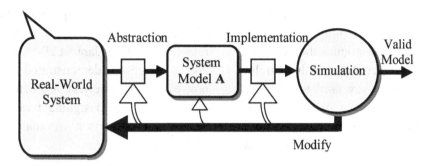

system itself. The simulation output may also be used include detail that may have not been considered in the previous abstraction, model, or the implementation, for example to collect additional or alternative types of data (Sinclair 2004, Law & Kelton 2000).

Another important use of simulation is as a tool to help validate an analytical approach to performance evaluation. In an analytical approach, the system model is implemented as a set of equations. The solution to these equations captures in some way the behavior of the model and thus optimistically of the system itself. Analytical modeling often requires simplifying assumptions that make the results suspect until they have been confirm by other techniques, such as simulation. Figure 2 illustrates the role of simulation in validating

results from an analytical model. The system models A and B in Figure 2 may actually be identical, or they may be quite different (Nutaro 2007, Chung 2004).

Computer simulation is widely-used in investigating the performance of existing and proposed systems in many areas of science, engineering, operations research, and management science, especially in applications characterized by complicated geometries and interaction probabilities, and for dealing with system design in the presence of uncertainty (Banks et. al. 2005). This is particularly true in the case of computer systems and computer networks (Forouzan 2007, Stallings 2005, Tanenbaum 2003). In order to study a system using simulation, first some features from the system are abstracted, which believe

Figure 2. The role of simulation in validating an analytical model

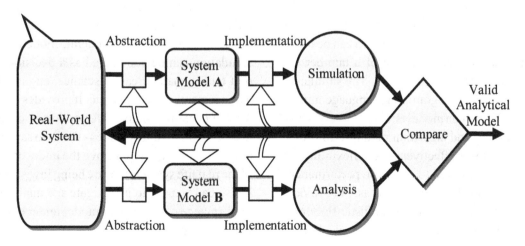

significant in determining its performance. This abstraction is called the system model. Next, the model is implemented by writing a computer program whose execution mimics the behavior of the model. Data collected during the simulation program's execution are used to compute estimates of the performance of the original system. The accuracy of these estimates depends on the fidelity of the model and the way in which the measurements are taken from the simulation programs (Sinclair 2004).

The principle objective for this work is to introduce the reader to the principles of computer simulation and how it can be used in computer networks analysis and design. Simulation models can be classified according to different criteria, however, in this work, we consider three widely-used criteria in classifying the different types of simulation models, and these are: time-variation of the state of the system variables, simulation termination procedure, and input-traffic pattern. According to first criteria, simulation models can be classified into continuous-valued, discrete-event, or a combination of the two. Discrete-event simulation can be implemented using one of the three methodologies: event-driven, process-oriented, and distributed simulation. Process-oriented is a well-approved and a powerful tool for evaluating the performance of computer networks in comparison with analytical modeling and experimental tests.

The process-oriented model is used in developing a computer network simulator, namely, MANSim (Al-Bahadili 2008), which can be used to investigate the performance of a number of flooding algorithms in MANETs. The simulator is written in C++ programming language and it consists of four main modules: network, mobility, computational, and algorithm modules. In order to demonstrate the effectiveness and flexibility of MANSim, it was used to study the performance of five flooding algorithms, these as: pure flooding (Bani-Yassein 2006), probabilistic flooding (Scott & Yasinsac 2004, Sasson et. al. 2003),

location-aided routing scheme 1 (LAR-1) (Ko & Vaidya 2000), LAR-1-probabilistic (LAR-1P) (Al-Bahadili et. al. 2007), the optimal multipoint relaying (OMPR) (Jaradat 2009, Qayyum et. al. 2002). The results demonstrated that simulation is an excellent cost-effective tool that can be used in analyzing and designing wireless computer networks in comparison with analytical modeling and experimental tests.

The rest of the chapter is organized as follows: The application of computer simulation is presented in Section 2. In Section 3, the main challenges to computer simulation are discussed. Section 4 provides a detailed discussion to the different classes of simulation models. Examples of simulation languages and network simulators and their main features are presented in Sections 5 and 6, respectively. Description of MANSim network simulator is given in Section 7. The different wireless environments and the computed parameters that are implemented in and computed by MANSim are defined in Sections 8 and 9, respectively. Section 10 presents an example of simulation results obtained from MANSim. Finally, in Section 11, conclusions are drawn and recommendations for future work are pointed-out.

THE APPLICATION OF COMPUTER SIMULATION

The application of computer simulation can potentially improve the quality and effectiveness of the system model. In general, modeling and simulation can be considered as a decision support tool in many areas of science, engineering, management, accountant, etc. It provides us with a more economical and safer option in order to learn from potential mistakes - that is to say, it can reduce cost, risk, and improve the understanding of the real life systems that are being investigated. It also can be used to investigate and analyze the performance of the system model under extreme working environment.

Computer simulation translates some aspects of the physical world into a mathematical model (description) followed by regenerating that model on a computer – which can be used instead of performing an actual physical task. For instance, simulations are widely used to evaluate the performance of routing protocols in wireless ad hoc networks characterized by presence of noise and high node mobility (Tseng et. al. 2002), measure packet delay in data networks (Fusk et. al. 2003), simulate TCP/IP applications (Ahmed & Shahriari 2001). In addition, computer modeling and simulation can be used as a computer network learning tool (Asgarkhani 2002).

A quick review of some of the projects that are employing computer simulation reveals various applications, such as:

- Training people to perform complex tasks.
- Designing better computer chips.
- Providing better weather forecasts.
- Performing predictions of the global economy.
- Studying social interaction.
- Analyzing financial risks.
- Compiling complex corporate plans.
- Designing complex computer networks.

Simulation modeling and analysis is one of the most frequently used operations research techniques. When used judiciously, simulation modeling and analysis makes it possible to (Maria 1997):

- Improve communication – e.g. standardizing the treatment of experimental data and the description of results to various interest research groups all over the world.
- Build a knowledge base of quantitative information.
- Characterize the data mathematically, by parameter fitting - rather than continually referring to the raw data.

- Validate a process - to increase understanding of the process.
- Study reproducibility - to determine those factors to which the process is sensitive and quantify their effect.
- Study process economics - to perform cost-effective and reliable analyses for different operational scenarios.
- Reduce experimental costs - to reduce trial-and-error experimentation over the long term.
- Study process optimization - to perform 'what-if' scenarios and investigate different possibilities, especially, extreme operating environment which may be difficult to experiment.

However, there are some pitfalls which need to be carefully considered in simulation. Simulation can be a time consuming and complex exercise, from modeling through output analysis that necessitates the involvement of resident experts and decision makers in the entire process. Following is a checklist of pitfalls to be considered.

- Unclear objective.
- Using simulation when an analytic solution is appropriate.
- Invalid model.
- Simulation model too complex or too simple.
- Erroneous assumptions.
- Undocumented assumptions. This is extremely important and it is strongly suggested that assumptions made at each stage of the simulation modeling and analysis exercise be documented thoroughly.
- Using the wrong input probability distribution.
- Replacing a distribution (stochastic) by its mean (deterministic).
- Using the wrong performance measure.
- Bugs in the simulation program.

- Using standard statistical formulas that assume independence in simulation output analysis.
- Initial bias in output data.
- Making one simulation run for a configuration.
- Poor schedule and budget planning.
- Poor communication among the personnel involved in the simulation study.

CHALLENGES TO COMPUTER NETWORKS SIMULATION

It is generally unfeasible to implement computer networks algorithms before valid tests are being performed to evaluate their performance. It is clear that testing such implementations with real hardware is quite hard, in terms of the manpower, time, and resources required to validate the algorithm, and measure its characteristics in desired realistic environments. External conditions also can affect the measured performance characteristics. The preferred alternative is to model these algorithms in a detailed simulator and then perform various scenarios to measure their performance for various patterns of realistic computer networks environments (e.g., connection media, node densities, node mobility, radio transmission range, transmission environment, size of traffic, etc.).

The main challenge to simulation is to model the process as close as possible to reality; otherwise it could produce entirely different performance characteristics from the ones discovered during actual use. In addition, the simulation study must carefully consider four major factors while conducting credible simulation for computer network research. The simulation study must be (Kurkowski et. al. 2006):

- Repeatable: The same results can be obtained for the same scenario every time the simulation is repeated.

- Unbiased: The results must not be biased to show a high performance for specific scenarios.
- Realistic: The scenarios used for tests must be of a realistic nature.
- Statistically sound: The execution and analysis of the experiment must be based on mathematical principles.

CLASSIFICATION OF SIMULATION MODELS

Simulation models can be classified according to several criteria, for example (Sinclair 2004, Roeder 2004, Hassan & Jain 2003):

- Time variation of the state of the system variables.
  - (1) Continuous-valued simulation
  - (2) Discrete-event simulation
- Simulation terminating.
  - (1) Terminating simulation
  - (2) Steady-state simulation
- Input traffic pattern.
  - (1) Trace-driven simulation
  - (2) Stochastic simulation

In what follows a description is given for each of the above simulation models.

Continuous-Valued versus Discrete-Event Simulation

Simulation models can be categorized according to the state of the system variables (events) in two categories; these are: continuous-valued and discrete-event simulations, which are described below.

Continuous-Valued Simulation

In a continuous-valued simulation, the values of the system states are continuously change with time. The various states of the system are usually represented by a set of differential-algebraic equations, differential equations (either partial or ordinary), or integro-differential equations. The simulation program solves all the equations, and uses numbers to change the state and output of the simulation. Originally, these kinds of simulations were actually implemented on analog computers, where the differential equations could be represented directly by various electrical components such as op-amps. By the late 1980s, however, most "analog" simulations were run on conventional digital computers that emulate the behavior of an analog computer.

To implement a continuous-valued model as a simulation program on digital computers, the equations represented the system are usually approximated by difference equations. In such simulations, time typically advances in fixed increments or clock ticks. When time is incremented, the simulation program computes new values for all system state variables. Often iteration is required to converge to a "correct" solution for the new values. If the time increment is too large, state variable values may not converge, or may violate some model-specific constraint between successive clock ticks. If this occurs, a simulator may try reducing the size of the clock tick and recomputing the new values. Continuous-valued simulation is widely used in many areas of science and engineering, such as: chemical process simulation, physical process simulation, electrical and electronic circuit simulation, control system simulation, etc (Nutaro 2007).

Discrete-Event Simulation

Discrete-event simulation deals with system models in which changes happen at discrete instances in time, rather than continuously. For example, in a model of a computer communication network, the arrival of a message at a router is a change in the state of the model; the model state in the interval between successive message arrivals remains constant. Since nothing of interest happens to the model between these changes, it is not necessary to observe the model's behavior (its state) except at the time a change occurs (Zeigler 2003).

Discrete-event simulations usually fit into one of three categories (Sinclair 2004):

i.   Event-driven simulation
ii. Process-oriented simulation
iii. Distributed simulation

In this section we present a detail description of the process-oriented simulation because it is the major focus of this chapter, but to understand how it works, we need to begin with a discussion of event-driven simulation. However, distributed simulation model is implemented as a set of processes that exchange messages to control the sequencing and nature of changes in the model state. The advantage of this approach is that it is a natural and perhaps the only practical way to describe a discrete-event simulation model to be executed in parallel (Nutaro 2004 & Nutaro 2003).

i.   **Event-driven simulation**

An event is a change in the model state. The change takes zero time; i.e., each event is the boundary between two stable periods in the model's evolution (periods during which the state variables do not change), and no time elapses in making the change. The model evolves as a sequence of events. To describe the evolution of the model, we need to know when the events occur and what happens to the model at each event.

The heart of an event-driven simulation is the event set. This is a set of (event, time) pairs, where event specifies a particular type of state change and time is the point in simulation time at which the event occurs. The event set is often implemented as a list, maintained in time-sorted order. The first entry (the head of the list) has an event time that is less than or equal to the event times of all other events in the list. An event-driven simulation also maintains a simulated time clock, the value of which is the time of the most recent event that has been processed.

The basic operation of an event-driven simulation with the event set implemented as a sorted list is as follows (Sinclair 2004):

1. Set the simulation clock to 0; place a set of one or more initial events in the event list, in time-sorted order.
2. Fetch the event E consisting of the ordered pair (E.type, E.time) at the head of the event list; if the event list is empty, terminate the simulation.
3. Set the simulation time to E.time. If E.time is greater than the maximum simulation time specified for the execution of the simulation model, terminate the simulation.
4. Use the event identifier E.type to select the appropriate event-processing code, called an event service routine.
5. Execute the selected code. During this execution, an event may update system information held in global data structures, and it may cause new events E' (with E'.time$\geq$E.time) to be inserted in the event list. Note that it does not change simulation time.
6. At the completion of execution of the event service routine, go to 2.

Often, an empty event list at step 2 indicates an error in the design of the simulation. Any simulation that is intended to describe the steady-state behavior of a system will, on average, add one event to the event set for each event removed from the event set. However, the length of the event list may vary during simulation execution.

The basic idea of the representation of an event can be extended to one that consists of a triple (E.type, E.time, E.info), where E.info is information that is specific to the particular event type. It might be a single value such as an identifier of a job that requires processing at a CPU, or it might

be a pointer to a structure containing several related pieces of information. The simulation driver, which is the part of the simulator responsible for maintaining the event list and checking for termination conditions based on simulation time, does not interpret the information in E.info; this is the responsibility of the event service routine.

The diagram in Figure 3 represents the overall structure of a simple event-driven simulation execution. The boxes labeled execute event *i* represent event service routines, which may be implemented as individual procedures or as part of a general event-processing module (or both). As noted above, an event service routine may cause zero or more new events to be inserted on the event list. If an event service routine inserts a new event on the event list, the type of the new event may be different from the event associated with the service routine. A key point is that events never change the simulation time directly; they can only affect simulation time by the creation of new events which are inserted on the event list.

Event-driven simulation is completely general; any discrete-event simulation may be implemented with this approach. However, it is not "user-friendly" in some respects. This is because each event stands alone - events by definition maintain no context because they only exist for zero simulation time. Process-oriented simulation provides an approach that allows related state changes to be combined in the context of a process.

ii. **Process-oriented simulation**

In process-oriented simulation, sets of related event types are grouped together in a process, which is similar to the concept of a process in an operating system. A process consists of a body of code, the resources (primarily memory) allocated to that code for its execution, and its state - the current point of execution in the code and the values of the variables accessed by the code. A process typically exists over a non-zero interval of simulation time, and may be active for the entire

Figure 3. Event-driven simulation

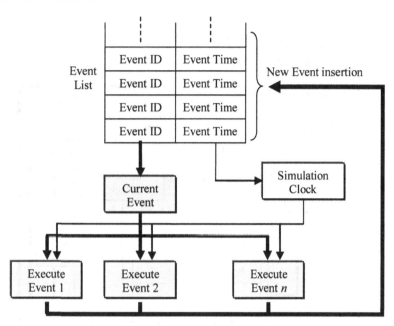

duration of the simulation. A process can execute and then be suspended pending the passage of a specified interval of simulation time or pending some interaction with another process.

The simulation driver is considerably more complicated than in the event-driven case. In addition to managing the event list, it must provide functions for:

- Process creation and activation/scheduling
- Process suspension
- Process termination
- Interprocess communication/synchronization

Readers with operating system experience can see the similarity between the simulation driver and process management in a conventional operating system. Indeed, process-oriented simulators could be written using the process management facilities available under an operating system such as UNIX, but the overhead in process-level context switching is too large to make this practical for many situations. Instead, the simulation

processes are usually lightweight threads within the context of a single UNIX-style process (Peek et. al. 2001).

We can take either of two viewpoints in structuring processes. A process can model some resource, such as a CPU, a disk, a channel, or a communications network. Jobs or customers that request service from these resources are represented as data structures that are passed from one process to another. Alternatively, jobs can be represented by processes, and resources in the system are described by shared data structures to which the jobs have access. In other words, the state of each component is represented by one or more global variables. The model is usually easier to implement with one of these approaches than the other, depending on how much the user can take advantage of the ability to group related events into a single process. The choice may also depend on the process interaction features provided by the simulation language.

The general structure of a process-oriented simulation is shown in Figure 4. The event list has been simplified; essentially, there is only one type

Figure 4. Process-oriented simulation

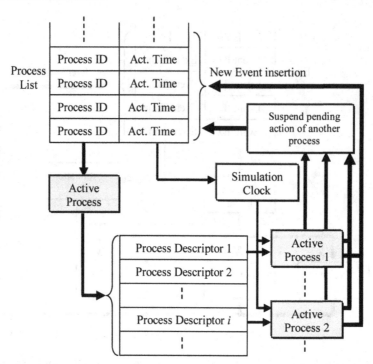

of event – start or wake up a process - eliminating the need for a field that identifies the event type. The E.info field mentioned above becomes the process ID field. It may point to a process descriptor in a table of descriptors for all active processes, or it may be the process descriptor itself. In this context, a process descriptor is an object that contains all of the information necessary to determine the state of a process whose execution is currently suspended. When the simulation driver gets the next event, it uses the process descriptor to find and restore the environment or context of that process and then starts the process at the point at which it suspended.

The process environment includes the process stack, register contents (including the program counter, stack pointer, and processor status word), and other process-specific information. In creating a process, the simulation driver must allocate memory for the process stack and initialize various register values. The per-process stack allocation is potentially a limitation in the use of process-oriented simulation.

As Figure 4 indicates, a process that has been activated can be suspended basically in two ways. First, the process can simply delay itself for a fixed interval of simulation time, in which case its descriptor is reinserted into the event list at the proper place. Second, the process can suspend itself for an indefinite period of time. For example, the process may wait on a semaphore. The process descriptor can only be reinserted into the event list due to the action of some other process, such as signaling a semaphore. Not indicated in Figure 4 is the possibility that a process will simply terminate and disappear.

The choice of process-oriented simulation over event-driven simulation is not one of modeling power but of implementation convenience. Process-oriented implementations group related events into a single process, using the normal flow of control within the execution of the process to define the sequencing of the events. Since the events within a process occur at different simulation times, the process exists over an interval of simulation time, unlike an event, which occurs at a single instant of time and then is gone. The ease of implementation and debugging with process-oriented simulation compared to event-driven simulation is gained at a cost of some additional overhead due to the need to switch contexts when a process suspends.

It is accurate to say that all discrete-event simulations are event-driven. Process-oriented simulation cloaks the basic event mechanism in higher level features that make writing, debugging, and understanding the simulation model easier, while distributed simulation replaces the event set completely with a mechanism that uses time-stamped messages that semi-autonomous parts of the simulation model exchange. In both cases, the user's view of the simulation model implementation and its execution is substantially different than in event-driven simulation.

Terminating versus Steady-State Simulation

Based on the simulation terminating criteria, computer simulation can be classified into two categories (Hassan & Jain 2003):

Terminating Simulation

A terminating simulation is used to study the behavior of a system for a well-defined period of time or number of events. Examples for such simulation may include:

- Evaluating the performance of a new TCP protocol stack only during the office hours 9 AM to 5 PM. A simulation is terminated after 8 hours of simulated time.
- Evaluating the performance of a new scheme for downloading 100 specific objects from a popular website. Simulation

terminated as soon as the last of the 100 objects is downloaded.

Steady-State Simulation

A steady-state simulation is used to investigate the steady-state behavior of a system. In such simulations, the simulation continues until the system reaches a steady-state; otherwise the simulation results can be significantly different from the true results. Example of such as simulation is:

- Measuring the long-term packet loss rate in congested router.
- Evaluating the average network reachability in MANET.

In such simulations, the simulation must be continued until the system reaches a steady-state; otherwise the mean packet-loss rate in the first example or average network reachability in the second example fluctuates as the system goes through the transient phase.

Trace-Driven versus Stochastic (Synthetic) Simulation

Computer and related systems are most often simulated using one of two types of input traffic patterns; these are (Hassan & Jain 2003):

Trace-Driven Simulation

Trace-driven simulation is an important tool in many areas. The idea is that model inputs are derived from a sequence of observations made on a real system. A classic example from computer engineering involves the design of new cache memory organizations. The designer uses a computer system, either in hardware or in software, to record the time-ordered sequence of memory accesses generated during the execution of some program(s). This ordered set, called the trace or address trace, contains the address of each memory reference and the type of access - read or write. Then the designer uses the trace as input to a trace-driven simulation implementation of a model of a cache memory system and from the model's outputs determines parameters of interest, such as the miss ratio, in judging the merits of the design. In computer networks trace-driven simulations, traces of packet arrival events (arrival time, packet size, etc.) are first captured from an operational network using a performance measurement tool (e.g., *tcpdump*). These traces are then processed to be converted in a suitable format, and used as input traffic for the simulation to produce the performance results.

The main advantage of trace-driven simulation is that the model inputs are real world; they are not approximations or "guesstimates" whose accuracy may be questionable, and the same trace can be used to evaluate and compare the performance of several algorithms and schemes. To achieve more credibility, many performance analysts use trace-driven simulation to evaluate the performance of a new algorithm. A major disadvantage is that this approach is not applicable to all types of systems. Limitations also exist if the system to be modeled invalidates the trace in some way. In the example of trace-driven simulation of a cache, the address trace generated by a uniprocessor may be misleading if applied to a model of a cache in a multiprocessor system.

Stochastic (Synthetic) Simulation

In stochastic simulation the system workload or the model input is characterized by various probability distributions, Poisson, exponential, On/Off, self-similar, etc. During the simulation execution, these distributions are used to produce random values which are the inputs to the simulation model. Most computer network simulation studies rely heavily on stochastic model in generating the input traffic pattern. In MANETs, a stochastic model is used to calculate node locations within the network area, direction of movement, probability of reception,

etc. The stochastically generated input traffic never matches 100% with the actual traffic observed on a given practical network.

SIMULATION LANGUAGES

A computer simulation language describes the operation of a simulation model on a computer. A simulation model can be implemented in a general-purpose programming language (e.g., C++, C#, Java, etc.) or in a language tailored specifically to describing simulation models (see below). The main features of the simulation languages are (Rorabaugh 2004, Maria 1997):

- Provide run-time environment.
- Develop with low-level programming languages such as C programming language.
- Provide a library of simulation-oriented functions to assist the user in implementing the simulation model.
- Include mechanisms for managing the simulation program execution and collecting data.
- Support parallel and distributed computing systems.
- Support both event and process-oriented simulations.
- Combine related events into a single process which makes the design, implementation, and, perhaps most importantly, debugging of the simulation model much easier.
- Has the advantage that users are likely to find many of its concepts familiar because of prior knowledge of operating system design and parallel programs.

Simulation languages can handle both major types of simulation: continuous and discrete-event though more modern languages can handle combinations of them. Most languages also have a graphical interface and at least simple statistical gathering capability for the analysis of the results.

An important part of discrete-event languages is the ability to generate pseudo-random numbers and varieties of probability distributions.

Discret- event simulation languages are viewing the model as a sequence of random events each causing a change in state. Examples are: AutoMod, eM-Plant, Rockwell Arena, GASP, GPSS, SimPy (an open-source package based on Python), SIMSCRIPT II.5 (a well established commercial compiler), Simula, Java Modelling Tools (an open-source package with graphical user-interface), Poses++, etc.

Continuous simulation languages are viewing the model essentially as a set of differential equations. Examples include: Advanced Continuous Simulation Language (ACSL) (supports textual or graphical model specification), Dynamo, SimApp (simple simulation of dynamic systems and control systems), Simgua (simulation toolbox and environment and it supports Visual Basic), Simulation Language for Alternative Modeling (SLAM), VisSim (a visually programmed block diagram language), etc.

Hybrid simulation languages handle both continuous and discrete-event simulations. Examples of such languages include: AMESim (simulation platform to model and analyze multi-domain systems and predict their performances), Any-Logic multi-method simulation tool (supports system dynamics, discrete-event simulation, agent-based modeling), Modelica (open-standard object-oriented language for modeling of complex physical systems), EcosimPro Language (EL) (continuous modeling with discrete-events), Saber-Simulator (simulates physical effects in different engineering domains, e.g., hydraulic, electronic, mechanical, thermal, etc.), Simulink, SPICE (analog circuit simulation), Z simulation language, Scilab (contains a simulation package called Scicos), XMLlab (simulations with XML), Flexsim 4.0 (powerful interactive software for continuous and discrete-event flow simulation), Simio software (for continuous, discrete-event, and agent-based simulation).

NETWORK SIMULATORS

There are a number of computer network simulators that have been developed throughout the years to support computer networks analysis and design. Some of them are of general-purpose use and other dedicated to simulate particular types of computer networks. A typical network simulator can provide the programmer with the abstraction of multiple threads of control and inter-thread communication. Functions and protocols are described either by finite-state machine, native programming code, or a combination of the two. A simulator typically comes with a set of predefined modules and user-friendly graphical user-interface (GUI). Some network simulators even provide extensive support for visualization and animation.

There are also emulators such as the NIST Network Emulation Tool (NIST NET). By operating at the IP level, it can emulate the critical end-to-end performance characteristics imposed by various wide area network (WAN) situations or by various underlying subnetwork technologies in a lab test-bed environment. Computer network simulators can also be classified as academic or commercial simulators (Chang 1999).

Some examples of academic simulators include:

- REAL: REAL is a simulator for studying the dynamic behavior of flow and congestion control schemes in packet switch data networks. Network topology, protocols, data and control parameters are represented by Scenario, which are described using NetLanguage, a simple ASCII representation of the network. About 30 modules are provided which can exactly emulate the actions of several well-known flow control protocols.
- INSANE: INSANE is a network simulator designed to test various IP-over-ATM algorithms with realistic traffic loads derived from empirical traffic measurements.

It's ATM protocol stack provides real-time guarantees to ATM virtual circuits by using rate controlled static priority (RCSP) queuing. A protocol similar to the real-time channel administration protocol (RCAP) is implemented for ATM signaling. A TK-based graphical simulation monitor can provide an easy way to check the progress of multiple running simulation processes.

- NetSim: NetSim is intended to offer a very detailed simulation of Ethernet, including realistic modeling of signal propagation, the effect of the relative positions of stations on events on the network, the collision detection and handling process and the transmission deferral mechanism. But it cannot be extended to address modern networks.

- Maisie: Maisie is a C-based language for hierarchical simulation, or more specifically, a language for parallel discrete-event simulation. A logical process is used to model one or more physical processes; the events in the physical system are modeled by message exchanges among the corresponding logical processes in the model.

Other examples also include ns-2 (ns Network simulator), VINT, U-Net, USC TCP-Vegas test-bed, TARVOS, NCTUns, WiredShark, Harvard simulator, and Network Workbench.

As to commercial simulator, examples include BONeS, COMNET III and OPNET. BONeS DESIGNER provides lots of building blocks, modeling capabilities, and analysis tools for development and analysis of network products, protocols, and system architectures. With its recent released ATM Verification Environment (AVE), it is specifically targeted for ATM architectural exploration and hardware sizing. COMNET III, a graphical, off-the-shelf package, lets you quickly and easily analyzes and predicts the performance of networks ranging from simple LANs to complex enterprise-wide systems (CACI). Starting with a library of network objects with one COMNET III object representing real world objects, The COMNET III's object-oriented framework and GUI gives user the flexibility to try an unlimited number of "what if" scenarios.

For maximum effectiveness, a simulation environment should be modular, hierarchical, and take advantage of the graphical capabilities of today's workstations. Optimized network engineering tool (OPNET) is an object-oriented simulation environment that meets all these requirements and is the most powerful general-purpose network simulator. OPNET provides a comprehensive development environment for the specification, simulation and performance analysis of communication networks. A large range of communication systems from a single LAN to global satellite networks can be supported. OPNET's comprehensive analysis tool is special ideal for interpreting and synthesizing output data. A discrete-event simulation of the call and routing signaling was developed using a number of OPNET's unique features such as the dynamic allocation of processes to model virtual circuits transiting through an ATM switch. Moreover, its built-in Proto-C language support provides it the ability to realize almost any function and protocol.

THE MANET SIMULATOR (MANSIM)

This section describes a process-oriented discrete-event MANET simulator, namely, MANSim (Al-Bahadili 2008). In fact, this section describes the philosophy behind the simulator, gives a brief outline of its history, explains its internal structure, and describes its use in computer network teaching and research. MANSim is especially developed to simulate and evaluate the performance of a number of flooding algorithms for MANETs, and it is a research-level and available to the academic community under no-cost license.

According to classification criteria discussed in Section 4, MANSim can be characterized as:

Figure 5. Regular-grid nodes distribution (4-node degree)

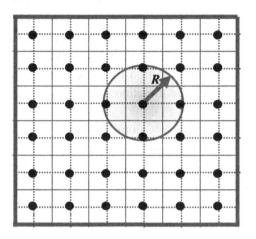

- Process-oriented discrete-event simulator
- Terminating simulation
- Stochastic input traffic pattern

It is written in C++ language, and it consists of four major modules:

(1) Network module (Geometrical configuration)
(2) Mobility module
(3) Computational module
(4) Algorithm module

In what follows a description is given to each of the above modules.

Network Module (Geometrical Configuration)

The network module is concerned with the distribution of mobile nodes within the network area. MANSim simulates two types of nodes distribution, these are:

Regular-Grid Nodes Distribution

In a regular-grid node distribution configuration, the network is considered as a regular-grid where nodes are placed at each intersection of the grid as illustrated in Figures 5 and 6. For this configuration, two node degrees are considered, namely 4-node degree and 8-node degree. In a 4-node degree (Figure 5), each node is allowed to communicate directly with its vertical and horizontal neighbors, and the radio transmission range of the node covers one-hop neighbor in each direction. In an 8-node degree (Figure 6), nodes are also allowed to communicate with the diagonal neighbors.

The regular-grid configuration is quite simplistic but it is useful for calculating benchmark analytical results for some computed network parameters for a specific network condition. These benchmark analytical results can be used to validate the simulation results. However, a more realistic configuration is required, that may consider random (non-regular) node distribution and produce variable node degrees.

Random Node Distribution

In a random node distribution configuration, the nodes are randomly placed on the X×Y network area as illustrated in Figure 7. They are placed according to a particular probability distribution function (PDF), such as linear distribution, Poisson's distribution, etc. For example, in a linear distribution, the x and y positions of the a node are calculated as follows:

$$x = X \bullet \xi \tag{1}$$

$$y = Y \bullet \xi \tag{2}$$

Where X and Y are the length and width of the network area, and ξ is a random number uniformly selected between 0 and 1 ($0 \leq \xi < 1$). Two nodes i and j are considered to be connected or neighbors if the Euclidean distance between these two nodes (r) is less than or equal to radio transmission range of the node (R), where r is given by:

Figure 6. Regular-grid nodes distribution (8-node degree)

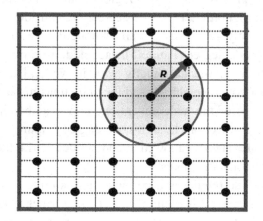

$$r = \sqrt{\left(x_i - x_j\right)^2 + \left(y_i - y_j\right)^2} \qquad (3)$$

One important point that must be carefully considered using random node distribution is to make sure that initially each node within the network should have at least one neighboring node.

Mobility Module

One of the main characteristics of MANETs is the mobility of their nodes. Mobility can be simulated using different mobility patterns (models). One

Figure 7. Random node distribution

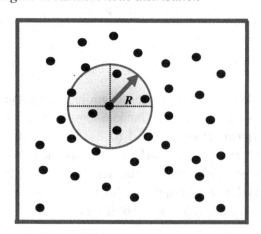

of the most widely-used patterns is the random-walk mobility pattern. In which, the direction of movement for a mobile node is randomly chosen from an appropriate PDF. In most applications, a node is allowed to move with equal probability in any direction within the geographical are of interest, i.e., the direction is sampled randomly from a uniform PDF.

The random walk mobility pattern is simulated as follows: each node is allowed to move around randomly within the network area during the simulation. The movement pattern of a node is simulated by generating a direction (θ), a speed (u), and a time interval (τ), which is also referred to as a pause time. The direction is sampled from a uniform PDF between 0 to 2π, thus

$$\theta = 2\pi\xi \qquad (4)$$

Nodes are either allow to move with a pre-assigned average speed (u_{av}), i.e., $u = u_{av}$, a pre-assigned maximum speed (u_{max}), i.e., $u = u_{max}$, or a node speed is sampled randomly between 0 and u_{max} (i.e., $u = \xi u_{max}$).

In order to consider node mobility, a simulation time (T_{sim}) must be setup; it is divided into a number of time intervals ($nIntv$) that allows the pause time to be calculated as:

$$\tau = T_{sim}/nIntv \qquad (5)$$

The distance traveled by the node is calculated as

$$d = u\tau \qquad (6)$$

Then, a new node location at time $t+\tau$ is calculated by:

$$x(t + \tau) = x(t) + d\,Cos(\theta) \qquad (7)$$

$$y(t + \tau) = y(t) + d\,Sin(\theta) \qquad (8)$$

Where $x(t)$, $y(t)$ and $x(t+\tau)$, $y(t+\tau)$ are the old and new locations of the node, respectively. This new node location must be checked to be within the network area, if it is not (i.e., the node leaves the network area), there are different ways to bring the node back to the network. In this model, a reduced weight approach is used to ensure that the node remains within the network area.

In the reduced weight approach the node is kept moving in the same direction, but the distance traveled (d) is reduced by multiplying it by descending weight until the new location be within the network area (i.e., $d = d \cdot \omega$). The weight ω is given by:

$$\omega = \frac{(I_{max} - k)}{I_{max}} \qquad (9)$$

An appropriate value for I_{max} is between 2 to 10, and k is set to zero and is incremented by 1 each time the node traveled outside the network area. However, other mobility patterns can be easily implemented in MANSim.

Computational Module

Many computational models start a simulation from a single source node positioned at the center of the network area, or from a single source node randomly selected within the network area. The simulation is repeated for S times, i.e., the source node is assumed to transmit S request messages. The results obtained from these simulations are averaged to give average values for the computed parameters. The results reflect the average behavior with regards to this particular source node, but they may not well reflect the average behavior of other nodes within the network.

But, a major feature of MANSim computational module is that it does not randomly pick a node and use it as a fixed source node. Instead, a loop is performed using all nodes within the network as a source node, then the computation for

the network parameters is performed sequentially over all node, except the source node, as destination nodes. The computed parameters for each source node are averaged over (n-1), and then these averaged values are averaged again over (n). In other words, the computed parameters are averaged over ($n(n$-1)). In this case, the computed parameters may well represent the average behavior of any of the nodes within the network.

Due to the probabilistic approach, in order to enhance the accuracy of the solution, the computation is repeated, in an inner loop, for each source and destination nodes for a number of runs, i.e., each source is allowed to initiate S requested messages. Once again, the computed parameters are averaged over S. However, it has been found that with small number of runs the solution is converged to a more stable solution, and for networks having no probabilistic behavior, i.e., p_t=1, S has no effect on the computed parameters and can be set to 1.

As it has been mentioned earlier, in order to consider node mobility, a simulation time (T_{sim}) is set. It is divided into a number of time intervals ($nIntv$) that yields a time interval or pause time (τ). The calculation is repeated, in an outer loop, for $nIntv$, and the results obtained for the computed parameters are averaged over $nIntv$. In general, it has been found that to obtain an adequate network performance, the pause time must be carefully chosen so that the distance traveled by the node, during location update interval, is less than the radio transmission range of the source node. For non-mobile nodes (fixed nodes) $nIntv$ has no effect on the computed parameters and can be set to 1. Figure (8) outlines the computational module of MANSim simulator.

Algorithm Module

In this module, the flooding optimization algorithm is implemented. In MANSim, until now, five flooding algorithms have been implemented, these are:

Figure 8. Computational module of the MANSim simulator

Computational Module.
Loop over the number of intervals (*nIntv*)
{
    Loop over the number of nodes as source nodes (*i*=1, *n*)
    {
        Loop over the number of nodes as destination nodes (*j*=1, *n*), except for *i*=*j*
        {
            Loop over the number of transmitted request message (*k*=1, *S*)
            {
                Compute IRec(*i*) and IRet(*i*) using a particular flooding algorithm, e.g., pure flooding,
                probabilistic, LAR-1, LAR-2, LAR-1P, OMPR, etc.
            }
            Compute the average values of the computed parameters (over *S*) for source node *i* and destination
            node *j*.
        }
        Compute the average values of the computed parameters (over *n*-1) for source node *i* and *n*-1
        destination nodes.
    }
    Compute the average values of the computed parameters (over *n*) for *n* source nodes and *n*-1 destination
    nodes.
}
Compute the average values of the computed network parameters (over *nIntv*).

- Pure flooding (Al-Bahadili & Jaradat 2007, Jaradat 2007)
- Probabilistic flooding (Al-Bahadili & Jaradat 2007, Jaradat 2007)
- Location-aided routing scheme 1 (LAR-1) algorithms (Al-Bahadili et. al. 2007, Al-Thaher 2007)
- A hybrid LAR-1 and probabilistic (LAR-1P) algorithm (Al-Bahadili et. al. 2007, Al-Thaher 2007)
- Optimal multipoint relaying (OMPR) algorithm (Al-Bahadili et. al. 2009, Jaradat 2009)

Discussion of the algorithms is beyond the scope of this chapter and details on each of the above algorithms can be found in the references mentioned next to each of them. In addition, more discussions on these algorithms can be found in (Bani-Yassein 2006, Ko & Vaidya 2000, Tseng et. al. 2002, Qayyum et. al. 2002). However, they all have a number of algorithm-dependent procedures to calculate:

- A node reception index vector iRec(*i*). This index is initialized with zero value and updated when a node receives a broadcast message. This occurs if the receiving node is within the radio transmission range of the transmitting node, and no error occurs during data transmission due to noise interference. Each time a node *i* successfully receives a request, an index iRec(*i*) is incremented by 1, where *i* represents the node ID. This index is used to calculate the network parameters such as: the average duplicate reception (ADR) and the reachability (RCH).

- A node retransmission index vector iRet(*i*). This index is initialized with zero value, except for the source and destination nodes and updated each time the node succeeded to retransmit the broadcast message. A node index iRet(*i*) is set to 1 if the node *i* retransmits a received message. This index is used to calculate the number of retransmission (RET) within the network.

WIRELESS NETWORK ENVIRONMENTS

In MANSim, two types of network environments can be simulated; these are:

1. **Noiseless (error-free) environment:** Noiseless (error-free) environment represents an ideal network environment, in which it is assumed that all data transmitted by a source node is successfully and correctly received by a destination node. It can be characterized by the following axioms or assumptions, which are still part of many MANET simulation studies, despite the increasing awareness of the need to represent noisy features (Kotz et. al. 2004):
   i. The world is flat
   ii. All radios have equal and circular radio transmission range
   iii. Communication link symmetry
   iv. Perfect link
   v. Signal strength is a simple function of distance.

2. **Noisy (error-prone) environment:** Noisy (error-prone) environment represents a realistic network environment, in which the received signal will differ from the transmitted signal, due to various transmission impairments, such (Kotz et. al. 2004):
   i. Wireless signal attenuation (p_{att})
   ii. Free space loss (p_{free})
   iii. Thermal noise (p_{therm})
   iv. Atmospheric absorption (p_{atm})
   v. Multipath effect (p_{mult})
   vi. Refraction (p_{ref})

All of these impairments are represented by a generic name, noise. The environment is called noisy environment. For modeling and simulation purposes, the noisy environment can be described by introducing a probability function, which referred to as the probability of reception (p_c). It defined as the probability that a wireless transmitted data is survived being lost and successfully delivered to a destination node despite the presence of all or any of the above impairments. Thus, p_c can be calculated as:

$$p_c = p_{att} \cdot p_{free} \cdot p_{therm} \cdot p_{atm} \cdot p_{mult} \cdot p_{ref} \ldots \ldots \quad (10)$$

For a noiseless environment p_c is set to unity.

COMPUTED PARAMETERS

MANSim calculates a number of network parameters to evaluate the performance of the implemented algorithms. These parameters were recommended by the IETF to judge the performance of flooding algorithms, such as (Ko & Vaidya 2000, Tseng et. al. 2002):

(1) **Number of retransmission (RET).** The percentage of nodes that retransmits the broadcast message. It is calculated as the number of node that actually retransmits the broadcast message divided by the total number of nodes within the network (n).

(2) **Average Duplicate Receptions (ADR).** The number of times the same broadcast message being received by each node within the network.

(3) **Reachability (RCH).** The probability of delivering a broadcast message between a source and a destination node within the network. It is calculated as the number of nodes that can be reached from a certain source node divided by n.

(4) **Average hop counts (AHC).** The average number of network segments in the route from source to destination node.

(5) **Saved rebroadcast (SRB).** The percentage reduction in the number of retransmission. It is calculated by dividing the difference between the number of nodes receiving the broadcast message and the number of nodes

that actually retransmitted the message by the number of nodes receiving the broadcast message.

(6) **Disconnectivity (DIS).** The probability of failing to deliver broadcast message to a certain destination node within the network. It is calculated as 1-RCH.

(7) **Average latency (LAT).** The interval from the time the broadcast was initiated to the time the last node finished its rebroadcasting.

In addition, MANSim can be used to investigate the effect of a number of input network parameters, such as:

(1) Node density (n_d). The number of nodes per unit area ($n_d = n/A$), where A is the network area ($A = X \times Y$).

(2) Node mobility or node speed (u). Nodes are assumed to move with either an average speed (u_{av}), maximum speed (u_{max}), or a randomly selected speed.

(3) Node transmission radius (R), which represents the area that can be covered by a certain node.

(4) Retransmission probability (p_t). The probability of retransmitting a received broadcast message.

(5) Reception probability (p_c). The probability of a broadcast message being successfully received by a destination node that located within the transmission range of the source node.

(6) Simulation time (T_{sim}). The total simulation time.

SIMULATION RESULTS

The discrete-event simulator MANSim has been used in a number of researches to evaluate the performance of flooding algorithms, such those mentioned in Section 7. It is approved as an efficient and flexible simulation tool that can be used to provide insight into the performance of these algorithms in ideal and realistic MANET environments.

In this work, we present results for one scenario. In this scenario, we compare the performance of six broadcast algorithms in noiseless and noisy environments. These algorithms are:

(1) Pure flooding
(2) Probabilistic flooding with fixed retransmission probability ($p_t = 0.8$)
(3) Probabilistic flooding with dynamic retransmission probability
(4) LAR-1 algorithm
(5) LAR-1P algorithm with fixed retransmission probability ($p_t = 0.8$)
(6) OMPR algorithm.

The performance is compared in terms of three parameters, these are: RET, ADR, and RCH. The input parameters for this scenario are summarized in Table 1.

The simulation results for RET, ADR, and RCH are shown in Figures 9, 10, and 11, respectively. Since the main objectives of this work is to demonstrate the use of discrete-event simulation in computer networks analysis and design, the simulation results are briefly discussed here, and a detail discussion can be found in the references mentioned next to each algorithm or in (Al-Bahadili et. al. 2009, Jaradat 2009).

The main points that are concluded from this scenario can be summarized as follows:

- Probabilistic flooding algorithm always achieves the highest possible RCH, but at the same time it introduces the low saving in RET and ADR, when it is compared with the other algorithms.
- LAR-1 and LAR-1P algorithms presents the highest reduction in RET and ADR but at the same time they provides the lowest RCH.
- The OMPR algorithm presents a moderate

Table 1. Input parameters

Parameters	Values
Geometrical model	Random node distribution
Network area	1000x1000 m
Number of nodes (n)	100 nodes.
Transmission radius (R)	200 m
Average node speed (u)	5 m/sec
Prob. of reception (p_c)	0.5 to 1.0 in step of 0.1
Simulation time (T_{sim})	300 sec
Pause time (τ)	30 sec

Figure 9. Variation of RET with p_c for various algorithms

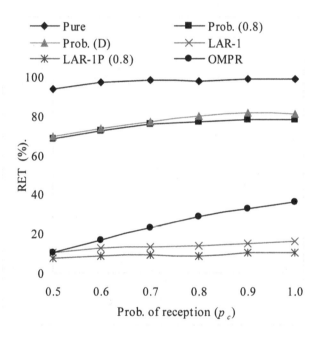

reduction in RET and ADR, when it is compared with probabilistic (fixed and dynamic p_t), LAR-1, and LAR-1P. It performs better than probabilistic and less than LAR-1 and LAR-1P for various network noise levels and nodes speeds. However, the RCH it achieves is higher than that of LAR-1 and LAR-1P algorithms.

Since the main objective of using flooding optimization is to achieve a cost-effective reachability, which means a highest possible reachability at a reasonable cost, in this work, cost is measured in terms of RET and ADR. The results obtained demonstrate that the OMPR algorithm provides an excellent performance as it can achieve the most excellent cost-effective reachability, for various network noise levels and nodes speeds,

Figure 10. Variation of ADR with p_c for various algorithms

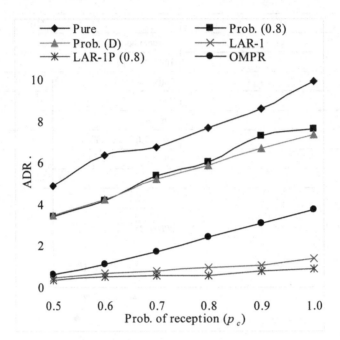

Figure 11. Variation of RCH with p_c for various algorithms

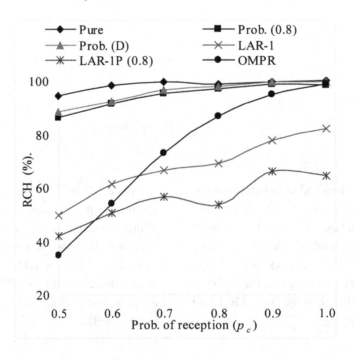

as compared to probabilistic (fixed and dynamic p_t), LAR-1, and LAR-1P algorithms.

Figures 9, 10, and 11 demonstrate that the OMPR algorithm provides an excellent network RCH in noisy environment when compared with LAR-1 and LAR-1P, at a significant reduction in RET and ADR. For example, for fixed nodes and p_c=0.5, it achieves a RCH of 47.1% compared with 33.9% and 23.8% for LAR-1 and LAR-1P (p_t=0.8), respectively. This is achieved at a cost of 11% RET compared with 6.6% and 4.2%, for LAR-1 and LAR-1P (p_t=0.8), respectively.

The figures also show that the probabilistic and OMPR algorithms provide almost a comparative performance in noiseless and low-noise environments (p_c>0.8). But, in terms of network reachability, the probabilistic approach overwhelmed the performance of the OMPR algorithm in noisy environment. For example, for mobile nodes with u=5 m/sec and p_c=0.5, the OMPR algorithm achieves a reachability of only 34.6%, while for the same environment, the probabilistic approach achieves over 85%. But, the probabilistic approach achieves this high network reachability at a very high cost of RET ($\approx$68%) and ADR ($\approx$3.5 duplicate reception per node) compared with RET=10.3% and ADR=0.587 for the OMPR algorithm.

CONCLUSION

This chapter presents a description of a newly developed research-level computer network simulator, namely, MANSim. It can be used to evaluate the performance of a number of flooding algorithms in ideal and realistic MANETs.

The main conclusions of this chapter can be summarized as follows:

- The simulator demonstrates an excellent accuracy, reliability, and flexibility in analyzing and designing wireless computer networks in comparison with analytical modeling and experimental tests as it

allows investigating various network and operation environments with minimum costs and efforts. For example various node densities, node speeds, node radio transmission range, noise-level, etc.

- The simulator can be learned quickly and it is sufficiently powerful, comprehensive, and extensible to allow investigation of a considerable range of complicated problems.
- Due to the flexible modular structure of the simulator, it can be easily modified to process other flooding algorithms, mobility models, probability density functions, etc.
- Many of its modules are design for easy re-use with other simulators.

For future work, it is highly recommended to implement more flooding algorithms, realistic mobility pattern, variable radio transmission range, various probability distribution functions for node distribution within the network area or to sample the direction of movement of mobile nodes. Furthermore, we suggest modifying the computational model to allow computing the power conservation using variable radio range adjustment methodologies.

REFERENCES

Ahmed, Y., & Shahriari, S. (2001). *Simulation of TCP/IP Applications on CDPD Channel*. M.Sc Thesis, Department of Signals and Systems, Chalmers University of Technology, Sweden.

Al-Bahadili, H. (2008). *MANSim: A Mobile Ad Hoc Network Simulator*. Personal Communication.

Al-Bahadili, H., Al-Basheer, O., & Al-Thaher, A. (2007). A Location Aided Routing-Probabilistic Algorithm for Flooding Optimization in MA-NETs. In *Proceedings of Mosharaka International Conference on Communications, Networking, and Information Technology* (MIC-CNIT 2007), Jordan.

Al-Bahadili, H., Al-Zoubaidi, A. R., Al-Zayyat, K., Jaradat, R., & Al-Omari, I. (2009). *Development and performance evaluation of an OMPR algorithm for route discovery in noisy MANETs.* To be published.

Al-Bahadili, H., & Jaradat, Y. (2007). Development and performance analysis of a probabilistic flooding in noisy mobile ad hoc networks. In *Proceedings of the 1st International Conference on Digital Communications and Computer Applications* (DCCA2007), (pp. 1306-1316), Jordan.

Al-Thaher, A. (2007). *A Location Aided Routing-Probabilistic Algorithm for Flooding Optimization in Mobile Ad Hoc Networks.* M.Sc Thesis, Department of Computer Science, Amman Arab University for Graduate Studies, Jordan.

Asgarkhani, M. (2002). *Computer modeling and simulation as a learning tool: A preliminary study of network simulation products.* Christchurch Polytechnic Institute of Technology (CPIT), Christchurch, New Zealand.

Bani-Yassein, M., Ould-Khaoua, M., Mackenzie, L., & Papanastasiou, S. (2006). Performance analysis of adjusted probabilistic broadcasting in mobile ad hoc networks. *International Journal of Wireless Information Networks, 13*(2), 127–140. doi:10.1007/s10776-006-0027-0

Banks, J., Carson, J. S., & Nelson, B. L. (1996). *Discrete-Event System Simulation* (2nd Ed.). Upper Saddle River, NJ: Prentice Hall.

Chang, X. (1999). Network simulation with OP-NET. In P. A. Farrington, H. B. Nembhard, D. T. Sturrock, & G. W. Evans (Eds.), *Proceedings of the 1999 Winter Simulation Conference*, (pp. 307-314).

Chung, A. C. (2004). *Simulation and Modeling Handbook: A Practical Approach.* Boca Raton, FL: CRC Press.

Forouzan, B. A. (2007). *Data Communications and Networking* (4th Ed.). Boston: McGraw-Hill.

Fusk, H., Lawniczak, A. T., & Volkov, S. (2001). Packet delay in models of data networks. *ACM Transactions on Modeling and Computer Simulation, 11*(3), 233–250. doi:10.1145/502109.502110

Hassan, M., & Jain, R. (2003). *High Performance TCP/IP Networking: Concepts, Issues, and Solutions.* Upper Saddle River, NJ: Prentice-Hall.

Jaradat, R. (2009). *Development and Performance Analysis of Optimal Multipoint Relaying Algorithm for Noisy Mobile Ad Hoc Networks.* M.Sc Thesis, Department of Computer Science, Amman Arab University for Graduate Studies, Jordan.

Jaradat, Y. (2007). *Development and Performance Analysis of a Probabilistic Flooding in Noisy Mobile Ad Hoc Networks.* M.Sc Thesis, Department of Computer Science, Amman Arab University for Graduate Studies, Jordan.

Ko, Y., & Vaidya, N. H. (2000). Location-Aided Routing (LAR) in Mobile Ad Hoc Networks. *Journal of wireless . Networks, 6*(4), 307–321.

Kotz, D., Newport, C., Gray, R. S., Liu, J., Yuan, Y., & Elliott, C. (2004). Experimental evaluation of wireless simulation assumptions. In *Proceedings of the 7th ACM International Symposium on Modeling, Analysis, and Simulation of Wireless and Mobile Systems*, (pp. 78-82).

Kurkowski, S., Camp, T., & Colagrosso, M. (2006). *MANET simulation studies: The current state and new simulation tools.* Department of Mathematics and Computer Sciences, Colorado School of Mines, CO.

Law, A., & Kelton, W. D. (2000). Simulation Modeling and Analysis (3rd Ed.). Boston: McGraw-Hill Higher Education.

Maria, A. (1997). Introduction to modeling and simulation. In S. Andradottir, K. J. Healy, D. H. Withers, & B. L. Nelson (Ed.) *Proceedings of the 1997 Winter Simulation Conference,* (pp. 7-13).

Nutaro, J. (2003). *Parallel Discrete Event Simulation with Application to Continuous Systems.* PhD Thesis, University of Arizona, Tuscon, Arizona.

Nutaro, J. (2007). Discrete event simulation of continuous systems. In P. Fishwick, (Ed.) *Handbook of Dynamic System Modeling.* Boca Raton, FL: Chapman & Hall/CRC.

Nutaro, J., & Sarjoughian, H. (2004). Design of distributed simulation environments: A unified system-theoretic and logical processes approach. *Journal of Simulation, 80*(11), 577–589. doi:10.1177/0037549704050919

Peek, J., Todin-Gonguet, G., & Strang, J. (2001). *Learning the UNIX Operating System* (5th Ed.). Sebastopol, CA: O'Reilly & Associates.

Qayyum, A., Viennot, L., & Laouiti, A. (2002). Multipoint relaying for flooding broadcast messages in mobile wireless network. *Proceedings of the 35th Hawaii International Conference on System Sciences,* (pp. 3866- 3875).

Roeder, T. M. K. (2004). *An Information Taxonomy for Discrete-Event Simulations.* PhD Dissertation, University of California, Berkeley, CA.

Rorabaugh, C. B. (2004). *Simulating Wireless Communication Systems: Practical Models in C++.* Upper Saddle River, NJ: Prentice-Hall.

Sasson, Y., Cavin, D., & Schiper, A. (2003). Probabilistic broadcast for flooding in wireless mobile ad hoc networks. *Proceedings of Wireless Communications and Networking Conference (WCNC '03), 2*(16-20), 1124-1130.

Scott, D., & Yasinsac, A. (2004). Dynamic probabilistic retransmission in ad hoc networks. *Proceedings of the International Conference on Wireless Networks,* (pp. 158-164).

Sinclair, J. B. (2004). *Simulation of Computer Systems and Computer Networks: A Process-Oriented Approach.* George R. Brown School of Engineering, Rice University, Houston, Texas, USA.

Stallings, W. (2005). *Wireless Communications and Networks* (2nd Ed.). Upper Saddle River, NJ: Prentice-Hall.

Tanenbaum, A. (2003). *Computer Networks* (4th Ed.). Upper Saddle River, NJ: Prentice Hall.

Tseng, Y., Ni, S., Chen, Y., & Sheu, J. (2002). The broadcast storm problem in a mobile ad hoc network. *Journal of Wireless Networks, 8,* 153–167. doi:10.1023/A:1013763825347

Zeigler, B. P. (2003). DEVS Today: Recent advances in discrete event-based information. *Proceedings of the 11th IEEE/ACM International Symposium on Modeling, Analysis and Simulation of Computer Telecommunications Systems,* (pp. 148-162).

KEY TERMS AND DEFINITIONS

Discrete-Event Simulation: In discrete-event simulation the operation of a system is represented as a chronological sequence of events. Each event occurs at an instant in time and marks a change of state in the system.

Continuous-Valued Simulation: In a continuous-valued simulation, the values of the system states are continuously change with time. The various states of the system are usually represented by a set of algebraic differential, or integro-differential equations. The simulation program solves the equations and uses the numbers to change the state and output of the simulation.

Process-Oriented Simulation: It is a type of simulation that allows related state changes to be combined in the context of a process.

Event-Driven Simulation: It is a type of simulation that allows the system model to evolve as a sequence of events, where an event represents a change in the model state. The change takes zero time; i.e., each event is the boundary between two stable periods in the model's evolution (periods during which the state variables do not change), and no time elapses in making the change.

Trace-Driven Simulation: It is an important tool in many simulation applications in which the model's inputs are derived from a sequence of observations made on a real system.

Stochastic Simulation: In stochastic simulation the system workload or the model input is characterized by various probability distributions, e.g., Poisson, exponential, On/Off, self-similar, etc. During the simulation execution, these distributions are used to produce random values which are the inputs to the simulation model

Simulation Language: Simulation language is a computer language describes the operation of a simulation model on a computer.

Network Simulator: It is a software tool develops to support computer networks analysis and design. Some of the network simulators are of general-purpose use and other dedicated to simulate particular types of computer networks.

MANSim: It is an academic, research-level computer network simulator, which can be used to evaluate, analyze, and compare the performance of a number of flooding algorithms in ideal and realistic MANET environments. It is written in C++ programming language, and consists of four main modules: network, mobility, computational, and algorithm modules.

MANET: A MANET, which stands for mobile ad hoc network, is defined as a collection of low-power wireless mobile nodes forming a temporary wireless network without the aid of any established infrastructure or centralized administration.

Flooding Algorithm: A flooding algorithm is an algorithm for distributing material to every part of a connected network. They are used in systems such as Usenet and peer-to-peer file sharing systems and as part of some routing protocols. There are several variants of flooding algorithm: most work roughly as follows: each node acts as both a transmitter and a receiver, and each node tries to forward every message to every one of its neighbors except the source node. This results in every message eventually being delivered to all reachable parts of the network.

Distribute Simulation: In a distributed simulation the model is implemented as a set of processes that exchange messages to control the sequencing and nature of changes in the model states.

Terminating Simulation: A terminating simulation is used to study the behavior of a system for a well-defined period of time or number of events.

Steady-State Simulation: A steady-state simulation is used to investigate the steady-state behavior of a system, where the simulation continues until the system reaches a steady-state. Otherwise the simulation results can be significantly different from the true results.

Chapter 20
Queuing Theory and Discrete Events Simulation for Health Care:
From Basic Processes to Complex Systems with Interdependencies

Alexander Kolker
Children's Hospital and Health Systems, USA

ABSTRACT

This chapter describes applications of the discrete events simulation (DES) and queuing analytic (QA) theory as a means of analyzing healthcare systems. There are two objectives of this chapter: (i) to illustrate the use and shortcomings of QA compared to DES by applying both of them to analyze the same problems, and (ii) to demonstrate the principles and power of DES methodology for analyzing both simple and rather complex healthcare systems with interdependencies. This chapter covers: (i) comparative analysis of QA and DES methodologies by applying them to the same processes, (ii) effect of patient arrival and service time variability on patient waiting time and throughput, (iii) comparative analysis of the efficiency of dedicated (specialized) and combined resources, (iv) a DES model that demonstrates the interdependency of subsystems and its effect on the entire system throughput, and (v) the issues and perspectives of practical implementation of DES results in health care setting.

INTRODUCTION: SYSTEM-ENGINEERING METHODS FOR HEALTHCARE DELIVERY

Modern healthcare achieved great progress in developing and manufacturing of medical devices, instruments, equipment and drugs to serve individual patients. This was achieved mainly by focusing

public and private resources on research in the life sciences, as well as on design and development of medical clinical and imaging devices.

At the same time, relatively little technical talent and material resources have been devoted to improving operations, quality and productivity of the overall health care as an integrated delivery system. According to the joint report of the National Academy of Engineering and Institute of Medicine (Reid et al, 2005), the cost of this collective inat-

DOI: 10.4018/978-1-60566-774-4.ch020

tention and the failure to take advantage of the methods that has provided quality and productivity breakthroughs in many other sectors of economy are enormous.

In this report system-engineering methods have been identified that have transformed the quality, safety and productivity performance of many other large-scale complex industries (e.g. telecommunications, transportation, manufacturing). (Reid et al, 2005). These system-engineering methods could also be used to improve efficiency of health care delivery as a patient-centered integrated system.

Ryan (2005) summarized system-engineering principles for healthcare. A system is defined as a set of interacting, interrelated elements (subsystems) - objects and/or people- that form a complex whole that behaves in ways that these elements acting alone would not. Models of a system enable one to study the impact of alternative ways of running the system, i.e. alternative designs, different configurations and management approaches. This means that system models enable one to experiment with systems in ways that cannot be used with real systems.

The models usually include a graphic representation of the system, which is a diagram showing the flow of items and resources. A mathematical description of the model includes objective functions, interrelationship and constraints. The components of the mathematical model can be grouped into four categories: (i) decision variables that represent possible options; (ii) variables, parameters and constants, which are inputs into the model, (iii) the objective functions, which are the output of the model, and (iv) constraints and logic rules that govern operation of the system.

Large systems are usually deconstructed into smaller subsystems using natural breaks in the system. The subsystems are modeled and analyzed separately, but they should be reconnected back in a way that recaptures the most important interdependency between them. Lefcowitz (2007) summarized, for example, that '...maximization of the output of the various subsystems should not be confused with maximizing the final output of the overall system'. Similarly, Goldratt (2004, p. 211) states that 'a system of local optimums is not an optimum system at all; it is a very inefficient system'.

Analysis of a complex system is usually incomplete and can be misleading without taking into account subsystems' interdependency (see section 3.3). Analysis of a mathematical model using analytic or computer algorithmic techniques reveals important hidden and critical relationships in the system that allows leveraging them to find out how to influence the system's behavior into desired direction.

The elements included in the system model and required information depends on the problem to be solved. For the output of the model to be useful, the model must mimic the behavior of the real system.

According to the already mentioned report by The National Academy of Engineering and Institute of Medicine (Reid et al, 2005), the most powerful system-analysis methods are Queuing Theory and Discrete Event Simulation (DES).

Both methods are based on principles of operations research. Operations research is the discipline of applying mathematical models of complex systems with random variability aimed at developing justified operational business decisions. It is widely used to quantitatively analyze characteristics of processes with random demand for services, random service time and available capacity to provide those services. Operations research methodology is the foundation of the modern management science.

Health care management science is applied to the various aspects of patient flow, capacity planning, allocation of material assets and human resources to improve the efficiency of healthcare delivery.

For the last 40 years, hundreds of articles have been published that demonstrate the power and benefits of using management science in healthcare. Several reviews have appeared that specifically examine DES applications in healthcare, such as Jun et al (1999), Carter (2002) and the recent review by Jacobson et al. (2006) that provides new updates that have been reported since 1999.

In contrast to these reviews that mainly listed DES publications without much discussion on how and why the models actually work and deliver, the objective of this chapter is to present a detailed description of the 'inner workings' of DES models for some healthcare processes starting from basic applications and proceeding to rather advanced models.

It is also a goal to demonstrate the fundamental advantage of DES methodology over queuing analytic (QA) models. This is demonstrated by comparative analysis of both DES and QA applied to the same problems.

The focus of this chapter is DES of the various aspects of random and non-random patient flow variability and its effect on process performance metrics. Using concrete examples and scenarios, it was demonstrated how simple DES models help to gain understanding of the basic principles that govern patient flow with random and non-random variability. It is further demonstrated how more advanced DES models have been used to study system behavior (output) changes with the change of the input data and/or process parameters.

QUEUING ANALYTIC (QA) MODELS AND DISCRETE EVENT SIMULATION (DES)

Queuing Analytic Models: Their Use and Limitations

The term 'queuing theory' is usually used to define a set of analytic techniques in the form of closed mathematical formulas to describe properties of the processes with a random demand and supply (waiting lines or queues). Queuing formulas are usually applied to a number of pre-determined simplified models of the real processes for which analytic formulas can be developed.

Weber (2006) writes that '…There are probably 40 (queuing) models based on different queue management goals and service conditions…' and that it is easy '… to apply the wrong model' if one does not have a strong background in operations research.

Development of tractable analytic formulas is possible only if a flow of events in the system is a steady-state Poisson processes. On definition, this is an ordinary stochastic process of independent events with the constant parameter equal to the average arrival rate of the corresponding flow. Time intervals between events in a Poisson flow are always exponentially distributed with the average inter-arrival time that is the inverse Poisson arrival rate. Service time is assumed to follow an exponential distribution or, rather rarely, uniform or Erlang distribution. Thus, processes with a Poisson arrival of events and exponential service time are Markov stochastic processes with discrete states and continuous time.

Most widely used queuing models for which relatively simple closed analytical formulas have been developed are specified as *M/M/s* type (Hall, 1990; Lawrence and Pasternak, 1998; Winston and Albright, 2000). (*M* stands for Markov since Poisson process is a particular case of a stochastic process with no 'after-effect' or no memory, known as continuous time Markov process). These models assume an unlimited queue size that is served by *s* providers.

Typically *M/M/s* queuing models allow calculating the following steady-state characteristics:

- probability that there are zero customers in the system
- probability that there are *K* customers in the system
- the average number of customers waiting in the queue

- the average time the customers wait in the queue
- the average total time the customer spends in the system ('cycle time')
- utilization rate of servers, i.e. percentage of time the server is busy

As more complexity is added in the system, the analytic formulas become less and less tractable. Analytic formulas are available that include, for example, limited queue size, customers leaving the system after waiting a specified amount of time, multiple queues with different average service time and different providers' types, different service priorities, etc (Lawrence and Pasternak, 1998; Hall, 1990).

However the use of these cumbersome formulas even built in Excel spreadsheets functions (Ingolfsson et al, 2003) or tables (Hillier, Yu, 1981; Seelen et al, 1985) is rather limited because they cannot capture complexity of most healthcare systems of practical interest.

Assumptions that allow deriving most queuing formulas are not always valid for many healthcare processes. For example, several patients sometimes arrive in Emergency Department at the same time (several people injured in the same auto accident), and/or the probability of new patient arrivals could depend on the previous arrivals when ED is close to its capacity, or the average arrival rate varies during a day, etc. These possibilities alone make the arrival process a non-ordinary, non-stationary with after-effect, i.e. a non-Poisson process for which queuing formulas are not valid. Therefore, it is important to properly apply statistical goodness-of-fit tests to verify that the null-hypothesis that actual arrival data follow a Poisson distribution cannot be rejected at some level of significance.

An example of a conclusion from the goodness-of-fit statistical test that is not convincing enough can be found, for instance, in Harrison et al (2005). The authors tried to justify the use of a Poisson process by using a chi-square goodness-of-fit test. The authors obtained the test p-values in the range from 0.136 to 0.802 for different days of the week. Because p-values were greater than 0.05 level of significance, they failed to reject the null-hypothesis of Poisson distribution (accepted the null-hypothesis).

On the other hand, the fundamental property of a Poisson distribution is that its mean value is equal to its variance (squared standard deviation). However, the authors' own data indicated that the mean value was not even close to the variance for at least four days of the week. Thus, the use of a Poisson distribution was not actually convincingly justified for the patient arrivals. Apparently, chi-square test p-values were not large enough to accept the null-hypothesis with high enough confidence (alternatively, the power of the statistical test was likely too low).

Despite its rather limited applicability to many actual patient arrival patterns, a Poisson process is widely used in operation research as a standard theoretical assumption because of its mathematical convenience (Gallivan, 2002; Green, 2006; Green et al, 1991; McManus et al, 2003).

The use of QA theory is often recommended to solve many pressing hospital problems of patient flow and variability, calculating needed nursing resources, the number of beds and operating rooms (IHI, 2008; Litvak, 2007; McManus et al, 2004; Haraden et al, 2003). However, such a recommendation ignores some serious practical limitations of QA theory for hospital applications. D'Alesandro (2008) summarized why QA theory is often misplaced in hospitals.

Some authors are trying to make queuing formulas applicable to real processes by fitting and calibration. For example, in order to use queuing formulas for a rather complex ED system, Mayhew and Smith (2008) made a significant process simplification by presenting the workflow as a series of stages. The stages could include initial triage, diagnostic tests, treatment, and discharge. Some patients experienced only one stage while others more than one. However, '… what constitutes a 'stage' is not always clear and can vary…and where one begins and ends may be blurred' (Mayhew and Smith, 2008). The authors assumed a Poisson arrival and exponential service time but then used actual distribution service time for 'calibration' purposes. Moreover, the authors observed that exponential service time for the various stages '…could not be adequately represented by the assumption that the service time distribution parameter was the same for each stage'. In the end, all the required calibrations, adjustments, fitting to the actual data made the model to lose its main advantage as a queuing model: its analytical simplicity and transparency. On the other hand, all queuing formulas assumptions and approximations still remained.

Therefore many complex healthcare systems with interactions and interdependencies of the subsystems cannot be effectively analyzed using analytically derived closed formulas.

Moreover, queuing formulas cannot be directly applied if the arrival flow contains a non-random component, such as scheduled arrivals (see sections 2.2.5, 2.3 and 3.2). Therefore, in order to use analytic queuing formulas, the non-random arrival component should be first eliminated, leaving only random arrival flow for which QA formulas could be used (Litvak, 2007).

Green (2004) applied *M/M/s* model to predict delays in the cardiac and thoracic surgery unit with mostly elective scheduled surgical patients assuming a Poisson pattern of their arrivals. The author acknowledged that this assumption could result in an overestimate of delays. In order to justify the use of *M/M/s* model the author argued that some '…other factors are likely to more than compensate for this'. However, it was not clear what those factors are and how much they could compensate the overestimated delays.

Still, despite their limitations, QA models have some place in operation research for application to simply structured steady-state processes if a Poisson arrival and exponential service time assumptions are accurate enough.

A number of specific examples that illustrate the use of simple QA models and their limitations are presented in the next sections.

Flu Clinic: Unlimited Queue Size with Steady State Operation

A small busy clinic provides flu shots during a flu season on a walk-in basis (no appointment necessary). The clinic has two nurses (servers). Average patient arrival rate is 54 patients per hour with about the same number of elderly and all others. Each shot takes on average about 2 min.

Usually there are quite a few people in the queue waiting for the shot. In order to reduce waiting time and the number of people in the queue, the staff conducted a brainstorming session. It was proposed to have one nurse to perform flu shots only for most vulnerable elderly patients, and another nurse to perform shots for all others. The staff began developing a pilot project plan to test this new operation mode on the clinic floor.

However, the clinic's manager decided first to test this idea using principles of management science and operations research. The manager assumed that analytical queuing formulas would be applicable in this case.

For the current operation mode, the following *M/M/s* analytical model with the unlimited queue size can be used:

Random patient arrivals are assumed to be a Poisson process with the total average arrival rate $\lambda=54$ pts/hr, average flu shot time $\tau=2$ min and the number of servers $N=2$.

The final (steady-state) probability that there are no patients in the system, p_0, is calculated using the formula (Hall, 1990; Green, 2006)

$$p_0 = [\sum_{n=0}^{N-1} \frac{a^n}{n!} + \frac{a^N}{N!(1-\rho)}]^{-1} \qquad (2.1)$$

where

$$a = \lambda * \tau, \; \rho = a / N$$

The average number of patients in the queue, L_q, is

$$L_q = a^{N+1} * p_0 / [N * N! * (1-\rho)^2] \qquad (2.2)$$

and the average time in the queue, t, is (the Little's formula)

$$t = L_q / \lambda \qquad (2.3)$$

Substituting in the formulas (2.1) to (2.3) $N=2$, $\lambda=54$ pts/hr, and $\tau=2$ min=0.033 hrs, we get average L_q =7.66 patients, and the average waiting time, t, about 8.5 min. The clinic's average utilization is 90%.

In practice, an excel spreadsheet is usually used to perform calculations using queuing formulas.

The new proposed system that is supposed to perform better will consist of two dedicated patient groups that would form two separate queues, one for elderly patients and another for all others (two separate subsystems with $N=1$). Arrival rate for each patient group is going to be $\lambda=54$ /2=27 pts/hr. Parameter: $\rho = a = \lambda * \tau = 27 pts / hr * 0.0333 \; hr = 0.9$.

Using formulas (2.1) to (2.3), we get the average number of patients in each queue Lq =8.1. Thus, the total queue for all patients will be 2*8.1=16.2 patients.

The average waiting time in the queue will be about 8.1/27=0.3 hours= 18 min.Thus, in the proposed 'improved' process the average waiting time and the number of patients in the queue will be about twice of those in the original process.

It should be concluded that the proposed improvement change that might look reasonable on the surface does not stand the scrutiny of the quantitative analysis.

The idea of separating one random patient flow with two servers on two separate random flows, each with one dedicated server, does not result in improvement because two separate servers cannot help each other if one of them becomes overworked for some time due to a surge in patient volume because of random variability of the patient flow.

This is an illustration of the general principle that the combined random work flow with unlimited queue size and no leaving patients is more efficient than separate work flows with the same total work load (see also section 2.3).

An example of using discrete events simulation (DES) to analyze the same process without resorting to analytical formulas will be given in section 2.

Flu Clinic: Unlimited Queue Size with Non-Steady-State Operation

The manager of the same clinic decided to verify that the clinic would operate smoothly enough with a new team of two less experienced nurses who would work only a little slower than the previous one. The average time to make a shot will be about 2.5 min (instead of average 2 min for more experienced staff, as in section 2.1.1). The manager reasoned that because this difference is relatively small it would not practically affect the clinic operation: the number of patients in the queue and their waiting time on the typical working day could be only a little higher than in the previous case or practically not different at all.

The manager plugged the average service time 2.5 min and the same arrival rate 54 pts/hr in the *M/M/s* queuing calculator. However the calculator returned no number at all, which means that no solution could be calculated. Why is that?

An examination of Equation (2.1) shows that if ρ becomes greater than 1 the last term in the sum becomes negative and the calculated p_0 also becomes negative, which does not make sense.

(If ρ is equal to 1, the term becomes uncertain and the calculations cannot be carried out at all). The average service time in this example is only slightly higher than it was in the previous case. However, this small difference made parameter ρ greater than 1 (ρ=1.125>1). This explains why the calculations cannot be done using this value.

Queuing analytical formulas with unlimited queue size are applicable only for steady-state processes, i.e. for the established processes whose characteristics do not depend on time. The steady-state condition is possible only if ρ < 1, otherwise the above formulas are not applicable and the queue grows indefinitely.

In section 2.2.2 it will be demonstrated how DES methodology easily handles this situation and demonstrates growth of the queue.

Flu Clinic: Time-Varying Arrival Rates

In the previous section 2.1.2 parameters of the queuing system (average arrival rate 54 patients per hour and average shot time 2.5 min) made a patient flow a non-steady-state one for which QA model with unlimited queue size could not be used.

However, the clinic's manager realized that the average patient arrival rate varies significantly during a day, and that 54 patients per hour was actually a peak arrival rate, from noon to 3 pm. In the morning hours from 8 am to 10 am the arrival rate was lower, 30 patients / hour. From 10 am to noon it was 40 patients / hour, and in the afternoon from 3 pm to 6 pm it was about 45 patients / hour.

Thus, the manager calculated the average arrival rate for these time periods for the day. It turned out to be (30+40+54+45)/4=42.25 patients/hour. He/she plugged this number in the queuing calculator (along with the average time to make a shot 2.5 min), and obtained the average number of patients in queue L_q =6.1 patients, and the average waiting time about 8.6 min. Because the calculator produced some numbers the manager made a conclusion that this clinic process will be in a steady-state condition and that the waiting time and the number of patients in the queue is acceptable.

But is it a correct conclusion? Recall that QA models assume that a Poisson arrival rate is constant during a steady-state time period (Hall, 1990; Lawrence et al, 2002; Green, 2006). If it is not constant, such as in this case, QA results could be very misleading. The wait time will be significantly greater in the mid-day period (and/or the steady-state condition will be violated). At the beginning and at the end of the day, though, the wait time will be much smaller. Because the arrival rate is included non-linearly in the exponential term of a Poisson distribution formula, the arrival rate cannot be averaged first and then substituted in the exponential term. (For non-linear functions, the average value of a function is not equal to the function of average values of its arguments).

As Green (2006) stated '…this illustrates a situation in which a steady-state queuing model is inappropriate for estimating the magnitude and timing of delays, and for which a simulation model will be far more accurate'.

It is tempting, as a last resort, to save the use of QA model by dividing the day into time periods in which arrival rate is approximately constant. Then a series of *M/M/s* models is constructed, one for each period. This approach is called SIPP (stationary independent period-by-period) (Green, 2006; Green et al, 1991).

If we apply this approach, the following results can be obtained:

- Time period 8 am to 10 am: L_q =0.8 patients in the queue, waiting time 1.6 min
- Time period 10 am to noon: L_q =3.8 patients in the queue, waiting time 5.7 min
- Time period noon to 3 pm: *no steady-state solution*
- Time period 3 pm to 6 pm: L_q =13.6 patients in the queue, waiting time 18.1 min

Notice how these results differ from those based on the averaging of the arrival rate for the entire day.

However this SIPP patch applied to QA models was found to be unreliable (Green, 2006; Green et al, 2001). This is because in many systems with time-varying arrival rates, the time of peak congestion significantly lags the time of the peak in the arrival rate (Green et al, 1991). These authors developed a modification called *Lag-SIPP* that incorporates an estimation of this lag. This approach has been shown to often be more effective than a simple SIPP (Green, 2006).

Even it is so, this does not make QA models application easier if there are many time periods with different constant arrival rates because many different *M/M/s* models need to be constructed accordingly to describe one process.

It will be demonstrated in section 2.2.4 how DES model easily and elegantly handles this situation with time-varying arrival rate.

ICU Waiting Time

This problem is presented by (Litvak 2007; Weber, 2006) to demonstrate how QA can be used to compare patient average waiting time to get into ICU if it has 5 beds and 10 beds and patient average arrival rate is 1 per day and 2 per day, accordingly. The average length of stay in ICU is 2.5 days. It is assumed that the length of stay in the ICU is exponentially distributed and, of course, that patient arrival is a Poisson process.

In order to apply QA formulas an additional assumption should be used that length of stay follows exponential distribution with the above average value.

Using *M/M/s* model it is easy to calculate that the average waiting time for 10 beds ICU is 0.43 hours, and that for 5 beds ICU is 3.1 hours. Average ICU utilization is 50%.

Thus, the waiting time for the larger unit is about 7 times shorter. Notice, however, that this result is valid only for exponential service and

inter-arrival time. If other distributions with the same average are used we should get a different result.

For example, length of stay could be in the range from 2 to 3 days with the average 2.5 days, and be described by a triangle distribution. Or the length of stay could follow a long-tailed lognormal distribution, also with the same average of 2.5 days and standard deviation of, say, 2 days (these values would correspond to log-normal parameters 3.85 and 0.703).

Thus, QA does not distinguish between different distributions with the same averages. This is a serious limitation of QA.

It will be demonstrated in section 2.2.7 how easy it is to use DES for different length of stay distributions with the same average.

DES Models: Basic Applications

In contrast to queuing formulas, DES models are much more flexible and versatile. They are free from assumptions of the particular type of the arrival process (Poisson or not), as well as the service time (exponential or not). They can be used for the combined random and non-random arrival flow. The system structure (flow map) can be complex enough to reflect a real system structure, and custom action logic can be built in to capture the real system behavior.

At the same time it should be noted that building a complex realistic simulation model sometimes requires a significant amount of time for custom logic development, debugging, model validation, and input data collection.

However, a good model is well worth the efforts because it becomes a powerful and practically the only real tool for quantitative analysis of complex hospital operations and decision-making.

Many currently available simulation software packages (ProcessModel, ProModel, Arena, Simula8, and many others) provide a user-friendly interface that makes the efforts of building a realistic simulation model not more demanding than

Table 1.

Inter-arrival time, min	Service time, min
2.6	1.4
2.2	8.8
1.4	9.1
2.4	1.8

the efforts to make simplifications, adjustments and calibrations to develop a rather complex but inaccurate queuing model.

Swain (2007), Abu-Taeh et al (2007), Hlupic (2000), Nikoukaran (1999) provided a review and a comparative study of dozens commercially available simulation packages.

A DES model is a computer model that mimics the dynamic behavior of a real process as it evolves with time in order to visualize and quantitatively analyze its performance. The validated and verified model is then used to study behavior of the original process and then identify the ways for its improvement (scenarios) based on some improvement criteria. This strategy is significantly different from the hypothesis-based clinical testing widely used in medical research (Kopach-Konrad et al, 2007).

DES models track entities moving through the system at distinct points of time (events). The detailed track is recorded of all processing times and waiting times. Then the system's statistics for entities and activities is gathered.

To illustrate how a DES model works step by step, let's consider a very simple system that consists of a single patient arrival line and a single server. Suppose that patient inter-arrival time is uniformly (equally likely) distributed between 1 min and 3 min. Service time is exponentially distributed with the average 2.5 min. (Of course, any statistical distributions or non-random patterns can be used instead). A few random numbers sampled from these two distributions are shown in Table 1.

Let's start our example simulation at time zero, t=0, with no patients in the system. We will be tracking any change or event that happened in the system.

A summary of what is happening in the system looks like Table 2.

These simple but tedious logical and numerical event-tracking operations (algorithm) are suitable, of course, only for a computer. However, they illustrate the basic principles of any discrete events simulation model, in which discrete events (changes) in the system are tracked when they

Table 2.

Event #	Time	Event that happened in the system
1	2.6	1st customer arrives. Service starts that should end at time= 4
2	4	Service ends. Server waits for patient
3	4.8	2nd patient arrives. Service starts that should end at time =13.6. Server is idle 0.8 min
4	6.2	3rd patient arrives. Joins the queue waiting for service
5	8.6	4th patient arrives. Joins the queue waiting for service
6	13.6	2nd patient (from event 3) service ends. 3rd patient at the head of queue (first in-first out) starts service that should end at time 22.7
7	22.7	Patient #4 starts service and so on.

occur over the time. In this particular example, we were tracking events at discrete points in time t=2.6, 4.0, 4.8, 6.2, 8.6, 13.6, 22.7.

Once the simulation is completed for any length of time, another set of random numbers from the same distributions is generated, and the procedure (called replication) is repeated. Usually multiple replications are needed to properly capture the system's variability. In the end, the system's output statistics is calculated, e.g. the average patient and server waiting time, its standard deviation, the average number of patients in the queue, the confidence intervals and so on.

In this example, only two patients out of four waited in the queue. Patient 3 waited 13.6-6.2=7.4 min and patient 4 waited 22.7-8.6=14.1 min, so the simple average waiting time for all four patients is (0+0+7.4+14.1)/4=5.4 min. Notice, however, that the first two patients did not wait at all while patient 4 waited 2.6 times longer than the average. This illustrates that the simple average could be rather misleading as a performance metric for highly variable processes without some additional information about the spread of data around the average (a so-called flaw of averages, see also concluding remarks for section 3.1).

Similarly, the simple arithmetic average of the number of waiting patients (average queue length) is 0.5. However a more informative metric of the queue length is the time-weighted average that takes into account the length of time each patient was in the queue. In this case it is (1*7.4+1*14.1)/22.7=0.95. Usually the time-weighted average is a better system's performance metric than the simple average.

DES models are capable of tracking hundreds of individual entities, each with its own unique set of attributes, enabling one to simulate the most complex systems with interacting events and component interdependencies.

Typical DES applications include: staff and production scheduling, capacity planning, cycle time and cost reduction, throughput capability, resources and activities utilization, bottleneck

finding and analysis. DES is the most effective tool to perform quantitative 'what-if' analysis and play different scenarios of the process behavior as its parameters change with time. This simulation capability allows one to make experiments on the computer, and to test different options before going to the hospital floor for actual implementation.

The basic elements (building blocks) of a simulation model are:

- Flow chart of the process, i.e. a diagram that depicts logical flow of a process from its inception to its completion
- Entities, i.e. items to be processed, e.g. patients, documents, customers, etc.
- Activities, i.e. tasks performed on entities, e.g. medical procedures, exams, document approval, customer check-in, etc
- Resources, i.e. agents used to perform activities and move entities, e.g. service personnel, equipment, nurses, physicians
- Entity routings that define directions and logical conditions flow for entities

Typical information usually required to populate the model includes:

- Quantity of entities and their arrival time, e.g. periodic, random, scheduled, daily pattern, etc. There is no restriction on the arrival distribution type, such as a Poisson distribution, required by the QA formulas
- The time that the entities spend in the activities, i.e. service time. This is usually not a fixed time but a statistical distribution. There is no restriction to an exponential service time distribution that is typically required by the QA formulas
- Capacity of each activity, i.e. the max number of entities that can be processed concurrently in the activity
- The maximum size of input and output queues for the activities

- Resource assignments: their quantity and scheduled shifts

Analysis of patient flow is an example of the general dynamic supply and demand problem. There are three basic components that should be accounted for in such problems: (i) the number of patients (or any items) entering the system at any point of time, (ii) the number of patients (or any items) leaving the system after spending some time in it, (iii) capacity of the system that defines the number of items that can be processed concurrently. All three components affect the flow of patients (items) that the system can handle (the system's throughput). A lack of the proper balance between these components results in the system's over-flow and gridlock. DES methodology provides invaluable means for analyzing and managing the proper balance.

It will be demonstrated in the following sections that even simple DES models have a significant advantage over QA models. To illustrate this advantage side by side, DES methodology will be applied to the same processes that have been analyzed using QA in previous sections 2.1.1 to 2.1.4

Comparative Analysis of QA and DES Methodologies

Unlimited Queue Size with Steady-State Operation

Let's consider a flu clinic that was analyzed using QA in section 2.1.1.

DES model structure is presented on Figure 1. It simply depicts the arrived patient flow connected to Queue, then coming to the flu clinic (box called Flu_Clinic), and then exit the system. These basic model elements are simply dragged down from the pallet and then connected to each other.

Next step is to fill in the process information: patients arrive periodically, one patient at a random exponentially distributed time interval with the

Figure 1.Layout of the simulation model of flu clinic. Information on the panel indicates patient arrival type (Periodic) that repeats on average every E(1.111) min (E stands for exponential distribution)

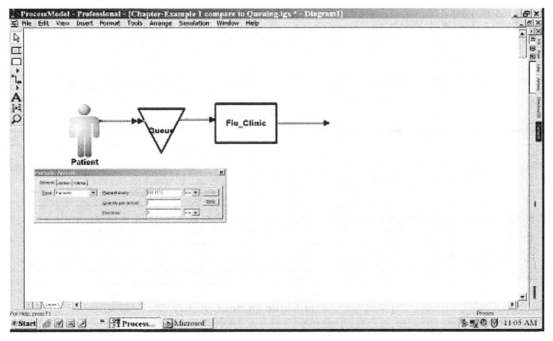

average inter-arrival time 60 min/54=1.111 min, E(1.111), as indicated on the data arrival panel on Figure 1 corresponds to Poisson arrival rate of 54 patients per hour (E stands for exponential distribution). In the Flu_Clinic data panel the capacity input was 2 (two patients served concurrently by two nurses), and the service time was exponentially random with the average value 2 min, E(2). This completes the model set-up.

The model was run 300 replications at which a statistically stable simulation output was reached. Multiple replications capture the variability of patient arrivals and service time. Results are presented on Figure 2.

It is seen that the number of patients in the queue steadily increases until a steady-state operation (plateau) is reached. The average steady-state number of patients in the queue is 7.7 with

some small fluctuations around this average (top plot).

The average waiting time is presented on Figure 2 (bottom plot). Similarly, the average steady-state waiting time 8.45 min was reached with some variations around the average. The average steady-state utilization is 89.8%.

Average number of patients in the queue (top) and average waiting time in the queue (bottom)

Thus, we received practically the same results with DES model as with QA model using about the same efforts. As an additional bonus with DES, though, we could watch how fast a steady-state operation was reached (a so-called warm-up period).

Figure 2. Unlimited queue size with steady-state operation

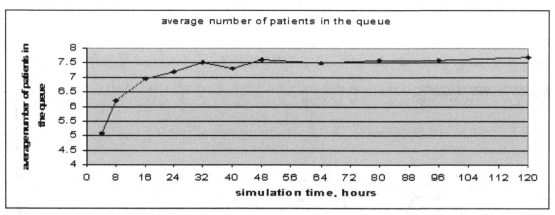

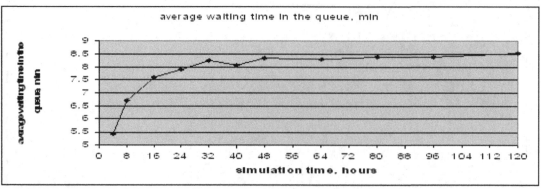

Unlimited Queue Size with Non-Steady State Operation

In section 2.1.2 QA model with the average service time 2.5 min could not produce results because a steady-state operation did not exist.

Using the same DES model described in the previous section we simply plug this average service time in the Flu_Clinic data panel making it E(2.5) min, and run the simulation model. Results are given on Figure 3.

Average number of patients in the queue (top) and average waiting time in the queue (bottom).

These plots demonstrate how the patient queue (top plot) and waiting time (bottom plot) grow with clinic operation time. The plots demonstrate no apparent trend to a steady-state regime (plateau). The growth goes on indefinitely with time.

This example also illustrates an important principle of 'unintended consequences'. An intuition that is not supported by objective quantitative analysis says that a small change in the system input (service time from the average 2 min to 2.5 min) would result in a small change in the output (small increase in the number of waiting patients and their waiting time). For some systems this is indeed true. Systems in which the output is always directly proportional to input are called linear systems. However, there are quite a few systems in which this simple reasoning breaks down: a small change in the value of the system's input parameter(s) results in a dramatic change (even qualitative change) in the system's outcome (behavior), e.g. from a steady-state regime to a non-steady-state regime. Such systems are called non-linear or complex systems despite the fact that they can consist of only a few elements.

Limited Queue Size with 'Inpatient' Patients Leaving the System

Unlimited queue size is not always a good model of real systems. In many cases patients wait in a waiting lounge that has usually a limited number of chairs (space). QA models designated *M/M/s/K* are available that include a limited queue size, *K*

Figure 3. Unlimited queue size with non-steady state operation

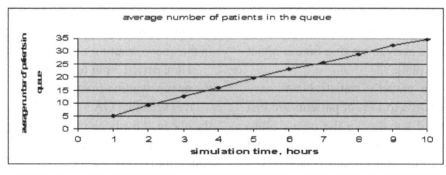

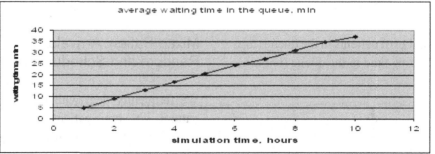

(Green, 2006; Lawrence and Pasternak, 1998; Hall, 1990). However analytic formulas become very cumbersome. If the QA model includes some patients that leave the system after waiting some time in the queue, the analytic formulas become almost intractable.

In contrast, DES models easily handle the limited queue size and patients leaving before the service began ('inpatient' patients).

To illustrate, we use the same DES model as in 2.2.1 with only a slight modification to include a new limited queue size and 'inpatient' patients.

Suppose that the queue size limit is 10 (the max number of chairs or beds) and patients leave after waiting 10 min (of course, these could be any numbers including statistical distributions). We put 10 in the field 'Input queue size', and draw a routing 'renege after 10 min'. The new model is now ready to go. Simulation results are presented on Figure 4.

The difference between an unlimited queue size (section 2.2.2) and a limited one with leaving patients is significant.

The plots suggest that limited queue size results in a steady-state solution (plateau). (It could be proved that a steady-state solution always exists if the queue size is limited). The steady-state average number of patients in the queue is about 4.5 (top plot) and the average waiting time is about 5.6 min (bottom plot).

However the model's statistics summary also shows that 10% to 11% of patients are lost because they did not stay in the queue more than 10 min. Thus, this simple DES model gives a lot of valuable information and serves as powerful tool to find out how to better manage the flu-clinic.

Average number of patients in the queue (top) and average waiting time in the queue (bottom).

Arrivals with Time-Varying Poisson Arrival Rate

In section 2.1.3 it was discussed why the use of QA model with a Poisson time-varying patient arrival rate is rather unreliable.

Let's see how easy it is to use DES model to address the same problem.

The DES model structure (layout) for time-varying arrival rate is the same as it was used in section 2.2.1. The only difference is a different arrival routing type: instead of periodic arrival with the random inter-arrival time, an input daily-pattern arrival panel should be used. We use one day of the week, and input 60 patients from 8 am to 10 am (30 pts/hour *2); 80 patients from 10 to noon (40 pts/hour*2); 162 patients from noon to 3 pm (54 pts/hour*3); and 135 patients from 3 pm to 6 pm (45 pts/hour * 3). The model of the entire day (from 8 am to 6 pm) is ready to go.

The following simulation results are obtained (compare with the approximated QA SIPP model results from section 2.1.3):

Time period 8 am to 10 am: L_q =0.6 patients in the queue, waiting time 0.84 min

Time period 10 am to noon: L_q =2.26 patients in the queue, waiting time 2.75 min

Time period noon to 3 pm: L_q =14.5 patients in the queue, waiting time 15.3 min

Time period 3 pm to 6 pm: L_q =20 patients in the queue, waiting time 25.5 min

It is seen that QA SIPP model over-estimates the queue at the beginning of the day and under-estimates the queue at the end of the day. Of course, only a DES model can provide results for the time period noon to 3 pm.

Mixed Patient Arrivals: Random and Scheduled

We frequently deal with mixed patient arrival pattern, i.e. some patients are scheduled to arrive on specific time while some patients arrive unexpectedly. For example, some clinics accept

Figure 4. Limited queue size with 'inpatient' patients leaving the system

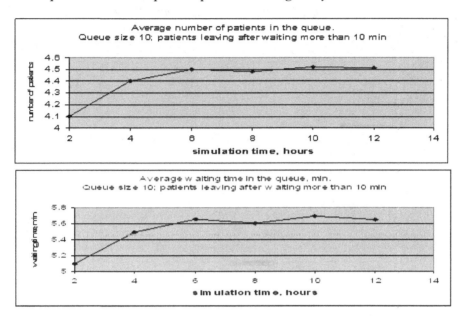

patients who made an appointment, but also accept urgent random walk-in patients. Operating room suites schedule elective surgeries while suddenly a trauma patient arrives and an emergency surgery is required. Such a mixed arrival pattern with a different degree of the variability requires a special treatment.

QA models should not be used if arrival flow contains a non-random component, i.e. it is not a Poisson random. Let's illustrate what happens if this principle is violated.

Suppose that there is one operating room (OR) and there are six scheduled surgeries for a day, at 7 am, 10 am, 1 pm, 4 pm, 7 pm, 10 pm. On this day six random emergency patients also arrived with the average inter-arrival time 4 hours, i.e. E(4) hours. Total number of patients for one day is 12.

If QA model is applied assuming that all 12 patients are random arrivals, then we would get arrival rate 12 pts/24= 0.5 pts per hour. Using the average surgery time 1 hour, E(1) hours, we get the average number of patients in the queue, $L_q =$

0.5, waiting time in queue, W_q=1 hour, and time in the system, W_s =2 hours.

Now, let's use a simple DES model with two arrival flows, one random, E(4) hours, and another one with scheduled six patients, as indicated on Figure 5.

Simulation length was 24 hours. The average number of patients in the queue was L_q = 0.3, waiting time in the queue W_q=0.33 hours, time in the system, W_s =0.55 hours.

Notice how badly QA model over-estimated the time: almost by a factor of 3 for waiting time in the queue, and almost by a factor of 4 for the time in the system !

Thus, QA models cannot account accurately enough for arrival variability that is lower than Poisson variability.

There are some approximate QA formulas that include a coefficient of variation of service time distribution but only for one server (Green, 2006).

Figure 5. Mixed patient arrivals: random and scheduled. Two arrival flows, one random, E(4) hours, and one with six patients scheduled at 7 am, 10 am, 1 pm, 4 pm, 7 pm, 10 pm, as indicated on the panel

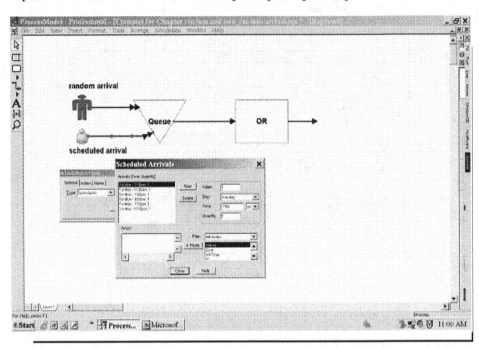

Effect of Added Variability on Process Flow and Delay

Let's now demonstrate how additional arrival variability, service time variability, and/or both would affect the throughput and waiting time in the system. We will be using a simple DES model similar to the model presented on Figure 1.

We consider five scenarios with consecutively added step-by-step patient flow variability:

- Scenario 1. No variability at all. Each patient arrives exactly every 2 hours. Service time (surgery) is exactly 2 hours.
- Scenario 2. There is arrival variability, i.e. a Poisson flow with the average arrival rate 0.5 pts/hr (average inter-arrival time is 2 hours, E(2) hrs). No service time variability, it is exactly 2 hours.
- Scenario 3. No arrival variability. There is a service time variability with the average service time 2 hours, E(2) hours.

- Scenario 4. There are both types of variability. Poisson arrival with the average arrival rate 0.5 patients per hour (average inter-arrival time 2 hours), and service time variability with the average service time 2 hours, E(2)
- Scenario 5. Poisson arrival variability with the average arrival rate 0.5 patients per hour (average inter-arrival time 2 hours). Service time variability is log-normally distributed with the distribution mean value 2 hours and standard deviation 4 hours (these values correspond to the lognormal parameters: location= -0.112 and scale=1.27).

Results for 24 hours simulation time are summarized in Figure 6. It follows from this table that as the variability steps are added to the process, patient throughput decreases, an overall waiting time increases and utilization decreases.

Figure 6. Five DES scenarios with consecutively added variability. Simulation performed for 24 hours period

INPUT		OUTPUT FOR ONE DAY (24 hours)				
Patient Arrival	Time in OR	average throughput (number of patients)	average number of patients waiting in queue	average time in the system, hrs	average waiting time in the system, hrs	average OR utilization,%
one patient every 2 hrs (no variability)	2 hrs (no variability)	12	0	2	0	100%
arrival variability: average inter-arrival time 2 hrs (Poisson arrival rate 0.5 pts/hr)	2 hrs (no variability)	10	1.4	4.1	2.1	86%
one patient every 2 hrs (no variability)	service time variability: average 2 hrs (exponential time distribution)	10	1	3.5	1.6	82%
arrival variability: average inter-arrival time 2 hrs (Poisson arrival rate 0.5 pts/hr)	service time variability: average 2 hrs (exponential time distribution)	9.4	1.6	4.2	2.3	78%
arrival variability: average inter-arrival time 2 hrs (Poisson arrival rate 0.5 pts/hr)	service time variability: average 2 hrs, standard deviation 4 hours (Log-normal distribution parameters: loc= -0.112; scale=1.27)	9.3	1.4	3.3	1.7	69%

At the same time, the variability distribution should not be characterized only by a single parameter, such as its coefficient of variation (CV). The overall shape of the variability distribution also plays a big role. For example, the coefficient of variation for the lognormal distribution service time (CV=4/2=2) is greater than that for exponential distribution (CV=1). Nonetheless, this did not result in increase of the wait time, as this would follow from an approximated queuing formula (Allen, 1978; Green, 2006). Only DES can accurately account for the effect of the distribution shape and skewness.

ICU Waiting Time

Analysis of ICU waiting time considered in section 2.1.4 using QA could be done using the same model as in the previous section (Figure 1). We simply use capacity 5 or 10, accordingly. Let's start with the exponential distribution of the length of stay with the average 2.5 days to compare with QA results (section 2.1.4).

Let's also use the average inter-arrival time as 1 day or 0.5 days, accordingly.

The following steady-state DES waiting times were obtained: 0.43 hours for 10 beds ICU and 2.94 for 5 beds ICU, accordingly. These are practically the same results as for QA (section 2.1.4).

Now, let's see how different distributions with the same average length of stay affect the waiting time. Recall, that QA cannot answer such practically important questions at all, and it is valid only for exponential distribution or, at best, for distributions with coefficient of variation close to 1 (Green, 2006).

For example, the triangle distribution limited between 2 days and 3 days with the average 2.5 days results in:

- for 10 beds ICU average waiting time is 0.27 hours while for 5 beds unit it is 1.72 hours. Notice, how significantly different these values are from the exponential length of stay with the same average.

Similarly, for the lognormal distribution with the same average 2.5 days and standard deviation, say, 2 days, we get:

- for 10 beds ICU average waiting time is 0.35 hours while for 5 beds unit it is 2.46 hours.

Thus, QA is severely limited in what it cannot account for different distributions of service time and always produces the same result if the same average is used regardless of the effect of different distributions with the same average.

Emergency and Elective Surgeries: Dedicated OR vs. Combined Service OR

In this section we will discuss the use of a simple DES model to address an issue that caused a controversy in literature on healthcare improvement. If patient flow into operating rooms consists of both elective (scheduled) and emergency (random) surgeries, is it more efficient to reserve dedicated operating rooms (OR) separately for elective and emergency surgeries, or to perform both types of surgeries in any available OR?

Haraden et al (2003) recommends that hospitals that want to improve patient flow should desig-

nate separate ORs for scheduled and unscheduled (emergency) surgeries. The authors state that in this arrangement '...Since the vast majority of surgeries is scheduled, most of the OR space should be so assigned. Utilization of the scheduled rooms becomes predictable, and wait times for unscheduled surgery become manageable'. The authors imply that this statement is self-evident, and provide no quantitative analysis or any other justification for this recommendation.

On the other hand, Wullink et al (2007) built DES model of OR suite for large Erasmus Medical Center hospital (Rotterdam, The Netherlands) to quantitatively test scenarios of using dedicated ORs for emergency and elective surgeries vs. combined use of all ORs for both types of surgeries. These authors concluded that based on DES model results '...Emergency patients are operated upon more efficiently on elective ORs instead of a dedicated emergency ORs. The results of this study led to closing of the emergency OR in this hospital'.

In contrast to the unsupported recommendation of Haraden et al (2003), Wullink et al (2007) presented specific data analysis to support their

Figure 7. Emergency and Elective surgeries: dedicated OR vs. combined service OR

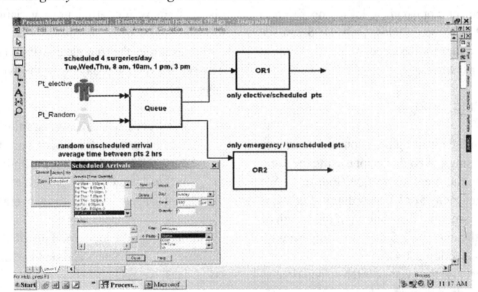

conclusions: combined use of all ORs for both types of surgery results in reduction of average waiting time for emergency surgery from 74 min to 8 min.

In this section we present a simple generic DES model to address the same issue and verify literature results. For simplicity, we consider an OR suite with two rooms, OR1 and OR2. Patient flow includes both emergency (random) and scheduled patients.

Let's first consider the situation when the majority of surgeries are emergency (random) ones. We assume a Poisson emergency patient arrival with the average inter-arrival time 2 hours, i.e. E(2) hours (Poisson arrival rate 0.5 pts/hr).

Four elective surgeries are assumed to be scheduled three days a week on Tuesday, Wednesday and Thursday at 8 am, 10 am, 1 pm and 3 pm. Both emergency and elective surgery duration is assumed to be random with the average value 2 hours, i.e. E(2) hours. (Wullink et al, 2007 used mean case duration 2.4 hours for elective and 2.1 hours for emergency surgeries)

Using these arrival and service time data, let's consider two scenarios.

Scenario 1: two ORs, one dedicated only for elective surgeries (OR1), and another dedicated only for emergency surgeries (OR2), as shown on Figure 7 If the dedicated OR is not available, then the new patient waits in the Queue area until the corresponding dedicated OR becomes available.

Scenario 2: also two ORs. However both emergency and elective patients go to any available OR, as indicated on Figure 8. If both ORs are not available, then the new patient waits in the Queue area until one of ORs becomes available.

Scenario 1 model layout: two ORs, one dedicated only for elective surgeries (OR1), and another dedicated only for emergency surgeries (OR2). Scheduled arrival pattern is indicated on the panel.

Simulation was run for 4 days (96 hours) Monday to Thursday (on Friday there were no scheduled elective surgeries) using 300 replications. DES results for these two scenarios are given in Figure 9.

Examination of the results is instructive. While the number of elective surgeries is the same for both scenarios, the number of performed emergency

Figure 8. Emergency and Elective surgeries: dedicated OR vs. combined service OR

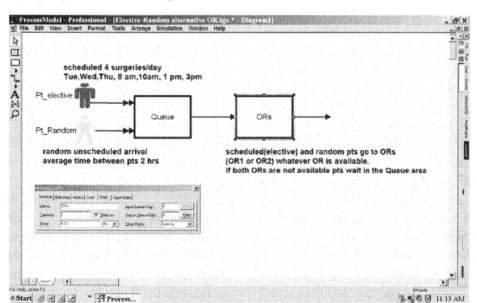

Figure 9. Simulation results: dedicated ORs vs. combined ORs. Most surgeries are emergency ones. Simulation performed for 4 days (96 hours) time period

Characteristics	dedicated OR		combined ORs	
	elective	emergency	elective	emergency
average number of surgeries	12	41.3	12	47.3
average waiting time in the system, hrs	0.7	7.1	1.3	1.06
average number of patients in Queue area	0.1	3.76	0.16	0.59
average OR utilization, %	24.2	85.8	62.7	

surgeries is higher for combined OR scenario. The average waiting time for elective surgery increases about 2 times for the combined OR scenario (from 0.7 to 1.3 hours); however, the average waiting time for emergency surgery drops dramatically from about 7 hours down to 1 hour ! (Compare this dramatic drop with Wullink et al (2007) result). The average number of patients waiting for emergency surgery is significantly lower for combined OR scenario. Dedicated elective OR is under-utilized (~24%) while dedicated emergency OR is highly utilized (~85%), resulting in a significant increase in waiting time for emergency surgeries. OR utilization in the combined OR scenario is a rather healthy 63%.

Scenario 2 model layout: two ORs. Both emergency and elective patients go to any available OR. Information of the panel indicates capacity of ORs (2) and the average surgery (service) time E(2) hr.

Now, let's consider the situation when the majority of surgeries are elective.

We have the same two scenarios with two ORs (dedicated and combined) with the average surgery duration 2 hours, E(2) hours.

However this time 6 daily elective surgeries are scheduled Monday to Thursday (no Fridays) at 7 am, 9 am, 11 am, 1 pm, 3 pm, 5 pm. Emergency (random) surgeries are less frequent with the average inter-arrival time 6 hours, E(6), i.e. Poisson arrival rate about 0.167 patients per hour.

Simulation results for 96 hours (4 days), 300 replications are given in Figure 10.

Notice that in this case the average waiting time for combined ORs drops about 3 to 4 times both for emergency and elective patients, as well as the average number of patients in the Queue area.

Overall, these DES results support the conclusions of Wullink et al (2007) that performing emergency surgeries in the combined OR scenario is more effective than in the reserved dedicated emergency OR. These authors provided a detailed instructive discussion on why dedicated OR scenario performs worse especially for emergency surgeries, while intuitively it seems that it should perform better, like Haraden et al (2003) assumed.

Wullink et al (2007) pointed out that besides reserving OR capacity for emergency surgeries arrivals, ORs need to reserve capacity to cope with the variability of surgery duration. In the combined OR scenario, reservation might be shared to increase the flexibility for dealing with unex-

Figure 10. Simulation results: dedicated ORs vs. combined ORs. Most surgeries are elective. Simulation performed for 4 days (96 hours) time period

Characteristics	dedicated OR		combined ORs	
	elective	emergency	elective	emergency
average number of surgeries	24	16.7	24	16.5
average waiting time in the system, hrs	1.3	0.8	0.32	0.3
average number of patients in Queue area	0.35	0.15	0.07	0.05
average OR utilization, %	49.6	34.6	42.2	

pected long case duration and emergency surgery, whereas the dedicated scenario does not offer the opportunity to use the overflow principle (compare this with two simplified scenarios considered earlier in section 2.1.1 using QA model).

On top of that, a dedicated OR scenario may cause queuing of emergency surgeries themselves because of their random arrival time. If emergency surgeries were allocated to all available ORs (combined scenario), then it would be possible to perform them simultaneously reducing thereby a waiting time.

Wullink et al (2007) acknowledge that '... interrupting the execution of the elective surgical case schedule for emergency patients may delay elective cases. However, inpatients are typically admitted to a ward before they are brought to the OR. Although delay due to emergency arrivals may cause inconvenience for patients, it does not disturb processes in the OR'.

As DES modeling indicates, delay in scheduled cases in the combined ORs (if the majority of surgeries are emergency) is usually not too dramatic (e.g. from 0.7 to 1 hour), while reduction of waiting time for emergency surgeries is very substantial (from 74 min to 8 min according to

Wullink's DES model, or from about 7 hours to 1 hour according to our simplified DES model with generic input data described in this section).

If the majority of surgeries are scheduled ones, then there is not much delay in combined ORs at all both for scheduled and emergency surgeries.

Examples presented in Section 2 illustrate a general fundamental principle: the lower variability in the system (both arrival and service), the lower delays (see also Green, 2006). In other words, lowering variability is the key to improving patient flow and to reduce delays and waiting times.

One of the root causes of why intuition usually fails to account for the effect of variability even in very simple systems is a general human tendency to avoid the complications of uncertainty in the decision making by turning it into certainty. Average procedure time or average number of arrived patients is typically treated as if they are fixed values ignoring the variability around these averages. This ignorance often results in erroneous conclusions. DES models, however, naturally handle complex variability using statistical distributions with multiple replications.

DES MODELS: ADVANCED APPLICATIONS

In this section more advanced features of DES models will be presented, such as custom-built action logic to capture fine details of system behavior, conditional and alternate routing types, multiple entities entries, multiple scheduled arrivals and highly skewed service time distributions that accurately reflect real data rather than assuming some hypothetical data distribution.

It will also be demonstrated how a specific problem statement leads to simulating different 'what-if' scenarios to address practically relevant issues for ED and ICU (sections 3.1 and 3.2), as well as interdependencies of patient flow for ED, ICU, OR and floor nursing units (NU) (section 3.3).

DES of Emergency Department Patient Flow: Effect of Patient Length of Stay on ED Ambulance Diversion

Emergency Department (ED) ambulance diversion due to 'no available beds' status has become a common problem in most major hospitals nationwide. A diversion status due to 'no available ED beds' is usually declared when the ED census is close to or at the ED beds capacity limit. ED remains in this status until beds become available when patients are moved out of ED (discharged home, expired, or admitted into the hospital as inpatients). Percent of time when ED is on diversion is one of the important ED patient performance metrics, along with the number of patients in queue in ED waiting room, or ED patient waiting time. ED diversion results in low quality of care, dissatisfaction of patients and staff, and lost revenue for hospitals.

Patients' length of stay (LOS) in ED is one of most significant factors that affect the overall ED throughput and ED diversion (Blasak et al, 2003; Gunal and Pidd, 2006; Garcia et al, 1995; Miller et al, 2003; Simon et al, 2003). There are generally two major groups of patients with different LOS distributions: (i) patients admitted as inpatients into the hospital (OR, ICU, floor nursing units), and (ii) patients stabilized, treated and discharged home. Mayhew and Smith (2008) also recognized a key difference between these two groups.

In order to effectively attack the problem of ED diversion reduction, the LOS of these two groups should be quantitatively linked to ED diversion. Then the target LOS limits can be established based on ED patient flow analysis.

A number of publications are available in which the importance of having ED LOS target was discussed. Kolker (2008) provided a detailed analysis of the literature.

One instructive article published recently by Mayhew and Smith (2008) evaluates the consequences of 4 hours LOS limits mandated by the UK National Health Services for the UK hospitals' Accident & Emergency Departments (A&ED). One of the main conclusions of this work was '... that a target should not only be demanding but that it should also fit with the grain of the work on the ground... Otherwise the target and how to achieve it becomes an end in itself'. Further, '... the current target is so demanding that the integrity of reported performance is open to question'. This work vividly illustrated the negative consequences of the administratively mandated LOS targets that have not been based on the objectives analysis of the patient flow and an A&ED capability to handle it.

Despite a considerable number of publications on the ED patient flow and its variability, there is not much in the literature that could help to answer a practically important question regarding the target patient LOS: what it should be and how to establish it in order to reduce ED diversion to an acceptable low level, or to prevent diversion at all? Therefore, a methodology that could quantitatively link the patient LOS limits and ED performance metrics would have a considerable practical value.

Description of the ED Patient Flow Model

Kolker (2008) described the entire ED system. It included a fast-track lane, minor care, trauma rooms and the main patient beds area. Total ED capacity was 30 beds.

Because the objective of this work was simulating an effect of patient LOS on diversion for the entire ED, the detailed model layout was significantly simplified. A widely recognized guideline in DES modeling is to keep the model as simple as possible while capturing the simulation objectives (Jacobson et al, 2006). This was reiterated by Dearie et al (1976) who stressed the importance of capturing only relevant performance variables when creating a simple but not necessarily the most complete model. Following this guideline, a simplified model is presented on Figure 11.

There are two modes of transportation by which patients arrive into ED indicated on Figure 11: walk-in and ambulance. When ED patients' census hit ED beds capacity limit (total 30 beds), an ambulance was bounced back (diverted), as it is indicated on Figure 11 Ambulance diversion continued until the time when the ED census dropped below the capacity limit. An action logic code was developed that tracked the percentage of time when the census was at the capacity limit. It was reported as percent diversion in the simulation output file.

All simulation runs start at week 1, Monday, at 12 A.M. (midnight). Because ED was not empty at this time, Monday midnight patients' census was used as the simulation initial condition on January 1, 2007: ED was pre-filled by 15 patients.

Each patient in the arrival flow was characterized by its week number, day of week, and admitting time on the record, as indicated on the panel on Figure 11. The following descriptive attributes (also indicated on the panel on Figure 11) were assigned to each patient on the arrival schedule to properly track each patient's routing and statistics in the simulation action logic:

Figure 11. Simplified ED structure used to simulate limiting length of stay for patients discharged home and patients admitted to the hospital

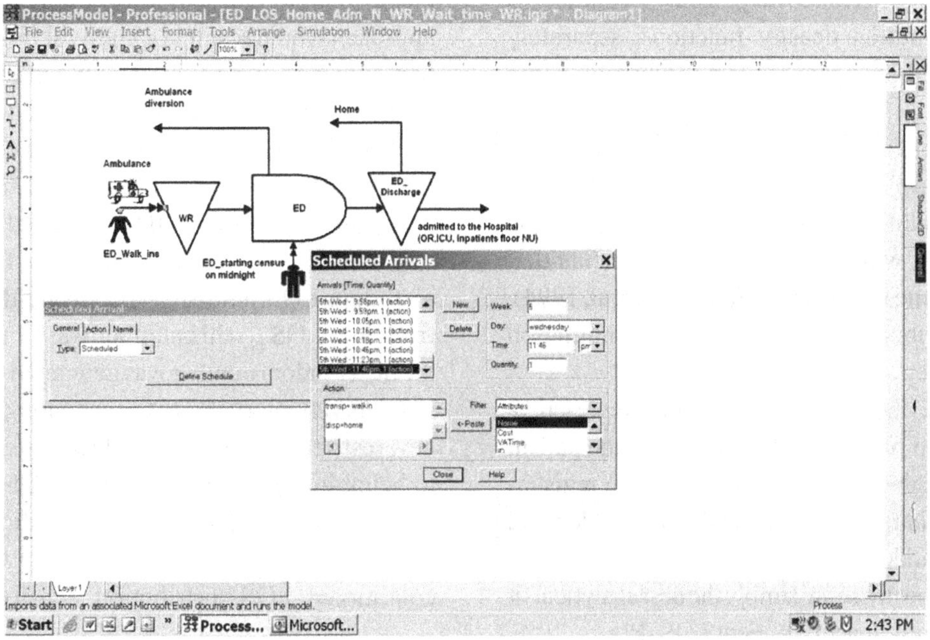

- Mode of transportation: (i) walk-in, (ii) ambulance.
- Disposition: (i) admitted as inpatient, (ii) discharged home

Arrived patients take available free beds reducing ED free capacity.

Discharged patients (released home or admitted as inpatients) moved out of the simulation system according to their disposition conditional routings. The patients' flow 'in and out' of the ED formed a dynamic supply and demand balance.

Total number of patients included in the simulation was 8411 for the two-month period from January 1 to February 28, 2007. This number of patients was representative enough to make results valid for subsequent months and years (Mayhew and Smith (2008) used three months 2002 database to calibrate the queuing model; however, the total number of patients was not given).

Overall Simulation Approach and LOS Distribution Density Functions

The critical element of the dynamics of the supply and demand balance was the time that the patients spent in ED. This time was fitted by a continuous LOS distribution density functions, separately for admitted as inpatients and discharged home patients.

The best fit distributions were identified using the Stat:Fit module built in the simulation package: admitted inpatients best fit LOS was log-logistic, while best fit LOS for patients discharged home was Pearson 6 (Johnson et al, 1994). These distributions were built into the simulation action logic.

Because these LOS distributions represent a combination of many different steps of the patient move through the entire ED process from registration to discharge (including both value-added and non-value-added steps and delays), there is no simple interpretation: these are simply the best analytical fit used to represent actual patient LOS data.

Random numbers drawn from these distributions were used to perform multiple replications in each simulation run. It was identified in 'cold' runs that about 100 replications were needed for each simulation in order to get a stable outcome.

Because the objective was to quantify the effect of the LOS limits (both for discharged home patients and admitted as inpatients) on the percent diversion, the LOS limits were used as two simulation parameters.

An overall simulation approach was based on a full factorial design of experiments (DOE) with two factors (parameters) at six levels, each imposed on the original (baseline) LOS distribution functions. Response function was the simulated percent diversion. Imposing LOS limits (parameters) on original (baseline) LOS distribution functions means that no drawn random LOS value higher than the given limiting value was allowed in the simulation run. Therefore, the original LOS distribution densities should have recalculated for each simulation run as functions of the LOS limits (parameters).

One might be tempted to assume that if a randomly drawn LOS number was higher than the given LOS limit value this number should be made equal to the LOS limit. However, such an approach would result in a highly skewed simulation output because a lot of LOS numbers would be concentrated at the LOS limit value.

Instead, a concept of conditional distribution density should be used. If a random LOS number was in the interval from 0 to LOS_{lim}, this number was used for a simulation replication. However if a random LOS number was outside the interval from 0 to LOS_{lim}, this number was not used, and the next random number was generated until it was in the given interval. This procedure generated a new restricted random variable that is conditional to being in the interval from 0 to LOS_{lim}.

Given the original LOS distribution density, $f(T)_{orig}$, and the limiting value, LOS_{limit}, the conditional LOS distribution density function of the new restricted random variable, $f(T)_{new}$ will be:

$$f(T)_{new} = \frac{f(T)_{orig}}{\int_0^{LOS_{lim}} f(T)_{orig} dT}, \text{ if T is less or equal to}$$

LOS.

$f(T)_{new} = \mathbf{0}$, if T is greater than LOS$_{lim}$.

Conditional distribution density $f(T)_{new}$ depicted on Figure 12 (bottom panel, dotted bold line) is a function of both original distribution density and the simulation parameter LOS$_{lim}$ (upper integration limit of the denominator integral).

These denominator integrals were preliminary calculated and then approximated by the 3-rd order polynomials that were built in the simulation action logic (Kolker, 2008).

The model's adequacy check was performed by running the simulation of the original baseline patients' arrival. The model's predicted percent diversion (~23.7%) and the reported percent di-

version (21.5%) are close enough (in the range of a few percentage points). Thus, the model captures dynamic characteristics of the ED patients' flow adequately enough to mimic the system's behavior, and to compare alternatives ('what-if' scenarios).

Along with the percent diversion calculation, a plot of ED census as a function of time (hours/weeks) was also simulated (Kolker, 2008). This instructive plot visualizes the timing when the ED census hits the capacity limit, and therefore ED diversion had to be declared. The plot also illustrated that at some periods of time (mostly late night time) the ED was actually at a low census.

A full factorial computer design of experiments (DOE) was performed with two factors: LOS$_{lim}$ (home) for discharged home patients and LOS$_{lim}$ (adm) for patients admitted into hospital. Each factor had six levels. Simulated percent diversion was a response function.

A summary of results is presented on Figure 13. It follows from this plot that several combinations

Figure 12. Distribution density function and imposed LOS limit

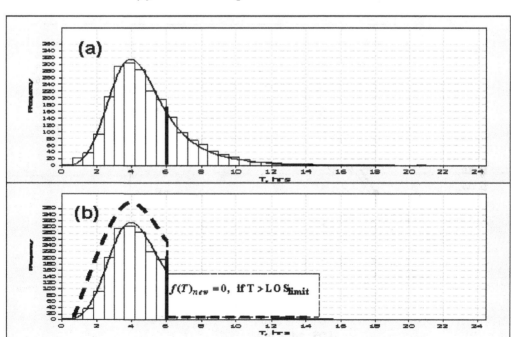

of parameters LOS $_{lim}$ (home) and LOS $_{lim}$ (adm) would result in low percent diversion.

For example, if LOS $_{lim}$ (home) stays at 5 hours (low curve) then LOS $_{lim}$ (adm) could be about 6 hours with the practically negligible diversion about 0.5%. Notice that Clifford et al (2008) established the goal for ED LOS 6 hours for inpatients to eliminate ambulance diversion and this metric is considered exceptional if less than 5% of patients exceed this limit. Any other combination of LOS $_{lim}$ (home) and LOS $_{lim}$ (adm) could be taken from the graph to estimate a corresponding expected percent diversion.

Thus, simulation helped to establish a quantitative link between an expected percent diversion and the limiting values of LOS. It has also suggested the reasonable targets for the upper limits LOS $_{lim}$ (home) and LOS $_{lim}$ (adm).

(a)   thin solid line: original LOS (top panel). Bold vertical line: imposed LOS limit 6 hrs

(b)   re-calculated restricted LOS: bold dotted line

Analysis of the LOS pattern in the study hospital indicated that a significant percentage of ED patients stayed much longer than the LOS targets suggested by the simulation. For example, ~24% patients of a study hospital exceeded LOS $_{lim}$ (adm) of 6 hours, and ~17% of patients exceeded LOS $_{lim}$ (home) of 5 hours. These long over-targets LOS for a significant percentage of patients were a root cause of ED closure and ambulance diversion.

Established LOS $_{lim}$ targets could be used to better manage a daily patient flow. The actual current LOS is being tracked down for each individual patient. If the current LOS for the particular patient at the moment is close to the target limiting LOS $_{lim}$ a corrective action should be implemented to expedite a move of this patient.

Multiple factors could contribute to the looming delay over the target LOS, such as delayed lab results or X-ray / CT, consulting physician is not

Figure 13. Summary plot representing simulated % diversion as a function of two parameters LOS lim (home) and LOS lim (adm)

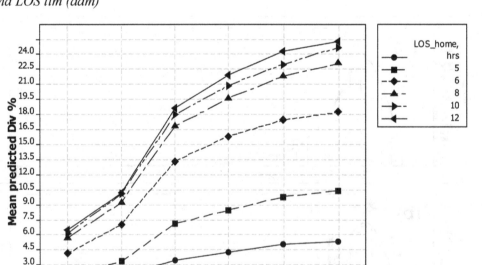

available, no beds downstream on hospital floor (ICU) for admitted patients, etc. Analysis and prioritizing the contributing factors to the over the target LOS $_{lim}$ is an important task.

Notice that the average LOS that is frequently reported as one of the ED patient flow performance metric cannot be used to manage a daily patient flow. In order to calculate the average LOS, the data should be collected retrospectively for at least a few dozens patients. Therefore, it would be too late to make corrective actions to expedite a move of the particular patient if the average LOS becomes unusually high (whatever 'high' means). In contrast, if the established upper limiting LOS $_{lim}$ targets were not exceeded for the great majority of patients, it would guarantee a low ED percent diversion, and the average LOS would be much lower than the upper limiting LOS $_{lim}$.

Marshall et al (2005) and de Bruin et al (2007) also discussed the shortcomings of reporting LOS only as averages (the flaw of averages) for the skewed (long tailed) data (see also an illustrative example in section 2.2).

EDs of other hospitals differ by their patient mix, their LOS distribution and bed capacity. However the overall simulation methodology presented here will be the same regardless of a particular hospital ED.

Such a general methodology would be more practically useful for other ED than some predetermined generalized 'one size fits all' target values.

The negative consequences of the 'one size fits all' approach were summarized by Mayhew and Smith, (2008): '…the practicality of a single target fitting all A&ED will come under increasing strain'.

DES of Intensive Care Unit (ICU) Patient Flow: Effect of Daily Load Leveling of Elective Surgeries on ICU Diversion

Intensive Care Unit (ICU) is often needed for the patients' care. Demand for ICU beds comes from emergency, add-on and elective surgeries. Emergency and add-on surgeries are random and cannot be scheduled in advance. Elective surgeries are scheduled ahead of time. However, they are often scheduled for the daily block-time driven mostly by physicians' priorities. (Daily block time is the time in the operating room that is allocated to the surgeon or the group of surgeons on the particular days of the week to perform a particular type of surgical services). Usually elective surgery scheduling does not take into account the competing demand for ICU beds from the emergency and add-on cases.

Because of the limited capacity of the ICU beds, such a disconnection often results in the Emergency Department (ED) closure (diversion) for patients due to no beds in ICU. This is a typical example of a system bottleneck caused by the interdependency and competing demands between the material (patient) flows in a complex system: the upstream problem (ED closure) is created by the downstream problem (no ICU beds) (see section 3.3).

Usually two types of variability affect the system's patient flow: natural process flow variability and scheduled (artificial) flow variability (Litvak et al, 2001; Litvak and Long, 2000; Haraden et al, 2003).

Patients can be admitted into ICU from the Emergency Department (ED), other local area hospitals, inpatient nursing units, and / or operating rooms (OR). Patients admitted into ICU from ED, other local area hospitals, and inpatient nursing units are primary contributors to the natural random flow variability because the timing of these admissions is not scheduled in advance and is unpredictable.

Admissions into ICU from the OR include emergency, add-on, and elective surgeries. Elective surgeries (cases) are defined as surgeries that could be delayed safely for the patient for at least more than 24 hrs (or usually much longer).

Emergency and add-on surgeries also contribute to the natural process flow variability. Because this type of variability is statistically random, it is beyond hospital control. It cannot be eliminated (or even much reduced). However, some statistical characteristics can be predicted over a long period of time that could help to manage it.

Elective surgeries that require post-operative admission into ICU contribute to the scheduled (artificial) flow variability. Elective surgery scheduling is driven mostly by individual priorities of the surgeons and their availability for other commitments (teaching, research, etc). This variability is usually within the hospital management control, and it could be reduced or eliminated by a proper management of the scheduling system.

It is possible to manage the scheduling of the elective cases in a way to smooth (or to daily load level) overall patient flow variability. A daily load leveling would reduce the chances of excessive peak demand for the system's capacity and, consequently, would reduce its diversion.

There are quite a few publications in which the issues of smoothing surgical schedules and ICU patient flow are discussed. Kolker (2009) provided a detailed analysis of the literature.

Nonetheless, there is not much in the literature that could help a scheduler to directly answer an important question: what maximum number of elective surgeries per day should be scheduled along with the competing demand from emergency surgeries in order to reduce ICU diversion to an acceptable low level, or to prevent diversion at all ?

Therefore, a methodology that could quantitatively link the daily number of elective surgeries and ICU patient flow throughput (or diversion) would have a considerable practical value.

Description of the ICU Patient Flow Model

Layout of the ICU model of the study hospital is represented on Figure 14.

The entire ICU system includes four specialized ICU units: Cardio ICU (CIC), Medical ICU (MIC), Surgical ICU (SIC) and Neurological ICU (NIC). Capacity (the number of beds) of each ICU unit was: CIC=8, MIC=10, SIC=21 and NIC=12. Total ICU capacity was 51 beds.

All simulation runs start at week 1, Monday, at 12 A.M. (midnight). Because ICU was not empty at this time, Monday midnight patients' census was used as the simulation initial conditions: CIC=8, MIC=9, SIC=20 and NIC=12.

Patients admitted into each ICU unit formed an entity arrival flow. The week number, day of the week and admitting time characterize each patient in the arrival flow.

Each discharged patient is also characterized by the week number, day of the week and discharge time.

Patient flow 'in and out' formed a dynamic supply and demand balance (supply of ICU beds and demand for them by patients). If there was no free bed at the time of admission in the particular primary ICU unit, then the patient moved into other ICU units using alternative type routings (depicted by the thin lines between the units, Figure 14).

Patient move followed the following action logic that simulated the established hospital's rules to deal with the overcapacity of the ICU units:

- if no beds available in CIC move to SIC
- if no beds available in MIC move to CIC else move to SIC else move to NIC
- if no beds available in NIC move to CIC else SIC

Panel indicates an example of scheduled SIC arrival: week number: 18; Day: Tuesday; Time: 2:00 pm. Patient attributes (bottom of the panel):

Figure 14. DES layout of the ICU patient flow model

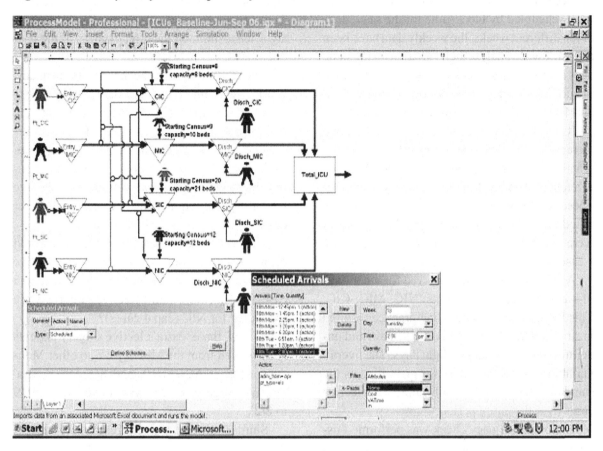

adm_from = OR (Operating Room); pt_type = els (elective scheduled)

When the patient census of the ICU system hit or exceeded a critical limit, then an ICU diversion was declared due to 'no ICU beds'. The critical limit in the study hospital was defined as the number of occupied beds, which is two beds less than the total capacity, i.e. 49 beds. The two 'extra' beds were left as a buffer in the anticipation of more admissions coming soon.

Diversion status was kept until the time when the ICU census dropped below the critical limit. An action logic code was developed that tracked the percentage of time when the census was at or exceeded the critical limit. It was reported as the percent diversion in the simulation output file.

The following descriptive attributes were as-signed to each patient on the arrival schedule to properly track each patient's routing and statistics in the simulation action logic:

- Patient type attribute: elective surgery (els) or emergency surgery (ems).
- Patient 'admitted from' attribute: emergency department (ED), operating room / recovery room (opr), external hospital, rehabilitation, any floor nursing unit.

The total number of admitted patients included into the ICU simulation model was 1847 during the 18 weeks period (about four months worth of data). The total number of elective cases was about 21% of all ICU admission for the 18 week period.

Because elective cases in the study hospital were scheduled by block-time for the same days of the different weeks, the weekly data have been drilled down to analyze their variation for the same days of the different weeks, i.e. from one Monday to another Monday of the following week, from one Tuesday to another Tuesday, and so on.

It follows from these data (Kolker, 2009) that there was a significant variability in the scheduling practice of elective surgeries from one Monday to another Monday, from one Tuesday to another Tuesday, and so on. For example, 8 cases were scheduled on Monday 6/5, 2007 while only 2 cases were scheduled on Monday 6/26, 2007, and only 1 case was scheduled for Monday 9/18, 2007.

A similar picture was observed for other days of week and other ICU units: NIC, MIC, CIC. This highly uneven scheduling practice resulted in straining the ICU system on busy days and underutilizing the system on light days. The overall variability of the schedule was quantified as the standard deviation of the daily number of elective cases over the entire period.

A model adequacy check was performed using the original baseline patient arrival database. The model's predicted percent diversion for the different time periods (from 1 month to 4 months long) was then compared with the actual percent diversion. The later was reported by the ED as the percent of time when the ED was closed to the ambulances due to 'no ICU beds'.

It could be concluded (Kolker, 2009) that the model captures dynamic characteristics of the ICU patient flow adequately enough (within 1 to 2 percent from the actually reported values) to mimic the system's behavior and to compare alternative ('what-if') scenarios.

Along with the percent diversion calculation, a plot of ICU census as a function of time (hrs/ weeks) was also simulated (Kolker, 2009). The plot visualizes the timing when the ICU census hits or exceeds the critical limit, and therefore ICU diversion had to be declared. The plot also illustrates that at some periods of time the ICU is actually underutilized having low census. These peaks and valleys of the census impose a significant strain on the effectiveness of the ICU operations.

Once the model was checked for its adequacy, it was used with enough confidence to simulate 'what-if' scenarios. The approach was to actively manipulate only the day and time of elective surgeries (leaving all emergency and add-on surgeries timing unchanged). The objective was to quantify the effect of the elective surgeries schedule smoothing (or, equivalently, daily leveling, or daily capping) on the ICU diversion.

The first 'what-if' scenario was: what would the percent diversion be if not more than 5 elective surgeries per day were scheduled for SIC (cap 5 cases) and not more than 4 elective surgeries were scheduled for NIC (cap 4 cases)?

For SIC three 'extra' elective surgery patients were moved from the Monday 6/5 to other Mondays, such as 6/26, 7/10, and 8/7. One 'extra' elective surgery patient was moved from 6/19 to 8/21.

Similarly, two 'extra' elective surgery patients were moved from Tuesday 6/13 to Tuesdays 6/27 and 9/5, accordingly, as illustrated on Figure 15.

Similar moves were performed for Wednesdays, Thursdays, and Fridays, as well as for NIC. As a result of these moves, new smoother schedules were obtained. Notice that the standard deviations of the new schedules were now much lower than they were for the original schedules (Kolker, 2009).

Simulation runs for the new smoothed schedules resulted in the much-reduced diversion: about ~3.5%. The simulated census clearly indicated that the critical census limit was exceeded less frequently and for a shorter period of time. This is the reason for the reduced diversion compared to the original un-smoothed schedule.

Notice that the total number of elective surgeries remains the same. Not a single surgery was dropped but rather 'extra' surgeries were

Figure 15. Diagram of the move of the number of elective surgeries for the daily level (cap) 5 cases (Mondays and Tuesdays shown)

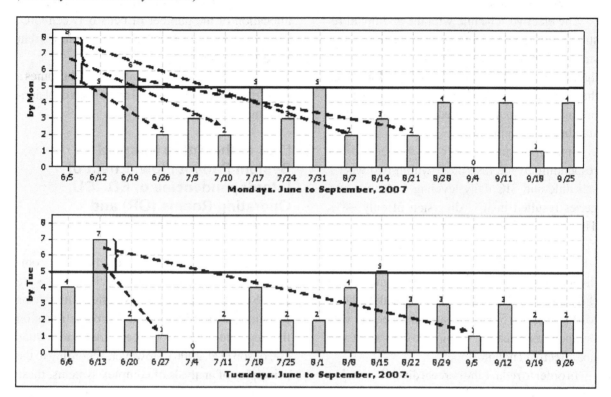

re-scheduled from the busy days to lighter later days to make the overall schedule for the same time period smoother.

Is it possible to lower diversion further?

The next 'what-if' scenario was: what will the percent diversion be if not more than 4 elective surgeries per day were scheduled, both for SIC and NIC (cap 4 cases)?

A similar move of the 'extra' surgeries from the days in which the daily level of 4 surgeries was exceeded to the later lighter days has resulted in the new schedule that was even smoother than the previous one with the leveling limit of 5 surgeries per day. Standard deviation was reduced by ~40% for Mondays, and ~35% for Tuesdays, Wednesdays, and Thursdays, respectively vs. the baseline original schedule. This should have helped to further reduce diversion. Indeed, the simulation runs

demonstrated that the diversion dropped down to the level of ~1.5%.

Is the predicted low ICU diversion ~1.5%, with the SIC and NIC daily leveling of not more than 4 elective surgeries per day an acceptable solution? Technically, it is. However, some 'extra' surgeries would have bumped to more than 2 months apart, e.g. from early June to early August (Figure 15). The problem is that not all patients could wait that long even though the surgery is elective. Also, from the practical standpoint, daily leveling of not more than 4 surgeries per day is sometimes too restrictive.

Therefore a next series of 'what-if' scenarios was considered: is it possible to get a low diversion about ~ 1% by bumping 'extra' cases to the block-time days which are not further than 2 weeks apart (Dexter et al, 1999) ? It was also considered increasing the daily leveling back to

5 elective surgeries per day in order to make the limit less restrictive.

The elective schedule with the additional restriction 'not more than two weeks apart' is less smooth. It has a higher standard deviation (1.59) than the schedule without restriction for which the standard deviation was 1.42. Notice that the original un-smoothed schedule had the highest standard deviation 1.97.

Simulation runs of the 'what-if' scenario corresponding to the restricted 'within two weeks' schedule and SIC daily leveling 5 elective surgeries resulted in ICU diversion of only ~8%. This is a relatively small gain compared to the original baseline un-smoothed schedule with ~10.5% diversion. This small reduction of the diversion was a reflection of a lower smoothness (higher standard deviation) of this schedule. Thus, load leveling to 5 elective surgeries per day with bumped 'extra cases' within 2 weeks apart was not effective enough alone.

In order to reduce the percent diversion back to low single digits while still keeping daily leveling at 5 elective surgeries per day and moving 'extra cases' within two weeks apart, an additional factor was considered. This factor was a more rigorous implementation of ICU admission and discharge criteria. It was suggested that patients with the likely LOS less than 24 hrs were excluded from ICU admission but moved to the regular nursing unit (see section 3.3). This scenario resulted in a significant reduction of ICU diversion, down to about ~ 1%.

There is a trade-off between these two scenarios. From the practical standpoint the higher level-loading elective schedule (5 surgeries per day) would be easier to implement than the lower level-loading one (4 surgeries per day) because the former is less restrictive. However, the former assumes that the ICUs admission criteria/exclusions are rigorously applied while the latter does not require exclusion from the current ICU admission practice.

One more valuable application of this DES model could be determining a more appropriate allocation of the number of beds between CIC, SIC, MIC, and NIC units, compared to the current historical allocation.

Once the DES model is validated, it becomes a powerful tool for the hospital operations decision-making.

DES of the Entire Hospital System Patient Flow: Effect of Interdependencies of ED, ICU, Operating Rooms (OR) and Floor Nursing Units (NU)

It was discussed in Introduction that large complex hospital systems or multi-facility clinics are usually deconstructed into smaller subsystems or units. Most published DES models focus on the separate analysis of these individual units (Jacobson et al, 2006). However, according to the principles of analysis of complex systems, these separate subsystems (units) should be reconnected back in a way that captures the most important interdependency between them. DES models that capture the interaction of major units in a hospital, and the information that can be obtained from analyzing the system as a whole, can be invaluable to hospital planners and administrators.

This section specifically illustrates a practical application of this system-engineering principle.

DES models of the ED and ICU patient flow have been described separately in details in sections 3.1 and 3.2. It is well known that these subsystems are not stand-alone units but they are closely interdependent, as well as the Operating Rooms (OR) and floor nursing units (NU).

A high-level patient flow map (layout) of the entire hospital system is shown on Figure 16 One output of the ED model for patients admitted into the hospital (ED discharge) now becomes an ICU, OR and NU input through ED disposition. About

62% of admitted patients were taken into operating rooms (OR) for emergency surgery, about 28% of admitted patients moved directly into ICU, and about 10% of patients admitted from ED into floor nursing units.

OR suite size was 12 interchangeable operating rooms used both for ED emergency and scheduled surgeries.. There were four daily scheduled OR admissions at 6 am, 9 am, 12 pm and 3 pm, Monday to Thursday (there were no scheduled surgeries on Fridays and weekends).

The best fit of the emergency surgery duration was found to be a Pearson 6 distribution.

Elective surgery duration depends on surgical service type, such as general surgery, orthopedics, neuro-surgery, etc. For the simplicity of this model, elective surgery duration was weighted by each service percentage. The best fit of the overall elective surgeries duration was found to be a Johnson SB distribution (Johnson et al, 1994).

About 14% of post surgery patients were admitted from OR into ICU (direct ICU admission)

while 86% were admitted into floor NU. However some patients (about 4%) were readmitted from floor NU back to ICU (indirect ICU admission from OR).

Patient length of stay (LOS) in NU was assumed to be in the range from 1 day to 10 days with the most likely 5 days represented by a triangle distribution. NU overall capacity was 420 beds. At the simulation start, NU was pre-filled with starting census 380 patients (see also sections 3.1 and 3.2).

Baseline DES resulted in ED diversion about 24%, ICU diversion about 11% (see sections 3.1 and 3.2), and floor NU diversion about 14.6%.

If limiting ED LOS had aggressive targets 5 hours for patients discharged home and 6 hours for patients admitted to the hospital (see section 3.1) then ED diversion became practically negligible (less than 0.5%). However because of interdependencies of patient flows, ICU diversion increased to 12.5% and floor NU diversion remained about the same, 14.9%. Thus, aggres-

Figure 16. DES layout of a high-level patient flow map of the entire hospital system

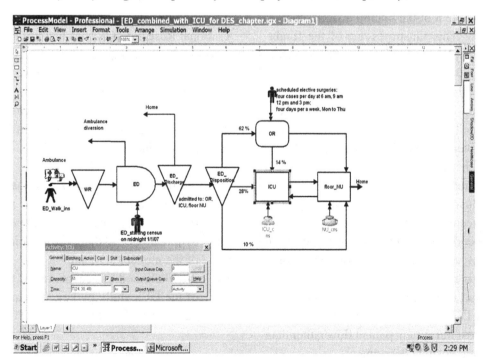

sive process improvement in one subsystem (ED) resulted in worsening situation in other interrelated subsystems (mostly, ICU).

If instead of the above aggressive limiting ED LOS a more relaxed target is used, say, LOS not more than 6 hours for discharged home and not more than 10 hours for admitted to the hospital, then simulated ED diversion would become about 7%, ICU diversion is about 11.1%, and floor NU diversion remained practically unchanged, 14.8%. While ED diversion now became worse, it is still better than it was at the baseline level by about a factor of 3. At the same time, this less aggressive ED target LOS did not, at least, make the ICU and floor NU diversion much worse.

Thus, from the entire hospital system standpoint the primary focus of process improvement activities should be on ED, and then on floor NU followed by ICU.

At the same time, ED patient target LOS reduction program should not be too aggressive and it should be closely coordinated with that for floor NU and ICU. Otherwise, even if ED reports a significant progress in its patient LOS reduction program, this progress will not translate into improvement of the overall hospital system patient flow. This illustrates one of the fundamental principles of the Theory of Constraints (Goldratt, 2004).

On the other hand, if ICU policy of declaring diversion is changed from 49 occupied beds to full capacity of 51 occupied beds, then ICU reported diversion will drop down to ~9.6%, leaving unchanged diversions of all other units in the system.

This illustrates that reported performance metric (percent of time at full capacity or some others) depends not only on physical capacity and patient flow variability but also on the hospital administrative policy.

Of course, many other scenarios could be analyzed using DES model to find out how to improve the entire hospital system patient flow rather than each separate hospital department.

PRACTICAL IMPLEMENTATION OF DES RESULTS IN HEALTHCARE: ISSUES AND PERSPECTIVES

As it was already pointed out and supported by extensive literature review (Jun et al, 1999; Jacobson et al, 2006), DES modeling as a methodology of choice in healthcare has been extensively used to quantitatively analyze healthcare delivery processes and operations and to help decision-makers to justify business decisions.

However, for DES to reach its full potential as the key methodology in healthcare, the results of simulation must be practically implemented. Unfortunately, the number of publications that report successful implementation of DES results is much lower than the number of publications that report successful development of DES models. For example, in the survey of two hundred papers reporting the results of DES studies in healthcare, only 16 reports of successful implementations were identified (Jacobson et al, 2006). Fone (2003) found that Operational Research has had limited success in the implementation of results in practice in the healthcare setting. Sachdeva et al (2006) also states that '...Healthcare Operational Research (OR) has had limited success in achieving an adequate level of acceptance by stakeholders, particularly physicians, leading to implementation of results'.

A likelihood of successful implementation or effectiveness of DES project (E) can be related to two major factors:

(i)   the likelihood that DES model adequately captures all relevant features of process (system) and properly verified and validated to actual clinical data, i.e. technical quality of the model (TQ), and

(ii) the likelihood of acceptance of the results of the DES study by key stakeholders and decision-makers (A), i.e., $E = TQ * A$.

A similar relationship in which acceptance term (A) also included accountability was presented by Mercy Medical Center (2007).

Most reported DES studies focus on TQ, and the likelihood of developing a good verified and validated DES model is high (although not guaranteed). However, if the likelihood of acceptance of the model results is low (for whatever reason), then the overall success and impact of the DES project measured by effectiveness of its implementation will also be low regardless of technical merits of the DES model itself.

A number of recommendations were developed to increase the likelihood of DES results implementation success. Some of these recommendations include (Jacobson, 2006): the system being simulated actually needs decision, the DES project must be completed before a deadline, data used for simulation are credible, and, most importantly, the key stakeholders and the decision-maker must actively participate in the project.

Lowery (1996) noted that involvement of the upper management in the project is critical for its success. Litvak (2007) argues that if hospital executives are not involved in the process (queuing theory or simulation), the analysts could do their calculations but they would not be used for decision-making.

Carter and Blake (2004) published an interesting summary of their experience in practical implementation of simulation projects. They have used four projects to highlight the practical lessons of applying operations research methodologies in health care: '...Experience suggests that OR techniques can be successfully applied in the health care setting. The secret is to understand the unique nature of the health care business and its impact on models, decision makers, and the development of implementation policies'. Further, '...decision making in hospitals is characterized by multiple players; ...incorporating the objectives of all decision makers is vital in this environment'.

Thus, procedure and methodology of applying DES requires decision-makers to work closely with the simulation analyst to provide details of the system, often for the first time. As a result, the decision-makers are likely to gain a new perspective on the relationship between the available resources and the capability of the system (Jacobson et al, 2006).

The experience of the author of this chapter has also shown that at least two main conditions are needed: (i) the stake-holder (project owner) must have a genuine incentive for process improvement and realize that there is no real alternative to DES modeling, and (ii) a dedicated and flexible data analyst must participate in the project. The data analyst must not only have a full access to raw data stored in various data bases but be also qualified enough to convert these data bases into a data file (usually Excel) with the fields that match the fields developed by a simulation specialist who designed the model. Thus, a successful DES project truly takes teamwork by the professionals.

Rakich et al (1991) studied the effect of DES on management development. The authors concluded that conducting a simulation study not only develops decision-making skills, but also forces to recognize the implication of system changes. It was noted that if decision-makers developed their own DES models, implementation occurred much more frequently. Mahachek (1992) noted that one of significant barriers in the implementation of DES is the decision-makers' perception that '... simulation is an additional layer of effort rather than an organizer of all your current efforts'. According to Lowery (1996), DES projects start as a means of documenting assumptions, organizing the decision-making process and identifying potential problem areas. She is quite right when she passionately writes that '...It is amazing how much time is spent in the planning process (especially in meetings) arguing over the differences in opinion, where these differences are due to disagreements over assumptions never actually acknowledged.... While disagreements may still ensue over the content of the assumptions, the arguments become focused when the assumptions... are in front of all participants'.

Healthcare has a culture of rigid division of labor. This functional division does not effectively support the methodologies that cross the functional areas, especially if they assume significant changes in traditional relationships (Kopach-Konrad et al, 2007). Furthermore, the role and status of DES professionals in healthcare delivery is not usually well defined and causes sometimes skepticism and fear.

Relatively few health care administrators are equipped to think analytically about how health care delivery should function as a system or to appreciate the relevance of system-engineering methods in healthcare. Even fewer are equipped to work with engineers to apply these tools (Reid et al, 2005). Thus, it is often difficult for many administrators to appreciate the DES approach contributions to the health care delivery process analysis. On the other hand, DES professionals often have little, if any, education in health care delivery. This sometimes results in the lack of clinically relevant factors related to patient care included in DES model, '...which are at the heart of physician decision-making' (Sachdeva et al, 2006).

This underscores the importance of considering social and communication issues in the acceptance and implementation of any socio-technical system (Kopach-Konrad, et al, 2007).

One approach proposed to overcome some of these issues was applied to pediatric ICU (Sachdeva et al, 2006). It includes a combination of 'hard' and 'soft' operations research. The initial simulation model of pediatric ICU patient flow was modified based upon input from the active participation of physicians working in this ICU. During interviews with stakeholders it was acknowledged that there are factors called 'soft' that are difficult to model in an objective unambiguous way. Therefore, soft OR was used to capture concerns that could not be captured using traditional DES methodology. Cognitive

mapping was chosen as the soft OR approach. Cognitive maps attempt to capture beliefs, values, and expertise of stakeholders by conducting structured interviews. Cognitive mapping was used for two main purposes: (i) to assist in the identification of issues that were previously not captured using traditional DES models, and (ii) comparing results from the outcomes research, hard and soft OR to enhance greater buy-in and acceptance by the key stakeholders.

The results of cognitive mapping helped not only identify new issues not captured by hard OR but also supported many of the results from hard OR that were counter-intuitive to pre-existing beliefs.

Thus, results from this study support the view that a combination of hard and soft OR allows a greater level of understanding leading to acceptance and willingness to implement DES results. This is consistent with the recommendations of the UK Engineering and Physical Science Research Council (EPSRC) (2004) regarding soft OR and application in healthcare. '...It has always been one of the main characteristics of OR to seek for opportunities to integrate soft and hard methods' (EPRSC, 2004).

CONCLUSION

This chapter covers applications of the most widely used system-engineering methods, such as queuing analytic theory and DES models, to healthcare,. It demonstrates the power of DES models for the analysis of patient flow with variability and subsystem interdependency.

Many health care organizations are making serious strategic decisions such as new construction to expand capacity, merging with other hospitals etc., without using system engineering and, particularly, DES modeling analysis to evaluate an impact of these decisions.

However, DES models and management science principles are widely used in other industries, and demonstrate a great value in providing important insights into operational strategies and practices.

Complex dynamics of delivery of care processes makes them an important area of application of DES modeling and management science methodologies to help identify both trends in capacity needs and the ways to use existing capacity more efficiently.

At the same time, it is acknowledged that one of the major current challenges is a relatively low acceptance of DES results by the medical community and hospital administration. Practical implementation of DES results in health care settings is sometimes rather slow and difficult.

There are various reasons for this situation, both technical and psychological. Some of them have been discussed in section 4.

Nonetheless, more and more healthcare organizations have started to recognize the value and predictive power of system engineering and DES models through concrete and realistic examples. The fast changing landscape of the healthcare industry will help promote the organizational changes needed for adoption improvement recommendations based on DES models. Hopefully this chapter contributes a little toward achieving this goal.

REFERENCES

Abu-Taieh, E., & El Sheikh, A. R. (2007). Commercial Simulation Packages: A Comparative Study. *International Journal of Simulation, 8*(2), 66–76.

Allen, A. (1978). *Probability, statistics and queuing theory, with computer science applications.* New York: Academic Press

Blasak, R., Armel, W., Starks, D., & Hayduk, M. (2003). The Use of Simulation to Evaluate Hospital Operations between the ED and Medical Telemetry Unit. In S. Chick, et al (Ed.), *Proceedings of the 2003 Winter Simulation Conference* (pp. 1887-1893). Washington, DC: IEEE.

Carter, M. (2002). Health Care Management, Diagnosis: Mismanagement of Resources. *Operation Research / Management Science (OR/MS) . Today, 29*(2), 26–32.

Carter, M., & Blake, J. (2004). Using simulation in an acute-care hospital: easier said than done. In M. Brandeau, F. Sainfort, & W. Pierskala, (Eds.), *Operations Research and Health Care. A Handbook of Methods and Applications*, (pp.192-215). Boston: Kluwer Academic Publisher.

Clifford, J., Gaehde, S., Marinello, J., Andrews, M., & Stephens, C. (2008). *Improving Inpatient and Emergency Department Flow for Veterans. Improvement report.* Institute for Healthcare Improvement. Retrieved from http://www.IHI.org/ihi

D'Alesandro, J. (2008). *Queuing Theory Misplaced in Hospitals.* Management News from the Front, Process Improvement. PHLO. Posted Feb 19, 2008 at http://phlo.typepad.com

de Bruin, A., van Rossum, A., Visser, M., & Koole, G. (2007). Modeling the Emergency cardiac inpatient flow: an application of queuing theory. *Health Care Management Science, 10,* 125–137. doi:10.1007/s10729-007-9009-8

Dearie, J., & Warfield, T. (1976, July 12-14). The development and use of a simulation model of an outpatient clinic. *Proceedings of the 1976 Summer computer Simulation Conference,* Simulation Council, Washington, DC, (pp. 554-558).

Dexter, F., Macario, A., Traub, R., Hopwood, M., & Lubarsky, D. (1999). An Operating Room Scheduling Strategy to Maximize the Use of Operating Room Block Time: Computer Simulation of Patient Scheduling and Survey of Patients' Preferences for Surgical Waiting Time. *Anesthesia and Analgesia, 89*, 7–20. doi:10.1097/00000539-199907000-00003

Engineering and Physical Sciences Research Council (EPSRC). (2004). *Review of Research Status of Operational Research (OR) in the UK,* Swindon, UK. Retrieved from www.epsrc.ac.uk

Fone, D., Hollinghurst, S., & Temple, M. (2003). Systematic review of the use and value of computer simulation modeling in population health and health care delivery. *Journal of Public Health Medicine, 25*(4), 325–335. doi:10.1093/pubmed/fdg075

Gallivan, S., Utley, M., Treasure, T., & Valencia, O. (2002). Booked inpatient admissions and hospital capacity: mathematical modeling study. *British Medical Journal, 324*, 280–282. doi:10.1136/bmj.324.7332.280

Garcia, M., Centeno, M., Rivera, C., & DeCario, N. (1995). Reducing Time in an Emergency Room via a Fast-track. In C. Alexopoulos, et al (Ed.), *Proceedings of the 1995 Winter Simulation Conference,* (pp. 1048-1053). Washington, DC: IEEE.

Goldratt, E., & Cox, J. (2004). *The Goal* (3rd Ed., p. 384). Great Barrington, MA: North River Press.

Green, L. (2004). *Capacity Planning and Management in Hospitals*. In M. Brandeau., F. Sainfort, W. Pierskala, (Eds.), *Operations Research and Health Care. A Handbook of Methods and Applications,* (pp.15-41). Boston: Kluwer Academic Publisher.

Green, L. (2006). Queuing Analysis in Healthcare. In R. Hall, (Ed.), *Patient Flow: Reducing Delay in Healthcare Delivery* (pp. 281-307). New York: Springer.

Green, L., Kolesar, P., & Soares, J. (2001). Improving the SIPP approach for staffing service systems that have cyclic demands. *Operations Research, 49*, 549–564. doi:10.1287/opre.49.4.549.11228

Green, L., Kolesar, P., & Svoronos, A. (1991). Some effects of non-stationarity on multi-server Markovian queuing Systems. *Operations Research, 39*, 502–511. doi:10.1287/opre.39.3.502

Green, L., Soares, J., Giglio, J., & Green, R. (2006). Using Queuing Theory to Increase the Effectiveness of Emergency Department Provider Staffing. *Academic Emergency Medicine, 13*, 61–68. doi:10.1111/j.1553-2712.2006.tb00985.x

Gunal, M., & Pidd, M. (2006). Understanding Accident and Emergency Department Performance using Simulation. In L. Perrone, et al (Ed.) *Proceedings of the 2006 Winter Simulation Conference* (pp. 446-452). Washington, DC: IEEE.

Hall, R. (1990). *Queuing methods for Service and Manufacturing.* Upper Saddle River, NJ: Prentice Hall.

Haraden, C., Nolan, T., & Litvak, E. (2003). *Optimizing Patient Flow: Moving Patients Smoothly Through Acute Care Setting* [White papers 2]. Institute for Healthcare Improvement Innovation Series, Cambridge, MA

Harrison, G., Shafer, A., & Mackay, M. (2005). Modeling Variability in Hospital Bed Occupancy. *Health Care Management Science, 8*, 325–334. doi:10.1007/s10729-005-4142-8

Hillier, F., & Yu, O. (1981). *Queuing Tables and Graphs* (pp.1-231). New-York: Elsevier, Hlupic, V., (2000). Simulation Software: A Survey of Academic and Industrial Users. *International Journal of Simulation, 1*(1), 1–11.

IHI - Institute for Healthcare Improvement. (2008). Boston, MA: Author. Retrieved from http://www. ihi.org/IHI/Programs/ConferencesAndSeminars/ ApplyingQueuingTheorytoHealthCareJune2008. htm

Ingolfsson, A., & Gallop, F. (2003). *Queuing ToolPak 4.0*. Retrieved from http://www.bus. ualberta.ca/aingolfsson/QTP/

Jacobson, H., Hall, S., & Swisher, J. (2006). Discreet-Event Simulation of Health Care Systems. In R. Hall, (Ed.), *Patient Flow: Reducing Delay in Healthcare Delivery*, (pp. 210-252). New York: Springer.

Johnson, N. Kotz., S., & Balakrishnan, N., (1994). *Continuous Univariate Distributions* (Vol.1). New York: John Wiley & Sons.

... *Journal of Medical Systems*, *31*(6), 543–546. doi:10.1007/s10916-007-9096-6

Jun, J., Jacobson, H., & Swisher, J. (1999). Application of DES in health-care clinics: A survey. *The Journal of the Operational Research Society*, *50*(2), 109–123.

Kolker, A. (2008). Process Modeling of Emergency Department Patient Flow: Effect of patient Length of Stay on ED diversion. *Journal of Medical Systems*, *32*(5), 389-401. doi: http://dx.doi. org/10.1007/s10916-008-9144-x

Kolker, A. (2009). Process Modeling of ICU Patient Flow: Effect of Daily Load Leveling of Elective Surgeries on ICU Diversion. *Journal of Medical Systems*. 33(1), 27-40. Doi: http://dx.doi. org/10.1007/s10916-008-9161-9

Kopach-Konrad, R., Lawley, M., Criswell, M., Hasan, I., Chakraborty, S., Pekny, J., & Doebbeling, B. (2007). Applying Systems Engineering Principles in Improving Health Care Delivery. *Journal of General Internal Medicine*, *22*(3), 431–437. doi:10.1007/s11606-007-0292-3

Lawrence, J., Pasternak, B., & Pasternak, B. A. (2002). *Applied Management Science: Modeling, Spreadsheet Analysis, and Communication for Decision Making*. Hoboken, NJ: John Wiley & Sons.

Lefcowitz, M. (2007, February 26). *Why does process improvement fail?* Builder-AU by Developers for developers. Retrieved from www.builderau. com.au/strategy/projectmanagement/

Litvak, E. (2007). A new Rx for crowded hospitals: Math. Operation management expert brings queuing theory to health care. *American College of Physicians-Internal Medicine-Doctors for Adults*, December 2007, ACP Hospitalist.

Litvak, E., & Long, M. (2000). Cost and Quality under managed care: Irreconcilable Differences? *The American Journal of Managed Care*, *6*(3), 305–312.

Litvak, E., Long, M., Cooper, A., & McManus, M. (2001). Emergency Department Diversion: Causes and Solutions. *Academic Emergency Medicine*, *8*(11), 1108–1110.

Lowery, J. (1996). Introduction to Simulation in Healthcare. In J. Charness, D. Morrice, (Ed.) *Proceedings of the 1996 Winter Simulation Conference*, (pp. 78-84).

Mahachek, A. (1992). An Introduction to patient flow simulation for health care managers. *Journal of the Society for Health Systems*, *3*(3), 73–81.

Marshall, A., Vasilakis, C., & El-Darzi, E. (2005). Length of stay-based Patient Flow Models: Recent Developments and Future Directions. *Health Care Management Science*, *8*, 213–220. doi:10.1007/ s10729-005-2012-z

Mayhew, L., & Smith, D. (2008). Using queuing theory to analyze the Government's 4-h completion time target in Accident and Emergency departments. *Health Care Management Science*, *11*, 11–21. doi:10.1007/s10729-007-9033-8

McManus, M., Long, M., Cooper, A., & Litvak, E. (2004). Queuing Theory Accurately Models the Need for Critical Care Resources. *Anesthesiology*, *100*(5), 1271–1276. doi:10.1097/00000542-200405000-00032

McManus, M., Long, M., Cooper, A., Mandell, J., Berwick, D., Pagano, M., & Litvak, E. (2003). Variability in Surgical Caseload and Access to Intensive Care Services. *Anesthesiology*, *98*(6), 1491–1496. doi:10.1097/00000542-200306000-00029

Mercy Medical Center. (2007). *Creating a Culture of Improvement*. Presented at the Iowa Healthcare Collaborative Lean Conference, Des Moines, IA, August 22. Retrieved from www.ihconline.org/toolkits/LeanInHealthcare/IHALeanConfCultureImprovement.pdf

Miller, M., Ferrin, D., & Szymanski, J. (2003). Simulating Six Sigma Improvement Ideas for a Hospital Emergency Department. In S. Chick, et al (Ed.) *Proceedings of the 2003 Winter Simulation Conference* (pp. 1926-1929). Washington, DC: IEEE.

Nikoukaran, J. (1999). Software selection for simulation in manufacturing: A review. *Simulation Practice and Theory*, *7*(1), 1–14. doi:10.1016/S0928-4869(98)00022-6

Rakich, J., Kuzdrall, P., Klafehn, K., & Krigline, A. (1991). Simulation in the hospital setting: Implications for managerial decision making and management development. *Journal of Management Development*, *10*(4), 31–37. doi:10.1108/02621719110005069

Reid, P., Compton, W., Grossman, J., & Fanjiang, G. (2005). *Building a better delivery system: A new engineering / Healthcare partnership*. Washington, DC: Committee on Engineering and the Health Care System, Institute of Medicine and National Academy of Engineering, National Academy Press.

Ryan, J. (2005). *Building a better delivery system: A new engineering / Healthcare partnership. System Engineering: Opportunities for Health Care* (pp.141-142). Washington, DC: Committee on Engineering and the Health Care System, Institute of Medicine and National Academy of Engineering, National Academy Press.

Sachdeva, R., Williams, T., Quigley, J., (2006). Mixing methodologies to enhance the implementation of healthcare operational research. *Journal of the Operational Research Society, advance online publication, September 6*, 1 - 9

Seelen, L., Tijms, H., & Van Hoorn, M. (1985). *Tables for multi-server queues* (pp. 1-449). New-York: Elsevier, Simon, S., Armel, W., (2003). The Use of Simulation to Reduce the Length of Stay in an Emergency Department. In S. Chick, et al (Ed.) *Proceedings of the 2003 Winter Simulation Conference* (pp. 1907-1911). Washington, DC: IEEE

Swain, J., 2007. Biennial Survey of discreet-event simulation software tools. *OR/MS Today, 34*(5), October.

Weber, D. O. (2006). Queue Fever: Part 1 and Part 2. *Hospitals & Health Networks, Health Forum*. Retrieved from http://www.IHI.org

Wullink, G., Van Houdenhoven, M., Hans, E., van Oostrum, J., van der Lans, M., Kazemier, G., (2007). Closing Emergency Operating Rooms Improves Efficiency.

KEY TERMS AND DEFINITIONS

Operations Research: The discipline of applying mathematical models of complex systems with random variability aimed at developing justified operational business decisions

Management Science: A quantitative methodology for assigning (managing) available material assets and human resources to achieve the operational goals of the system based on operations research.

Non-Linear System: A system that exhibits a mutual interdependency of components and for which a small change in the input parameter(s) can result in a large change of the system output

Discrete Event Simulation: One of the most powerful methodologies of using computer models of the real systems to analyze their performance by tracking system changes (events) at discrete moments of time

Queuing Theory: Mathematical methods for analyzing the properties of waiting lines (queues)

in simple systems without interdependency. Typically uses analytic formulas that must meet some rather stringent assumptions to be valid.

Simulation Package (also known as a simulation environment): A software with user interface used for building and processing discrete event simulation models

Flow Bottleneck / Constraint: A resource (material or human) whose capacity is less than or equal to demand for its use.

Chapter 21
Modelling a Small Firm in Jordan Using System Dynamics

Raed M. Al-Qirem
Al-Zaytoonah University of Jordan, Jordan

Saad G. Yaseen
Al-Zaytoonah University of Jordan, Jordan

ABSTRACT

The Jordanian banks and the risk analysts in particularly are seeking to adapt and buy new analytical techniques and information systems that help in identifying, monitoring and analysing the credit risk especially for the small firms that represents the biggest firms' base in the Jordanian markets. This chapter supports that what analysts need is a thinking tool that allow the user to simulate, understand and control different policies or strategies. It will then enable better decision to be made. A simulator based on system dynamics methodology is the thinking tool produced by this chapter. The system dynamics methodology allows the bank to test "What If" scenarios based on a model which captures the behaviour of the real system over time. The objectives of this chapter is to introduce new performance measures using systems thinking paradigm that can be used by the Jordanian banks to assess the credit worthiness of firms applying for credit.

LITERATURE REVIEW

System Dynamics was developed in the second half of the 1950s by Jay W. Forrester at the Alfred P. Sloan School of Management at the Massachusetts Institute of Technology. Forrester's main study was the activities in Operations Research (or Management Science) that aimed to support managerial decision making through mathematical and scientific methods. According to his studies, he found that operations research was not effective in helping to solve many strategic problems inside the organisations. It was too mathematically oriented and focused too much on optimisation and analytical solutions. It neglected non-linear phenomena and relationships between corporate functions.

Forrester (1961) proposed to move towards closed-loop thinking in order to enhance the decision making process where the decision are seen as a means to affect the environment and changes in

DOI: 10.4018/978-1-60566-774-4.ch021

the environment also provide input to decisions which aim to influence the connection with this environment. This led Forrester to start studying decision making in social systems from the view point of information feedback control systems, so he made system dynamics more useful and relevant to the study of managerial problems. Forrester developed a method to study and simulate social systems as information feedback systems.

The method was first applied to corporate problems and was called Industrial Dynamics. Forrester (1961) defines Industrial Dynamics as "the study of the information feedback Characteristics of industrial activity to show how organizational structure, amplification (in policies), and time delays (in decision and actions) interact to influence the success of the enterprise. It treats the interactions between the flows of information, money, orders, materials, personnel, and capital equipment in a company, an industry, or a national economy". Lane (1997) summarises Forrester's method to modelling and understanding management problems as "social systems should be modelled as flow rates and accumulations linked by information feedback loops involving delays and non-linear relationships. Computer simulation is then the means of inferring the time evolutionary dynamics endogenously created by such system structures. The purpose is to learn about their modes of behaviour and to design policies which improve performance".

Because social systems contain lots of non-linear relationships, Forrester choose an experimental, or simulation, approach to be utilised in System Dynamics (Vennix 1996). Following Forrester's studies and publications, the method came to be applied to a large variety of problems and its name changed into the more general System Dynamics.

System dynamics is applied currently by both academic researchers and practitioners from all over the world. Applications of system dynamics have reached most of fields such as: health care, commodity production cycle, economic fluctuations, energy and project management and many more fields. Finally, there is an international system dynamics society at MIT, holding a yearly international system dynamics conference. In addition there is the society's journal (System Dynamics Review) and a huge number of chapters and literature on the system dynamics subject published in the conferences and journals around the world.

THE APPROACH OF SYSTEM DYNAMICS

System Dynamics is a systems thinking approach that uses a perspective based on information feedback and delays to understand the dynamic behaviour of complex physical, biological and social systems. It also helps the decision maker untangle the complexity of the connections between various policy variables by providing a new language and set of tools to describe. Then it does this by modelling the cause and effect relationships among these variables. Furthermore, System Dynamics method enables the decision makers or the modeller via its tools in any system to identify the underlying structure of their system or issue and how this structure determines the system's behaviour (see figure 1). The left arrow symbolizes the relationship while the right arrow indicates the deeper understanding that happens from analysing a system structure. System Dynamics can also be used to study the changes in one part of a system in order to observe its affect on the behaviour of the system as a whole (Martin 1997; Anderson and Johnson 1997; Brehmer 1992). Sterman (2000) gives an insight that the real value of an SD model should be to eliminate problems by changing the underlying structure of the system rather than anticipating and reacting to the environment. This allows the model to interact with the environment and gives/alerts feedback for structure changes. This is what the term (Dynamics) refers to: the

Figure 1. The link between structure and behavior (Adapted from Sterman, 2000)

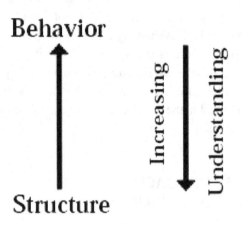

Feedback in System Dynamics

Feedback is one of the core concepts of System Dynamics. Yet our mental models often fail to include the critical feedbacks determining the dynamics of our systems (Sterman, 2000).

Much of the art of system dynamics modelling is to discover and represent the range of different feedback processes in any complex systems that enable the modeller to understand the dynamics of these systems because all complex behaviour arise from the interactions (feedbacks) among the variables of the system. It's not only dynamics that rise from feedback, but all learning too depends on feedback. As Sterman (2000) states "we make decisions that alter the real world; we gather information about the real world and uses the new information to revise our understanding of the world and the decisions we make to bring our perception of the state of the system closer to our goals" .

All the dynamics in any system arise from the interaction of just two feedback loops, a positive loops (or self reinforcing loops) and negative loops (self correcting loops).

Positive loop creates or reinforce actions which increases the state of the system (whatever is happening in the system) which in turn leads to more action further increasing the system state, this is why it's called self reinforcing. For example: Higher wages lead to higher prices, which in turn increase the wages etc.

On the other hand a negative loop is a goal seeking. It counteracts and opposes change to stabilize behaviour. An example of negative feedback is; the more attractive a city, the greater the immigration from other areas which will increase unemployment, housing price, crowding in the schools until it is no more attractive to move to.

It is important to notice that a positive feedback loop is not associated with good and a negative feedback loop is not associated with bad. Either type of loop can be good or bad, depending on which way it is operating and on the content. The

changes in the system's variables while interacting which stimulate changes over time?

By applying SD, one can enhance the usefulness of the model to address and analyse problems and provide more significant, rational and pertinent policy recommendations.

Lyneis (2000) stresses the importance of System Dynamic Models and its power to forecast a market demand for instance and compares this with a statistical forecast. He mentioned that a SD Model provides more reliable forecasts than the statistical (non-structural) models and tries to understand the underlying structure that created the data stream.

In summary, the process is to "observe and identify problematic behaviour of a system over time and to create a valid diagrammatic representation of the system, capable of reproducing (by computer simulation) the existing system behaviour and facilitating the design of improved system behaviour. For example; changing behaviour from decline to growth or from oscillation to stability" (Wolstenholme, 1990).

analysis of these feedback loops can facilitate our understanding of the process, its organisational boundaries, delay, information and strategies which interact to create its behaviour.

Dealing with Complexity

As the world becomes more complex, many people and organisations find themselves bombarded with lots of problems to solve, less time to solve them, and very few chances to learn from their mistakes. Managers will need to deal with complexity and with these changes. Also they need to develop their systems thinking capabilities and to be able to create an effective learning process in complex dynamic systems to overcome the different barriers to learning which are created by complex dynamics systems. Many philosophers, scientist and managers have been calling for a fundamental new ways of thinking that improve the ability to see the world as a complex system. As Sterman stated, "a system in which we understand that you can't just do one thing and that everything else is connected to everything else. He argued that it's crucial to develop new ways of system thinking. He states that "if people had a holistic worldview, they would then act in consonance with the long term best interest of the system as a whole, identify the high leverage points in systems and avoid policy resistance" (Sterman, 2000). This actually can be done using System Dynamics tools such as Virtual world (formal models, Microworld, management flight simulators, computer simulation) in which decision makers and managers can refresh decision making skills, test their scenarios and strategies and conduct experiments (Bianchi and Bivona 1999; Bach 2003).

SYSTEM DYNAMICS TOOLS

System Dynamics method uses different types of diagrammatic representations. These representations and tools can be implemented in response to the identification of a problem. These are respectively Causal loop diagrams, Stock and flows diagrams and computer simulation which all considered being important steps in building a system dynamics model. We will briefly explain them as follows:

Causal Loop Diagrams (CLD)

"Causal loop diagrams provide a framework for seeing interrelationships rather than things, for seeing patterns of change rather than static snapshots" (Senge, 1990). Causal loop diagrams constitute a powerful way to express concisely causal statements and to identify feedback structure of complex systems. In a causal loop diagram a causal relationship between two variables is represented by means of an arrow. The variable at the tail is supposed to have a causal effect on the variable at the point. Also a distinction can be made between two types of causal relationships: positive and negative. A positive causal relationship implies that both variables will change in the same direction while a negative causal loop implies that both variables change in opposite directions.

Causal loop diagrams are excellent tools for capturing our hypotheses about the causes of dynamics, eliciting and capturing individuals and team's mental models and finally its helpful for communicating the important feedbacks we believe are responsible for the problem under analysis. It can be very useful in the early stage of a project, when the modeller need to work with the client team to elicit and capture their mental models. They are effective in presenting the results of modelling work in a non technical fashion as we will see when studying the causal loop diagrams for my project.

Figure 2 shows a simple example of a causal loop diagram; it shows the effect of quality improvements of a firm's reputation, revenue and profit, market share which increases the firm's capacity for training and further improvements in quality.

Figure 2. Causal loop diagram for quality improvement

Causal loop diagrams have some limitations if they are used alone. The most important limitations of causal loop diagrams that they do not distinguish and capture the stocks and flows of systems which sometimes might be helpful to show. System dynamics method uses the second diagrammatic representation which is Stock and flow diagram.

Stocks and Flows

Stocks and Flows represent one of the essential features of a system dynamics model in analysing any system by describing it in terms of stocks (another meaning is levels), flows (or rates), converters (auxiliaries) and the feedback loops formed by these variables. The way in which these variables represent a system is critical to the dynamics of the system. Many system dynamics experts say that after understanding the feedback structure of the system in a model, it is important to further elaborate by building a computer simulation designed to represent its dynamic behaviour (Jackson 2003).

Stock and flow diagram is usually constructed from a causal loop diagram that is familiar to us.

The balance in our bank account is a stock. The number of employed people in a firm is a stock.

Stocks are altered by inflows and outflows. The employees in a firm increases via hiring rate and decreases via layoff, retirements and the rate of leavers. Our bank account increases by our deposits and decreases through our spending. Although they are familiar to us, lots of people can not distinguish clearly between them which lead to underestimation of time delays, policy resistance and other related issues.

Figure 3 is a simple example of stock and flows diagram showing the typical symbols used in the stock and flows diagram.

The stock in this example is the number of employees in a firm. This is shown as a rectangle. The hiring rate is the inflow represented by a pipe (arrow) adding to the stock with a kind of valve controlling the inflow. People leaving the firm is another flow which subtract from the stock of employees with a valve controlling the outflow of employees. Clouds represent the source (the stock from which a flow originating outside the boundary of the model arises), and the sinks (the stocks into which the flows leaving the model boundary drain) for the flows. Sterman (2000) addressed the contribution of stocks to dynamics. He explained how stocks can be critical in generating the dynamics of systems. We will summarize his reasons as follows:

Stocks Characterize the State of the System and Provide the Basis for Actions

Stocks provide the decision makers in any system about the state of their systems providing them with the needed information to act. For example; the balance sheet summarize the financial health of a firm by proving the decision makers with reports about the value of cash, inventory, account receivable and debts etc than can be helpful for future decisions such as issuing new loans, paying dividends and controlling other variables.

Figure 3. Stock and flows diagram

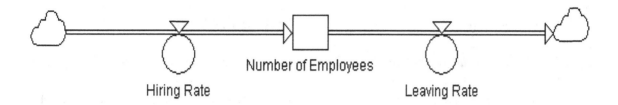

Stocks Provide Systems
with Inertia and Memory

Because stocks accumulate past events, these events persist only if there is no changes happen to the stock through its inflow and outflow. Our beliefs and memories are stocks that show our mental states. They persist over time, generating inertia and continuity in out attitudes and behaviours.

Stocks are the Source of Delays

There is a difference between the time we mail a letter and the time it is received. During this interval, my letter resides in a stock of letters. There is a lag between the letters send (input) and the letters received (output). This is the delay. All delays involve stocks.

Stocks Create Disequilibrium Dynamics

Inflows and outflows usually not equals because they are governed by different decisions which lead to disequilibrium dynamics in the system. Sterman argued that understanding the nature and stability of these dynamics is one of purposes of a system dynamics model. He states "whenever two coupled activities are controlled by different decision makers, involve different resources, and are subject to different random shocks, a buffer or stock between them must exist, accumulating the difference. As these stocks vary, information about the size of the buffer will feed back in various ways to influence the inflows and outflows. Often, these feedbacks will operate to bring the stock into balance. Whether and how equilibrium is achieved cannot be assumed but is an emergent property of the whole system as its many different feedback loops interact simultaneously "(Sterman 2000).

SYSTEM DYNAMICS SOFTWARE

There is lots of user friendly software available now that allows conversion of causal loop diagram and stocks and flows diagram into sophisticated computer simulation of the problems or issues being investigated. Examples of these different kinds of software are DYNAMO, STELLA, ITHINK, VENSIM and POWERSIM (the latest is being used in this research chapter).

Initial values are identified for the stocks, variables values are also identified for the relationships, and the structural relationships are determined between the variables using constants, graphical relationships and mathematical functions where appropriate.

THE PROCESS OF BUILDING SYSTEM DYNAMICS MODEL

Modelling purpose is to solve a problem and also to gain insight into the real problem to design effective policies in a real world, with all its ambiguity, messiness, time pressure and inter-personal conflict. It is a feedback process, not a linear sequence of steps.

Models are very important tools for managers that enable them to design their organisations, shaping its structure, strategies and design rules and enable them to take different decisions in their organisations. It is an effective tool in promoting system thinking in an organisation.

In order to be in a position to employ that tool it is necessary that managers and modellers at least understand the basic principles in designing and building a system dynamics model. Some authors (Sterman 2000 Vennix 1996) distinguished several stages in building a system dynamics model.

These stages are summarized as follows.

Problem Identification

It is the most important step in the building process. We need a clear purpose in order to build any model and we should focus on the problem rather than a system. The modeller must ask: what is the problem? Why is it a problem? What are the main concepts and variable we must consider? Problem starts time and how far in the future should we consider? What is the historical and future behaviour of the variables under investigation?

Dynamic Hypothesis Formulation

The next step is to formulate a dynamic hypothesises that explain both the current theories of the problem and as endogenous feedback interactions and structure. Also the modeller should construct different maps based on the previous analysis such as causal loop diagram, stock and flows diagram, model boundary diagram and other tools.

Simulation Model

This step is to formulate the simulation model and test it for consistency with the purpose and estimate the parameters, equations and studying the system structure to improve our understanding of the system.

Testing the Model

Testing the model is about comparing the model behaviour after simulation with the actual behaviour of the system to make sure that all variables correspond to a meaningful concept in the real world and to test whether our model is robust through testing it under extreme conditions (conditions that never exist in the real world) which enable the modeller to discover the flaws in his model and set the stage for improved understanding.

Design and Evaluate Policies for Improvement

After developing confidence in the model in terms of its structure and behaviour, the modeller can design and evaluate different policies and create strategies and decision rules and study the effect of the policies and their interactions and examine the strength of policies under different scenarios which is known as sensitivity analysis.

Figure 4 recasts the previous modelling stages. These stages are iterative and represent a continual process.

CONSTRUCTING THE SIMULATOR USING A SYSTEM DYNAMICS MODEL

Introduction

The aim of this section is to develop, model and understand the critical influences of the variables which determine the basic characteristics of any small firm. The main motivations is to bring dynamic perspectives and better understanding and analysis of small companies and enable the risk analyst to gain a deeper insight of how this

Figure 4. Modelling process

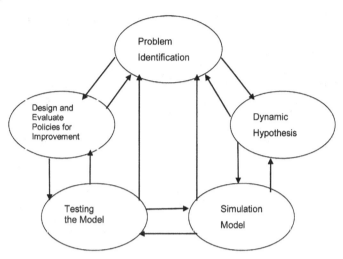

company would react under certain conditions and different scenarios.

The first part in building the Simulator is constructing the system dynamics model. This model replicates the current method in calculating the financial ratios based on system dynamics features such as Delays, feedback and causal relations which are included in the model to help the analyst to understand the interactions between the company's variables. The model was constructed using Powersim Studio 2005.

Model Boundary

Setting the model boundary is very important tool in system dynamics. It helps the modeller to represent the model's causal structure and summarizes the scope of the model. Sterman (2000) said "A broad model boundary that captures important feedbacks is more important than a lot of details in the specification of individual component".

Figure 5 depicts the Boundary of the System Dynamics model boundary which captures the scope of my study.

Three types of factors are distinguished in this section. Endogenous factors (arising from within) are the key variables that are embodied within the feedback structure. Exogenous factors

(arising from without) are the constant factors in the model that cannot change by themselves over the simulation. These factors are controlled and changed by the analyst himself according to a set of "What if" scenarios when he interacts with the Simulator to test the result of his actions and decisions on the firm's future performance.

The above figure shows a list of factors that have not been included in the model. These are factors that are outside our control and their effects are reflected in the values given to the exogenous factors. For example the interest rate would reflect any inflation.

Model Description

In this section, a simplified generic system dynamics model of a small firm has been built. This model is of firms which import or buy finished goods and sells these goods without doing any production processes.

It replicates the current method used in the Jordanian banks in calculating the financial ratios which is considered a very important performance measures for assessing a firm's financial position, but this prototype model is better than the current methods in generating the financial ratios because it has an interactive user interface that allows

Figure 5. The system dynamics model boundary

Excluded Factors	Exogenous Factors	Endogenous Factors
• Rival's actions	• Work force Productivity	• Major Financial Ratios (Net profit, Return on Equity....etc)
• Government's actions	• Interest Rate	
• Other stockholder's actions	• Tax Rate	
• International laws for Export	• Raw material's Price	• Firm's Assets and Liabilities
• Inflation Rate	• Selling price	
	• New loans	• Increasing Bank Credit
	• Sales Orders	• Cash Flow
	• Loan Repayment	• Cash Deficit
	• Credit given to Customers	
	• Credit given to the firm	

the analyst not only to get the ratios and analyse them, but also to have the chance to analyse the main variables that affect and changes these ratios over time. These variables are considered in the model as exogenous factors (arising from without) and they do not change by themselves over the simulation.

The next sections will describe the financial model contents such as causal loop diagram, stock and flows diagram and the model's simulator and interface.

Causal Loop Diagram

Figure 6 shows the Causal Loop Diagram of the firm which is consists of four Reinforcing Loops (R) and Six Balancing Loops (B). These loops represent the major Feedback structure of any small production firm .Each causal loop is explained in the following figures.

Figure 7 shows the first three reinforcing loops. They depict the effect of increasing sales orders in the firm. Simulating any increase in the firm's sales orders will increase the sales and eventually increases the cash in the firm. The firm's bank balance will increase which provides more liquidity to the firm. It also improves its financial

solvency which makes the firm optimistic about its future sales orders, so it motivates its customers and brings new customers. This can be done by giving them credit facilities in paying the price of their purchases which creates the first reinforcing loop (R1). Improving the firm's solvency is a good indication of the firm's eligibility for new loans or for an increase in the line of credit which causes the cash to increase another time (R2).

The third reinforcing loop represents another effect of increasing the sales which is reducing the total cost per product as the fixed cost will still the same while the sales increase. This of course will cause a decrease in the product price which makes the product attractive in the market and attract new buyers to place more orders

The financial cost will increase because the firm will pays the bank more interests as it is getting new loans (or withdrawing from its line of credit) which decrease the cash and creates the first balancing loop(B1) in figure 8. Another balancing one in the figure is when the account receivables increases as the firm offers more credit facilities to its customers, this increase will have two effects, it decreases the cash as the collected cash will decrease (B2), it also will increase the risk of bad debts which decreases both the col-

Figure 6. The causal loop diagram of a production firm

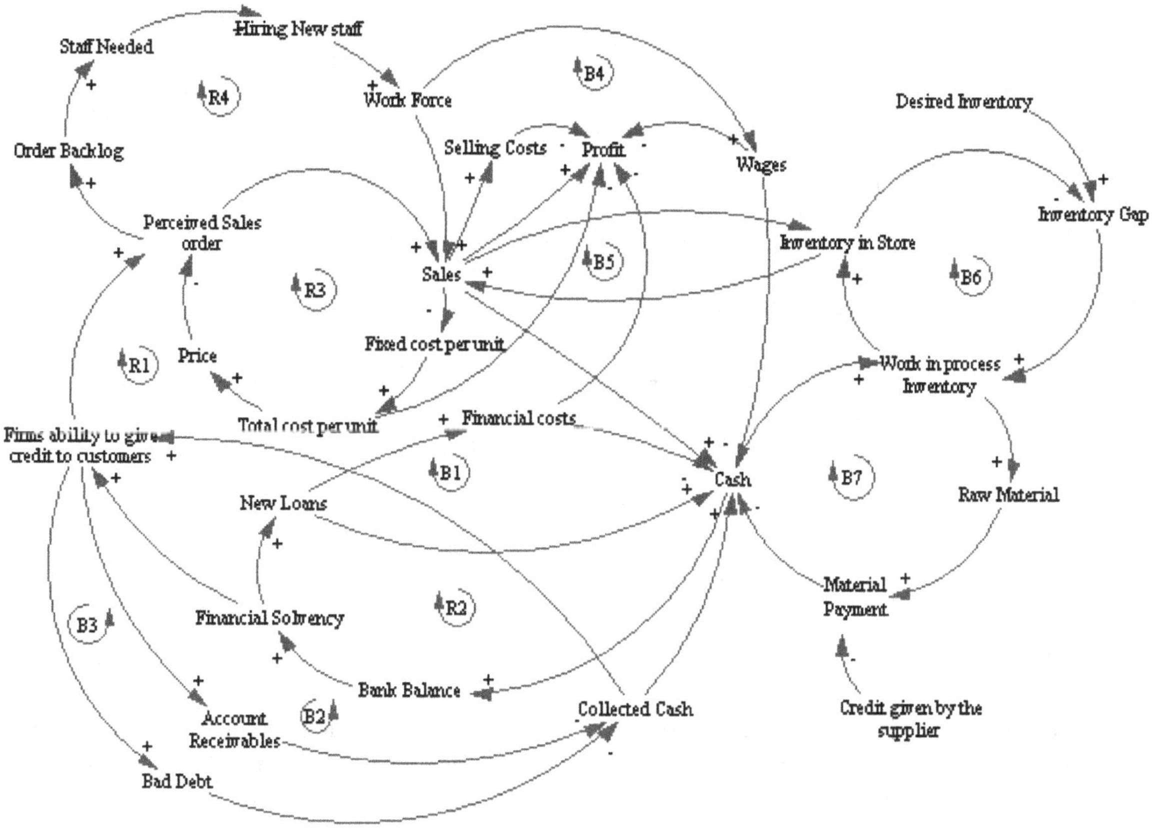

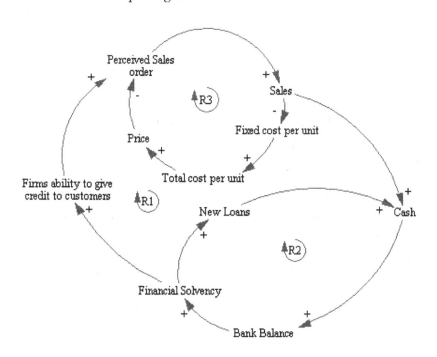

Figure 7. R1, R2 and R3 causal loops diagram

Figure 8. B1, B2 and B3 causal loops diagram

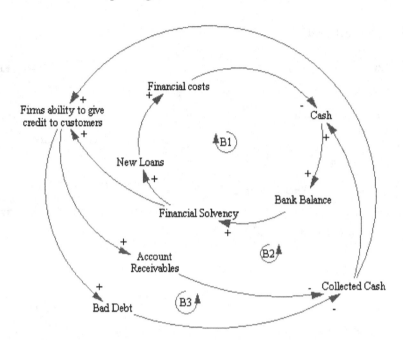

lected cash from customers and the cash balance in the firm (B3).

Receiving more sales orders will create a backlog as the firm needs more capacity and more staff to fulfil these new orders, so the firm will start hiring new staff to work at the firm which increases the sales and the financial solvency again and encourages the customers to place more and more orders by giving them credit facilities as the capacity is improving by hiring new staff. This is the fourth reinforcing loop (R4). But this reinforcing loop is not continuous as the firm cannot keep hiring staff always without any consequences.

Actually increasing the Workforce will increase the wages paid by the firm which decreases the cash and tighten the credit facilities given to the customer which in turn decreases the sales orders and reduces hiring new staff and so on. This is the balancing loop (B4) in figure 9.

Cash is considered the main variable in the firm as the firm uses cash to pay its loan repayment, wages, cost of its purchases and running the operations in the firm without any liquidity problems. Increasing the cash will push the firm to expand and buy more materials from suppliers and convert these materials into finished goods, these purchases reduces the cash as the firm has to pay its purchases cost to the supplier. These payments depend on the credit given to the firm by its suppliers of how much the percentage of cash sales. For instant, if the firm have to pay 100% of its purchases in cash, the cash will decrease and then the firm's purchases from the supplier will be less that the case in which the firm have to pay nothing to receive its material purchases. This is the balancing loop (B7).

The balancing loop (B5) represents the relation between sales and the inventory in stores. The more products in the firm's store the more completed sales. Delivering the sales to the buyers will decrease the inventory in store which creates a inventory gap between the quantity of products are available in the firm's store and the desired inventory level (B6). Figure 10 shows these three balancing loops.

Figure 9. R4 and B4 causal loops diagram

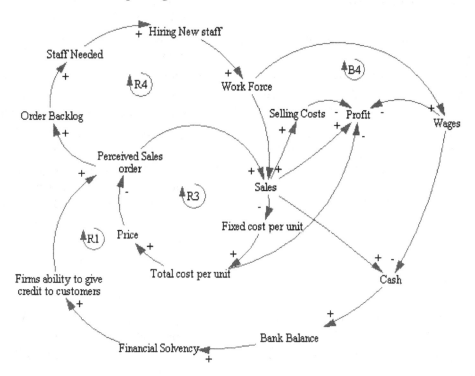

Figure 10. B5, B6 and b7 causal loop diagram

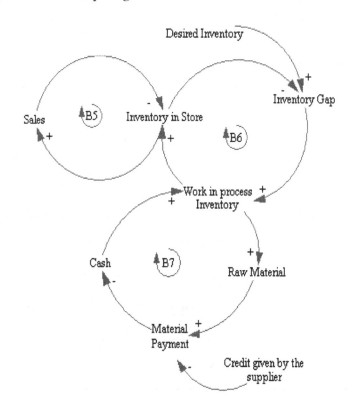

Stocks and Flows Diagram

The production firm model as mentioned before is an enlargement and enhancement of the prototype model which consists of several sectors which considered the main variables in each small manufactures firm that produce finished goods to the market.

Figure 11 represents the sales orders structure which is basically the market demand on the firm's product. The sales orders level was set to be a constant in the model to enable the credit analyst to simulate the tested or assumed level and to observe the impact of any simulated sales orders on the different variables and financial measures, and this the main objective for the varying types of parameters in the model.

The structure shows also the sales orders backlog in the firm which is increased by receiving new orders and decreases by selling and shipping products to the customers.

The expected orders stock represents the future expectations about the sales orders level that eventually will determines the desired finished goods inventory level and the desired production rate to make sure that the production and the inventory levels are constraint by the expected future demand.

The future demand expectations establish the need to produce more finished goods from materials inventory to fulfil these orders and ship the sales to the customers. As shown in Figure 12, starting the production is limited of the materials inventory in stock, staff capacity and the desired production rate, while selling new products is limited of how much finished products there are in stores and on the firm's capacity to fulfil the existing demand.

Figure 13 represents the workforce structure which increases by hiring new staff and decreases by staff leaving the firm. The desired level of workforce is determined by what is the desired level of production and the productivity of its staff in producing finished goods and sells them.

As the firm starts its production processes, the supply of materials starts as well according to the production level and the level of the desired and actual material inventory as shown in Figure 14

Figure 11. Sales orders structure

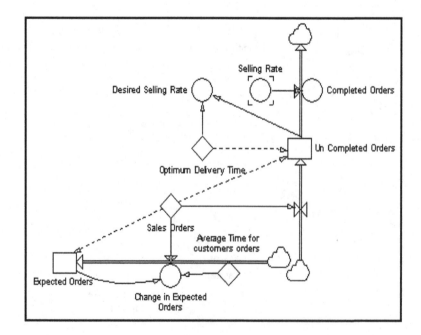

Figure 12. Production structure

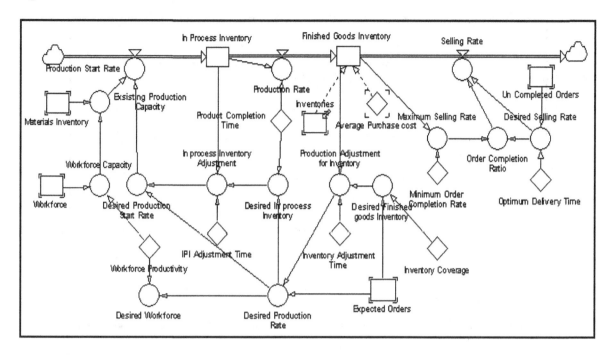

Figure 13. Workforce structure

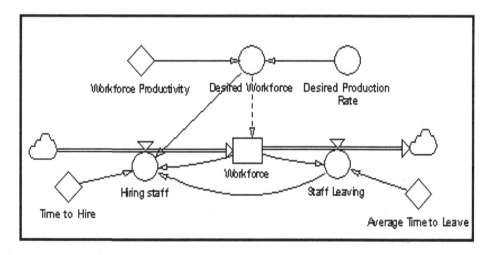

to run the productions without any disruption. Therefore, the analyst should consider all the variables that might affect supplying the material at the right time. For example, materials order completion rate and the delay in receiving the purchased materials.

The firm pays for its materials purchases according to the credit given by the supplier which determines the payments schedule. As shown in Figure 15, new material purchases from supplier increases the account payable, while the payments to supplier decrease it.

Figure 14. Raw material inventory structure

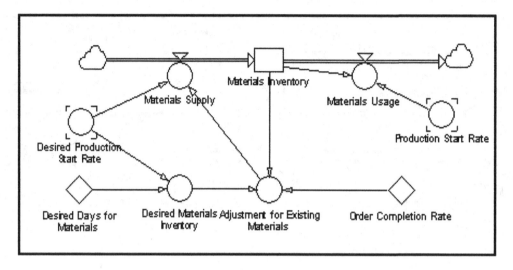

Figure 15. Account payable structure

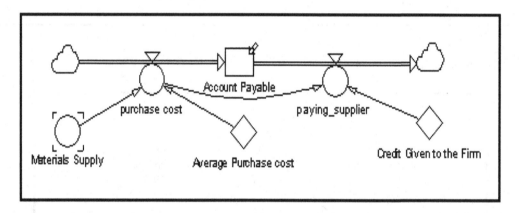

Figure 16 shows the account receivable structure which represents the total monies owed the firm by its customers on credit sales made to them. It depends mainly on the credit policy given to the customer to encourage them to increase their purchases from the firm. The effect of credit policy on the firm is explained in next sections in many aspects.

Collecting the sales revenue from the customers, new loans and the owner's investment are the main income to the firm which increases the cash as shown in figure 17. The cash is the most liquid asset in the firm that is always ready to be used to pay bills, pay supplier, repayment of bank loans and much more expected and unexpected outlays.

If the cash is not enough to meet the firm's obligations, the firm will withdraw cash from its line of credit increasing the bank credit stock. Figure 18 represents the bank credit structure which decreases by the firm's repayments of loan and increases by using more cash from the bank credit which is constraint by its line of credit which Gitman (2000) defined as "An agreement between a commercial bank and a business specifying the amount of un secured short-term borrowing the

Figure 16. Account receivables structure

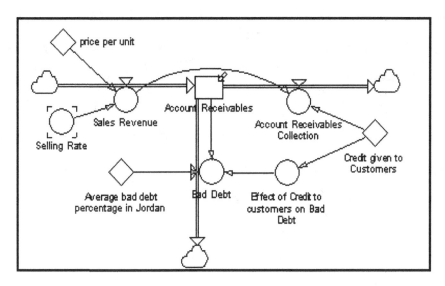

Figure 17. Cash structure

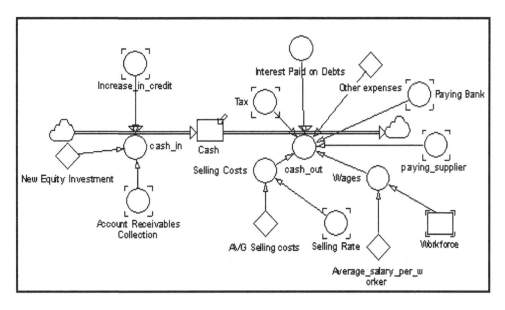

bank will make available to the firm over a given period of time"

A financial summary of the firm's operating results during each period is shown in figure 19 which represents the income structure for the firm which could be provided to the analyst as an income statement report as shown in the final Simulator.

Another significant part in measuring the firm's performance is to analyse the firm's cash flow. Gitman (2000) divided the firm's cash flow into three main flows which are shown in figure 20. These flows are: operating flows which are cash inflows and outflows related to the production and sales. Secondly are the investment flows which are the cash flows related to purchase or sale of

Figure 18. Bank credit structure

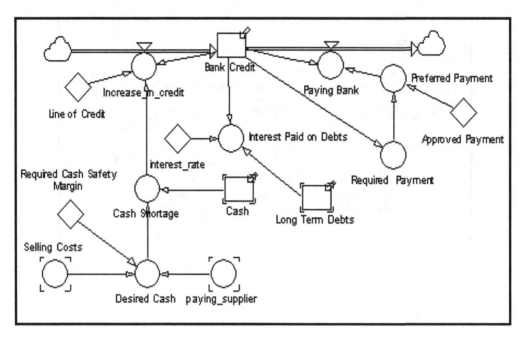

Figure 19. Income structure

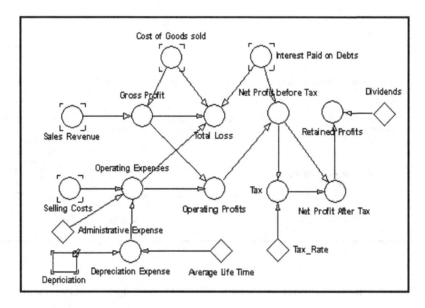

the firm's assets and finally the financing flows which are the cash flows related to debt and equity and the transactions related to them.

The Statement of cash flows would be available as a report to credit analyst to enable him to assess whether any development have occurred in the firm that are contrary to the firm's policy and to evaluate progress in the firm towards projected goals. To be able to provide financial reports to the credit analyst in the Simulator, some few

Figure 20. Cash flow structure

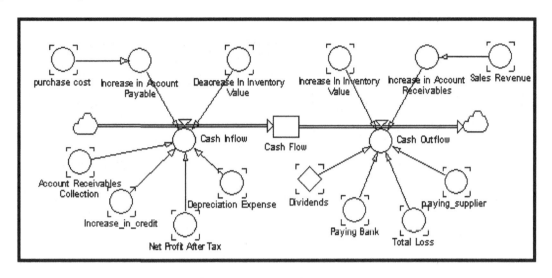

Figure 21. Assets & liabilities structure

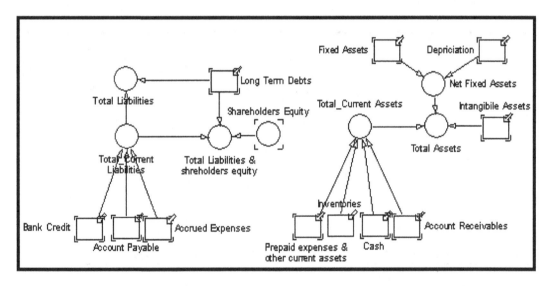

structures are produced such as figure 21 which represents the main variables in the balance sheet which are the assets and the liabilities structures as shown in the next figure.

Figure 22 illustrates the inventory value structure. The inventory in the firm includes raw materials, in process inventory and the finished goods inventory held by the firm. The structure for each type of inventory was shown in previous figures.

As a part of the performance measures which the credit analyst used to analyse the firm's performance is calculating and interpreting the common financial ratios. The inputs to ratio analysis are mainly the figures in both the financial statement and the income statement.

In the next figures, four categories of financial ratios are shown which are: Profitability ratios, activity ratios, liquidity ratios and debt ratios.

Figure 22. Inventory value structure

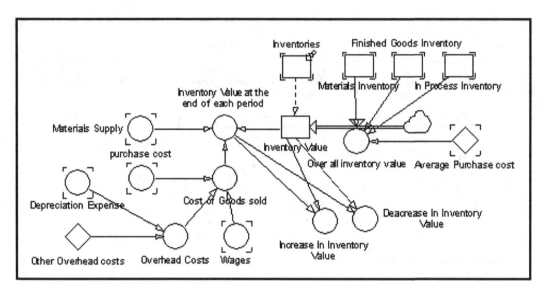

Figure 23. Profitability ratios

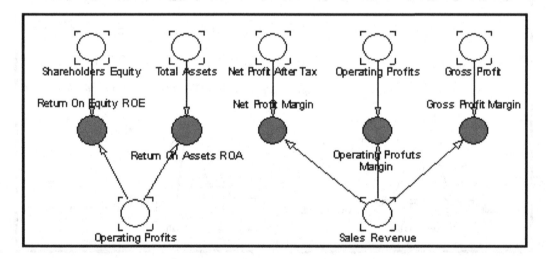

Figure 23 shows the basic profitability ratios which measure the return and evaluate the firm's earning with respects to the level of sales, level of assets, or the owners. The banks are always concern about the firm's future so they pay a close attention to any changes in the profit level during the year.

The next category is represented in figure 24 which are the activity ratios that "Measure the speed with which the various accounts are converted into sales or cash" (Gitman 2000). The main activity ratios in this part are the inventory turn over, average collection period and account payable turnover.

In figure 25, the basic liquidity ratios are shown to help the credit analyst to measure the firm's ability to meet its short-term commitments as they come due which refer mainly to the solvency of

Figure 24. Activity ratios

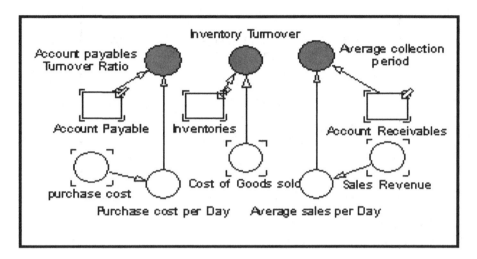

Figure 25. Liquidity ratios

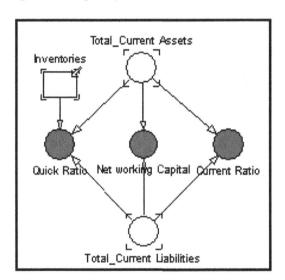

the firm's overall financial situation. The liquidity ratios used in the model are current ratio, quick ration and net working capital.

The last category of the financial ratios is the debt ratios which are shown in figure 26. Two debt ratios were used in the model to assess the debt position of the firm under investigation. These ratios are significant for the bank analyst, because the bank is usually concerns about the firm indebtedness and its ability to satisfy the claims of all its creditors.

Data

The data in this model is from these main sources:

The initial value for all the stocks in the model are the same as the values in the firm's last balance sheet which consists of the Assets (Cash, Inventory, Account Receivables, Prepaid expenses & other current assets, Fixed assets, Intangible Assets and Depreciation) and the Liabilities (Bank Credit, Account Payable, Accrued Expenses, Long Term Debts, Retained Earnings and so on)

Some of the Data are given by the firm it self such as selling Price, Material purchase cost, Usual sales orders, selling costs, Tax Rate, Interest Rate, or from other financial statement such as Income statement or profit and loss statement.

The Simulator

Currently, the analyst doesn't interact and doesn't have the access to change the model it self, but he will check the financial ratios and to test the effect of his decision on the financial ratios, whether

Figure 26. Debt ratios

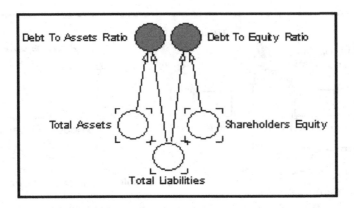

Figure 27. The user interface of the simulator

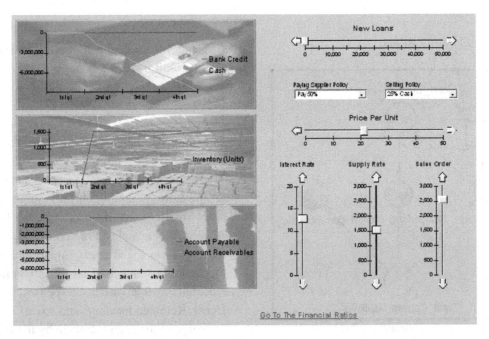

it's improving or not. In the first model, there are some variables that can be changed through interacting with the model's interface and observing the changes to the firm's performance over time. The changeable variables included in the interface are price per unit, new loans given to the firm, interest rate on loans, supply rate, sales orders, changing the payment policy whether the one given to the firm's customers or the one given to firm by its suppliers. Through this Simulator, the user would be able to switch between three main pages. The interface in which he can change the variables and display the main variables graphs, the financial ratio's page which shows the changes that might happen to each ratio every time step. Figure 27 shows the model's interface with the changing parameters and the graphs that help the user to get a better insight and to take his decision efficiently, while figure 28 displays the financial ratios report over the simulation period

Figure 28. The financial ratios report

Financial Ratios

Time	Quick Ratio	Return On Assets ROA	Return On Equity ROE	Debt To Equity Ratio	Debt To Assets Ratio	Current Ratio
01/02/2007	1.26	0.00 %	0.00 %	95.25 %	54.17 %	2.70
01/03/2007	1.23	1.20 %	2.17 %	99.67 %	55.29 %	2.55
01/04/2007	1.42	1.11 %	2.17 %	104.10 %	53.12 %	2.63
01/05/2007	1.58	1.03 %	2.17 %	108.52 %	51.27 %	2.70
01/06/2007	1.72	0.95 %	2.17 %	112.94 %	49.67 %	2.76
01/07/2007	1.84	0.89 %	2.17 %	117.36 %	48.28 %	2.81
01/08/2007	1.94	0.84 %	2.17 %	121.78 %	47.06 %	2.86
01/09/2007	2.03	0.79 %	2.17 %	126.20 %	45.98 %	2.90
01/10/2007	2.12	0.75 %	2.17 %	130.62 %	45.01 %	2.93
01/11/2007	2.19	0.71 %	2.17 %	135.04 %	44.15 %	2.96
01/12/2007	2.26	0.67 %	2.17 %	139.47 %	43.36 %	2.00
01/01/2008	2.32	0.64 %	2.17 %	143.89 %	42.66 %	3.02

Back to the Interface

and the changes that happened to each of these ratios every month. This Simulator switches to the new paradigm as discussed in chapter three. It switches from static to dynamic, reductionism to holism and from linear to non-linear thinking. It allows the analyst to observe the performance of the firm over the simulation time and analyse the significant interactions inside a firm.

The next figure 29 is the excel sheet table that provides the system dynamics model with the firm's past balance sheet. The variables in this table are connected directly to the model, and any changes happen on this sheet will immediately be transferred to the Simulator in case of changing the firm under investigation.

CONCLUSION

This chapter found that using new types of thinking in analysing small firms in Jordan is an effective method in gaining a deeper insight into any firm. A simulator has been built based on a system dynamics model which has been used by the analyst to interact with.

We found that the analyst got a better understanding of various interactions inside small firms through his ability to test different scenarios by interacting with the simulator's interface. The simulator enabled the analysts to get a deeper insight into the firm, predict the future behaviour under any potential shock and simulate and analyse any decision or policy that the firm will implement in the future before it is implemented in the real world.

This chapter found that if the bank's credit officer used the Simulator at the time of approving the loan; his would make better credit decision based on deep understanding of the interconnections inside the firm and the organisational structure assessment.

Figure 29. The Excel sheet

Balance Sheet	
Assets	
Cash	400
Account Receivables	400
Inventories	600
Prepaid expenses & other current assets	600
Fixed Assets	2500
Depreciation	1300
Intangible Assets	0
Total Assets	3200
Liabilities	
Account Payable	700
Bank Credit	600
Accrued Expenses	100
Long Term Debts	600
Common Stock	600
Additional Paid In Capital	0
Retained Earnings	600
Total Liabilities	3200

REFERENCES

Anderson, V., & Johnson, L. (1997). *Systems thinking tools: from concepts to causal loops.* Waltham, MA: Pegasus Communications, Inc.

Bach, M. (2003). Surviving in an environment of financial indiscipline: a case study from a transition country. *System Dynamics Review, 19*(1), 47–74. doi:10.1002/sdr.253

Bianchi, C., & Bivona, E. (1999). Commercial and financial policies in small and micro family firms: the small business growth management flight simulator. *Simulation and gaming.* Thousand Oaks, CA: Sage publications.

Brehmer, B. (1992). Dynamic decision making: human control of complex systems. *Acta Psychologica, 81*, 211–241. doi:10.1016/0001-6918(92)90019-A

Breierova, L. & Choudhari, M. (1996). An introduction to sensitivity analysis. *MIT system dynamics in education project.*

Cebenoyan, A., & Strahan, P. (2004). Risk management, capital structure and Lending at banks. *Journal of Banking & Finance, 28*, 19–43. doi:10.1016/S0378-4266(02)00391-6

Forrester, J. (1961). *Industrial Dynamics.* New York: MIT Press and Wiley Inc.

Forrester, J. (1992). System dynamics, systems thinking, and soft OR. *System Dynamics Review, 10*(2).

Gitman, L. (2000). *Managerial Finance: Brief.* Reading, MA: Addison-Wesley.

Jackson, M. (2003). *System Thinking: Creative Holism for Managers.* Chichester, UK: Wiley.

Jimenez, G. & Saurian, J. (2003). Collateral, type of lender and relationship banking as determinants of credit risk. *Journal of banking and finance.*

Lane, D. (1997). Invited reviews on system dynamics. *The Journal of the Operational Research Society, 48*, 1254–1259.

Lyneis, J. (2000). System dynamics for market forecasting and structural analysis. *System Dynamics Review*, *16*(1), 3–25. doi:10.1002/(SICI)1099-1727(200021)16:1<3::AID-SDR183>3.0.CO;2-5

Maani, K., & Cavana, R. (2000). S*ystems thinking and modelling: understanding change and complexity.* New Zealand: Pearson Education, New Zealand.

Martin, L. (1997). Mistakes and Misunderstandings. *System Dynamics in Education Project.* System Dynamics Group, Sloan School of Management, Massachusetts Institute of Technology, Cambridge, MA.

Senge, P. (1990). *The Fifth Discipline, The art & practice of learning organisation.* New York.

Sterman, J. (1992). *Teaching Takes Off, Flight Simulator for Management Education, the Beer Game.* Sloan school of Management, Massachusetts Institute of Technology, Cambridge, MA.

Vennix, J. (1996). *Group model building: facilitating team learning using system dynamics.* Chichester, UK: Wiley

Wolstenholme, E. (1990). *System Enquiry: a system dynamics approach.* Wiley: New York.

KEY TERMS AND DEFINITIONS

Causal Loop Diagram: Causal loop diagrams (CLDs) are a kind of systems thinking tool. These diagrams consist of arrows connecting variables (things that change over time) in a way that shows how one variable affects another

Financial Ratios: Financial ratios are a valuable and easy way to interpret the numbers found in statements. It can help to answer critical questions such as whether the business is carrying excess debt or inventory, whether customers are paying according to terms, whether the operating expenses are too high and whether the company assets are being used properly to generate income. When computing financial relationships, a good indication of the company's financial strengths and weaknesses becomes clear. Examining these ratios over time provides some insight as to how effectively the business is being operated.

Simulator: A computer simulation is an attempt to model a real-life or hypothetical situation on a computer so that it can be studied to see how the system works. By changing variable, prediction and testing different scenarios.

Simulator's Interface: The interface or the user interface is the aggregate of means by which the user interacts with the system, a particular machine, device, computer program or other complex tools. The simulator in this research is constructed based on the simulation model. It is interactive and provides managers with a user interface that allows them to experiment with the model.

Stock and Flows Diagram: Stock and flow diagrams provide a bridge to system dynamics modeling and simulation. Basically Stock and flow diagrams contain specific symbols and components representing the structure of a system. Stocks are things that can accumulate—(Think of a stock as a bathtub.) Flows represent rates of change—(Think of a flow as a bathtub faucet, which adds to the stock, or a bathtub drain, which reduces the stock.) These diagrams also contain "clouds," which represent the boundaries of the problem or system in question

System Dynamics Model: It's a computer simulation model based on system dynamics features that aim to confirm that the structure hypothesized can lead to the observed behaviour and to test the effects of alternative policies on key variables over time. Modeling purpose is to solve a problem and also to gain insight into the real problem to design effective policies in a real world, with all its ambiguity, messiness, time pressure and interpersonal conflict. It is a feedback process, not a linear sequence of steps. System dynamics models are very important tools for managers that enable them to design their organizations, shaping its structure, strategies and design rules and enable them to take different decisions in their organizations. It is an effective tool in promoting system thinking in an organization.

System Dynamics: System dynamics is an approach to understanding the behaviour of over time. It deals with internal feedback loops and time delays that affect the behaviour of the entire system. It also helps the decision maker untangle the complexity of the connections between various policy variables by providing a new language and set of tools to describe. Then it does this by modeling the cause and effect relationships among these variables

Systems Thinking: Systems thinking, in contrast, focuses on how the thing being studied interacts with the other constituents of the system—a set of elements that interact to produce behaviour—of which it is a part. This means that instead of isolating smaller and smaller parts of the system being studied, systems thinking works by expanding its view to take into account larger and larger numbers of interactions as an issue is being studied. This results in sometimes strikingly different conclusions than those generated by traditional forms of analysis, especially when what is being studied is dynamically complex or has a great deal of feedback from other sources, internal or external. Systems thinking allows people to make their understanding of social systems explicit and improve them in the same way that people can use engineering principles to make explicit and improve their understanding of mechanical systems.

Chapter 22
The State of Computer Simulation Applications in Construction

Mohamed Marzouk
Cairo University, Egypt

ABSTRACT

Construction operations are performed under different working conditions including (but not limited to) unexpected weather conditions, equipment breakdown, delays in procurement, etc. As such, computer simulation is considered an appropriate technique for modeling the randomness of construction operations. Several construction processes and operations have been modeled utilizing computer simulation such as earthmoving, construction of bridges and tunnels, concrete placement operations, paving processes, and coordination of cranes operations. This chapter presents an overview of computer simulation efforts that have been performed in the area of construction engineering and management. Also, it presents two computer simulation applications in construction; earthmoving and construction of bridges' decks. Comprehensive case studies are worked out to illustrate the practicality of using computer simulation in scheduling construction projects, taking into account the associated uncertainties inherited in construction operations.

INTRODUCTION

Simulation is one of the techniques that has been used to model uncertainties involved in construction operations. Although simulation is a powerful tool for modeling construction operations, the application of simulation is still limited in the construction domain. This has generally been attributed to the

difficulty in learning and applying simulation languages to industry (Sawhney and AbouRizk 1996, Oloufa et al 1998, Touran 1990). The simulation process is an iterative process which involves different steps. It has been defined as "imitation of a real-world process or system over time" (Banks et al 2000). Modeling construction operations utilizing discrete event simulation, requires the modeler to define three main elements (Schriber and Brunner 1999): project, experiments and replications (see

DOI: 10.4018/978-1-60566-774-4.ch022

Figure 1). A "*project*" is performed to study a certain operation which has specific characteristics, for example, an earthmoving operation that contains a definite scope of work and specific road characterisitics. An "*experiment*" represents one alternative of the project under consideration by changing the resources assigned for the execution of the project and/or its individual activities. A "*replication*" represents one execution of an experiment within the project.

Modeling utilizing simulation can be applied either in a general or special purpose simulation environment. General purpose simulation (GPS) is based on formulating a simulation model for the system under study, running the simulation and analyzing the results in order to decide whether the system is acceptable or not. In case of being unacceptable, the process is re-iterated and a new alternative system is considered. Different GPS software systems have been developed for a wide range of industries: AweSim (Pritsker et al 1997) and GPSS/H (Crain 1997); for construction: Micro-CYCLONE (Halpin and Riggs 1992) and STROBOSCOPE (Martinez 1996). Special

Figure 1. Elements of discrete event simulation

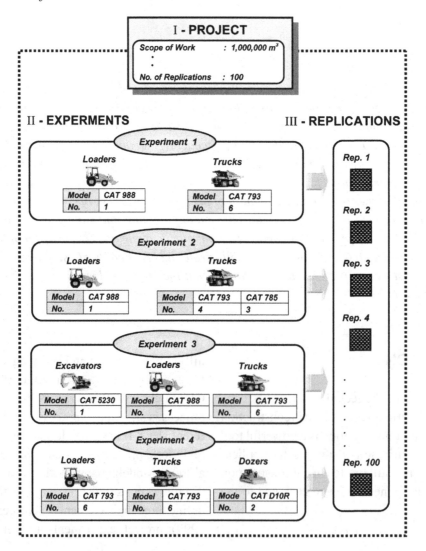

purpose simulation (SPS) is based on creation of a platform or a template for a specific domain of application (Marzouk and Moselhi 2000, AbouRizk and Hajjar 1998). The steps for simulation, in this case, are the same as in the GPS case except for the first step (construct simulation model) since the platform has the characteristics and behavior of the system under study. Also, the modification is limited to the input parameter(s) of a pre-defined system and not to the characteristics and behavior of the system. This chapter presents a state of computer simulation applications in construction. Then, it describes in details two construction applications that have been modeled using computer simulation. These applications are earthmoving and construction of bridges decks.

Background

Considerable efforts have been made to model construction operations utilizing simulation. These include Halpin (1977), Paulson (1978), Ioannou (1989), Oloufa (1993), Tommelein et al (1994), Sawhney and abouRizk (1995), Shi (1995), Martinez (1996), McCabe (1997), Oloufa et al (1998), Hajjar and AbouRizk (1999). CYCLONE, CYCLic Operation Network (Halpin 1977), is a modeling system that provides a quantitative way of viewing, planning, analyzing and controlling construction processes and their respective operations. CYCLONE is a network simulation language that models construction activities which have a cyclic or repetitive nature. CYCLONE consists of six basic elements (see Figure 2): 1) *NORMAL* which represents an unconstrained work task; 2) *COMBI* which represents a constrained work task; 3) *QUEUE* which represents a waiting location for resources; 4) *FUNCTION* which describes a process function (generation or consolidation); 5) *COUNTER* which controls the iterations of the cyclic operation; and 6) *ARCS* which represent the flow logic.

Different simulation implementations have been developed utilizing the CYCLONE which

include INSIGHT (Paulson 1978), UM_CYLONE (Ioannou 1989), and Micro-CYCLONE (Halpin and Riggs 1992). Several construction processes and operations have been modeled utilizing CYCLONE: selecting loader-truck fleets (Farid and Koning 1994); construction of cable-stayed bridges (Abraham and Halpin 1998, Huang et al 1994); resolving construction disputes (AbouRizk and Dozzi 1993); concrete placement operations (Vanegas et al 1993); placing and finishing slab units (Hason 1994); and paving processes (Lluch and Halpin 1982, Gowda at al 1998). Oloufa (1993) proposed an object-oriented approach for simulating construction operations. In this approach, the system at hand is modeled by creating objects of classes which represent the system's resources and entities. These objects are interacting and communicating amongst one another via message transfer. He developed a simulation language (MODSIM) dedicated to earthmoving operations.

Tommelein et al (1994) developed an object-oriented system (CIPROS) that models construction processes by matching resource properties to those of design components. Two types of resources were distinguished in this model: product components and construction resources. Product components are design element classes which form the process being modeled. They are defined for the contractor by plans and specifications. On the other hand, construction resources are temporary equipment and material that are used during construction. In order to create a simulation model utilizing the CIPROS, the user has to go through different steps: 1) define project design and specification; 2) create activity-level plan and relate activity; 4) initialize product components; 5) identify construction resources; 6) construct simulation network (formation of the elemental simulation networks which describe the methods of construction); and finally, 7) run simulation.

HSM (Sawhney and AbouRizk 1995, Sawhney and AbouRizk 1996) is a hierarchical simulation modeling for planning construction projects which combines the concepts of work breakdown struc-

Figure 2. CYCLONE Modeling Elements (adapted from Halpin 1977)

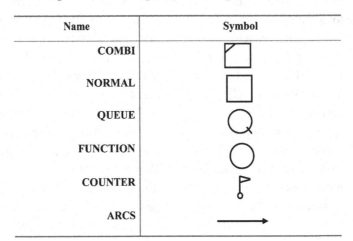

Name	Symbol
COMBI	
NORMAL	
QUEUE	
FUNCTION	
COUNTER	
ARCS	

ture and process modeling. Modeling a project via HSM requires performing different stages: 1) divide the project into hierarchical structure (project, operations, and processes); 2) create a resource library for the project (names, quantity, cost, etc.); 3) identify the sequence of operations and links (serial, parallel, cyclic, or hammock links); 4) perform process modeling utilizing the CYCLONE modeling elements along with added ones dedicated to resources and linkages of process; and finally 5) extend the model to a common level in order to run simulation.

RBM (Shi 1995, Shi and AbouRizk 1997) is a resource-based modeling for construction simulation which defines the operating processes into atomic models. For developing a model utilizing RBM, three steps should be performed: 1) define resource library and specify different atomic models along with their input and output ports; 2) define project specifications including system specifications (involving r-processes "process-task level" and their connectivity, resource assignment and termination conditions); 3) model generation by formatting different r-processes into SLAM II network statements along with linkage transition among these r-processes whether direct (where entities can be routed directly to the following r-process) or indirect (where there is a need for a

conversion). Martinez and Ioannou (1999); and Martinez (1996) developed a general purpose simulation programming language (STROBO-SCOPE). To model construction operations utilizing STROBOSCOPE, the modeler needs to write a series of programming statements that defines the network modeling elements. STROBOSCOPE has different advantages including: 1) ability to access the state of the simulation (e.g. simulation time, number of entities waiting in their queues, etc.) and 2) ability to distinguish involved resources and entities. Several construction processes and operations have been modeled utilizing STROBO-SCOPE including: earthmoving (Ioannou 1999, Martinez 1998); location of temporary construction facilities (Tommelein 1999); and the impacts of changes for highway constructions (Cor and Martinez 1999).

McCabe (1997 and 1998) developed an automated modeling approach which integrates computer simulation and belief networks. Computer simulation is used to model construction operations, whereas, belief networks are utilized as a diagnostic tool to evaluate project performance indices such as: 1) queue length (QL); 2) queue wait (QW); 3) server quantity (SQ); 4) server utilization (SU); and 5) customer delay (CD). These indices are calculated from the simulation statistics, subsequently, the performance of the system is evaluated by the believe network in order to reach a corrective action. This corrective action includes modifying the number and/or capacity of the involved servers or entities in the model. Oloufa et al (1998) proposed a set of resource-based simulation libraries as an application of special purpose simulation (SPS). In this approach, simulation was performed by first selecting construction resources from the developed libraries, then linking the resources to define the logic which describes the interaction among the resources used. Different resource libraries are required to be defined in order to serve different applications. For example, the resource library for the shield tunneling (the selected implementation for their approach) contains different resources including TBM (tunnel boring machine), trains, trucks, different rail types, vertical conveyor, etc. Simphony (Hajjar and AbouRizk 1999) is a computer system for building special purpose construction simulation tools. Different simulation tools were implemented in the Simphony environment (AbouRizk and Hajjar 1998) including AP2-Earth for earthmoving analysis, CRUISER for aggregate production analysis, and CSD for optimization of construction dewatering operations. Chandrakanthi et. al. (2002) presented a model to predict waste generation rates, as well as to determine the economic advantages of recycling at construction sites. The model was developed to achieve the following:

- estimate the amount of waste that one specific project will generate using its project plan (stochastic activity schedule),
- quantify the reusable fraction of waste material,
- optimize the methods to sort, store and to transport the collected reusable or recyclable materials,
- identify the capacity, locations, and number of recycle bins required for a site, and

- identify costs for these operations and to optimize resource utilization in terms of labor and equipment for waste management.

Appleton et. al. (2002) presented a special purpose simulation template, dedicated for the tower crane operations. They modeled on-site management of the tower crane resource based on prioritized work tasks that need to be performed within a specified period of time. Elfving and Tommelein (2003) presented a model that uses various input scenarios to show how sensitive the procurement time is to the effects of multitasking and merge bias. The model determines the time required to procure complex equipment and to locate and size time buffers in the procurement process. Song and AbouRizk (2003) developed a system for building virtual fabrication shop models that can perform estimating, scheduling, and analyze production. The system is capable to define conceptual models for product, process, and the fabrication facility itself. It offers tools, such as product modeling, process modeling and planning, and a special purpose facility modeling tool, which allow users to implement these conceptual models. Lu and Chan (2004) modeled the effects of operational interruptions upon the system performance by applying Simplified Discrete Event Simulation Approach (SDESA). The developed SDESA modeling was illustrated with an application of earthmoving operation.

Lee and Pena-mora (2005) explored the use of system dynamics in identifying multiple feedback processes and softer aspects of managing errors and changes. The developed system was applied in a design-build highway project in Massachusetts. They concluded that the system dynamics approach can be an effective tool in understanding of complex and dynamic construction processes and in supporting the decision making process of making appropriate policies to improve construction performance. Boskers and AbouRizk (2005) presented a simulation-based model for assessing uncertainty associated with capital infrastructure projects. The proposed model accounts for expected fluctuations in the costs and durations of various work packages. Also, it accounts for the inflation of costs over time based on when the work packages occur. Zhang and Hammad (2007) presented a simulation model based on agents to coordinate crane operations where two cranes are working together. The model can dynamically control the kinematic action of two cranes, taking into consideration the functional constraints for safety and efficiency of operations. Hanna and Ruwanpura (2007) proposed simulation model that is capable to optimize resource requirements for a petrochemical project, based on standard discipline requirements and involvements. All above listed efforts are geared towards the use of computer simulation in construction. The following sections describe the developments made in two construction applications that have been modeled using computer simulation.

MODELING EARTHMOVING OPERATIONS

Problem Background

Earthmoving operations are commonly encountered in heavy civil engineering projects. In general, it is rare to find a construction project free of these operations. For large-scale projects (e.g. dams, highways, airports and mining), earthmoving operations are essential, frequently representing a sizable scope of work. Earthmoving operations are frequently performed under different job conditions, which may give rise to uncertainty. This includes equipment breakdown, inclement weather and unexpected site conditions. Traditional scheduling using network techniques (critical path method (CPM), precedence diagram method (PDM) and line of balance (LOB) does not directly take into account such uncertainties (Sawhney and AbouRizk 1995). Also, earthmoving operations have a cyclic nature which can

ideally be represented by simulation (Touran 1990). In fact, it is essential, in modeling these operations, to consider the dynamic interaction among the individual pieces of equipment in a production fleet.

System Description

A simulation system (*SimEarth)* has been designed and implemented in Microsoft environment as a special purpose tool for estimating time and cost of earthmoving operations (Marzouk and Moselhi 2004-a, Marzouk and Moselhi 2004-b, Marzouk and Moselhi 2003-a, Marzouk and Moselhi 2003-b, Marzouk and Moselhi 2002-a, Marzouk and Moselhi 2002-b, Marzouk 2002). The system consists of several components including EarthMoving Simulation Program (*EMSP*) which has been designed utilizing discrete event simulation (DEVS) (Banks 1998) and object-oriented modeling (Quatrani 1998, Deitel and Deitel 1998, Skansholm 1997). Different features of object-orientation have been employed including classes, objects, dynamic data structure, and polymorphism. The three-phase simulation (Pidd 1995) was employed instead of process interaction in order to control the dynamics of *EMSP* by tracking the activities of the simulated process. The three-phase simulation approach is considered most appropriate for object oriented simulation (OOS), specially when there are too many entities involved in the process being modeled to avoid synchronicity loss (Pidd 1995). The utilization of three-phase simulation and object-orientation in the developed engine are described subsequently.

EMSP tracks activities in three phases: phase 1 which advances simulation time to the next simulation event; phase 2 which carries out all due Bs; and phase 3 which carries out all possible Cs. Figure 3 depicts a number of activities being tracked by *EMSP* for an earthmoving operation that contains the main activities of load, haul, dump, and return. In Phase 1, *EMSP*'s first activity is removed and the simulation time is advanced to the next time. In Phase 2, all due B activities (bound to happen) are carried out. In Phase 3, all possible C activities (conditional) are performed. It should be noted that an activity (e.g. haul) may exist more than one time since it may be carried out by different entities (e.g. hauler ID = 2 and 3) as shown in Figure 3. In the design of *EMSP*, different types of classes have been defined to capture the properties of key objects in earthmoving operations. This includes objects of entities, resources, activities and stored simulation statistics. The classes are coded in Microsoft Visual C++ 6.0. The classes used in the design of *EMSP* are of two types: auxiliary and main (see Figure 4).

Auxiliary classes are connected to the main classes through either association or aggregation relationships, whereas, the main classes are connected to each other through inheritance relationships. The main classes of *EMSP* capture different situations according to the activities involved. Therefore, they represent different combinations of earthmoving activities. Figure 5 depicts the sequence diagram that shows the progression of message sending to the other classes in order to

perform a complete simulation run.

The main classes of *EMSP* represent an earthmoving operation that contains any combination of main and secondary activities, allowing interaction between equipment. The eight main classes which are: OPY_Simulate, OPE_Simulate, OSD_Simulate, OCT_Simulate, PS_Simulate, PC_Simulate, PSC_Simulate and SC_Simulate. The OPY_Simulate class represents an earthmoving operation that consists of the four main activities: load, haul, dump and return. It has been designed to act as a base class for the main classes used in *EMSP* (see Figure 4), benefiting from the inheritance feature of object-orientation. It also has both association and aggregation relationships with the auxiliary classes. The association relationship is used with the M_Queue, Activity, Activity_List, M_Activity, Hauled_Earth and Haul_Equip classes, whereas, the aggregation relationship is used with the Queue class (see Figure 4). Creating an object of the OPY_Simulate class and invoking its member functions provide a complete replication of a simulation experiment. During simulation replication, the follow-

Figure 3. Tracking of activities in EMSP

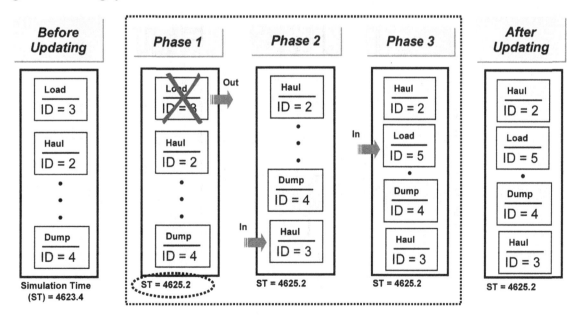

ing tasks are carried out: 1) importing input data from external files; 2) creating objects of haulers (entities) and loaders (resources); 3) initializing simulation and setting entities and resources into their queues; 4) defining the probability distributions for the duration of the activities involved; 5) adding and removing objects from the current activity list (*CAL*); 6) checking the termination condition for the replication (e.g. all earth has

been hauled); and 7) storing simulation statistics for further analysis.

Initiating simulation replication of an earth-moving operation that contains the four main activities, causes *EMSP* to allocate a memory space for an object of OPY_Simulate class. Seven member functions (principal functions) of that class will be called consecutively (see Figure 6):

Figure 4. EMSP main and auxiliary classes

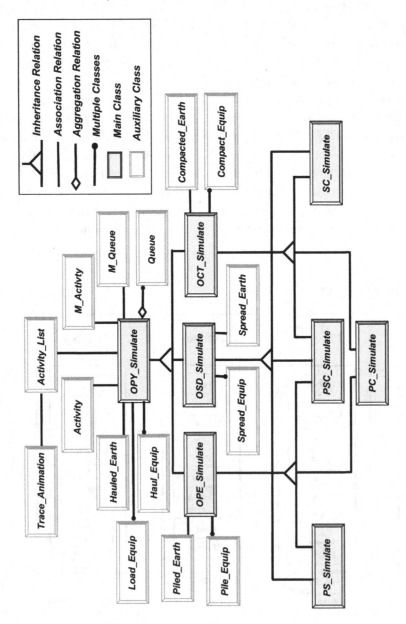

Figure 5. sequence diagram for message transfer from principal function

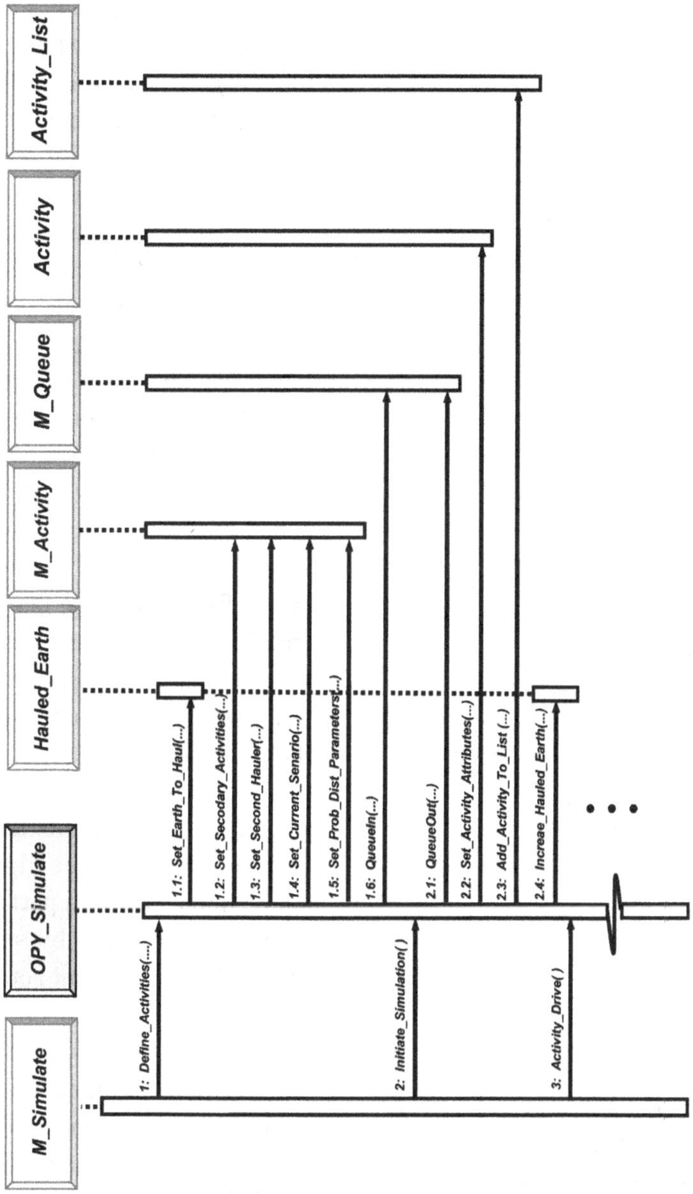

1) Define_Activities(..);
2) Initiate_Simulation();
3) Activity_Drive();
4) Store_QueueLength_Statistics(..);
5) Store_WaitTime_Statistics(..);
6) Store_Activities_Duration_Statistics(..);
7) Store_SecondHauler_Activities_ Statistics(..).

It should be noted that the last principal function is called only in the case of second hauler model existence.

Case Study

This case study considers the construction of Saint-Margurerite-3 (SM-3) dam. The dam is the

Figure 6. Flow of the principal functions

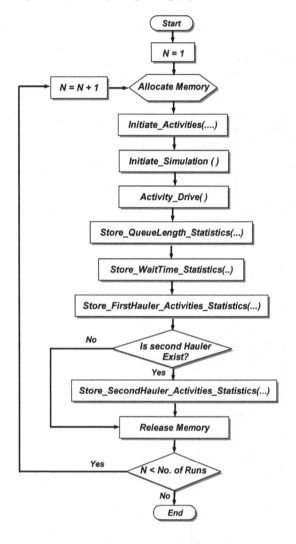

highest rockfill dam in the province of Quebec - Canada, located on "Saint-Marguerite" river, 700 km northeast of Montreal. SM-3 is a $2 billion project, developed to generate 2.7 terawatthours (TWh) of electricity annually. The project consists of four main components (Hydro-Quebec 1999): 1) a rockfill dam, 2) an 882-megawatt (MW) power station, 3) a headrace tunnel to direct water to the power station and 4) a spillway to discharge excess water from the reservoir. The dam location was chosen to benefit from a 330 m water head, seven times the height of Niagara Falls. The owner targeted the completion of the dam construction

in three years. To model the rockfill dam, the following were considered: 1) the quantities and type of soils used to fill the body of the dam (i.e. scope of work), 2) the locations of soils' borrow bits, 3) the target three-year construction duration, 4) the constraints paused by the relatively short construction season, 5) the equipment used to perform the work, and 6) the indirect cost components. The dam consists of several soil types with different size and compaction requirements. For simplicity, three soil types were considered in the modeling of the dam: 1) compacted moraine (clay), 2) granular (sand and gravel) and 3) rock. The total volume of the soil considered in the modeling was 6.3 million m^3 (Hydro-Quebec 1999). The actual excavated natural soil from the riverbed was estimated to be 1,038,000 m^3 (Peer 2001). In view of the relatively short construction season and the targeted project duration, the project was phased in three stages, each spanning a construction season as shown in Figure 7. Upon entering the input data to *SimEarth* and requesting the fleet that provides minimum total duration, *SimEarth* first triggers its simulation engine (*EMSP*) to perform pilot runs (see Figure 8). Subsequently, simulation analysis is performed for each of the recommended fleets by specifying the number of simulation runs and activating the *"Analyze"* function (see Figure 8). Different reports can then be generated in a graphical form (see Figure 9). Tables 1 and 2 list the estimated durations obtained from the simulation analysis and their associated direct cost. Table 3 provides the total cost, direct and indirect, of the project.

MODELING BRIDGES DECK CONSTRUCTION

Problem Background

Bridge construction projects are classified as infrastructure construction projects, which encompass also tunnels, airports, dams, highways,

Figure 7. typical cross section of the dam

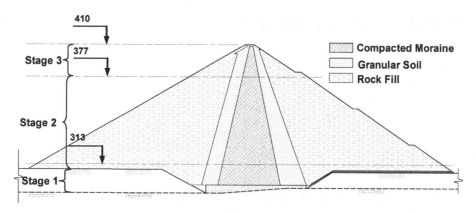

Figure 8. Results of pilot simulation

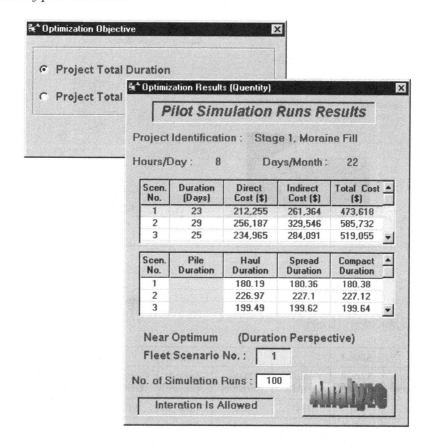

etc. Infrastructure projects are those which are characterized by long duration, large budget, and complexity. New construction methods have been developed to improve constructability, such as "Segmental" construction which eliminates falsework system. Segmental construction is executed in a cyclic manner which elites computer simulation as a best modeling technique. Such new construction methods can be modeled utilizing computer simulation.

Figure 9. EMSP graphical report

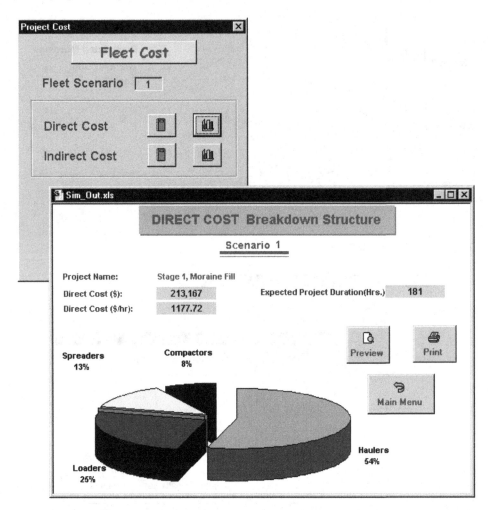

Table 1. Estimated durations (hours)

Scope	Stage 1			Stage 2			Stage 3		
	Main Activities	Spread Activity	Compact Activity	Main Activities	Spread Activity	Compact Activity	Main Activities	Spread Activity	Compact Activity
Moraine	181	181	181*	857	857	857*	1000	1000	1000*
Granular	101	101	101*	746	746	746*	722	722	722*
Rock	452	516	532*	1505	1505	1505*	1253	1430	1476*
Excavated Clay	458*	812	---	---	---	---	---	---	---
Total Duration	1272 hrs. = 159 Days = 7.2 Months			3108 hrs. = 195 Days = 7.5 Months			3198 hrs. = 200 Days = 7.7 Months		

Table 2. Estimated Direct Cost (Dollars)

Fleet Name	Stage 1	Stage 2	Stage 3
Moraine	213,167	3,113,601	1,603,620
Granular	118,950	1,672,883	1,004,064
Rock	645,577	15,638,049	8,837,741
Excavated Clay	3,117,007	---	---
Total Direct Cost	4,094,701	20,424,532	11,445,424

Table 3. Project Total Cost

Fleet Name	Direct Cost	Indirect Cost	
		Time Related	Lump sum
Stage 1	4,094,701	1,800,000	
Stage 2	20,424,532	3,750,000	53,973,233
Stage 3	11,445,424	3,850,000	
Total	35,964,657	63,373,233	
Markup (2.5%)	2,331,572		
Total Cost	101,669,462		

System Description

A framework (*Bridge_Sim*) has been developed to aid contractors in planning of bridge deck construction (Marzouk et. al. 2008-a, Marzouk et. al. 2008-b, Marzouk et. al. 2007, Marzouk et. al. 2006-a, Marzouk et. al. 2006-b, Zein 2006). The developed framework performs two main functions; deck construction planning and optimizing deck construction using launching girder method. These two functions are performed by *Bridge_Sim*'s main component modules; Bridge Analyzer Module, Simulation Module, Optimization Module, and Reporting Module. Figure 10 depicts a schematic diagram for the proposed framework that shows the interaction between its components.

Bridge Analyzer Module is considered the coordinator of the planning function, provided by *Bridge_Sim*. This module analyzes the project and breaks it down into construction zones. Dividing the bridge into zones is done taking into account:

1. The construction methods that is used in construction. For each construction method, a zone representing it is created and defined.
2. The set of assigned resources in each construction method. For a given construction method, resources can be assigned differently in two different construction locations, these two locations are defined as two separate zones using the same construction method.
3. General sequence of construction. If two parts are constructed using the same construction method by the same set of resources and are required to be executed simultaneously or successively, then, these two parts are defined as two separate zones with a specific relationship between them.

The procedure followed by the Bridge Analyzer Module to perform a planning session of deck construction can be summarized as following (see Figure 11):

Figure 10. Interaction amongst Bridge_Sim components

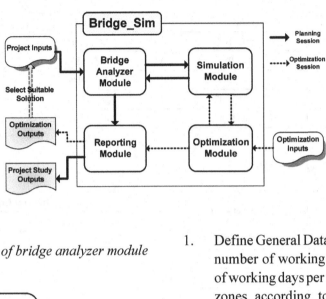

Figure 11. Flowchart of bridge analyzer module processes

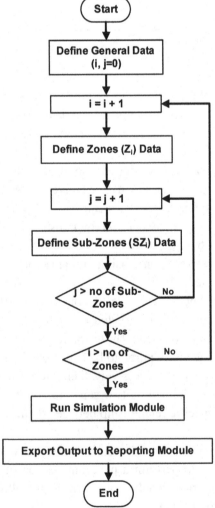

1. Define General Data. General data involves number of working hours per day, number of working days per week, number of bridge zones according to contractor plan, and estimated indirect costs. The framework provides numerous indirect cost items falling into two main categories; time-dependent and time-independent indirect costs.

2. Define Zones Data. For each zone, the contractor selects the applied construction method, define number of sub-zones, and assign labor crews and equipment. The sub-zone may be a pier or a segment depending on the type of construction method.

3. Define Sub-Zones data. For each sub-zone within a zone, the contractor estimates the durations of involved tasks and materials costs. The framework provides the contractor with five probability density functions to estimate task duration.

4. Run Simulation Module. The Bridge Analyzer Module sends input data to the Simulation Module to estimate the total duration and cost for each zone and/or sub-zone. The contractor have to define two simulation parameters; number of simulation runs and confidence level.

5. Export output to Reporting Module. Once the Simulation Module estimates the total duration and cost for each zone and/or sub-

zone, Bridge Analyzer Module retrieves output obtained from Simulation Module and exports it to the Reporting Module. The Reporting Module processes the output to get the total duration and cost of the whole deck.

Simulation Module is responsible for estimating the total duration and total cost of bridge deck construction. The proposed Simulation Module utilizes STROBOSCOPE (Martinez 1996), a general purpose simulation language. The simulation module is developed in Microsoft Visual Basic 6.0 to control STROBOSCOPE program. There are fourteen simulation models built-in the developed Simulation Module as listed in Figure 12. Figure 13 lists STROBOSCOPE elements utilized to build up the simulation models.

According to the method of construction, Simulation Module selects the simulation model that represents the case and it modifies the selected model to account for the input data. The input data are: 1) the work size (i.e. number of segments), 2)

numbers of the assigned resources, 3) number of replications, 4) number of working hours per day, and 5) estimated durations for construction tasks. After modifying the template simulation input file, simulation module launches STROBOSCOPE to run this input file. The output (i.e. durations) is exported to a text file to be retrieved by the simulation module to perform cost calculations.

Developing a simulation model, representing a specific construction operation, needs special skills to be acquired by the modeler like programming logic and engineering knowledge. The procedure of designing and building a simulation model can be summarized as following:

1. Study the operation under consideration to analyze it and determine its main components, specifying its technical limitations.

2. Break-down the considered operation into main processes that have their respective tasks. For each task, the involved resources (materials, labor, and/or equipments) are defined.

Figure 12. Developed simulation models for bridge deck construction

File name	Description
CastinSitu	Cast-in-place of falsework method.
Steel	Steel span construction
Carriage(1)	Cantilever carriage method using pump line technique for typical segments only
TotalCarriage(1)	Cantilever carriage method using pump line technique for typical and stump segments
Carriage(2)	Cantilever carriage method using truck mixers technique for typical segments only
TotalCarriage(2)	Cantilever carriage method using truck mixers technique for typical and stump segments
ClosingSegment	Cantilever carriage method for closing segment construction
Precast(1)	Pre-cast balanced cantilever method using mobile cranes technique
Precast(2)	Pre-cast balanced cantilever method using Beam-Winch technique
DeckPushing(1)	Segments fabrication operation (Deck pushing method) using single form technique
DeckPushing(2)	Segments fabrication operation (Deck pushing method) using multi-forms technique
DeckPushingTotal	Deck pushing method including all operations
SteppingFormwork	Stepping formwork method
LaunchingGirder	Launching girder method

3. Determine the type of each task, either *Normal* or *Combi*, depending on the need for resources. A *Combi* task is required to be preceded by a Queue for each involved resource.

4. Determine execution sequence and relationships between tasks by using *Arcs* to produce the network.

5. Create control statements to add more control and model logical conditions which cannot be modeled using normal arcs and tasks.

6. Code the developed network and control statements in a form of simulation language.

7. Verify the simulation model and test it by running it via real cases to determine any bugs or errors.

The following section describes cast-in-place on falsework method as an example of the developed simulation models.

Cast-in-Place on Falsework Method

Cast-in-place on falsework technique operation involves four main processes for each span: 1) false-work system erection, 2) bottom flange construction, 3) top flange and webs construction, and 4) stressing and dismantling of formwork and false-work. Table 4 lists processes and tasks of deck construction using cast-in-place on false-work method. Figure 14 depicts the elements of the network that capture the subject construction method. False-work system erection process is done by four tasks: i) setting of pads, ii) constructing bents, iii) setting stringers, and iv) rolling out soffit (see Figure 15). Falsework system erection starts by setting of timber pads, which act as a means of transferring dead and live loads of the structure under construction to the ground prior to post tensioning (see Figure 16). Setting of pads is represented by *Combi* element, named *SettingPads*, which needs two types of resources:

Figure 13. STROBOSCOPE simulation elements (adapted from Martinez 1996)

Symbol	Name	Description
▭	NORMAL	Unconstrained in its starting logic and indicates active processing of (or by) resource entities.
⬠	COMBI	Logically constrained in starting, otherwise similar to the NORMAL work task modeling element.
◯	QUEUE	Represents a queuing up or waiting for use of passive state resources.
→	ARC	Used to model the direction of resource entity flow between the various active state nodes and the passive state nodes.
◉	FORK	Node used to divide the resource path in the model where multi branches follow it and the resource must move through one branch only.
(A)	ASSEMBLER	Node used to break up a compound resource into its main components.
(D)	DISASSEMBLER	Node used to assemble various resources into a compound resource.
⬭	Fusion QUEUE	Represents the queue which bears its name
▱	CONSOLIDATOR	Activities that start and finish their instances depending exclusively on resources they receive.

Table 4. Processes and Tasks of falsework method

Process	Task	Description
False-Work Erection	*SettingPads*	Setting of falsework pads
	BentsErection	Falsework bents erection
	SettingStringers	Setting of falsework stringers
	RollingSoffit	Falsework soffit rolling
Bottom Flange & Webs	*ExternalFormwork*	Erection of webs external formwork
	Rebar1	Placing of bottom flange and webs reinforcement
	InstallDucts1	Placing of stressing ducts
	InternalFormwork	Erection of webs internal formwork
	Casting1	Bottom flange and webs casting
	Curing1	Bottom flange and webs curing
Top Flange	*Dismantle1*	Dismantling of webs internal formwork
	FlangeFormwork	Erection of top flange formwork
	Rebar2	Placing of top flange reinforcement
	InstallDucts2	Placing of stressing ducts
	Casting2	Top flange casting
	Curing2	Top flange curing
Stressing & Dismantling	*Stressing*	Inserting and stressing of stressing cables
	CompleteDismantle	Dismantling of all falsework and formwork

formwork crew, and dummy resource, which is used to maintain the logic flow and dependency between activities. To allow resource tracing, each resource path is referenced with identity letters. The two resources; formwork crew and dummy; are drawn to *SettingPads* through links; *F1*, and *L1*, respectively. After pads setting, vertical bents (steel or timber) are erected to serve as a support for the stringers and transfer stringers loads to the bottom pads as shown in Figure 16. Vertical bents erection is represented by *Normal* element named *BentsErection* which has same resources required by the previous task. The third task in falsework erection is setting stringers which are made of either timber or steel. Stringers are set in place one by one and spaced as determined in the false-work design. *SettingStringers* is a *Normal* element that receives its resources (formwork crew) from *BentsErection*. Once the stringers are set, rolling out soffit task takes place. The soffit

consists of two main elements; timber joists and plywood sheets. Timber joists are set perpendicular to the stringers, whereas, plywood sheets are placed on the timber joists, to serve both as the bottom form for the bottom flange of the bridge. *RollingSoffit* is a *Normal* element that draws its resources (formwork crew and crane) from *SettingStringers*.

The process of bottom flange and webs construction starts by the erection of the external formwork of webs (*ExternalFormwork*). This task is a normal task where it derives its resource (i.e. *Formcrew*) immediately from preceding *RollingSoffit* task. This task is followed by five tasks to finish up the process of bottom flange and webs construction: *Rebar1*, *InstallDucts1*, *InternalFormwork*, *Casting1*, and *Curing1*. Each task requires its own resources except *Curing1*, which is a normal task requires only the dummy resource from preceding task. The third process

Figure 14. Simulation model of cast-in-place on falsework method

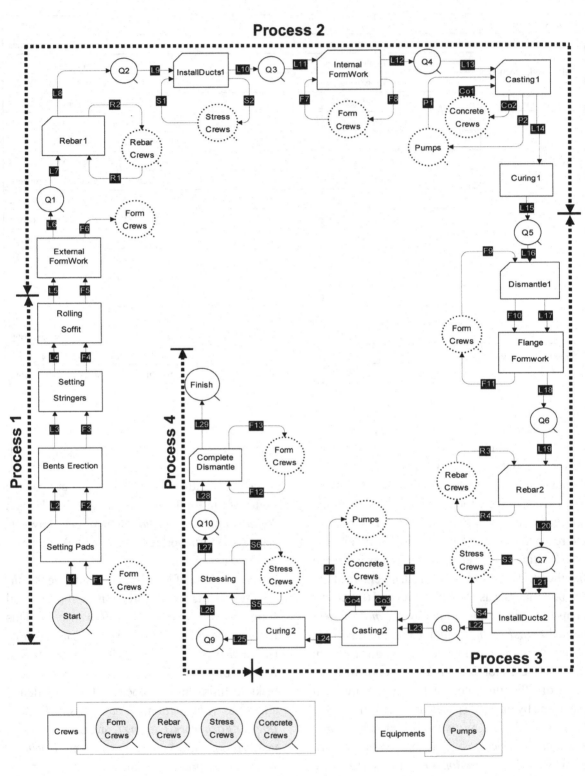

Figure 15. Typical False-work Structure and Components

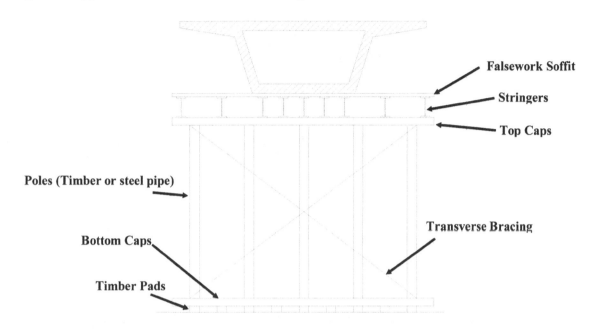

Figure 16. Falsework Components (adapted from Tischer and Kupre 2003)

named top flange construction involves same tasks of the previous process, but preceded by additional task named *Dismantle1*. This task is to dismantle the inner formwork of webs to clear space for the top flange formwork.

Until this moment, the whole section is constructed, but cannot sustain its own self weight unless the last process is accomplished. This process involves only two tasks: *Stressing*, and *CompleteDismantle*. The first task of the fourth

Figure 17. El-Warrak bridge layout and construction zones

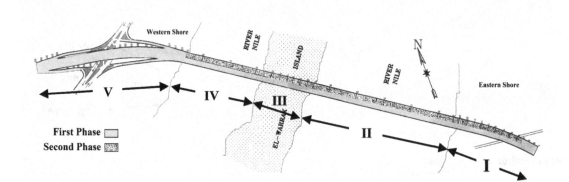

Table 5. Bridge zones vs. number of spans

ID	Zone	No. of spans	Total Length (m)
I	Eastern Shore	13	400
II	Eastern Nile Branch	6	600
III	El-Warrak Island	6	230
IV	Western Nile Branch	4	360
V	Western Shore	22	670

process is to thread the stressing cables into empty ducts and stress them to the design load. The last task is to dismantle all erected formwork and falsework systems after the superstructure is considered self-supported. The simulation model represents the construction of single span. The *Start* Queue is initiated in the beginning of the simulation session by one dummy resource. The simulation model runs until the dummy resource reaches the *Finish* Queue. The simulation run stops as there is no more Dummy resource to initiate *SettingPads*. This termination of simulation is named "lake of resources" termination.

Case Study

This case study considers the deck construction of El-Warrak Bridge, which is a part of the Ring Road of Cairo - Egypt. It links Basos city to El-Warrak city over the River Nile and it crosses El-Warrak Island. The Ring Road crosses the River Nile at two locations: El-Warrak Island in the north and El-Moneeb in the south. The total length of the bridge is 2,250 meters, whereas, the length of its outlet and inlet ramps is 600 meters. The bridge width varies from 42 meters to 45 meters while the ramps have a width of 9 meters. The total contract value of the bridge is L.E 170 millions and it was planned to be executed in 55 months. The contract scope of work includes the execution of bridge foundations, piers, deck, and finishes. The bridge consists of five main zones (see Figure 17): i) Eastern Shore (Basos shore), ii) Eastern Nile Branch, iii) El-Warrak Island, iv) Western Nile Branch, and v) Western Shore (El-Warrak shore). Eastern shore, El-Warrak Island, and Western Shore Zones were constructed using a traditional cast-in-place on falsework method. Eastern Nile Branch and Western Nile Branch Zones were constructed using cantilever carriage method. The number of spans and the length of each zone are listed in Table 5. The outlet and inlet ramps, which exist on western shore zone, have four ramps.

Once the case data are fed to the developed *Bridge_Sim* system, the system provides its outputs in a form of minimum expected duration, maximum expected duration, mean expected duration, and standard deviation for each subzone. *Bridge_Sim* adopts Central Limit theorem to estimate zones and project durations. Minimum, maximum and mean expected durations, for each zone, are estimated by summing up sub-zones' values (see Table 6). Falsework sub-zones are summed up considering the overlap period between casting segments.

Construction of the Eastern and Western Shores forms the longest path which controls the total duration. The mean expected total duration for deck construction of El-Warrak Bridge is estimated to be 544 working days, which corresponds to 635 calendar days. The difference between the estimated total duration and actual duration (the 3 years listed is the contract) represents the duration of mobilization, sub-structure construction, piers construction and finishes. The associated total cost of the deck is 66,875,526 L.E which consists of 57,791,708 L.E. as direct costs and 9,083,818 L.E. as indirect costs.

Future Trends

Future research on the use of computer simulation in construction encompasses several areas. Although simulation optimization has been applied in construction domain (Marzouk et. al. 2008, Marzouk and Moselhi 2004-b, Marzouk and Moselhi 2003-a), several opportunities exist to be challenged such as multi-objective optimization, constraint optimization, and evolutionary algorithms. Also, integrating computer simulation in Building Information Modeling (BIM) is a promising trend in the area construction engineering and management future research. That can be done by: 1) developing an easy-to-use 3D modeling approach that simplifies exploration, navigation, and analysis on construction operations, 2) formulating an advanced estimating system that allows users to produce faster and more accurate cost estimates, reports, and bids, and 3) providing a scheduling tools that automatically generate multiple project schedules based on customized scheduling logic, taking into consideration the uncertainties inherited in construction projects.

CONCLUSION REMARKS

This chapter reviewed the application of computer simulation in construction. Several general purpose simulation (GPS) software systems and special purpose simulation (SPS) platforms have been introduced in construction. Such systems and tools were extensively reviewed and described in the chapter. The chapter also presented two computer simulation applications in construction. The first application models earthmoving operation (*SimEarth*), whereas, the second one models the

Table 6. Expected durations for El-Warrak bridge zones (days)

Zones	Shortest Duration	Mean Duration	Longest Duration	Standard Deviation	Variance
Eastern Shore	121.68	122.75	123.82	3.34	11.13
Eastern Nile Branch	379.74	381.33	382.92	4.19	17.60
El-Warrak Island	89.84	90.61	91.35	2.98	8.90
Western Nile Branch	373.7	375.41	377.08	4.31	18.55
Western Shore	402.34	405.93	409.52	7.65	58.59

construction of bridges' decks (*Bridge_Sim*). The simulation engine of *SimEarth*, named EarthMoving Simulation Program (*EMSP*), was designed utilizing discrete event simulation (DEVS) and object-oriented modeling. Different features of object-orientation have been employed including classes, objects, dynamic data structure, and polymorphism. *Bridge_Sim* has been developed to aid contractors in planning of bridge deck construction. The developed framework performs two main functions; deck construction planning and optimizing deck construction using launching girder. The designated tasks of *Bridge_Sim*'s components (Bridge Analyzer Module and Simulation Module) were described. Two comprehensive case studies, that were modeled using *SimEarth* and *Bridge_Sim*, were presented.

REFERENCES

AbouRizk, S. M., & Dozzi, S. P. (1993). Application of computer simulation in resolving construction disputes. *Journal of Construction Engineering and Management, 119*(2), 355–373. doi:10.1061/(ASCE)0733-9364(1993)119:2(355)

AbouRizk, S. M., & Hajjar, D. (1998). A framework for applying simulation in construction. *Canadian Journal of Civil Engineering, 25*(3), 604–617. doi:10.1139/cjce-25-3-604

Abraham, D. M., & Halpin, D. W. (1998). Simulation of the construction of cable-stayed bridges. *Canadian Journal of Civil Engineering, 25*(3), 490–499. doi:10.1139/cjce-25-3-490

Appleton, B. J. A., Patra, J., Mohamed, Y., & AbouRizk, S. (2002). Special purpose simulation modeling of tower cranes. *Proceedings of the 2002 Winter Simulation Conference*, San Diego, CA, (pp. 1709-1715).

Banks, J. (1998). *Handbook of simulation*. New York: John Wily & Sons, Inc.

Banks, J., Carson, J. S., Nelson, B. L., & Nicol, D. M. (2000). *Discrete-Event System Simulation*. Upper Saddle River, NJ: Prentice Hall, Inc.

Boskers, N. D., & AbouRizk, S. M. (2005). Modeling scheduling uncertainty in capital construction projects. *Proceedings of the 2005 Winter Simulation Conference*, Orlando, FL, (pp. 1500-1507).

Chandrakanthi, M., Ruwanpura, J. Y., Hettiaratchi, P., & Prado, B. (2002). Optimization of the waste management for construction projects using simulation. *Proceedings of the 2002 Winter Simulation Conference*, San Diego, CA, (pp. 1771-1777).

Cor, H., & Martinez, J. C. (1999). A case study in the quantification of a change in the conditions of a highway construction operation. *Proceedings of the 1999 Winter Simulation Conference*, Phoenix, AZ, (pp. 1007-1009).

Crain, R. C. (1997). Simulation using GPSS/H. *Proceedings of the 1997 Winter Simulation Conference*, Atlanta, GA, (pp. 567-573).

Deitel, H. M., & Deitel, P. J. (1998). *C++ how to program*. Upper Saddle River, NJ: Prentice Hall.

EBC Web site (2001). *EBC achievements: civil engineering/earthworks*. Retrieved from http://www.ebcinc.qc.ca/

Elfving, J. A., & Tommelein, I. D. (2003). Impact of multitasking and merge bias on procurement of Complex Equipment. *Proceedings of the 2003 Winter Simulation Conference*, New Orleans, LA, (pp. 1527-1533).

Farid, F., & Koning, T. L. (1994). Simulation verifies queuing program for selecting loader-truck fleets. *Journal of Construction Engineering and Management, 120*(2), 386–404. doi:10.1061/(ASCE)0733-9364(1994)120:2(386)

Gowda, R. K., Singh, A., & Connolly, M. (1998). Holistic enhancement of the production analysis of bituminous paving operations. *Construction Management and Economics*, *16*(4), 417–432. doi:10.1080/014461998372204

Hajjar, D., & AbouRizk, S. M. (1999). Simphony: an environment for building special purpose simulation. *Proceedings of the 1999 Winter Simulation Conference*, Phoenix, AZ, (pp. 998-1006).

Halpin, D. W. (1977). CYCLONE-method for modeling job site processes. *Journal of the Construction Division*, *103*(3), 489–499.

Halpin, D. W., & Riggs, L. S. (1992). *Planning and analysis of construction operations*. New York: John Wiley & Sons, Inc.

Hanna, M., & Ruwanpura, J. (2007). Simulation tool for manpower forecast loading and resource leveling. *Proceedings of the 2007 Winter Simulation Conference*, Washington, DC, (pp. 2099-2103).

Hason, S. F. (1994). *Feasibility and implementation of automation and robotics in Canadian building construction operation*. M.Sc.Thesis, Center for Building Studies, Concordia University, Portland, OR.

Huang, R., Grigoriadis, A. M., & Halpin, D. W. (1994). Simulation of cable-stayed bridges using DISCO. *Proceedings of the 1994 Winter Simulation Conference*, Orlando, FL, (pp. 1130-1136).

Hydro-Quebec (1999). *Sainte-Marguerite-3 hydroelectric project: in harmony with the environment*.

Ioannou, P. G. (1989). *UM-CYCLONE user's manual*. Division of Construction Engineering and Management, Purdue University, West Lafayette, IN.

Ioannou, P. G. (1999). Construction of dam embankment with nonstationary queue. *Proceedings of the 1999 Winter Simulation Conference*, Phoenix, AZ, (pp. 921-928).

Lee, S., & Pena-mora, F. (2005). System dynamics approach for error and change management in concurrent design and construction. *Proceedings of the 2005 Winter Simulation Conference*, Orlando, FL, (pp. 1508-1514).

Lluch, J., & Halpin, D. W. (1982). Construction operations and microcomputers. *Journal of the Construction Division*, *108*(CO1), 129–145.

Lu, M., & Chan, W. (2004). Modeling concurrent operational interruptions in construction activities with simplified discrete event simulation approach (SDESA). *Proceedings of the 2004 Winter Simulation Conference*, Washington, DC, (pp. 1260-1267).

Martinez, J. C. (1996). *STROBOSCOPE-state and resource based simulation of construction process*. Ph.D. Thesis, University of Michigan, Ann Arbor, MI.

Martinez, J. C. (1998). EarthMover-simulation tool for earthwork planning. *Proceedings of the 1998 Winter Simulation Conference*, Washington DC, (pp. 1263-1271).

Martinez, J. C., & Ioannou, P. J. (1999). General-purpose systems for effective construction simulation. *Journal of Construction Engineering and Management*, *125*(4), 265–276. doi:10.1061/(ASCE)0733-9364(1999)125:4(265)

Marzouk, M. (2002). *Optimizing earthmoving operations using computer simulation*. Ph.D. Thesis, Concordia University, Montreal, Canada.

Marzouk, M., & Moselhi, O. (2000). Optimizing earthmoving operations using object-oriented simulation. *Proceedings of the 2000 Winter Simulation Conference*, Orlando, FL, (1926-1932).

Marzouk, M., & Moselhi, O. (2004-a). Multi-objective optimization of earthmoving operations. *Journal of Construction Engineering and Management, 130*(1), 105–113. doi:10.1061/(ASCE)0733-9364(2004)130:1(105)

Marzouk, M., & Moselhi, O.(2004-b). Fuzzy clustering model for estimating haulers' travel time. *Journal of Construction Engineering and Management, 130*(6), 878–886. doi:10.1061/(ASCE)0733-9364(2004)130:6(878)

Marzouk, M., & Moselhi, O.(2003-a) Constraint based genetic algorithm for earthmoving fleet selection. *Canadian Journal of Civil Engineering, 30*(4), 673–683. doi:10.1139/l03-006

Marzouk, M., & Moselhi, O.(2003-b). An object oriented model for earthmoving operations. *Journal of Construction Engineering and Management, 129*(2), 173–181. doi:10.1061/(ASCE)0733-9364(2003)129:2(173)

Marzouk, M., & Moselhi, O.(2002-a). Bid preparation for earthmoving operations. *Canadian Journal of Civil Engineering, 29*(3), 517–532. doi:10.1139/l02-023

Marzouk, M., & Moselhi, O.(2002-b). Simulation optimization for earthmoving operations using genetic algorithms. *Construction Management and Economics, 20*(6), 535–544. doi:10.1080/01446190210156064

Marzouk, M., Said, H., & El-Said, M. (2008b). Special purpose simulation model for balanced cantilever bridges. *Journal of Bridge Engineering, 13*(2), 122–131. doi:10.1061/(ASCE)1084-0702(2008)13:2(122)

Marzouk, M., Zein, H., & El-Said, M. (2006a). Scheduling cast-in-situ on falsework bridges using computer simulation. *Scientific Bulletin, Faculty of Engineering . Ain Shams University, 41*(1), 231–245.

Marzouk, M., Zein, H., & El-Said, M. (2006b). BRIGE_SIM: framework for planning and optimizing bridge deck construction using computer simulation. *Proceedings of the 2006 Winter Simulation Conference*, Monterey, CA, (pp. 2039-2046).

Marzouk, M., Zein, H., & El-Said, M. (2007). Application of computer simulation to construction of deck pushing bridges. *Journal of Civil Engineering and Management, 13*(1), 27–36.

Marzouk, M., Zein El-Dein, H., & El-Said, M. (2008a. (in press). A framework for multiobjective optimization of launching girder bridges. *Journal of Construction Engineering and Management.*

McCabe, B. (1997). *An automated modeling approach for construction performance improvement using computer simulation and belief networks.* Ph.D. Thesis, Alberta University, Canada.

McCabe, B. (1998). Belief networks in construction simulation. *Proceedings of the 1998 Winter Simulation Conference*, Washington DC (pp. 1279-1286).

Oloufa, A. (1993). Modeling operational activities in object-oriented simulation. *Journal of Computing in Civil Engineering, 7*(1), 94–106. doi:10.1061/(ASCE)0887-3801(1993)7:1(94)

Oloufa, A., Ikeda, M., & Nguyen, T. (1998). Resource-based simulation libraries for construction. *Automation in Construction, 7*(4), 315–326. doi:10.1016/S0926-5805(98)00048-X

Paulson, G. C. Jr. (1978). Interactive graphics for simulating construction operations. *Journal of the Construction Division, 104*(1), 69–76.

Peer, G. A. (2001). Ready to Serve. *Heavy Construction News*, March 2001, 16-19.

Pidd, M. (1995). Object orientation, discrete simulation and three-phase approach. *The Journal of the Operational Research Society, 46*(3), 362–374.

Pritsker, A. A. B., O'Reilly, J. J., & LaVal, D. K. (1997). *Simulation with visual SLAM and Awesim.* New York: John Wiley & Sons, Inc.

Quatrani, T. (1998). *Visual modeling with rational rose and UML.* Reading, MA: Addison-Wesley.

Sawhney, A., & AbouRizk, S. M. (1995). HSM-Simulation-based planning method for construction projects. *Journal of Construction Engineering and Management, 121*(3), 297–303. doi:10.1061/(ASCE)0733-9364(1995)121:3(297)

Sawhney, A., & AbouRizk, S. M. (1996). Computerized tool for hierarchical simulation modeling. *Journal of Computing in Civil Engineering, 10*(2), 115–124. doi:10.1061/(ASCE)0887-3801(1996)10:2(115)

Schriber, T. J., & Brunner, D. T. (1999). Inside discrete-event simulation software: how it works and how it matters. *Proceedings of the 1999 Winter Simulation Conference*, Phoenix, AZ, (pp. 72-80).

Shi, J. (1995). *Optimization for construction simulation.* Ph.D. Thesis, Alberta University, Canada.

Shi, J., & AbouRizk, S. M. (1997). Resource-based modeling for construction simulation. *Journal of Construction Engineering and Management, 123*(1), 26–33. doi:10.1061/(ASCE)0733-9364(1997)123:1(26)

Skansholm, J. (1997). *C++ From the beginning.* Harlow, UK: Addison-Wesley.

Song, L., & AbouRizk, S. M. (2003). Building a virtual shop model for steel fabrication. *Proceedings of the 2003 Winter Simulation Conference*, New Orleans, LA, (pp. 1510-1517).

Tischer, T. E., & Kuprenas, J. A. (2003). Bridge falsework productivity – measurement and influences. *Journal of Construction Engineering and Management, 129*(3), 243–250. doi:10.1061/(ASCE)0733-9364(2003)129:3(243)

Tommelein, I. D. (1999). Travel-time simulation to locate and staff temporary facilities under changing construction demand. *Proceedings of the 1999 Winter Simulation Conference*, Phoenix, AZ (pp. 978-984).

Tommelein, I. D., Carr, R. I., & Odeh, A. M. (1994). Assembly of simulation networks using designs, plans, and methods. *Journal of Construction Engineering and Management, 120*(4), 796–815. doi:10.1061/(ASCE)0733-9364(1994)120:4(796)

Touran, A. (1990). Integration of simulation with expert systems. *Journal of Construction Engineering and Management, 116*(3), 480–493. doi:10.1061/(ASCE)0733-9364(1990)116:3(480)

Vanegas, J. A., Bravo, E. B., & Halpin, D. W. (1993). Simulation technologies for planning heavy construction processes. *Journal of Construction Engineering and Management, 119*(2), 336–354. doi:10.1061/(ASCE)0733-9364(1993)119:2(336)

Zein, H. (2006). *A framework for planning and optimizing bridge deck construction using computer simulation.* M.Sc. Thesis, Cairo University, Cairo, Egypt.

Zhang, C., & Hammad, A. (2007). Agent-based simulation for collaborative cranes. *Proceedings of the 2007 Winter Simulation Conference*, Washington, DC. (pp. 2051-2056).

KEY TERMS AND DEFINITIONS

General Purpose Simulation: is based on formulating a simulation model for the system under study, running the simulation and analyzing the results in order to decide whether the system is acceptable or not.

Special Purpose Simulation: is based on creation of a platform or a template for a specific domain of application.

Object-Oriented Modeling: is a modeling paradigm mainly used in computer programming by considering the problem not as a set of functions that can be performed but primarily as a set of related, interacting objects.

B Activity: bound to happen activity.

C Activity: conditional activity

Building Information Modeling: digital representation of the physical and functional characteristics of a facility.

Simulation Optimization: the process of maximizing information retrieval from simulation analysis without carrying out the analysis for all combinations of input variables.

Compilation of References

AbouRizk, S. M., & Dozzi, S. P. (1993). Application of computer simulation in resolving construction disputes. *Journal of Construction Engineering and Management, 119*(2), 355–373. doi:10.1061/(ASCE)0733-9364(1993)119:2(355)

AbouRizk, S. M., & Hajjar, D. (1998). A framework for applying simulation in construction. *Canadian Journal of Civil Engineering, 25*(3), 604–617. doi:10.1139/cjce-25-3-604

Abraham, D. M., & Halpin, D. W. (1998). Simulation of the construction of cable-stayed bridges. *Canadian Journal of Civil Engineering, 25*(3), 490–499. doi:10.1139/cjce-25-3-490

Abu-Taieh, E., & El Sheikh, A. R. (2007). Commercial Simulation Packages: A Comparative Study. *International Journal of Simulation, 8*(2), 66–76.

ACIMS. (2000). *DEVS/HLA software*. Retrieved September 1st, 2008, from http://www.acims.arizona.edu/SOFTWARE/software.shtml. Arizona Center for Integrative Modelling and Simulation.

ACIMS. (2003). *DEVSJAVA modeling & simulation tool*. Retrieved September 1st, 2008, from http://www.acims.arizona.edu/SOFTWARE/software.shtml. Arizona Center for Integrative Modeling and Simulation.

Adamski, M. (2001). A Rigorous Design Methodology for Reprogrammable Logic Controllers. In *Proc. DESDes'01*, (pp. 53 – 60), Zielona Gora, Poland.

Adelsberger, H. H., Bick, M., & Pawlowski, J. M. (2000, December). *Design principles for teaching simulation with explorative learning environments*. In J. A. Joines, R.

R. Barton, K. Kang & P. A. Fishwick (Eds.), *Proceedings of the 2000 Winter Simulation Conference*, Piscataway, NJ (pp. 1684-1691). Washington, DC: IEEE.

Agarwal, S., Handschuh, S., & Staab, S. (2005). Annotation, Composition and Invocation of Semantic Web Services. *Journal of Web Semantics, 2*(1), 1–24.

Agostini, A., & De Michelis, G. (2000, August). A Light Workflow Management System Using Simple Process Models. *Computer Supported Cooperative Work, 9*(3-4), 335–363. doi:10.1023/A:1008703327801

Ahmed, Y., & Shahriari, S. (2001). *Simulation of TCP/IP Applications on CDPD Channel*. M.Sc Thesis, Department of Signals and Systems, Chalmers University of Technology, Sweden.

Al Hudhud, G., & Ayesh, A. (2008, April 1-4). Real Time Movement Cooredination Technique Based on Flocking Behaviour for Multiple Mobile Robots System. In *Proceedings of Swarming Intelligence Applications Symposium*. Aberdeen, UK.

Al-Bahadili, H. (2008). *MANSim: A Mobile Ad Hoc Network Simulator*. Personal Communication.

Al-Bahadili, H., & Jaradat, Y. (2007). Development and performance analysis of a probabilistic flooding in noisy mobile ad hoc networks. In *Proceedings of the 1st International Conference on Digital Communications and Computer Applications* (DCCA2007), (pp. 1306-1316), Jordan.

Al-Bahadili, H., Al-Basheer, O., & Al-Thaher, A. (2007). A Location Aided Routing-Probabilistic Algorithm for Flooding Optimization in MANETs. In *Proceedings of*

Mosharaka International Conference on Communications, Networking, and Information Technology (MIC-CNIT 2007), Jordan.

Al-Bahadili, H., Al-Zoubaidi, A. R., Al-Zayyat, K., Jaradat, R., & Al-Omari, I. (2009). *Development and performance evaluation of an OMPR algorithm for route discovery in noisy MANETs.* To be published.

Alberts, D. S., & Hayes, R. E. (2003). Power to the Edge, Command and Control in the Information Age. *Department of Defense Command and Control Program; Information Age Transformation Series.* Washington, DC.

Alesso, H. P., & Smith, C. F. (2005). *Developing Semantic Web Services.* Wellesley, MA: A.K. Peters, Ltd.

Alexander, S. E. (1982). Radio propagation within buildings at 900 MHz. *IEE Electronics Letters, 18*(21), 913–914. doi:10.1049/el:19820622

Al-Hudhud, G. (2006, July 10-12). Visualising the emergent behaviour of a multiagent communication model. In *Proceedings of the 6th International Conference on Recent Advances in Soft Computing,* (pp. 375–381). Canterbury, UK: University of Kent.

Allen, A. (1978). *Probability, statistics and queuing theory, with computer science applications.* New York: Academic Press

Alnoukari, M., & Alhussan, W. (2008). Using data mining techniques for predicting future car market demand. *International Conference on Information & Communication Technologies: From Theory to Applications, IEEE Conference,* Syria.

Alnoukari, M., Alzoabi, Z., & Hanna, S. (2008). Using applying adaptive software development (ASD) agile modeling on predictive data mining applications: ASD-DM methodology. *International Symposium on Information Technology,* Malaysia.

Al-Thaher, A. (2007). *A Location Aided Routing-Probabilistic Algorithm for Flooding Optimization in Mobile Ad Hoc Networks.* M.Sc Thesis, Department of Computer Science, Amman Arab University for Graduate Studies, Jordan.

Altiok, T. (2001, December). Various ways academics teach simulation: are they all appropriate? In B. A. Peters, J. S. Smith, D. J. Medeiros, and M. W. Rohrer (Eds.), *Proceedings of the 2001 Winter Simulation Conference,* Arlington, VA, (pp. 1580-1591).

Analytica. (2006). *Lumina.* Retrieved 2008, from Analytica: www.lumina.com

Anand, S. S., Bell, D. A., & Hughes, J. G. (1995). The Role of Domain Knowledge in Data Mining. *CIKM'95,* Baltimore, MD, (pp. 37–43).

Anderson, V., & Johnson, L. (1997). *Systems thinking tools: from concepts to causal loops.* Waltham, MA: Pegasus Communications, Inc.

Appleton, B. J. A., Patra, J., Mohamed, Y., & AbouRizk, S. (2002). Special purpose simulation modeling of tower cranes. *Proceedings of the 2002 Winter Simulation Conference,* San Diego, CA, (pp. 1709-1715).

Asgarkhani, M. (2002). *Computer modeling and simulation as a learning tool: A preliminary study of network simulation products.* Christchurch Polytechnic Institute of Technology (CPIT), Christchurch, New Zealand.

Ashby, W. R. (1970). Analysis of the system to be modeled. *The process of model-building in the behavioral sciences* (pp. 94-114). Columbus, OH: Ohio State University Press.

Asperti, A., & Busi, N. (1996, May). *Mobile Petri Nets* (Tech. Rep. No. UBLCS-96-10). Bologna, Italy: Università degli Studi di Bologna.

Astrachan, O., & Rodger, S. H. (1998). Animation, visualization, and interaction in CS1 assignments. In *The proceedings of the 29th SIGCSE technical symposium on computer science education* (pp. 317-321), Atlanta, GA. New York: ACM Press.

Astrachan, O., Selby, T., & Unger, J. (1996). An object-oriented, apprenticeship approach to data structures using simulation. In *Proceedings of frontiers in education* (pp. 130-134).

Aulin, T. (1979). A modified model for fading signal at a mobile radio channel. *IEEE Transactions on*

Vehicular Technology, 28(3), 182–203. doi:10.1109/T-VT.1979.23789

Avatars and agents in immersive virtual environments. (2004). Technical Report, The Engineering and Physical Sciences Research Council. Retrieved from http://www.equator.ac.uk/index.php/articles/697.

Axelrod, R., & Cohen, M. D. (2000). *Harnessing complexity: Organizational implications of a scientific.* New York: Basic Books.

Baars, H., & Kemper, H. G. (2007). Management Support with Structured and Unstructured Data-An Integrated Business Intelligence Framework. *Information Systems Management, 25,* 132–148. doi:10.1080/10580530801941058

Babich, F., & Lombardi, G. (2000). Statistical analysis and characterization of the indoor propagation channel. *IEEE Transactions on Communications, 48*(3), 455–464. doi:10.1109/26.837048

Bach, M. (2003). Surviving in an environment of financial indiscipline: a case study from a transition country. *System Dynamics Review, 19*(1), 47–74. doi:10.1002/sdr.253

Badouel, E., & Darondeau, P. (1997, September). Stratified Petri Nets. In B. S. Chlebus & L. Czaja (Eds.), *Proceedings of the 11th International Symposium on Fundamentals of Computation Theory (FCT'97)* (p. 117-128). Kraków, Poland: Springer.

Badouel, E., & Oliver, J. (1998, January). *Reconfigurable Nets, a Class of High Level Petri Nets Supporting Dynamic Changes within Workflow Systems* (IRISA Research Report No. PI-1163). IRISA.

Baecker, R. M. (1998). Sorting out sorting: A case study of software visualization for teaching computer science. In M. Brown, J. Domingue, B. Price, & J. Stasko (Eds.), *Software visualization: Programming as a multimedia experience* (pp. 369–381). Cambridge, MA: The MIT Press.

Baker, R. S., Boilen, M., Goodrich, M. T., Tamassia, R., & Stibel, B. A. (1999). Testers and visualizers for teaching data structures. In *Proceedings of the 30th SIGCSE technical symposium on computer science education* (pp. 261-265), New Orleans, LA. New York: ACM Press.

Balch, T. (2000, 4). *TeamBots.* Retrieved 10 2008, from Carnegie Mellon University - SCholl of Computer science: http://www.cs.cmu.edu/~trb/TeamBots/

Balci, O. (1995). Principles and techniques of simulation validation, verification. In *Proceedings of the 1995 Winter Simulation Conference,* eds. C. Alexopoulos, and K. Kang, 147-154. Piscataway, New Jersey: Institute of Electrical and Electronics Engineers, Inc.

Balci, O. (1998). Verification, Validation and Testing. In J. Banks (Ed.) *Handbook of Simulation.* Hoboken, NJ: John Wiley & Sons

Balci, O. (1998). Verification, validation, and accreditation. In *Proceedings of the 1998 Winter Simulation Conference,* eds. D. J. Medeiros, E. F. Watson, J. S. Carson and M. S. Manivannan, 41-48. Piscataway, New Jersey: Institute of Electrical and Electronics Engineers, Inc.

Banitsas, K. A., Song, Y. H., & Owens, T. J. (2004). OFDM over IEEE 802.11b hardware for telemedical applications. *International Journal of Mobile Communications, 2*(3), 310–327.

Bani-Yassein, M., Ould-Khaoua, M., Mackenzie, L., & Papanastasiou, S. (2006). Performance analysis of adjusted probabilistic broadcasting in mobile ad hoc networks. *International Journal of Wireless Information Networks, 13*(2), 127–140. doi:10.1007/s10776-006-0027-0

Bankes, S. C. (2002). Agent-based modeling: A revolution? *Proceedings of the National Academy of Sciences of the United States of America, 99*(10), 7199–7200. doi:10.1073/pnas.072081299

Banks, J. (1998). *Handbook of simulation.* New York: John Wily & Sons, Inc.

Banks, J. (2000, December 10-13). *Introduction to Simulation.* In J. A. Joines, R. R. Barton, K. Kang, & P. A. Fishwick (Eds.), *Proceedings of the 2000 Winter Simulation Conference,* Orlando, FL, (pp. 510-517). San Diego, CA: Society for Computer Simulation International.

Banks, J. (2001, December). Panel session: Education for simulation practice – five perspectives. In B. A. Peters, J. S. Smith, D. J. Medeiros, & M. W. Rohrer (Eds.) *Proceedings of the 2001 Winter Simulation Conference*, Arlington, VA, (pp. 1571-1579).

Banks, J., Carson, J. S., II, Nelson, B. L., & Nicol, D. M. (2005). *Discrete event simulation* (4th Ed.). Upper Saddle River, NJ: Pearson Prentice Hall.

Banks, J., Gerstein, D., & Searles, S. P. (1998). Modeling Processes, Validation, and Verification of Complex Simulations: A Survey. *Methodology and Validation*: *Simulation Series, 19*(1), 13–18.

Barlas, Y., & Carpenter, S. (1990). Philosophical roots of model validation: Two paradigms. *System Dynamics Review, 6*(2), 148–166. doi:10.1002/sdr.4260060203

Bäsken, M., & Näher, S. (2001). GeoWin a generic tool for interactive visualization of geometric algorithms. In S. Diehl (Ed.), *Software visualization: International seminar* (pp. 88-100). Dagstuhl, Germany: Springer.

Battista, G. D., Eades, P., Tamassia, R., & Tollis, I. (1999). *Graph drawing: Algorithms for the visualization of graphs*. Upper Saddle River, NJ: Prentice Hall.

Bečvář, M., Kubátová, H., & Novotný, M. (2006). Massive Digital Design Education for large amount of undergraduate students. [Royal Institute of Technology, Stockholm.]. *Proceedings of EWME, 2006*, 108–111.

Benford, S., Burke, E., Foxley, E., Gutteridge, N., & Zin, A. M. (1993). Ceilidh: A course administration and marking system. In *Proceedings of the 1st international conference of computer based learning*, Vienna, Austria.

Bernardi, S., Donatelli, S., & Horvàth, A. (2001, September). Implementing Compositionality for Stochastic Petri Nets. *Journal of Software Tools for Technology Transfer, 3*(4), 417–430.

Bertoni, H. L., Honcharenko, W., Macel, L. R., & Xia, H. H. (1994). UHF propagation prediction for wireless personal communications. *IEEE Proceedings, 82*(9), 1333–1359. doi:10.1109/5.317081

Best, E. (1986, September). COSY: Its Relation to Nets and CSP. In W. Brauer, W. Reisig, & G. Rozenberg (Eds.), *Petri Nets: Central Models and Their Properties, Advances in Petri Nets (Part II)* (p. 416-440). Bad Honnef, Germany: Springer.

Better, M., Glover, F., & Laguna, M. (2007). Advances in analytics: Integrating dynamic data mining with simulation optimization. *IBM . Journal of Research and Development (Srinagar), 51*(3/4).

Bian, Y., Poplewell, A., & O'Reilly, J. J. (1994). Novel simulation technique for assessing coding system performance. *IEE Electronics Letters, 30*(23), 1920–1921. doi:10.1049/el:19941297

Bianchi, C., & Bivona, E. (1999). Commercial and financial policies in small and micro family firms: the small business growth management flight simulator. *Simulation and gaming*. Thousand Oaks, CA: Sage publications.

Bianchi, G. (2000). Performance analysis of the IEEE 802.11 distributed coordination function. *IEEE Journal on Selected Areas in Communications, 18*(3), 535–547. doi:10.1109/49.840210

Binzegger, T., Douglas, R. J., & Martin, K. A. C. (2004). A quantitative map of the circuit of cat primary visual cortex. *The Journal of Neuroscience, 24*(39), 8441–8453. doi:10.1523/JNEUROSCI.1400-04.2004

Birta, L. G. (2003). A Perspective of the Modeling and Simulation Body of Knowledge. *Modeling & Simulation Magazine, 2*(1), 16–19.

Birta, L. G. (2003). *The Quest for the Modeling and Simulation Body of Knowledge*. Keynote presentation at the Sixth Conference on Computer Simulation and Industry Applications, Instituto Tecnologico de Tijuana, Mexico, February 19-21, 2003.

Blasak, R., Armel, W., Starks, D., & Hayduk, M. (2003). The Use of Simulation to Evaluate Hospital Operations between the ED and Medical Telemetry Unit. In S. Chick, et al (Ed.), *Proceedings of the 2003 Winter Simulation Conference* (pp. 1887-1893). Washington, DC: IEEE.

Bologna Process (2008). Strasbourg, France: Council of Europe, Higher Education and Research. Retrieved August 15, 2008, from http://www.coe.int/t/dg4/ higher-education/EHEA2010/BolognaPedestrians_en.asp

Boroni, C. M., Eneboe, T. J., Goosey, F. W., Ross, J. A., & Ross, R. J. (1996). Dancing with Dynalab. In *27th SIGCSE technical symposium on computer science education* (pp. 135-139). New York: ACM Press.

Boskers, N. D., & AbouRizk, S. M. (2005). Modeling scheduling uncertainty in capital construction projects. *Proceedings of the 2005 Winter Simulation Conference*, Orlando, FL, (pp. 1500-1507).

Boumans, M. (2006). The difference between answering a 'why' question and answering a 'how much' question. In G. K. Johannes Lenhard, & T. Shinn (Eds.), *Simulation: Pragmatic construction of reality; sociology of the sciences yearbook* (pp. 107-124). Dordrecht, The Netherlands: Springer.

Brade, D. (2000). Enhancing M&S Accreditation by Structuring V&V Results. *Proceedings of the Winter Simulation Conference*, (pp. 840-848).

Brade, D. (2003). *A Generalized Process for the Verification and Validation of Models and Simulation Results*. Dissertation, Universitüt der Bundeswehr München, Germany.

Brade, D., & Lehmann, A. (2002). Model Validation and Verification. In *Modeling and Simulation Environment for Satellite and Terrestrial Communication Networks– Proceedings of the European COST Telecommunication Symposium*. Boston: Kluwer Academic Publishers.

Brader, J. M., Senn, W., & Fusi, S. (2007). Learning real-world stimuli in a neural network with spike-driven synaptic dynamics. *Neural Computation, 19*(11), 2881–2912. doi:10.1162/neco.2007.19.11.2881

Bradu, B., Gayet, P., & Niculescu, S.-I. (2007). A Dynamic Simulator for Large-Scale Cryogenic Systems. In R. K. B. Zupančič (Ed.), *Proc. EUROSIM*, (pp. 1-8).

Braun, W. R., & Dersch, U. (1991). A physical mobile radio channel model. *IEEE Transactions on Vehicular Technology, 40*(2), 472–482. doi:10.1109/25.289429

Brehmer, B. (1992). Dynamic decision making: human control of complex systems. *Acta Psychologica, 81*, 211–241. doi:10.1016/0001-6918(92)90019-A

Breierova, L. & Choudhari, M. (1996). An introduction to sensitivity analysis. *MIT system dynamics in education project.*

Bremermann, H. J. (1962). Optimization through evolution and recombination. In F. T. J. M.C. Yovits, & G.D. Goldstein (Eds.), *Self-oganizing systems* (pp. 93-106). Washington D.C.: Spartan Books.

Brette, R., Rudolph, M., Carnevale, T., Hines, M., & Beeman, D., Bower et al. (2007). Simulation of networks of spiking neurons: A review of tools and strategies. *Journal of Computational Neuroscience, 23*, 349–398. doi:10.1007/s10827-007-0038-6

Bridgeman, S., Goodrich, M. T., Kobourov, S. G., & Tamassia, R. (2000). PILOT: An interactive tool for learning and grading. In *Proceedings of the 31st SIGCSE technical symposium on computer science education* (pp. 139-143). New York: ACM Press. Retrieved from http://citeseer.ist.psu.edu/bridgeman00pilot.html

Broadcom. (2003). *IEEE 802.11g: the new mainstream wireless LAN standard*. Retrieved May 23 2007, from http://www.54g.org/pdf/802.11g-WP104-RDS1

Brown, M. H. (1988). *Algorithm animation.* Cambridge, MA: MIT Press.

Brown, M. H., & Hershberger, J. (1992). Color and sound in algorithm animation. *Computer, 25*(12), 52–63. doi:10.1109/2.179117

Brown, M. H., & Raisamo, R. (1997). JCAT: Collaborative active textbooks using Java. *Computer Networks and ISDN Systems, 29*(14), 1577–1586. doi:10.1016/S0169-7552(97)00090-1

Brown, P. J. (1980). *Writing Interactive Compilers and Interpreters*. Chichester, UK: John Wiley & Sons.

Brown, R. (1988). Calendar queues: A fast 0(1) priority queue implementation for the simulation event set problem. *Journal of Communication ACM, 31*(10), 1220–1227. doi:10.1145/63039.63045

Bullington, K. (1977). Radio propagation for vehicular communications. *IEEE Transactions on Vehicular Technology, 26*(4), 295–308. doi:10.1109/T-VT.1977.23698

Burks, A. W., & Neumann, J. v. (1966). *Theory of self-reproducing automata*. Urbana and London: University of Illinois Press.

Cabac, L., Duvignau, M., Moldt, D., & Rölke, H. (2005, June). Modeling Dynamic Architectures Using Nets-Within-Nets. In G. Ciardo & P. Darondeau (Eds.), *Proceedings of the 26th International Conference on Applications and Theory of Petri Nets (ICATPN 2005)* (p. 148-167). Miami, FL: Springer.

Cairo, O., Aldeco, A., & Algorri, M. (2001). Virtual Museum's Assistant. In *Proceedings of 2nd Asia-Pacific Conference on Intelligent Agent Technology*. Hackensack, NJ: World Scientific Publishing Co. Pte. Ltd.

Cali, F., Conti, M., & Gregori, E. (2000). IEEE 802.11 protocol: design and performance evaluation of an adaptive backoff mechanism. *IEEE Journal on Selected Areas in Communications, 18*(9), 1774–1786. doi:10.1109/49.872963

Capra, L., & Cazzola, W. (2007, December). Self-Evolving Petri Nets. *Journal of Universal Computer Science, 13*(13), 2002–2034.

Capra, L., & Cazzola, W. (2007, on 26th-29th of September). A Reflective PN-based Approach to Dynamic Workflow Change. *In Proceedings of the 9th International Symposium in Symbolic and Numeric Algorithms for Scientific Computing (SYNASC'07)* (p. 533-540). Timisoara, Romania: IEEE CS.

Capra, L., & Cazzola, W. (2009). An Introduction to Reflective Petri Nets. In E. M. O. Abu-Atieh (Ed.), *Handbook of Research on Discrete Event Simulation Environments Technologies and Applications*. Hershey, PA: IGI Global.

Capra, L., & Cazzola, W. (2009). Trying out Reflective Petri Nets on a Dynamic Workflow Case. In E. M. O. Abu-Atieh (Ed.), *Handbook of Research on Discrete Event Simulation Environments Technologies and Applications*. Hershey, PA: IGI Global.

Capra, L., De Pierro, M., & Franceschinis, G. (2005, June). A High Level Language for Structural Relations in Well-Formed Nets. In G. Ciardo & P. Darondeau (Eds.), *Proceeding of the 26th international conference on application and theory of Petri nets* (p. 168-187). Miami, FL: Springer.

Carson, J. S., II. (2004, December). *Introduction to Modeling and Simulation*. Paper presented at 2004 Winter Simulation Conference (pp. 1283-1289).

Carter, M. (2002). Health Care Management, Diagnosis: Mismanagement of Resources. *Operation Research / Management Science (OR/MS) . Today, 29*(2), 26–32.

Carter, M., & Blake, J. (2004). Using simulation in an acute-care hospital: easier said than done. In M. Brandeau, F. Sainfort, &W. Pierskala, (Eds.), *Operations Research and Health Care. A Handbook of Methods and Applications*, (pp.192-215). Boston: Kluwer Academic Publisher.

Casti, J. L. (1995). *Complexification: Explaining a paradoxical world through the science of surprise* (1st Ed.), New York: HarperPerennial.

Cattaneo, G., Italiano, G. F., & Ferraro-Petrillo, U. (2002, August). CATAI: Concurrent algorithms and data types animation over the internet. *Journal of Visual Languages and Computing, 13*(4), 391–419. doi:10.1006/jvlc.2002.0230

CAVIAR project website (n.d.). Available at http://www.imse.cnm.es/caviar/.

Cazzola, W. (1998, July 20th-24th). Evaluation of Object-Oriented Reflective Models. In *Proceedings of ecoop workshop on reflective object-oriented programming and systems (ewroops'98)*. Brussels, Belgium.

Cazzola, W., Ghoneim, A., & Saake, G. (2004, July). Software Evolution through Dynamic Adaptation of Its OO Design. In H.-D. Ehrich, J.-J. Meyer, & M. D. Ryan (Eds.), *Objects, Agents and Features: Structuring Mechanisms for Contemporary Software* (pp. 69-84). Heidelberg, Germany: Springer-Verlag.

Cebenoyan, A., & Strahan, P. (2004). Risk management, capital structure and Lending at banks. *Journal of Banking & Finance, 28,* 19–43. doi:10.1016/S0378-4266(02)00391-6

Cellier, F., & Kofman, E. (2005). *Continuous system simulation.* Berlin: Springer.

Cercas, F. A. B., Cartaxo, A. V. T., & Sebastião, P. J. A. (1999). Performance of TCH codes with independent and burst errors using efficient techniques. *50th IEEE Vehicular Technology Conference,* Amsterdam, Netherlands, *(VTC99-Fall),* (pp. 2536-2540).

Cercas, F. A., Tomlinson, M., & Albuquerque, A. A. (1993). TCH: A new family of cyclic codes length 2m. *International Symposium on Information Theory, IEEE Proceedings,* (pp. 198-198).

Chandrakanthi, M., Ruwanpura, J. Y., Hettiaratchi, P., & Prado, B. (2002). Optimization of the waste management for construction projects using simulation. *Proceedings of the 2002 Winter Simulation Conference,* San Diego, CA, (pp. 1771-1777).

Chang, X. (1999). Network simulation with OPNET. In P. A. Farrington, H. B. Nembhard, D. T. Sturrock, & G. W. Evans (Eds.), *Proceedings of the 1999 Winter Simulation Conference,* (pp. 307-314).

Chiola, G., Dutheillet, C., Franceschinis, G., & Haddad, S. (1990, June). On Well-Formed Coloured Nets and Their Symbolic Reachability Graph. In *Proceedings of the 11th international conference on application and theory of Petri nets,* (p. 387-410). Paris, France.

Chiola, G., Dutheillet, C., Franceschinis, G., & Haddad, S. (1993, November). Stochastic Well-Formed Coloured Nets for Symmetric Modeling Applications. *IEEE Transactions on Computers, 42*(11), 1343–1360. doi:10.1109/12.247838

Chiola, G., Franceschinis, G., Gaeta, R., & Ribaudo, M. (1995, November). GreatSPN 1.7: Graphical Editor and Analyzer for Timed and Stochastic Petri Nets. *Performance Evaluation, 24*(1-2), 47–68. doi:10.1016/0166-5316(95)00008-L

Cho, Y. K., Hu, X. L., & Zeigler, B. P. (2003). The RT-DEVS/CORBA environment for simulation-based design of distributed real-time systems. *Simulation Transactions, 79*(4), 197–210. doi:10.1177/0037549703038880

Choi, S., Park, K., & Kim, C. (2005). *On the performance characteristics of WLANs: revisited.* Paper presented at the 2005 ACM SIGMETRICS international conference on Measurement and modeling of computer systems (pp. 97–108).

Chow, J. (1999). Development of channel models for simulation of wireless systems in OPNET. *Transactions of the Society for Computer Simulation International, 16*(3), 86–92.

Chrysanthou, Y., Tecchia, F., Loscos, C., & Conroy, R. (2004). *Densely populated urban environments.* The Engineering and Physical Sciences Research Council. Retrieved from http://www.cs.ucl.ac.uk/research/vr/Projects/Crowds/

Chung, A. C. (2004). *Simulation and Modeling Handbook: A Practical Approach.* Boca Raton, FL: CRC Press.

Chung, W., Chen, H., & Nunamaker, J. F. Jr. (2005). A Visual Framework for Knowledge Discover on the web: An Empirical Study of Business Intelligence Exploration. *Journal of Management Information Systems, 21*(4), 57–84.

Clarke, R. H. (1968). A statistical theory of mobile radio reception. *The Bell System Technical Journal, 47,* 957–1000.

Claverol, E., Brown, A., & Chad, J. (2002). Discrete simulation of large aggregates of neurons. *Neurocomputing, 47,* 277–297. doi:10.1016/S0925-2312(01)00629-4

Clifford, J., Gaehde, S., Marinello, J., Andrews, M., & Stephens, C. (2008). *Improving Inpatient and Emergency Department Flow for Veterans. Improvement report.* Institute for Healthcare Improvement. Retrieved from http://www.IHI.org/ihi

Cody, F., Kreulen, J. T., Krishna, V., & Spangler, W. S. (2002). The Integration of Business Intelligence and Knowledge Management. *Systems Journal, 41*(4), 697–713.

Coloured Petri Nets at the University of Aarhus (2009). Retrieved from http://www.daimi.au.dk/CPnets/

Cor, H., & Martinez, J. C. (1999). A case study in the quantification of a change in the conditions of a highway construction operation. *Proceedings of the 1999 Winter Simulation Conference*, Phoenix, AZ, (pp. 1007-1009).

Corbitt T. (2003). Business Intelligence and Data Mining. *Management Services Magazine*, November 2003.

Council of Graduate Schools. (2007). *Findings from the 2006 CGS International Graduate Admissions Survey, Phase III Admissions and Enrolment Oct. 2006, Revised March 2007*. Council of Graduate Schools Research Report, Council of Graduate Schools, Washington DC.

Crain, R. C. (1997). Simulation using GPSS/H. *Proceedings of the 1997 Winter Simulation Conference*, Atlanta, GA, (pp. 567-573).

Crews, W. (n.d.). *Gwinnett County Public Schools*. Retrieved 2008, from Gwinnett County Public Schools, http://www.crews.org/curriculum/ex/compsci/8thgrade/stkmkt/index.htm

CRONOS project website (n.d.). Available at www.cronosproject.net.

Crosbie, R. E. (2000, December). Simulation curriculum: a model curriculum in modeling and simulation: do we need it? Can we do it? In J. A. Joines, R. R. Barton, K. Kang & P. A. Fishwick, (Eds.) *Proceedings of the 2000 Winter Simulation Conference*, Piscataway, NJ, (pp. 1666-1668). Washington, DC: IEEE...

Czerwinski, T. (1998). *Coping with the Bounds: Speculations on Nonlinearity in Military Affairs*. Washington, DC: National Defense University Press.

D. Molkdar, D. (1991). Review on radio propagation into and within buildings. *IEEE Proceedings, 138*(11), 61-73.

D'Alesandro, J. (2008). *Queuing Theory Misplaced in Hospitals*. Management News from the Front, Process

Improvement. PHLO. Posted Feb 19, 2008 at http://phlo.typepad.com

Dahmann, J., Salisbury, M., Turrel, C., Barry, P., & Blemberg, P. (1999). *HLA and beyond: Interoperability challenges*. Paper no. 99F-SIW-073 presented at the Fall Simulation Interoperability Workshop Orlando, FL, USA.

Davis, P. K. (1992). *Generalizing concepts and methods of verification, validation, and*. Santa Monica, CA: RAND.

Davis, P. K., & Blumenthal, D. (1991). *The base of sand problem: A white paper on the state of military*. Santa Monica, CA: RAND.

de Bruin, A., van Rossum, A., Visser, M., & Koole, G. (2007). Modeling the Emergency cardiac in-patient flow: an application of queuing theory. *Health Care Management Science, 10*, 125–137. doi:10.1007/s10729-007-9009-8

Dearie, J., & Warfield, T. (1976, July 12-14). The development and use of a simulation model of an outpatient clinic. *Proceedings of the 1976 Summer computer Simulation Conference*, Simulation Council, Washington, DC, (pp. 554-558).

Dehaene, S., & Changeux, J.-P. (2005). Ongoing spontaneous activity controls access to consciousness: A neuronal model for inattentional blindness. *Public Library of Science Biology, 3*(5), 910–927.

Deitel, H. M., & Deitel, P. J. (1998). *C++ how to program*. Upper Saddle River, NJ: Prentice Hall.

Delorme, A., & Thorpe, S. J. (2003). SpikeNET: An event-driven simulation package for modeling large networks of spiking neurons. *Network: Computational in Neural Systems, 14*, 613–627. doi:10.1088/0954-898X/14/4/301

Department of Defense. (1996). *Modeling & Simulation Verification, Validation, and Accreditation* (US DoD Instruction 5000.61). Washington, DC: Author.

Desel, J., & Esparza, J. (1995). *Free Choice Petri Nets* (Cambridge Tracts in Theoretical Computer Science Vol. 40). New York: Cambridge University Press.

DEVS-Standardization-Group. (2008). *General Info.* Retrieved September 1st, 2008, from http://cell-devs. sce.carleton.ca/devsgroup/.

Dexter, F., Macario, A., Traub, R., Hopwood, M., & Lubarsky, D. (1999). An Operating Room Scheduling Strategy to Maximize the Use of Operating Room Block Time: Computer Simulation of Patient Scheduling and Survey of Patients' Preferences for Surgical Waiting Time. *Anesthesia and Analgesia, 89,* 7–20. doi:10.1097/00000539-199907000-00003

Diesmann, M., & Gewaltig, M.-O. (2002). NEST: An environment for neural systems simulations. In V. Macho (Ed.), *Forschung und wissenschaftliches rechnen.* Heinz-Billing-Preis, GWDG-Bericht.

Digilent, (2009). Retrieved from http://www.digilentinc. com

Dobrev, P., Kalaydjiev, O., & Angelova, G. (2007). *From Conceptual Structures to Semantic Interoperability of Content.* (LNCS Vol. 4604, pp. 192-205). Berlin: Springer-Verlag.

EBC Web site (2001). *EBC achievements: civil engineering/earthworks.* Retrieved from http://www.ebcinc. qc.ca/

Elfving, J. A., & Tommelein, I. D. (2003). Impact of multitasking and merge bias on procurement of Complex Equipment. *Proceedings of the 2003 Winter Simulation Conference,* New Orleans, LA, (pp. 1527-1533).

Ellis, C., & Keddara, K. (2000, August). ML-DEWS: Modeling Language to Support Dynamic Evolution within Workflow Systems. *Computer Supported Cooperative Work, 9*(3-4), 293–333. doi:10.1023/A:1008799125984

Engineering and Physical Sciences Research Council (EPSRC). (2004). *Review of Research Status of Operational Research (OR) in the UK,* Swindon, UK. Retrieved from www.epsrc.ac.uk

English, J., & Siviter, P. (2000). Experience with an automatically assessed course. In *Proceedings of the 5th annual SIGCSE/sigcue conference on innovation and technology in computer science education, iticse'00* (pp. 168-171), Helsinki, Finland. New York: ACM Press.

ENOVIA. (2007, September). *Dassault systèmes plm solutions for the mid-market* [white-paper]. Retrieved from http:/www.3ds.com/fileadmin/brands/enovia/pdf/ whitepapers/CIMdata-DS_PLM_for_the_MidMarket-Program_review-Sep2007.pdf)

Epstein, J. M., & Axtell, R. (1996). *Growing artificial socieities: Social science from the bottom up.* Washington, DC: Brookings Institution Press.

Erhard, W., Reinsch, A., & Schober, T. (2001). Modeling and Verification of Sequential Control Path Using Petri Nets. In *Proc. DESDes'01,* (pp. 41 – 46) Zielona Gora, Poland.

Erl, T. (2005). *Service-Oriented Architecture Concepts, Technology and Design.* Upper Saddle River, NJ: Prentice Hall.

Ester, M., Kriegel, H. P., Sander, J., Wimmer, M., & Xu, X. (1998). Incremental clustering for mining in a data warehousing environment. *Proceedings Of The 24th Vldb Conference,* New York.

Everett, J. E. (2002). A decision support simulation model for the management of an elective surgery waiting system. *Journal for Health Care Management Science, 5*(2), 89–95. doi:10.1023/A:1014468613635

Ewing, G., Pawlikowski, K., & McNickle, D. (1999, June). *Akaroa 2: exploiting network computing by distributed stochastic simulation.* Paper presented at European Simulation Multiconference (ESM'99), Warsaw, Poland, (pp. 175-181).

Fall, K., & Varadhan, K. (2008). *The ns manual. The VINT project.* Retrieved February 10, 2008, from http:// www.isi.edu/nsnam/ns/doc/

Family of Standards for Modeling and Simulation (M&S) High Level Architecture (HLA) – (a) IEEE 1516-2000 Framework and Rules; (b) IEEE 1516.1-2000 Federate Interface Specification; (c) IEEE 1516.2-2000 Object Model Template (OMT) Specification IEEE 1516-2000, *IEEE Press.*

Fang, X., Sheng, O. R. L., Gao, W., & Iyer, B. R. (2006). A data-mining-based prefetching approach to caching for network storage systems. *INFORMS Journal on Computing, 18*(2), 267–282. doi:10.1287/ijoc.1050.0142

Fantacci, R., Pecorella, T., & Habib, I. (2004). Proposal and performance evaluation of an efficient multiple-access protocol for LEO satellite packet networks. *IEEE Journal on Selected Areas in Communications, 22*(3), 538–545. doi:10.1109/JSAC.2004.823437

Farid, F., & Koning, T. L. (1994). Simulation verifies queuing program for selecting loader-truck fleets. *Journal of Construction Engineering and Management, 120*(2), 386–404. doi:10.1061/(ASCE)0733-9364(1994)120:2(386)

Farwer, B., & Moldt, D. (Eds.). (2005, August). *Object Petri Nets, Process, and Object Calculi.* Hamburg, Germany: Universität Hamburg, Fachbereich Informatik.

Fayyad, U., Piatetsky-Shapiro, G., & Smyth, P. (1996). From data mining to knowledge discovery in databases, American Association for Artificial Intelligence. *AI Magazine*, 37–54.

Feinstein, A. H., & Cannon, H. M. (2002). Constructs of simulation evaluation. *Simulation & Gaming, 33*(4), 425–440. doi:10.1177/1046878102238606

Feinstein, A. H., & Cannon, H. M. (2003). A hermeneutical approach to external validation of simulation models. *Simulation & Gaming, 34*(2), 186–197. doi:10.1177/1046878103034002002

Ferber, J. (1999). *Multi-agent systems: An introduction to distributed artificial intelligence.* Harlow, UK: Addison-Wesley

Feuerstein, M. J., Blackard, K. L., Rappaport, T. S., Seidel, S. Y., & Xia, H. H. (1994). Path loss, delay spread, and outage models as functions of antenna height for micro-cellular system design. *IEEE Transactions on Vehicular Technology, 43*(3), 487–489. doi:10.1109/25.312809

Filippi, J. B., & Bisgambiglia, P. (2004). JDEVS: an implementation of a DEVS based formal framework for environmental modelling. *Environmental Modelling & Software, 19*(3), 261–274. doi:10.1016/j.envsoft.2003.08.016

Fishman, G. S., & Kiviat, P. J. (1968). The statistics of discrete-event simulation. *Simulation, 10*, 185–195. doi:10.1177/003754976801000406

Fishwick, P. (2002). The Art of Modeling. *Modeling & Simulation Magazine, 1*(1), 36.

Fleischer, R., & Kucera, L. (2001). Algorithm animation for teaching. In S. Diehl (Ed.), *Software visualization: International seminar* (pp. 113-128). Dagstuhl, Germany: Springer.

Fone, D., Hollinghurst, S., & Temple, M. (2003). Systematic review of the use and value of computer simulation modeling in population health and health care delivery. *Journal of Public Health Medicine, 25*(4), 325–335. doi:10.1093/pubmed/fdg075

Fong, J., Li, Q., & Huang, S. (2003). Universal data warehousing based on a meta-data modeling approach. *International Journal of Cooperative Information Systems, 12*(3), 318–325. doi:10.1142/S0218843003000772

Forouzan, B. A. (2007). *Data Communications and Networking* (4th Ed.). Boston: McGraw-Hill.

Forrester, J. (1961). *Industrial Dynamics.* New York: MIT Press and Wiley Inc.

Forrester, J. (1992). System dynamics, systems thinking, and soft OR. *System Dynamics Review, 10*(2).

French, R. C. (1979). The effect of fading and shadowing on channel reuse in mobile radio. *IEEE Transactions on Vehicular Technology, 28*(3), 171–181. doi:10.1109/T-VT.1979.23788

Frigg, R., & Reiss, J. (2008). *The philosophy of simulation: Hot new issues or same old stew?* Gershenson, C. (2002). Complex philosophy. *The First Biennial Seminar on the Philosophical, Methodological.*

Fujimoto, R. (1998). Time management in the High-Level Architecture. *Simulation: Transactions of the Society for Modeling and Simulation International, 71*(6), 388–400. doi:10.1177/003754979807100604

Fujimoto, R. (2000). *Parallel and distributed simulation systems.* Mahwah, NJ: John Wiley and Sons, Inc.

Furber, S. B., Temple, S., & Brown, A. D. (2006). High-performance computing for systems of spiking neurons. In *Proceedings of the AISB'06 Workshop on GC5: Architecture of Brain and Mind,* (Vol. 2, pp 29-36). Bristol: AISB.

Fusk, H., Lawniczak, A. T., & Volkov, S. (2001). Packet delay in models of data networks. *ACM Transactions on Modeling and Computer Simulation, 11*(3), 233–250. doi:10.1145/502109.502110

Gallivan, S., Utley, M., Treasure, T., & Valencia, O. (2002). Booked inpatient admissions and hospital capacity: mathematical modeling study. *British Medical Journal, 324,* 280–282. doi:10.1136/bmj.324.7332.280

Gamez, D. (2007). SpikeStream: A fast and flexible simulator of spiking neural networks. In J. M. de Sá, L. A. Alexandre, W. Duch & D. P. Mandic (Eds.) *Proceedings of ICANN 2007,* (Vol. 4668, pp. 370-79). Berlin: Springer Verlag.

Gamez, D. (2008). Progress in machine consciousness. *Consciousness and Cognition, 17*(3), 887–910. doi:10.1016/j.concog.2007.04.005

Gamez, D. (2008). *The Development and analysis of conscious machines.* Unpublished doctoral dissertation. University of Essex, UK. Available at http://www.davidgamez.eu/mc-thesis/

Gamez, D., Newcombe, R., Holland, O., & Knight, R. (2006). Two simulation tools for biologically inspired virtual robotics. *Proceedings of the IEEE 5th Chapter Conference on Advances in Cybernetic Systems* (pp. 85-90). Sheffield, UK: IEEE.

Garcia, M. N. M., Roman, I. R., Penalvo, F. J. G., & Bonilla, M. T. (2008). An association rule mining method for estimating the impact of project management policies on software quality, development time and effort. *Expert Systems with Applications, 34,* 522–529. doi:10.1016/j.eswa.2006.09.022

Garcia, M., Centeno, M., Rivera, C., & DeCario, N. (1995). Reducing Time in an Emergency Room via a Fast-track. In C. Alexopoulos, et al (Ed.), *Proceedings of the 1995 Winter Simulation Conference,* (pp. 1048-1053). Washington, DC: IEEE.

Gartner Group. (1996, September). Retrieved November 12, 2005, from http://www.innerworx.co.za/products.htm.

Gass, S. I. (1999). Decision-Aiding Models: Validation, Assessment, and Related Issues for Policy Analysis. *Operations Research, 31*(4), 601–663.

Gatfield, T., Barker, M., & Graham, P. (1999). Measuring Student Quality Variables and the Implications for Management Practices in Higher Education Institutions: an Australian and International Student Perspective. *Journal of Higher Education Policy and Management, 21*(2). doi:10.1080/1360080990210210

Gerstner, W., & Kistler, W. (2002). *Spiking neuron models.* Cambridge, UK: Cambridge University Press.

Girault, C., & Valk, R. (2003). *Petri Nets for Systems Engineering.* Berlin: Springer-Verlag.

Girija, N., & Srivatsa, S. K. (2006). A Research Study-Using Data Mining in Knowledge Base Business Strategies. *Information Technology Journal, 5*(3), 590–600. doi:10.3923/itj.2006.590.600

Gitman, L. (2000). *Managerial Finance: Brief.* Reading, MA: Addison-Wesley.

Gleick, J. (1987). *Chaos: Making a new science.* New York: Viking.

GloMoSim. (2007). *GloMoSim Manual.* Retrieved April 20, 2007, from http://pcl.cs.ucla.edu/projects/glomosim/GloMoSimManual.html

Gloor, P. A. (1998). User interface issues for algorithm animation. In M. Brown, J. Domingue, B. Price, & J. Stasko (Eds.), *Software visualization: Programming as a multimedia experience* (pp. 145–152). Cambridge, MA: The MIT Press.

Gödel, K. (1931). Über formal unentscheidbare sätze der principia mathematica und verwandter. *Monatshefte Für Mathematik Und Physik,* (38), 173-198.

Goldratt, E., & Cox, J. (2004). *The Goal* (3rd Ed., p. 384). Great Barrington, MA: North River Press.

Gomes, L., & Barros, J.-P. (2001). Using Hierarchical Structuring Mechanism with Petri Nets for PLD Based System Design. In *Proc. DESDes'01* (pp. 47–52), Zielona Gora, Poland.

Gorgone, J. T., Gray, P., Stohr, E. A., Valacich, J. S., & Wigand, R. T. (2006). MSIS 2006. Model Curriculum and Guidelines for Graduate Degree Programs in Information Systems. *Communications of the Association for Information Systems, 17*, 1–56.

Gowda, R. K., Singh, A., & Connolly, M. (1998). Holistic enhancement of the production analysis of bituminous paving operations. *Construction Management and Economics, 16*(4), 417–432. doi:10.1080/014461998372204

Graco, W., Semenova, T., & Dubossarsky, E. (2007). Toward Knowledge-Driven Data Mining. *ACM SIGKDD Workshop on Domain Driven Data Mining (DDDM2007)*, (pp. 49-54).

Green, D. B., & Obaidat, M. S. (2003). Modeling and simulation of IEEE 802.11 WLAN mobile ad hoc networks using topology broadcast reverse-path forwarding (TBRPF). *Computer Communications, 26*(15), 1741–1746. doi:10.1016/S0140-3664(03)00043-4

Green, L. (2004). *Capacity Planning and Management in Hospitals*. In M. Brandeau., F. Sainfort, W. Pierskala, (Eds.), *Operations Research and Health Care. A Handbook of Methods and Applications*, (pp.15-41). Boston: Kluwer Academic Publisher.

Green, L. (2006). Queuing Analysis in Healthcare. In R. Hall, (Ed.), *Patient Flow: Reducing Delay in Healthcare Delivery* (pp. 281-307). New York: Springer.

Green, L., Kolesar, P., & Soares, J. (2001). Improving the SIPP approach for staffing service systems that have cyclic demands. *Operations Research, 49*, 549–564. doi:10.1287/opre.49.4.549.11228

Green, L., Kolesar, P., & Svoronos, A. (1991). Some effects of non-stationarity on multi- server Markovian queuing Systems. *Operations Research, 39*, 502–511. doi:10.1287/opre.39.3.502

Green, L., Soares, J., Giglio, J., & Green, R. (2006). Using Queuing Theory to Increase the Effectiveness of Emergency Department Provider Staffing. *Academic Emergency Medicine, 13*, 61–68. doi:10.1111/j.1553-2712.2006.tb00985.x

Griffin, A., Lacetera, J., Sharp, R., & Tolk, A. (Eds.). (2002). *C4ISR/Sim Technical Reference Model Study Group Final Report (C4ISR/Sim TRM)*, (SISO-Reference Document 008-2002-R2). Simulation Interoperability Standards Organization, Orlando, FL.

Grigori, D., Casati, F., Castellanos, M., Sayal, U. M., & Shan, M. C. (2004). Business Process Intelligence. *Computers in Industry, 53*, 321–343. doi:10.1016/j.compind.2003.10.007

Grillmeyer, O. (1999). An interactive multimedia textbook for introductory computer science. In *The proceedings of the thirtieth SIGCSE technical symposium on computer science education* (pp. 286–290). New York: ACM Press.

Gunal, M., & Pidd, M. (2006). Understanding Accident and Emergency Department Performance using Simulation. In L. Perrone, et al (Ed.) *Proceedings of the 2006 Winter Simulation Conference* (pp. 446-452). Washington, DC: IEEE.

Ha, T. T. (1990). *Digital satellite communications* (2nd Ed.). New York: McGraw-Hill.

Hagmann, C., Lange, D., & Wright, D. (2008, 1). *Cosmic-ray Shower Library (CRY)*. Retrieved 10 2008, from Lawrence Livermore National Laboratory, http://nuclear.llnl.gov/

Hajjar, D., & AbouRizk, S. M. (1999). Simphony: an environment for building special purpose simulation. *Proceedings of the 1999 Winter Simulation Conference*, Phoenix, AZ, (pp. 998-1006).

Hall, R. (1990). *Queuing methods for Service and Manufacturing*. Upper Saddle River, NJ: Prentice Hall.

Halpin, D. W. (1977). CYCLONE-method for modeling job site processes. *Journal of the Construction Division, 103*(3), 489–499.

Halpin, D. W., & Riggs, L. S. (1992). *Planning and analysis of construction operations*. New York: John Wiley & Sons, Inc.

Hanna, M., & Ruwanpura, J. (2007). Simulation tool for manpower forecast loading and resource leveling. *Proceedings of the 2007 Winter Simulation Conference*, Washington, DC, (pp. 2099-2103).

Hansen, F., & Meno, F. I. (1977). Mobile fading-Rayleigh and lognormal superimposed. *IEEE Transactions on Vehicular Technology*, 26(4), 332–335. doi:10.1109/T-VT.1977.23703

Hansen, S. R., Narayanan, N. H., & Schrimpsher, D. (2000, May). Helping learners visualize and comprehend algorithms. *Interactive Multimedia Electronic Journal of Computer-Enhanced Learning, 2*(1).

Haq, F., & Kunz, T. (2005). *Simulation vs. emulation: Evaluating mobile adhoc network routing protocols*. Paper presented at the International Workshop on Wireless Ad-hoc Networks (IWWAN 2005).

Haraden, C., Nolan, T., & Litvak, E. (2003). *Optimizing Patient Flow: Moving Patients Smoothly Through Acute Care Setting* [White papers 2]. Institute for Healthcare Improvement Innovation Series, Cambridge, MA

Harmon, S. Y. (2002, February-March). Can there be a Science of Simulation? Why should we care? *Modeling & Simulation Magazine, 1*(1).

Harrison, G., Shafer, A., & Mackay, M. (2005). Modeling Variability in Hospital Bed Occupancy. *Health Care Management Science*, 8, 325–334. doi:10.1007/s10729-005-4142-8

Hasenauer, H. (2006). *Sustainable forest management: growth models for europe*. Berlin: Springer.

Hashemi, H. (1979). Simulation of the urban radio propagation channel. *IEEE Transactions on Vehicular Technology*, 28(3), 213–225. doi:10.1109/T-VT.1979.23791

Hashemi, H. (1993). Impulse response modelling of indoor radio propagation channels. *IEEE Journal on Selected Areas in Communications*, 11(7), 967–978. doi:10.1109/49.233210

Hashemi, H. (1993). The indoor radio propagation channel. *Proceedings of the IEEE*, 81(7), 943–968. doi:10.1109/5.231342

Hason, S. F. (1994). *Feasibility and implementation of automation and robotics in Canadian building construction operation*. M.Sc.Thesis, Center for Building Studies, Concordia University, Portland, OR.

Hassan, M., & Jain, R. (2003). *High Performance TCP/IP Networking: Concepts, Issues, and Solutions*. Upper Saddle River, NJ: Prentice-Hall.

Hata, M. (1990). Empirical formula for propagation loss in land mobile radio services. *IEEE Transactions on Vehicular Technology*, 29(3), 317–325. doi:10.1109/T-VT.1980.23859

Haydon, P. (2000). Neuroglial networks: Neurons and glia talk to each other. *Current Biology*, 10(19), 712–714. doi:10.1016/S0960-9822(00)00708-9

Haykin, S. (2001). *Communication systems* (4th Ed.). Chichester, UK: John Wiley & Sons, Inc.

Heidemann, J., Bulusu, N., Elson, J., Intanagonwiwat, C., Lan, K., & Xu, Y. (2001). *Effects of detail in wireless network simulation*. Paper presented at the SCS Multiconference on Distributed Simulation (pp. 3–11).

Helstrom, C. W. (1984). *Probability and stochastic processes for engineers* (1st Ed.). New York: MacMillan.

Henry, R. R., Whaley, K. M., & Forstall, B. (1990). The University of Washington illustrating compiler. In *Proceedings of the ACM SIGPLAN'90 conference on programming language design and implementation* (pp. 223-233).

Heusse, M., Rousseau, F., Berger-Sabbatel, G., & Duda, A. (2003, March 30-April 3). *Performance anomaly of 802.11b*. Paper presented at the IEEE INFOCOM'03 (pp. 836-843).

Hicheur, A., Barkaoui, K., & Boudiaf, N. (2006, September). Modeling Workflows with Recursive ECATNets. In *Proceedings of the Eighth International Symposium on Symbolic and Numeric Algorithms for Scientific Computing (SYNACS'06)* (p. 389-398). Timisoara, Romania: IEEE CS.

Higgins, C., Symeonidis, P., & Tsintsifas, A. (2002). The marking system for CourseMaster. In *Proceedings of the 7th annual conference on innovation and technology in computer science education* (pp. 46–50). New York: ACM Press.

Hilen, D. (2000). *Taylor Enterprise Dynamics (User Manual)*. Utrecht, The Netherlands: F&H Simulations B.V.

Hill, R. R., McIntyre, G. A., Tighe, T. R., & Bullock, R. K. (2003). Some experiments with agent-based combat models. *Military Operations Research, 8*(3), 17–28.

Hiller, L., Gosnell, T., Gronberg, J., & Wright, D. (2007, November). *RadSrc Library and Application Manual*. Retrieved October 2008, from http://nuclear.llnl.gov/

Hillier, F., & Yu, O. (1981). *Queuing Tables and Graphs* (pp.1-231). New-York: Elsevier, Hlupic, V., (2000). Simulation Software: A Survey of Academic and Industrial Users. *International Journal of Simulation, 1*(1), 1–11.

Hoare, C. A. R. (1985). *Communicating Sequential Processes*. Upper Saddle River, NJ: Prentice Hall.

Hodges, J. S. (1991). Six or so things you can do with a bad model. *Operations Research, 39*(3), 355–365. doi:10.1287/opre.39.3.355

Hodgkin, A. L., & Huxley, A. F. (1952). A quantitative description of membrane current and its application to conduction and excitation in nerve. *The Journal of Physiology, 117*, 500–544.

Hoffmann, K., Ehrig, H., & Mossakowski, T. (2005, June). High-Level Nets with Nets and Rules as Tokens. In G. Ciardo & P. Darondeau (Eds.), *Proceedings of the 26th International Conference on Applications and Theory of Petri Nets (ICATPN 2005)* (pp. 268-288). Miami, FL: Springer.

Holland, J. H. (1995). *Hidden order: How adaptation builds complexity*. Cambridge, MA: Helix Books.

Huang, R., Grigoriadis, A. M., & Halpin, D. W. (1994). Simulation of cable-stayed bridges using DISCO. *Proceedings of the 1994 Winter Simulation Conference*, Orlando, FL, (pp. 1130-1136).

Huang, Y. (2002). *Infrastructure, query optimization, data warehousing and data mining for scientific simulation*. A thesis, University of Notre Dame, Notre Dame, IN.

Hürsch, W., & Videira Lopes, C. (1995, February). *Separation of Concerns* (Tech. Rep. No. NUCCS- 95-03). Northeastern University, Boston.

Hundhausen, C. D., Douglas, S. A., & Stasko, J. T. (2002, June). A meta-study of algorithm visualization effectiveness. *Journal of Visual Languages and Computing, 13*(3), 259–290. doi:10.1006/jvlc.2002.0237

Hundhausen, C., & Brown, J. (2005). What you see is what you code: A "radically-dynamic" algorithm visualization development model for novice learners. In *Proceedings IEEE 2005 symposium on visual languages and human-centric computing*.

Huyet, A. L. (2006). Optimization and analysis aid via data-mining for simulated production systems. *European Journal of Operational Research, 173*, 827–838. doi:10.1016/j.ejor.2005.07.026

Hydro-Quebec (1999). *Sainte-Marguerite-3 hydroelectric project: in harmony with the environment*.

Hyvönen, J., & Malmi, L. (1993). TRAKLA – a system for teaching algorithms using email and a graphical editor. In *Proceedings of hypermedia in Vaasa* (pp. 141-147).

IEEE. (2000). *HLA Framework and Rules* (Version IEEE 1516-2000). Washington, DC: IEEE Press.

Ihde, D. (2006). Models, models everywhere. In G. K. Johannes Lenhard, & T. Shinn (Eds.), *Simulation: Pragmatic construction of reality; sociology of the sciences yearbook* (pp. 79-86). Dordrecht, The Netherlands: Springer.

IHI - Institute for Healthcare Improvement. (2008). Boston, MA: Author. Retrieved from http://www.ihi.org/IHI/Programs/ConferencesAndSeminars/ApplyingQueuingTheorytoHealthCareJune2008.htm

Ikegami, F., Yoshida, S., Takeuchi, T., & Umehira, M. (1984). Propagation factors controlling mean field on urban streets. *IEEE Transactions on Antennas and Propagation, 32*(8), 822–829. doi:10.1109/TAP.1984.1143419

Ilachinski, A. (2000). Irreducible semi-autonomous adaptive combat (ISAAC): An artificial-life approach to land warefare. *Military Operations Research, 5*(3), 29–47.

Ingolfsson, A., & Gallop, F. (2003). *Queuing ToolPak 4.0.* Retrieved from http://www.bus.ualberta.ca/aingolfsson/QTP/

Ioannou, P. G. (1989). *UM-CYCLONE user's manual.* Division of Construction Engineering and Management, Purdue University, West Lafayette, IN.

Ioannou, P. G. (1999). Construction of dam embankment with nonstationary queue. *Proceedings of the 1999 Winter Simulation Conference,* Phoenix, AZ, (pp. 921-928).

ITU-R, P.341-5, (1999). *The concept of transmission loss for radio links,* [Recommendation].

Izhikevich, E. M. (2003). Simple model of spiking neurons. *IEEE Transactions on Neural Networks, 14,* 1569–1572. doi:10.1109/TNN.2003.820440

Izhikevich, E. M., & Edelman, G. M. (2008). Large-scale model of mammalian thalamocortical systems. *Proceedings of the National Academy of Sciences of the United States of America, 105,* 3593–3598. doi:10.1073/pnas.0712231105

Jackson, D., & Usher, M. (1997). Grading student programs using ASSYST. In *Proceedings of 28th ACM SIGCSE symposium on computer science education* (pp. 335-339).

Jackson, M. (2003). *System Thinking: Creative Holism for Managers.* Chichester, UK: Wiley.

Jacobson, H., Hall, S., & Swisher, J. (2006). Discreet-Event Simulation of Health Care Systems. In R. Hall, (Ed.), *Patient Flow: Reducing Delay in Healthcare Delivery,* (pp. 210-252). New York: Springer.

Jakes, W. C. (1974). *Microwave mobile communications* (1st Ed.). Washington, DC: IEEE Press.

Jaradat, R. (2009). *Development and Performance Analysis of Optimal Multipoint Relaying Algorithm for Noisy Mobile Ad Hoc Networks.* M.Sc Thesis, Department of Computer Science, Amman Arab University for Graduate Studies, Jordan.

Jaradat, Y. (2007). *Development and Performance Analysis of a Probabilistic Flooding in Noisy Mobile Ad Hoc Networks.* M.Sc Thesis, Department of Computer Science, Amman Arab University for Graduate Studies, Jordan.

JarpPetri Nets Analyzer Home Page (2009). Retrieved from http://jarp.sourceforge.net/

Jaschik, S. (2006). Making Sense of 'Bologna Degrees.' *Inside Higher Ed.* Retrieved November 15, 2008 from http://www.insidehighered.com/news/ 2006/11/06/bologna

Jensen, K., & Rozenberg, G. (Eds.). (1991). *High-Level Petri Nets: Theory and Applications.* Berlin: Springer-Verlag.

Jensen, P. A., & Bard, J. F. (2003). *Operations research models and methods.* Hoboken, NJ: John Wiley & Sons.

Jermol, M., Lavrac, N., & Urbanci, T. (2003). Managing business intelligence in a virtual enterprise: A case study and knowledge management lessons learned. *Journal of Intelligent & Fuzzy Systems, 14,* 121–136.

Jeruchim, M., Balaban, P., & Shanmugan, K. S. (2000). *Simulation of communication systems – modelling methodology and techniques* (2nd ed.). Amsterdam, The Netherlands: Kluwer Academic.

Jimenez, G. & Saurian, J. (2003). Collateral, type of lender and relationship banking as determinants of credit risk. *Journal of banking and finance.*

Johnson, A. (2006). The shape of molecules to come. In G. K. Johannes Lenhard, & T. Shinn (Eds.), *Simulation: Pragmatic construction of reality; sociology of the sciences yearbook* (pp. 25-39). Dordrecht, The Netherlands: Springer.

Johnson, G. W. (1994). *LabVIEW Graphical Programming.* New York: McGraw-Hill.

Johnson, N. Kotz., S., & Balakrishnan, N., (1994). *Continuous Univariate Distributions* (Vol.1). New York: John Wiley & Sons.

Jukic, N. (2006). Modeling strategies and alternatives for data warehousing projects. *Communications of the ACM, 49*(4), 83–88. doi:10.1145/1121949.1121952

Jun, J., Jacobson, H., & Swisher, J. (1999). Application of DES in health-care clinics: A survey. *The Journal of the Operational Research Society, 50*(2), 109–123.

Kabal, P. (1993). *TEXdraw – PostScript drawings from TEX.* Retrieved from http://www.tau.ac.il/cc/pages/docs/ tex-3.1415/ texdraw_toc.html

Kaipainen, T., Liski, J., Pussinen, A., & Karjalainen, T. (2004). Managing carbon sinks by changing rotation length in European forests. *Environmental Science & Policy, 7*(3), 205–219. doi:10.1016/j.envsci.2004.03.001

Karavirta, V., Korhonen, A., Malmi, L., & Stålnacke, K. (2004, July). MatrixPro – A tool for on-the-fly demonstration of data structures and algorithms. In *Proceedings of the third program visualization workshop* (pp. 26–33). Warwick, UK: Department of Computer Science, University of Warwick, UK.

Kavi, K. M., Sheldon, F. T., Shirazi, B., & Hurson, A. R. (1995, January). Reliability Analysis of CSP Specifications Using Petri Nets and Markov Processes. In *Proceedings of the 28th Annual Hawaii International Conference on System Sciences (HICSS-28)* (p. 516-524). Kihei, Maui, HI: IEEE Computer Society.

Keating, B. A., P. S. (2003). An overview of APSIM, a model designed for farming systems simulation. *European Journal of Agronomy, 18*(3-4), 267–288. doi:10.1016/ S1161-0301(02)00108-9

Kelton, W. D., Sadowski, R. P., & Sadowski, D. A. A. (1998). *Simulation with Arena*. Boston: McGraw-Hill.

Kerdprasop, N., & Kerdpraso, K. (2007). Moving data mining tools toward a business intelligence system. *Enformatika, 19*, 117–122.

Kheir, N. A. (1988). *Systems Modeling and Computer Simulation*. Basel, Switzerland: Marcel Dekker Inc.

Kim, Y. J., Kim, J. H., & Kim, T. G. (2003). Heterogeneous Simulation Framework Using DEVS BUS. *Simulation Transactions, 79*, 3–18. doi:10.1177/0037549703253543

Kincaid, H. (1998). Philsophy: Then and now. In N. S. Arnold, T. M. Benditt & G. Graham (Eds.), (pp. 321-338). Malden, MA: Blackwell Publishers Ltd.

Kindler, E. (Ed.). (2004). Definition, Implementation and Application of a Standard Interchange Format for Petri Nets. In *Proceedings of the Workshop of the satellite event of the 25th International Conf. on Application and Theory of Petri Nets*, Bologna, Italy.

Klein, E. E., & Herskovitz, P. J. (2005). Philosophical foundations of computer simulation validation. *Simulation \& Gaming, 36*(3), 303-329.

Kleindorfer, G. B., & Ganeshan, R. (1993). The philosophy of science and validation in simulation. In *Proceedings of the 1993 Winter Simulation Conference*, ed. G.W. Evans, M. Mollaghasemi, E.C. Russell, and W.E. Biles, 50-57. Piscataway, New Jersey: Institute of Electrical and Electronic Engineers, Inc.

Kleindorfer, G. B., O'Neill, L., & Ganeshan, R. (1998). Validation in simulation: Various positions in the philosophy of science. *Management Science, 44*(8), 1087–1099. doi:10.1287/mnsc.44.8.1087

Knuuttila, T. (2006). From representation to production: Parsers and parsing in language. In G. K. Johannes Lenhard, & T. Shinn (Eds.), *Simulation: Pragmatic construction of reality; sociology of the sciences yearbook* (pp. 41-55). Dordrecht, The Netherlands: Springer.

Ko, Y., & Vaidya, N. H. (2000). Location-Aided Routing (LAR) in Mobile Ad Hoc Networks. *Journal of wireless . Networks, 6*(4), 307–321.

Kolker, A. (2008). Process Modeling of Emergency Department Patient Flow: Effect of patient Length of Stay on ED diversion. *Journal of Medical Systems, 32*(5), 389-401. doi: http://dx.doi.org/10.1007/s10916-008-9144-x

Kolker, A. (2009). Process Modeling of ICU Patient Flow: Effect of Daily Load Leveling of Elective Surgeries on ICU Diversion. *Journal of Medical Systems.* 33(1), 27-40. Doi: http://dx.doi.org/10.1007/s10916-008-9161-9

Kopach-Konrad, R., Lawley, M., Criswell, M., Hasan, I., Chakraborty, S., Pekny, J., & Doebbeling, B. (2007). Applying Systems Engineering Principles in Improving Health Care Delivery. *Journal of General Internal Medicine, 22*(3), 431–437. doi:10.1007/s11606-007-0292-3

Korhonen, A., & Malmi, L. (2000). Algorithm simulation with automatic assessment. In *Proceedings of the 5th annual SIGCSE/SIGCUE conference on innovation and technology in computer science education, IT-iCSE'00* (pp. 160–163), Helsinki, Finland. New York: ACM Press.

Korhonen, A., Malmi, L., Myllyselkä, P., & Scheinin, P. (2002). Does it make a difference if students exercise on the web or in the classroom? In *Proceedings of the 7th annual SIGCSE/SIGCUE conference on innovation and technology in computer science education, ITICSE'02* (pp. 121-124), Aarhus, Denmark. New York: ACM Press.

Kotz, D., Newport, C., Gray, R. S., Liu, J., Yuan, Y., & Elliott, C. (2004). Experimental evaluation of wireless simulation assumptions. In *Proceedings of the 7th ACM International Symposium on Modeling, Analysis, and Simulation of Wireless and Mobile Systems*, (pp. 78-82).

Kreutzer, W. (1986). *System Simulation - Programming Styles and Languages*. Reading, MA: Addison Wesley Publishers.

Krichmar, J. L., Nitz, D. A., Gally, J. A., & Edelman, G. M. (2005). Characterizing functional hippocampal pathways in a brain-based device as it solves a spatial memory task. *Proceedings of the National Academy of Sciences of the United States of America, 102*(6), 2111–2116. doi:10.1073/pnas.0409792102

Kubátová, H. (2003, June). Petri Net Models in Hardware. [Technical University, Liberec, Czech Republic.]. *ECMS, 2003*, 158–162.

Kubátová, H. (2003, September). Direct Hardware Implementation of Petri Net based Models. [Linz, Austria: J. Kepler University – FAW.]. *Proceedings of the Work in Progress Session of EUROMICRO, 2003*, 56–57.

Kubátová, H. (2004). Direct Implementation of Petri Net Based model in FPGA. In *Proceedings of the International Workshop on Discrete-Event System Design - DESDes'04*. Zielona Gora: University of Zielona Gora, (pp. 31-36).

Kubátová, H., & Novotný, M. (2005). Contemporary Methods of Digital Design Education. *Electronic Circuits and Systems Conference*, (pp. 115-118), Bratislava FEI, Slovak University of Technology.

Küppers, G., & Lenhard, J. (2005). Validation of simulation: Patterns in the social and natural sciences. *Journal of Artificial Societies and Social Simulation, 8*(4), 3.

Küppers, G., & Lenhard, J. (2006). From hierarchical to network-like integration: A revolution of modeling. In G. K. Johannes Lenhard, & T. Shinn (Eds.), *Simulation: Pragmatic construction of reality; sociology of the sciences yearbook* (pp. 89-106). Dordrecht, The Netherlands: Springer.

Küppers, G., Lenhard, J., & Shinn, T. (2006). Computer simulation: Practice, epistemology, and social dynamics. In G. K. Johannes Lenhard, & T. Shinn (Eds.), *Simulation: Pragmatic construction of reality; sociology of the sciences yearbook* (pp. 3-22). Dordrecht, The Netherlands: Springer.

Kuhlmann, A., Vetter, R. M., Lubbing, C., & Thole, C. A. (2005). Data mining on crash simulation data. *Proceedings Conference MLDM 2005, Leipzig/Germany*.

Kummer, O. (1998, October). Simulating Synchronous Channels and Net Instances. In J. Desel, P. Kemper, E. Kindler, & A. Oberweis (Eds.), *Proceedings of the Workshop Algorithmen und Werkzeuge für Petrinetze* (Vol. 694, pp. 73-78). Dortmund, Germany: Universität Dortmund, Fachbereich Informatik.

Kurkowski, S., Camp, T., & Colagrosso, M. (2005). MANET simulation studies: the incredibles. *ACM SIGMOBILE Mobile Computing and Communications Review, 9*(4), 50–61. doi:10.1145/1096166.1096174

Kurkowski, S., Camp, T., & Colagrosso, M. (2006). *MANET simulation studies: The current state and new simulation tools*. Department of Mathematics and Computer Sciences, Colorado School of Mines, CO.

Kvaale, H. (1988). A decision support simulation model for design of fast patrol boats. *European Journal of Operational Research*, 37(1), 92–99. doi:10.1016/0377-2217(88)90283-4

Laakso, M.-J., Salakoski, T., Grandell, L., Qiu, X., Korhonen, A., & Malmi, L. (2005). Multi-perspective study of novice learners adopting the visual algorithm simulation exercise system TRAKLA2. *Informatics in Education*, 4(1), 49–68.

Lake, T., Zeigler, B., Sarjoughian, H., & Nutaro, J. (2000). *DEVS Simulation and HLA Lookahead,* (Paper no. 00S-SIW-160). Presented at Spring Simulation Interoperability Workshop Orlando, FL, USA.

Lane, D. (1997). Invited reviews on system dynamics. *The Journal of the Operational Research Society*, 48, 1254–1259.

Lange, K. (2006). Differences between statistics and data mining. *DM Review*, 16(12), 32–33.

Langton, C. G. (1989). Artificial life. *Artificial Life*, 1–48.

Latane, B. (1996). Dynamic social impact: Robust predi-tions from simple theory. In U. M. R. Hegselmann, & K. Triotzsch (Eds.), *Modelling and simulatiion in the social sciences fromthe philosophy of science point of view*. New York: Springer-Verlag.

Lau, K. N., Lee, K. H., Ho, Y., & Lam, P. Y. (2004). Mining the web for business intelligence: Homepage analysis in the internet era. *Database Marketing & Customer Strategy Management*, 12, 32–54. doi:10.1057/palgrave.dbm.3240241

Law, A. M., & Kelton, W. D. (1991). *Simulation Modeling and Analysis*. San Francisco: McGraw-Hill.

Lawrence, J., Pasternak, B., & Pasternak, B. A. (2002). *Applied Management Science: Modeling, Spreadsheet Analysis, and Communication for Decision Making*. Hoboken, NJ: John Wiley & Sons.

Lee, S., & Pena-mora, F. (2005). System dynamics approach for error and change management in concurrent design and construction. *Proceedings of the 2005 Winter Simulation Conference*, Orlando, FL, (pp. 1508-1514).

Lee, W. C. Y. (1989). *Mobile cellular telecommunications systems*. New York: McGraw-Hill.

Leevers, D., Gil, P., Lopes, F. M., Pereira, J., Castro, J., Gomes-Mota, J., et al. (1998). An autonomous sensor for 3d reconstruction. In *3rd European Conference on Multimedia Applications, Services and Techniques (ECMAST98)*, Berlin, Germany.

Lefcowitz, M. (2007, February 26). *Why does process improvement fail?* Builder-AU by Developers for developers. Retrieved from www.builderau.com.au/strategy/projectmanagement/

Lehmann, A., Saad, S., Best, M., K.ster, A., Pohl, S., Qian, J., Walder, C., Wang, Z., & Xu, Z., (2005). *Leitfaden für Modelldokumen-tation, Abschlussbericht* (in German). ITIS **e.V.**

Levy, S. (1992). *Artificial life: A report from the frontier where computers meet*. New York: Vintage Books.

Li, H., Tang, W., & Simpson, D. (2004). Behavior based motion simulation for fire evacuation procedures. In *Conference Proceedings of Theory and Practice of Computer Graphics*. Washington DC: IEEE.

Ligetvári, Zs. (2005). *New Object's Development in DES LabVIEW* (in Hungarian). Unpublished Master's thesis, Budapest University of Technology and Economics, Hungary.

Liski, J., Palosuo, T., Peltoniemi, M., & Sievanen, R. (2005). Carbon and decomposition model Yasso for forest soils. *Ecological Modelling*, 189(1-2), 168–182. doi:10.1016/j.ecolmodel.2005.03.005

Litvak, E. (2007). A new Rx for crowded hospitals: Math. Operation management expert brings queuing theory to health care. *American College of Physicians-Internal Medicine-Doctors for Adults*, December 2007, ACP Hospitalist.

Litvak, E., & Long, M. (2000). Cost and Quality under managed care: Irreconcilable Differences? *The American Journal of Managed Care*, 6(3), 305–312.

Litvak, E., Long, M., Cooper, A., & McManus, M. (2001). Emergency Department Diversion: Causes and Solutions. *Academic Emergency Medicine, 8*(11), 1108–1110.

Lluch, J., & Halpin, D. W. (1982). Construction operations and microcomputers. *Journal of the Construction Division, 108*(CO1), 129–145.

Lombardi, S., Wainer, G. A., & Zeigler, B. P. (2006). *An experiment on interoperability of DEVS implementations* (Paper no. 06S-SIW-131). Presented at the Spring Simulation Interoperability Workshop Huntsville, AL, USA.

Lönhárd, M. (2000). *Simulation System of Discrete Events in Delphi* (in Hungarian). Unpublished Master's thesis, Budapest University of Technology and Economics, Hungary.

Lönnberg, J., Korhonen, A., & Malmi, L. (2004, May). MVT — a system for visual testing of software. In *Proceedings of the working conference on advanced visual interfaces* (AVI'04) (pp. 385–388).

Loscos, C., Marchal, D., & Meyer, A. (2003, June). Intuitive crowd behaviour in dense urban environments using local laws. In *Proceedings of the conference of Theory and Practice of Computer Graphics, TP.CG03*, University of Birmingham, Birmingham UK. Washington DC: IEEE.

Lowery, J. (1996). Introduction to Simulation in Healthcare. In J. Charness, D. Morrice, (Ed.) *Proceedings of the 1996 Winter Simulation Conference,* (pp. 78-84).

Lu, M., & Chan, W. (2004). Modeling concurrent operational interruptions in construction activities with simplified discrete event simulation approach (SDESA). *Proceedings of the 2004 Winter Simulation Conference,* Washington, DC, (pp. 1260-1267).

Lucio, G. F., Paredes-Farrera, M., Jammeh, E., Fleury, M., & Reed, M. J. (2008). *OPNET Modeler and Ns-2: comparing the accuracy of network simulators for packet-level analysis using a network testbed.* Retrieved June 15, from http://privatewww.essex.ac.uk/~gflore/

Lutz, E., Cygan, D., Dippold, M., Dolainsky, F., & Papke, W. (1991). The land mobile satellite communication channel – recording, statistics, and channel model. *IEEE Transactions on Vehicular Technology, 40,* 375–386. doi:10.1109/25.289418

Lyneis, J. (2000). System dynamics for market forecasting and structural analysis. *System Dynamics Review, 16*(1), 3–25. doi:10.1002/(SICI)1099-1727(200021)16:1<3::AID-SDR183>3.0.CO;2-5

Maani, K., & Cavana, R. (2000). *Systems thinking and modelling: understanding change and complexity.* New Zealand: Pearson Education, New Zealand.

Maas, W., & Bishop, C. M. (Eds.). (1999). *Pulsed neural networks.* Cambridge, MA: The MIT Press.

Macal, C. M., & North, M. J. (2006). Tutorial on agent-based modeling and simulation part 2: How to model. In *Proceedings of the 2006 Winter Simulation Conference,* eds. L. R. Perrone, F. P. Wieland, J. Liu, B. G. Lawson, D. M. Nicol, and R. M. Fujimoto, 73-83. Piscataway, New Jersey: Institute of Electrical and Electronics Engineers, Inc.

Madewell, C. D., & Swain, J. J. (2003, April-June). The Huntsville Simulation Snapshot: A Quantitative Analysis of What Employers Want in a Systems Simulation Professional. *Modelling and Simulation (Anaheim), 2*(2).

Maes, P. (1987, October). Concepts and Experiments in Computational Reflection. In *N. K. Meyrowitz (Ed.), Proceedings of the 2nd conference on object-oriented programming systems, languages, and applications (OOPSLA'87)* (Vol. 22, pp.147-156), Orlando, FL.

Mahachek, A. (1992). An Introduction to patient flow simulation for health care managers. *Journal of the Society for Health Systems, 3*(3), 73–81.

Malmi, L., & Korhonen, A. (2004). Automatic feedback and resubmissions as learning aid. In *Proceedings of 4th IEEE international conference on advanced learning technologies, ICALT'04* (pp. 186-190), Joensuu, Finland.

Malmi, L., Karavirta, V., Korhonen, A., & Nikander, J. (2005, September). Experiences on automatically assessed algorithm simulation exercises with different resubmission policies. *Journal of Educational Resources in Computing, 5*(3). doi:10.1145/1163405.1163412

Malmi, L., Karavirta, V., Korhonen, A., Nikander, J., Seppälä, O., & Silvasti, P. (2004). Visual algorithm simulation exercise system with automatic assessment: TRAKLA2. *Informatics in Education, 3*(2), 267–288.

Malmi, L., Korhonen, A., & Saikkonen, R. (2002). Experiences in automatic assessment on mass courses and issues for designing virtual courses. In *Proceedings of the 7th annual SIGCSE/SIGCUE conference on innovation and technology in computer science education, ITiCSE'02* (pp. 55–59), Aarhus, Denmark. New York: ACM Press.

Mandelbrot, B. B. (1982). *The Fractal Geometry of Nature*. New York: W.H. Freeman.

Mannila, H. (1997). Methods and problems in data mining. *Proceedings of International Conference on Database Theory*, Delphi, Greece.

Maria, A. (1997). Introduction to modeling and simulation. In S. Andradottir, K. J. Healy, D. H. Withers, & B. L. Nelson (Ed.) *Proceedings of the 1997 Winter Simulation Conference*, (pp. 7-13).

Marian, I. (2003). *A biologically inspired computational model of motor control development*. Unpublished MSc Thesis, University College Dublin, Ireland.

Markram, H. (2006). The Blue Brain project. *Nature Reviews. Neuroscience, 7*, 153–160. doi:10.1038/nrn1848

Marshall, A., Vasilakis, C., & El-Darzi, E. (2005). Length of stay-based Patient Flow Models: Recent Developments and Future Directions. *Health Care Management Science, 8*, 213–220. doi:10.1007/s10729-005-2012-z

Martin, L. (1997). Mistakes and Misunderstandings. *System Dynamics in Education Project*. System Dynamics Group, Sloan School of Management, Massachusetts Institute of Technology, Cambridge, MA.

Martinez, J. C. (1996). *STROBOSCOPE-state and resource based simulation of construction process*. Ph.D. Thesis, University of Michigan, Ann Arbor, MI.

Martinez, J. C. (1998). EarthMover-simulation tool for earthwork planning. *Proceedings of the 1998 Winter Simulation Conference*, Washington DC, (pp. 1263-1271).

Martinez, J. C., & Ioannou, P. J. (1999). General-purpose systems for effective construction simulation. *Journal of Construction Engineering and Management, 125*(4), 265–276. doi:10.1061/(ASCE)0733-9364(1999)125:4(265)

Marzouk, M. (2002). *Optimizing earthmoving operations using computer simulation*. Ph.D. Thesis, Concordia University, Montreal, Canada.

Marzouk, M., & Moselhi, O. (2000). Optimizing earthmoving operations using object-oriented simulation. *Proceedings of the 2000 Winter Simulation Conference*, Orlando, FL, (1926-1932).

Marzouk, M., & Moselhi, O. (2004). Multiobjective optimization of earthmoving operations. *Journal of Construction Engineering and Management, 130*(1), 105–113. doi:10.1061/(ASCE)0733-9364(2004)130:1(105)

Marzouk, M., & Moselhi, O. (2002). Bid preparation for earthmoving operations. *Canadian Journal of Civil Engineering, 29*(3), 517–532. doi:10.1139/l02-023

Marzouk, M., & Moselhi, O. (2002). Simulation optimization for earthmoving operations using genetic algorithms. *Construction Management and Economics, 20*(6), 535–544. doi:10.1080/01446190210156064

Marzouk, M., & Moselhi, O. (2003) Constraint based genetic algorithm for earthmoving fleet selection. *Canadian Journal of Civil Engineering, 30*(4), 673–683. doi:10.1139/l03-006

Marzouk, M., & Moselhi, O. (2003). An object oriented model for earthmoving operations. *Journal of Construction Engineering and Management, 129*(2), 173–181. doi:10.1061/(ASCE)0733-9364(2003)129:2(173)

Marzouk, M., & Moselhi, O. (2004). Fuzzy clustering model for estimating haulers' travel time. *Journal of Construction Engineering and Management, 130*(6), 878–886. doi:10.1061/(ASCE)0733-9364(2004)130:6(878)

Marzouk, M., Said, H., & El-Said, M. (2008). Special purpose simulation model for balanced cantilever bridges. *Journal of Bridge Engineering, 13*(2), 122–131. doi:10.1061/(ASCE)1084-0702(2008)13:2(122)

Marzouk, M., Zein El-Dein, H., & El-Said, M. (2008. (in press). A framework for multiobjective optimization of launching girder bridges. *Journal of Construction Engineering and Management.*

Marzouk, M., Zein, H., & El-Said, M. (2006). BRIGE_SIM: framework for planning and optimizing bridge deck construction using computer simulation. *Proceedings of the 2006 Winter Simulation Conference*, Monterey, CA, (pp. 2039-2046).

Marzouk, M., Zein, H., & El-Said, M. (2006). Scheduling cast-in-situ on falsework bridges using computer simulation. *Scientific Bulletin, Faculty of Engineering . Ain Shams University, 41*(1), 231–245.

Marzouk, M., Zein, H., & El-Said, M. (2007). Application of computer simulation to construction of deck pushing bridges. *Journal of Civil Engineering and Management, 13*(1), 27–36.

Mason, D. V., & Woit, D. M. (1999). Providing mark-up and feedback to students with online marking. In *The proceedings of the thirtieth SIGCSE technical symposium on computer science education* (pp. 3-6), New Orleans, LA. New York: ACM Press.

Mattia, M., & Del Guidice, P. (2000). Efficient event-driven simulation of large networks of spiking neurons and dynamical synapses. *Neural Computation, 12*, 2305–2329. doi:10.1162/089976600300014953

Mayhew, L., & Smith, D. (2008). Using queuing theory to analyze the Government's 4-h completion time target in Accident and Emergency departments. *Health Care Management Science, 11*, 11–21. doi:10.1007/s10729-007-9033-8

McCabe, B. (1997). *An automated modeling approach for construction performance improvement using computer simulation and belief networks.* Ph.D. Thesis, Alberta University, Canada.

McCabe, B. (1998). Belief networks in construction simulation. *Proceedings of the 1998 Winter Simulation Conference*, Washington DC (pp. 1279-1286).

McHaney, R. (1991). *Computer simulation: a practical perspective.* San Diego, CA: Academic Press.

McManus, M., Long, M., Cooper, A., & Litvak, E. (2004). Queuing Theory Accurately Models the Need for Critical Care Resources. *Anesthesiology, 100*(5), 1271–1276. doi:10.1097/00000542-200405000-00032

McManus, M., Long, M., Cooper, A., Mandell, J., Berwick, D., Pagano, M., & Litvak, E. (2003). Variability in Surgical Caseload and Access to Intensive Care Services. *Anesthesiology, 98*(6), 1491–1496. doi:10.1097/00000542-200306000-00029

Mei, L., & Thole, C. A. (2008). Data analysis for parallel car-crash simulation results and model optimization. *Simulation Modelling Practice and Theory, 16*, 329–337. doi:10.1016/j.simpat.2007.11.018

Mercy Medical Center. (2007). *Creating a Culture of Improvement.* Presented at the Iowa Healthcare Collaborative Lean Conference, Des Moines, IA, August 22. Retrieved from www.ihconline.org/toolkits/LeanIn-Healthcare/IHALeanConfCultureImprovement.pdf

Miller, B. P. (1993). What to draw? When to draw? An essay on parallel program visualization. *Journal of Parallel and Distributed Computing, 18*(2), 265–269. doi:10.1006/jpdc.1993.1063

Miller, J. H., & Page, S. E. (2007). *Complex adaptive systems: An introduction to computational models of social life.* Princeton, NJ: Princeton University Press.

Miller, M., Ferrin, D., & Szymanski, J. (2003). Simulating Six Sigma Improvement Ideas for a Hospital Emergency Department. In S. Chick, et al (Ed.) *Proceedings of the 2003 Winter Simulation Conference* (pp. 1926-1929). Washington, DC: IEEE.

Mitchell, M., Crutch, J. P., & Hraber, P. T. (1994). Dynamics, computation, and the "edge of chaos": A re-examination. In G. Cowan, D. Pines, & D. Melzner (Eds), *Complexity: Metaphors, Models and Reality.* Reading, MA: Addison-Wesley.

Mittal, S., & Risco-Martin, J. L. (2007). DEVSML: Automating DEVS Execution over SOA Towards Transparent Simulators Special Session on DEVS Collaborative Execution and Systems Modeling over SOA. In *Proceedings of the DEVS Integrative M&S Symposium, Spring Simulation Multiconference, Norfork, Virginia, USA,* (pp. 287–295). Washington, DC: IEEE Press.

Molnar, I., Moscardini, A. O., & Breyer, R. (2009). Simulation – Art or Science? How to teach it? *International Journal of Simulation and Process Modelling, 5*(1), 20–30. doi:10.1504/IJSPM.2009.025824

Molnar, I., Moscardini, A. O., & Omey, E. (1996, June). Structural concepts of a new master curriculum in simulation. In A. Javor, A. Lehmann & I. Molnar (Eds.), *Proceedings of the Society for Computer Simulation International on Modelling and Simulation ESM96,* Budapest, Hungary, (pp. 405-409).

Montgomery, D. C. (Ed.). (2005). *Design and Analysis of Experiments.* New York: John Wiley & Sons.

Morbitzer, C., Strachan, P., & Simpson, C. (2004). Data mining analysis of building simulation performance data. *Building Services Engineers Res. Technologies, 25*(3), 253–267.

Morrison, A., Mehring, C., Geisel, T., Aertsen, A., & Diesmann, M. (2005). Advancing the boundaries of high-connectivity network simulation with distributed computing. *Neural Computation, 17,* 1776–1801. doi:10.1162/0899766054026648

Morrison, M., & Morgan, M. S. (1999). Models as mediating instruments. In M. S. Morgan, & M. Morrison (Eds.), *Models as mediators* (pp. 10-37). Cambridge, UK: Cambridge University Press.

Mosca, R., & Giribone, P. (1982). An application of the interactive code for design of o.r. simulation experiment to a slabbing-mill system. In M.H. Hamza (Ed.), *IASTED International Symposium on Applied Modelling and Simulation* (pp. 195-199). Calgary, Canada: ACTA Press.

Mosca, R., & Giribone, P. (1982). An interactive code for the design of the o.r. simulation experiment of complex industrial plants. In M.H. Hamza (Ed.), *IASTED Interna-tional Symposium on Applied Modelling and Simulation* (pp. 200-203). Calgary, Canada: ACTA Press.

Mosca, R., & Giribone, P. (1982). A mathematical method for evaluating the importance of the input variables in simulation experiments. In M.H. Hamza (Ed.), *IASTED International Symposium on Modelling, Identification and Control* (pp. 54-58). Calgary, Canada: ACTA Press.

Mosca, R., & Giribone, P. (1982).Optimal length in o.r. simulation experiments of large scale production system. In M.H. Hamza (Ed.), *IASTED International Symposium on Modelling, Identification and Control* (pp. 78-82). Calgary, Canada: ACTA Press.

Mosca, R., & Giribone, P. (1983). O.r. muliple-objective simulation: experimental analysis of the independent varibales ranges. In M.H. Hamza (Ed.), *IASTED International Symposium on Applied Modelling and Simulation* (pp. 68-73). Calgary, Canada: ACTA Press.

Mosca, R., & Giribone, P. (1986). Flexible manufacturing system: a simulated comparison between discrete and continuous material handling. In M.H. Hamza (Ed.), *IASTED International Symposium on Modelling, Identification and Control* (pp. 100-106). Calgary, Canada: ACTA Press.

Mosca, R., & Giribone, P. (1986). FMS: construction of the simulation model and its statistical validation. In M.H. Hamza (Ed.), *IASTED International Symposium on Modelling, Identification and Control* (pp. 107-113). Calgary, Canada: ACTA Press.

Mosca, R., & Giribone, P. (1988). Evaluation of stochastic discrete event simulators of F.M.S. In P. Breedveld et al. (Ed.), *IMACS Transactions on Scientific Computing: Modelling and Simulation of Systems* (Vol. 3, pp. 396-402). Switzerland: Baltzer AG.

Mosca, R., & Giribone, P. (1993). Critical analysis of a bottling line using simulation techniques. In M.H. Hamza (Ed.), *IASTED International Symposium on Modelling, Identification and Control* (pp. 135-140). Calgary, Canada: ACTA Press.

Moya, L., & Weisel, E. (2008) The Difficulties with Validating Agent Based Simulations of Social Systems. *Proceedings Spring Multi-Simulation Conference, Agent-Directed Simulation*, Ottawa, Canada.

Muguira, J. A., & Tolk, A. (2006). Applying a Methodology to Identify Structural Variances in Interoperations. *Journal for Defense Modeling and Simulation*, 3(2), 77–93. doi:10.1177/875647930600300203

Muhdi, R. A. (2006). Evaluation Modeling: Development, Characteristics and Limitations. *Proceedings of the National Occupational Research Agenda* (NORA), (pp. 87-92).

Mund, M., Profft, I., Wutzler, T., Schulze, E.D., Weber, G., & Weller, E. (2005). Vorbereitung für eine laufende Fortschreibung der Kohlenstoffvorräte in den Wäldern Thüringens. Abschlussbericht zur 2. *Phase dem BMBF-Projektes "Modelluntersuchungen zur Umsetzung des Kyoto-Protokolls"*. (Tech. rep., TLWJF, Gotha).

MVASpike [computer software] (n.d.). Available from http://mvaspike.gforge.inria.fr/.

Myers, B. A., Chandhok, R., & Sareen, A. (1988, October). Automatic data visualization for novice Pascal programmers. In *IEEE workshop on visual languages* (pp. 192-198).

Myers, R. H., & Montgomery, D. C. (Eds.). (1995). *Response Surface Methodology*. New York: John Wiley & Sons.

Nabuurs, G. J., Pussinen, A., Karjalainen, T., Erhard, M., & Kramer, K. (2002). Stemwood volume increment changes in European forests due to climate change-a simulation study with the EFISCEN model. *Global Change Biology*, 8(4), 304–316. doi:10.1046/j.1354-1013.2001.00470.x

Nagel, J. (2003). *TreeGrOSS: Tree Growth Open Source Software - a tree growth model component*.

Nagel, J., Albert, M., & Schmidt, M. (2002). Das waldbauliche Prognose- und Entscheidungsmodell BWINPro 6.1. *Forst und Holz*, 57(15/16), 486–493.

Nance, R. E. (2000, December). Simulation education: Past reflections and future directions. In J. A. Joines, R. R. Barton, K. Kang & P. A. Fishwick, (Eds.) *Proceedings of the 2000 Winter Simulation Conference*, Piscataway, NJ (pp. 1595-1601). Washington, DC: IEEE.

Nance, R. E., & Balci, O. (2001, December). Thoughts and musings on simulation education. In B. A. Peters, J. S. Smith, D. J. Medeiros, & M. W. Rohrer (eds.), *Proceedings of the 2001 Winter Simulation Conference*, Arlington, VA (pp. 1567-1570).

Naps, T. L., Rößling, G., Almstrum, V., Dann, W., Fleischer, R., & Hundhausen, C. (2003, June). Exploring the role of visualization and engagement in computer science education. *SIGCSE Bulletin*, 35(2), 131–152. doi:10.1145/782941.782998

National Research Council. (2002). *Modeling and Simulation in Manufacturing and Defense Acquisition: Pathways to Success*. Washington, DC: Committee on Modeling and Simulation Enhancements for 21st Century Manufacturing and Defense Acquisition, National Academies Press.

National Research Council. (2006). *Defense Modeling, Simulation, and Analysis: Meeting the Challenge*. Washington, DC: Committee on Modeling and Simulation for Defense Transformation, National Academies Press.

National Science Board. (2008). *Science and Engineering Indicators 2008*. Arlington, VA: National Science Foundation.

Navarro-Serment, L., Grabowski, R., Paredis, C. & Khosla, P. (2002, December). Millibots. *IEEE Robotics & Automation Magazine*.

Nayak, R., & Qiu, T. (2005). A data mining application: analysis of problems occurring during a software project development process. *International Journal of Software Engineering and Knowledge Engineering*, 15(4), 647–663. doi:10.1142/S0218194005002476

Naylor, T. H., & Finger, J. M. (1967). Verification of computer simulation models. *Management Science*, 14(2), 92–106. doi:10.1287/mnsc.14.2.B92

Nelson, B. L. (2002). Using Simulation To Teach Probability. In C.-H. C. E. Yücesan (Ed.), *Proceedings of the 2002 Winter Simulation Conference* (p. 1815). San Diego, CA: informs-cs.

NEST [computer software] (n.d.). Available from http://www.nest-initiative.org.

Network Simulator 2 (2008). Retrieved September 15, 2008, from www.isi.edu/nsnam/ns/

Newcombe, R. (2007). *SIMNOS virtual robot* [computer software]. More information available from www.cronosproject.net.

Ng, P. C., & Liew, S. C. (2007). Throughput analysis of IEEE 802.11 multi-hop ad hoc networks. *IEEE/ACM Transactions on Networking, 15*(2), 309-322.

NI LabVIEW Developer Team. (2007). *LabVIEW 8.5 User Manual.* Austin, TX: National Instruments.

Nicopoliditis, P., Papadimitriou, G. I., & Pomportsis, A. S. (2003). *Wireless Networks.* Hoboken, NJ: Wiley, Jonn Wiley & Sons Ltd.

Nigash, S. (2004). Business Intelligence. *Communications of the Association for Information Systems, 13,* 177–195.

Nikoukaran, J. (1999). Software selection for simulation in manufacturing: A review. *Simulation Practice and Theory, 7*(1), 1–14. doi:10.1016/S0928-4869(98)00022-6

Nonaka, I., Toyama, R., & Konno, N. (2000). SECI, Ba and aeadership: a unified model of dynamic knowledge creation. *Long Range Planning, 33,* 5–34. doi:10.1016/S0024-6301(99)00115-6

North Atlantic Treaty Organization. (2002). *NATO Code of Best Practice for Command and Control Assessment.* Revised ed. Washington, DC: CCRP Press

North, M. J., & Macal, C. M. (2007). *Managing business complexity: Discovering strategic solutions with.* New York, NY: Oxford University Press.

NSF-Panel. (2006, May). *Revolutionizing Engineering Science through Simulation.* Retrieved 2008, from Report of the National Science Foundation Blue Ribbon Panel on Simulation-Based Engineering Science, http://www.nsf.gov/pubs/reports/sbes_final_report.pdf

Nutaro, J. (2003). *Parallel Discrete Event Simulation with Application to Continuous Systems.* PhD Thesis, University of Arizona, Tuscon, Arizona.

Nutaro, J. (2007). Discrete event simulation of continuous systems. In P. Fishwick, (Ed.) *Handbook of Dynamic System Modeling.* Boca Raton, FL: Chapman & Hall/CRC.

Nutaro, J. J. (2005). *Adevs.* Retrieved Jan 15, 2006, from http://www.ece.arizona.edu/ nutaro/

Nutaro, J., & Sarjoughian, H. (2004). Design of distributed simulation environments: A unified system-theoretic and logical processes approach. *Journal of Simulation, 80*(11), 577–589. doi:10.1177/0037549704050919

NVIDIA PhysX [computer software] (n.d.). Available from http://www.nvidia.com/object/nvidia_physx.html.

Odersky, M. (2000, March). Functional Nets. In G. Smolka (Ed.), *Proceedings of the 9th European Symposium on Programming (ESOP 2000)* (p. 1-25). Berlin, Germany: Springer.

Okuhara, K., Ishii, H., & Uchida, M. (2005). Support of decision making by data mining using neural system. *Systems and Computers in Japan, 36*(11), 102–110. doi:10.1002/scj.10577

Oloufa, A. (1993). Modeling operational activities in object-oriented simulation. *Journal of Computing in Civil Engineering, 7*(1), 94–106. doi:10.1061/(ASCE)0887-3801(1993)7:1(94)

Oloufa, A., Ikeda, M., & Nguyen, T. (1998). Resource-based simulation libraries for construction. *Automation in Construction, 7*(4), 315–326. doi:10.1016/S0926-5805(98)00048-X

OMNEST (2007). Retrieved September 15, 2007, from www.omnest.com

OMNeT++ (2008). Retrieved September 15, 2008, from http://www.omnetpp.org/

OPNET Technologies. (2008). Retrieved September 15, 2008, from www.opnet.com

OR/MS. (2003). *OR/MS.* Retrieved from OR/MS, www.lionhrtpub.com/orms/surveys/Simulation/Simulation.html

Oren, T. I. (2002, December). Rationale for a Code of Professional Ethics for Simulationists. In E. Yucesan, C. Chen, J. L. Snowdon & J. M. Charnes (Eds.), *Proceedings of the 2002 Winter Simulation Conference,* San Diego, CA, (pp. 13-18).

Oren, T. I. (2008). *Modeling and Simulation Body of Knowledge.* SCS International. Retrieved May 31 2008 from http://www.site.uottawa.ca/~oren/MSBOK/MSBOK-index.htm#coreareas

Ören, T. I., & Numrich, S. K. S.K., Uhrmacher, A.M., Wilson, L. F., & Gelenbe, E. (2000). Agent-directed simulation: challenges to meet defense and civilian requirements. In *Proceedings of the 32nd Conference on Winter Simulation,* Orlando, Florida, December 10 – 13. San Diego, CA: Society for Computer Simulation International.

Page, E. H., Briggs, R., & Tufarolo, J. A. (2004). Toward a Family of Maturity Models for the Simulation Interconnection Problem. In *Proceedings of the Spring Simulation Interoperability Workshop.* New York: IEEE CS Press.

Painter, M. K., Erraguntla, M., Hogg, G. L., & Beachkofski, B. (2006). Using simulation, data mining, and knowledge discovery techniques for optimized aircraft engine fleet management. *Proceedings of the 2006 Winter Simulation Conference,* 1253-1260.

Palosuo, T., Liski, J., Trofymow, J. A., & Titus, B. D. (2005). Litter decomposition affected by climate and litter quality - Testing the Yasso model with litterbag data from the Canadian intersite decomposition experiment. *Ecological Modelling, 189*(1-2), 183–198. doi:10.1016/j.ecolmodel.2005.03.006

Papajorgji, P., Beck, H. W., & Braga, J. L. (2004). An architecture for developing service-oriented and component-based environmental models. *Ecological Modelling, 179*(1), 61–76. doi:10.1016/j.ecolmodel.2004.05.013

Papoulis, A. (1984). *Probability, random variables, and stochastic processes* (2nd Ed.). New York: McGraw-Hill, Inc.

Parsons, J. D. (1992). *The mobile radio propagation channel* (1st Ed.). Chichester, UK: John Wiley & Sons, Inc.

Paul, R. J., Eldabi, T., & Kuljis, J. (2003, December). Simulation education is no substitute for intelligent thinking. In S. Chick, P. J. Sanchez, D. Ferrin & D. J. Morrice (Eds.), *Proceedings of the 2003 Winter Simulation Conference,* New Orleans, LA, (pp. 1989-1993).

Paulson, G. C. Jr. (1978). Interactive graphics for simulating construction operations. *Journal of the Construction Division, 104*(1), 69–76.

Pawlikowski, K. (1990). Steady-state simulation of queuing processes: a survey of problems and solutions. *ACM Computing Surveys, 1*(2), 123–170. doi:10.1145/78919.78921

Pawlikowski, K., Jeong, H.-D. J., & Lee, J.-S. R. (2002). On credibility of simulation studies of telecommunication networks. *IEEE Communications Magazine, 40*(1), 132–139. doi:10.1109/35.978060

Pawlikowski, K., Yau, V. W. C., & McNickle, D. (1994). *Distributed stochastic discrete event simulation in parallel time streams.* Paper presented at the Winter Simulation Conference. pp. 723-730.

Peek, J., Todin-Gonguet, G., & Strang, J. (2001). *Learning the UNIX Operating System* (5th Ed.). Sebastopol, CA: O'Reilly & Associates.

Peer, G. A. (2001). Ready to Serve. *Heavy Construction News,* March 2001, 16-19.

Peltoniemi, M., Mäkipää, R., Liski, J., & Tamminen, P. (2004). Changes in soil carbon with stand age - an evaluation of a modelling method with empirical data. *Global Change Biology, 10*(12), 2078–2091. doi:10.1111/j.1365-2486.2004.00881.x

Phillips, D. C. (2000). Constructivism in education. opinions and second opinions on controversial issues. *99ᵗʰ yearbook of the national society for the study of education (Part 1).* Chicago: The University of Chicago Press.

Phillips-Wren, G., & Jain, L. C. (Eds.). (2005). *Intelligent Decision Support Systems in Agent-Mediated Environments.* The Netherlands: IOS Press.

Phillips-Wren, G., Ichalkaranje, N., & Jain, L. C. (Eds.). (2008). *Intelligent Decision Making –An AI-Based Approach.* Berlin: Springer-Verlag.

Pidd, M. (1995). Object orientation, discrete simulation and three-phase approach. *The Journal of the Operational Research Society, 46*(3), 362–374.

Pidd, M. (2003). Tools for thinking: Modelling in management science. (2nd Ed., pp. 289-312) New York: John Wiley and Sons.

Pierson, W., & Rodger, S. (1998). Web-based animation of data structures using JAWAA. In *Proceedings of the 29th SIGCSE technical symposium on computer science education* (pp. 267-271), Atlanta, GA. New York: ACM Press.

Pohl, J. G., Wood, A. A., Pohl, K. J., & Chapman, A. J. (1999). IMMACCS: A Military Decision-Support System. *DARPA-JFACC 1999 Symposium on Advances in Enterprise Control,* San Diego, CA.

Porté, A., & Bartelink, H. H. (2002). Modelling mixed forest growth: a review of models for forest management. *Ecological Modelling, 150,* 141–188. doi:10.1016/S0304-3800(01)00476-8

Potter, S. S., Elm, W. C., & Gualtieri, J. W. (2006). Making Sense of Sensemaking: Requirements of a Cognitive Analysis to Support C2 Decision Support System Design. *Proceedings of the Command and Control Research and Technology Symposium.* Washington, DC: CCRP Press.

Power, D. J. (2007). A Brief History of Decision Support Systems. *DSSResources.com.* Retrieved from http://DSS-Resources.COM/history/dsshistory.html, version 4.0.

Power, D. J., & Sharda, R. (2007). Model-driven decision support systems: Concepts and research directions. *Journal for Decision Support Systems, 43*(3), 1044–1061. doi:10.1016/j.dss.2005.05.030

Price, B. A., Baecker, R. M., & Small, I. S. (1993). A principled taxonomy of software visualization. *Journal of Visual Languages and Computing, 4*(3), 211–266. doi:10.1006/jvlc.1993.1015

Pritsker, A. A. B., O'Reilly, J. J., & LaVal, D. K. (1997). *Simulation with visual SLAM and Awesim.* New York: John Wiley & Sons, Inc.

Proakis, J. G. (2001). *Digital communications* (4th Ed.). New York: McGraw- Hill.

Program for International Student Assessment (PISA). (2006). *Highlights from PISA 2006.* Retrieved August 15, 2008 from Web site: http://nces.ed.gov/surveys/pisa/

Pullen, J. M., Brunton, R., Brutzman, D., Drake, D., Hieb, M. R., Morse, K. L., & Tolk, A. (2005). Using Web Services to Integrate Heterogeneous Simulations in a Grid Environment. *Journal on Future Generation Computer Systems, 21,* 97–106. doi:10.1016/j.future.2004.09.031

Qayyum, A., Viennot, L., & Laouiti, A. (2002). Multipoint relaying for flooding broadcast messages in mobile wireless network. *Proceedings of the 35ᵗʰ Hawaii International Conference on System Sciences,* (pp. 3866- 3875).

Qiu, Z.-M., & Wong, Y. S. (2007, June). Dynamic Workflow Change in PDM Systems. *Computers in Industry, 58*(5), 453–463. doi:10.1016/j.compind.2006.09.014

Quatrani, T. (1998). *Visual modeling with rational rose and UML.* Reading, MA: Addison-Wesley.

Rakich, J., Kuzdrall, P., Klafehn, K., & Krigline, A. (1991). Simulation in the hospital setting: Implications for managerial decision making and management development. *Journal of Management Development, 10*(4), 31–37. doi:10.1108/02621719110005069

Rappaport, T. S. (2002). *Wireless communications principles and practice* (2nd Ed.). Upper Saddle River, NJ: Prentice Hall.

Rappaport, T. S., Seidel, S. Y., & Takamizawa, K. (1991). Statistical channel impulse response models for factory and open plan building radio communication system design. *IEEE Transactions on Communications, 39*(5), 794–806. doi:10.1109/26.87142

Reek, K. A. (1989). The TRY system or how to avoid testing student programs. In [New York: ACM Press.]. *Proceedings of SIGCSE, 89*, 112–116. doi:10.1145/65294.71198

Reichert, M., & Dadam, P. (1998). ADEPTflex - Supporting Dynamic Changes in Workflow Management Systems without Losing Control. *Journal of Intelligent Information Systems, 10*(2), 93–129. doi:10.1023/A:1008604709862

Reid, P., Compton, W., Grossman, J., & Fanjiang, G. (2005). *Building a better delivery system: A new engineering / Healthcare partnership.* Washington, DC: Committee on Engineering and the Health Care System, Institute of Medicine and National Academy of Engineering, National Academy Press.

Reisig, W. (1985). *Petri nets: An introduction* (EATCS Monographs in Theoretical Computer Science Vol. 4). Berlin: Springer.

Remondino, M., & Correndo, G. (2005). Data mining applied to agent based simulation. *Proceedings 19th European Conference on Modelling and Simulation.*

Resnyansky, L. (2007). *Integration of social sciences in terrorism modelling: Issues, problems.* Edinburgh, Australia: Australian Government Department of Defence, DSTO Command and Control.

Reutimann, J., Giugliano, M., & Fusi, S. (2003). Event-driven simulation of spiking neurons with stochastic dynamics. *Neural Computation, 15*, 811–830. doi:10.1162/08997660360581912

Rice, S. O. (1958). Distribution of the duration of fades in radio transmission: Gaussian noise model. *The Bell System Technical Journal, 37*(3), 581–635.

Robertson, N., & Perera, T. (2001). Feasibility for Automatic Data Collection. In *Proceedings of the 2001 Winter Simulation Conference.*

Robinson, S. (2008). Conceptual modelling for simulation Part I: definition and requirements. *The Journal of the Operational Research Society, 59*, 278–290. doi:10.1057/palgrave.jors.2602368

Roeder, T. M. K. (2004). *An Information Taxonomy for Discrete-Event Simulations.* PhD Dissertation, University of California, Berkeley, CA.

Rogers, R. V. (1997, December) What makes a modelling and simulation professional? The consensus view from one workshop. In S. Andradottir, K. J. Healy, D. A. Whiters & B. L. Nelson (Eds.), *Proceedings of the 1997 Winter Simulation Conference*, Atlanta, GA (pp. 1375-1382). Washington, DC: IEEE.

Rohl, J. S. (1986). *An Introduction to Compiler Writing.* New York: Macdonald and Jane's.

Rohrmeier, M. (1997). *Telemanipulation of robots via internet mittels VRML2.0 and Java.* Institute for Robotics and System Dynamic, Technical University of Munchen, Munich, Germany.

Rorabaugh, C. B. (2004). *Simulating Wireless Communication Systems: Practical Models in C++.* Upper Saddle River, NJ: Prentice-Hall.

Ross, M. D. (n.d.). *3-D Imaging In Virtual Environment: A Scientific, Clinical And Teaching Tool.* Retrieved from United States National Library of Medicine- National Institiute of Health, http://biocomp.arc.nasa.gov/

Ross, M. S. (1987). *Introduction to probability and statistics for engineers and scientists.* Chichester, UK: John Wiley & Sons, Inc.

Rößling, G., Schüler, M., & Freisleben, B. (2000). The ANIMAL algorithm animation tool. In *Proceedings of the 5th annual SIGCSE/SIGCUE conference on innovation and technology in computer science education, ITiCSE'00* (pp. 37-40), Helsinki, Finland. New York: ACM Press.

Roxburgh, S. H., & Davies, I. D. (2006). COINS: an integrative modelling shell for carbon accounting and general ecological analysis. *Environmental Modelling & Software, 21*(3), 359–374. doi:10.1016/j.envsoft.2004.11.006

Ruardija, P., J. W.-B. (1995). SESAME, a software environment for simulation and analysis of marine ecosystems. *Netherlands Journal of Sea Research, 33*(3-4), 261–270. doi:10.1016/0077-7579(95)90049-7

Russell, S. (2007, May). *Open Dynamics Engine*. Retrieved October 2008, from Open Dynamics Engine, http://www.ode.org/

Ryan, J. (2005). *Building a better delivery system: A new engineering / Healthcare partnership. System Engineering: Opportunities for Health Care* (pp.141-142). Washington, DC: Committee on Engineering and the Health Care System, Institute of Medicine and National Academy of Engineering, National Academy Press.

Sachdeva, R., Williams, T., Quigley, J., (2006). Mixing methodologies to enhance the implementation of healthcare operational research. *Journal of the Operational Research Society, advance online publication, September 6*, 1 - 9

Saikkonen, R., Malmi, L., & Korhonen, A. (2001). Fully automatic assessment of programming exercises. In *Proceedings of the 6th annual SIGCSE/SIGCUE conference on innovation and technology in computer science education, ITiCSE'01* (pp. 133-136), Canterbury, UK. New York: ACM Press.

Salah, K., & Alkhoraidly, A. (2006). An OPNET-based simulation approach for deploying VoIP. *International Journal of Network Management, 16*, 159–183. doi:10.1002/nem.591

Salimifard, K., & Wright, M. B. (2001, November). Petri Net-Based Modeling of Workflow Systems: An Overview. *European Journal of Operational Research, 134*(3), 664–676. doi:10.1016/S0377-2217(00)00292-7

Sampaio, A., & Henriques, P. (2008). Visual simulation of Civil Engineering activities:Didactic virtual models. *International Conferences in Central Europe onComputer Graphics, Visualization and Computer Vision*. Czech Republic: University of West Bohemia.

Sargent, R. G. (1996). Some Subjective Validation Methods Using Graphical Displays of Data. *Proc. of 1996 Winter Simulation Conf.*, (pp. 345–351).

Sargent, R. G. (1996). Verifying and Validating Simulation Models. *Proc. of 1996 Winter Simulation Conf.*, (pp. 55–64).

Sargent, R. G. (2000). Verification, Validation, and Accreditation of Simulation Models. *Proceedings of the Winter Simulation Conference*, (pp. 50-59).

Sargent, R. G. (2000, December). Doctoral colloquium keynote address: being a professional. In J. A. Joines, R. R. Barton, K. Kang and P. A. Fishwick (Eds.), *Proceedings of the 2000 Winter Simulation Conference*, Piscataway, NJ, (pp. 1595-1601). Washington, DC: IEEE.

Sarjoughian, H., & Zeigler, B. (2000). DEVS and HLA: Complementary paradigms for modeling and simulation? *Simulation Transactions, 17*(4), 187–197.

Sarkar, N. I., & Halim, S. A. (2008, June 23-26). *Simulation of computer networks: simulators, methodologies and recommendations*. Paper presented at the 5th IEEE International Conference on Information Technology and Applications (ICITA'08), Cairns, Queensland, Australia, (pp. 420-425).

Sarkar, N. I., & Halim, S. A. (2008, June 23-26). *Simulation of computer networks: simulators, methodologies and recommendations*. Paper presented at the 5th IEEE International Conference on Information Technology and Applications (ICITA'08), Cairns, Queensland, Australia (pp. 420-425).

Sarkar, N. I., & Lo, E. (2008, December 7-10). *Indoor propagation measurements for performance evaluation of IEEE 802.11g*. Paper presented at the IEEE Australasian Telecommunications Networks and Applications Conference (ATNAC'08), Adelaide, Australia, (pp. 163-168).

Sarkar, N. I., & Petrova, K. (2005, June 27-30). *WebLanDesigner: a web-based system for interactive teaching and learning LAN design*. Paper presented at the 3rd IEEE International Conference on Information Technology Research and Education, Hsinchu, Taiwan (pp. 328-332).

Sarkar, N. I., & Sowerby, K. W. (2006, November 27-30). *Wi-Fi performance measurements in the crowded office environment: a case study*. Paper presented at the

10th IEEE International Conference on Communication Technology (ICCT), Guilin, China (pp. 37-40).

Sarkar, N. I., & Sowerby, K. W. (2009, April 4-8). *The combined effect of signal strength and traffic type on WLAN performance.* Paper presented at the IEEE Wireless Communication and Networking Conference (WCNC'09), Budapest, Hungary.

Sasson, Y., Cavin, D., & Schiper, A. (2003). Probabilistic broadcast for flooding in wireless mobile ad hoc networks. *Proceedings of Wireless Communications and Networking Conference (WCNC '03), 2*(16-20), 1124-1130.

Sawhney, A., & AbouRizk, S. M. (1995). HSM-Simulation-based planning method for construction projects. *Journal of Construction Engineering and Management, 121*(3), 297–303. doi:10.1061/(ASCE)0733-9364(1995)121:3(297)

Sawhney, A., & AbouRizk, S. M. (1996). Computerized tool for hierarchical simulation modeling. *Journal of Computing in Civil Engineering, 10*(2), 115–124. doi:10.1061/(ASCE)0887-3801(1996)10:2(115)

Scalable Network Technologies. (2007). *QualNet Developer.* Retrieved 20 April, 2007, from http://www.qualnet.com/products/developer.php

Schafer, T. M., Maurer, J., & Wiesbeck, W. (2002, September 24-28). *Measurement and simulation of radio wave propagation in hospitals.* Paper presented at IEEE 56th Vehicular Technology Conference (VTC2002-Fall), (pp. 792-796).

Schelling, T. C. (2006). *Micromotives and macrobehavior* (2nd Ed.). New York: WW Norton and Company.

Schmeiser, B. (2004, December). *Simulation output analysis: A tutorial based on one research thread.* Paper presented at 2004 Winter Simulation Conference, (pp. 162-170).

Schmid, A. (2005). What is the truth of simulation? *Journal of Artificial Societies and Social Simulation, 8*(4), 5.

Schmidt, D. C. (2006). *Real-time CORBA with TAO.* Retrieved September 5th, 2008, from http://www.cse.wustl.edu/ schmidt/TAO.html.

Schriber, T. J., & Brunner, D. T. (1999). Inside discrete-event simulation software: how it works and how it matters. *Proceedings of the 1999 Winter Simulation Conference*, Phoenix, AZ, (pp. 72-80).

ScienceDaily. (2006). Digital Surgery with Touch Feedback Could Improve Medical Training. *ScienceDaily.*

Scott, D., & Yasinsac, A. (2004). Dynamic probabilistic retransmission in ad hoc networks. *Proceedings of the International Conference on Wireless Networks*, (pp. 158-164).

Searle, J., & Brennan, J. (2006). General Interoperability Concepts. In *Integration of Modelling and Simulation* (pp. 3-1 – 3-8), (Educational Notes RTO-EN-MSG-043). Neuilly-sur-Seine, France

Sebastião, P. J. A. (1998). *Simulação eficiente do desempenho dos códigos TCH através de modelos estocásticos* [Efficient simulation to obtain the performance of TCH codes using stochastic models], (Master Thesis, Instituto Superior Técnico – Technical University of Lisbon, 1998), Lisboa, Portugal.

Sebastião, P. J. A., Cercas, F. A. B., & Cartaxo, A. V. T. (2002). Performance of TCH codes in a land mobile satellite channel. *13th IEEE International. Symposium on Personal, Indoor and Mobile Radio Communication., (PIMRC2002)*, Lisbon, Portugal, (pp. 1675-1679).

Seelen, L., Tijms, H., & Van Hoorn, M. (1985). *Tables for multi-server queues* (pp. 1-449). New-York: Elsevier, Simon, S., Armel, W., (2003). The Use of Simulation to Reduce the Length of Stay in an Emergency Department. In S. Chick, et al (Ed.) *Proceedings of the 2003 Winter Simulation Conference* (pp. 1907-1911). Washington, DC: IEEE

Sen, A., & Sinha, A. P. (2005). A comparison of data warehousing methodologies. *Communications of the ACM, 48*(3), 79–84. doi:10.1145/1047671.1047673

Senge, P. (1990). *The Fifth Discipline, The art & practice of learning organisation.* New York.

Shanahan, M. P. (2008). A spiking neuron model of cortical broadcast and competition. *Consciousness and Cognition, 17*(1), 288–303. doi:10.1016/j.concog.2006.12.005

Shanmugam, K. S. (1979). *Digital and analog communication systems.* Chichester, UK: John Wiley & Sons.

Shariat, M., & Hightower, R. Jr. (2007). Conceptualizing Business Intelligence Architecture. *Marketing Management Journal, 17*(2), 40–46.

Shi, J. (1995). *Optimization for construction simulation.* Ph.D. Thesis, Alberta University, Canada.

Shi, J., & AbouRizk, S. M. (1997). Resource-based modeling for construction simulation. *Journal of Construction Engineering and Management, 123*(1), 26–33. doi:10.1061/(ASCE)0733-9364(1997)123:1(26)

Shi, Y., Peng, Y., Kou, G., & Chen, Z. (2005). Classifying Credit Card Accounts For Business Intelligence And Decision Making: A Multiple-Criteria Quadratic Programming Approach. *International Journal of Information Technology & Decision Making, 4*(4), 581–599. doi:10.1142/S0219622005001775

Shinn, T. (2006). When is simulation a research technology? practices, markets, and. In G. K. J. Lenhard, & T. Shinn (Eds.), *Simulation: Pragmatic construction of reality; sociology of the sciences yearbook* (pp. 187-203). Dordrecht, The Netherlands: Springer.

Shnayder, V., Hempstead, M., Chen, B., Allen, G., & Welsh, M. (2004). *Simulating the power consumption of large-scale sensor network applications.* Paper presented at the 2nd international conference on Embedded networked sensor systems, (pp. 188-200).

Silver, R., Boahen, K., Grillner, S., Kopell, N., & Olsen, K. L. (2007). Neurotech for neuroscience: Unifying concepts, organizing principles, and emerging tools. *The Journal of Neuroscience, 27*(44), 11807–11819. doi:10.1523/JNEUROSCI.3575-07.2007

Simbad Project Home. (2007, Dec). Retrieved 1 2008, from Simbad Project Home: http://simbad.sourceforge.net/

Simon, H. A. (1962). The architecture of complexity. *Proceedings of the American Philosophical Society, 106*(6), 467–482.

Simon, H. A. (1996). *The sciences of the artificial* (3rd Ed.). Cambridge, MA: The MIT Press.

Simon, M. K., & Alouini, M. (2000). *Digital communication over fading channels.* Chichester, UK: John Wiley & Sons.

Simulation Interoperability Standards Organization (SISO). (2006). *The Base Object Model Standard; SISO-STD-003-2006: Base Object Model (BOM) Template Standard; SISO-STD-003.1-2006: Guide for Base Object Model (BOM) Use and Implementation.* Orlando, FL: SISO Documents.

Simulations, D. O. D. *Improved Assessment Procedures Would Increase the Credibility of Results,* (1987). Washington, DC: U. S. General Accounting Office, PEMD-88-3.

Sincich, T. (Ed.). (1994). *A Course in Modern Business Statistics.* New York: Macmillan College Publishing Company.

Sinclair, J. B. (2004). *Simulation of Computer Systems and Computer Networks: A Process-Oriented Approach.* George R. Brown School of Engineering, Rice University, Houston, Texas, USA.

Siringoringo, W., & Sarkar, N. I. (2009). Teaching and learning Wi-Fi networking fundamentals using limited resources. In J. Gutierrez (Ed.), *Selected Readings on Telecommunications and Networking* (pp. 22-40). Hershey, PA: IGI Global.

Skansholm, J. (1997). *C++ From the beginning.* Harlow, UK: Addison-Wesley.

Slater, M., Steed, A., & Chrysanthou, Y. (2002). *Computer Graphics and Virtual Environments: from Realism to Real-Time.* Reading, MA: Addison Wesley.

Smith, W. (2005). Applying data mining to scheduling courses at a university. *Communications Of AIs, 16,* 463–474.

Song, L., & AbouRizk, S. M. (2003). Building a virtual shop model for steel fabrication. *Proceedings of the 2003 Winter Simulation Conference,* New Orleans, LA, (pp. 1510-1517).

Spieckermann, A., Lehmann, A., & Rabe, M. (2004). Verifikation und Validierung: berlegungen zu einer integrierten Vorgehensweise. In K. Mertins, & M. Rabe, (Hrsg), *Experiences from the Future Fraunhofer IRB, Stuttgart,* (pp. 263-274). Stuttgart, Germany.

SpikeSNNS [computer software] (n.d.). Available from http://cortex.cs.may.ie/tools/spikeNNS/index.html.

SpikeStream [computer software] (n.d.). Available from http://spikestream.sf.net.

Srivastava, B., & Koehler, J. (2003). Web Service Composition - Current Solutions and Open Problems. *Proceedings ICAPS 2003 Workshop on Planning for Web Services.*

Srivastava, J., & Cooley, R. (2003). Web Business Intelligence: Mining the Web for Actionable Knowledge. *INFORMS Journal on Computing, 15*(2), 191–207. doi:10.1287/ijoc.15.2.191.14447

Stallings, W. (2005). *Wireless Communications and Networks* (2nd Ed.). Upper Saddle River, NJ: Prentice-Hall.

Stanislaw, H. (1986). Tests of computer simulation validation: What do they measure? *Simulation & Games, 17*(2), 173–191. doi:10.1177/0037550086172003

Stasko, J. T. (1991). Using direct manipulation to build algorithm animations by demonstration. In *Proceedings of conference on human factors and computing systems* (pp. 307-314), New Orleans, LA.

Stasko, J. T. (1997). Using student-built algorithm animations as learning aids. In *The proceedings of the 28th SIGCSE technical symposium on computer science education* (pp. 25-29), San Jose, CA. New York: ACM Press.

Stasko, J. T. (1998). Building software visualizations through direct manipulation and demonstration. In M. Brown, J. Domingue, B. Price, & J. Stasko (Eds.), *Software visualization: Programming as a multimedia experience* (pp. 103-118). Cambridge, MA: MIT Press.

Steele, R. D. (2002). *The New Craft of Intelligence: Personal, Public and Political.* VA: OSS International Press.

Sterman, J. (1992). *Teaching Takes Off, Flight Simulator for Management Education, the Beer Game.* Sloan school of Management, Massachusetts Institute of Technology, Cambridge, MA.

Stolba, N., & Tjoa, A. M. (2006). The relevance of data warehousing and data mining in the field of evidence-based medicine to support healthcare decision making. *Enformatika, 11*, 12–17.

SUN. (2006). *JDK-ORB.* Retrieved September 1st, 2008, from http://java.sun.com/j2se/1.5.0/docs/guide/idl/

Suzuki, H. (1977). A statistical model for urban radio propagation. *IEEE Transactions on Communications, 25*(7), 673–680. doi:10.1109/TCOM.1977.1093888

Swain, J., 2007. Biennial Survey of discreet-event simulation software tools. *OR/MS Today, 34*(5), October.

Szczerbicka, H., et al. (2000, December). Conceptions of curriculum for simulation education (Panel). In J. A. Joines, R. R. Barton, K. Kang & P. A. Fishwick (Eds.), *Proceedings of the 2000 Winter Simulation Conference,* Piscataway, NJ (pp. 1635-1644). Washington, DC: IEEE.

Takai, M., Martin, J., & Bagrodia, R. (2001, October). *Effects of wireless physical layer modeling in mobile ad hoc networks.* Paper presented at MobiHOC, Long Beach, CA, (pp. 87-94).

Tanenbaum, A. S. (2003). *Computer networks* (4th ed.). Upper Saddle River, NJ: Prentice Hall.

Tang, W., Wan, T., & Patel, S. (2003, June 3-5). Real-time crowd movement on large scale terrains. In *Theory and Practice of Computer Graphics.* Washinton, DC: IEEE Computer Society.

Tani, J., Nishimoto, R., & Paine, R. W. (2008). Achieving "organic compositionality" through self-organization: Reviews on brain-inspired robotics experiments. *Neural Networks, 21*(4), 584–603. doi:10.1016/j.neunet.2008.03.008

Tecchia, F., Loscos, C., Conroy, R., & Chrysanthou, Y. (2003). Agent behaviour simulator (abs): A platform for urban behaviour development. In *Conference Proceed-*

ings of Theory and Practice of Computer Graphics. Washington, DC: IEEE.

Teccia, F., & Chrysanthou, Y. (2001). *Agent behavior simulator.* Web Document, University College London, Department of Computer Science.

Technologies, O. P. N. E. T. (2009). Retrieved January 20, 2009, from www.opnet.com

Tetcos. (2007). *Products.* Retrieved 20 April, 2007, from http://www.tetcos.com/software.html

Tickoo, O., & Sikdar, B. (2003). On the impact of IEEE 802.11 MAC on traffic characteristics. *IEEE Journal on Selected Areas in Communications, 21*(2), 189–203. doi:10.1109/JSAC.2002.807346

Tischer, T. E., & Kuprenas, J. A. (2003). Bridge falsework productivity – measurement and influences. *Journal of Construction Engineering and Management, 129*(3), 243–250. doi:10.1061/(ASCE)0733-9364(2003)129:3(243)

Tolk, A. (1999). Requirements for Simulation Systems when being used as Decision Support Systems. [), IEEE CS press]. *Proceedings Fall Simulation Interoperability Workshop, I,* 29–35.

Tolk, A., & Diallo, S. Y. (2008) Model-Based Data Engineering for Web Services. In Nayak R. et al. (eds) *Evolution of the Web in Artificial Intelligence Environments,* (pp. 137-161). Berlin: Springer.

Tolk, A., & Jain, L. C. (Eds.). (2008). *Complex Systems in the Knowledge-based Environment.* Berlin: Springer Verlag.

Tolk, A., Diallo, S. Y., & Turnitsa, C. D. (2008). Implied Ontological Representation within the Levels of Conceptual Interoperability Model. [IDT]. *International Journal of Intelligent Decision Technologies, 2*(1), 3–19.

Tolk, A., Diallo, S. Y., Turnitsa, C. D., & Winters, L. S. (2006). Composable M&S Web Services for Net-centric Applications. *Journal for Defense Modeling and Simulation, 3*(1), 27–44. doi:10.1177/875647930600300104

Tommelein, I. D. (1999). Travel-time simulation to locate and staff temporary facilities under changing construc-tion demand. *Proceedings of the 1999 Winter Simulation Conference,* Phoenix, AZ (pp. 978-984).

Tommelein, I. D., Carr, R. I., & Odeh, A. M. (1994). Assembly of simulation networks using designs, plans, and methods. *Journal of Construction Engineering and Management, 120*(4), 796–815. doi:10.1061/(ASCE)0733-9364(1994)120:4(796)

Tonfoni, G., & Jain, L. C. (Eds.). (2003). *Innovations in Decision Support Systems.* Australia: Advanced Knowledge International.

Tonnelier, A., Belmabrouk, H., & Martinez, D. (2007). Event-driven simulations of nonlinear integrate-and-fire neurons. *Neural Computation, 19,* 3226–3238. doi:10.1162/neco.2007.19.12.3226

Tools, C. P. N. (2009). Retrieved from http://wiki.daimi.au.dk/cpntools/cpntools.wiki

Tosic, V., Pagurek, B., Esfandiari, B., & Patel, K. (2001). On the Management of Compositions of Web Services. In *Proceedings Object-Oriented Web Services (OOPSLA).*

Touran, A. (1990). Integration of simulation with expert systems. *Journal of Construction Engineering and Management, 116*(3), 480–493. doi:10.1061/(ASCE)0733-9364(1990)116:3(480)

Truong, T. H., Rothschild, B. J., & Azadivar, F. (2005) Decision support system for fisheries management. In *Proceedings of the 37th Conference on Winter Simulation,* (pp. 2107-2111).

Tseng, Y., Ni, S., Chen, Y., & Sheu, J. (2002). The broadcast storm problem in a mobile ad hoc network. *Journal of Wireless Networks, 8,* 153–167. doi:10.1023/A:1013763825347

Turban, E., Aronson, J. E., Liang, T. P., & Sharda, R. (2007). *Decision Support and Business Intelligence Systems,* (8th Ed.). Upper Saddle River, NJ: Pearson Prentice Hall.

Turner, M. J., Richardson, R., Le Blanc, A., Kuchar, P., Ayesh, A., & Al Hudhud, G. (2006, September 14). Roboviz a collaborative user and robot. In *CompuSteer*

Workshop environment network testbed. London, UK: Oxford University.

Uzam, M., Avci, M., & Kürsat, M. (2001). Digital Hardware Implementation of Petri Nets Based Specification: Direct Translation from Safe Automation Petri Nets to Circuit Elements. In *Proc. DESDes'01,* (pp. 25 – 33), Zielona Gora, Poland.

Vaduva, A., & Vetterli, T. (2001). Metadata management for data warehousing: an overview. *International Journal of Cooperative Information Systems, 10*(3), 273. doi:10.1142/S0218843001000357

Valk, R. (1978, July). Self-Modifying Nets, a Natural Extension of Petri Nets. In G. Ausiello & C. Böhm (Eds.), *Proceedings of the Fifth Colloquium on Automata, Languages and Programming (ICALP'78),* (p. 464-476). Udine, Italy: Springer.

Valk, R. (1998, June). Petri Nets as Token Objects: An Introduction to Elementary Object Nets. In J. Desel & M. Silva (Eds.), *Proceedings of the 19th International Conference on Applications and Theory of Petri Nets (ICATPN 1998)* (p. 1-25). Lisbon, Portugal: Springer.

van Dam, A. (1999). Education: the unfinished revolution. [CSUR]. *ACM Computing Surveys, 31*(4). doi:10.1145/345966.346038

van der Aalst, W. M. P. (1996). *Structural Characterizations of Sound Workflow Nets* (Computing Science Reports No. 96/23). Eindhoven, the Netherlands: Eindhoven University of Technology.

van der Aalst, W. M. P., & Basten, T. (2002, January). Inheritance of Workflows: An Approach to Tackling Problems Related to Change. *Theoretical Computer Science, 270*(1-2), 125–203. doi:10.1016/S0304-3975(00)00321-2

van der Aalst, W. M. P., & Jablonski, S. (2000, September). Dealing with Workflow Change: Identification of Issues and Solutions. *International Journal of Computer Systems, Science, and Engineering, 15*(5), 267–276.

Vanegas, J. A., Bravo, E. B., & Halpin, D. W. (1993). Simulation technologies for planning heavy construction processes. *Journal of Construction Engineering and Management, 119*(2), 336–354. doi:10.1061/(ASCE)0733-9364(1993)119:2(336)

vanguardsw. (n.d.). *vanguardsw.* Retrieved 2008, from vanguardsw: www.vanguardsw.com

Varga, A. (1999). Using the OMNeT++ discrete event simulation system in education. *IEEE Transactions on Education, 42*(4), 1–11. doi:10.1109/13.804564

Varga, A. (2001, June 6-9). *The OMNeT++ discrete evenet simulation system.* Paper presented at the European Simulation Multiconference (ESM'01), Prague, Czech Republic.

Vennix, J. (1996). *Group model building: facilitating team learning using system dynamics.* Chichester, UK: Wiley

Verbeke, J. M., Hagmann, C., & Wright, D. (2008, February 1). http://nuclear.llnl.gov/simulation/fission.pdf. Retrieved October 1, 2008, from Computational Nuclear Physics, http://nuclear.llnl.gov/simulation/

Vinoski, S. (1997). CORBA - Integrating diverse applications within distributed heterogeneous environments. *IEEE Communications Magazine, 35*(2), 46–55. doi:10.1109/35.565655

VMware Player [computer software] (n.d.). Available from http://www.vmware.com/products/player/.

Walfish, J., & Bertoni, H. L. (1988). A theoretical model of UHF propagation in urban environments. *IEEE Transactions on Antennas and Propagation, 36,* 1788–1796. doi:10.1109/8.14401

Wan, T. R., & Tang, W. (2003). An intelligent vehicle model for 3d visual traffic simulation. In *IEEE International Conference on Visual Information Engineering, VIE.*

Wan, T., & Tang, W. (2004). Agent-based real time traffice control simulation for urban environment. *IEEE Transactions on Intelligent Transportation Systems.*

Wang, Z., & Lehmann, A. (2008). *Verification and Validation of Simulation Models and Applications.* Hershey, PA: IGI Global.

Watson H. J., Wixom B. H., Hoffer J. A., Lehman R. A., & Reynolds A. M. (2006). Real-Time Business Intelligence: Best Practices at Continental Airlines. *Journal of Information Systems Management*, 7–18.

Weaver, W. (1948). Science and complexity. *American Scientists, 36.*

Weber, D. O. (2006). Queue Fever: Part 1 and Part 2. *Hospitals & Health Networks, Health Forum.* Retrieved from http://www.IHI.org

Weiss, S. M., Buckley, S. J., Kapoor, S., & Damgaard, S. (2003). Knowledge-Based Data Mining. [Washington, DC.]. *SIGKDD, 03,* 456–461.

Wheeler, D. A. (n.d.). *SLOCCount* [computer software]. Available from http://www.dwheeler.com/sloc/.

Wilton, D. (2001). The Application Of Simulation Technology To Military Command And Control Decision Support. In *Proceedings Simulation Technology and Training Conference* (SimTecT), Canberra, Australia.

Winsberg, E. (1999). Sanctioning models: The epistemology of simulation. *Science in Context, 12*(2), 275–292. doi:10.1017/S0269889700003422

Winsberg, E. (2001). Simualtions, models, and theories: Complex physical systems and their. *Philosophy of Science, 68*(3), 442–454. doi:10.1086/392927

Winsberg, E. (2003). Simulated experiments: Methodology for a virtual world. *Philosophy of Science, 70,* 105–125. doi:10.1086/367872

Winsberg, E. (2006). Handshaking your way to the top: Simulation at the nanoscale. In G. K. J. Lenhard, & T. Shinn (Eds.), *Simulation: Pragmatic construction of reality; sociology of the sciences yearbook* (pp. 139-151). Dordrecht, The Netherlands: Springer.

Winsberg, E. (2006). Models of success versus the success of models: Reliability without. *Synthese, 152,* 1–19. doi:10.1007/s11229-004-5404-6

Wixom, B. H. (2004). Business Intelligence Software for the Classroom: Microstrategy Resources on the Teradata University Network. *Communications of the Association for Information Systems, 14,* 234–246.

Wolfram, S. (1994). *Cellular Automata and Complexity: Collected Papers.* Reading, MA: Addison-Wesley Publishing Company.

Wolstenholme, E. (1990). *System Enquiry: a system dynamics approach.* Wiley: New York.

Wu, D., Olson, D. L., & Dong, Z. Y. (2006). Data mining and simulation: a grey relationship demonstration. *International Journal of Systems Science, 37*(13), 981–986. doi:10.1080/00207720600891521

Wullink, G., Van Houdenhoven, M., Hans, E., van Oostrum, J., van der Lans, M., Kazemier, G., (2007). Closing Emergency Operating Rooms Improves Efficiency.

Wutzler, T. (2008). Effect of the Aggregation of Multi-Cohort Mixed Stands on Modeling Forest Ecosystem Carbon Stocks. *Silva Fennica, 42*(4), 535–553.

Wutzler, T., & Mund, M. (2007). Modelling mean above and below ground litter production based on yield tables. *Silva Fennica, 41*(3), 559–574.

Wutzler, T., & Reichstein, M. (2007). Soils apart from equilibrium – consequences for soil carbon balance modelling. *Biogeosciences, 4,* 125–136.

Wutzler, T., & Sarjoughian, H. S. (2007). Interoperability among parallel DEVS simulators and models implemented in multiple programming languages. *Simulation Transactions, 83*(6), 473–490. doi:10.1177/0037549707084490

Xilinx, (2009). Retrieved from http://www.xilinx.com/f

Xu, D., Yin, J., Deng, Y., & Ding, J. (2003, January). A Formal Architectural Model for Logical Agent Mobility. *IEEE Transactions on Software Engineering, 29*(1), 31–45. doi:10.1109/TSE.2003.1166587

Yacoub, M. D. (2000). Fading distributions and co-channel interference in wireless systems. *IEEE Antennas & Propagation Magazine., 42*(1), 150–159. doi:10.1109/74.826357

Yacoub, M., Baptista, J. E. V., & Guedes, L. G. R. (1999). On higher order statistics of the Nakagami-m distribution. *IEEE Transactions on Vehicular Technology, 48*(3), 790–794. doi:10.1109/25.764995

Yegani, P., & McGillem, C. D. (1991). A statistical model for the factory radio channel. *IEEE Transactions on Communications, 39*(10), 1445–1454. doi:10.1109/26.103039

Yilmaz, L. (2007). Using meta-level ontology relations to measure conceptual alignment and interoperability of simulation models. In *Proceedings of the Winter Simulation Conference*, (pp. 1090-1099).

Yilmaz, L., Ören, T., & Aghaee, N. (2006). Intelligent agents, simulation, and gaming. *Journal for Simulation and Gaming, 37*(3), 339–349. doi:10.1177/1046878106289089

Youzhi, X., & Jie S. (2004). The agent-based model on real-time data warehousing. *Journal of Systems Science & Information, 2*(2), 381–388.

Zack, J., Rainer, R. K., & Marshall, T. E. (2007). Business Intelligence: An Analysis of the Literature. *Information Systems Management, 25*, 121–131.

Zeigler, B. P. (1986) Toward a Simulation Methodology for Variable Structure Modeling. In Elzas, Oren, Zeigler (Eds.) *Modeling and Simulation Methodology in the Artificial Intelligence Era.*

Zeigler, B. P. (2003). DEVS Today: Recent advances in discrete event-based information. *Proceedings of the 11th IEEE/ACM International Symposium on Modeling, Analysis and Simulation of Computer Telecommunications Systems,* (pp. 148-162).

Zeigler, B. P., & Hammonds, P. E. (2007) *Modeling & Simulation-Based Data Engineering: Introducing Pragmatics into Ontologies for Net-Centric Information Exchange.* New York: Academic Press.

Zeigler, B. P., & Sarjoughian, H. S. (2002). Implications of M&S Foundations for the V&V of Large Scale Complex Simulation Models, Invited Paper. In *Verification & Validation Foundations Workshop Laurel, Maryland, VA.*, (pp. 1–51). Society for Computer Simulation. Retrieved from https://www.dmso.mil/public/transition/vva/foundations

Zeigler, B. P., Praehofer, H., & Kim, T. G. (2000). *Theory of modeling and simulation* (2nd Ed.). New York: Academic Press.

Zeigler, B. P., Sarjoughian, H. S., & Praehofer, H. (2000). Theory of quantized systems: DEVS simulation of perceiving agents. *Cybernetics and Systems, 31*(6), 611–647. doi:10.1080/01969720050143175

Zein, H. (2006). *A framework for planning and optimizing bridge deck construction using computer simulation.* M.Sc. Thesis, Cairo University, Cairo, Egypt.

Zhang, C., & Hammad, A. (2007). Agent-based simulation for collaborative cranes. *Proceedings of the 2007 Winter Simulation Conference*, Washington, DC. (pp. 2051-2056).

Zhu, C., Wang, O. W. W., Aweya, J., Oullette, M., & Montuno, D. Y. (2002). A comparison of active queue management algorithms using the OPNET Modeler. *IEEE Communications Magazine, 40*(6), 158–167. doi:10.1109/MCOM.2002.1007422

About the Contributors

Evon M. O. Abu-Taieh is a Ph.D. holder in Simulation. A USA graduate for both her Master of Science and Bachelor's degrees with a total experience of 19 years. Author of many renowned research papers in the Airline and IT, PM, KM, GIS, AI, Simulation, Security and Ciphering. Editor/author of Book: Utilizing Information Technology Systems Across Disciplines: Advancements in the Application of Computer Science.IGI, USA. Editor/author Handbook of Research on Discrete Event Simulation Environments: Technologies and Applications, IGI, USA. Guest Editor, Journal of Information Technology Research (JITR) Editorial Board Member in: International Journal of E-Services and Mobile Applications (IJESMA and International Journal of Information Technology Project Management (IJITPM) and International Journal of Information Systems and Social Change (IJISSC). Editor/author of Book: Simulation and Modeling: Current Technologies and Applications. IGI, USA. Developed some systems like: Ministry of transport databank, auditing system for airline reservation systems and Maritime Databank among others in her capacity as head of IT department in the ministry of transport for 10 years. Furthermore worked in the Arab Academy in her capacity as Assistant Professor, Dean's Assistant and London School of Economics (LSE) Director. Appointed many times as track chair, reviewer in many international conferences: IRMA, CISTA, and WMSCI. Enjoys both the academic arena as well as the hands on job. (abutaieh@gmail.com)

Asim Abdel Rahman El Sheikh got a BSc (honors) from University of Khartoum (Sudan),an MSc and a PhD from University of London (UK). El Sheikh worked for University of Khartoum, Philadelphia University (Jordan) and The Arab Academy for Banking & Financial Sciences (Jordan). El Sheikh is currently the dean of the faculty of information systems & technology at the Arab Academy for Banking & Financial Sciences. El Sheikh's areas of research interest are computer simulation and software engineering. Email Address : a.elsheikh@aabfs.org.

* * *

Sattar J Aboud is a Professor at Middle East University in Jordan. He received his education from United Kingdom. Dr. Aboud has served his profession in many universities and he was awarded the Quality Assurance Certificate of Philadelphia University, Faculty of Information Technology. His research interests include the areas of both symmetric and asymmetric cryptography, area of verification and validation, and performance evaluation.

Jeihan Abu-Tayeh attend school at the Rosary School in Amman, then she acquired her bachelor's in Pharmaceutical Science and Management from Al-Ahlyya Amman University. Furthermore, in 2002, she got her M.B.A. with emphasis on "International Marketing & Negotiations Technique", with outstanding G. P. A. of 3.87 out of 4 (with honors) from Saint Martin's College, State of Washington; U.S.A. Currently, Jeihan Abu-Tayeh is a Head of the International Agencies & Commissions Division at the Jordanian Ministry of Planning and International Cooperation. In her capacity, she has the opportunity to maintain sound cooperation relations with the World Bank Group, as well as the UN Agencies, in order to extend to Jordan financial and technical support for developmental projects through setting appropriate programs and plans, building and improving relations with those organizations. This is achieved through loans and aids programs, by means of designing project proposals, conducting Problem & Needs Assessment for the concerned Governmental and Non-Governmental Jordanian entities, followed by active participation in extensive evaluation processes, conducted by either the UN Country Team, or the World Bank Group Country Team.

Hussein Al-Bahadili is an associate professor at the Arab Academy for Banking & Financial Sciences (AABFS). He earned his M.Sc and PhD from the University of London (Queen Mary College) in 1988 and 1991, respectively. He received his B.Sc in Engineering from the University of Baghdad in 1986. In addition to his academic activities at the University of Baghdad, he worked for the Iraqi Atomic Energy Commission (IAEC) for more than 15 years. He was head of the Department of Software at the Centre of Engineering Design, and then he became Director of the Centre of Information Technology. He was the INIS Liaison Officer for Iraq at the International Atomic Energy Agency (IAEA) from 1997 to 2000. Dr. Al-Bahadili is a member of the Wireless Networks and Communications Group (WNCG) at the School of Engineering, University of Brunel, United Kingdom. He is also a visiting researcher at the Centre of Osmosis Research and Applications (CORA), University of Surrey, United Kingdom. He has published many papers in different fields of science and engineering in numerous leading scholarly and practitioner journals, and presented at leading world-level scholarly conferences. His research interests include parallel and distributed computing, wireless communication, data communication systems, computer networks, cryptography, network security, data compression, image processing, data acquisition, computer automation, electronic system design, computer architecture, and artificial intelligence and expert systems.

Mohammad A. Al-Fayoumi is a Professor at Middle East University in Jordan, and now he is the dean of Information technology faculty. He received his education from Romania. Dr. Fayoumi has served his profession in many Universities and he awarded many prices and certificates from different Universities in Arab nation. His research interests include the methodology areas of Information Security and Simulation and modeling.

Ghada A.K. Al-Hudhud holds a PhD from De Montfort University/ United Kingdom. Ghada serves as the head of Department of Software Engineering at Al-Ahliya Amman University, Jordan. Ghada is interested in modelling systems within virtual environments. Ghada is also interested in working on image compression. Ghada has been working as a key partner in an EPSRC project funded by Computational Steering Network.

Mouhib Alnoukari: Currently preparing a PhD in Management Information Systems (MIS) at The Arabic Academy for Banking and Financial Sciences, Damascus, Syria. Holds MBA from Damascus University, MS in Mathematics from Damascus University, and MS in Computer Engineering from Montpellier University, France. Currently working as the ICT director at the Arab International University. Published papers in different conferences and journals such as: ITSim 2008 Malaysia, ICTTA'08 Syria, EQAF 2008 Budapest, Damascus University Journal, and others.

Mohamed Alnuaimi is a Professor at Middle East University in Jordan, and now he is the Vice President of the University. He received his education from Krakoff University, Poland. Dr. Alnuaimi has served his profession in many Universities and he awarded many prices, medals and certificates from different Universities in Arab nation. His research interests include the methodology areas of Applied Statistic and Simulation and modeling.

Raed Musbah Al-Qirem has a PhD in Management Information system from the University of Sunderland-United Kingdom. His research focused on some of systems thinking methodologies which are System Dynamics and Viable System model (Managerial Cybernetics). Because his experience was in Banking and finance, he constructed a Decision Support System using systems thinking to evaluate the credit worthiness of firm's applying for credit in the Banks. He is now an assistant Professor in the MIS department at Al-Zaytoonah University of Jordan.

Zaidoun Alzoabi: Currently preparing a PhD in (Management Information Systems) at the Arab academy for Banking and Finance Science, Damascus, Syria. Holds Master in Computer Applications (MCA) from J.M.I University, New Delhi, India. Currently working at Arab International University as the Quality Assurance director. Also as an Information and Communication Consultant at the Modernization of Ministry of Finance project (an EU funded project). Published papers in the different conferences and journals such as: ITSim 2008 Malaysia, ICTTA'08 Syria, EQAF 2008 Budapest, and others.

Lorenzo Capra was born in Monza (Italy), and went to the University of Milan, where he obtained his Laurea degree in Computer Science. After collaborating with the Automation Research Center at the National Electric Power Provider (ENEL), he moved to the University of Turin, where he received a Ph.D in Computer Science. He is currently assistant professor at the Dept. of Informatics and Communication (DICO) of the University of Milano, Italy. His research interests include High-Level Petri Nets analysis/simulation and formal methods in software engineering.

Adolfo Cartaxo received the degree of "Licenciatura" in Electrical and Computer Engineering, and the Ph. D. in Electrical and Computer Engineering in 1985, and 1992, respectively, from Instituto Superior Técnico (IST). He is currently Associate Professor at the Electrical and Computer Engineering Department of IST. He joined the Optical Communications Group (OCG) of IST as a researcher in 1992, and he is now the leader of the OCG conducting research on optical fibre telecommunication systems and networks. He is a senior member of the IEEE Laser and Electro-Optics Society. He has authored or co-authored more than 65 journal publications (15 as first author) as well as more than 90 international conference papers. He is co-author of two international patents. His current research areas of interest include fiber optic communication systems and networks, and simulation of telecommunication systems.

Lucia Cassettari earned her degree in management engineering in 2004 at the University of Genoa. Currently she is a researcher at DIPTEM, University of Genoa, in the field of simulator-based applications for industrial plants; particular attention is focused on the application of DOE and Optimization techniques to industrial plant problems using Simulation.

Walter Cazzola (Ph.D.) is currently an assistant professor at the Department of Informatics and Communication (DICo) of the University of Milano, Italy and the chair of the ADAPT research group (http://adapt-lab.dico.unimi.it). His research interests include reflection, aspect-oriented programming, programming methodologies and languages. He has written and has served as reviewer of several technical papers about reflection and aspect-oriented programming. Details can be read from his home page http://homes.dico.unimi.it/~cazzola.

Francisco Cercas received his Licenciatura, M.Sc., and Ph.D. degrees from Instituto Superior Técnico (IST), Technical University of Lisbon, Portugal, in 1983, 1989 and 1996, respectively. He worked for the Portuguese Industry as a research engineer and developed the work of his M.S. and Ph.D. theses as an invited researcher at the Satellite Centre of the University of Plymouth, UK. This resulted in new contributions for the characterization of DDS (Direct Digital Frequency Synthesizer) signals and in a new class of codes named TCH after Tomlinson, Cercas and Hughes. He lectured during 15 years at IST and became Associate Professor in 1999 at ISCTE, Lisbon, where he is the Head of the Department of Sciences and Technologies of Information. He has over 100 international publications with referees including conferences, magazines, book chapters and a patent. His main research interests focus on mobile and personal communications, satellite communications, channel coding and ultra wide band communications.

David Gamez completed his BA in natural sciences and philosophy at Trinity College, Cambridge, and took a PhD in Continental philosophy at the University of Essex. After converting to IT, he worked on the EU Safeguard project, which developed an agent system to protect electricity and telecommunications management networks against attacks and accidents. When the Safeguard project ended he took up a PhD position on Owen Holland's CRONOS project. During this PhD he developed a theoretical framework for machine consciousness, developed the SpikeStream neural simulator and made predictions about the representational and phenomenal states of a spiking neural network.

Brian L. Heath is a DAGSI Fellow and currently a Ph.D. Candidate in Engineering with focus in Industrial and Human Systems at Wright State University (Dayton, OH, USA). In 2008 he received a M.S. in Industrial and Human Factors Engineering from Wright State University and in 2006 he received a B.S. in Industrial Engineering from Kettering University (Flint, MI, USA). He is a member of INFORMS and the Institute of Industrial Engineering (IIE). His research interests include agent-based modeling, simulation, validation philosophy, scientific model building, work measurement, and statistics.

Raymond R. Hill is a Professor of Operations Research with the Air Force Institute of Technology. He has a Ph.D. in Industrial and Systems Engineering from The Ohio State University. His research interests are in the areas of applied statistics and experimental design, mathematical modeling and combinatorial optimization and simulation to include agent-based modeling. He is a member of INFORMS and the Institute of Industrial Engineering (IIE) and an associate editor for the Journal of Simulation, Military Operations Research and the Journal of Defense Modeling and Simulation.

Alexander Kolker is currently Outcomes Operations Project Manager in Children's Hospital of Wisconsin, Milwaukee, Wisconsin. He has been extensively involved in the various applications of Healthcare management science and Operations research using discrete event simulation: from hospital capacity expansion planning to patient flow improvement and optimized staff utilization. He actively publishes in peer reviewed journals and speaks at conferences in the area of simulation and management science applications for health care. Previously he has been with Froedtert Hospital, and with General Electric Co, Healthcare Division, as a simulation specialist and reliability engineer. Alex holds a PhD in applied mathematics from the Moscow Technical University, and is an ASQ certified Reliability engineer.

Ari Korhonen has been Adjunct Professor of Computer Science (specialising in Software Visualization) since 2006. He is currently Lecturing Researcher of the Faculty of Information and Natural Sciences in the Helsinki University of Technology. He holds M.Sc. (Tech), Lic.Sc. (Tech), and D.Sc. (Tech) in Computer Science, all from the Helsinki University of Technology, Finland. His previous positions include research positions and acting professor at the same university. He established the Software Visualization Group at the Helsinki University of Technology in 2000 and has been its leader since. He has been the manager of several research projects, including AAFAS (2005-2008), funded by the Academy of Finland. A former secretary of The Finnish Society for Computer Science (1999-2001), he is currently the editor of its journal Tietojenkäsittelytiede (2002-). At present he belongs to the board in IEEE Education Society Chapter for the Joint Norway/Denmark/Finland/Iceland/Sweden Sections. He has constantly refereed major journals and conferences including ACM Journal on Educational Resources in Computing, Educational Technology & Society journal, The Baltic Sea Conference on Computing Education Research, the ACM Annual Conference on Innovation and Technology in Computer Science Education, and the ACM Technical Symposium on Computer Science Education. In addition, he has served on the Program Committees for the 7th and 8th Baltic Sea Conferences on Computing Education Research, and the 3rd, 4th, and 5th Program Visualization Workshops. His research interests include data structures and algorithms in software visualization. Especially various applications of computer aided learning environments in computer science education. Current work is concerned with software tools and principles in the area of automatic assessment systems.

Hana Kubatova received her Ph.D. (CSc.) degree in Computer Science and Engineering at the Czech Technical University in Prague (CTU) in 1987. She currently works as an associate professor and as a deputy head of the Department of Computer Science and Engineering at the CTU. She is a leader of the VLSI research group with 20 members and with following areas of interest: Petri Nets in modelling, simulation and hardware design, design and evaluation of heuristic techniques for selected problems in VLSI systems, reconfigurable computing, HW/SW co-design methodologies, embedded processor cores for FPGA, design for testability, BIST on circuit and system level, design and modeling of fault-tolerant and dependable systems.

György Lipovszki was born in Miskolc, Hungary and finished his study at Budapest University of Technology and Economics, where he was graduated in 1975 in electronics sciences. He is now Associate Professor at the Department of Mechatronics, Optics and Engineering Informatics and his research field is the development of simulation frame systems in different programming environments. He is a member of the Editorial Board of International Journal for the Scholarship of Teaching and Learning.

Mohamed Marzouk, Ph.D., PMP is Associate Professor in the Structural Engineering Department, Faculty of Engineering, Cairo University. He has 12 years of experience in the Civil Engineering. His expertise has been in the fields of structural engineering, project management, contract administration, and construction engineering and management. His experience covers different phases of projects including design, construction, monitoring, research, consulting, and project management. Dr. Marzouk is certified Project Management Professional (PMP®). He authored and co- authored over 40 scientific publications. His research interest includes simulation and optimization of construction processes, object-oriented simulation, fuzzy logic and its applications in construction, risk analysis, and decision analysis. Dr. Marzouk is currently involved in several academic and scientific committees.

Richard Membarth received the postgraduate diploma in computer and information sciences from the Auckland University of Technology, Auckland, New Zealand in 2007, and the Diploma degree in computer science from the University of Erlangen-Nuremberg, Erlangen, Germany in 2008. Richard is currently working toward his Ph.D. degree in computer science in the Department of Computer Science at the University of Erlangen-Nuremberg, Erlangen, Germany. His research interests include parallel computer architectures and programming models for medical imaging as well as invasive computing.

Istvan Molnar was born in Budapest and educated at the Budapest University of Economic Sciences (currently, Corvinus University), where he received his MSc. and PhD. He has completed his postdoctoral studies in Darmstadt, Germany. In 1996 he has received his CSs. degree from the Hungarian Academy of Sciences. Currently, he is an Associate Professor at the Bloomsburg University of Pennsylvania. His main fields of interest are microsimulation, simulation optimization, simulation software technology, and simulation education. Dr. Molnar is a member of the Editorial Board of International Journal of Mobile Learning and Organization, published by Inderscience Publishers.

Roberto Mosca is Full Professor of "Industrial Plants Management" and "Economy and Business Organization" at the DIPTEM (Department of Industrial Production, Thermoenergetics and Mathematical Modelling), University of Genoa. He has worked in the simulation sector since 1969 using discrete and stochastic industrial simulators for off-line and on-line applications. He has been more time national coordinator of research projects of national relevant interest His research work focuses on original application of DOE and RSM to simulation experiment. He is author of about 200 scientific papers published for International Conferences and International Journals . Currently he is Director of DIPTEM in University of Genoa.

Roberto Revetria earned his degree in mechanical engineering at the University of Genoa. He completed his PhD in Mechanical Engineering in 2001. He is currently involved, as Associate Professor, in the DIPTEM of Genoa University, working on advanced modeling projects applied to ERP integration and maintenance planning applied to industrial case studies. He is active in developing projects involving simulation with special attention to HLA (High Level Architecture).

Hessam S. Sarjoughian is Assistant Professor of Computer Science and Engineering at Arizona State University in Tempe, Arizona. Sarjoughian is Co-Director of the Arizona Center for Integrative Modeling & Simulation (ACIMS). His research focuses on modeling and simulation methodologies, model composability, distributed co-design modeling, visual simulation modeling, and agent-based simulation. He led the development of the Online Masters of Engineering in Modeling & Simulation in the Fulton School of Engineering at ASU in 2004. He was among the pioneers who established the Modeling & Simulation Professional Certification Commission in 2001. His research has been supported by NSF, Boeing, DISA, Intel, Lockheed Martin, Northrop Grumman, and US Air Force.

Nurul Sarkar is a Senior Lecturer in the School of Computing and Mathematical Sciences at AUT University, Auckland, New Zealand. He has more than 13 years of teaching experience in universities at both undergraduate and postgraduate levels and has taught a range of subjects, including computer networking, data communications, computer hardware, and eCommerce. His first edited book entitled "Tools for Teaching Computer Networking and Hardware Concepts" has been published by IGI Global Publishing in 2006. Nurul has published more than 80 research papers in international refereed journals, conferences, and book chapters, including the IEEE Transactions on Education, the International Journal of Electrical Engineering Education, the International Journal of Information and Communication Technology Education, the International Journal of Business Data Communications and Networking, Measurement Science & Technology, and SIGCSE Bulletin. Nurul was the recipient of Academic Staff Doctoral Study Award, and co-recipient of the 2006 IRMA International Conference Best Paper Award for a fundamental paper on the modelling and simulation of wireless networks. Nurul's research interests are in multi-disciplinary areas, including wireless network architecture, performance modelling and evaluation of wireless networks, radio propagation measurements, network security, simulation and modelling, intelligent agents, and tools to enhance methods for teaching and learning computer networking and hardware concepts. Nurul is a member of various professional organisations and societies, including IEEE Communications Society, Information Resources Management Association (IRMA), and ACM New Zealand Bulletin. He served as Associate technical editor for the IEEE Communications Magazine; Associate editor for Advances in Business Data Communications and Networking book series; editor for Encyclopaedia of Information Technology Curriculum Integration book series; Chairman of the IEEE New Zealand Communications Society Chapter, and Executive peer reviewer of the Journal of Educational Technology & Society.

Pedro Sebastião received the BSc degree in Electronic and Telecommunication and Computing, ISEL, Polytechnic Institute of Lisbon, Portugal, in 1992. He graduated in Electrical and Computing Engineering and received the MSc degree in Electrical and Computer Science from IST, Technical University of Lisbon, Portugal, in 1995 and 1998, respectively. From 1992 to 1998, he was with the Department of Studies in the Portuguese Defence Industries. In 1995, he joined with the IT, Portuguese Telecommunication Institute. From 1998-2000, he was with the Communication Business unity, in Siemens. Also, from 1999 to 2005, he was a lecturer in the Department of Information and Communication Technologies in ISG, High Management Institute. Since 2005, he is a lecturer in the Department of Sciences and Information Technologies in Lisbon University Institute - ISCTE. He has authored more than 40 international publications including conferences, magazines and book chapters. His current research interests are stochastic models, efficient simulation algorithms, satellite, mobile and personal communication systems and planning tools.

Andreas Tolk is Associate Professor for Engineering Management and Systems Engineering at Old Dominion University in Norfolk, VA, USA. He received has Ph.D. and M.S. in Computer Science from the University of the Federal Armed Forces in Munich, Germany. More than 25 of his conference papers were awarded for outstanding contributions. He is affiliated with the Virginia Modeling Analysis and Simulation Center in Suffolk, VA, USA. His research targets at the integration of Engineering Management, Modeling and Simulation, and Systems Engineering methods and principles, in particular for Complex Systems and System of Systems applications.

Thomas Wutzler is a junior researcher at the Max Planck Institute for Biogeochemistry in Jena, Germany. His research focuses on understanding and modelling the carbon cycle of terrestrial ecosystems with emphasis on soil carbon processes, uncertainties, and problems of scales. He graduated as a master of computer science at the technical university in Dresden, Germany. Then he continued with research in earth system sciences and earned a PhD in natural science. He strives to provide communication and interfaces between the research communities of simulation computer science and earth system sciences. His research has been supported by the German Environmental Foundation.

Saad Ghaleb Yaseen has a PhD in Management Information Systems. He is an associate Professor and head of the MIS Department in the Faculty of Economics and Administrative Sciences as Al-Zaytoonah University of Jordan. He had conducted over 40 specialized studies in many fields such as IT, IS, e Management and knowledge management. He is a renowned expert in the management of IT projects and a professional academician in the Middle East.

Index